Bishop Edward Thomas O'Dwyer of Limerick, 1842–1917

'An able man, a strong man, for Ireland an unusual man'
H.W. Cleary to Monsignor O'Riordan, 1917.

'Brilliant he was and looked,
Edward Thomas O'Dwyer … our difficult bishop'
Kate O'Brien.

Bishop
Edward Thomas O'Dwyer
of Limerick, 1842–1917

THOMAS J. MORRISSEY, SJ

with a foreword by Professor Emmet Larkin

FOUR COURTS PRESS

Set in 10.5 pt on 12 pt Bembo
by Carrigboy Typesetting Services for
FOUR COURTS PRESS LTD
7 Malpas Street, Dublin 8, Ireland
e-mail: info@four-courts-press.ie
http://www.four-courts-press.ie
and in North America for
FOUR COURTS PRESS
c/o ISBS, 920 N.E. 58th Street, Suite 300, Portland, OR 97213.

© Thomas Morrissey 2003

A catalogue record for this title
is available from the British Library.

ISBN 1-85182-772-2

Printed in Great Britain
by MPG Books, Bodmin, Cornwall

Contents

PART FOUR
THE PRELATE, THE MAN, THE EDUCATIONALIST

PART FIVE
CHALLENGES IN THE NEW CENTURY, 1900–1917

Foreword

Edward Thomas O'Dwyer (1842–1917), the celebrated bishop of Limerick, was for most of his episcopal career disliked by his people, feared by his priests, and distrusted by his episcopal colleagues. In the final year of his life, however, he became a popular idol and died a national hero. How did this strange redemption come to pass? That is the story of this very fine biography by Thomas J. Morrissey.

Edward Thomas O'Dwyer was at one and the same time an unusually able and gifted man, who was also a deeply flawed and conflicted human being. His gifts included a strong, versatile, and agile intelligence, accompanied by a wonderful facility to articulate that mind, and a singular tenacity in implementing its will. On the debit side, O'Dwyer exhibited a dogmatic and authoritarian strain that apparently could brook no opposition once his mind was made up. He also had an unfortunate tendency to be unscrupulous with regard to his means when he believed a salutary end to be at stake. Finally, he had an unhappy penchant for invective that was very unattractive, especially in a man of the cloth.

For more than thirty years, from 1886 to 1917, O'Dwyer governed the diocese of Limerick with an iron hand. He was an excellent administrator and over that period he achieved a great deal of spiritual and material good. He attended meticulously to visitations, conferences, retreats, missions, catechesis, sodalities and confraternities, increased the number of secular and regular clergy, and was assiduous in refurbishing sacred space. He also provided significantly for the social needs of his people by promoting temperance, improving housing, expanding nursing, alleviating poverty, and upgrading the educational facilities of his diocese. The effecting of much of this good, however, was marred by innumerable and often very bitter controversies, confrontations, and quarrels with all and sundry who had the temerity to contradict what he believed was the right course to pursue. He clashed not only with local Protestants, accusing them of fraud and proselytizing in administering educational endowments, but also with the communities of Christian Brothers and the Society of Jesus for flouting his authority in educational matters. The vehemence and mode of dealing with his antagonists and their motives, moreover, were most disconcerting. The worst aspect of this lack of charity, however, was to be found less in O'Dwyer's public quarrels than in the ruthless treatment of old friends who had the misfortune to fall from his favour.

But what was it that caused such a radical ambivalence in this remarkably gifted and conflicted man? Certainly, on one level, his local and ordinary jurisdiction, O'Dwyer exhibited an extraordinary need for imposing order and control. Both his strengths and his weaknesses reflected this need. Indeed, his obvious achievements as an administrator were as true a witness to this need as his over-reactions to being thwarted were an authentic testimony to his deep desire for that order and control. Still, while this deep psychological need explains much about O'Dwyer's behaviour, it does not account for all. How is one to explain, for example, his extraordinary conduct in matters where he had little jurisdiction and no real control? Why did he confront the Irish bishops as a body on all the great national issues of the day almost immediately on succeeding as a bishop, and then continue to remain a thorn in the side of the body with a breathtaking self-sufficiency as long as those issues remained real? Whether it was University Education, the Plan of Campaign, or the Fall of Parnell, O'Dwyer assumed a position contrary to that of the bishops as a body, and in the process acquired among the Irish people an unenviable reputation of being a 'Castle bishop' and a political outcast.

Two questions emerge as crucial, therefore, in this very convincing effort by Fr Morrissey to explain O'Dwyer's extraordinary behaviour. Why did O'Dwyer do what he did, and how did he manage to persevere in doing it for nearly thirty years? Because the how leads to a better understanding of the why in Fr Morrissey's presentation, it is perhaps more appropriate here to deal with it first. What Fr Morrissey makes perfectly clear is that in playing the great game of high politics in the Irish Church, O'Dwyer quickly learned that the Roman card was trumps. For thirty years he carefully cultivated the Roman authorities, and in the process he earned and retained the confidence of three successive popes. His influence at Rome became his effective counter-weight to the enormous pressure brought to bear on him by the Irish bishops as a body, and provided him with very considerable room for both manoeuvre and survival in the face of his episcopal colleagues.

The confidence of Rome, therefore, not only explains how O'Dwyer was able to sustain himself for so long, but also to a considerable degree, why he chose to do so. Certainly, a splendid ego, a sublime self-confidence, and an unintimidatible will, all contributed psychologically to his motivation. Even more important to his psyche, however, was his need to play the great game of high politics on his own terms, and when his episcopal colleagues insisted on his subordination in the interests of the priorities of the body, he decided to enter the game in the name of the Roman constituency, and thus become its representative and a significant player, in spite of his colleagues. The supreme irony, of course, is that in denouncing the British government in the person of its military governor, General Maxwell, after the Easter Rising in May 1916, for executing the leaders of that Rising, O'Dwyer became, after thirty years in the Irish political wilderness, a national hero overnight.

Once again, it only remains to say, all those who are interested in the history of the modern Irish Church are deeply indebted to Thomas J. Morrissey for this richly detailed and analytically impressive biography of one of most significant and difficult makers and shakers of that Church.

EMMET LARKIN

5 April 2003 The University of Chicago

Preface

Edward Thomas O'Dwyer was a figure of controversy in Ireland during the last quarter of the nineteenth and the first quarter of the twentieth century. Appointed bishop when quite young, a 'mere curate', frail and partly deaf, he was determined not to be taken lightly. He asserted himself almost immediately on the issues of university education and the methods employed by the Land League, defying, in the process, most of his fellow bishops, the Irish parliamentary party, and nationalist feeling. As a result, he was hailed by unionists for his honesty and courage, and spurned by nationalists as a 'Castle' and 'landlord' bishop. In his own diocese his assertiveness in educational matters led to public disputes with the Protestant community in regard to control of two schools, with the Jesuits in connection with Mungret College, and with the Christian Brothers over their school in Bruff and in relation to collections for the upkeep of their schools in the city. Others to experience his waspish assertiveness were Limerick businessmen, Limerick corporation, and the British government. What gave his criticisms particular strength were his fluency and power of language, his undoubted ability, and his readiness to challenge and insult powerful opponents. The most celebrated example was his defiant public letter to General Maxwell following the 1916 executions, a letter which stirred the nation, made him a national hero, and had people queuing to purchase copies of his pastoral letters. He died in the glow of popularity.

O'Dwyer's life, however, had not been characterised only by controversy. He devoted his energy and ability to improving the physical well-being of his people, to relieving the lot of the poor, to achieving better educational opportunities for the Irish people at primary, secondary and university level, to extending opportunities for teacher training, to providing improved hospital care in Limerick, and to reforming the system of workhouses throughout the country. In addition, he won papal recognition for his writing on theological matters, promoted the Irish language movement, and was a stout supporter of Horace Plunkett in his work for agricultural cooperation and improved farming methods. Despite his pugnacity, he had a lively sense of humour, was a gifted raconteur, and good company.

All in all, therefore, Bishop O'Dwyer was a far more complicated personality than he has frequently been depicted. In the view of one clergyman, writing from London, after the bishop's death in 1917, he was 'an able man, a strong man, for Ireland an unusual man'. His forthrightness was part of what made him unusual. He had little time for the usual Irish anxiety to please, the anodyne words to avoid offence. For Kate O'Brien, the novelist, whose family knew him well and who personally admired him, he was an 'autocrat', hard on his clergy, 'a man of iron principle and courage', a 'just man', and 'brilliant he was and looked, Edward Thomas O'Dwyer ... our difficult bishop'.[1]

A balanced picture of so controversial a person requires the compilation of a large amount of material from a wide range of sources. 'Be warned', Ecclesiastes declared (ch. 12), 'that writing books involves endless hard work.' In the present instance, the 'hard work' was greatly lightened by the pioneering research enshrined in two outstanding MA theses: 'Bishop Edward Thomas O'Dwyer and the Course of Irish Politics, 1870–1917' by Edward P. O'Callaghan, OFM, and 'Bishop O'Dwyer of Limerick 1886–1917 and the Educational Issues of his Time' by John Rushe. I am indebted to both authors for making their theses available to me, and to John (Sean) Rushe, in addition, for his articles on O'Dwyer in the *Old Limerick Journal* and for much additional background information on the bishop and his family. Research for this book has also been forwarded by the generous assistance of Jerome aan de Wiel during his time in Limerick. During the past three years research has been conducted in many archives. In Ireland, I am particularly indebted to the interest and support of Bishop Donal Murray, custodian of the O'Dwyer papers in the Limerick diocesan archives, to Bishop William Walsh and the archivist of the Killaloe diocese, to Archbishop Sean Brady for permission to work in the Armagh diocesan archives, to David Sheehy, yet again, for his assistance during my work in the Dublin diocesan archives over many years, to Fergus. O'Donoghue, SJ, archivist of the Irish Jesuit province, to Sr Elizabeth Ryan, FCJ, provincial, and Sr Eileen Keane, FCJ, for making available the Laurel Hill school chronicles and annals, and to Mark Tierney, OSB, for introducing me to the Glenstal Abbey archives. My thanks are also due to the librarians and officers of the National Library of Ireland, of Dublin University, and of University College Dublin, and to the most helpful officials of the National University of Ireland. Outside of Ireland the main centres of attention were the Irish College Rome, the central archives of the Irish Christian Brothers, Rome, and the archives of Propaganda Fide. The work in the archives of the Irish College and at Propaganda was undertaken with the gracious assistance and organisation of Monsignor John Fleming (now bishop of Killala) and Monsignor John Hanly. The important research at the Christian Brothers well-structured Roman archives was made possible by the General of the Brothers and facilitated by the welcoming archivist, Br Peter Fogarty. In Oxford, relevant material was unearthed in the diaries of Sir Horace Plunkett. I am indebted to Dr Trevor West of TCD for bringing this to my attention, and to Ms Kate Targett, Oxford, for her specialised knowledge of the diaries and her readiness to transcribe and share her knowledge.

---

1 'Christmas in the Presentation parlour', in *Old Limerick Journal*, 5.

This work, and my previous books, could not have been written without the abiding interest and encouragement of the Jesuit provincial, and of the members of my religious community. The search for books and extraneous knowledge was furthered as usual by Brendan Woods, SJ, of the Miltown Park library; copying, at a critical moment was readily performed by Eileen Toomey and Valerie Corrigan; assistance in computer expertise was generously provided by Conor Flynn, and by Conall O'Cuinn, SJ. I wish to acknowledge, too, the permission of Mr Justin Keating and the Keating family to avail of the striking painting by Sean Keating which adorns the cover, to thank the president of Maynooth College for permission to reproduce a painting of the young Bishop O'Dwyer, and to express my gratitude to Tom Keogh, Limerick City Museum, who kindly made available to me his remarkable collection of historical postcards. Once again I am deeply indebted to Professor Emmet Larkin, University of Chicago, for reading the manuscript, sharing his unique knowledge of the period, affirming the work, and agreeing to write the Foreword. Any mistakes remaining in the book are solely of my making.

Publication has been made possible by a generous grant-in-aid from Limerick diocese and from Bishop O'Dwyer's own foundation, Mary Immaculate Training College. There has also been welcome assistance from Limerick City Council. The result of these contributions is a publication worthy of the customary high standards of the Four Courts Press.

THOMAS J. MORRISSEY, SJ

List of illustrations

appearing between pages 212 and 213

CREDITS

Illustrations 1 and 2: courtesy Rt Revd Monsignor Dermot Farrell, president, St Patrick's College, Maynooth; 3 courtesy National Gallery of Ireland; all other illustrations save 4–6 and 11: courtesy Tom Keogh collection, Limerick City Museum.

PART ONE

Prelude to episcopacy, 1842–1886

Boyhood to early priesthood, 1842–1868

Edward Thomas O'Dwyer was born on 25 January 1842, at Holy Cross, Co. Tipperary,[1] into a family with a strong sense of history. The O'Dwyers of Kilnamanagh, in the south riding of Co. Tipperary, were one of the four septs, or forms of Gaelic clans, in the county – the O'Kennedys, O'Dwyers, O'Mulryans, and O'Meaghers – whose members included landowners, army officers and prominent clergymen. Extant records for the O'Dwyers go back to the thirteenth century. Among the clergy of note were two abbots of Holy Cross monastery, one in the fifteenth century and one who resigned in 1534 shortly before Henry VIII's suppression of the monasteries, and a bishop of Limerick, Edmund O'Dwyer, who sat as a spiritual peer on the supreme council of the Irish Confederacy, was present at the siege of Limerick by the Cromwellians in 1651, and escaped in the uniform of a soldier. He died at Brussels three years later.[2] His story was researched with interest by his nineteenth-century successor, Edward Thomas O'Dwyer.

The latter's father was named John Keatinge-O'Dwyer, a double-barrelled surname which suggested pride in another celebrated family connection. Arthur Young in his *Tour of Ireland* (1779),[3] wrote of a Keatinge estate as one of the greatest farms in Ireland, and the seventeenth-century author, Geoffrey Keatinge, published in the Irish language a celebrated history of Ireland up to the Norman invasion. John Keatinge-O'Dwyer took the Keatinge part of his name from his mother, the daughter of General Richard Keatinge of Bansha Castle, Co. Tipperary, and the sister of General Sir Henry Sheehy-Keatinge, KCB, who was governor of Mauritius for thirty years and who had a son, Sir Henry Keatinge, who was to be appointed a member of the privy council in 1887.[4] On the O'Dwyer side, John Keatinge-O'Dwyer's father, and Edward Thomas' grandfather, was Morgan O'Dwyer, JP, an extensive landowner at Cullen, Co. Tipperary, and one of the first Catholic magistrates appointed after the Act of Catholic Emancipation, 1829. Described as the 'owner of many horses', he brought the produce of his lands to the markets in Cork, and had many business interests.[5] It was said of the O'Dwyers that they 'hunted their own hounds in their own grounds';[6] and the future bishop was likely to have acquired his well-documented love of horses and his skill as a horseman from his father's side of the family.

Morgan O'Dwyer had at least two other sons and one daughter. One of the sons, Thomas Morgan O'Dwyer, after some time at Trinity College, Dublin, studied for the priesthood at the college of Propaganda Fide in Rome, where he was class-fellow of the future pope, Leo XIII. The other brother, Roger Keatinge-O'Dwyer, was said to have declined the offer of governor of Vancouver Island in order to stay on the family estate.[7] Their sister, Jane, married Michael Doheny, the Young Ireland revolutionary and song writer, who subsequently acted as editor of the *Phoenix* newspaper, which he founded with James Stephens and John O'Mahony, the inspirers of the Fenian movement. Doheny died in the United States in 1862; his wife, who also had strong nationalist views, died at Cashel in 1885.[8]

John Keatinge-O'Dwyer, the future bishop's father, also appears to have held strong patriotic views. His obituary in the *Limerick Recorder and Tipperary Vindicator,* on 20 February 1872, noted that in 1832–3 he was among the 'tithe martyrs', those Catholics who actively opposed having to pay tithes to the Established Church and endured 'a protracted imprisonment'.[9] He had studied for the priesthood at the Irish College, Paris, where he was reputed to have been gifted academically and to have been styled 'the silver tongue' because of his eloquence.[10] He left the seminary, having taken minor orders, and became an excise officer. He married Anne Quinlivan,[11] a cultured, self-assured young Limerick woman,[12] whose family were engaged in the flour-milling and corn trade. Their prosperity was indicated by the fact that her brother, Laurence Quinlivan, was mayor of Limerick in 1850, and later high sheriff; positions, especially that of mayor, which were held at that period only by men of considerable fortune.[13] Another brother, Michael Quinlivan, became a priest of the Killaloe diocese and died in 1904 as parish priest of Kilkee, Co. Clare.[14]

The forebears, then, of Edward Thomas O'Dwyer belonged to a section of the population who considered themselves of higher status than the ordinary working people and distinct from the planter ascendancy, though, like other Catholics of their class, they sometimes took on the loud-voiced assurance and even *hauteur* of the Ascendancy, and became like some of those Anglo-Irish gentry and squireens in their hard-riding, half-picturesque, irresponsible behaviour. These, 'at their best, were attractive, wilful perhaps, and quick-tempered, but generous too and fearless' – qualities that some recognised in Bishop O'Dwyer, but which were, in him, elevated and tempered by high ideals, religious commitment, and intellectual ability.[15]

Shortly after Edward Thomas' birth, his father was assigned to Limerick city. There the family settled. There were two other children, both girls. Kate, of whom little is known and who died in 1870, and Annie, who was two years older than her brother and entered the Congregation of the Sisters of Charity of St Paul the Apostle in September, 1857, taking the name Sr Mary Gonzaga. She was situated for many years at St Paul's Convent, Selly Park, Birmingham, where the congregation had its novitiate and a teacher-training college. Following her noviceship, she taught at the college. Later she resided at Banbury, near Oxford.[16]

Annie and her brother appear to have grown up together, and were very close. Their relationship reveals much about him. They corresponded regularly and she shared with him on her reading, the comments of visitors on political and church matters, and various aspects of convent and college life. On 21 April 1877, having chided him for not writing for some time, she confessed she could not stay angry with her 'old playfellow and brother' in whose love for her she had 'more faith than in anything save the Creed'.[17] Eleven years later, his importance in her life evoked the admission: 'One little word from you, spoken in any kind of tone, has more influence on my thoughts and conduct than all the books I have ever read.'[18] He, for his part, confident of her abiding support, disclosed to her what he would tell no other, and of this she was immensely proud.[19] He was also at hand to respond to her feelings of hurt or resentment,[20] and to smooth the way with her superior and members of her community. While he was still a curate, she asked him to write to the Revd Mother, observing shrewdly: 'The attention will please her immensely and do her good as well. She has a strong gift of faith as well as a natural liking for 'outward trappings' of rank. She often speaks of the French bishops, … of their state, their princely way of life etc and she thinks that the Irish bishops best resemble them in this.' As an added inducement, she included the Revd Mother's laudatory comment in his regard – 'I like him. Holiness and purity are stamped on his face.' O'Dwyer's letter and his subsequent visits to the convent made a life-long ally of the Revd Mother, even to her prescribing a report of one of his Sunday sermons as spiritual reading in the community.[21] He also wrote to other nuns at his sister's request, and on his visits to her convent went out of his way to chat with and charm all he met for her sake. She, in turn, had him, or their mother, send on copies of his Sunday sermons and, later, copies of his pastorals, and cuttings of his public letters and speeches, which she circulated in the community and distributed to interested visitors and outside acquaintances.

Annie's letters reflect also an extensive family kinship. Various family relations are mentioned, but none more often than their mother. Their father, who was dead before the first of Annie's extant letters,[22] is seldom mentioned and then, usually, as 'poor Pipity'. On 2 June 1890, on the occasion of Edward Thomas's visit to the Irish College, Paris, Annie remarked regretfully at what might have been – if only poor Pipity could 'have foreseen that a son of his a Bishop would one day give Orders in the college where he was spending the best years of his life'. It cannot have been easy for John Keatinge-O'Dwyer in an Ireland where a returned seminarian was viewed as 'a spoiled priest' and carried something of a stigma as a result. Annie's letters suggest something unfulfilled, something missing, where their father was concerned. The suggestion is heightened by the enigmatic, sparse newspaper reference to their sister Kate's death, on 27 October 1870. It merely reported: 'Deaths. O'Dwyer, at the residence of her father, Mallow, Co. Cork, Kate, daughter of John Keatinge O'Dwyer Esq.'.[23] The omission of any reference to other members of the family, or to relations, and the mention of the father's residence at Mallow, rather than Limerick, raises questions about Edward's and Annie's family life and whether their parents were separated.

Their affection for their mother, *née* Anne Quinlivan, is very evident. Annie mentions her regularly and is concerned for her. Edward brought her to live with him when he was made bishop, and she furnished the episcopal residence and oversaw its day-to-day running. Some twelve letters of hers, which have survived, indicate that she was a cultured woman of strong views and a strong religious faith. She also seems to have had a good business head. The Limerick diocesan archives have a number of documents in her name dealing with stocks and shares.[24] Her son, it may be noted, had extensive dealings of a similar nature. He appears, moreover, to have been quite punctilious in business matters to judge from the manner in which he took to task the very able archbishop of Dublin, Dr William Walsh, on 18 October and 2 November 1886, over the 'careless' manner in which the Training College account was kept. He even suggested that the person responsible, Bishop Francis McCormack, should be reported to Propaganda Fide.[25]

John Keatinge-O'Dwyer's 'failure' to complete his studies for the priesthood, and his subsequent position as excise officer, ensured that his family was not wealthy like other related branches of the O'Dwyers, but they retained their family pride and sense of distinction. If the parents separated, there is no evidence that the children were neglected. Edward, indeed, as the only boy in a house of three women, appears to have been a focus of attention, and this, combined with his evident intelligence and fluency, bolstered his self-esteem. His later life, not surprisingly, gave testimony to a strong self-assurance, a desire to be a centre of attention and to have his own way. In his home he also received, however, deep Christian values, which included concern for those who were poor in material possessions and opportunity. Hence, self-centred insensitivity tended to vie with generosity and sympathy in his treatment of others.

EDUCATION

Edward received his primary schooling from the Irish Christian Brothers at Sexton Street, Limerick. His ability and application earned the distinction of 'the gold watch prize', and he also gained a reputation for energy and fearlessness in coping with aggression from an older boy.[26] For secondary or intermediate education he was sent to a school in the small town of Doon, Co. Limerick, in the diocese of Cashel and Emly. There, he seems to have attended as a boarder, and had as his Classics teacher Fr John Ryan, subsequently bishop of Limerick.[27] When Edward indicated that he wished to become a priest, he was accepted for the Limerick diocese by Bishop Ryan.[28] This required him to attend for a while at the diocesan college of St Munchin, at Hartstonge Street, Limerick, which had just been entrusted by the bishop to the care of the Jesuits. He was one of the first students under the new management.[29] In that first year, 1859–60, the school was finding its way and had not a rhetoric or senior class. The curriculum available included the Ancient Classics, Mathematics, English, French, and an introduction to German. First place in the overall aggregate was secured by O'Dwyer.[30] Nothing else is recorded of his time at the school. It is possible that his future hostility towards the Society of Jesus, especially in his own diocese, had its roots in this year.[31] In 1860, at eighteen years of age, he moved on to Maynooth College.

At Maynooth, he showed conspicuous ability, coming in the first three or four places in each subject without unduly extending himself. The professor of Humanity in Maynooth at the time, Edward O'Brien, recalling him years later, observed somewhat elliptically that he was 'a clever accomplished man who could dig six feet down into any subject with perfect ease and security, but if he went an inch lower the whole structure fell on him. He had the good sense, however, to know where to stop.'[32]

O'Dwyer appears to have read widely and deeply, particularly in areas which interested him. He could never abide, Bishop Michael Fogarty of Killaloe remarked, 'mere summaries of knowledge'. He went to the sources, and as a student his favourite readings were in Scriptural Studies and the Fathers of the Church, especially Augustine and Ambrose.[33] O'Dwyer's academic results during his years at Maynooth read as follows. In 1860–1, when there was a range of studies under the heading 'Rhetoric', he obtained second place overall. The following year, when the subjects were fewer and more closely studied, he gained second place in Logic, and third in 'Gallican Languages'. In 1862–3, when the year's subjects were Mathematics and Natural Philosophy, he obtained first in each. In 1863–4 he was third in Dogmatic and Moral Theology, but first in Ecclesiastical History. The next year, when there were four main subject areas, he was fourth in Dogmatic and Moral Theology, second in Ecclesiastical History, third in Irish Language, and second in Catechetics/Sacred Eloquence. In 1865–66 he gained first place in Sacred Eloquence, third in Dogmatic and Moral Theology, and third in Sacred Scripture. In his final year, 1866–7, he did not figure in the prize list because he was called home for early ordination in February 1867.[34]

In O'Dwyer's class there were Peadar Ua Laoghaire (Peter O'Leary), subsequently a distinguished Irish language scholar and author, and four others who became bishops: James Browne of Ferns (1884–1919), Robert Browne of Cloyne (1894–1935), Joseph Hoare of Ardagh (1895–1927), and John Healy, who became coadjutor bishop of Clonfert in 1884, and archbishop of Tuam (1895–1918). Of these, Healy and O'Dwyer were the leading figures academically, and overall, with the exception of James Murphy of Dublin, a rather eccentric man of great ability but poor judgment,[35] they were the most successful scholars in their year. It is, perhaps, indicative of O'Dwyer's standing at Maynooth that his closest friend there, and for some years afterwards, was a brilliant student two years ahead of him academically, William J. Walsh, soon to become a professor, and subsequently president of the college and archbishop of Dublin.

Called home by his bishop, George Butler, who had succeeded Dr Ryan in 1864, O'Dwyer was ordained in St John's Cathedral, Limerick, on 10 February

1867. Having his theological studies curtailed, seemed in no way to undermine his confidence in himself or his assurance in theological matters. A month after his ordination the Fenian rising took place. All his life he was reputed to have empathised with the hopeless daring of the scattered Fenian bands.[36] The following year he became caught up in a bitter controversy related to politics and to his former Jesuit teachers.

POLITICS, EDUCATION, AND THE JESUITS

By the time of O'Dwyer's ordination some tension appeared to have arisen between Bishop Butler and the Limerick Jesuits, who had moved their school to a more central location nearby, the Crescent, Limerick. Dr Butler had waged a successful campaign against the government-supported primary school in the city, the Model School. He discouraged parents from sending their children, and to cater for these mainly poorer children he prevailed on the Jesuits to agree to open a special school at Bedford Row. The problem for the Jesuits, apart from manpower, was finance, as only a very small fee could be charged. The bishop refused to contribute financially, but, according to the then Jesuit rector, Fr Edward Kelly, had talked of setting up a rival Latin school to their St Munchin's College if they did not undertake the new school.[37] The Jesuit provincial, Fr Edmund O'Reilly, a former priest of the diocese and a highly esteemed professor at Maynooth, wrote to the bishop on 4 February 1864, regretting that the school had been undertaken by the Order and giving notice of future withdrawal.[38] The institution lasted only from March 1864 to June 1865, and did not successfully cater for the class of pupil the bishop had in mind; instead, its low fees were availed of by reasonably well off parents who sought to use the school as a preparatory academy for St Munchin's College. In 1865 the Jesuits announced their withdrawal, declaring their inability to continue and suggesting that the pupils in need could now be catered for in the recently expanded Christian Brothers' school.[39]

Two years later, without any apparent connection or sign of conflict with the Order, Dr Butler decided to open his own seminary college.[40] The decision led to tension between some of the local clergy and the Jesuits, and this came very much to the fore late in 1868 on the occasion of a general election. The candidates in Limerick were: Major Gavin and William Francis Russell on the Liberal side, supporting Gladstone's disestablishment of the Anglican church in Ireland, and opposing them a combination of the Tory, Peter Tait, mayor of the city and a major employer, and Richard Piggott, who, a short time previously, had been editor of a Fenian newspaper. The bishop called together his clergy to decide whom to support. In the era before the introduction of the secret ballot, 1872, the decision of the bishop and his clergy carried considerable weight with the voting Catholic population. The decision was for the Liberal candidates. The Jesuits, for some reason, perhaps fear of the disenfranchised mob supporting Peter

Tait or disagreement as to which side to support, decided unwisely not to vote. In an election marked by intense feeling, and by riots resulting in the death of one man,[41] the diocesan clergy were incensed by the neutrality of the Jesuits, which, other matters aside, was taken as a reflection on their decision. 'The Limerick priests are so vexed with Ours for not voting', the then Jesuit rector, Thomas Kelly, reported, 'that they have offered and urged to open an opposition school at the Crescent.' 'Our pupil O'Dwyer', he added, 'is at the head' of the critics.[42] Two years later, on 3 August 1870, Kelly was to announce that the diocesan priests were 'cutting off' from the Crescent boys from the country and the city, and that very few of the senior class might attend in September. 'Many in Limerick dislike the way we are treated,' he explained, 'and send away their children unwillingly.'[43] In the event, such a large number of pupils had moved already by 1869 to the new diocesan college that it had a full complement of students, whereas the Jesuit school languished.[44] O'Dwyer's prominence as a leading opponent, so soon after his ordination, indicated an exceptional strength of personality and a capacity to verbalise opposition. These were not qualities, however, that guaranteed popularity in a parish.

2

The curate. A difficult apprenticeship, 1867–74

Edward O'Dwyer's early years as a priest appear to have been troubled and unsure. In eight years he was in eight different parishes. The precise reason for so many changes has not been established, but anecdotal evidence suggests that his loud, assertive manner (linked, perhaps, to his poor hearing), fluency, wit and wilfulness created problems for parish priests and fellow curates. One such anecdote, which persisted in clerical memory, underlined his reputation for getting his own way. Finding that his bedroom in a rural parish was cold, he requested that he might have a fire in his room. The parish priest refused. Thereafter for some nights the pastor was unable to sleep because of thunderous sound in the room above his. On enquiring the cause of this noise, his young curate informed him that he had to jump up and down before going to bed in order to get his feet warm![1] He got his fire, but he was moved before long.

O'Dwyer's curacies in the first eight years were: St Patrick's parish, Limerick city, in the spring of 1867;[2] Rathkeale, Co. Limerick, summer 1867; Capagh, autumn 1867; Bruff, February 1868; St Patrick's, Limerick city, again, November 1868; Adare, 1870; Newcastle West, 1872; Shanagolden, 1874.[3]

Initially, prospects looked very good. His striking appearance, ready charm and intelligence were in his favour. In the summer of 1867, while he was on holiday in Kilkee, Co. Clare, where his family, like many Limerick families, holidayed, and where he enjoyed the reputation of being a strong swimmer and daring diver,[4] he met with the parish priest of Rathkeale, Dr James O'Shea. The latter was much taken by him. His admiration grew when, in the course of a debate with a Protestant minister staying in the same hotel, O'Dwyer displayed a mastery of subject, keenness of argument, and clarity of exposition. O'Shea determined to request the bishop to appoint him to Rathkeale. The bishop agreed. Young O'Dwyer's practical judgment, however, did not match his academic sharpness. He undertook his work as curate with energy and zeal, but introduced novelties that tried the patience of his well-disposed pastor. Within a short time he was moved to the small parish of Cappagh, and from there to Bruff. There, too, he seems to have alienated the parish priest as, after eight months, he was moved once more. He spent the Christmas of 1868 back in St Patrick's parish in the city. In 1870 he found a favourable haven.[5] He was appointed to Adare, a picturesque village and parish some nine miles south west of Limerick city, where the pastor was not one towards whom he could feel intellectually or socially superior, and where, indeed, the social ambience was superior to that of the most exalted members of his family. The parish priest, John Stanislaus Flanagan (1821–1905), had been prominent in his youth in social life and on the hunting field, and then had gone to study for the priesthood at Saint Sulpice in Paris. He joined the Oratorians in 1848 and two years later was ordained at Oscott. He remained with the Oratorians until 1865, during which time he showed himself 'a sound and well read theologian' and became friendly with John Henry Newman.[6] In 1865 he returned to Ireland as chaplain to Lord Dunraven, whose main residence was in Adare and who, together with two other gentry in West Limerick, the poet Aubrey de Vere and William Monsell, later Lord Emly, had been part of the Oxford Movement, friends of Newman, and converts to Catholicism. Flanagan's cultivated social graces, intellectual ability, friendship with Newman, and wide reading made him a welcome addition to the Dunraven circle and he became confidant and friend to members of the Dunraven family as well as to Monsell, de Vere, and others. Through Dunraven's influence he was made parish priest of Adare. Taken by O'Dwyer's ability and manners, he became something of a father figure to the young man. He encouraged his reading, keeping him up to date over the years with new publications, especially in theology, promoted his interest in the writings of Newman, introduced him to Dunraven, de Vere and Monsell, with whom, and other members of the gentry, O'Dwyer was to become friendly and, in the eyes of his critics, over-identified. The curate's interest in horses was also fostered by Flanagan, and he soon showed himself a fearless rider and a keen judge of horseflesh.

In 1870, also, O'Dwyer displayed his political sympathies in a very open manner. That year, Isaac Butt stood as a parliamentary candidate for the city of Limerick. For years he had been a prominent unionist and barrister and then had acquired standing with the nationalist population by his legal defence of the leaders of the 1848 and of the Fenian rebellions. His political sympathies, moreover, underwent change and he became the founder of the Home Rule movement. Of special significance, too, for O'Dwyer was the fact that Butt's grandfather, also Isaac Butt, lived in Adare, that his father, a pastor of the Established Church, had been born there, and that Butt himself as a boy had spent holidays in the village. Butt's policies, his intelligence, political and social prominence, and Adare connection, made a combination with a powerful appeal for O'Dwyer, and he became an enthusiastic supporter at a time when few priests indicated any interest. He stood on the same hustings with Butt in 1871, and they became close friends.

In 1872 O'Dwyer was promoted to Newcastle West as curate to the elderly Dean Richard O'Brien, who was respected as a scholar and patriot. He settled in well, became friendly with the other curate, John Carrick, who was also a native of Limerick city, and acquired a reputation throughout the locality as a preacher.[7] His well-prepared sermons, imaginatively presented, and delivered quickly in a 'twanging, high pitched, but clear and cultivated voice',[8] attracted large congregations. His learning was admired and his strong patriotic sentiments respected. He was on the crest of a wave, and then his very eloquence, in its cutting and forthright form, helped to alienate large sections of the parish. The occasion was the parliamentary vacancy caused by elevation to the peerage in 1873 of William Monsell, who for many years had represented the county of Limerick at Westminster.

UNPLEASANT POLITICAL INTERLUDE

The campaign to fill the seat took place in the context of the general election of 1874. To select an appropriate candidate was important. Dr Butler called a meeting of his priests to discuss the matter. One candidate, John James Kelly, Rockstown Castle, whose father had been a member of the Repeal Association many years earlier, had issued his manifesto on 23 December 1873.[9] He was a young man of good social position and well-educated. The clergy were favourably disposed towards him, and the advocacy of the 'young, boyish looking' O'Dwyer on behalf of Kelly made a strong impression.[10] A resolution in support of Kelly was passed by 80 votes to 3, and the clergy's support was made public.[11] William Monsell, now Lord Emly, also expressed support for Kelly. The latter's manifesto placed denominational education at the head of his priorities, followed by Home Rule, 'further amelioration' of the conditon of tenant farmers, and the release of Fenian prisoners.[12]

Another aspirant, William Henry O'Sullivan, a shopkeeper-publican and a tenant farmer in Kilmallock, was a prominent and popular nationalist, but without Kelly's education and social standing. He put forward much the same priorities as Kelly but in different order. He placed Home Rule first and denominational education second, and he was more definite in his aims for the tenant farmers, and more persuasive in his promise to work for the release of prisoners in that he was able to point to his own experience of prison as a Fenian. He added a further promise, namely, to work to alleviate the miserable condition of the labouring class.[13] The Limerick Farmers Club decided to support O'Sullivan as most likely to represent their interests. The stage was thereby set for a bitter struggle. It became virtually a class struggle, with churchmen and landlords seen as supporting Kelly, and the ordinary people and 'true nationalists' the other candidate. O'Dwyer added to the bitterness. His vehement support for Kelly appears to have rested on two considerations: that Kelly was a more fitting replacement for Monsell and more likely to hold his own among the well educated, sophisticated members at Westminster than O'Sullivan, and the second consideration, it may be surmised from his later emphasis on education, was that Kelly made denominational education his top priority.

O'Dwyer took sides with characteristic forthrightness. On 3 January 1874, the day O'Sullivan's manifesto appeared, he had a letter in the *Munster News*, which announced that O'Sullivan was 'not qualified to represent this great country' and that in terms alone of 'personal unfitness' his election to parliament would be 'most disastrous'. He was not in the same class as Butt, Shaw, Martin or Blennerhasset, who had represented the Irish cause with distinction.[14] Turning to one of O'Sullivan's strong points with the popular electorate, namely, his having been imprisoned as a Fenian, O'Dwyer asserted that his arrest had been the result of an error – that, far from taking an active part in the 1867 rising, O'Sullivan had publicly abjured any connection with the Fenians. He went on to point out that 'nationalist' covered Home Rulers as well as Fenians, and that he, while respecting the political views of Fenians, was a convinced Home Ruler. In deference to truth and honesty, O'Dwyer acknowledged that Kelly's father had to answer for the unjust treatment of his tenants in the past and that some of the responsibility for this descended on his son. He proposed that a court of inquiry be set up for the purpose of assessing the amount of restitution that should be paid to those tenants so that J.J. Kelly's name might be fully cleared.[15]

The clergy in their public pronouncement on 10 January made it clear that they did not in any way wish to dictate, only to offer their honest opinion. Their pronouncement coincided in essentials, however, with what O'Dwyer had already stated. It was important that Limerick elect to parliament 'a man of education, intelligence, position and ability'. They judged Kelly to be such, while the election of O'Sullivan would be 'a complete disaster' for Limerick and, indeed, for Home Rule since he was known to represent 'extreme views', separation rather than Home Rule. To the charge that Kelly's father had been an 'exterminator', the priests claimed that this was much exaggerated and that in Kelly's own case it did not apply.[16]

In the contest neither side spared the other. On the day after O'Dwyer's letter, O'Sullivan happened to be holding a political meeting at Newcastle West where O'Dwyer was curate. He availed of the occasion to criticise him in turn. This was followed by a scathing, personalised letter from O'Dwyer in which he referred to O'Sullivan's poor command of the English language at the Newcastle West meeting. His style, he pronounced, was 'better known in stable yards than in the society in which Mr O'Sullivan is trying to get pitch-forked'.[17] A week later at a meeting in his native Kilmallock, O'Sullivan referred to O'Dwyer as 'the Newcastle slanderer', which, predictably, drew another broadside from the 'slanderer'. This time he focussed on O'Sullivan's claims to Fenian connections. He was not worthy, declared O'Dwyer, 'to be named on the same day' with those who had risked their lives in 1867. He had in open court, O'Dwyer alleged, disowned on oath the cause for which he claimed he had suffered, and that 'solely for the paltry profits of a public house'.[18]

Kelly, as might be expected, used O'Dwyer's cutting sarcasm to his own advantage.[19] As the campaign progressed there were occasions when priests were hooted, and other occasions when priests led mobs against O'Sullivan's supporters.[20] At Askeaton and Rathkeale there were riots, and at the former town, where there was strong support for O'Sullivan, the parish priest was openly insulted, and a man named O'Donoghue lost his life in a clash with the police.[21]

On 7 February in the *Munster News*, O'Dwyer criticised the violence manifested in O'Sullivan's campaign, claiming that 'raging mobs' followed him round, from meeting to meeting, and turned peaceful towns into 'bear gardens'. He also made use in the same letter of the old argument that those who supported O'Sullivan were 'going in the teeth' of their bishops and priests, and, moreover, were effectively associating themselves with known bigots like the landowner, Delmege, and Church of Ireland Archdeacon Gould. Any support for O'Sullivan, he maintained, gave 'sanction and help to violence and tyranny'.[22]

Despite O'Dwyer's view that O'Sullivan was unsuitable on social and educational grounds, Butt appears to have favoured O'Sullivan to Kelly, and to have suggested to him, in the first instance, to go forward. He rightly judged that he had the better chance of being elected.[23] He declined, however, to make his views public, though he attended a Farmers Club meeting in Kilmallock at which O'Sullivan was present, as also a considerable number of clergy from the archdiocese of Cashel and Emly.[24] As voting time drew near he departed for England until all was over. In the outcome, O'Sullivan was successful; and his victory was represented as a victory for advanced nationalism over liberal unionism, and as a defeat for the priest and the landlord in politics.

When the results were announced, O'Dwyer wrote to the *Munster News* and, though he alluded to some remarks made about him by O'Sullivan after the election, he made it clear that he had no hard feelings. He called for peace, and expressed the hope that there would be a united nationalist front in Limerick for the future.[25] Years later, on his first episcopal visit to Kilmallock, he went out of his way to call on O'Sullivan, who was then retired from politics. Subsequently, he granted the rare concession of allowing O'Sullivan's body be interred in the grounds of the parish church.[26] From petty vituperation to magnanimity – a reflection of O'Dwyer's complex personality.

Shortly after these events, in April 1874, he was transferred to Shanagolden, Co. Limerick. His many admirers in Newcastle West rallied round and at 'a large meeting' in Foynes presented him, as a mark of their regard, with a purse of sovereigns representing 'numerous subscriptions'.[27] Less benign memories of him, however, were retained by many tenant farmers and radical republicans. They identified him with the educated and the well-to-do, judging that he had little concern for their rights and needs and was but a half-hearted nationalist Their assumptions later found expression during O'Dwyer's opposition to the tenants' scheme of collective bargaining on individual estates known as the Plan of Campaign, and were to be reflected also in the vigour and venom of the opposition to him during a long dispute over the withdrawal of the Christian Brothers from Bruff. The defeat of O'Dwyer's candidate in 1874 remained a persistent memory. At a public meeting in Limerick at the time of his episcopal opposition to the Plan of Campaign, William O'Brien, MP, sensing the mood of the crowd, remarked, to loud applause, that it was 'a most singular thing' that the bishop seemed to possess the special faculty for being on the wrong side in politics 'in every action of his life'.[28]

Despite O'Dwyer's political activities and unsettled record, he remained well regarded by his bishop. On 3 June 1874, following an apology from O'Dwyer for his delay in obtaining signatories for a particular memorial, Butler assured him that he did not feel surprised at not hearing from him, 'being well aware that with you no time will be lost'.[29] Within months of O'Dwyer's arrival at Shanagolden, a vacancy occurred at St Michael's parish in Limerick, which the bishop considered particularly suitable for him. It was an important appointment. O'Dwyer's travels were over. At St Michael's, a city parish, he found scope for his immense energy and many talents, and demonstrated that he had learned something from his protracted apprenticeship. There, he made the impact that led to his choice as bishop by his fellow priests.

3

St Michael's parish: meeting needs,
1874–1886

St Michael's parish is one of the five Limerick city Catholic parishes that have
survived from medieval times.[1] After 1838 it became a bishop's parish, with an
administrator rather than a parish priest Edward O'Dwyer was sent to the parish
when the administrator, John Mulqueen, fell ill. He soon made his mark in the
church by his eloquent sermons which drew large congregations, and by his
energetic involvement in the social needs of the parish.

CONCERN FOR TEMPERANCE

One of the first of these needs was to counter the desolation being caused by
alcohol, especially among the working-class population. To provide an alternative to the public house a temperance hall had been established, but it had had
little effect.[2] O'Dwyer, a teetotaller all his life, with a deep awareness of the
degradation occasioned by alcoholic indulgence,[3] set about making the hall a
centre of attraction. His enthusiasm infected a group of young men, and these
became his co-organisers in developing both indoor amusements and an outdoor athletic club.

Not content with such measures, however, he lobbied for the Sunday closing
of public houses, and became a spokesman for a resolution, backed by the
Catholic and Protestant bishops and clergy, calling on 'the legislature to pass into
law next session a bill to close public houses on Sunday uniformly throughout
Ireland'. It was not a resolution likely to appeal to members of the Home Rule
party, which received funding from the brewing interests and the Vintners
Association. At Limerick courthouse on 13 November 1877, a public meeting,
presided over by the mayor, James Spaight, JP, was held to debate the resolution.
A large gathering of clergy and of the working class attended, and also,
unexpectedly, a considerable number of publicans, led by the secretary of the
Vintners Association from Dublin.

The atmosphere in the courthouse was tense. O'Dwyer, as spokesman for the
resolution, pleaded in his opening remarks for reasoned argument, not clamour.
Soon, however, he added to the tension himself. He accused the mayor of
rigging the meeting in favour of the publicans by inviting so many of them to

attend, and declared that had 'the temperance people' known about this they could have had 'a far more respectable crowd' present. Amid some disorder, the mayor denied the accusation. O'Dwyer then explained that he would not support the Sunday closing if he were not convinced it would benefit the people. He was shouted down, and the vintners' representative, Mr Godsel, called him 'a humbug', and demanded 'fair play'. O'Dwyer responded defiantly that he was prepared 'to stand there till night if he would not be allowed to proceed (cheers)'. He then proceeded to describe the horror and misery caused by excessive drinking which he had encountered in St Michael's parish. He had seen people of the city 'reduced to the lowest depths of degradation' in this court. A publican shouted at him to confine himself to the facts of the case. O'Dwyer, according to the *Limerick Reporter and Tipperary Vindicator* of 14 November 1877, replied by taking off his coat, to the cheers of the crowd, and asserting that 'Sunday closing would not be an effectual cure for drunkenness, but it would break its back' (laughter). Amid cries of 'Shut up' he referred at length to the evidence given before a committee of the House of Commons on the Sunday Closing Bill, and challenged the crowd –

> Will you vote for yourselves and sobriety or will you vote for Whisky interests? (Confusion). That is the issue.

A voice shouted 'Shut up', and 'at this juncture', as the report observed obscurely, 'a very disgraceful scene occurred, and a man in the crowd pointed a stick at the speaker'.

O'Dwyer remained undeterred, and eventually won out when an amendment to the resolution was lost. Several people then sought to speak but were prevented by the uproar until the meeting broke up.[4] The boyish, frail-looking curate had demonstrated that he would not be steamrolled or intimidated. Nearly a hundred years later, Dean Punch, ordained in 1910, and noted for his own fearlessness during his long life, observed summarily – 'The man was afraid of nothing.'[5]

IMPROVING EDUCATIONAL AND CULTURAL STANDARDS

As well as improving conditions for mainly working-class people, O'Dwyer determined to provide opportunities for self-improvement to those on a slightly higher social level – such as the drapers' and grocers' assistants, many of whom lived in lodgings in the city. There was already in existence at the Dominican church and residence a literary society, run by the prior, Fr J.J. Carbery, aided by Maurice Lenihan, editor of the *Limerick Reporter and Tipperary Vindicator*, which catered for such young men. Debates were held and papers presented, which were published in the *Reporter*. The clergy of St Michael's parish, however, notably O'Dwyer, believed that they should be catering for such young men themselves. Learning that the Munster and Leinster Bank was moving from its extensive premises at the junction of Sarsfield Street and Henry Street, O'Dwyer managed to purchase the site 'in his own account and with the credit of his uncle, Laurence Quinlivan, corn merchant'.[6] There, he established the Limerick Catholic Literary Institute, a venture that manifested in many ways O'Dwyer's wide horizons and idealistic hopes.

'During my time on the mission,' he informed a meeting of the Limerick Catholic Institute in October, 1900, referring to his time as a curate, 'I tried to take part in every movement for the social and intellectual improvement of the city, and it is my wish to see the clergy always act on the same principle. In an especial manner it should be their aim to lead the people in intellectual and educational movements.'[7] In keeping with this, he had arranged at the foundation of the Institute that it be governed by a council consisting of a president, vice-president, spiritual director, treasurer, two secretaries, and fifteen other members, and that three of the council, exclusive of the spiritual director, should be priests, and not subject to popular vote like the other members. He sought, moreover, to have the council 'constituted, if possible, of the very cream of our Catholic laymen';[8] and, as a headline to such participation, the first president of the Institute was his good friend Richard O'Shaughnessy, BA, BL, MP, the son of an eminent Limerick surgeon, a graduate of Trinity College Dublin, a committed Catholic, and a highly respected public figure.

O'Dwyer's conception of his literary institute was a place where 'facilities for self-improvement' were 'joined to reasonable amusement',[9] but his emphasis was on self-improvement. He thought of the venture as primarily engaged in 'the promotion of literary and scientific study, and the cultivation of artistic taste among the Catholic young men of Limerick' by means of 'lectures, private classes in various subjects, as the number may require, and by means of a library, consulting and circulating.'[10] Young women were also welcome, for O'Dwyer, as the novelist Kate O'Brien recalled, 'was a man with an unexpected regard for the brains of women'.[11] O'Shaughnessy, however, in his inaugural lecture, with unconscious condescension, made it clear that the women's role was to be restricted and ancillary. They might avail of the library where there were 'readable books … within the literary range which is dearest to a lady's mind', but they might not 'enter on any masculine enterprise' or 'become advocates of women's rights' but might rather engage 'in works of charity' and, in general, by their presence and decorum, exert a refining influence in the Institute which sought 'the cultivation and happiness of the young men of this city'![12] The president in his address emphasised, as was to be expected, the Institute's dual objectives of cultural development and amusement. The main opportunities for the latter were: indoor – billiards, chess, and the use of a gym; and outdoor – cricket, some athletics and other sports. The cultural side, as indicated, included a library, reading room, classes, and public lectures. To O'Dwyer's and O'Shaughnessy's regret the demand for the cultural aspect was to prove disappointing.

An extensive library was built up, but was little used. The membership of the Institute attained 350 in its first year, and rose to a peak of 570 in 1878, but at no stage did more than one fifth of these become subscribers to the library.[13] The main attention was elsewhere – the billiard room, the gymnasium, and the reading room, which, already in 1876, was supplied with almost all the leading Irish and English papers and periodicals.[14] The poor demand for the library was, perhaps, not surprising considering that only a small number of the members had secondary education.

The greatest disappointment from O'Dwyer's point of view was the poor demand for further education. Subjects such as History, Science, English, Irish, French, Commerce and so on were offered, with an examination and certificate available for some of them, but few people availed of them. The areas which achieved some success were those requiring less application: tonic sol-fa, ladies' callisthenics and, to a lesser degree, essay and debating classes. From these last developed in time annual concerts and a lively dramatic society. The one other area of some success was that of public lectures. Prominent figures from the world of politics, law, religion, education, science, medicine, and some major literary figures, addressed public audiences over many years. An analysis of some 101 lectures given at the Institute, demonstrates that 21 dealt with aspects of history, 18 with travel, 10 with some aspect of religion, 8 with education, 8 with science and medicine, 8 with literature, and 5 with music.[15] The topics chosen appealed to a more sophisticated audience, and the lecturers were recognised leaders in their fields, and usually Catholics – all of which added lustre to the Institute.

Down the years the cultural side was challenged by the need to meet popular demand and the Institute's financial needs by expanding the amusement side. This led to differences between lay and clerical members of the council, and to a gradual lack of interest on the part of the clergy and of those seeking the more cultural aspects of the Institute. The venture required dynamic leadership and much commitment, and this was not available from Dr O'Dwyer after his election to the episcopacy; it is doubtful, indeed, if he would have committed himself continually to the Institute as a priest in the absence of interest in learning. His interest in education always vied with more immediately pastoral desires, and he was not prepared to devote himself exclusively to teaching, or the administration of teaching, especially when students were poorly motivated and not gifted intellectually. In 1900, on the 25th anniversary of the Institute, he expressed with typical forthrightness and some exaggeration, his disappointment at the failure of his original vision.

> From the commencement one of the greatest difficulties with which we had to contend in this Institute was to keep it from sinking into a mere social club. It was often a wearisome and almost hopeless task to try and get our members to devote themselves to anything in the nature of continuous work or study. We began classes of various kinds, got excellent masters, did what we could to make them attractive, and yet they always

dwindled down to very small proportions and finally vanished. Why this
was so I cannot tell. We found a deplorable want of education amongst the
young men in the shops. I do not speak of anything approaching scientific
or literary culture, but the very rudiments of the English language
were unknown to many of them. As for foreign languages – French or
German – they were quite outside our reach. Still nothing we could do
could keep our classes together. I fear there is something deficient in our
national character. We want perseverance; we are impatient of labour; we
are unwilling to wait for results.[16]

This want of perseverance and unwillingness to wait for results that he applied
to students might, perhaps, have been applied to himself by his own bishop after
he appointed him to teach and administer the diocesan college of St Munchin.

FIRST INVOLVEMENT IN SCHOOL WORK. THE BACKGROUND

A brief history of the college is essential to an understanding of that appointment and of future events. On 10 March 1859 St Munchin's diocesan college,
which had virtually collapsed during the 1850s, was reopened at No. 1
Hartstonge Street, Limerick, as already noticed, as a day school under Jesuit
management. The aim of the college was outlined in its prospectus: 'In this
college ... young gentlemen receive a sound, refined and Catholic education.
They are prepared for the university and the ecclesiastical college; for the learned
professions; for public service – civil and military; and for the departments of
mercantile and commercial life.'[17] The basic reason for which St Munchin's was
founded, namely the education of students for the priesthood, was now being
fulfilled within a wider context and at the intermediate or secondary level of
education. In 1862 the Jesuits bought Richmond House at the centre of the
Crescent, Limerick, quite near to the original college at 1 Hartstonge Street,
which was at the corner of the Crescent. The school now functioned on the two
sites. Before long it became evident that the Jesuits, who also had opened a
public church at the Crescent, were finding it difficult to combine the work of
school, church, and the many demands they were receiving for retreats. They
undertook a school at Bedford Row unwillingly, as has been seen, and had to
withdraw from it. There was no prospect of additional men being provided by
the Jesuit provincial. The province was over-stretched. A school had been opened
at Galway, shortly after Limerick, and in 1865 the Irish Jesuit mission to Australia
was undertaken. When, therefore, a diocesan priest, Fr Joseph Bourke, proposed
in 1867 that he assume responsibility for 1 Hartstonge Street, and train students
for the diocese there, both the bishop and the Jesuits were relieved. There were
not lacking, it may be assumed, priests other than O'Dwyer to advise the bishop
that a number of his best prospective candidates were likely to be enticed to join
the Jesuits in a college under Jesuit management. After all, ever since the days of

the highly popular Jesuit, Peter Kenney, as vice-president of Maynooth, many secular priests and students had joined the Society of Jesus, and three of the current Jesuit community at Limerick, as well as the provincial, were former Maynooth men. Archbishop Paul Cullen was later to observe that in Dublin, contrary to his expectations, the schools of the various religious orders – Carmelites, Augustinians, Marists, Jesuits, Vincentians, and Holy Ghosts – provided scarcely any vocations to the diocese. Instead, as he wrote to Monsignor Tobias Kirby in Rome, 'the religious orders get all'.[18]

Fr Bourke financed his project from his own resources, and launched it with the aid of one diocesan priest It was advertised in the *Irish Catholic Directory* of 1872 as Limerick Diocesan Seminary, but it continued as previously to cater for a wide range of subjects and careers. Within a few years it outshone the Jesuit school at the Crescent. This was largely occasioned, as mentioned previously, by the stormy parliamentary election of 1868 when the Liberals, George Gavin and William Francis Russell, were opposed by a Scots Presbyterian and Tory, Peter Tait, and the former editor of a Fenian newspaper, Richard Piggott, and the Jesuits' decided not to vote in the election. Already, by 1876/77, Bourke was able to announce that students of his college had 'passed for ecclesiastical colleges, attorneys' apprentices, Apothecaries' Hall, and the College of Surgeons'. By 1879 there were four diocesan priests on the staff and three laymen, together with Mons. l'Abbé l'Heritier, chaplain to Lord Emly's French wife, who taught French, chemistry, and practical science, and a Herr Printzen, formerly of the University of Münster. The diocesan priests changed fairly frequently, because the bishop did not wish to keep any one in the college who did not desire to remain.[19] The college was doing so well by 1880 that Bourke decided to lease Mungret Agricultural College, which had just become vacant.

Mungret Agricultural College had originated as a result of a partial famine in 1825, for which large sums were collected in England, and a reproductive loan fund was established. In 1852 the loans given through this fund were called in, and a levy of £4,079. 9s. 7d. was put on Co. Limerick as the amount to be repaid. Through the influence of Lord Monteagle, however, a bill was passed in the House of Commons, which allowed the sums of money to be vested in trustees to establish an agricultural college to serve the county. Portion of an estate had come on the market at Mungret, situated some three to four miles from Limerick city, consisting of seventy acres of land, together with some buildings. This was purchased and vested in five trustees, two of whom were Lord Emly and the Protestant bishop of Limerick. In 1853 the trustees leased the property to the National Board with a view to the setting up an agricultural college. The college opened in 1858. It did not prove successful and was closed in September 1878.

The trustees were bound by act of parliament either to run the college themselves or get someone to run it for them. A necessary requirement was that the college provide some agricultural training. A subsequent bill enabled the lord lieutenant to decide to whom the property should be committed and also to approve its purpose. Relieved by this flexibility, Lord Emly set about finding new tenants. Bourke's application was viewed favourably because of the success of his college, and also because Bishop George Butler and Lord Emly were close friends, and l'Abbé l'Heritier was on the staff of St Munchin's College. Mungret College, as a result, opened its doors as part of St Munchin's College, Limerick, on 23 September 1880.

During the academic year 1880–1, the teachers who taught at Hartstonge Street had also to travel to take class at Mungret on a regular basis. Even in the era of the motorcar this would represent a daily problem. In the 1880s it put serious strain on the teaching resources of the college, and by the end of the year it was clear that from an educational and financial point of view the arrangement could not continue. During the summer of 1881, Fr Bourke was obliged to terminate the project, return to Hartstonge Street, and face a debt. To clear the debt he proposed to dispose of the assets of the Hartstonge Street College to pay his bills. At this there was considerable murmuring amongst the clergy, who claimed he had no right to dispose of any part of the property, that it belonged to the diocese. Prominent among these was one whom Bourke had viewed as a friend and colleague, Edward Thomas O'Dwyer. Incensed, Bourke took the unusual step of publishing 'A Letter addressed to the Lord Bishop and the Clergy of the Diocese of Limerick',[20] in which he pointed out that the entire project of re-establishing a diocesan college in 1867 was undertaken at his personal initiative and with his own resources, and that while the college was under the patronage of the bishop and the clergy it was not supported by the diocese and did not belong to the diocese. Hence, he claimed the right to dispose of the assets in order to pay his bills. In the end, the disagreement was settled. He sold the furniture of the college to meet the expenses he had incurred.[21] He then resumed parish life in the diocese.

The presidency of St Munchin's College passed, meantime, to Bourke's former friend, O'Dwyer, who had entered the college as a part-time teacher in 1880. It was not a task for which he felt prepared and at ease, to judge by his evidence in 1901 before the Royal Commission on University Education chaired by Lord Robertson. In 1881, Dr Butler offered him the full-time post of principal or president. He hoped, in the view of one contemporary, that O'Dwyer would live at Hartstonge Street and 'have regular charge', but O'Dwyer would not consent. 'He agreed to give two or three hours teaching' there but 'he wished to hold his curacy at St Michael's, be responsible for sick calls etc.'[22] This rendered him less than genuine in the view of Joseph Bourke, who observed pointedly and ironically in his public letter

> The Revd Gentleman who now conducts the Crescent school, retains his curacy and superintends the school duties from without – to my mind a most significant proof of his faith in what he had undertaken to achieve.[23]

That Bishop Butler was not happy with the situation was soon indicated by his casting his lot once more with the Jesuits. Fr William Ronan, rector of the Jesuit college at the Crescent, had started a missionary school for 'apostolic students', young men who wished to become priests but had no funds to pay for their education and who were financed, through Ronan's arrangements with bishops from English speaking foreign regions – such as North America, South Africa, Australia, New Zealand, even India – on condition that they committed themselves to work in those countries. Butler introduced Ronan to the idea of moving to Mungret College and of catering there also for the students of the diocese. Lord Emly added his support. The Jesuit provincial at the time refused permission, but on Ronan appealing to Rome the Jesuit General approved the project. As a result, St Munchin's College became absorbed in a new Mungret College, and all arrangements appear to have been conducted by Dr Butler without reference to Fr O'Dwyer.

This slight by the bishop did little to improve O'Dwyer's attitude towards a Jesuit managed seminary. His hostility seems to have been well known to judge by a letter from Fr John Baptist Réné, the president of Mungret College, following Bishop Butler's death in 1886. He wrote to William Ronan, then in America collecting funds for the expansion of the Mungret apostolic-cum-seminary college, expressing his fears for the future if Fr O'Dwyer were made bishop. Ronan, a former diocesan priest, and an optimistic man, popular with clergy and bishops throughout the country, who had evidently sought to establish friendly relations with O'Dwyer, assured Réné that he had nothing to fear, that O'Dwyer knew 'the difficulty of working a seminary with secular priests' and had been glad that the Jesuits had got Mungret but 'was hurt because Dr Butler told him nothing of the transfer of the seminary until it was accomplished'.[24] Ronan, like so many, failed to read the future bishop's many-sided personality.

O'Dwyer was quite capable of telling Ronan frankly of the difficulties he experienced in running a school with secular priests, after all, he was to announce publicly before the Robertston Commission in 1901 that the clergy teaching in the Catholic diocesan seminaries throughout Ireland had 'never received a true education', and that he himself, when he was teaching, was 'absolutely unfitted for the work' and that, deprived of any university training in the classics, he had had to work very hard at night to keep ahead of his pupils.[25] Furthermore, in his desire to make a case for university education for Catholics, and out of an idealistic vision of Newman's *Idea of a University*, he exaggerated to the point of stating that many of the priests teaching in Ireland came out of Maynooth 'deficient in all classical education, and in all scientific and mathematical education, and above all ... deficient in that indefinable thing that is not knowledge but culture – the character of the man that is formed when he goes through the process of real university education'. Such open criticism of his fellow clergy, however, did not mean that he was glad that the Jesuits, or doubtless any other religious order, had control of the diocesan seminary. He was to make this clear quite soon after he became bishop.

A HOUSING PROBLEM

There was another issue during his years at St Michael's, which moved O'Dwyer to emphatic, and even precipitous action, namely, the housing conditions of many of the working population. He instituted a campaign for better housing, founding for the purpose the Artisans' Dwelling Company. The more he experienced the misery and health hazards endured by so many, the more his anger grew against the wealthy employers of the city, who showed no signs of compassion or of practical intent to remedy conditions. Consequently, when he obtained permission to address the members of the Limerick Harbour Board, composed mainly of wealthy merchants, he was not in a conciliatory mood. He told them that, with the possible exception of the mayor, Dr W.T. O'Sullivan, they had no 'adequate idea of the miserable way in which their workers were housed'. Then, singling out one member, he declared vehemently that when he went one morning to the house of a poor working man in the employment of that merchant, the man's 'poor wife and children were sitting crouched around a meagre fire, the roof was broken in and the snow was falling through. The poor children were trying to warm themselves as best they could ... and the poor wife was shivering ... and cried to him, "O, Father, the cold is going through me."' 'That', O'Dwyer added, 'was only one out of hundreds of cases' of the working men of the city in the employment of the gentlemen who constituted the Board. He then proceeded to lecture them and quoted the section of the government act that, in his view, empowered the Harbour Board to erect labourers' dwellings. Not surprisingly, the Board's reaction was hostile. When he had withdrawn, his words and manner were vigorously criticised.

O'Dwyer himself realised that he had been offensive and tactless. In the *Limerick Chronicle* of 5 April 1881, he had the grace and common sense to apologise. 'I should consider it a great misfortune', he wrote, 'if by mistaken zeal I should have weakened the force of my own advocacy.' He did not intend, he explained, to rebuke the members of the Harbour Board, whose generosity and genuine desire to promote the well being of the people he well knew. He finished, nevertheless, with the reminder that 'a master is not a mere task-master, and his workman is not as a beast of burden. They are both men – made in the image of the same God, and are bound to love one another'. And to take the 'lowest view' of the matter, he added, just as 'a man makes a stable comfortable for his horse that he may get more work out of him', so an employer 'ought to make a fairly decent home for his men, to keep them in health, to withdraw them from the public house, and to give them the self-respect which is a strong stimulant of honesty and energy'.[26]

At this time, 1880–1, the *Limerick Chronicle* was testifying to the inadequate wages of many workmen in the city, some of them with large families.[27] Largely through O'Dwyer's social concern, and his political and social influence with the corporation and wealthy classes, first as a priest, and then as bishop, hundreds of working families were provided with better housing,[28] though the problem remained far from solved. Thirty years later, some 31.7 percent of the population of Limerick city were said to be still living in overcrowded, unhealthy conditions.[29]

In the light of his evident concern for the welfare of youth and of the less well-off members of society, and his readiness on their behalf to face down local authorities and the wealthy, O'Dwyer became a revered and popular figure to a large section of the population of the city and in parts of the county. Even those he challenged could not but respect his zeal and whole-hearted solicitude for those in need, and they were conditioned to accept even his lectures and abuse by the fact that he was a hardworking priest, who spoke in a cultured accent and came from a respectable family. His very genuineness and forthrightness earned him admirers. 'Never ... hesitate to impress me with your opinions', his friend Richard O'Shaughnessy, MP, requested on 1 January 1877. 'They are of high and valuable [*sic*], because they come from an honest man that understands thoroughly what he desires.'[30]

O'Dwyer was seen, inevitably, as a valuable adherent to the cause of Home Rule. His links with the Home Rule movement and its leaders, which were already extensive prior to his coming to St Michael's and continued during much of his time there, added to his conspicuousness and to his local reputation. They set the scene, too, for his later encounters as bishop with some of those leaders, particularly those who helped to orchestrate the land agitation. His early involvement with the Home Rule movement, therefore, requires special consideration.

4

Home Rule enthusiast and Land
League critic, 1870–1886

O'Dwyer's interest in the political aims of Isaac Butt had brought him, as seen earlier, into active involvement in politics, especially in the Limerick area. The fact that Butt stood for Limerick, however, meant that O'Dwyer became acquainted with many of Butt's main followers. With his usual thoroughness he studied Butt's policies and reflected on the country's main social and political issues.

At the end of the 1860s the two main issues agitating the country were land reform, expressed in a movement seeking increased rights for tenants, and amnesty for Fenian prisoners. Although the agitators for each of these goals did not always agree, they recognised in the Protestant lawyer, Isaac Butt, a figure embracing both causes. Like Daniel O'Connell, whom he sought to emulate, Butt endeavoured to bring the various strands of Irish life under one leadership, and, like O'Connell, he had also come to believe that the only hope for the country lay in Home Rule. In 1870 he produced a pamphlet on home government and founded the Home Government Association. The pamphlet bore the self-revealing title: *Home government for Ireland, Irish federalism: its objects and Its hopes*. After seventy years of union, Ireland, he declared, was the 'most discontented' and 'the poorest country in Europe'. It was time, therefore, to unite all sectors of society in a form of self-government. Nothing else would meet the country's needs, and, if granted, would cement relations with Britain and, in Ireland, would encourage public spirit, self-reliance and national pride, the prerequisites for good government.[1] His views on education also appealed to O'Dwyer. He favoured the establishment of a Catholic university college, which, although endowed by the authorities, would be governed solely by the Catholic hierarchy. He intended the setting up of such an institution to be one of the first acts of a Home Rule government. His support of denominational education was such that he viewed the arguments of those who wished to remove education from the control of churchmen as 'the most contemptible of all cants – the cant of the most intolerant and narrow-minded of all bigotries, that of the 'liberality' which is intolerant of every earnest and deep conviction of men ...'[2]

Despite this, the bishops and the majority of the clergy remained suspicious of the new movement and placed their trust in Gladstone, who, by 1870, had disestablished the Anglican Church in Ireland and seemed determined to solve the land and university questions. Butt's initial political steps, moreover, did not inspire confidence. He had a distrust of popular agitation and irrationality and, hence, imposed a £1 entry fee to the Home Government Association as a deterrent to popular membership. He evidently viewed the Association as essentially a body of gentlemen exerting pressure in parliament in support of Home Rule.

In 1871 Butt travelled to Limerick city to contest the parliamentary seat vacated by the death of Francis William Russell, MP. At the meeting that adopted him as the formal Home Rule candidate, he placed second after Home Rule the setting up of a Catholic university, and the establishment of religious equality and denominational education. He did not emphasise the land issue, perhaps because dissatisfaction with the Land Act of 1870 had not yet been widely expressed.

Much of what he advocated in respect of Home Rule, and especially education, were reflected in O'Dwyer's subsequent aims and writing. Shortly before his death, Bishop O'Dwyer made clear his esteem for Butt and his support of him at a time when his own bishop and nearly all the clergy were opposed.

> I began my career in the year 1870 as a supporter of Isaac Butt ... I may mention that I was the only priest in the diocese of Limerick to stand on the hustings when the standard of Home Rule was raised by Isaac Butt, and furthermore that I was honoured by that great man up to his death.[3]

O'Dwyer, indeed, was present at Butt's nomination in the Court House, Limerick, on 20 September 1871, and, although there were some clergy from elsewhere in attendance, he was the only one from Limerick.[4] Moreover, he addressed the gathering explaining why 'a simple priest in the County of Limerick' had come to support Butt. He was there as a man like themselves, he announced, but he stood, too, for the interests of religion, for which if the test came he hoped he would have the strength to give his life. These interests, he explained, were closely connected with the granting of Home Rule. Then, having adverted to the dangers of 'liberalism, socialism and communism' obtaining a foothold among the disgruntled working class population, he gave it as his opinion that 'until they were a nation they would be in a moveable discontented element open to bad and pernicious influences'.[5] He wished, he added, to work for the unification of the diverse elements in the country, because only thus united would good be achieved for the Irish people. Mr Gladstone had done well with the disestablishment of the Established Church, O'Dwyer continued, and his Land Act seemed to have removed the most glaring defects of the land system, but 'the just claims of the national mind' remained unsatisfied. Material prosperity of itself would not make a nation. Peace and order would only flourish when self-government was conceded.[6]

Following Butt's victory in the election, which the *Daily Express* described as 'a victory for the rabble' and a sign that the initiative had passed from the clergy, the *Pall Mall Gazette* observed that the only priests who supported Butt 'were men notoriously independent of Episcopal restraint'. O'Dwyer was clearly one of the priests embraced by that comment, though it was most unlikely that Bishop George Butler had sought to restrain his political adherence. O'Dwyer spoke at the celebrations to mark the election victory, and was hailed by the *Nation* newspaper, together with Fr Patrick Quaid, parish priest of O'Callaghan's Mills, Co. Clare, as 'worthy priests and patriots' who had received a rapturous reception from the people, gladdened to see priests once more in their 'accustomed place', namely, 'in the van of the struggle for Irish freedom'.[7] It was a reception very different from what O'Dwyer would experience some sixteen years later.

Butt's stance on denominationalism and equality in education, his marked reserve towards mass agitation, and his opposition to violence and intimidation – which occasioned a certain distance from the tenants' movement, all appealed to O'Dwyer and helped establish a bond of friendship between them. Even Butt's early elitist view of being represented by gentlemen in parliament appealed to O'Dwyer, as was seen in his approach to the 1874 election in Co. Limerick.

At the end of 1873 the Home Government Association changed its name to the Home Rule League and opened itself to a wider public. It also obtained increased support from the Catholic hierarchy and clergy, many of whom had been annoyed by Gladstone's open criticism of aspects of Catholic teaching, and by his University bill of 1873 that had proposed a Catholic university college within Dublin University. The League was but three weeks old, however, when Gladstone sprung an election. Its position was further weakened by the Liberals now claiming to be Home Rulers, while the tenant farmers, disillusioned by the loopholes found by the landlords in the 1870 Land Act, sought candidates who would put land issues first – hence the contest between O'Sullivan and Kelly in Co. Limerick, where O'Dwyer contributed to the division. Division was almost endemic under Butt. He made no attempt to impose unity from the top, as Parnell was to do later. He appealed for unity but left the constituencies free to make their own choices. Despite all this, the League did well in the election. Fifty-nine Home Rulers, of varying degrees of commitment, were elected. But, as the Tory party was victorious, the prospect of achieving Home Rule during their term of office appeared hopeless. Butt turned his attention to the formation of public opinion by means of lectures and discussions in the various cities and town throughout the country. The *Nation* supported him in this policy and urged that every town should have a centre, with a library and reading room, where young men could inform themselves on matters regarding the well being of the country. It seems more than a coincidence that, shortly after coming to St Michael's parish in 1874, O'Dwyer set about purchasing a premises to house his Catholic Literary Institute, to which he invited Butt and other Home Rulers as speakers.

In parliament, meantime, the government's neglect of the views of the Irish Home Rule members created a frustration that resulted in certain Irish members deliberately obstructing the business of parliament in order to compel attention to Irish issues. The leaders in this endeavour were Joseph Biggar and Charles Stewart Parnell. Their behaviour made the headlines, and evoked wide interest in Ireland, even among extreme nationalists there and in North America. Butt, however, strongly disapproved. He had a deep respect for the 'Mother of Parliaments', and the practice of obstructing the business of the House, delaying business on English and international issues in order to draw attention to Ireland's grievances, seemed to him disrespectful to parliament and unworthy of gentlemen and parliamentarians. The issue grew large as the case for obstruction was canvassed through the country by Parnell, and by former Fenians such as O'Connor Power.

By the autumn of 1877, the pressure of those he termed the 'obstructives' had undermined Butt's already frail health. He was unable to fulfil a number of engagements. On 18 September he wrote to O'Dwyer to apologise for not being able to to lecture at the Catholic Literary Institute. He went on to confide about his state of health and to give expression to the sense of depression and gloom he was experiencing. He was weighed down by the demands of meetings and the questioning of his policy, and annoyed by the reports in the newspapers that he was suffering from 'a disease of the heart'. The truth of the matter was that for many years he had been subjected 'to an irregular action of the heart'. Latterly, however, he had had 'a very sensible and painful oppression of the heart and (a) gasping or almost so for breath'. His doctor in London, after a thorough examination, had declared his heart perfectly sound and judged that the symptoms that oppressed him were the result of turmoil and anxiety arising from his fights with the obstructives. All medical men, moreover, had told him that the irregularities of his heart were not likely to shorten his life. 'Still,' he added frankly, 'I am not well and I am far from sure I ever will be – and it is Biggar and Parnell.' He had spent over six years building up the Irish Parliamentary party, and now believed that achievement was being undermined by treasonable, idiotic behaviour. The Home Rule party, not only in parliament but also in the country, was 'irretrievably broken up'. For himself, it was only a question of 'at what stage' he would retire from the leadership of the party and most probably from public life. Then, as if standing back from himself, he observed that he would be glad to think, 'that these were the delusions of physical weakness inducing despondency'. Perhaps if he had his old energy he might yet stop the break-up. 'Your letter telling me of the good effect of my manifesto', he continued, 'ought to make me more cheery. After all, things may come right.' 'I have perfect faith', he assured O'Dwyer, 'in Ireland's destiny and in the Providence that guards it, and if it be his will that I should not do the things my foolish heart had thought he intended me to do, I must be content even if I do not live to see them done by anyone else.'

Asking to be excused for imposing his gloominess on him, Butt assured him that, even if resigned his position as member for Limerick, he would hold himself bound to go and lecture for him. O'Dwyer, in a letter to him, had evidently tried to comfort him against the increased popularity acquired by the obstructives. In a postscript, Butt commented – 'I was greatly amused at your statement that the most popular man in Ireland would be the man who would knock down a couple of ministers on the floor of the House of Commons. There is too much truth in it.'[8]

The division in the party over policy and leadership was such by December 1877 that it was agreed to hold a national conference. At a special meeting of the conference committee on Christmas Eve, 1877, the conference date was fixed for Monday, 14 January 1878, by eight votes to four. The minority, who were Butt supporters, had sought to postpone the conference until Tuesday, 15 January, at 11 a.m., in order to allow the clergy time to come up from the country.[9] The clergy were now among Butt's strongest supporters, partly because they feared the Fenian element on Parnell's side. In Limerick, as might be expected, clerical support was particularly strong. In May 1877, indeed, the bishop, George Butler, and his clergy had been active promoters of a Butt Testimonial Fund.[10]

On Christmas Day, 1877, the day after the committee's vote, Butt wrote again to O'Dwyer. The previous day, he announced, two of his close followers called on him to present their resignation. 'It is the beginning of the end,' he declared. 'Unless the obstructives are defeated at the conference every man of character and position in the ranks of Home Rule will follow their example and leave us, and every effort to advance the cause of self-government (will) be thrown back for years as hopelessly and completely as was the case in the Young Ireland schism.' 'I need not say', he added, 'of what value your presence at the conference will be. I hope nothing will prevent you coming.' 'The obstructives', he concluded, 'do not hesitate to say now that they fixed Monday to throw difficulties in the way of the attendance of the priests.'[11]

The day before the national conference, Butt wrote again. 'A great and decisive majority', he maintained, was necessary at the conference. He would not be surprised if the obstructives opposed Archdeacon O'Regan's proposal of a vote of confidence in him, and he thought that John Dillon might press the resolution of which he had given notice. 'If you can *without great inconvenience* be here,' Butt continued, 'I would certainly press you to come. Circumstances may arise in which a speech from you would be of the greatest value.' 'Any of our Limerick friends whom you can influence', he concluded, 'press them to come up. The result of this conference will determine a great deal of the national cause.'[12]

The issues at the conference were party unity and the policy to be adopted in parliament with respect to obstruction. This last had been given added relevance by the threat of war between Russia and Turkey in the Balkans, which had led the Commons to postpone the consideration of Irish matters, much to the intense annoyance of many Irish members, some of whom now felt that the menacing international situation provided the opportunity for a campaign of obstruction which would focus world attention on Ireland's grievances. This attitude found expression in the resolution pressed by John Dillon to which Butt had referred. Dillon, a vocal upholder of Parnell's 'more vigorous policy', called on the six hundred delegates at the conference, among whom were 39 members of parliament and 130 Catholic clergymen,[13] to support his proposal

> That this conference is of opinion that should the question of intervention in the present war [between Russia and Turkey] be brought before the House of Commons the Irish party ought, through its leader, to repudiate all sympathy with England on this question, and the party ought to empha- sise this declaration by leaving the House in a body before the division.

This would bring home to the English people, Dillon maintained, 'the reality of our demand for Home Rule, and the sternness of our demand to have it.'[14] The resolution was seconded by Joseph Biggar, who emphasised the priority of Irish interests while yet professing loyalty to Butt.

Butt subjected the resolution to a telling analysis, pointing out that it contradicted a resolution passed two hours earlier and already made public. The earlier McCabe Fay resolution declared that 'upon all imperial questions the Irish members are to consult together (applause), and to endeavour to arrive at united action (renewed applause)', yet 'having passed that resolution, within two hours afterwards you pass another resolution that they are not to meet to consult together, but that the matter is to be determined here.' This was to dictate to the members, tying their hands and leaving no flexibility to deal with changing situations. 'If you look to the real interest of Ireland in this matter', Butt advised, 'we should keep ourselves free.'[15] He requested Dillon to withdraw the confusing and divisive resolution.

O'Dwyer, who, with John Redmond, stood by Butt, succeeded in getting a hearing, despite attempts to prevent him. He made a rousing speech in support of the leader and of his call for the withdrawal of the resolution. Dillon, however, refused to withdraw, until Parnell put forward an amendment[16] stating that in the case of the Eastern Question it would 'be the duty of the Irish party to consult together, and to carry out as a party a united line of policy and action'. This received scarcely any support; the senior members, in particular, balking at 'the duty' aspect, seeing it as a denial of their freedom of action by turning of them into delegates rather than representatives.[17]

Following this, Parnell and Butt came together, and the chairman announced that they had come up with a revised amendment that would, he was confident, satisfy all concerned. Before Parnell could rise to move his new amendment, however, the young curate from Limerick intervened. 'Every member of the conference', O'Dwyer insisted defiantly in his ringing voice amidst cries for Parnell, 'who has anything to say on any question that turns up should get a fair hearing, and he claimed it as not a privilege but as a right (Hear, hear).' 'When he heard the proposition of Mr John Dillon', O'Dwyer explained, '... he sent word to the chairman that, if no one else did so, he would propose an amendment to it. Then he found an amendment proposed that almost substantially embodied his own views, and he made up his mind not to speak at all about it, for his individual opinion was worth very little; but he found that under the amendment and under the resolution as before the meeting there was a great fundamental question at stake (Hear, hear).'

'The question now before the conference is', O'Dwyer continued, 'to decide whether we are to send our members – whom we have accepted in solemn exercise of the franchise to represent us as carrying our confidence – to carry out our views in the House of Commons, or take them before a desk and write down for them what they are to do, and send them tied hand and foot to the House of Commons (No, no). That was the issue. (A voice – It is not).' 'Now, he believed there was a way out clearly of the difficulty,' O'Dwyer asserted, ' a plain middle course that they might take.' 'He thought', referring to Parnell's amendment, 'that by putting in ['] as far as possible they should follow a united action ['], and some words to this effect, a certain majority of them, with Mr Butt as their leader, should bind the minority (No, no).'[18] Parnell, without reference to O'Dwyer's intervention, then proposed his altered amendment leaving out the word 'duty', thereby, as he said, getting rid 'of the idea of dictation'. Now the amendment merely read: 'We recommend the Irish party (loud applause) to consult together and to carry out as a party a united line of policy and action (cheers).' It was carried with enthusiasm.

Analysing the debate in considerable detail, Professor Emmet Larkin observed, in *The Roman Catholic Church and the emergence of the modern Irish political system, 1874–78* (Dublin, 1996, p. 497), that 'the only person of all those who discussed Parnell's original amendment, and who apparently realised what was really at stake, was Father O'Dwyer'. That amendment instructed the members of the parliamentary party that it was their *duty* to consult and to *carry out* a united line of action. O'Dwyer was as opposed as Butt and other senior members to the idea of 'duty', of being made mere delegates, but he also understood that behind the amendment was the necessary implication that to *carry out* a united line of action it was essential that the principle be accepted that the majority should bind the minority. He wanted this expressed rather than implied and he also made it clear that it be expressed under Mr Butt's leadership!

Parnell remained content to leave the matter implied, though later as leader he would not only adopt the principle but also would require a written pledge, binding all members, to vote and act with the party or resign their seats. 'The supreme irony', as Larkin noted, 'was that it was this same Father O'Dwyer, who was among the earliest to articulate explicitly the principle on which the effective power of the party in the modern Irish political system was to come to rest, who was to become the bishop of Limerick in 1886, and who for more than thirty years after was to prove to be the most persistent and bitter critic of the party among the Irish bishops.'[19]

By April 1878 the pressure on Butt was such that he wrote to his election committee in Limerick requesting that they draw up and circulate an address of confidence in the way he was handling Irish affairs. O'Dwyer undertook to speak on his behalf at the diocesan conference, and to encourage the bishop and clergy to add their signatures to the address. Subsequently, he reported to the election committee that most of the clergy had complied with his request[20] He further proposed that a sub-committee be set up to draft another address in support of Butt which would be adapted to the views of the mayor, and of all the public bodies, and of 'all the electors' in the constituency.[21] These proposals adapted to everyman were also accepted, and he was elected himself on to the sub-committee.

Butt's position by the summer of 1878 seemed strong, and then on 2 August he made a critical mistake. In a debate in the House of Commons when a motion of censure was being pressed against the government by the Liberal party on its handling of the Eastern crisis, and particularly on its concluding various secret treaties without consultation with parliament, Butt spoke in support of the government's policy, and even signified that he would vote in its favour – this without convening a meeting of the Home Rule members to decide how they would deal with the motion of no confidence in the government, as had been agreed at the national conference in January. His action split the party: 17 voted with him, 10 against, and 30, including Parnell and Biggar, abstained. It was the turning point in the struggle for power in the Home Rule Association.[22]

Early in November Butt issued a manifesto to his own constituents that confirmed that there were serious divisions in the party. The obstructives, if they succeeded with their 'policy of sustained action', he declared, would bring about 'the total and complete breaking up of the existing Irish parliamentary party' and his own exclusion from parliament and from political life. He called for support for his own policies, and for the methods he was using at Westminster, and urged that those who refused to adopt them be censured.[23] In the *Cork Examiner*, on 21 November, O'Dwyer responded to the manifesto on behalf of the Limerick constituents. He began by examining the nature of the quarrel between Parnell and Butt. Much was made of the vigorous policies of Parnell, but that was not the central issue. The question was what did Parnell stand for? He needed to make his position clear. It was evident what Butt stood for – that in the prosecution of the Irish cause 'the constitution was his limit'. It was not evident with Parnell, he declared pointedly, echoing rumours of his links to Fenianism. If his policy led 'immediately or indirectly into a fight with the House of Commons', it was unlikely to win the support of 'the thinking and truly responsible classes'. If, however, while demanding greater energy at Westminster, he confined himself to constitutional action, then it was difficult to see any fundamental difference between himself and Butt, and little reason why there should not be a cordial union for the sake of the country.

Three days later, however, a new development precipitated events. On 24 November the government announced that parliament was to be convened two months earlier, on 5 December, to consider the mounting crisis in Afghanistan.

What would be the stand of the Irish Parliamentary party? Butt made it clear by letter that, while unable to attend parliament for reasons of health, he opposed any pressing of Irish claims at this time when matters of 'vital importance to the United Kingdom' were being deliberated.[24] On reading this, John Dillon, T.D. Sullivan, and Francis Hugh O'Donnell wrote to the *Freeman's Journal*, repudiating Butt's leadership.[25] The following day, a long letter from Parnell in the same paper lamented that 'the apathy of the leader' had again resulted in another lost opportunity of vital importance. On 6 December, O'Connor Power went so far as to denounce Butt as a traitor to the Home Rule party and to the Irish cause.[26]

On that date, in the *Cork Examiner*, O'Dwyer came to Butt's defence, criticising not only the unconstitutional actions of Parnell and Biggar, but especially their attitudes towards their leader. Parnell, he declared, was sadly lacking in any sense of gratitude to Butt and, moreover, was forgetting that his quarrel was not just with his leader but 'with the majority of the Home Rule party, as at present constituted'. He concluded by censuring Parnell and his followers for hounding and humiliating Butt. At a meeting of the Limerick Farmers' Club, he vigorously defended Butt before an audience made restless by successive harvest failures in 1877 and 1878, and by a serious decline in the price of agricultural produce because of increased competition from America and the Antipodes. Writing to O'Dwyer on 14 December, a grateful Butt remarked:

> I seize the first leisure day to write to thank you for your splendid defence of me at the Farmers' Club. I would willingly accept a great deal of abuse and misrepresentation to have such a speech made by you.

He wished he had back the energy to do something for the country. He was quite sure, he added, that the government ministers would bring in 'a *liberal* university bill' – not framed on the principles he had advocated but still conferring a great boon on the country. This was the Royal University Act, brought in the following year, in which the principle of indirect subsidy in the Intermediate Education Act was applied at university level. Butt was very conscious of O'Dwyer's interest in university education, and his regret that a university education had not been available to him. He also made it clear that his efforts were bearing fruit in other fields. 'We may also get a measure transforming the management of county affairs from grand juries to elective councils,' he announced, and even the equalisation 'of our borough franchise to that of England might follow.'[27]

On the day of Butt's letter, the *Freeman's Journal* carried a devastating criticism of him by Dillon. He was accused of putting the interests of the British Empire before those of Ireland. It was time, Dillon declared, for a change of leadership. A meeting of the Home Rule League was called for February 1879 to deal with the evident divisions. At the meeting, T.D. Sullivan, editor of the *Nation*, moved what was, in effect, a vote of no confidence in Butt. Dillon supported the motion with a strongly worded denunciation of the leader, adding that he had gone back on the principles enunciated at the 1874 conference. In his reply, Butt failed to impress the meeting. He was a very ill man. He survived Sullivan's no confidence vote by a mere majority of eight. Parnell, Biggar, and Dillon voted against him.

Shortly afterwards, the equalisation of the Irish borough franchise with that of the English and Scottish boroughs, to which Butt had referred in his letter to O'Dwyer, was moved by a good friend of Butt, Charles Meldon, the senior member for Co. Kildare. The English and Scottish Liberals supported the motion, but it was defeated by 256 to 187 votes.[28] One of the strongest opponents of the motion was Randolph Churchill, who had become familiar with the Irish political scene, and had done much for education, while serving as private secretary to his father, the current viceroy, the duke of Marlborough. Mr Butt, he asserted in the course of his address, 'had the support of the educated the industrious, and the loyal classes who had the franchise; while the enthusiastic audience' which were said to rally round 'that interesting quartet, the members for Meath (Parnell), Cavan (Joseph Biggar), Mayo (John Dillon), and Dungarvan (John O'Connor Power), were composed as every impartial Irishman would admit, almost entirely of the ignorant, idle and drunken ... to whom it was now proposed to give votes'.[29]

Much as O'Dwyer might empathise with Churchill's description of Parnell and his supporters, it was no help to Butt to be supported by Churchill. His concerns, however, were soon to cease. On 5 May 1879 his heart failed. He was buried at his request in Stranorlar, Co. Donegal, in a private funeral. On Saturday morning, 10 May, his remains were conveyed from his residence in George's Street, Dublin, to the Amiens Street station for the long journey by train to Stranorlar.[30] Some 150 mourners, besides the immediate family, made up the funeral cortege. Parnell made sure to be prominent among the mourners. A handful of priests attended the funeral, many others were deterred, it seems, by the private nature of the occasion.[31] One priest made his way from Limerick to pay his final respects to a man he regarded as political leader and friend. Such letters between them as have survived indicate their mutual respect and esteem. It was the end of an era for Edward Thomas O'Dwyer. Before long he was to abandon all active involvement in party politics. His attitude became almost entirely reactive.

O'Dwyer's work for Butt's party had made him a figure of much influence. This continued for a while longer. Later in May 1879 he strongly supported his friend, Daniel F. Gabbett, as a Home Rule candidate for Butt's seat in Limerick, and subsequently described him from the victorious platform as 'the friend of the people' and his election as 'a great national stroke'.[32] His influence over Gabbett was reflected some months later in a letter from London in which the latter apologised for voting in the publicans' interest in a bill about closing hours. 'If you had intimated to me the slightest wish, I need hardly say I would have voted in compliance with your desire.'[33] His influence outside Limerick is suggested by a letter from the senior member for Kildare, Charles Meldon, who, in response to a request for a speaker on temperance, replied from London – 'Kindly let me know which of our men now in Ireland you wish to go to Limerick and when. I need not assure you that any personal action of mine will cheerfully be given for the asking.'[34]

Such influence among party members faded as leadership passed to Parnell and his followers, men whom O'Dwyer, and almost all the bishops and clergy viewed with suspicion because of their links to persons and organisations associated with violence: the persons included ex-Fenians such as Michael Davitt in Ireland and the influential John Devoy in America; the organisations, mainly those involved in land agitation, like the Land League. A succession of events was to bring about a major change in the attitude of many bishops and clergy, but not in O'Dwyer. Where the new leaders of the Irish party were concerned, it suited them to identify his independent voice with that of Butt, now discredited as pro-establishment, and not truly nationalist and Irish.

O'DWYER AND THE LAND LEAGUE

By 1879, successive years of bad harvests and widespread agricultural depression had left many tenants unable to pay their rents, and this, in turn, led to the eviction of over one thousand families in that year. This occasioned reprisals. Cattle were maimed, hay and buildings burned, landlords and 'land grabbers' attacked. Michael Davitt coordinated the protest by means of an organisation, called the Land League, which also helped to provide shelter and assistance for evicted tenants. Financial assistance was made available through John Devoy and his supporters in the United States. Davitt, moreover, persuaded Parnell that his power base and political standing would advance if he abandoned obstruc-tionism in parliament and made himself the voice of the Irish tenantry. In October 1879 Parnell accepted presidency of the Irish National Land League. He presented a voice of moderation, but outrages continued. Moreover, as time passed some of his lieutenants, notably John Dillon, became active in promoting a policy of boycotting to deter 'land grabbers', those who rented land whence a tenant had been evicted. At a meeting in Tipperary Parnell gave a vivid description of the working of this policy. 'If you meet him (the 'land grabber') in the fair, walk away silently. Do him no injury, offer him no violence, but let no man have any dealings with him. In the same way, when he lives in the country, let everyman's door be shut against him.'[35]

Faced with so much suffering on the part of numerous tenants, and under pressure to side with them, many priests identified with their cause. A number of bishops, including Thomas Croke, archbishop of Cashel, Patrick Duggan of Clonfert, and to some extent George Butler of Limerick, and prominent churchmen like William J. Walsh, president of Maynooth and future archbishop of Dublin, supported the Parliamentary party in its efforts to contain the violence and to seek a just constitutional solution to the tenants' problems.

Meanwhile, branches of the Land League had sprung up in many parts of the country. In Co. Limerick branches were formed in nearly every parish. Abbeyfeale in west Limerick was reputed to be the first town to set up its own branch. The parish priest, William Casey, led it. In August 1882 he was to inform O'Dwyer that he had spent the day at the scene of the eviction of thirty-two families. 'Such scenes', he added sorrowfully, 'may I never witness again.'[36] The tenant farmers in the area combined to provide huts for the evicted families. Experiences like these generated bitter feeling, and a general strike against the payment of rents.

A relation of O'Dwyer was among the prominent supporters of the agrarian struggle. Fr Eugene Sheehy, a curate at Kilmallock, was eventually arrested and imprisoned. In Limerick, as elsewhere in Ireland, the land war reached its peak in October 1881 with the arrest of Parnell and some of the other leaders. In response, crime and outrage expanded at an alarming rate. By the end of that year there were as many as 30,000 soldiers in the country, and 12,000 constabulary, endeavouring to preserve a semblance of law and order.

During this period, O'Dwyer showed little sympathy for the Land League. He remained strongly opposed to violence, and the League's association with Davitt, and with Parnell, Biggar, and Dillon, encouraged him to keep his distance. He deeply distrusted the three parliamentarians because of the way they had treated Butt. His coolness towards the League, however, did not indicate support for government policy. This he made clear in a harsh, extreme way at the expense of his 'former champion and fast friend', Daniel Gabbitt, MP. The latter had stated in the *Limerick Chronicle* of 30 October 1880 that he viewed with dismay the daily accounts of outrages and destruction of property associated with the Land League's campaign. The only hope for the country was an alliance with the Liberal government [Gladstone had come back to power in the 1880 election]. He looked to the authorities to restore a feeling of security to all classes in the country 'without (if possible) adopting coercive measures'. This tacit acceptance of the policy of coercion, O'Dwyer chose to view as 'a terrible literary thunderbolt'.[37] Although he did not approve of the policies of the League, nor with the impudent dictation by a 'clique of strangers' then operating politically in Limerick, he felt it necessary to protest publicly against Gabbitt's 'outrageous letter'. He would have preferred to remain in the background since he could not support either side, but he felt obliged to condemn Gabbitt's 'anti-national conduct'. He could not support anyone who invoked 'the pains and penalties' of the English government, which, as far as Irishmen were concerned, was the 'common enemy' and 'the author of all our wrongs'. Gabbitt had failed in his duties towards his constituents, O'Dwyer concluded, and consequently no longer deserved to represent them. Such an extreme, unreserved reaction evokes the suspicion that a rift had already occurred between the two men, and that, perhaps, Gabbitt's vote on the closing hours issue had been viewed as a betrayal, and as an assertion of independence now that he was elected.

The *Limerick Chronicle*, in its editorial that same day, mused in a revealing way on O'Dwyer's outburst. Although Gabbitt was the occasion for 'dragging the incensed clergymen once more before the public', the said clergyman, the paper noted, had availed of the occasion to express his displeasure with 'the ultra-Parnellite faction' which, the *Chronicle* suggested, was the 'clique of strangers' mentioned in his letter. The editorial concluded with the observation that it was at a loss as to the real nature of the dispute between the Parnellites and O'Dwyer, especially as both had criticised Gabbitt's letter for the same reasons.[38]

A few days later Parnell was conferred with the freedom of Limerick city. Many priests attended the civic ceremony. O'Dwyer's name was not among them.[39] His name was also absent in the list of clergy who attended a large public meeting of the Land League in March 1881.[40] The absence of such a prominent clerical figure did not pass unnoticed. In fact, he was in an unhappy state of mind about the way in which both Irish political and church leaders were acting.

Two months earlier, he had given pointers to a future public stance in a private letter to Aubrey de Vere, in which he expressed his reservations about the Land League and its clerical supporters. The excesses that the League was encouraging, he observed, were doing great damage to the moral fibre of the people, and the clergy were largely to blame. The basic principles of religion were being put aside 'by those who were bound to be their defenders and expounders'. The repudiation of contracts, the refusal to pay rent, and all other excesses, were being weighed not against the laws of morality, but against the end in view. He did not blame the masses. 'Rough-minded peasants' could not be expected to work out the intricacies of moral argument. The clergy had not asserted themselves and thereby gave tacit sanction to Land League agitation and immoral methods. He expressed himself puzzled by the absence of any official pronouncement 'from any body entitled to give it for the whole country'. He did not feel in a position, however, to query the hierarchy's policy. He bowed to their 'great wisdom and experience'. Perhaps their way of acting, he concluded, namely avoiding 'an open conflict with an excited people' was, in the long run, the best course.[41] In a further letter to his poet friend he complained that the people were acting blindly from passion and self-interest, and were being misled by the silence of those who should restrain and guide them. In the current climate it was virtually impossible 'to get even a hearing' for the cause of justice. Anyone who dared bring before the public mind the basic principles of justice and honesty was likely to be branded a landlord advocate. This had happened when Archbishop McCabe of Dublin had ventured to make his views known on the general situation. It was a great pity, O'Dwyer asserted, that the 'Catholic advocates of justice' did not strike out more boldly and continuously.[42]

That autumn, 1881, O'Dwyer emerged once more in the role of an 'incensed clergyman', but this time his target was the police. A large concourse of people had gathered in Limerick in October to protest against the imprisonment of Parnell. During the proceedings the police had fired into the crowd. O'Dwyer, who was present with his solicitor friend, John Dundon, demanded an official inquiry into the incident, alleging that nothing had occurred to justify such a show of force, and he openly charged the police with brutality. He pleaded the People's case in open court stating that while he would never condone riotous behaviour, he took this action in order 'to put down violence on the part of those in authority'.[43] When he failed to have those responsible brought to justice in his first bid, he continued to press his plea, with characteristic doggedness, at several subsequent sittings of the court. When this too proved futile he resorted to a public letter, which gave rise to a seemingly interminable correspondence with a local official, Ambrose Hall. The latter maintained that the shots had been fired in self-defence, while O'Dwyer treated the police actions, and the support for them, with biting sarcasm, and was strongly critical of all those responsible for preserving law and order.

Gladstone and Parnell arrived at an agreement in April 1882, whereby Gladstone agreed to amend the Land Act to the benefit of the lease holders and, in effect, to drop the policy of coercion, and Parnell agreed to support the amended Land Act, to use his influence against intimidation and outrage in Ireland, and 'to cooperate cordially for the future with the Liberal party in forwarding liberal principles and measures of general reform'.[44] By the end of the year the outlawed Land Leagues was superseded by a new organisation, the Irish National League. The new body was controlled by Parnell, was not agrarian, and was committed to Home Rule. This, however, appeared to make no difference to O'Dwyer. In 1883, when there was an enthusiastic popular response to a testimonial for Parnell, which was supported by Drs Croke of Cashel and Butler of Limerick, the *Limerick Chronicle*, which opposed the testimonial, drew attention to the fact that there was 'a popular and energetic clergyman' who had refused to associate himself with the scheme. He was alleged to have said, moreover, that 'the Land League began badly, and would end badly' and that the majority of the people of Limerick would have nothing to do with the testimonial because of Parnell's connection with 'communistic leaders' and with 'atheism'.[45]

The following year, the Catholic bishops enlisted the aid of the parliamentary party in forwarding their views on education, and in 1885 the rank-and-file of the clergy were involved in the local conventions of the party. The party led by Parnell had been accepted by the clerical church. In Limerick, Butt's old constituency, there was almost a complete swing in favour of Parnell by November 1885. At a national convention in the city's Theatre Royal, which had come together to select candidates for the coming general election, there were 90 priests among 363 delegates. O'Dwyer, who had been so prominent, was not present. He had distanced himself, it seemed, from clerical political involvement and from the activities of the Irish parliamentary party.

Hence, viewing Edward Thomas O'Dwyer on the threshold of his career as an influential bishop, one sees a person with strong nationalist, but not separatist, views, who considers England 'the common enemy', and hopes to acquire self government or Home Rule by constitutional means. He is strongly opposed to the use of violence to achieve ends, and blames priests for a silence that condones violence. He is puzzled by the hierarchy's absence of leadership on moral issues. In his view, a churchman's duty was to enunciate the principles of the Catholic religion irrespective of popularity or political expediency. Finally, he has little liking for or trust in Parnell, Biggar, and Dillon, who he viewed as betrayers and subverters of Butt. The dogmatic assertive zeal of Dillon provoked in him a particularly strong reaction, and he was to remain unrelenting towards the member for Mayo for the rest of his life. Dillon, for his part, gave him little reason to relent!

O'Dwyer's zeal, wide abilities, and high profile, and his popularity with many of the ordinary people, led to his being spoken of as a likely future bishop. A further requirement, however, before he would be seriously considered as *episcopabilis*, or suitable for episcopal office, was a reputation for sound learning. This, too, as will appear, he had acquired to a notable degree in the years since his ordination.

5

Scholar and public communicator

Despite his involvement in many and varied activities, O'Dwyer kept up his reading in theology and embarked on a number of reviews and articles on theological subjects which earned him a reputation as a theologian.

On 21 April 1880, William J. Walsh, president of Maynooth College, informed his friend O'Dwyer that the following month would be time enough for his article in the *Irish Ecclesiastical Record*.[1] He had called confidently on him to contribute a review article on William George Ward's book of essays on *The Church's doctrinal infallibility*, a compendium of articles previously published in the *Dublin Review*. Ward, who was highly regarded in Rome as a philosopher, taught theology at Westminster seminary, and enjoyed a reputation as a formidable apologist. An Anglican convert to Rome and a fellow of Balliol College, Oxford, he had contacts across Britain. That Walsh asked O'Dwyer to write the review said much of his confidence in O'Dwyer's ability, and the latter, for his part, determined to fulfil the task as competently as possible. He turned to his mentor in Adare, the 'bald pated, red faced PP',[2] John S. Flanagan, the friend of John Henry Newman.

Flanagan replied at length on the subject of infallibility on 20 April. He sent a number of references, and some relevant writings in his own possession. Three days later he forwarded two books written since the Vatican Council, at which the pronouncement on papal infallibility had been made: 'One … a volume of Hugo Hurter, SJ, professor at Innsbruck; the other by Camillo Mazella, SJ, … superior at the Gregorian University, Rome'. Both books were in Latin. He also enclosed some pamphlets, and added wonderingly:

> It surprises me how you can pass from the very roughest political work to a study of this nature. Your brain must be splendidly organised, when as the Limerick poet says, on another subject, it can apply itself today to politics – home-rule – land tenure, and tomorrow to metaphysics and theology, – in fact 'Every whole damned thing'.[3]

On 13 May Flanagan lamented that his own grasp of theology had been choked by the thorns of daily life, and then went on to consider further queries of O'Dwyer – as to what was *now* the certainty of the doctrine of the assumption of the Blessed Virgin into heaven, what theological note would he attach to it?

And was it more certain than the Immaculate Conception was before its definition? Flanagan quoted Suarez, the Jesuit theologian of the seventeenth century,
to the effect that the Assumption might not be denied without temerity. Suarez,
Flanagan noted, attached the same note to the doctrine on the Immaculate
Conception. He went on to examine Suarez's teaching in some detail, and the
following day returned to the topic with reference to an article in the *Dublin
Review*, and to a consideration of Newman's teaching on the development of
doctrine and on how decrees of infallibility were based on what was in the deposit
of faith handed on by the apostles. He had a manuscript of Newman, Flanagan
continued informatively, 'written by himself for me, about 10 or 12 years ago, in
which he shows what *he* means by a truth being in the *depositum* implicitly, and
in what sense it would be known to the apostles, but unfortunately Lord Emly
carried it off and has never returned it, so I can't show it to you.'[4]

Thus carefully prepared, O'Dwyer's review appeared in two parts in the *Irish
Ecclesiastical Record*, August and September 1880. He praised Ward's mastery and
exposition of his subject and his literary power, and fully assented to most of the
author's content. On certain points, however, he expressed criticism, notably, on
Ward's claim of infallibility for the Church's ordinary magisterium, so that
Pius IX might be said 'never to have ceased from issuing one continuous
infallible pronouncement'.[5] O'Dwyer substantiated his own comments with
references to various authors – to St Robert Bellarmine (d. 1621), to Dr Joseph
Fessler, secretary to the Vatican Council (1869–70), and to John Henry Newman.
Newman's works became a life-long source of interest and study for O'Dwyer,
so much so that when Modernist theologians would later claim Newman in
their support, Wilfrid Ward, then editor of the *Dublin Review*, and son of William
George Ward, called on O'Dwyer to defend the great Oratorian. The defence
won special praise from the Holy See. O'Dwyer's friend of student days, William
J. Walsh, was also an admirer of Newman. On 24 March 1884 Walsh sent him a
paper he had received from Newman,[6] and three days later corresponded on the
question of inspiration and the genuineness of the Scriptures as developed by
Newman. Interestingly, this last letter betrayed an almost juvenile literary
belligerence similar to that of O'Dwyer – telling his friend 'to look out next
week in the *Freeman*' for his case against University College Cork, and asking
'Did you observe the hit I gave Trevelyan about his injudicial mode of acting in
a case in which he is to be judge of appeal'.[7]

During his remaining years as curate, O'Dwyer continued to write for the
Ecclesiastical Record, sharpening his style, and holding forth with a confidence and
even an abandon that eventually left him open to devastating criticism. In
November 1883 he challenged a Fr E.A. Shelley, OSA, who, in the September
issue of the *Record*, had written on 'Papal Benediction in *Articulo Mortis*'[Papal
blessing on the point of death]. Shelley had claimed that the papal blessing,
which carried a plenary indulgence, might be given only once to the same
person in the same illness.[8] O'Dwyer challenged this by examining the precise
application of the original Latin text, especially as to what was meant by 'the

same illness', and then, with reference to Shelley's putting aside the views of other authors, set about demolishing his case in racy style. 'Two birds with one stone was always considered good shooting', O'Dwyer observed, 'but Father Shelley brings down a bag full ... of higher game' and he might also 'have mentioned nine out of ten of the working priests on the mission'. But 'the consciences of priests who cannot look into authorities for themselves ought not to be disturbed unless under necessity, and by one entitled to speak with authority', and he ventured to judge 'Father Shelley's conclusion quite wrong, and his reasoning a total misapprehension of the decrees to which he appeals'. He then went on to develop his argument at length.[9] His writings at this stage were encouraged by the then editor of the *IER*, Professor John Healy, destined to become a friend and supportive colleague as bishop of Clonfert and then archbishop of Tuam.[10]

O'Dwyer's interest in problems relating to moral theology and canon law brought him to the question of the possible use of the telephone in relation to the sacrament of penance. He wrote of this in the *Record* for January 1883,[11] was challenged by a Redemptorist priest, Thomas Levius in February,[12] and their interchange continued month after month until November 1883. O'Dwyer, indeed, was still writing on the subject in December 1885: referring with seeming authority to scientific developments in electricity, the transmission of sound, acoustics and vibratory theory, and making reference to various works, including those of a 'Professor J. Ryan', all of which justified his position against that of Levius. In the issue of January 1886, however, he was pulled up sharply by Professor Ryan.[13] The latter, addressing the question of 'The Telephone in Relation to the Sacrament of Penance', accused O'Dwyer of being unscientific in his approach, of accepting 'the figurative expositions of popular lectures with childlike confidence' and 'undiscriminating credulity'. He disavowed, he declared, the views attributed to him by O'Dwyer in the November 1885 issue. He had been misquoted and misrepresented. O'Dwyer was not guilty of 'premeditated unfairness', Ryan continued mercilessly, he just had a tendency to misrepresent. He had 'with considerable imagination and tact created an unreal opponent' whose views he then exposed 'to his play of humour and resource of argument'. That seems to have ended O'Dwyer's public interest in the subject! It was the year in which he was to be proposed for bishop and then made bishop. It would have been foolhardy to endeavour to continue a controversy likely to lower the dignity of the episcopal office, a dignity of which he was to show himself very conscious.

In addition to such academic writings, O'Dwyer, as has been seen, wrote to the newspapers on more popular topics. Many dealt with political and educational issues and were, not infrequently, confrontational. He revealed something of his pragmatic policy with respect to such public lectures in the course of a comment on a published letter of Aubrey de Vere, which he ventured to convey to the poet on 1 April 1881.

In a newspaper these days your letter (You will allow me to say) was too long and too abstract. These are the days of post cards, telegrams, and personalities. The only expedient that would reconcile newspaper readers to so long a letter is hard hitting personality, of course you could not descend to that; yet it was pleasant to see you had arrested the attention of the bishops and made them advert to aspects of the controversy which were in danger of being overlooked.[14]

O'Dwyer did not appear to have had any difficulty himself to descending to 'hard-hitting personality'.

His creativity also found expression, of course, in his sermons. His reputation as a preacher grew steadily in the early years of his priesthood. He began to be called on to preach for special occasions. In July 1874, for example, while a curate in Shanagolden, he was invited to give a charity sermon in Kilkee, Co. Clare. The fact that the parish priest was his uncle may have played a part in the invitation, but the considerable collection of £180[15] justified the choice of preacher. The quality of his regular preaching also continued to impress. It drew increased numbers to St Michael's as it had done earlier at Newcastle West

From Newcastle West, on 20 April 1884, he received a light-hearted, warm letter from a relation, George Sheehy, which referred to some of his public correspondence but also bore nuances for the future. Sheehy was not aware, it seems, of O'Dwyer's virtual withdrawal from political affairs. He and his wife had been concerned about O'Dwyer's health when they had not seen his name mentioned with respect to a recent national demonstration. Instead, the dominant clerical figure had been Fr Robert Ambrose, 'a grand type of nationalist' who spared no one that deserved censure. He was a strong supporter of the tenants, and if O'Dwyer had had him by his side during the late riots in the city the peelers would not dare bludgeon the people as they did. 'He would help you', Sheehy continued, referring to O'Dwyer's correspondence on police brutality, 'to stop the flippant and noisy tongue of the recreant Ambrose Hall.' He then reminded him that 'the Newcastle people … are proud of the gifted young saggart who bids fair in God's own time to don the mitre'. 'God's own time', however, was expected to be a considerable distance away, for Sheehy ended his letter with the ardent wish that he would see him as dean living in St Ita's presbytery, Newcastle West[16]

The thought of a premature death for Bishop George Butler was far from everyone's thoughts. Two years later, however, he contracted a cold that became fatal. To the sorrow of clergy and people, he died on 3 February 1886.

PART TWO

Defying the popular trend, 1886–1891

6

The arrival of the new bishop.
Assured beginnings, 1886–1888

Bishop Butler's death came as a shock to his people and to his fellow prelates. Dr Croke expressed the sense of loss in a letter to Monsignor Kirby in Rome on 14 February 1886. He mourned 'a personal friend ... faithful and sagacious' whose weighty words were always respected by the bishops. 'The country at large looked up to him', Croke maintained, 'and in the diocese of Limerick he was simply idolised ... He lived like a hermit, and, dying, left all he had to the poor.'[1]

The news of the death had scarcely been absorbed, however, before thoughts of a successor began to occupy people's minds. Soon it became clear, even before Dr Butler was buried, that a curate, without administrative experience, was being spoken of as the popular choice of clergy and people. This remarkable development was recalled vividly more than thirty years later by Richard Canon O'Kennedy as he reminisced about the cold Sunday in February 1886 when, amid showers of sleet, large numbers came to the episcopal palace, Corbally, Limerick, to accompany the remains of George Butler to the cathedral. 'One of those preceding me', O'Kennedy recalled,

> was a young priest in biretta and soutane. His surplice was under his arm ... He ... walked alone. He was slight and barely of middle-height. He was extremely pale. I was then chaplain at the Limerick Union, and with my hospital eye I counted the priest very delicate. Indeed, I thought he was not long for earth; and to myself I said, what do they want making a bishop of that poor delicate priest? for his name was in the ear of the public.

'That was Father Edward Thomas O'Dwyer', O'Kennedy explained. 'The face was white, but it was an intellectual face. No portrait did it justice ... ' This very delicate looking man was to pass the same route as Dr Butler, but not until thirty-one years had passed, which, in O'Kennedy's view, indicated what strong reserves of character he must have had. 'Though handicapped in health, as he then was, handicapped in sight and hearing', yet he 'stood out head and shoulders beyond all his competitors'.[2]

The frail curate was not prominent at the funeral, but a month later his reputation as an orator led to his being chosen as the preacher at the Month's Mind for the dead bishop. His powerful sermon on 3 March 1886, which was later published as a pamphlet, was preached to a packed church and followed with wrapt attention.[3] The earnestness and feeling with which he spoke of Dr Butler moved many to tears. He told of the late bishop's commitment to the poor from his earliest days as a priest,[4] and of his 'true episcopal spirit in providing not only a school, but a home for the orphans of the diocese'. Where his priests were concerned he had a singular power in drawing out their zeal and in encouraging them to do good, and towards them he was never narrow but always 'broad-minded and manly'. With all the religious orders 'he was at home', and he helped to make the convents 'truly schools of Christian perfection'. Essentially, Bishop Butler was a man of warm, impulsive, ardent nature, but 'he never allowed any human sympathy to usurp the place of religious duty', especially his main duty as bishop, to be 'the guardian of God's children' and 'to feed the members of God's household' over which he had been placed by God. In all he did, O'Dwyer observed, he sought no praise; indeed 'he had a dread of the appetite of praise which creeps into the souls of good men'.[5]

To O'Dwyer's audience, his presentation also suggested that he himself was a man of deep humanity and spirituality, who appreciated both the exalted office of bishop and the dignity of each human being as a child of God and brother/sister of Christ. Only in retrospect did his emphasis on 'religious duty' and the primary duty of the bishop take on added significance. His assertion that the bishop's main concern was to feed his flock with the food of spirit and truth, and to guard them against corruption and falsehood, and that no considerations of sympathy or popularity should be allowed to usurp that duty, foreshadowed the guiding considerations of his own time as bishop.

APPOINTMENT PROCESS

Later on the day of the Month's Mind, Archbishop Croke presided at a meeting of the parish priests of the diocese to choose a successor to Bishop George Butler. Beforehand, the most likely candidate was thought to be Dr Thomas Hammond, parish priest of Newcastle West, who for most of his life as a priest had been dean at Maynooth College. Another candidate spoken of was Fr Joseph Bourke, the former president of the diocesan college. When the votes were counted, however, O'Dwyer had secured 20 votes, Hammond 12, and Bourke 4. Edward Thomas O'Dwyer, therefore, was deemed ('*dignissimus*' the most worthy) in the *terna* commended to Rome.[6] The enthusiasm of some of his supporters led at least one parish priest to press his case in a letter to Monsignor Kirby, the agent of the Irish bishops in Rome. The Revd Cornelius P. Kenny, parish priest of Fedamore, Co. Limerick, rhapsodised in favour of the choice of the majority of the parish priests to fill the vacant office. 'No worthier selection could be made in all Ireland,' he assured Kirby on 30 March 1886.

> He is to my mind the very man of all men wanting to us at this critical time. He is supreme in knowledge of theology and philosophy. He is a ripe scholar; an ardent student; he has a large comprehensive mind and cultivates it to the utmost. In any spare hour he is sure to be found amongst his books. Apart from that, he is the very – if I ought use the expression – incarnation and embodiment of missionary work, ever on the alert to raise the poor, to enlighten the middle class, and attract the patronage and practical support of the higher classes.

'His organising power is simply Napoleonic,' Kenny argued relentlessly, indicating that he would bring about 'strict discipline among the clergy', who were 'becoming more radical every day', and would curb the younger clergy, who 'dressed like fops', and would 'keep them to their studies and make them preach'. With increasing laudation, the writer claimed that O'Dwyer was both intimate and familiar with every priest in the diocese and knew 'the right man for the right place'. Among the episcopacy he would be 'a bright particular star' who would be an honour not only to Limerick but to all Ireland. 'In disposition', Kenny affirmed, 'he is gentle and generous, full of love and charity for every human being.' As a preacher he was unrivalled. Kirby, Kenny advised, should dismiss any criticisms of O'Dwyer that might be sent to him during the interregnum. They were 'all lies'. 'I implore you to use your utmost influence to carry out the wishes of the P.Ps', Kenny pleaded, adding, scarcely credibly, 'I am no party of Fr O'Dwyer. I seldom see him. I speak *solely, entirely, absolutely* in the interests of religion in our great and important diocese.'[7]

Such a reference as that of Fr Kenny might appear so overdrawn as not to merit serious consideration, yet, not long after his inflated letter, the archives of Propaganda Fide display Cardinal William Massajo, in the course of presenting proposals for the vacant see of Limerick, commenting in a most complimentary manner on 'Edoardo O'Dwyer', the choice of the clergy of 'a flourishing diocese'. He noted that he 'received great praise for philosophy and theology at Maynooth', and that as a priest he was 'known for integrity of behaviour, piety, zeal and doctrine', and apart from English, he knew 'Latin, Greek, French, German and Italian'. He was '45 years of age, 19 years as a priest'.[8] Rome moved more quickly than usual in making the appointment. On Monday, 10 May 1886, Denis Hallinan, curate at Newcastle West, noted in his diary: 'Telegram received announcing the appointment of Fr O'Dwyer as Bishop of Limerick. Great rejoicing in the city.'[9] The celebrations there were marked by blazing tar barrels and the sound of marching bands.[10] The reference to 'rejoicing in the city', without reference to the author's county area, may suggest less than enthusiasm among tenant farmers, who recalled the disagreements of 1874.

CONGRATULATIONS, CONSECRATION, CELEBRATION

Congratulations were received from many quarters, including Monsignor Kirby at the Irish College, Rome. O'Dwyer replied on 14 May, thanking him for his kind words of congratulation and encouragement, and asking his prayers that he might not shame the line of saintly bishops of whom he was the unworthy successor, 'nor disappoint the hopes of those who, as your Grace, generously expect good things from me'. He adroitly reminded Kirby of his kindness to him ten years previously when he visited Rome and Kirby had kindly asked Pope Pius IX to bless his ears. He trusted that he might count on the same kindness to aid him in the future.[11] On a more business-like note O'Dwyer wrote to Bishop James McCarthy of Cloyne to ask if it were in order to have two names on his episcopal seal, and whether it was permitted to have the family arms and family motto quartered with the episcopal ones. McCarthy replied affirmatively on 13 June.[12] The chosen family motto was '*Virtuti non armis fido*' (I trust in courage, not in force of arms),[13] which was to have a particular relevance on a number of occasions during his episcopate.

O'Dwyer's consecration took place on a very warm 29 June, the feast of Sts Peter and Paul, a holy day of obligation. The cathedral, as a result, was 'crammed' with people long before the mass and ceremony began. Fr Hallinan noted in his diary that there were eleven bishops present, and numerous priests, most of them from the diocese. Archbishop Croke was the consecrating prelate, assisted by James McCarthy of Cloyne and Andrew Higgins of Kerry. The preacher for the occasion was Thomas Carr, bishop of Galway. The mass was not a high mass. The ceremony concluded at 1.30 p.m.[14] The *Limerick and Clare Advocate* told of Mrs O'Dwyer, and an uncle of the bishop, a Mr E. O'Dwyer from Cashel, and the members of the corporation in their robes, occupying seats in the sanctuary; of banners and bannerettes and draped pillars; of hundreds outside the church who could not get in; and of an atmosphere of jubilation 'at the elevation of one who had so much endeared himself to the hearts of all'. The wonderful enthusiasm for him of the people, the paper continued, 'can be accounted for by the sincerity with which he has entered into their dearest concerns whenever his valuable counsel and aid were sought, making their interests his own, and sparing no effort to serve them, no matter what the sacrifice to himself. There is nothing they could do for him they would not do.' The regard of his fellow priests, the report continued, was shown by their choice of a curate to be their bishop; and the unprecedently quick appointment by Rome was further acknowledgement that he had been an exceptional candidate. The report added that O'Dwyer had always been a Home Ruler, but had 'exercised an independent judgment with regard to political questions – not seeking popularity, but doing just what he thought right himself'. The writer recalled his sympathy with the agitation for the amnesty of the political prisoners in 1869, and 'the remarkably able, eloquent and moving speech he made at the great meeting held in Bruff ' in support of the prisoners. Finally, the paper drew attention to a particular question put to the new bishop as part of the consecration ceremony, a question which, as time would show, O'Dwyer took very seriously: 'Wilt thou bear fidelity, subjection and obedience according to canonical authority, in all things to the Blessed Peter the Apostle, to whom God gave the power of binding and losing, to his vicar the Lord Pope Leo XIII, and to his successors, the Roman Pontiffs?'

After the ceremony, all the guests assembled at a reception in the Athenaeum Hall, where food and liquid refreshments were provided at O'Dwyer's expense. John S. Flanagan, parish priest of Adare, read an address on behalf of the clergy, to which the bishop replied appropriately. Then there was an address on behalf of the laity, to which his Lordship's response was, according to Fr Hallinan, 'equally good'. At a subsequent dinner there were 400 guests, and speeches by Dr O'Dwyer, Lord Emly, Bishop Healy of Clonfert, and others. All, apparently, well delivered. The 'Health of the Diocese' was 'cleverly proposed' by the teetotaller Bishop O'Dwyer. Finally, Archbishop Croke spoke, and the occasion drew to a close.[15]

THE EXTENT OF THE CHALLENGE

The diocese of Limerick over which the young bishop was to rule followed the contours of the county to the north, west, and south. To the north it crossed the Shannon and jutted into Co. Clare; to the west it bordered Co. Kerry; to the south, Co. Cork; but to the east it encountered the archdiocese of Cashel and Emly, which extended into Co. Limerick to within nine or ten miles of Limerick city.

A wide range of people participated in operating the various institutions and works of the diocese. There were 110 diocesan clergy, in 49 parishes, with 94 parochial and district churches. They also served as chaplains to hospitals, to two gaols, five workhouses, and various convents and charitable institutions. In addition, there were some 40 clergy drawn from the following religious orders: Augustinians, Dominicans, Franciscans, Redemptorists, and Jesuits. Women religious were particularly prominent: 26 Presentation sisters served mainly in schools; of the Sisters of Mercy, there were seven convents involving 116 sisters, who worked throughout the diocese in orphanages, and hospitals, but mainly in education; the Faithful Companions of Jesus, numbers not available, ran two schools 'for young ladies', one at Laurel Hill, Limerick, the other at Bruff, Co. Limerick; the Good Shepherd Convent of 48 sisters looked after 100 women in a 'Magdalene asylum' and 30 in a female reformatory; and the Convent of Mary Reparatrice, with a smaller number of sisters, provided a house of continuous prayer. In terms of educational provision: convent schools, in city and county, provided primary education for 5,466 pupils, mainly girls, while Christian Brothers' schools catered for 6,000 boys. The Brothers also ran an industrial school. Secondary education for girls from 'the higher classes' was provided by the Faithful Companions of Jesus at Laurel Hill and Bruff; while boys were provided for by 8 Jesuits at the Crescent, Limerick, while another eight Jesuits educated 90 boarders, preparing for the priesthood, and some other students, at Mungret College three miles outside the city.[16]

All in all, a considerable area of responsibility for a frail looking, young man, who previously had not even had responsibility for a parish. Yet, there was an air of assurance about the new bishop. He had a natural distinction that seemed appropriate to his exalted office.[17] He was, as remembered by Archdeacon John Begley, author of *The Diocese of Limerick*, 'a young priest of presentable appearance and fascinating manner'.[18] The new bishop's assurance and aplomb, however, appears to have raised questions in Archbishop Croke's mind from the very beginning. Eighteen months later, on 12 January 1887, following disagreements between O'Dwyer and many of the bishops, he observed to his friend Archbishop Walsh of Dublin: 'I knew well, ever since the display at his consecration dinner, that + E.T. would give trouble ... He must be put down ...'[19] Edward Thomas O'Dwyer, for his part, was conscious both of his youthful appearance and of the dignity of his office, and was determined not to be taken for granted. Responding to an address from his former class fellows at Maynooth shortly after his consecration, he remarked – 'Entering on my episcopacy, when I feel our lives henceforth have separate lines, and never can be one again, it will be a comfort to know that I bear with me your affection, your sympathy and your prayers ...'[20] The response was not that different from the popular anecdote that when some of his fellow curates said to him, just prior to his consecration, that they would find it difficult to get used to calling him 'My Lord', the brief reply was – 'You better get used to it'![21] This stern side to him was fairly widely experienced within a short time. Archbishop Croke, some six months after the new bishop's consecration, reported to Archbishop Walsh: 'In the Limerick side of my diocese, where I have spent the last few days, I learned that there is 'a caution' already amongst the priests and that they are afraid of (their) skin of him. 'Tis well our fellows do not shiver before us.'[22] The volatility and self-will that were present in the priest, were to become more obvious in the exalted position of bishop, where his swings of mood were joined to authority and affected far more people. To many, however, such failings, in addition to the infirmity of his deafness, made him a more sympathetic and appealing figure, and they readily appreciated his human qualities, his pastoral zeal and personal gifts.

ASSURED BEGINNINGS

There was a bustling start to his episcopate: a round of visits to parishes, hospitals, orphanages, schools, convents, the arch-confraternity at the Redemptorist church, various sodalities and confraternities at other churches, and other social and religious groupings. Of the various organisations in the diocese, the arch-confraternity run by the Redemptorist priests already held an honoured place in O'Dwyer's esteem. It brought 2000 to 3000 men to evening devotions each Monday, and similar number on Tuesday evenings. There was also a successful boys' confraternity attached to the main body. The effect of these practices on numerous homes over many years was immense. Shortly after his consecration, he expressed pride in the Holy Family Confraternity, as it was called, and subsequently he promoted and encouraged its work again and again.[23] His early activities also included a visit, with his mother, to his sister, Annie, at St John's priory in Bambury, England.[24]

After some time, O'Dwyer arranged for certain changes of clergy, and in September conducted his first diocesan conference.[25] The conference made his priests aware of his clear mind, his high ideals, and his capacity to communicate in a lively and interesting manner. 'Dr. O'Dwyer was the ablest man I ever met in my life,' Dean Punch recalled towards the close of his long life. 'At conferences, he asked a question and for two hours he deduced everything he said from that first question.'[26]

Dr Butler had commenced the custom of holding diocesan conferences during Easter week at four venues on successive days – Newcastle West, Rathkeale, Bruff and Limerick. At each of these places conferences were held four times a year. This meant sixteen conferences attended by the bishop, and four by the priests. The aim was to provide the clergy with the opportunity of 'common consultancy on matters affecting religion in the diocese'. The subjects for study and consideration were Church History, Sacred Scripture, and Moral Theology. Dr Butler adapted his own wide reading and ability to the lower all round level of his priests with much success, but O'Dwyer, especially in the area of moral theology, adopted a more erudite textbook for discussion.[27] Canon Richard O'Kennedy, in the *Irish Monthly,* shortly after the bishop's death, recalled aspects of his life. Among these recollections was the impact made by O'Dwyer's conferences.[28] 'He was particularly anxious', O'Kennedy recalled, 'to see all his priests well grounded on the questions of justice and ownership and restitution.'[29] During the conferences individual priests were set particular cases to solve, and their resolution or approach was then open to comment by all present. The bishop's sensitivity towards justice was paralleled by sensitivity towards the observation of rubrics in administering the sacraments, and above all in the celebration of the Mass. Justice was a matter between man and man, but rubrics he viewed as between man and God. Hence, he did not just ask questions about rubrics at his conferences, he requested priests to stand at the altar and go through the physical actions. In his visitation of the parishes, moreover, he scrutinised carefully the observance of the rubrics at the public Masses.

All this emphasis on knowledge and practice, and the examination of both, must have occasioned strain, even fear, among some of his priests; but with respect to the conduct of the conferences, it is clear that quite a number found them of interest and value. Canon O'Kennedy described the process:

Sitting at conference, with all of us sitting in a semi-circle about him because of his deafness, he at the beginning gave you a *resume* of the matter to be discussed, the whys and wherefores ... He did it with such knowledge of the question that the whole thing became simplicity itself, and with such a wealth of illustration, humorous as a rule, and even boyish, that you saw it was almost a plaything in his hands.

'Three hours was generally the length of the sitting,' O'Kennedy added. 'With another that might be long and wearisome; but with him, while you were glad at the end to stand up and stretch your legs, you felt that he had given the sitting a great élan, and had robbed it of all tediousness.'[30]

The fascination of the bishop was linked to his humour, his gifts as a raconteur, and his range of knowledge and interests. He had a mind stored with theology, classical and English literature, and he had more than a passing acquaintance with French, Italian, German, science, history, accountancy, art, politics, and music, and, on a more earthy note, with practical experience of horses as a rider and breeder. His portrait from these early years, viewed retrospectively, reflected his coiled energy, and his eyes with their bright, direct gaze manifested the sharp intelligence, which so many noted.

Some insight into his literary and cultural interests may be gathered from his sister Annie's letters to him. The interests and experiences she mentioned to him suggest that they were held in common. On 27 November 1884 she wrote of Macauley, Mrs Sheridan, Reynolds and Haydn, expressed a wish to hear Ruskin's lectures at Oxford, and added – 'You don't forget our *delightful readings* last year, how we discussed Giotto etc.' On 18 October 1874 she had looked forward to *La Somnambula* at the musical festival in Leeds; and many years later, on 6 February 1898, she devoted most of her letter to the celebrated Spanish coloratura singer, Madame Patti. An undated letter announces that she had just finished *Coriolanus*, and she asks him to send on *French history* by Guizot. On Easter Sunday 1892 she recommended 'a nice book', *Le Recit d'une Soeur*, by Mrs Craven, and urged him to get the original. 'The English translation by Lady Fullerton is very good but it goes without saying it is inferior to the French.' 'I wish you could read it aloud to me,' she added, 'and then we might talk it over.' Much earlier, on 21 April 1877, when she had eventually heard from him, after a long silence, she declared in humorous exasperation: 'It's all very well to be quoting Aeneas to me. I wonder what he would say to your barbarous treatment of your older sister and she a nun!'[31]

In accordance with the high ideals of his office, O'Dwyer planned not only to raise religious standards among his priests but also to promote knowledge, spiritual devotion, and education among his people. Education in all its aspects was an abiding interest. Primary education, he viewed as the basis for the future, and he soon made a habit of frequently visiting primary schools and encouraging the teachers. Indeed, within days of his consecration as bishop he responded to an address from the national teachers of the diocese by expressing publicly his recognition of the value of their work and their lack of proper remuneration. He promised to work hard on their behalf.[32]

Before long, on the basis of advice from diocesan officials, personal contact, and correspondence, he became intimately informed on happenings and needs in various parishes. Among the matters mentioned, in extant letters from parish priests, were: financial affairs, a sexual scandal in a parish, alms for the support of a school, a dispensation to marry where there was an obstacle of consanguinity, church collections. There was also evidence of the bishop acting firmly, even threateningly, in a letter from a priest who acknowledged his Lordship's just reprimand and requested humbly: 'I must only throw myself on your mercy, and ask for the sake of a friendship that began many years since, not to throw me on the world.' He had made 'a solemn vow to avoid certain things' for the rest of his life. The bishop appears to have heeded his request. The priest continued in the same parish until his death in 1895.[33] There were also, as will be evident in later chapters, numerous letters dealing with aspects of education.

Such activities and correspondence, however, were but as background to the wider issues which involved him in the first two years of his episcopate – those concerning university education, land agitation, and the visit of the papal representative, Archbishop Ignatius Persico. In facing these he was afflicted, initially, not only with deafness but with a deficiency in sight. He sought advice about the best eye specialists to consult, and was given the name of specialists in London, Freiburg and Dublin.[34] It is not clear which he consulted, but the news was better than expected. His sister, Annie, responded joyfully on 15 August 1887: 'It is delightful to hear that we have good grounds for hoping that the disease in your eye maybe totally arrested. A great deal, I think,' she counselled, 'depends on your general health and you should do all you can to improve it … At any rate take a good long holiday out of your friends reach.'[35]

Of the 'friends' from whom she advised a holiday, two of those closest to him from student days had been Thomas Carr, who became bishop of Galway, and William J. Walsh, archbishop of Dublin. Carr sent his farewells on 2 October 1886, as he set out for the archbishopric of Melbourne, thanking him for his friendship and great kindness and asking his prayers.[36] O'Dwyer's friendship with Walsh was to be weakened by differences of view on the university question. Both men were educationalists, both had strong opinions on the best way of dealing with the university issue. Walsh was used to being the leading voice of the hierarchy on educational matters and probably resented presumption of equality on the part of a recently appointed prelate, while O'Dwyer felt he was being patronised and dictated to by Walsh. Their differences had their origins in how best to go about securing a satisfactory university education for the majority population following the failure of Newman's Catholic University.

7

University education and the Senate appointment. Defying the Episcopal Standing Committee, 1886–1888

The development of the university question in the years following the failure of the Catholic University greatly influenced Dr Walsh. He took a stand during the years 1880 to 1884 which influenced many people, and which altered his relationship with Edward Thomas O'Dwyer.

THE BACKGROUND

The Catholic University failed through lack of recognised qualifications and of adequate funding. In 1873 Gladstone sought to solve the problem of university education for Catholics by introducing a bill that would open up Dublin University, as distinct from Trinity College, in order to comprise within it not only Trinity College but also the Catholic University, the Queen's Colleges of Belfast and Cork, and any other college that fulfilled conditions in the bill entitling a college to university status. The measure was narrowly defeated and resulted in the ousting of the Liberals from office. Gladstone's plan, however, was to remain the basis of Dr Walsh's ideal solution up to the foundation of the National University in 1908. Disraeli's Conservative government offered a solution in August 1879, which sought to meet some of the Catholics' needs without alienating the strong Non-Conformist vote in Britain. The Royal University of Ireland was established, based on the principle of indirect subsidy that had been followed in the Intermediate Education Act. It was a purely examining body, which, however, enabled Catholic colleges to compete for recognised degrees, and which had a senate empowered to draw up a scheme of exhibitions, prizes and scholarships, and to allocate fellowships, as a form of indirect endowment. This benefit to Catholic colleges occasioned a controversy among Catholics. It was generated through Dr Walsh, then president of Maynooth College.

THE UNIVERSITY SENATE CONTROVERSY

In 1881 it was announced that of the 26 proposed fellowships, half were to go to Catholics. Each carried £400. The holders were to be official examiners of the Royal University and were to teach in an educational institution approved by the senate of that university. The following year, October 1882, the bishops decreed that the Catholic University, now reduced to a handful of students, be handed over to Edward, Cardinal McCabe, archbishop of Dublin. The latter, after advice, decided that henceforth the Catholic University would be but a moral body with six constituent colleges, of which one, University College, St Stephen's Green, would occupy the buildings of the Catholic University and have centralised in it all the fellowships allotted to Catholics.[1] With this endowment of Catholic fellows, who would teach the students of University College and also serve as their examiners, it was hoped that applications to the college would greatly increase and that the college would become a force in university education. A year later, however, in the face of little success and financial problems, the bishops, on the proposal of Archbishop Thomas Croke of Cashel, voted that the college be handed over to the Jesuits, with William Delany as president.[2] Delany had demonstrated in a small college in the midlands, St Stanislaus College, Tullabeg, that Catholic students could obtain good results in the London University examinations.

On 26 October 1883, Delany, on behalf of the Society of Jesus, signed an agreement with the episcopal trustees of the Catholic University. What appealed to Delany was the concentration of all the Catholic fellows at University College, with the one exception, because of its difficult location, of St Malachy's College, Belfast. He saw the concentration as the means of surpassing all the Queen's Colleges and of proving, through the success of his students in examinations, that the case for a recognised university for Catholics was overwhelming. Dr Walsh, then president of Maynooth College and a member of the senate of the Royal University, supported Delany's case to the bishops; and then a year later, to Delany's astonishment, came up with a proposal that required that some fellowships be given to the highly successful college at Blackrock run by the Holy Ghost Fathers. The ensuing fellowship controversy ran from January to December 1884.[3]

Dr James Kavanagh, president of Carlow College, gave notice that if the Blackrock proposal were approved he would apply for a similar concession for Carlow. The argument in favour of the concentration of teaching power in one central college was endangered. The senate turned down Dr Walsh's proposal. Complaining at the injustice of this monopoly, he resigned, and accused the chairman of the senate, Lord Emly, of neglect of duty as a senator and committee man. His stance led to criticism from Dr Kavanagh and from bishops who had been his admirers. Archbishop Croke thought it unrealistic to have 'two competing establishments in or near Dublin ... both certain to lack vigour, because both lacking funds'.[4] Bishop Butler of Limerick was trenchant. It surprised him that Dr Walsh would advocate the 'fritting away of the teaching power of the Catholic fellows by dividing it between several schools'. He had always understood him to favour concentration 'so as to create, in Dublin, a great centre of Catholic thought and feeling, and educational work, which by its eminent success in connection with the Royal University, should of necessity, and in the not very distant future, force recognition and endowments at the hand of the government'. He reminded Walsh, as Dr Kavanagh had done, that University College was the bishops' college, that the Jesuits could be removed if not satisfactory or if the government was prepared to subsidise a Catholic college but not one run by the Jesuits. The bishops had considered three possibilities, 'but in all of them', Butler declared, 'the concentration of the fellows at St Stephen's Green was a central factor', and 'if the Jesuits took it up they were to have all the fellows'. Finally, he quietly defended his Limerick friend. 'I am puzzled', he chided, 'by your reference to Lord Emly in connection with neglect of duty as a senator or committee man. I think you will find on enquiry that he has been constant in his attendance at senate and committee meetings.'[5] Dr Walsh remained unmoved by the arguments of Croke, Kavanagh, and Butler.

In November and December 1884 he brought his quarrel into the public arena with contributions to the *Tablet* and the *Freeman's Journal*. His criticisms were eagerly publicised by the Belfast *Morning News*. Not surprisingly, one of the first matters on which O'Dwyer sought advice after his appointment as bishop was the concentration of fellows. Hence, it may be presumed, he had followed the correspondence with interest, seeing that Walsh was a close friend and that his own bishop took an opposing view; never thinking that the controversy was to influence Walsh's future attitude to the Royal University and its senate, and to O'Dwyer himself.

The controversy was eventually brought to an end by a formidable response from a prominent lay member of the senate, Dr Francis Cruise. His long letter in the *Freeman's Journal* of 2 December 1884 ranged over the history of the fellowships and the background to Dr Walsh's opposition, and left Walsh feeling publicly humiliated. Speaking as a Catholic member of the senate, Cruise regretted Walsh's charging the senate with a policy 'essentially based on unfairness and injustice' just because it was not prepared to accept his *ipse dixit*. It was a puzzle to him as a layman, he continued, how Walsh could claim his withdrawal from the senate was on a point of principle, seeing that the cardinal and several other prominent churchmen found no problem in staying on. As to his concern over 'the supposed iniquity' of 'monopoly', this came strangely from the president of Maynooth College, for was not Maynooth a monopoly, and a very big one?

Walsh was upset and deeply stung. On 5 December he responded in a rather evasive and deflated letter, which concluded with the mortifying request that Cruise would now 'have the propriety to let the matter drop'. Cruise closed the public controversy two days later. He was desisting out of respect, he declared, while restating his belief in the accuracy of the picture he had drawn of Walsh's policy and its effect on the bishops' college. 'I deeply regret', he added, 'the grave imprudence which originated such a controversy and conducted it so strangely.'[6] A few days later when Delany called on Cardinal McCabe, the latter observed that he had informed Dr Walsh that his letter of resignation 'was most uncalled for and inopportune'.[7] McCabe, annoyed that Walsh had resigned without consulting him, invited John Healy, professor at Maynooth, to allow his name be proposed for the vacant place. On Healy questioning the propriety of this, he being a member of Walsh's staff, he was informed that he was to be appointed coadjutor to the bishop of Clonfert. Healy, having consulted Walsh, accepted appointment to the senate.[8] An independent, forceful personality, Healy was to prove a staunch supporter of the St Stephen's Green College, a critic of Walsh and a friend to O'Dwyer.

Walsh, though a large-minded man, never got over his sense of public humiliation, and the blame for it was firmly linked to the senate of the university. Thereafter, his attitude to the Royal University and its senate was dismissive or openly hostile. University College, as the institution favoured by the senate, experienced, inevitably, some of his disapproval. He had 'closed his eyes', as Bishop Butler commented to Delany on 24 November, to the consequences of his actions in the fellowship business.[9] His hostility to the senate and the Royal University took on magnified dimensions with his appointment to the archbishopric of Dublin in 1885. The grounds for disagreement with O'Dwyer became evident when the latter was offered a seat on the senate!

O'Dwyer for many years, certainly from his association with Isaac Butt, viewed the provision of satisfactory university education for the Catholic majority as a political and social priority, prior even to the land question. The establishment of the Royal University, in his view, was a big step forward. It brought about what he later termed 'a momentous change' in that it signified the dissolution of the Queen's University, the acknowledgement of the validity of the Catholic objection to frequenting the Queen's colleges, and the provision of an indirect endowment for Catholic colleges. The Queen's colleges were no longer autonomous. Now, together with the Catholic colleges, they were placed under the senate of the Royal University. Despite the 'momentous change', however, and the value he recognised in using the Royal University Act to develop the Catholic colleges and to increase third-level educational opportunities for the Catholic population, O'Dwyer, like the other bishops, wanted much more than an examining institution. His vision and theirs was for a residential university on par, at least, with Trinity College, and they viewed this as an inalienable right. Unlike many of his colleagues, however, O'Dwyer was not prepared to allow other objectives take priority over the university question.[10]

He made this clear at one of his early public functions. At a prize-giving ceremony at the Crescent College, Limerick, in mid-October 1886, he distanced himself from views expressed publicly by Archbishop Walsh some days earlier. Walsh had emphasised the importance of the alliance of the Irish party with the Liberals for the attainment of Home Rule, and advised that issues, which might upset the prevailing cordial relations, such as the demand for a Catholic university, should be shelved for the time being. In this, Walsh announced, he felt he was echoing the sentiments of his episcopal colleagues. O'Dwyer was definite. The university question was 'too sacred', he asserted, 'to be postponed to any consideration of political expediency or the exigencies of a political party'.[11] In a letter to Walsh on 18 October, he deplored any suggestion of postponing the education question and could not see how it could interfere with the broader question of Home Rule.[12] On 2 November he informed the archbishop that he had grounds for believing that the Tories were prepared to treat the education question independently, and that this was an opportunity that should not be lost. It was the duty of the bishops as spiritual leaders of the people to seek a settlement of this important matter 'from any quarter', irrespective of whether it was Whig or Tory. This was not inconsistent with supporting the movement for self-government.[13] The Irish political leaders sought land reform while seeking Home Rule. The question of higher education was every bit as pressing as land reform. Both were national issues and should be given equal attention by the Irish leaders. He chose to ignore the hard political fact that the land issue was more important to politicians in terms of votes and public support than the more peripheral university question.

The priorities of Isaac Butt, and the memory of how he had been treated by the current Irish leaders, remained with O'Dwyer, and lurked behind a striking assertion in the course of his address at the Crescent College prize-giving. As long as the Irish leaders strove to put the land question before all other national demands, he declared, he personally would feel obliged to use his influence to further what he considered to be 'religiously and politically the most important question' committed to his care, namely, that of providing a university for the Catholic majority.[14]

O'Dwyer's Limerick speech brought a letter from Walsh on 20 October that opened with the comment – 'You have done splendid service by Monday's address.' He went on to explain that by reason of his being in the capital he had close contacts with Liberals and Tories, and had hopes of development in the area of education. If the Protestant press construed from O'Dwyer's address that he was 'in favour of pressing on the education question' and that Walsh was 'for keeping it in the background', then they were in for a surprise. He was against, however, putting forward proposals to the government. 'If we propose anything definite,' he declared, in what was to become a personal refrain, 'they will simply fall back on a criticism of details.' 'Just now', he added, 'it will be easy to force them to take the initiative in proposing. Then we can criticise it from our side with a much better chance of good results.'[15]

Another letter responding to his address came from John Healy, coadjutor bishop of Clonfert. It opened up an interesting prospect. 'I was very much pleased with the report of your speech'; he observed, 'something of the kind was very much wanting.' He agreed that the education question could be better settled at this time than it would be in the future. He then observed calculatingly: 'There are two Catholic vacancies on the senate, one for a cleric and one for a lay-man. I dare say the former vacancy would be offered to you if it were thought your Lordship would accept it.' 'I should be very glad', he added, 'if you could see your way to accept the place, because I think you would be able to give invaluable assistance in settling the question.' There had been a resolution passed sometime ago, he further explained, that two bishops should be placed on the senate, but he had not taken the place as a bishop. He was not a bishop when appointed and never considered himself as a representative of the *coetus episcoporum* or bishops' standing committee. At one time, as a result, there were three bishops – Cardinal McCabe, Dr Woodlock, and himself. The cardinal's place was still vacant. 'I think', he concluded, 'if you telegraphed to Propaganda and asked their sanction … all would be right.' He mentioned this, of course, 'only in case the vacancy should be offered'.[16]

It was a clear invitation to express his interest in accepting a place on the senate, and implied that this might be accomplished without the approval of the bishops' standing committee by an appeal to Rome. It was a tempting offer to someone with O'Dwyer's ambitions to make an impact on the educational scene, and this was evident to both Healy and Lord Emly. The latter was destined to play a large part in O'Dwyer's life over the next several years. William Monsell, Lord Emly, had been a close friend of O'Dwyer's two predecessors, Bishops John Ryan and George Butler, and his strong religious faith, and wide theological reading, his personal friendship with John Henry Newman, and his links with Lacordaire, Montalambert, and other European Catholic intellectuals, were all likely to render him a figure of interest and influence to the new bishop of Limerick. Eight years later, O'Dwyer would acknowledge with feeling that one of the privileges the office of bishop had brought him was 'first to know, and then greatly to value, and finally to love one of the most lovable, one of the most beautiful, and one of the noblest characters' he had ever met. Emly's stance on a number of political issues might not have been popular, but in these, O'Dwyer observed approvingly, he 'exercised the inalienable right of every free man to think for himself, and to act for himself in a purely political question'.[17] Besides, he added significantly, Emly, as vice-chancellor of the Royal University, considered it his duty to obtain for his fellow Catholics 'as large a measure [of] the benefits of the existing university as it was in his power to acquire,' and by practically redressing some existing abuses he had brought home 'the blessings of a higher education to thousands of Irish Catholics.'[18]

From the start, everything induced O'Dwyer to take a far more positive view of Emly than his friend Walsh. Hence, after his appointment to Limerick was announced, and before his consecration, it was to Emly he wrote to enquire about the Royal University and the concentration of fellowships in one Catholic college. Emly, in reply, pointed out first that his own position *vis-à-vis* the Royal University did not mean that he viewed that institution as a solution to the university question. As a member of parliament he had urged, and still considered it the best solution, 'that a great Catholic college should be founded in

Dublin University'. Gladstone's measure, though imperfect principally 'in not providing direct endowment for a Catholic college, was sound in principle'. Then, speaking of the Royal University, he explained that the powers of the senate were executive, not legislative. They 'had 13 Catholic fellowships at £400 a year each to dispose of'. This was the only approximation to endowment at their disposal. Common sense dictated that there should be a concentration of fellows so as to make the strongest possible case for a university for Catholics. Catholic fellows, besides, were in very short supply. It would be even more difficult to attract them if they were to be scattered in 'obscure colleges' around the country. Limited though resources were, the concentration of teaching fellows was, Emly believed, 'on the way' to making 'our college great and distinguished', and was also playing an important role 'by training up a highly educated class'. With such teachers, he added, 'we shall soon have a college worthy to be united to Trinity College as a college worthy of the University of Dublin, one with which it would be proud to be united'. To accomplish this, however, there was need for a rich endowment. He and Bishop Healy had been active in seeking to obtain this from the government.[19]

That Emly, knowing O'Dwyer's interest and personality, set about preparing for his election to the senate of the university, seems likely. In conjunction with him, Healy planted the seed in O'Dwyer's mind. On Emly's role, Archbishop Croke had a story for Dr Walsh on 14 January 1887. His cousin, Fr Robert Carbery, SJ, during a visit to Thurles, Co. Tipperary, had told him that 'about three months ago Lord Emly canvassed for + E.T.'s (Croke's partly derisive way of referring to Edward Thomas O'Dwyer's appointment.' Amongst others, he called on John Thomas Ball, vice-chancellor of Dublin University, a member of the senate, and on Christopher Palles, lord chief baron of the exchequer in Ireland, also a senator. 'Ball refused, at first, to countenance' O'Dwyer's appointment, 'on the grounds that he was an *advanced nationalist* and recommended the appointment of [Robert] Browne of Maynooth instead. But, on being assured *by Lord Emly that E.T. was an orthodox loyalist*, he fell in with his Lordship's views, and in furtherance of them canvassed Palles – or rather spoke to him approvingly of the proposed appointment.' 'So,' Croke concluded, 'the thing was well managed and secured.'[20] By the date of Croke's letter, O'Dwyer had made his decision. In the intervening months he had corresponded with and sounded many people on university matters.

On 1 November two very different letters were sent to him. Dr Walsh informed him pointedly that in anything he said in public he spoke for the bishops as a body. 'Where no corporate policy has been decided on, I keep clear of the point.' 'Your declaration', he reminded O'Dwyer, 'could only be for yourself as an individual.'[21] The other correspondent was W.H. Keating, a frequent contributor to the press on educational matters. He forwarded the content of a long letter of Dr William Delany, SJ, on the university question. The Irish party, Keating claimed, had no interest in the university project and most of them held 'unCatholic views about education'. The hierarchy were failing in their duty by giving over, 'by formal resolution', the conduct of education to the party. Now was the time, he urged, to press the Catholic demand in its entirety.[22]

Something of Keating's and his own doubts about Parnell and his party must have been conveyed to Dr Walsh, as five days later the archbishop assured O'Dwyer that 'the education question' was 'all right' and that Parnell's attitude was 'one of perfect harmony with ours'. In the same letter, he mentioned that he had arranged to have 'the first meeting of the episcopal committee of 13 (of which the Munster bishops elected you as representative member) on the occasion of the reopening of Marlborough Street [school] on the 8th December.' 'So, you see', he added lightly, 'you will have to come to town for the occasion.'[23] O'Dwyer had been selected to preach the reopening sermon!

Next day, almost on cue, Keating wrote again. He assured O'Dwyer in honeyed tones that he had 'very special advantages in taking a leading part' in a great cause. 'At the head of a great community, representing a vast Catholic population, perfectly untrammelled by previous engagements, a new departure is perfectly open to you.' 'And a grander role', he maintained, 'cannot be conceived than for your Lordship to take your stand on the inalienable *rights* of your flock to have their educational claim satisfied in the fullest and highest manner.' He believed that if his Lordship using his 'freedom' and exercising his 'clear right' followed up his first declaration he would have the nation behind him. It was the kind of message that an ambitious part of O'Dwyer wanted to hear, and that predisposed part was further stimulated by Keating's criticism of the party's attempts 'to place Mr T.P. O'Connor in the front rank in educational matters'. There could be no clearer indication, Keating observed, 'of the rapidity with which we are sinking'. Mr O'Connor was said, 'with too many evidences of its truth, to have abandoned not the practice only, but the bare profession of Catholicism.'[24]

Other voices were also pointing O'Dwyer towards an important, virtually independent role in education. One of these was Captain William H. O'Shea, MP for Clare, largely remembered because of his wife's relations with Parnell, but who was also well known to O'Dwyer. On 20 November 1886, O'Shea informed O'Dwyer, that, following his meeting with him in Limerick three weeks previously, he had taken 'opportunities of ascertaining the real position of the Irish education question and the views of statesmen as to the possibility and advisability of dealing with it in the immediate future'. If the Irish bishops made up their mind once for all on a programme, O'Shea advised, and 'concentrated their attention on education as a question altogether apart from nationalism' much might be achieved, and people like Randolph Churchill might become interested.[25]

Two days later, O'Shea described a letter O'Dwyer had sent him as 'an important document'. He had enclosed it in a memo to Churchill. A further letter from O'Shea on the same date, 22 November 1886, observed that Archbishop Walsh's recent speech -calling for a college in Dublin University while criticising Trinity College — had created a situation which made an initiative from the government impossible. He went on to underline, by contrast, the good impression being made by O'Dwyer. 'It is with the greatest gratification', he assured him, 'that I hear you everywhere spoken of with very unusual emphatic kindness and esteem.' Recently he had dined with Fr John Healy, parish priest of Little Bray, and the latter, and many of his guests, concurred, 'that the friendly interest taken in you is widespread. The Lord Chancellor told me this afternoon that he had heard the greatest praise of you in many quarters.'[26]

About this time, too, the bishop of Limerick heard from William Delany, president of University College. At the request of Mr W.H. Keating, Delany explained, he forwarded to O'Dwyer a copy of a letter which he had written in urgent haste the previous January for the perusal of Archbishops Walsh and Croke. Their Graces were meeting in Thurles to discuss the university question, and his letter was brought to them by Dr James Kavanagh of Carlow College. The latter agreed with Delany's purpose, namely to put clearly and emphatically before the archbishops 'the objections against merging our Catholic Colleges *in one institution with Trinity College*, which once done, could not easily be undone'. Delany added that Keating had sent him a letter he had received from O'Dwyer, and his Lordship's views commanded his ' notice and most cordial assent', but he wished to make clear that he dissented from a number of Keating's views and from his 'personal attacks' on opponents.

The 'urgency' of his letter in January, Delany explained, 'was due to two causes: 1. Dr Walsh seemed to have put forward amalgamation with Trinity as the ultimate and final object to be sought, and to be sought at once. 2. Lord Carnarvon [the viceroy], in two long conversations had given me clearly to understand that', in his opinion, 'amalgamation with Trinity presented insuperable difficulties; but that the government were favourably disposed, he himself *thoroughly* so, to giving the Catholics an independent Catholic university – with Cork and Galway colleges made Catholic, and a great central Catholic college in Dublin suitably equipped and endowed as compared with Trinity College.'

'There was, besides', Delany added, 'the pressing consideration which was often forgotten, that when full rights are obtained we shall find ourselves unable to fill the chairs of the new university unless we make preparation now at once.' He was endeavouring now 'under crushing difficulties to create a sure supply in these departments'. If University College had 'suitable help through scholarships and equipment they could in 5 or 6 years turn out a number of men to meet the needs of a great university, distinctly Catholic, and under exclusively Catholic management.' These were the principal alternatives he had in mind when writing, he concluded, 'the Tories being still in power, and the queen's speech still unmade'. 'In that speech,' Delany observed, 'there was *at that time* included a reference to the Irish education question. It did not appear in the speech at the opening of parliament, thanks, I am told, to Dr Walsh's Thurles speech, declaring war against Trinity.'[27] This was the speech, given prior to the perusal of Delany's letter, in which the archbishop made his much quoted statement that no educational settlement could be accepted which would leave Trinity College –

'that standing monument of conquest' – in its privileged position.[28] Delany added that although he believed that for religious and patriotic, as well as educational reasons, 'we ought to aim at establishing a great national university, distinctly Catholic and under Catholic management', he was nevertheless clearly of the opinion 'that we ought to secure *now* anything that we can obtain consistently with our principles, and without prejudice to the realisation of that ultimate aim'.

The concurrence of views confirming his own, and presenting Dr Walsh as an obstacle on the way, helped fuel O'Dwyer's desire to be a leader in education. He had made it clear, it would seem, that he was open to an invitation to accept a senate seat, and the invitation came during November. On 25 November he informed the viceroy, Lord Londonderry, that he accepted, and he thanked him for the nomination to the senate of the Royal University, adding, however: 'I think it right to say, before my name is submitted to her Majesty that I do not regard the Royal University as it is, or in any development of it I can conceive, to be a satisfaction of the just claims of the Catholics of Ireland which it should be my duty as a bishop to urge.'[29]

Proud, perhaps, of his qualified response to the viceroy, O'Dwyer ingenuously shared with his friend Walsh his letter of acceptance, adding, 'I suppose in succession to Dr McCabe.'[30] The position of senator would put him 'in reach of information', he maintained, 'and in communication with people', which would make him more useful in the 'working of a settlement'. The question needed to be agitated and meetings should be organised to that end. In Limerick he could 'easily get together fine and influential Catholics', representative of all shades of political opinion, 'to promote our higher interests'. Then, referring insensitively to a recent speech by Walsh, he remarked – 'I have been told that the cabinet are still prepared to deal with the question in a broad way but that they regard that speech as a *non-possumus*[31] on the part of the Irish bishops.' Could his Grace remove the impression said to be present in the government, O'Dwyer asked, 'that an offer on their part now would be regarded as a bribe to corrupt the Catholic hierarchy'? In conclusion, with reference to the fact that since July 1886 the Conservatives were in office and favoured denominational education, and that their chief secretary, Sir Michael Hicks-Beach, was sympathetic to the Catholic case, O'Dwyer commented: 'I am convinced that in our lifetime we shall not get so great a chance of a large measure as is offered by the peculiar position of a government holding the principles of the present one on education, even from an Irish parliament if such comes in our time.'[32]

Walsh, used to being the authoritative spokesman for the bishops on education, was not disposed to being instructed by a very recent bishop, one, besides, who seemed ill-informed on episcopal appointments to the senate. He replied on 26 November that if O'Dwyer were appointed senator, it was not as the bishops' senator.[33] The following day O'Dwyer responded with a defensive sharpness: 'I quite understand that my appointment on the senate had no representative character and was quite a personal thing. Not likely the bishops would have me for their representative … I would regard such an honour as more than counterbalanced by its restraints.'[34]

Four days after O'Dwyer's acceptance, Captain O'Shea replied to his request for advice on how best to move forward the university question. He had spoken on the matter with Randolph Churchill and Joseph Austin Chamberlain. His advice was to 'induce the bishops … to come to a decision among themselves as to the acceptable minimum' they required from the government. He presumed that they would agree not to interfere with the Protestants and Trinity College. Having agreed on 'the acceptable minimum', the bishops should keep its content secret, and then 'speak out at once, the louder the better, so long as the note is kept distinct'. 'You mention', O'Shea observed, 'an expression of Catholic opinion which would raise the demand out of party politics. That is exactly what is wanted. Let the reform be demanded on its own merits, and no delay. It would be a false step just at present to accentuate the exclusive solidarity of the Parnellites with the question. In other words, let the demand, for the present at least, be rather national than nationalist.' O'Shea then added: 'You know my views and myself so well that I need not trouble with many reasons for advising you in the first place to establish a reasonable minimum, and to get it on paper.' The implication that he and O'Dwyer were well acquainted suggests perhaps a family connection. Certainly there was opportunity for boyhood acquaintance. O'Shea's father had been mayor of Limerick. He went on, pandering to O'Dwyer's vanity, 'You are the very man, young, energetic, possessing Dr Walsh's friendship, to draft such a plan – and to get it initialled. I do not underestimate the difficulties of the enterprise but I hope your day is come.'[35]

He did underestimate the difficulty, and the commanding position of Walsh among the Irish hierarchy. In the estimation of the archbishops of Dublin and Cashel, and in that of most of the bishops, education, land issues, and Home Rule were all intertwined, and they cherished unity between themselves and the Irish party as the vital means of achieving these objectives, and viewed the unionists in their various guises as plotting to break up that alliance. Hence, a policy of singling out the university question for settlement and without agreement with the Irish party was viewed as a mistaken and dangerous policy. When word came of O'Dwyer's acceptance of Lord Londonderry's invitation, the bishops' standing committee, under Walsh's leadership, were in no mood to consider 'a reasonable minimum' of agreement; rather did they view the invitation to O'Dwyer as an attempt to undermine episcopal authority by inviting an individual prelate to accept a position on the senate without prior consultation with the body of bishops. Their mind towards the senate was already one that demurred at having any bishops on it. O'Dwyer came under immediate pressure to withdraw his acceptance when he attended the standing committee meeting in Dublin on 8 December. The argument that the government was going against a former practice and bypassing the hierarchy, and his sense of loyalty to fellow bishops, induced him to promise to withdraw.

On his return to Limerick, he drafted a letter of resignation to the chief secretary, Sir Michael Hicks-Beach. 'I learned for the first time on Thursday last, at a meeting of the bishops in Dublin,' he announced, 'that an understanding had existed since the foundation of the Royal University that representative bishops, elected by their own body, would have seats on the Royal University. I immediately informed their lordships that I will at once try and stop my own appointment to which I had given my assent, and in as much as the ... understanding had not been observed.' 'However, on my return to Limerick', he explained, 'I find that the appointment has been actually made, and I take the earliest opportunity of writing to you – in the absence of the Lord Lieutenant – to say, that however disagreeable to me to take such a step, that I do not see what other course is open to me but to resign under the circumstances.'[36]

His obvious reluctance to resign resulted in his postponing the sending of the letter. Strangely, perhaps in hope of dissuasion, he did send a letter of resignation to Lord Emly. The latter showed the letter to Bishop John Healy, who then wrote to O'Dwyer. Emly and he had talked over the matter, Healy announced. They both considered that it would be better that he 'should not actually resign, at least for the present'. After all, there was no need to hurry. Healy's personal wish was that he remain on the senate in view of the subsequent discussions that might arise on the university question. Then, his position as senator would lend weight to his opinions. 'Meantime', Healy further advised, 'you might let your name remain, even if you did not attend any meetings as several other senators do.' Lord Emly 'said he would take no action in reference to your Lordship's letter', Healy concluded, 'until he or I heard from you again.'[37]

In the temporary breathing space thus provided, O'Dwyer sought further support for his desire to stay on the senate. He wrote to Walsh for advice. The latter forwarded his letter to Croke. On 13 December Croke returned the letter with the comment: 'There is plainly only one course open to him – that which you have suggested. Having undertaken to decline the honour, he cannot possibly accept it.'[38] O'Dwyer wrote also to Michael Logue, bishop of Raphoe, for advice. He replied on 13 December 1886 in a similar vein. It was unfortunate, Logue commented, 'that your Lordship's appointment has been completed before you had time to take the action you intended'. The government, no doubt, was interested in fostering 'any little want of union it finds among the bishops', he warned, and the surest means ' of succeeding in this evil design' was 'to pick out individual bishops and appoint them to representative positions independent of the general body of the episcopate'. It was mentioned after the bishops' meeting, Logue confided 'in strict confidence', that 'your Lordship sought the appointment with full knowledge of the views of the bishops and without making any account of them, and that you did so acting under the advice of some particular bishop, whose name was withheld from me'. He had reason to fear, moreover, that this was 'believed by some at least of the Castle authorities', who, of course, 'would be delighted if it were so'. Hence, Logue explained, it was his candid opinion that it would be better for O'Dwyer to refuse the appointment despite 'the difficulty of doing so, now that things have gone so far'. The best plan would be to give honestly 'the real reason, i.e. the strong feeling you found among the bishops as to appointments to representative positions made without any regard to their wishes. This is how the thing strikes me ...'[39]

To Logue's surprise, O'Dwyer's response was sharp. Logue assured him on 21 December that he had not believed the construction put on his acceptance of a senate seat, and that he had said to the person who made the statement that 'I knew your Lordship since you were a student, and that you were not the kind of person to sacrifice a principle for any personal ends'. O'Dwyer, not surprisingly, had assumed from Logue's letter that the remarks about him were made by a fellow bishop. In his reply, Logue assured him that the person who made the comment was not a bishop, and that it had probably been made 'only as a matter of chit chat', and that he, Logue, was, as far as he knew, the only one of the bishops who heard the remark. After this humbling retraction, he went on to give a history of the senate's dealings with the bishops, as related by the less than objective Archbishop Walsh. In the light of 'this abstract of the history of the question,' Logue explained, it was 'very doubtful whether the bishops would consent to elect any of their body to represent them in the senate.' There was no question of the bishops not considering O'Dwyer qualified for the office, Logue concluded. It was 'not a question of persons, but a question of principle'.[40]

Walsh, meantime, had reason to feel aggrieved at the implication that he was not concerned about solving the university question. He was very active in sensitive negotiations with Hicks-Beach on the whole range of educational matters. On 19 December he informed Monsignor Kirby that he believed there were good prospects of 'working out a full settlement of the education question to make it 'denominational' and to give us full equality of endowments for our Catholic schools and colleges, in all three departments, primary, intermediate and university.'[41] Three weeks later he was sufficiently confident to inform Cardinal Manning that the education question was 'on the high road to settlement'.[42] In these hopeful circumstances, about which Walsh could not speak openly, O'Dwyer's concern about a place on the senate with a view to helping to solve the university question must have seemed an unnecessary irritant, but one, nevertheless, which involved an important principle relating to episcopal authority and influence.

The absence of any definite indication of O'Dwyer's intentions, led Walsh to write in exasperation to Croke that it still was not clear that O'Dwyer had resigned. Croke replied somewhat ambiguously on 23 December that '+ E.T. is a nice fellow. He is 'cutting' up curiously. But people who know him best prophesied all this, and plenty more to come.' As to resignation, Croke thought he would not resign. 'The "Pet" [Dr Healy] will surely advise him, or has advised him not to do so. He must be tamed, and will, please God, in due course.'[43] Still seeking support for what he personally desired, but loathe to take the step which might seem to put him on the side of the government against the body of bishops, O'Dwyer turned once more for advice and assistance to Walsh, as an old friend, pointing out that the situation had changed since the standing committee meeting in that the appointment had been actually made before he could withdraw. Walsh replied on 30 December that he would not like 'to interfere in a matter' which 'was settled in our last meeting'.[44]

As the new year commenced, the *Freeman's Journal* announced that the Bishop of Limerick had resigned from the senate of the Royal University. Taken aback, O'Dwyer had his secretary, Fr Andrew Murphy, complain to Edmund Dwyer Gray, MP, proprietor of the *Journal*. The latter replied on 5 January that his source for the information was an announcement in some paper, probably the *Irish Times*, but he could not be positive in this and had not time himself to look it up.[45] This cavalier response evoked an angry letter from O'Dwyer, which accused the paper of 'improper conduct' on this and on previous occasions in respect of his lordship. Dwyer Gray replied that the item was inserted 'without the slightest notion of giving offence', adding – 'If the statement was untrue and you so inform me I shall be happy to have it contradicted. If it was not untrue, I am at a loss, as a plain man, to understand wherein lies the offence.' He was not aware of any occasion in which the paper was guilty of 'improper conduct' in relation to his Lordship. The same day, their letters crossing, O'Dwyer, through his secretary, Fr Andrew Murphy, declared that Gray's letters would have been satisfactory if, like the *Evening Mail*, he had quoted the source of his information, but they were not satisfactory as an explanation 'of the apparently authoritative announcement' that he undertook to make 'in a form that must have led the public to believe' he 'had had definite and authoritative information on the subject'.[46] On 9 January, pushed into a corner by Gray's query whether the statement was true or untrue, O'Dwyer decided to state it was 'untrue', and that he had not resigned. 'His Lordship desires me say', Andrew Murphy wrote, 'that the announcement in the *Freeman* was utterly untrue, and went far beyond the information which you can allege in support of it, while you must have known that accurate information was quite within your reach.' 'In regard to the general tone of the *Freeman* towards him, for which you make yourself responsible', Murphy added lamely, 'his Lordship desires me say, he has only to hope that at some future time he may be able to convince you of its impropriety.'[47]

Walsh, meanwhile, was continuing his negotiations with Hicks-Beach, and also quietly arranging to situate his own candidate on the senate in O'Dwyer's place. His desire was to have no official episcopal representative on the body, and to prevent O'Dwyer's non-representative presence as a bishop since he, with Dr Healy, was likely to be an independent voice on university matters, prepared, perhaps, to propose policies different from his. Once O'Dwyer had resigned, he planned to have him replaced by a non-bishop, a Dublin priest friend. He wrote to Croke after meeting with Hicks-Beach on 6 January, and Croke, replying five days later, congratulated him on the progress being made in the negotiations, and then issued a warning regarding Walsh's friend, Dr Gerald Molloy, rector of the Catholic University, whom the archbishop had chosen to succeed O'Dwyer.

'There is great prejudice against Molloy throughout the country,' he observed. 'He is invariably regarded as an unmitigated Whig, and a Jump-Jim-Crowe man in politics.'[48]

Walsh shortly afterwards brought Croke up to date with a further communication. His letter enclosed a significant letter from O'Dwyer to him. This last appears to have been the final written communication between O'Dwyer and Walsh on the senate question. It had been written in response to a letter from Walsh, which had hinted at the appointment of a successor to O'Dwyer on the senate. On 8 January 1887 O'Dwyer had replied:

> I am not sure that I understand the purport of your letter, which I have just received. You say that 'arrangements were considered for filling up the vacancy'. Does this mean a vacancy to be created by my resignation or one already in existence? If the first, I should think the negotiations had progressed too rapidly; and the assumption that it was essential that no bishop should be put on, the ostensible grounds on which I have been asked to resign being that faith was broken by not having a bishop selected in a particular way put on, seems to me inadvisable. But to prevent any further misconception, I wish to say explicitly that, notwithstanding the announcement in the *Freeman*, I have not resigned, and as things have gone, it is less likely than ever that I shall.[49]

Despite the awkwardness of expression in the letter, the final sentences were clear. Dwyer-Gray had precipitated a decision, and the confused thinking of many of the bishops with respect to the senate, and anger at Walsh's manoeuvre to have him resign in order to appoint his own candidate in his place, helped O'Dwyer to justify his decision.

Sharing Walsh's annoyance at O'Dwyer's letter, Croke observed on 12 January: 'I knew well, ever since the display at his consecration dinner that + E.T. would give trouble. He must be put down, and will not, I apprehend, except by the interposition of Propaganda.' 'At our meeting' in the steering committee, he reminded Walsh, 'we went distinctly on the grounds that we had ruled to have only two bishops on the senate, and that no bishop should be on it except as a nominee of … our aggregate body.' O'Dwyer 'promised unmistakably to resign forthwith'. 'How practically', Croke asked, 'had we better approach + E.T.?' *'Frappez et frappez vite'* [Strike and strike quickly], he suggested pugnaciously, 'should be the word.'[50] The very next day Croke wrote again, this time saying – 'I have just had a letter from Gray', referring to the owner and publisher of the *Freeman's Journal*, 'in which he tells me that he got a fearful rating from + E.T., through his secretary, because of the *Freeman* paragraph about his resignation'. 'I do not think we can do anything', he advised, 'until we meet in Dublin.'[51]

Without informing Croke, Dr Walsh followed his recommendation to have O'Dwyer 'put down' by 'the interposition of Propaganda'. On 22 January 1887 he marked 'Confidential' on his letter to Archbishop Kirby, the Irish bishops agent in Rome, adding, 'Kindly destroy this when read'.

'I think it well to let your Grace know', he began, 'that in the opinion of several of our leading bishops we are at least in some danger of a reopening of the old dissensions within the episcopal ranks.' 'The Royal University, an institution which many of us have from the very start regarded with serious misgivings, is the present source of the trouble.' At its opening, he explained, the bishops only decided by a bare majority to nominate two members to the senate. Those named were Cardinal McCabe and Dr Woodlock, 'and the Lord Lieutenant, as a matter of course, nominated them'. 'When the cardinal died, no bishop was appointed in his place.' 'But a month or two ago, to the surprise of the whole country,' Walsh continued histrionically, 'it was announced that the Lord Lieutenant had appointed *Dr O'Dwyer* of *Limerick* – the junior member of our body! Great annoyance was, of course, felt at this – the more so as the young prelate had shown on several occasions in public a strongly marked disposition to break off from his brethren and to act for himself.' 'At a recent meeting of our Episcopal Standing Committee', Walsh added, 'a strong expression of opinion' resulted in his promising 'to resign the seat on the ground that faith had not been kept with this body, in thus making an appointment of a bishop to the senate without any reference to them'. 'That promise, however,' he emphasised, 'he has not even as yet kept. *There is reason to fear he will not do so.*' 'Now we feel,' he went on relentlessly, 'that if government can thus pick and choose for such positions on education boards individual members of our body, who may be altogether out of harmony with the body general, the influence of the bishops in the matter of education is at an end.'

Having thus presented his version of events, Walsh came to the object of his letter. 'It will, in fact, be necessary', he insisted

> to refer this case to the Holy See. But meanwhile it would be well for Y. G. [Your Grace] to mention the matter in a general way to Card. Simeoni, or even to the Holy Father himself, saying that I have some fear that seeds of dissension may have been skilfully sown amongst us. Thus the authorities will be on their guard.[52]

On the day Walsh wrote to Rome, Croke sent him the letter, quoted in an earlier chapter, in which he mentioned that on his visitation to the Limerick part of his diocese he learned that O'Dwyer's clergy were afraid of him. O'Dwyer presently was 'keeping very quiet', he remarked.[53]

In Rome, Kirby, having received Walsh's disturbing letter, deliberated about what to do, and then, about mid-February, addressed a paternal letter to O'Dwyer urging him to resign. O'Dwyer, who had been in England for an extended visit, replied on 22 February that he would respond 'tomorrow' to Kirby's confidential communication.[54] Walsh, at the same time, remained friendly with his Limerick colleague, continuing to like him personally. 'I am sorry you could not come out for a day or two on your way through,' Walsh wrote on 20 February 1887, and then referred to educational issues and to his negotiations with Sir Michael Hicks-Beach. He concluded on a caring and personal note: 'Dr Murphy tells me you have to wear heavy 'goggles', but thank God that your eyes are safe and sound.'[55]

O'Dwyer's 'tomorrow' extended over two weeks. It was only on 9 March that he replied to Kirby, but his delay proved tactically important. By the time his letter reached Rome, Walsh's standing and that of Croke had been seriously weakened there. On 7 March Hicks-Beach had resigned as chief secretary, and with him went the high hopes for educational reform that Walsh had raised at Rome and among his fellow bishops. In addition, his support for the Plan of Campaign and the non-payment of rent, and Croke's unwise statement exculpating the non-payment of taxes, provided ample ammunition for the prominent English and Irish Catholic laymen who were leveling heavy criticisms at the Vatican against the two archbishops. In this context, O'Dwyer's wily defence, and his strong assertion of loyalty to Rome and of support for law and order, placed him in a favourable light.

With all the desired marks of deference to Archbishop Kirby, O'Dwyer not only firmly stood his ground, but took the offensive.

> Having given the best consideration in my power to your most kind and affectionate advice, I regret that I cannot see my way at present, to take the course that your Grace has been so good as to suggest.

'I do not think', he explained, 'that the interests of higher Catholic education or the influence of the episcopal body would be served by an action which, as regards myself personally, should be marked by levity and fecklessness, and would be accepted as an affront by the government which meant to act fairly by the bishops in the matter. The difficulty in the case,' he continued reasonably, 'does not lie with me. I am of opinion that a representative bishop chosen by his colleagues would be infinitely preferable to one chosen as I have been by the government, and I am satisfied from my correspondence with the Chief Secretary on this point that the government will easily accept a practical understanding to give effect to such an arrangement; and if the bishops direct their representations towards this end I shall gladly put my resignation at their disposal: but, unless under the direction of Propaganda, I will not throw up a place, where as a Catholic bishop there are immense and yearly growing Catholic interests to be protected, as a mere isolated act, and without reference to some definite and reasonable policy.'

'Dr Walsh ought to be our representative,' he observed pointedly. 'I have no doubt that the government would gladly appoint him, and as a matter of course the bishops would elect him, and if he consents to go on the senate, or failing him, if any other bishop is selected, I will resign my place in his favour. But the difficulty is that Dr Walsh, having left the senate of the Royal University on some side issue, does not wish, I presume, to go back and consequently there is a deadlock. But the Royal University counts its Catholic students now by hundreds and almost thousands and cannot be allowed for personal considerations to drift out of episcopal influence. 'Pursuing the attack, O'Dwyer informed Kirby:

> Dr Walsh wrote to me some time ago that he had arranged with the Chief Secretary for my successor, laying it down as essential that he should *not* be a bishop, and it was the assumption of such authority as regards myself, and the mistake of such a policy as regards the bishops, that determined me to retain my place at least until the next meeting of the general body of the bishops.

'I wish to add finally', he stated adroitly, 'as your Grace has honoured me with so confidential a communication, that I fear that there is underlying the pressure that has been brought to bear on me from many sides, the spirit of general resistance to civil authority which has been growing in Ireland, and if encouraged will produce the same results to religion that the revolution has produced in every country in which it has triumphed.' 'In my humble opinion', he pressed on, 'we are abandoning the principles of obedience, of reverence, and of charity that were the traditions of our predecessors, and for the sake of mere favour allowing the people to follow methods of violence and disobedience.' 'As long as the priests of the Church', O'Dwyer warned, 'are useful political agents for the leaders of this system, they will be applauded, and appear to hold in influence: but when the time comes, as come it must, that we can no longer pander to popular passions, I fear the reaction will show that our power has been undermined.' 'I write this to your Grace with great sorrow, and diffidence in my own judgment,' he concluded, 'but with the most intimate conviction of its truth.'[56]

O'Dwyer followed up this masterly letter, with a circumspect and carefully weighted note on 13 March. 'I am sure that it is unnecessary for me to convey to your Grace that my letter of last week was entirely confidential, and written under the influence of the extremely kind and affectionate advice which your Grace has been so good as to tender to me.' Then, in exoneration of his temerity in criticising the eminent Archbishop of Dublin, he artfully confessed: 'I shall be very sorry, however deeply I deplore a good deal that is being said and done in Ireland, to express my views generally in [a] way that might seem wanting in deference to those who are charged with weightier responsibilities and are so well qualified to bear them.' 'But', he added, 'when I have to express my own opinions in confidence I can only feel regret that I find that in the attempt to be candid, I have to assume a tone of self-sufficiency.'[57]

Two months later, on 16 May, he informed Kirby that he was sure he would be glad to hear that 'the standing committee of the bishops unanimously approved my stand on the university'. On 27 May, however, Walsh explained that the 'approval' was that O'Dwyer had not finally accepted the appointment to the senate up to the time of the meeting and no action was to be taken until the general meeting in June.[58] In fact, no action was taken. O'Dwyer's position had faded in significance before the wave of coercion and violence in the country and the rumours of condemnation from Rome.[59]

Despite his struggle to retain his seat on the senate, O'Dwyer attended its meetings very seldom. He kept in touch with its deliberations, it may be presumed, through Lord Emly, and certainly by means of correspondence with such senate members as William Delany and Bishop John Healy. The most likely reason for his poor attendance record at the senate, and to a lesser extent at episcopal meetings, was his difficulty in hearing. With a small familiar group he could manage effectively, but in a larger meeting he felt at sea. In February 1901, following a senate meeting at which he played an important part, he wrote revealingly to William Delany: 'I fear I was a great bother to you on Thursday on account of my deafness, and for myself it was most disagreeable not to be able to follow the discussion'.[60] The affliction for one so able, and so keen to participate, was particularly acute.

In all, O'Dwyer attended only five meetings of the senate in over twenty years. The first was as late as 21 February 1901, the meeting referred to in his letter to Delany. On that occasion he moved the motion for a Royal Commission to enquire into the standing and operation of the Royal University. It resulted in the influential Robertson Commission. He attended again on 26 July to monitor, it would seem, the progress of his motion. On 14 May 1903 he handed in notice of motion calling on the government to implement the recommendations of the Robertson Commission, and on 29 October he was present as the motion of 14 May was debated and passed. Three years later, on 8 February 1906, he once more called for the implementation of the recommendations of the Robertson Commission, and his final attendance was on 7 March 1906, at a special meeting which debated and passed the motion of 8 February.[61] Thus, all his attendances were related to the Robertson Commission, which he had helped to initiate. The sparse attendance over twenty years was partly redeemed by the establishment of that influential commission, and by the fact that he used his position as senator, and the private information it made available to him, to make effective public pronouncements on the university question.

Meanwhile, the 'junior member' of the hierarchy, in his first year as bishop, had stood out successfully against the powerful episcopal standing committee and had questioned Dr Walsh's leadership in educational affairs. In the same period he had signalled a recalcitrant stand also with regard to the methods used by the land agitators, and had won sympathy at Rome and earned the praise of prominent Catholic noblemen in Britain and Ireland. His stand with respect to land agitation, however, also led to sustained public abuse and ridicule for his views, and during those dark days and months of trial he was to find no support from Walsh, Croke, and most of the body of bishops. It was the price of his independent dissent.

8

The Plan of Campaign, 1886–1888.
The bishop and the papal condemnation

AGRARIAN DISTRESS

In the final months of Bishop Butler there was an increase in distress and turmoil in many parts of rural Ireland, mainly because of a depression in trade and a decline in agricultural prices. Tenants who enjoyed 'judicial rents' in line with the land act of 1881 now found themselves in difficulties, while those outside that system were in even worse straits. In these situations, the landlords either lowered their rents to assist their tenants, or else they pursued their right under the law to confiscate their tenants' goods and even to evict. This last option was also resorted to by a number of landlords who had lowered their rents but found their tenants still unable to pay. The local priest in some locations helped to organise the tenants to agree on a rent they could afford and to offer this reduced rent to the local landlords. If accepted, harmony prevailed; if not, there were, not infrequently, evictions, followed by reactions involving violence against the landlords' animals, property, and agents. More militant members of the National League, the wider grass-roots body supporting the Irish Parliamentary party, were prominent in stirring the agitation and injecting it with an explosive mixture of class, religious and national hostility. The tenants were Catholic, the landlords, almost all, Protestant; the tenants were peasants, the landlords either titled or upper middle class; the tenants blamed their ills on the British government, the landlords were identified with the government, especially a Conservative government.

Bishop O'Dwyer, mindful of the violence and irrational fervour which he had encountered during the Land League, was determined to do all he could to preserve peace in his own diocese. It was not to be an easy task. His diocese was bordered on three sides by areas of intense disorder to which many clergy contributed: Kerry, where the bishop, Andrew Higgins, had little or no control over his priests; Clare, where a similar situation prevailed under the ailing bishop of Killaloe, Michael Flannery, and his coadjutor, James Ryan; and Tipperary and the parts of Co. Limerick that were included in the archdiocese of Cashel and Emly under Archbishop Thomas Croke, who was openly supportive of the tenants' movement and of his priests involvement. O'Dwyer felt sympathy for the tenants' cause, but he had reason to remember how agrarian problems could be used to vent spleen and gain power, and how life could be made intolerable for those farmers who wished to pay their rent or those who voiced criticism of the movement. He decided for the present to stand back from the situation and to avoid public comment. His eventual involvement was to be choreographed, at least in part, by his old adversary, John Dillon.

While Home Rule was in prospect during 1885–6, Parnell, the Irish Parliamentary party, and other prominent members of the National League, avoided overt support for the land struggle lest it alienate their Liberal supporters. This kept a rein on rural agitation. With the defeat of the Home Rule bill in June 1886, however, and the replacement of the Liberals by a Conservative government, the prospects for order became bleak. The land question was now the central focus. It became the Irish question.

At their conference at Maynooth, early in September 1886, the Irish Catholic hierarchy expressed anxiety at the inability of many tenants to pay their rents and at the increasing number of evictions. They feared that 'social evils of the gravest character' would result, and they urged the government to act.[1] In the House of Commons, Parnell sought a similar result. He warned that unless remedial legislation was introduced, neither he, nor the Irish members, would be able to control the frustration of the tenants during the coming winter. He proposed a Tenants' Relief Bill that empowered the Land Commission to reduce judicial rents which were fixed before 1884, if tenants paid half the rent due in the current year and half their previous arrears. The bill also empowered the courts to suspend all eviction proceedings on payment of half the rent and arrears. The measure was defeated. It was clear that the tenants could expect little sympathy from a Tory-controlled House of Commons. A furious Dillon informed the assembly that he would 'tell the people of Ireland to continue in that course of persistent and determined agitation by which in the past they' had 'won every single liberty and every single concession that' had 'been granted them.'[2]

EMERGENCE OF PLAN OF CAMPAIGN

On 17 October 1886, Dillon proposed a new policy for the National League. It involved a system of collective bargaining on individual estates, which became known as the Plan of Campaign. It proposed that the tenants on each estate should combine and offer the landlord a reduced rent. If the landlord refused, the tenants were to put the proffered rent in the hands of trustees chosen by themselves, and, if the landlord proceeded to evict, the money in trust would be used to fight the evictions and to support those who suffered eviction. Tenants were assured that if their campaign fund was not sufficient, if would be supported by the resources of the National League. Basic to the Plan was the idea that the tenants fixed their own rents, and that if anyone bid for and occupiedthe farm of an evicted tenant he and his family would be boycotted.[3]

The new movement was conducted during its five-year existence with extraordinary energy, courage and passion by John Dillon and William O'Brien. It was assisted by a wide range of less prominent leaders, all of whom came from the more radical wing of the parliamentary party and several of whom had connections with Fenianism, but Dillon and O'Brien set the tone. Both preached against landlords and landlordism in a sweeping manner that allowed no exceptions and fomented hatred.[4] O'Brien publicly accused the Irish gentry of remaining 'as distinctly foreigners in race and language and sympathy as when their ancestors came over, throat-cutting and psalm-singing, with Cromwell';[5] while to Dillon they were 'the curse of Ireland' and 'parasites',[6] and the tenants' campaign was, as he proclaimed in a celebrated speech at Castlerea, Co. Mayo, on 5 December 1886, 'a holy struggle' having as its aim 'to destroy the tyranny of landlordism' and 'to hand over the possession of the soil of Ireland to the class who labour in that soil'.[7] Not surprisingly, Dillon's biographer, F.S.L. Lyons, observed that 'for a true understanding of his career' it was important 'to be clear that for him a steady, unrelenting hatred of landlordism was the most potent force driving him into politics and keeping him there.'[8]

It is also important to an understanding of O'Dwyer in these years to realise that he, and many other bishops, had to cope with members of the clergy using language about landlords not only unbecoming their station but every bit as combustible as that of Dillon. It ranged from a priest in Co. Armagh urging Lord Londonderry to follow his ancestor's example and cut his own throat,[9] to Matthew Ryan, of Herbertstown, Co. Limerick, popularly known as 'the general' for his marshalling of tenants, who declared unreservedly that no rent was a fair rent,[10] and to Fr William Casey, parish priest of Abbeyfeale, Co. Limerick, in O'Dwyer's diocese, who delivered the ultimate outburst in biased indiscriminate condemnation:

> I don't care who the landlord is, no matter what sort he is, if he was an angel from heaven, he is a bad man provided he is a landlord.

Even if offered 'a thousand acres for half a farthing', Casey continued, 'I say join the Plan of Campaign and ask a reduction of fifty per cent.'[11]

The one-sided, aggressive declarations of the supporters of the Plan, not least their sweeping condemnations of landlords, were unwelcome to O'Dwyer, but it was the use of physical violence, the fear generated by dire threats, and by boycotting, that were most reprehensible. Intimidation was promoted by militaristic language. Dillon, in April 1888, used it in a chilling manner, when he delivered a warning to the tenants of The O'Grady estate at Herbertstown, Co. Limerick. 'Going into this struggle', he announced, 'is very like going into a battle, and in a battle when a man turns tail his officer will shoot him through the head. You know perfectly well what I mean. I don't say we should use personal violence, but it is a principle of the army or of any body of disciplined men that ... the man who turns tail on the rest is looked on as a traitor.'[12]

The O'Grady estate in question was well known to O'Dwyer, and, as will later appear, he was deeply concerned at the palpable injustice and calculated ruthlessness applied there by leaders of the Plan of Campaign. It was an outstanding example of how the Plan was used in support of tenant opportunism against a man, known as a kindly landlord, because of his financial vulnerability. Indeed, it has been remarked by the author of *The Plan of Campaign, 1886–1891*, that 'the evidence suggests that the majority of estates in which the Plan was implemented were carefully chosen and that landlord vulnerability, rather than obduracy, was the determining factor'.[13]

The use of boycotting as an essential weapon occasioned misgiving on the part of many prelates. O'Dwyer appreciated the reasoning behind it as a deterrent against someone bidding for a farm from which a tenant had been evicted, but the injustice it inflicted in practice made it unacceptable to him. The subject of the process was to be, in Parnell's words at Ennis in September 1880, 'isolated from the rest of his kind, as if he were a leper of old', shunned by his neighbours 'even in the house of worship.'[14] He found himself and his family not served in the shops, his cattle un-saleable at fairs, his horses unshod, his children 'hooted at the village school', and he and his family set apart 'like an outcast in his usual place of public worship.'[15]

O'DWYER HOLDS BACK

Against this complex background, O'Dwyer's position gradually clarified. As a new bishop testing the ground, his approach was largely reactive. Faced with the emphasis on the land question as the top priority, and Archbishop Walsh's remarks that the university issue should be shelved for the present, he had countered on 18 October 1886, at the Crescent College prize giving, as has been seen, by stating that he would use his influence to further what he considered to be 'religiously and politically the most important question' committed to his care, namely, providing a satisfactory university for the Catholic population.[16] Two months later, following Dillon's intemperate denunciations of landlordism and his call to the people at Castlerea to fight to destroy the landlord system, O'Dwyer surprised the Limerick corporation by his response to their inflated address commemorating his episcopal consecration. The mayor had praised his links with the people 'in every national effort' and expressed confidence that he would give his support 'to any movement for the advancement of nationality'.

The address itself praised his many achievements and how he had helped to keep the banner of Home Rule 'flying above the heads of the Irish race.' O'Dwyer, replying, assured the Corporation that he would always be with them 'in the vindication of our national rights as Irishmen', but then reminded those present that his primary duty was the spiritual direction of his flock. In a clear reference to the current political scene, he remarked that he did not think his place was with the 'recognised leaders'. He was convinced of the need for Home

Rule, and he was concerned for the tenant farmers and the hardships they were experiencing, but he could best serve their cause by working 'to regulate their ardour in looking for reform'. He would be most useful to his countrymen, he continued, 'by acting as a brake upon the machine, rather than as a boiler to supply steam'.[17]

Another person concerned with 'acting as a brake' and regulating the agitation, but in a wider context, was Archbishop Walsh. Fearing that the movement could fall into radical hands and create a situation which would alienate large sections from the church, as had happened in mainland Europe, he determined to support constitutional figures such as Dillon and O'Brien, knowing that their leader, Parnell, disapproved of any violence being associated with the campaign. At the beginning of December 1886, Walsh gave an important interview to W.T. Stead, editor of the *Pall Mall Gazette*, in which he stated that, after reflecting on the land acts of 1870 and 1881, it was clear to him that the system of land tenure in Ireland was 'no longer a system of landlord ownership exclusively'. The tenant now was recognised by law as having his ownership as well. In this situation of dual ownership the landlord could no longer be sole arbiter of the rent to be paid, and this applied even to old contracts.[18]

The interview gave standing to the Plan of Campaign. Even the Tablet, the organ of English Catholics, which was often critical of the national movement and agitation in Ireland, acknowledged that it was now evident that land tenure in England was quite different from Ireland, and that given dual ownership and the steep fall in prices in Ireland the fixed rents were no longer equitable, and the tenants were entitled to a readjustment. The government, however, by declining to intervene had decided in favour of the landlords and had ignored the implications of the land acts. The leaders of the National League, in consequence, had advised the tenants to treat the decision of the legislature as ill informed, and to act on their own judgment and knowledge. The question was were they justified in so acting? *The Tablet* thought not, for 'such doctrines amount to anarchy and revolution'.[19]

It is not clear how O'Dwyer viewed Walsh's intervention. The indications are that he was still reflecting on the rights and wrongs of the over all conflict. His colleague in Clonfert, John Healy, coadjutor bishop, however, held views that in some respects echoed those of the *Tablet*. In a letter to Cardinal Simeoni, papal secretary of state, on 6 December, he virtually accused Walsh of fomenting civil war by his interview, and complained that none of the bishops had 'dared to speak' against him. On the general atmosphere of intimidation associated with the Plan of Campaign, he observed that 'that nefarious system, the boycott – a social excommunication which disregards all justice and charity – almost every-where obtains, especially in the south and the west, and terrifies everybody, even the bishops themselves and the priests, who hardly venture to absent themselves from the meetings of the National League. This system we see daily in operation with our own eyes.'[20] An attempt was to be made on his life because of his criticism of boycotting in the dispute between the Earl of Clanrickarde, Hubert George de Burgh Canning, one of the severest landlords, and his tenants.

On 19 December 1886, the Plan of Campaign was declared an illegal conspiracy. Four days later, John MacEvilly, archbishop of Tuam, observed: 'The government seems determined to drive the people to extremes. If they suppress legal associations, secret societies will grow.'[21]

With the New Year, the first fruits of O'Dwyer's reflections appeared in a frank and perceptive letter to the poet and landlord, Aubrey de Vere. 'In my opinion,' he commented on 12 January 1887, 'Ireland is halfway down an inclined plane and equilibrium is impossible until we reach the bottom. The faster the old order changeth now the better.' 'I fully agree with you', he continued acutely, 'as [to] the danger of demoralisation and consequent irreligion: but taking the facts as they are, without regard to the further question of the conduct of those who have brought them to their present condition, it seems to me that no reconstruction can be attempted, nor any conservative principle be operative *until the feud between the landlord and tenant classes is ended by the abolition of the former.*'[22] O'Dwyer went on: 'I do not regard this as an ideal: I do not regard the methods by which it is being worked out just: I do not think that religion can go through such a crisis without loss: but I think all these have now become necessary evils, and peace will be reached only through them.' 'It is very strange', he concluded in the same hard-headed vein, 'how Irish politics have proceeded. Mr Gladstone's land legislation has been, I think, 'the leaven that leavened the whole mass' and made order possible only through a social revolution.'[23] This was a far cry from the charges that would later be cast at him as a 'Castle bishop', and as pro-landlord and unionist in outlook. On 31 March 1887, indeed, he conveyed to Aubrey de Vere something of the difficulty he was experiencing as a bishop seeking to give a lead to his people. 'However you approach them,' he observed, 'Irish politics are a sad tangle; and between the wrong-doing of the government and the excesses of the people, it is not easy for one who wishes to be a Catholic 'before all things' to make a choice.'[24]

O'Dwyer's independent stand on the university question, and his alliance on that issue with BishopHealy, and his response to Limerick corporation, induced Archbishop Croke to see him and Healy as hostile to the Plan of Campaign and pro-landlord. Archbishop Walsh, to some extent, shared similar views. On 9 March 1887, Croke wrote in exasperation to Walsh, in the wake of a reprimand from Rome in relation to an unwise statement of his advocating the non-payment of taxes. Monsignor Kirby had written to him, he complained, as if he were 'still a student in the Irish College Paris', adding: 'It is quite possible that Portumna (Healy) and + *E.T. may have written to Rome*[25] disassociating themselves from the bulk of the bishops; but I do not believe that anyone else of their lordships would think of taking such a step.'[26]

There is no evidence of O'Dwyer writing to Rome on the land question at this time, but he was increasingly being viewed as pro-landlord, even though he had made no public statement critical of the tenant movement. His known association with a number of Limerick landowners gave grounds for suspicion, even as it had in Land League days. It is appropriate, therefore, to examine, at this stage, his relations with a number of the key landlords in his diocese, and how his friendship with them gave him a very different perspective from that of his Fedamore parish priest, Fr Casey.

CONCERNED AND PERCEPTIVE LANDLORDS

O'Dwyer's high regard for William Monsell, Lord Emly, has been noted in the previous chapter. The latter's wide learning and culture was associated in the bishop's mind with the benefits of a true university education, and he, with Aubrey de Vere, Fr Flanagan of Adare, and his secretary, Fr Andrew Murphy, provided oases of intellectual stimulation not otherwise readily available in the diocese. Emly frequently lent him books and articles on writers such as Von Hugel, on mystical theology and biblical criticism, Loisy, on new developments in scripture studies, and the duc de Broghlie, on morality and Catholic educa-tion,[27] while frequently exchanging views on the writings of Cardinal Newman. As to Emly's political and social views, O'Dwyer observed after his friend's death, 'that Lord Emly did what he believed was the best for his faith, what was best for the people amongst whom he lived and amongst whom he died.'[28]

Aubrey de Vere had helped O'Dwyer as a priest when he was establishing his Literary Institute. He continued to share with him as bishop his views on religion, politics, and literature. On the land situation, he informed Emly on 22 December 1885 that he had a letter from Fr Flanagan who mentioned that he had arranged matters between Lord Dunraven and his tenants, and that Lord Monteagle, in the Foynes area, would 'get in most of his March rent' and would 'give 30 percent off the September' rent. 'But', de Vere concluded, 'we are all living on sufferance and from hand to mouth.'[29] The 'hand to mouth' reappeared six months later, 25 June 1886, when he wrote Emly: 'I have been forced to give £5 to the new bishop's testimonial – much against my wish. Anything I give now is subtracted from *food and clothing!*'[30]

Aubrey de Vere wrote about Ireland, its history and its problems, in poetry and prose. He thought of himself as profoundly Irish and was interested in the well-being of all its people. As a Catholic he took a deep interest in the church's teaching and history, and was proud to be of assistance to his bishop. It was so also with Emly, who was prepared to assist O'Dwyer in his struggles with some local schools,[31] as well as on university matters. O'Dwyer's contacts with these Catholic gentlemen, and Emly's brother-in-law, Edwin Wyndham-Quin, earl of Dunraven, all converts of Newman, brought him into touch with non-Catholic gentry like Monteagle and Sir Stephen de Vere, and with influential contacts in the government in Ireland and in Britain. All these O'Dwyer saw as a means of greater influence for himself, his diocese, his projects, and the Catholic Church. Monteagle became a staunch supporter in O'Dwyer's projects for orphaned children, but Sir Stephen de Vere was, perhaps, the most interesting of his landlord acquaintances. Ready to support a range of worthy causes, he refused to aid O'Dwyer's Literary Institute because it was confined to Catholic young men, but later readily gave advice on a number of issues, including the running of local hospitals concerning which O'Dwyer had particular plans. Unlike his brother, Stephen de Vere remained a member of the Anglican church and he was one of the most caring and committed landowners in the country. During the great Famine he travelled to North America in one of the 'coffin ships' to experience what the people were suffering so as to be able to speak from experience when he raised their plight in parliament. His thinking as a landlord and an Irishman found expression in a long but magisterial letter to Emly on 11 April 1882. It merits attention as, in itself, a refutation of the indiscriminate denunciation of landlords on the part of Dillon and O'Brien, and many of their lay and clerical supporters.

'The experiment of foreign rule has been tried in Ireland for 6 or 7 centuries, and has failed,' de Vere commenced. 'True it is that the experiment has been unwisely carried out. The attempt has been made to establish a foreign social garrison which ... scorned the sympathy of the people; and since the Reformation to set up a religion antagonistic to the faith of the entire nation. The result has been social confusion and political disloyalty ... Throughout those long years this false system of government has produced its only possible result, a seething substratum of discontent kept down by military force and uncon-stitutional coercion.'

'Gladstone was the only statesman', de Vere continued, 'unless we may except Pitt (I speak of Pitt's opinions and not his actions), who saw that political and religious enfranchisement was the only remedy.' He tried it in 1870 and 1881, but it all came too late. 'The heart of the people was too entirely poisoned to be influenced by gratitude, justice, or even self-interest.' In time, no doubt, things will quieten down, and 'rents, with large reductions will be paid, but', he ventured, 'I am not so sanguine as to expect that there will ever be, under the present system, a real union between the two nations. You will still have chronic discontent, with occasional outbursts again to be smothered, not overcome, by violent suspensions of constitutional law.' The changes of 1870 and 1881 were statesmanlike but imperfect, and introduced 'an imperfect revolution' which only aggravated discontent. 'The old feudal system has been uprooted, and what is substituted is lame and incomplete.' It was now no longer possible, de Vere feared, 'to maintain the old relations of society', even on a purely commercial basis, because 'mutual confidence and mutual faith' were lacking. He regretted the change. He cherished an ideal, which, unfortunately, had not been exercised in Ireland.

'If the mutual relations of owners and occupiers', he mused, ' had been more assimilated to those of 'the family', – if absenteeism had been put an end to, – if the landlord had learned to sympathise with the domestic life of his tenant, to share his losses with cheerful generosity, to assist him by his capital, to instruct him by his example, to make him feel, in short, that they had a common hope, a common interest, and a mutual love, then indeed, I should say with firm belief that the Irishman with his impulsive, indolent, weak but affectionate nature would be happier and better as a tenant than as a small proprietor.' 'But', he added, 'you cannot galvanise a dead social system.'

As matters stood, what had to be done to restore peace in Ireland?

> We must do what Stein and Hardenburg[33] did. We must complete and consolidate the new regime we have introduced but not set up in working order. We must, acting in unison with the sentiment of the Irish people, transfer proprietorship in land from the *present head-renters* to the *occupiers*.

'It is a fearful but inevitable experiment', he acknowledged. 'One almost shudders to contemplate the disruption of old ties, affections, and associations. But we must fix our eyes steadily on the alternative – on a land where, as now, the law is defied, where human life is not sacred, where the rights of property are openly violated, where the moral conscience of a fine people is, under nefarious guidance, daily and hourly fading or rather rotting away. We dare not hesitate as to our choice.'

And what would be the probably result of this choice? 'I believe', he asserted in prophetic vein, 'judging from the present character, habits, and circumstances of the country, that the effects of the change for the first two generations will be an increase of suffering, but a suffering involving a moral education.' Later, 'a new social system will, we may hope, have struck root, and may give fair promise ... The people will have become more patient, more industrious, more just, more rational – in short more fit to govern themselves. Many of the causes which produced Ireland's hatred of England will have ceased. The 'landlord garrison', the alien church, will have passed away. A people taught by suffering, which they can no longer attribute to any but themselves, or the dispensation of providence, will become wiser by experience and more prosperous by independence and self-reliance. The day may then have come when it may be possible without danger to the state to entrust to Ireland a more direct and responsible share in the government of the United Empire, and to cap the pyramid of salutary revolution by establishing political self-government of a federal union.'

'I have not time to enter into details', de Vere concluded, 'nor do I feel competent to do so ... I do not mean to lay down a scheme, or even to speak with certainty of results,' but, he added:

> Unless we complete the revolution which we have begun, and to whose principles we stand committed, Ireland will see no lasting peace, and will make no industrial progress, but will continue to be, as she has been since the times of Henry II and Pope Adrian, a curse and a weakness to England. Some great change must be made. We cannot go on for ever, and

that without reasonable hope of success, with military occupation, suspended *habeas corpus*, and civil obligations enforced by the bayonet.[34]

On 1 May 1882, after he had heard from Emly, de Vere replied. 'I am glad you like my letter on Ireland. I am not ashamed to say I like it too, and I look upon it as *my legacy.*'[35]

The 'legacy' remained virtually undisturbed in the Monsell papers until the present time. It was assumed by the 'nefarious leadership' that such people had nothing to offer. They were made feel aliens in their own country, even as the Ulster Protestant tenants were in the face of a Plan of Campaign that identified the cause of Ireland with the Catholic majority. Fortunately, something of the thinking of de Vere and of the circle of landlords to the west of Limerick was to persist for a while longer and to make its contribution, in the person of a Dunraven, to the Land Act of 1903 and in the deliberations leading up to the National University Act of 1908. O'Dwyer's life, as noted, was enhanced in many ways by his landlord friends, and they influenced and supported him in his concern at the manner in which 'nefarious leadership' was undermining and deadening 'the moral conscience of a fine people'.

During the early months of 1887, nevertheless, O'Dwyer continued to maintain his silence. Meantime, a new coercion law was enacted and by February some of the leaders of the Plan of Campaign, including Dillon, were in jail. This brought Parnell out of his elected silence to lend support to Dillon and the movement. Before long, the government began to consider suggestions about seeking papal aid to bring about an ecclesiastical ban on the agitation.

THE COMING OF A PAPAL LEGATE

The idea was mooted as early as September 1885 by Captain John Ross (later Sir John Ross of Bladensburg, and then earl of Ross), whom O'Dwyer came to know through Lord Emly.[36] He was an Irishman, born in Italy, a Tory in politics, a devout Catholic, and a captain in the Coldstream Guards. He served on Lord Carnarvon's staff in 1885 and 1886 when Carnarvon was Irish viceroy. He was persistent in promoting Catholic issues, while opposing Home Rule; and was a close friend of the duke of Norfolk, who had similar aims. He had also cultivated the Secretary of Propaganda, Dominico Jacobini, and Abbot Bernard Smith, an Irish Benedictine long resident in Rome. Ross sought three particular objectives: 1. To have the pope send a delegate to Ireland 'to correct, enforce, and preserve religion', because the bishops were failing in their duties; 2. To increase English Catholic influence by promoting the establishment of diplomatic relations between Rome and Britain, something sought by Pope Leo XIII, and opposed by the Irish bishops, who feared it would increase British influence at Rome; 3. To solve the university question for Irish Catholics, which he believed to be a distinct possibility under a Tory administration, and this increased his interest in and support for O'Dwyer and Healy and, on the other hand, induced him to see Archbishop Walsh as an obstacle and as more of a political agent than a churchman.[37]

On 15 September 1885, Ross impressed on Norfolk the 'absolute necessity for an Apostolic Delegate to visit Ireland', and that he have full powers 'to correct, enforce, and preserve religion'. He suggested the name of Monsignor Ignatius Persico as the man most fitted to head such a mission.[38] Persico had worked as a priest in England, and had been papal representative in India. He spoke English well. In the final months of 1886 the duke of Norfolk and his supporters pressed their case in Rome. Those associated with Norfolk, apart from Ross of Bladensburg, included Lord Emly,[39] Herbert Vaughan, bishop of Salford and proprietor of the *Tablet* newspaper, and probably Bishop Healy of Clonfert. On 18 June 1887, Michael Verdon, vice-rector of the Irish College Rome, wrote to Archbishop Walsh that it was 'in contemplation to send Monsignor Persico, accompanied by Fr Gualdi, as Apostolic Visitor to Ireland'.[40] The fact that the appointment was associated with the intercession of Norfolk and English Catholics, and that the Irish bishops had not been consulted, gave rise to suspicion among Irish nationalists as to the purpose of the mission, and even to opposition to it, an attitude partly shared by Archbishops Walsh and Croke.

On 8 July 1887, Ignatius Persico and Enrico Gualdi arrived in Dublin and were greeted by the archbishop who insisted that they stay with him. Walsh set about trying to invigilate the mission. He kept an eye on whom Persico interviewed, and cultivated Gualdi, who proved more garrulous and indiscreet than Persico wished. The latter resented Walsh's manoeuvring, though outwardly he preserved appearances.[41] He had 'the Italian gift', George Errington, unofficial government representative in Rome, informed Gladstone, 'of making the people whom he saw on both sides believe that he is firmly convinced that their views are the right ones: a useful gift I suppose for a commissioner in search of information.'[42] After two weeks in Dublin, Persico decided to move to other parts of Ireland and then return to Dublin. Shortly before his departure he attended a reception at Lucan, Co. Dublin. Among the guests was Colonel Alfred Turner, a special commissioner of the Royal Irish Constabulary for the very troublesome areas of Kerry and Clare. On 25 July Turner informed Sir Redvers Buller, under secretary for Ireland: 'I had a great opportunity last night with Mons. Persico and his secretary Gualdi – and I told them fully about the priests in Kerry and Clare.' 'The Bishop of Limerick (RC)', Turner added, 'had already told them that the parts of Limerick near Clare were made a perfect hell through boycotting and intimidation and that had made a great impression on him [Persico], which I added to by telling him that all Clare was in the same state, and that most of the priests helped in producing that state of things.' 'They go to Limerick tomorrow', he concluded, 'and then proceed to Kerry and Clare.'[43]

They did proceed to Limerick the following day, 26 July, but did not go on to Kerry and Clare. Their journey south was in the nature of a private visit to

Lord Emly at Tervoe, some four miles west of Limerick. A press report noted that they were accompanied by an Italian servant and that at Limerick station they were met by Emly and his party, Emly being 'immediately recognised by Monsignor Persico'. Subsequently, Emly was careful to make it clear to a newspaper representative that the visit was 'purely a private one and altogether unconnected with Monsignor Persico's mission in Ireland'.[44] The envoys stayed two or three nights and were likely to have met other resident and improving landlords such as Sir Stephen de Vere and Edwin Wyndham-Quin, earl of Dunraven, as well as Aubrey de Vere, Fr Flanagan, and Edward Thomas O'Dwyer. The visit necessarily provided the papal legate with different views from those readily available in Dr Walsh's immediate surroundings. The company at Tervoe, it may be presumed, would have made clear the orthodoxy of their bishop, who, in turn, might be expected to have exercised his considerable charm and intellectual gifts for the benefit of the important visitor. Persico and Gualdi journeyed from Limerick to Armagh, where they arrived on 30 July.

The following day, Archbishop Croke waxed indignant in a letter to Archbishop Walsh at being by-passed in his own archdiocese by Monsignor Persico, and went on to assert that the agitation in the country was constitutional unlike what went on under Garibaldi or Mazzini in Persico's homeland. ''Tis all bosh,' he exclaimed vehemently. 'England has deprived us of arms – the right of every free citizen. We have invented a weapon that serves our turn instead. It is called "boycotting"!' 'If we have no means of shooting our enemy, we may have the privilege of leaving him "severely alone".'[45] On 4 August, still brooding, he commented sweepingly: 'Great indignation loudly expressed here, and generally felt in south, at Monsignor Persico's extraordinary manoeuvre in passing me by here, and going to meet Lord Emly and his gang.'[46] O'Dwyer, it would appear, was bracketed in his mind as part of Emly's 'gang'. In September, this impression was deepened and also became fixed in Dillon's mind, and in that of Wilfrid Scawen Blunt, the colourful English Liberal supporter of Home Rule, even though O'Dwyer had made no public pronouncement concerning the Plan of Campaign.

BRANDED AS ANTI-TENANT FARMER

The occasion of Blunt's judgment was his visit to Limerick, with Dillon, for a convention attended by 'about one hundred delegates from various parts of Ireland, convened to discuss ways and means for the coming campaign'.[47] O'Dwyer, endeavouring to keep his own clergy aloof from the Plan of Campaign, had instructed them not to attend the convention. He was annoyed subsequently to read in the *Cork Examiner* of 21 September that a number of priests from the Cashel diocese had been present. He complained to Croke that same day and asked that the priests, pastors and curates, be punished by the archbishop.[48] The latter, having remarked that O'Dwyer was not acting like his predecessor who gave his priests a free hand in political matters, promised that he would bring O'Dwyer's complaint to the notice of his priests in so far as he could.[49] Meanwhile, after the meeting of the convention, Blunt and Dillon went to call on the new bishop of Limerick, who they met 'walking out with his chaplain to his country house'. O'Dwyer invited them into tea, and then there ensued what Blunt termed 'a curious conversation'. It concerned the activities of the Plan of Campaign against the estate mentioned earlier, that of The O'Grady, at Herbertstown, Co. Limerick, in the diocese of Cashel and Emly. Blunt later admitted that he was informed by a Limerick priest, a Fr Higgins, that not only were the tenants on the estate not rack-rented, The O'Grady was the best landlord in the country;[50] a view partly confirmed by contemporary police reports, which maintained that the agitation on the The O'Grady property 'was probably the least justified of all those started in 1886–7.'[51]

On 13 August 1887, pending evictions on the estate, The O'Grady had issued a circular appealing to his tenants to save themselves. A copy reached O'Dwyer. The author reminded his tenants that he was a resident landlord, whose ancestors had dwelt among them for more than four hundred years. He knew his tenants personally, and the friendliest relations had always existed between them. Evictions were unknown on the estate. In 1885, recognising the fall in the price of stock and produce, he had reduced judicial rents by 15 per cent and the non-judicial rents by 25 per cent. In October 1886, similar abatements were offered but the tenants demanded an all-round reduction of 40 per cent. This he rejected, as he considered it to be 'unreasonable and unjust', whereupon the tenants adopted the Plan of Campaign, refused to pay rents, compelled his agent to resign by threats of boycotting, and persisted, he added, in 'boycotting myself and household, preventing my servants attending chapel, and driving my labourers away'. He made further concessions, but these, too, were rejected.[52]

The O'Grady estate was heavily encumbered. The income from the 400-acre demesne was essential to survival. The cynical nature of the campaign was indicated by the admission of the secretary of the local National League branch, a man named McGuire, to a visiting American lawyer, George Pellew, that they were aware that the property was heavily mortgaged, that the encumbrancers would have to foreclose and put the estate up for sale, and that there would be no one to buy it but the tenants pretty cheaply. 'That is what we all expect', McGuire is alleged to have declared.[53]

At his meeting with Blunt and Dillon, the bishop, not surprisingly, took Dillon to task for his Plan of Campaign at Herbertstown, which he spoke of as 'highway robbery and plunder' and The O'Grady as a much injured man. Dillon, according to Blunt, defended himself by stating 'that he, or rather O'Brien, had taken up the case on the assurance as to facts of the priests, and that on them the responsibility lay of any injustice that might have been done. He could not, however, now, just or unjust, back out of the matter and retire in the face of the enemy, even supposing the bishop's case to be correct. All that he could do would be to accept any offer of a compromise honourable to the tenants which should be offered.' 'On this,' Blunt continued, 'the bishop put forward a feeler, and I think very likely he has been commissioned by The O'Grady to effect a settlement. All the same, it is most unfortunate that the diocese should have fallen into such hostile hands.'

On the basis of this criticism of the operation of the Plan of Campaign on one estate, and because he had not permitted his clergy attend the convention, and perhaps because of his emphasis on university education, O'Dwyer was seen as 'hostile', and Blunt went on to the sweeping judgment – 'Dr O'Dwyer, whom I remember last year as a shaky kind of patriot, has now gone over bag and baggage to the enemy', adding, he 'is a dangerous little man, and it appears he is heading a reactionary movement in the episcopacy which may yet bring evil.'[54]

O'Dwyer provided further grounds for Croke to think of him in 'reactionary' terms on 2 November 1887, when he protested to the archbishop at the appearance in Limerick of a Cashel priest at a political meeting, at which he even spoke, without his permission as bishop of Limerick. To make matters worse, the priest in question was Matthew Ryan, 'the general', a director of the campaign against The O'Grady, and a man whom Croke himself found difficult to control.[55] To O'Dwyer's subsequent embarrassment he learned that one of his own priests, Fr Eugene Sheehy, who had been imprisoned during the Land League troubles and was a relation of his, had assured Ryan that his bishop had given permission to priests to attend the meeting![56] O'Dwyer apologised to Croke.

While the campaign against The O'Grady was at its height and evictions taking place, Monsignor Persico paid his official visit to Limerick, a circumstance which, perhaps, explains a remark of Wilfrid Blunt that the Herbertstown case was later used 'with great damage' in Rome against the agitators.[57] The *Limerick Chronicle* of 1 September 1887 noted that the papal envoy was met on arrival in the city by the mayor, Francis A. O'Keefe, the bishop, and a considerable number of clergy. They processed through the main streets, where 'a vast multitude of the people' had turned out to greet the pope's representative. Two days later, O'Dwyer introduced Persico to one of his great sources of pride, the Archconfraternity of the Holy Family, and availed of the occasion to address personally the great assembly of men on the theme of loyalty to the Holy See.[58] Persico was impressed by the state of the church in Limerick and by the young bishop, in whom henceforth he took a paternal interest.

As the weeks of autumn passed, Balfour's policy of coercion took an emotional toll of the Irish clergy, many of whom were fearful that the violence of the people could not be contained in the face of such provocative policy and the prospect of a hard winter. By 5 November 1887, the bishop of Cork, T.A. O'Callaghan, was reporting to Monsignor Kirby: 'The strain on the country is simply terrible. We fear the struggle will be long, as the present government has thrown aside all restraint and excited a determined opposition which no coercion can suppress.'[59] Walsh and Croke, dreading a collapse into anarchy and Fenianism, struggled to preserve the clerical-nationalist alliance, and were exercised lest some of their colleagues, influenced by O'Dwyer and Healy, might waver and be drawn towards working with the Conservative administration in order to obtain educational improvements. There was also the burden of prevailing fears and rumours that Persico's impending report to Rome would be unfavourable, which, if it happened, might lead to action from the papacy which could have serious implications for the clerical-nationalist alliance and the peace of the country.

DEFYING CRITICS

At this tense, unfavourable juncture, O'Dwyer chose to trail his coat in defiance of the land agitators. In the popular mind it placed him definitely in the enemy camp. The occasion was once again a prize-giving function at the Sacred Heart College, the Crescent, at the beginning of November. The report in the *Limerick Chronicle* on 5 November observed that he commenced by stating that it was his considered opinion that, both for the spiritual and temporal welfare of the people, it was essential that adequate provision be made for their religious education. This was of more consequence than 'that the land be reformed, or even self-government achieved ...' He was not advocating any weakening in the campaign for Home Rule, he added carefully, but the situation was developing to the point where the land question was 'disputing precedence' with the national question. The farmers, by the strength of their voting power, had succeeded in forcing both the leaders and those who supported the movement for self-government 'to accommodate ... to their needs'. Addressing his episcopal colleagues, he appealed to them either to withdraw their support for a Catholic university college altogether or else press on with it wholeheartedly. On the question of denominational education he felt sure there was agreement on fundamentals between Catholics and Protestants. Irish education, as a result, was not part of the political game, and it was most desirable that it be treated as 'a non-contentious, non-political question'. He advised that negotiations be opened as soon as possible with the present government, for more was to be gained from a Tory administration, which had always upheld the principle of denominational education, than from a Liberal government.[60]

Dr Croke, harassed, in addition to the social and political tensions, by a financial crisis in his diocese, the impending death of dean of the diocese, and by the letter from O'Dwyer condemning the presence of 'the general' at the Limerick meeting, wrote angrily to Walsh on reading of the Limerick speech. 'What an insidious and, indeed, thoroughly dishonest speech he made yesterday in Limerick in reference to educational affairs. One would imagine that religious education was neglected in Ireland, or that our youth in consequence were going straight to perdition. His trickery and treachery will soon be shown up or I am very much mistaken.'[61] More damaging to O'Dwyer's public image, however, was the fact that the *Tablet* congratulated him on his insight, and availed of his speech to emphasise that the worthwhile alliance for the Irish people lay with the Tories and Liberal Unionists, and that they should strive for the realisation of their aims in education, instead of wasting energy on a land settlement and on the 'remote and doubtful contingency' of Home Rule. It advised the Irish leaders to take their cue from the bishop of Limerick, and to be 'content to forget the enmities of politics for a little while for the winning of so great a good.'[62]

Shortly after this, Persico, now staying in the Capuchin monastery in Cork, requested O'Dwyer to visit him before the end of the week.[63] As a close watch was maintained on visitors to the papal envoy, rumours soon began to circulate of intrigues between Persico and O'Dwyer, as representing the more unionist-inclined bishops. The explanation was otherwise, as Persico was later to make clear to Archbishop Walsh.[64] It was part, however, of the raft of rumours and suspicions now circulating around O'Dwyer in November and December 1887. On 28 November the papal envoy wrote advising him to be on his guard 'against any attempt that may be made to drag you out on the education question'. 'I have heard this', he explained, 'in a way I cannot mention.'[65] That this did not indicate a decline of confidence on his part, however, was indicated on 10 December by his inviting himself to stay with O'Dwyer on 26 December,[66] and by a further letter on 15 December thanking O'Dwyer for his Christmas wishes and requesting him in confidence to obtain all the information he could about 'the list of the candidates for the Kilmore diocese, and also that of Achonry', which he enclosed, and concerning which O'Dwyer might communicate during his visit to Limerick.[67] But four days later the situation had changed. Insinuations, prognostications, and allegations in the *Pall Mall Gazette*, quoted provocatively in the *Freeman's Journal* and *United Ireland*, led him to cancel his visit. 'No doubt Y.L. must have read all the fine articles on the 'startling rumour' and the *Pall Mall Gazette*,' he wrote on 19 December, 'and hence you will easily understand that it would be neither wise nor prudent for me to pay you the promised visit. Certainly it would have been a sincere pleasure for me and also a nice recreation to spend a few days with you, but I must forego all that. Indeed my going to Limerick in the present state of excitement would do no good, on the contrary harm to Y.L.'[68]

Characteristically, O'Dwyer's method of defence was to attack. The following day, 20 December 1887, the *Freeman's Journal* carried a long letter from the bishop of Limerick headed – 'The Alleged Unionist Coercion Intrigue', in which he disclaimed vigorously the allegations against him in the *Pall Mall Gazette*, the *Freeman's Journal*, and *United Ireland*. He had been accused, he declared, of being 'in political intrigues with the government for certain purposes – that I have been using my influence as a bishop in the interests of the landlords as against the farmers – and that as a unionist I have been trying to defeat the national movement for Home Rule.' All of these charges, he insisted, 'whether openly stated or insinuated in offensive epithets … are utterly and entirely false'. Even the strongest opponent he ever had in Limerick, politically or otherwise, would never believe that he 'would stoop to the methods of political intrigue'. He then addressed the separate charges. He had not been in any plot with the government about education. As to his being a unionist, he pointed to the long record of his support for Home Rule. To the charge that he was a 'landlord bishop' he responded at greater length, because it was 'more malicious' than the other allegations and was made at a 'moment of intense feeling on the part of the people'. The previous October he had impressed on his priests their duty 'to stand by their people and to show them sympathy in the difficulties of the situation'. He considered the struggle for the 'radical reform of the land system' to be just and legitimate, and he approved heartily of priests and people involving themselves in agitation, so long as their methods were in keeping with the law of God. He had told his own priests, moreover, that where he could not go along with his people he would hold back and not join their enemies and his. He had resolved, in short, to stand by as long as he could. Now, however, he felt he could no longer keep silent about certain aspects of the agrarian struggle. Boycotting was always accompanied by a 'terrible risk of crime' when it was used with 'an excitable people'. Hence, however defensible in theory, it was sinful in practice, and he had directed his priests that they could not be party to boycotting. The Plan of Campaign as such was justifiable only as a last resort, when it was the only means available for resisting injustice. In conclusion, he declared disparagingly, 'the guidance of the agitation was not only politically stupid', it was 'morally wrong', and he asked his readers to believe him when he said, 'without corrupt motive of any kind', that he firmly believed that both boycotting and the Plan, because they offered violent resistance to the law, were 'bad and sinful'.[69]

The day the letter appeared, O'Dwyer wrote to Persico asking his opinion. The latter assured him that he could not have remained silent under the imputations in the *Pall Mall Gazette* and the *Freeman* that compromised him with his people. He would have preferred, however, the letter to have been 'shorter and less detailed'. Then speaking of his own vulnerable position, he observed that he 'must remain silent under the imputation of playing the part of intriguer and barterer of the Irish cause' even though it was all 'a tissue of calumnies to prejudice' his 'mission in the eyes of the Irish people at home and abroad.' 'May God forgive the slanderers,' he concluded.[70]

The 'slanderers' continued active in O'Dwyer's case. Following his published letter, the *Freeman* published other letters criticising his views as alien to the sentiments of the Irish church and deficient in national spirit;[71] and one 'respectful' contribution from W.F. Dennehy, editor of the *Irish Catholic*, pointed, not surprisingly, to an apparent contradiction in his lordship's letter, namely, that if the methods of the Plan of Campaign were 'sinful', as he claimed, how could he, the custodian of the conscience of his people, 'stand aside'? It must mean that he did not regard the methods of which he complained 'as being in any proper sense of the word "sinful".'[72]

O'Dwyer, however, did receive some messages of approval, and a number of English publications praised his letter. Early in January 1888, moreover, the priests of the Limerick diocese in assembly assured him of their loyalty and support. The bishop's written response was read to the assembly by the vicar-general, Dr William Moloney. In it he explained why he felt that his office and his personal honour had obliged him to respond to the accusations made against him. One of these imputations was that he had used his episcopal authority to hinder his clergy from identifying themselves with the political and social actions of the people. He now called on the present gathering to answer whether or not they had ever had such a communication from him. As to the *Freeman*, 'its vile correspondence or its slanders at second hand' would never terrorise him into submission. His recent letter to the paper, he insisted, reflected his 'own personal attitude' with respect to the agrarian struggle, he had no intention of forcing his viewpoint on anyone else. He did claim the right, however, to put his views before his clergy and the people of the diocese when there was a question of morality involved. When the address had been read, Archdeacon John Halpin, on behalf of the vicars of the diocese, through whom the alleged communication would have been passed on to the rest of the clergy, emphatically denied the existence of any such communication.[73]

What seemed clear to his lordship, was not always clear to others. That he was conveying his 'own personal attitude' rather than a binding moral instruction must have come as a surprise to many of his clergy. Similar confusion surrounded his claim that he had not hindered his clergy from identifying themselves with the political and social actions of the people. After all, he had forbidden his priests to attend certain meetings involving the Plan of Campaign, yet there were political meetings with which he made no effort to interfere. In November 1887 priests from Limerick cathedral were present at a banquet in honour of some Home Rule politicians, and both secular and regular clergy attended a public lecture by Michael Davitt, the hero of the Land League;[74] and the following January, at a greeting accorded to the inflammatory Fr Matthew Ryan, 'the general', on his release from prison, most of the priests from the Cathedral parish were present; and at the end of that month, four parish priests and eight curates from the diocese attended a large gathering at Rathkeale addressed by Michael Davitt and John Redmond, at which one of the curates spoke from the platform.[75]

Despite his protestations, rumours continued of O'Dwyer's arrangements and intrigues with the British government. In the nationalist press, by the spring of 1888, he was firmly stigmatised as a unionist, and, protest his innocence as he might, his opposition to the methods used in the agrarian struggle were sufficient to brand him as an enemy, a 'Castle bishop'.

THE PAPAL DECREE

On 20 April 1888 the dreaded condemnation of the Plan of Campaign came from Rome over the signature of Cardinal Raphaele Monaco. It took the form of criticising such aspects of the Plan as had been delated to the Vatican, and giving reasons for the condemnation. The reasons given reflected little knowledge of the Irish situation.[76]

The decree was issued without consulting the Irish bishops, or notifying Archbishop Walsh, though he was in Rome at the time, and contrary to the advice given in Persico's report. Croke, fearful of the reaction among the nationalist leaders, arranged a meeting with Dillon. On 2 May he wrote to Walsh that they had agreed that, as the reasons given 'as a basis for the decree' were ill founded, the decree did not apply in the Irish situation.[77] Already, on 29 April, Dillon had explained this to a meeting of the tenants at Herbertstown, Co. Limerick. The papal pronouncement did not refer to them, he announced, because in their case there was no freedom of contract, the land courts were run by the landlords and, therefore, not impartial, and the Plan, besides, was not operated, as stated, 'by force and intimidation'.[78] On 17 May the Catholic members of the Irish Parliamentary party, summoned by the lord mayor of Dublin, Thomas Sexton, MP, passed resolutions critical of the decree, and concluded that although they 'acknowledged unreservedly the spiritual jurisdiction of the Holy See, they could recognise no right in the Holy See to interfere in their political affairs'.[79] Before long, the reaction against the papal document moved beyond polite resolutions. The leaders of rural agitation, Dillon and O'Brien, conducted a campaign of vehement public criticism across the country, which depicted the pope as siding with their traditional enemy against his own Catholic people. Yet, to O'Dwyer's annoyance, the bishops as a body remained silent and did not publish the papal rescript to priests or people.

DR O'DWYER AND PAPAL TEACHING. DEFIED IN HIS CATHEDRAL CITY

Before considering O'Dwyer's response to the papal condemnation, it is important to view it in the context of the Church of the time.

Mise en scène

When he was a young man, the Roman Catholic Church was under attack from many sides and seemed in decline. Garibaldi announced that he would make Rome the capital of Freemasonry. At Geneva a congress of anarchists heard Bakunin and others proclaim the end of Christianity. Then, came a rallying around the beleaguered pope, the summoning of the first Vatican Council, and its defiant proclamation of papal infallibility. With this, the scene changed. The pope was no longer a condemner of errors, he was the illuminator of the paths that men and women should follow. The entire church looked to him as the assured guardian of Christ's message. There was a new sense of assurance, despite the loss of the Papal States. Many were predisposed to enlarge the authority of papal statements, to extend infallibility to papal encyclicals and pronouncements, and virtually to identify the church with the pope and the clerical teaching authorities. The institutional church, under the pope, held the truth, and stood against the world.

Much of this outlook was reflected in O'Dwyer. He allowed for little or no flexibility in interpreting papal pronouncements. Bishop Healy was of similar mind, as was O'Dwyer's English friend, Bishop Vaughan of Salford. Cardinal Manning, on the other hand, although one of the architects of the decree of infallibility, had the precise scope of the definition ever in mind, and was far more aware of the inner workings in Rome, of the various, even conflicting pressures that influenced papal pronouncements, and hence he empathised with Walsh, and even with the impatient, outspoken Croke, and was prepared to speak for them at Rome. Healy and O'Dwyer, for their part, seemed to feel obliged to apply the papal criticism and condemnation literally and quickly, irrespective of the hostility this was likely to arouse, and the division and bitterness they were likely to generate in the Irish church. Had all the Irish bishops acted that way, then, in Walsh's and Croke's view, a schism would most likely have occurred, and the country would have been divided between a nationalist majority and an official church seen as West-British and on the side of the oppressive government. The spectre of what had happened in France haunted Walsh and Croke with good reason. For O'Dwyer, it would seem, the issue was simpler. The pope had spoken. He was Christ's representative. His way had to be the right one.

The response

The first to make a public and positive response to the papal rescript was the bishop of Kerry, who issued a comment on the papal rescript to his clergy, and ordered that it be read at all public masses on the following Sunday.[80] The second to act was O'Dwyer, who readily found confirmation of his own views in the papal document. Typically, he only moved when the public outcry against the papal decree impinged directly on his own diocese, the area for which he had spiritual responsibility. A public demonstration to consider the decree was to be held in Limerick. Instead of quietly arranging a meeting with the mayor, Francis A. O'Keefe, or addressing a private letter to him, as most bishops would have done, he determined to go public. Like Archbishop Walsh in Dublin, though without his subtlety, he was coming to see the press as his pulpit, his way of bringing to bear the authority of his office, and his undoubted power of communication, against opponents, who, for their part, viewed such an approach as episcopal intimidation.

He informed the mayor by public letter on 25 May that the papal decree bound 'the conscience of those whom it concerns', and, sweepingly, that it was a 'grievous sin for any Catholic to disobey it, and a much more grievous sin, under any pretext, for anyone to deny the pope's authority to issue it'. Because of that, and the likely outcome of the meeting, he had decided, he declared, that none of his clergy would attend the demonstration. 'With this official intimation,' he added, 'I have discharged my duty.' Then, craving the mayor's indulgence, he issued the 'political remark' that there was a real danger in the present situation 'of rending the whole Irish to its very base at home and abroad', adding determinedly, if somewhat melodramatically: 'If we are driven to defend the prerogatives of the Holy See, I trust we shall follow those who, before us, sustained more serious persecution that, thank God, our opponents can yet inflict on us.'[81] The mayor, in response, assured him that there was no intention of attacking the pope. The meeting, like similar meetings throughout the country, sought to point out that the rescript, though having certain validity and binding force, did not actually apply to Ireland. It was not based 'on evidence sufficient to warrant its issue'.[82] This was to continue a main point of difference at this stage.

From Modena, Italy, on 28 May, Walsh, who was on his way home, observed to Monsignor Kirby that it was regrettable that the bishops did not speak as a body. He hoped that O'Dwyer's letter would have effect, but he would have more confidence if it came from someone in whom the people had more trust.[83] The lack of trust was exploited, in fact, by leaders of the agitation, most notably by William O'Brien. On the morning of the Limerick meeting, 27 May, impressed by the welcome he had received, O'Brien announced that he was proud to find the nationalists of Limerick no more intimidated 'by the proclamation from the palace of Corbally' than either he or they would be 'by a proclamation from Mr Balfour', thereby linking O'Dwyer once more with the Tory administration. He then described the bishop's direction to the people and clergy as 'the rashest and most unjust' that ever came from the pen of an Irish ecclesiastic. He had rushed into print at a time when the rest of the hierarchy were 'remonstrating and respectfully protesting at Rome'. 'He left Limerick the previous day', O'Brien declared, adding cowardice to the bishop's failings, but 'taking care to supply his manifesto to every Orange paper.' Then, having recalled O'Dwyer's part in the election of 1874, and accused him of always being on the wrong side, O'Brien concluded by linking him with the anti-nationalist, even with the anti-Catholic factions in the country, who were the allies of the repressive Tory administration.[84] John Dillon joined the chorus with 'a slashing attack' at a meeting in Kildare, warning his hearers that O'Dwyer was the 'champion of rack-renting and land-grabbing in Ireland',[85] while Michael Davitt, though not a supporter of the Plan of Campaign, described the bishop of Limerick's letter as written in a 'spirit of reckless ultra-montanism' and exhibiting 'the very worst form of clerical dictatorship' which had done so much harm to the church in Ireland. He, Davitt, was taking his stand with ninety-nine out of every hundred lay-nationalist Catholics in Ireland in not obeying the rescript.[86]

The size and enthusiasm of the Limerick meeting was hailed in the nationalist papers, and played down by the English press. *The Times*, indeed, as reported in the *Limerick Chronicle* of 29 May 1888, observed that William O'Brien, despite the large crowds, would have gladly 'exchanged a few thousand of his audience for a handful of priests', and it deplored the sad fact that 'the courageous Bishop of Limerick' could be abused with impunity. The force of the observation was indirectly acknowledged by O'Brien on the same date when, in pointed defiance of the bishop, he went to Glensharrold in the Limerick diocese, where the Plan of Campaign was being waged against the Delmege family estate, and a remarkable 57 per cent reduction was being sought by the tenants. Addressing the latter, he described O'Dwyer's statement as 'a heavy blow' against them by preventing Fr Robert Ambrose, one of their local leaders, from attending the meeting. The bishop's letter, he complained, had 'gagged and shackled' all the priests of the diocese. Then, in an aggressive vein, he proclaimed that the meeting in the city had marked the end of the papal rescript 'as a matter of practical politics' and, he assured his audience, that both the Plan and boycotting would continue to be used and the land grabber continue to be treated 'as a public pest and a public enemy'.[87]

On the encouraging side for O'Dwyer was support from some Episcopal colleagues; Herbert Vaughan, bishop of Salford,[88] Nicholas Donnelly, auxiliary bishop of Dublin,[89] and John Healy of Clonfert, who expressed himself 'pained and humiliated by the temporising policy of those who ought to know better' and grandiloquently assured O'Dwyer that 'Catholics yet unborn' would thank him for his letter to the mayor of Limerick.[90] A meeting of the Irish hierarchy was scheduled for Clonliffe College, Dublin, on Wednesday 30 May. O'Dwyer was pleased and relieved to find that they had before them a letter from Walsh, still in Rome, addressed to the primate, Michael Logue. The pope, Walsh reported, wanted his decree communicated at once to the clergy for their guidance, and expressed his regret that it had not been done before this. The reasons stated by Cardinal Monaco were not to be seen as limiting the sense of the decree which was an official act of the Holy Office, confirmed by his holiness. Finally, the people should be instructed, Walsh insisted, that the decree was a decision on morals and not an act of political interference.[91]

The bishops followed the instruction. They announced that the decree was for the domain of morals alone, that the Holy Father remained deeply interested in 'the temporal welfare of our country', that 'hasty or irreverent language' should not be used 'with reference to the sovereign pontiff or the sacred congregation through which he usually issues his decrees', and that the pope had an inalienable and divine right to speak with authority on all questions pertaining to faith and morals.[92]

'We did substantially what we were told to do', Croke informed Walsh on 31 May, and made it understood 'that what we had done was done with bad grace'. Later, on 14 June, in a further letter to Walsh, he stressed that at the meeting it was agreed that no written communication would be issued to the priests or to the press. Directions were to be given orally by the bishop to his priests. O'Dwyer was 'very quiet and conciliatory', Croke observed, and 'took part in drafting the resolutions' with himself and Bishop Patrick O'Donnell of Raphoe.[93] The episcopal resolutions, Dr O'Callaghan, of Cork, assured Kirby on 2 June, 'had a calming effect on the country'. 'The feeling throughout the country', he explained, had been 'most intense'. 'Cursing the pope was quite common. Women threw his likeness out of their houses and the excitement extended even to the children.'[94] Croke on 6 June confirmed that there were to be 'no more "big meetings".' 'If no further provocation be given to the people', he added, 'the past will be forgiven and forgotten.'[95]

He reckoned without his Limerick colleague's volatile temperament and his tendency to strike back vigorously when attacked. O'Dwyer smarted at the insults offered him in his own city and diocese, and readily linked his grievance to the insults offered to the pope by the members of the Irish party, who defied the papal decree and declared that as Catholics that they could recognise 'no right in the Holy See to interfere with the Irish people in the management of their political affairs'.[96] This seemed tantamount to asserting that there was such a thing as politics without morals. He determined defiantly, with his readiness for public confrontation, to present the papal teaching to the full glare of publicity, conscious that his doing so would be approved in Rome.

A LETTER TO THE CLERGY: THE 'LIMERICK MANIFESTO'

O'Dwyer's 'provocation' was given at a synod of the regular and secular clergy of the diocese, in St John's Cathedral, on 11 June 1888. It took the form of a long and remarkable letter, which he had read out to the assembled priests, and of which copies were sent to Rome and to the British and Irish press. As he expected, it caused a major stir. The *Spectator*, for the week ending 16 June, commented:

> On Monday, Bishop O'Dwyer addressed a synod of his clergy at Limerick in a speech of singular and masculine ability; indeed, as a mere piece of English, we have hardly read its equal for a long time.

In order to appreciate this document, at once ingenious and caustic, it is necessary to consider it at some length.

'It is my duty as bishop of this diocese', O'Dwyer began, 'to bring to your knowledge officially the decree recently issued by the Holy Office, and sanctioned by the Holy Father, in condemnation of the practices known as the Plan of Campaign and Boycotting.' After this attention-catching opening, he went on to explain that there was some doubt at first among theologians about the application of the decree because of the reasons attached to it by Cardinal Monaco, but that now, after a letter sent by Archbishop Walsh conveying the pope's clear direction, it was evident that 'these practices of boycotting and the Plan of Campaign as they actually exist in Ireland stand condemned as violations of the moral law of charity and justice', and that it was 'now a settled and certain law of the Catholic Church, which all the faithful of this diocese are bound to take from me as their bishop, that these practices are sinful.' And it was 'even more sinful, as being against faith, to deny or impugn under any pretext the right of the pope to condemn them.'

Then, having pointed out that there was no difference of opinion amongst Irish bishops 'as to the meaning or binding force of this decree', he noted pungently that the decree had been made 'a matter of public agitation and the subject of consideration, not only by that curious body, the conciliabulum of laymen, that sat on the pope in Dublin, but by public boards in the country down to the little village branches of the League', so that it was clear that the sooner 'the plain truth' was 'put before the people the better'. 'To my mind', he insisted vigorously, 'there never has been in Ireland since St Patrick planted the Faith here a greater scandal or more injury done to religion than this most deplorable agitation. Whatever may have been the intention of the leaders, and God alone can judge that, the general tendency of the speeches … has been to impair the … childlike, and undoubting faith and confidence with which the hearts of our countrymen have ever turned to the Chair of Peter.'

'A series of resolutions', he went on relentlessly, 'have been hawked about the country telling the Holy Father that we will take no interference in politics from him. But just consider what this comes to. The pope, as the supreme teacher of morals, tells us authoritatively that certain practices are violations of the fifth and seventh commandments. Are the commandments of God within his jurisdiction? Has he a commission to teach his people whether certain practices are violations of the virtues of justice and charity?' If he has, then 'every man, politicians as well as the rest, must obey' when he speaks. The pope has nothing to say to politics as politics, but he has 'a divine and inalienable right to interfere in all questions in which faith and morals are involved.'

'This is not the place to talk politics', the bishop then avowed, and he only did so to prevent a misunderstanding of his position at the present crisis. He explained:

> I am a nationalist, I believe, as true and as sound as the best of you. I have never wavered in my belief in Home Rule for Ireland. I am a land reformer. I detest as earnestly as any man the oppression of heartless landlords, and would go any length sanctioned by religion to restrain them. I believe there never will be peace in Ireland or prosperity until every farmer is the owner of his own farm, and am prepared to give every legitimate aid, according to my position, to any political agitation for these ends. But from that agitation must be eliminated whatever is against God's law – I don't care what advantage it brings to the farmers or others – if it put a gold mine in the heart of every farm and abolished all rent for ever, if it is condemned by the Church I will not have it.

He did not think, he added, 'that a state of equilibrium, social or political', would 'ever be reached as long as the centre of government' was 'outside Ireland'; but, even for 'all the blessings which Home Rule would bring', he would not sanction 'the violation of God's law, much less the repudiation of the authority of the vicar of Christ'.

Turning to criticisms of a personal character, he noted that it had been said repeatedly that he had 'habitually associated with the aristocracy, and for years, as a priest, took sides with the rich against the poor, and with the landlords against their tenants'. 'There was not one particle of truth in these statements', he insisted, taking them together, 'nor a shadow of foundation for them'. They were 'simply malicious inventions ... lies concocted by the leaders of the agitation for the purpose of prejudicing the poor people' against him, 'and thus weakening' his 'authority in teaching them all their duty'. 'Such methods', he added, 'may succeed for a time, but they are not the methods of honourable men.' Then turning rhetorically to his priests, as he had done at the previous gathering, he put the question – 'Is there in your whole body, secular and regular, a priest less open to such a charge?' 'But the making of that reckless charge has done a great deal of good', he added, because many men recognising that that statement was a lie were less disposed to believe other statements of the agitators.

Finally, O'Dwyer assured his listeners that he did not 'retain one atom of rancour' against his traducers. He could 'make allowances as well as any man for excitement or political passion'. 'These men had got into a most trying position, and although much of their language was wrong', it was 'easy to understand how they were betrayed into it.' 'Let the whole matter drop now', he declared magnanimously, as he brought his carefully crafted letter to an end. 'Let it pass away as a painful incident, and if again priests and people stand together upon the same platform, I can promise you that no remembrance of the personal ill-treatment which I have received will interfere to disturb the harmony of the reunion.'[97]

Writing to Dr Donnelly, auxiliary bishop of Dublin, the following day, O'Dwyer commented: 'If ever O'Brien and Co. have power, I suspect, after my performance yesterday, that I had better get my soul in order.' 'Very probably', he continued, 'some of our brethren may object to my action: but looking to my own diocese, I am convinced that it would be a serious blow to religion if the defiance of these men were to go unrebuked.' 'Then', he explained, 'I wanted to put myself right, after all their falsehoods, with those of the public who yet can think.' 'I am so much obliged to your Lordship', he concluded, 'for your kindness and sympathy all through.'[98]

Some of his 'brethren' did object to his action. 'The Limerick manifesto came on the country with surprise', Croke reported to Walsh on 14 June. 'He took part in drafting the resolutions' at our meeting. 'There was to be *no writing*. And yet see what the little cur has done!' 'It is unaccountable', Croke confessed. 'The general impression is that he has lost his head. How else account for his eccentricity and audacious egotism?' 'Tis hard to hold one's tongue under the circumstances', he concluded, but ''tis better to be silent than to further offend the public conscience by shivering a lance over his head.'[99] The *Irish Catholic* warned, however, – 'if the agitation is revived, ... if there be more heart-burning discussions and dissensions, this address of his Lordship will be the proximate cause.'[100]

The lay nationalist leadership, however, demonstrated unexpected moderation in allowing the 'provocation' given by O'Dwyer to pass, influenced, perhaps, by

Croke. O'Dwyer's defiance was further strengthened by supportive communications from parts of Ireland and from overseas. Among these last was one from
Captain O'Shea in Madrid, which praised his moral courage, assured him of his
'sincere friendship' and of his 'deepest appreciation' of his efforts 'in the cause of
honesty and of the deluded people'.[101] Bishop Donnelly, as usual, gave support.
Writing to thank him on 16 June, O'Dwyer commented vehemently that when
it was a question of 'leading Catholic (?) politicians' scouting 'the solemn
decision of the pope on a question of morals and almost stating they had the
approval of the bishops', then, if he 'were to be chopped in pieces, instead of
being covered with dirt', he 'would not let such a challenge go unanswered.' In
the same letter, he remarked deprecatingly – 'It is hard to have to appear as if
assuming a place and authority amongst my betters when I am simply doing
what I think is the obvious duty of any man in my position.'[102]

Before the end of June, news came of the pope's approval of O'Dwyer's stand.
Despite such approbation, O'Dwyer was left under no illusion as to how many
of the farming community in his diocese viewed him. His old mentor and
friend, Fr T.S. Flanagan, had the courage to tell him. 'I'm very glad', Flanagan
observed to Lord Emly on 29 June with reference to his bishop, 'that the pope
has noticed his action. He is simply hated by the farmers. I rode up last week to
the southern part of the county – I was to Rockhill, Charleville and Effin, and
the feeling against him in those parts was vehemently strong. He knows from me
that this is so – but', he added revealingly, 'no one else would tell him.' The
bishop had just returned from the meeting of the hierarchy at Maynooth. 'There
will be something from them about the land and their sympathy with the
tenants etc.,' Flanagan commented, but nothing about the decree, 'no public
manifesto'. Emly, forwarding the letter to Ross, noted in the margin against the
concluding sentence – 'Is this not monstrous?'[103]

DR WALSH AND THE CLERICAL-NATIONALIST ALLIANCE

The bishops, under the guidance of Walsh, recently returned from Rome, were
determined not to let the papal decree lead to a breach in the clerical-nationalist
alliance. Walsh did not approve of O'Dwyer's public letter, nor of the pope's
praise of it, which he believed was likely to foment a rift between priests and
people. Hence, in an address to the Dublin municipal corporation and other
dignatories, on 17 July, he set about building bridges with sensitivity and
diplomatic skill. It was not until he returned to Ireland, he declared, that he was
able to realise 'the painful intensity of the crisis through which our people had,
thank God, safely passed, and the fearful narrowness of their escape from a
disaster in which, but for the unyielding firmness of their Catholic faith, and of
their loyalty to the See of Peter, that faith might have been brought to ruin'. The
resolutions passed by members of the party, 'and reiterated by the corporation
had', he declared, 'been grievously misrepresented and misunderstood'.

Sometimes the 'misrepresentation' was due to malice, and in one case, referring indirectly to O'Dwyer, to 'a somewhat over zealous and altogether self-constituted guardian and defender ... who took it upon himself to declare that your action upon these resolutions was nothing short of an insult to me'. 'For myself,' Walsh asserted, 'I can only say that I fail to see it.'[104]

The archbishop was acutely conscious that what mattered was the nationalist people's perception. As he viewed it, the harsh words against the decree and the pope, uttered under popular excitement, reflected not so much hostility to the pope as spiritual ruler but rather anger that his holiness had entered into an alliance with their hereditary enemy against them. While that perception remained, the decree, in Walsh's view, could not be enforced without destroying the clerical-nationalist alliance, and with it, the church's power and influence with the greater part of the people.

O'DWYER'S MOTIVATIONS?

To Sir George Errington, also recently back from Rome, Walsh's speech of 17 July was a scandalous minimising of 'all the pope's orders and strong expressions' and an indirect defence of 'those who attacked the pope'.[105] But what of O'Dwyer? If Walsh was motivated mainly by the desire to preserve the clerical-nationalist alliance for the sake of the church in Ireland, what were the factors motivating O'Dwyer? They appear to have been many, and difficult to place in order of priority. He was activated by a sense of episcopal duty to uphold religious and moral values in his own diocese, and was also moved by a zealous reverence for papal authority, and a dislike of physical violence and intimidation. He was influenced, too, by a deep-seated suspicion and distrust of John Dillon and other leaders of the Irish party, especially where the church's standing and teaching were concerned. In this respect, he was at one with Emly, O'Shea, and, as will appear, Monsignor Persico, in considering Archbishop Walsh's desire for close links with the parliamentary party as likely to create a situation, especially in a Home Rule Ireland, in which the church would become subservient to the party. 'If some steps are not taken to shake the church free from the agitators', he apprised Bishop Donnelly on 11 July 1888, 'they will crush us in the end';[106] and he was disposed to accept O'Shea's estimation that there were 'many phases of anti-clericalism amongst the present leaders of the people' and 'that if their day ever came' they would 'and must direct their organisation against the church. They will submit to no such *imperium in imperio* [empire within an empire].'[107] Then, there were the imponderable factors rooted in his own personality: the desire to lead, to control, to display ability and knowledge through the public press, and that 'unconscious claim to infallibility' which, as his admirer Richard Canon O'Kennedy admitted, was manifested in holding 'that his own opinion could not be wrong' and in clinging to his views 'with greater tenacity' when faced with opposition.[108]

Meanwhile, the leaders of the Plan of Campaign, in their public outcry against the papal decree, had attributed much of the blame to Monsignor Persico and his report to Rome.

THE PERSICO REPORT

In fact, his report, which was sent on 14 December 1887, had recommended that there should not be condemnation of abuses and troubles as this would increase rather diminish active agitation. His advice was that Rome 'act directly on the bishops and through them', for with their full agreement and support the carrying out of remedies would be possible and even 'easy'. As a further step in the process, the four archbishops should be called to Rome, together with one or two bishops from each province. He expressly mentioned O'Dwyer as one of the bishops.[109]

Long before the papal decree was published in April 1888, however, and even before his own report was completed, Persico, as has been seen, was the subject of hostile suspicions and calumnies. Poor weather and declining health, partly occasioned by adverse pressure, led to his going to Devon in mid-January 1888. He intended returning to Ireland, but never did. The reaction to the papal decree determined this. He, moreover, was likely to have contributed to the emphasis in the decree by a series of agitated letters to Cardinal Rampolla, papal secretary of state, before and after going to Devon, which were increasingly critical of the situation in Ireland and of the Irish bishops, particularly Archbishops Walsh and Croke.[110] In his official report, too, he had been critical of the two men, if less so, as 'the two standard bearers' of the Irish hierarchy, who had compromised themselves 'by giving open support to the National League, and, what is worse, to the Plan of Campaign'.[111]

On the overall situation, Persico in his report showed himself close to O'Dwyer's thinking in his judgment that the conduct of the clergy could not be allowed continue and that the bishops were at fault 'in tolerating things manifestly opposed to justice and Christian charity, especially when they permitted priests take part in the Plan of Campaign and boycotting'.[112] Again, he found fault with the bishops 'putting themselves in the hands of the political party without thinking that the politicians' had 'different ideas' to them 'and so should not inspire blind trust and confidence.' 'The politicians', he added, 'have acquired such power in the country as to exclude the influence and power of the clergy and put at risk the trust of the Irish people in their clergy and church.'[113] As well as Walsh's espousal of the cause of the National League and of that of the Plan of Campaign, it was noted that he had imposed himself on the body of bishops and that, although some criticised him, none had 'the courage to resist him in their meetings'.[114] Of Croke, the papal envoy shrewdly observed that he was 'of impetuous character' and 'often commits acts of imprudence and does not know how to hold himself within the limits of moderation'. His 'mania about political things', Persico added, 'destroys all his good qualities'.[115]

Against this censorious background, O'Dwyer and his diocese came out well. 'The spirit of the population in general is good', Persico reported, 'and the condition of the diocese is satisfactory from all aspects.' The bishop, 'who governed the diocese only for a year and six months, is a man of tender conscience and of right principles, alien to politics and animated by zeal'. He presented 'a true type of bishop'. He was 'young' and in 'need of experience and also of prudence and discretion', the envoy observed, but it would 'be easy for him to acquire these qualities because he is docile and open to reason. He should be one of the bishops to be called to Rome as one of the province of Cashel.'[116] Needless to say, Persico's portrait of the bishop of Limerick was far from what Walsh or Croke would have drawn!

O'Dwyer cultivated his links with Persico. The latter wrote him on 1 August 1888 from Birmingham, prior to his return to Italy, thanking him for his kindness in writing to him on his departure from England, and concluding – 'It is for me to thank you, for you have always been kind to me, and I shall never cease to pray for Y.L. (your Lordship.)'[117] Persico, as the unofficial authority on Ireland, continued influential at Rome and helped to establish O'Dwyer's favourable standing there. He was appointed general secretary of the Congregation of the Oriental Rite, and in 1893 was created cardinal and became prefect of the Sacred Congregation of Indulgences. He died two years later.

FURTHER PRESSURE FROM ROME

In July 1888 a letter from the pope expressed anger at the lack of support for his decree, and conveyed further dissatisfaction with the Plan of Campaign and boycotting, without any balancing criticism of the landlords.[118] This was followed in September by a strong communication from Cardinal Rampolla to Archbishop Walsh, at the direction of his holiness, which conveyed the pope's 'grief and surprise' at the manner in which his encyclical letter to the Irish bishops regarding the decree of the Holy Office had been received in Ireland. Neither from the people, nor the episcopate, had come the expected 'dutiful manifestation of sincere adhesion'. Walsh replied that the bishops would make a fitting response to His Holiness at their meeting on 9 October.[119]

Following that meeting, Walsh and Croke circulated a draft letter for the consideration of the bishops, which explained the complexity of the Irish situation at some length and why they had acted as they did. O'Dwyer took umbrage at the document. 'I would put my hand in the fire before signing this document drawn up by his Grace and Dr C.' he informed Donnelly on 15 November. 'It teems over with offence to the Holy See', telling them in Rome, in effect, 'You ... are an ignorant lot.'[120] He wrote to a number of bishops to seek their support in rejecting the draft letter, but without success. A number of his colleagues, however, called for some amendments.[121] On 10 November an even stronger letter came from Rampolla, which made many charges against the clergy based largely on newspaper reports. Archbishop MacEvilly complained to Kirby on 22 November that the cardinal's charges were 'quite unfounded' where his diocese was concerned, and that 'the most frightful lies' were reported in the papers.[122] The archbishops, concerned at the reaction Rampolla's letter might generate, decided not to mention it even to their clergy. O'Dwyer disagreed. He expressed surprise that Walsh could not see that the letter was an indication 'of the currents in Rome',[123] and that it closed all the openings made in the draft letter and rendered it useless.[124] On 24 November, after Bishop Higgins of Kerry had refused to join his protest, he poured out his frustration once more to Bishop Donnelly. The arguments in the draft letter might have had some validity prior to the papal rescript, he protested, but not once the pope had spoken. 'I cannot for the life of me', he exclaimed, 'see how nay bishop can ask the pope in the interests of religion to allow him to stand by inactively while the … magisterial voice of the Church is being treated with contempt.' To do so would be to 'simply ask for tolerance for Mr W. O'Brien to boast on the part of the Irish people in the House of Commons that they knew how to resist Balfour, the evictions, and the Holy Inquisition, (and) for Dr Kenny to declare that he would not accept the condemnation of the Plan from "a foreign potentate".' 'In a word', it was 'a demand to allow the faith of Ireland not merely to be undermined insidiously but openly overthrown.' 'It is a sad crisis', he concluded, 'but those who hold with the pope may, I trust, have some assurance that they are right.'[125]

AN AUTHORITATIVE, ASSERTIVE PRELATE

Such 'assurance' ensured that he stood out against fellow bishops as against lay agitators. When the bishops' joint letter, much shorter and more precise than in its original form, was finally being got ready for Rome on 7 December 1888, two prelates still refused to sign any form of it, O'Dwyer of Limerick and Healy of Clonfert.[126]

Thus, the bishop of Limerick ended the year on a note of defiance. It was as if he relished doing so, and, where lay opponents were concerned, almost enjoyed combining defiance with a manifestation of episcopal power. Successively, in letters to Donnelly on 3 and 9 December, he told of people leaving a church *en masse* when a land-grabber came in. Some members of parliament had been exhorting people in the area. O'Dwyer sent his vicar-general to the church the next Sunday to warn that the parish would be placed under interdict if this behaviour persisted. 'I am glad to say', he wrote on 3 December, 'that yesterday that fellow came to Mass and no notice was taken of him. I am almost sorry, as, if they persisted, I would have written a public letter that would warm some of their ears'.[127] Six days later the story and his bravado had become embellished. If they had not obeyed, he declared, 'I was determined to denounce them, MPs and all, and to publish the most of Rampolla's letter.' On this last, he added how odd it was that important letters were coming from Rome 'on matters affecting the condition of the church in Ireland and that not even our clergy are allowed to know of their existence.'[128]

Rampolla's letter had become the final defiance as Christmas drew near. On 23 December, having thanked Donnelly for his invitation to join him on a journey to Italy, which he declined because it coincided with his visitation of the convents in his diocese, he moved on, with his usual sniping wit, to areas of contention. 'I suppose I shall be denounced again', he observed, 'for trying to re-instate the university question', adding wryly – 'What an odd comment on the past it is that his Grace of Dublin, who *was kept at home from Sydney in the interests of that question, should have manoeuvred it most effectually almost out of range of practical politics.*' Then, fittingly, in an individualistic and belligerent diapason to the year, he remarked: 'I have not yet sent my answer to Cardinal Rampolla's letter; but as soon as I get any definite information of the despatch of the joint document I shall then send mine.'[129]

On this note of provocative, mischievous, almost insolent challenge, the stormy first two years of Thomas Edward O'Dwyer's episcopacy came to a close. It was as if he had come to see himself in the role of a Cardinal Cullen, whom he greatly admired, and to whom Herbert Vaughan of Salford had consolingly and immoderately compared him – 'Do you remember how years ago they used to abuse Cardinal Cullen for his plain speaking, but they could not help respecting him for it, and then they began to feel that he was master?'[130] The stubborn assured zeal, the pugnacity, the mischievous and seeming righteous *hauteur* that he had displayed thus far were to be tested to the limit in the next three years, a momentous time for the country even more than for himself.

9

Confronting the Plan of Campaign: from its zenith to its decline, 1889–1891

The New Year opened sadly for Edward Thomas O'Dwyer. His mother, to whom he was devoted, died. On 6 January 1889, Archbishop Croke wrote in a spirit of sympathy and assured him that he would leave for Limerick the following day, go to Corbally, and subsequently attend the obsequies.[1] Three days later he divulged to Archbishop Walsh:

> I was in Limerick yesterday at the funeral of E.T.'s mother. Poor woman, she felt the bishop's isolation and eccentricities very much and had her days shortened accordingly. She was greatly respected by all classes, and had a grand funeral. The little gentleman himself felt the shock very much and showed signs of deep and genuine grief.[2]

Meantime, the work of the diocese continued and the agrarian struggle kept intruding, sometimes in unusual forms. One such was mentioned to Lord Emly by Fr Flanagan, of Adare, on 8 January 1889. It indicated a kind and merciful side to the bishop, an aspect seldom noted by the public press. It concerned a Fr O'Mahony, an agitated curate. Flanagan quoted a reply from O'Dwyer regarding the priest: 'I allowed him to continue on the mission, although with a considerable doubt as to whether I am right, lest a sudden shock should unhinge his reason and make him a permanent lunatic ... but meanwhile I do not think that I offend God by leaning to the side of mercy, and sparing him as long as I can.' Flanagan went on to mention that O'Mahony had been in a lunatic asylum, and was 'in certain subjects out of his mind'. 'I remember', he added, the bishop 'having him before him at Newcastle West some six or eight months ago, and his having then warned him against taking part in any political movement whatever, and told [him] to attend to his spiritual duties. He afterwards abused Dr O'Dwyer unmercifully all about the west.'[3]

The previous day, Flanagan had sent Emly a copy of Cardinal Rampolla's letter to the bishops of Ireland, which, presumably, he had received from O'Dwyer. 'Nothing could be clearer', Flanagan commented. He could not understand how Archbishop Walsh allowed William O'Brien speak out as he did, or how any bishop could in conscience allow the Plan of Campaign be established in his diocese. 'As to our own bishop,' Flanagan continued, 'he is prepared of course to enforce it vigorously if any disobedience to the decree is manifest in his diocese – and that, I imagine, by ecclesiastical penalties if necessary.'[4]

The fact that O'Dwyer's determination was known, and the shortage of funds among campaigners, helped to produce something of a lull in the Limerick area. On 18 February 1889, the bishop informed Monsignor Kirby that, 'in spite of some unhappy incidents here and there, the country as a whole is advancing towards peace'.[5] The 'unhappy incidents' included boycott activity in Knockea parish, Co. Limerick. On 1 December 1888, he had informed Kirby that he had 'a great trouble' in one parish 'where the whole congregation on 2 successive Sundays' had 'left the church in order to "boycott" an obnoxious person.'[6] This was evidently the parish about which he had boasted to Donnelly on 9 December that he had restored order by firm measures. In May and June 1889, nevertheless, the 'boycott' flared up with a new intensity.

The *Tipperary Vindicator*, on 21 June 1889, provided an account of the incidents. The cause of the problem in Knockea parish was the occupation of the widow Clune's evicted farm by one Michael Ryan. The latter had been boycotted by the local people as a land-grabber, and prominent members of the community, such as Fr Marinan, Messrs Finucane and Sheehy, MPs, and Mr J.H. Moran, solicitor, were prosecuted and imprisoned for speeches that were held to constitute a conspiracy against the taking of evicted farms. The boycotting continued. Eventually it entered the local church. The congregation in Ryan's part of the building moved to another part. The bishop sent his vicar-general, William Moloney, a former parish priest of the area, to address the people and to warn that if the boycott continued in church 'the divine service would be suspended in the chapel'. For a time Dr Moloney's advice was followed, but then the boycotting recurred. On the instructions of the bishop, Timothy Halpin, the parish priest, announced that after that Sunday the church would be closed if the boycotting continued. It continued, and the next Sunday it was announced at the two masses that henceforth there would be no masses in the church, no sacraments administered in the parish, with the exception of baptism and extreme unction; there would be no confessions, and in the case of death the priest would not be allowed to attend at the grave and women of the parish after confinement would not be churched. To add to the upset of the occasion, the previous Friday night the pew that Ryan occupied, and the kneeler he used, were cut away with a saw by intruders. This, the priest at the Sunday mass, Daniel Crotty, condemned as a sacrilegious act and announced that it would be reported to the bishop.

The bishop, as he tended to do when he wished to emphasise an issue or situation, resorted to a public letter. He addressed it to the parish priest, Timothy Halpin, and took pains to outline all the procedures he had taken in order to avoid this 'extreme step' of closing the church. 'For week and months,' he declared, 'I have waited patiently in the hope that the religious spirit of the people would of itself relieve me from so painful a necessity.' He had sent his vicar-general to put before them in 'the most fatherly language the evils of their conduct'; at his request the parish priest had gone about from house to house for weeks, trying by remonstrance and persuasion to work upon them individually; and, finally, for the last three Sundays they had been formally warned of the measures which he would take if they persevered in their action. 'Now,' he continued, 'as all these efforts have failed, I must take steps within my power to prevent God's house and God's worship from being made the instruments of a wicked and irreligious combination for the attainment of its ends.' Boycotting, he explained yet again, had been condemned by the supreme head of the Church, and was sinful everywhere; 'but if there were never a decision by competent authority on the point, the ... religious instincts of a Catholic people ought to teach them the outrageous impropriety of fighting out in God's house, and in the presence of the awful sacrifice of the Mass, their quarrels about land or politics or any other secular interest.' He was aware of the extenuating fact that some acted under the influence of sheer terror, and he quoted a notice served on some of the parishioners – 'Take Warning. If you enter the grabber's gallery, you do so at your peril. Take this notice, or, by heaven, you will suffer. By Order.' 'This is one of the methods', the bishop stated defiantly, 'by which your parish is being disturbed; but however it is brought about, ... as long as I am bishop of this diocese, by God's help, I, and I alone, shall determine who shall and who shall not be excluded from the house of God, and I am not prepared to abdicate to any set of men.' 'When the people of Knockea were induced to begin this system of boycotting', O'Dwyer remarked, 'they did not expect that they would be led or driven to the lengths to which they have gone.' Now, not only had they brought misconduct into the church, but they had gone so far as to withdraw their children from instructions for First Communion in order to cause the parish priest to exclude from the table of the Lord the children of those whom they wished to shun; 'and finally, this series of misdeeds culminated on Friday in the sacrilegious breaking into the church and the destruction of its furniture.' 'It is all sad and deplorable', he concluded, 'and especially so as I know that up to this there has not been a more peaceable, orderly, or religious com- munity in the whole diocese.' He trusted that after this a better sense would prevail among them, and that they would return to their ordinary good conduct, and that tomorrow as they thought of the faithful throughout the world, gathered round the altars of the Church to keep the solemn feast of Corpus Christi, they would feel the loneliness of their own church, unblessed by the Divine Presence, and put to themselves the question – 'What will it profit a man to gain the whole world and suffer the loss of his soul.'[7]

As might be expected, the unionist press praised O'Dwyer's stand. The nationalist papers were critical, if not as freely as before. Fr Flanagan commented to Emly on 21 June that 'since Archbishop Walsh has condemned boycotting in church, it was a mistake of the Knockea Leaguers to carry the system into church as they have – and what the bishop of Limerick has done any bishop might have done, though the anti-nationalist papers pat him on the back as having done what no one else except a man of their own part would have had the courage to do.'[8]

The bishop's interdict continued throughout the summer and almost to Christmas. The *Limerick Chronicle*, of 10 December 1889, announcing the reopening of Knockea church after an interdict lasting over six months, stated, inaccurately, that Michael Ryan did not attend the Sunday mass which marked the reopening. The *Times* added further inaccuracy. On 15 August 1890, the bishop's secretary, Andrew Murphy, sent the following clarifying letter to *The Times*. It was reproduced in the *Limerick Chronicle* on 19 August 1890:

> Sir,
> I am directed by the Bishop of Limerick to inform you that the letter which appeared in the issue of yesterday signed C.H.W. in ref. to the boycotting of Michael Ryan is a tissue of libellous falsehoods. The church was reopened by V. Rev. Dr Moloney, VG, on receiving from the parishioners a distinct undertaking that there should be no repetition of the boycotting which led to its being closed … Michael Ryan attended Mass there on that day and repeatedly since without the least manifestation of feeling against him on the part of the people, and on the occasion of the episcopal visitation, when the Bishop in very strong language rebuked the boycotting that had gone on,

Similar misrepresentations were to be part of O'Dwyer's experience with the other more celebrated Plan of Campaign exercise in his diocese, that concerning the Delmege family estate, Glensharrold, Co. Limerick.

As noted earlier, the Delmege property had been made an issue for a considerable time. The fact that it was in O'Dwyer's diocese gave the enterprise a particular savour for the agitators. When, indeed, a meeting took place near the Glensharrold estate late in October 1889, and none of the Limerick clergy attended, it was rumoured that the bishops had circulated a letter to the parish priests and to the superiors of religious communities instructing that it was a reserved sin for anyone to defend or advocate the Plan of Campaign.[9] O'Dwyer in this, and in other landlord cases, found himself in the dilemma between landlord rights and the compassionate claims of the tenants. He sought to get as much as seemed possible for the tenants, but if they refused what seemed a fair offer he considered the landlord within his rights in evicting. It was a most unpopular stand with those proclaiming tenant rights, but it was the right response, he believed, and he stood stolidly by it. In a response to Lord Emly on 19 October 1888 he put his position starkly: 'I do not see what course is open to the landlord but to use his legal rights. It's a sad thing that tenants will not take the liberal offer which he makes. For myself, I shall have no more to say to it. I'm inclined to think that the leaders amongst them must be reckless bankrupts whose condition would be exposed if a settlement were made.'[10]

On 24 October 1889 a new Tenants Defence Association, quite distinct from the Plan of Campaign, had been formed to counteract the combination of landlords started by Mr A.H. Smith-Barry to support the encumbered Ponsonby estate, Co. Cork.[11] Right up to the formal foundation of the new Tenants Defence Association, O'Dwyer had remained strongly opposed to the Plan of Campaign. The Tenants Defence Association, however, was presented by Parnell as a 'peaceful movement', and it was supported by him and many members of the party who had not been associated with the Plan. Archbishop Walsh described it as non-political and having as its sole purpose the defence of the tenants and their property.[12] Many bishops quickly contributed to it as a defence against what Archbishop MacEvilly believed to be a powerful landlord confederacy determined to 'exterminate' the Catholic people.[13]

This seemingly new venture, acceptable to bishops and the nationalist majority, attracted O'Dwyer, though his ingrained suspicion of Irish party leaders remained. Knowing that a meeting of the Association was scheduled for Limerick at the start of December, he had his secretary, Fr Murphy, write to Redmond, as chairman of the meeting, to learn if, according to Parnell's public letter, there would be 'no open or covert advocacy of the Plan of Campaign', as it was only on this express condition that he could allow the clergy of the diocese be present at the convention.[14] Redmond responded carefully, sending a copy of the constitutions of the Association and assuring Fr Murphy that the Association did not 'involve or contemplate the advocacy of any particular combination amongst the Irish tenant farmers' but sought merely to defend tenant farmers 'and to protect them against attack by combinations of landlords or by any landlords engaged in such combinations.'[15] A further letter from the bishop sought assurance that all would be kept well controlled at the convention, to which Redmond firmly replied by telegram that while as chairman he would use his authority to substantially meet the case he could not undertake what was impossible, namely, 'determining matters which' he was 'neither authorised nor competent to decide'. On the back of the telegram, the bishop or Murphy wrote: 'Thanks for telegram, which is entirely satisfactory and sufficient.'[16]

The meeting in Limerick was attended by several Irish members of parliament and by a clerical representation that included five parish priests from the county and several city curates.[17] The *Freeman's Journal* of 4 December 1889 claimed that the country had waited with 'much concern' for Dr O'Dwyer's reaction to the Defence Association. His lordship's support had resulted in every parish being represented, and this placed the Limerick meeting 'among the first and best' of such gatherings in the country. O'Dwyer, concerned at such praise from such a source, and fearing, perhaps, that he might be accused of changing his values and standards, made public his cautious correspondence with Redmond, a revelation which also showed Redmond in a good light.

Thus, a difficult, eventful year came to a relatively peaceful end: a year marked by deaths, discomfort, some bitter disappointment, and some occasions of satisfaction and hope. O'Dwyer's mother's death had been followed later in the year by that of Sr Mary Joseph Croke, of the Mercy Congregation, a woman of wit and strong personality who had nursed in the Crimean War and whose brother, the archbishop, with his fondness for nicknames, termed the 'abbess'. O'Dwyer had been unable to attend the funeral because of an accident to his foot that left him disabled for several weeks.[18] Croke's letter to him at the time indicated the personal bond between them despite their political differences. 'I should have wished greatly to have had you at our sad ceremony of yesterday', the archbishop wrote on 10 November, 'but was reconciled to your absence by the conviction that in spirit and sympathy you were with me, and that some strong controlling circumstance alone kept you otherwise away. Your letter, received this morning, confirms me in that view and I thank you sincerely for it. The respect generally entertained for the poor abbess was manifested yesterday in a remarkable manner.'[19]

Of a more joyful nature were the appointments of a number of new bishops. Consulted about the candidates for Kerry by Cardinal Simeoni, prefect of Propaganda, O'Dwyer unreservedly proposed John Coffey as an experienced, pious, learned and prudent priest, who belonged to no political party and would be, if elected, 'indifferent to them all and would restrain the disturbed minds of the people within just limits'.[20] He was appointed bishop of Kerry on 28 July 1889, a choice considered 'deplorable' by Archbishop Walsh.[21] O'Dwyer was also consulted about the vacancy in the diocese of Killaloe. His good friend, Thomas McRedmond, was appointed in September.[22] The following month, a life-long friend of McRedmond was appointed to Waterford. John Egan had been a lecturer in the Royal University and was an unexpected choice. The influence of Persico seems to have been at work in all three,[23] and also that of prominent English Catholics, and of Lord Emly and Capt. John Ross of Bladensburg.[24] Then there was the bitter disappointment, the hopes raised and dashed of a solution to the university problem. In August, Balfour in the House of Commons agreed 'that something ought to be done to give higher education to the Roman Catholics in Ireland' and suggested the possibility of a new scheme to solve the question without a university bill.[25] O'Dwyer and Bishop Healy supported the project in defiance of the main body of bishops and the Irish party. Their sense of betrayal was intense when Balfour, under Non-Conformist pressure, reneged on his promise to Catholics.[26] O'Dwyer's reaction was almost violent in its vehemence. On 20 December 1889, in the most unseasonable of moods, he denounced Balfour's dishonest evasion of his pledges, and went so far as to proclaim 'nothing can be extorted from England except by fear'.[27]

Returning, however, to the local scene: eviction decrees were obtained against a number of tenants on the estate of John Christopher Delmege, Glensharrold, in January 1890. O'Dwyer decided to intervene personally to effect a settlement. He engaged the service of a friend, J. Greene Barry, a former land commissioner, to make an independent assessment of the land. The land court had already recommended a thirty per cent reduction in the annual rent, and Greene Barry concurred in the ruling of the court. As a result of these findings, the bishop went to the local church at Connekerry on 15 January and 'impressed upon the tenants the desirability of accepting the terms proposed by the court'.[28] He also offered to contribute £100 from his own means towards the payment of arrears. He urged the tenant farmers to avail themselves of these terms, which he considered just and fair, and appealed to them to avoid the bleak prospect of eviction. When the offer was put to a vote it was defeated. The tenants, bolstered by promises of aid through the Defence Association, opted to hold out for a forty per cent reduction. The bishop, because they had refused his solution, withdrew his offer to help with the payment of arrears.

O'Dwyer's efforts met with an immediate critical response from the Irish party member for Monaghan, P. O'Brien, who at a meeting in Glensharrold early in February charged that the bishop was 'actuated not so much with a desire to help the tenants but rather to break up their organisation'.[29] His actions, as well as his overall policy on the land question, were 'totally opposed' to that of the bishops and priests who followed Archbishops Walsh and Croke in fully backing the Defence Association. O'Dwyer's money offer he presented as a 'bribe to the poor people to induce them to break away from their combination'.

Glensharrold faded from the news for a number of weeks, and O'Dwyer, too, became preoccupied with other demands. In March three major issues in Limerick city claimed his attention. A long drawn-out bacon dispute reached the point where mediation was sought. An independent mediator was suggested. Two names were mentioned. Michael Davitt and Dr O'Dwyer. The majority favoured the bishop. He effected a satisfactory settlement,[30] dispensing his verdict from horseback, it is popularly alleged, before the assembled participants in Perry Square, Limerick. Four days later, the bishop's request that the city magistrates be called together to discuss aspects of the licensing trade was granted by T.A. Purcell, QC. The magistrates met on 14 March. The long report on the meeting showed them agreeing to limit the granting of licenses, as proposed by the bishop.[31] On 18 March a projected public meeting drew from his Lordship an open letter to the mayor. The occasion was a protest against the ill treatment in prison of the Limerick fenian, John Daly. The bishop cautioned against using language that might be taken as indicating toleration of the 'abominable and murderous crime called 'dynamitism'.' He also warned the young men of Limerick against 'the danger of secret societies of all kinds'. Such societies, he pronounced insultingly, were composed of 'a gang of fools with a money-making fool' at the head. Since the protest, however, was against the ill treatment of a prisoner, he thought there was no reason why people should not participate.[32]

In May, the Glensharrold estate became the focus of attention once more. In the middle of the month 'the receiver of the property offered a clear receipt, to August 1899, to all tenants who, before 27 May 1890, paid a year's rent, less thirty per cent. The question of arrears, which averaged three and one-half year's rent, would thus be disposed of.' In a letter addressed to Archdeacon John Halpin on 24 May, which was to be read to the tenants, O'Dwyer made 'a last appeal, as their friend and bishop,' to accept the land court's generous offer and save themselves from eviction. It was understandable that tenants would combine against 'rapacious and oppressive landlords', but the highest tribunal in the land had arrived at its decision with the aid of a landvaluer, who was a most honourable man. His own policy, O'Dwyer continued, had been to help people get as large a reduction as possible, but in this case a 30 percent reduction was the most that could be obtained, and eviction was too high a price to pay for a difference of ten per cent between their demands and the decision by the court. He condemned those who, with 'mischievous cruelty', were urging on the tenants to destruction; and he warned the tenants that to turn down the offer would be to be guilty of reckless folly, and they would be unable to persuade anyone thereafter that they were the victims of rapacious landlords.[33]

Unfortunately, the day the letter was made public coincided with the first of the evictions, and this provided some of the Leaguers with the opportunity to interpret the bishop's letter as just another attack on boycotting and the Plan of Campaign;[34] and a week later, at a meeting of the National League Council in Dublin, Timothy Harrington described the bishop's communication as a 'deliberate attempt to deprive' the evicted tenants 'of the sympathy of the Irish people'. It was an open secret, he added, that the bishop of Limerick was not considered to be 'a friend of the national cause'. He was 'at the side of the court and of the landlords', and if the Irish farmers accepted the logic of his arguments they would certainly end up as paupers.[35] He also accused the bishop of inconsistency in urging the tenants to accept a 30 percent reduction, even though he had agreed to argue for a rent reduction of 35 percent.

O'Dwyer refused to allow the allegations go unchallenged. In the course of another open letter to Archdeacon Halpin, he criticised Harrington for being consistently inaccurate in his public statements and pointed out that it was William O'Brien who proposed the 35 percent reduction, and that all he had agreed to do was to act as a go-between the tenants and the court and to press to have the offer accepted. He called on Harrington to apologise for his calculated mistakes.[36] Some days later, the *Limerick Chronicle* published some letters that passed between O'Dwyer's solicitor, John Dundon, and Harrington, which demonstrated that Dundon had earlier passed on to the National League Council the bishop's views on the Glensharrold dispute, and that Harrington had deliberately suppressed a letter that indicated that it was Dillon and O'Brien who moved from 40 percent to 35 percent.[37] Harrington, in the *Freeman's Journal* of 14 June, protested against this waste of public time in discussing such 'ridiculous quibbles', and returned to the original charge that O'Dwyer was seeking to prejudice the claims of the 'unfortunate victims of rack-rent', adding, more revealingly than he realised, that though O'Dwyer might be able to influence 'castles and courts and landlords', in the final analysis the people would turn to their political leaders who were with them in their struggle.[38] His words were an acknowledgement that the excessive reaction to O'Dwyer on the part of some leaders of the Irish party was a measure of the threat they perceived in him.

ATTACKED IN THE HOUSE OF COMMONS AND IN HIS OWN CITY

The Glensharrold dispute found its way into the House of Commons on 11 July 1890 in a manner hostile to the bishop of Limerick. The author was John Dillon. Claiming to speak on behalf of the Catholics of Ireland, he declared 'that he and his co-religionists were as independent of Rome and of the agents of his Holiness in all political matters as any Nonconformist on those benches (cheers)'. Then, in an intemperate outburst, he accused Balfour and his uncle, Lord Salisbury, of 'crawling to the court of Rome and offering bribes to his Holiness to aid them in crushing the people of Ireland (loud cheers)'; and he went on to charge, in respect of university education, that 'the right hon. gentle-man had succeeded by his promises and schemes in capturing two Irish bishops, one of whom, the Right Reverend Dr O'Dwyer, bishop of Limerick, has gone so far as to write one of the most infamous, cowardly, dastardly letters ever penned by ecclesiastical hand,' and he did this 'as a servant of the government of Ireland'. That letter 'appeared in the press of Ireland on the same day that a number of wretched people were evicted'.[39] Following an objection from the chief secretary that an attack on the bishop was out of order, Dillon responded that he would say no more, and then added that 'as an Irish Catholic, that gentleman [the bishop of Limerick] had done his worst against the Irish church, and he was exceedingly glad he stood alone among the episcopacy of Ireland with his scandalous conduct (cheers).'[40] Parnell, conscious of the bishops' increasing nervousness about the headstrong leadership of the land agitation, attempted to calm the disturbed water. He suggested that methods of mediation might be used to terminate the strife where the Plan of Campaign was still in operation.

O'Dwyer was deeply disturbed by the unfairness of such a savage attack in the privileged setting of the House of Commons, and the fact that it was made by Dillon made it all the more unacceptable. He determined to strike back in kind, while using the defence of the honour of his Holiness as his justification. His cutting language was unworthy of both his office and of the proclaimed subject of his defence.

In the *Freeman's Journal*, on Monday, 14 July, his long letter to the editor announced that he had no wish to engage in 'a contest in billingsgate' with Mr Dillon, but felt he had to defend his own simple and matter of fact letter on the Glensharrold case against Mr Dillon's 'outburst of outrageous language'. He then proceeded to out-do that outburst. Mr Dillon had of late, he declared, been engaged collecting money, ostensibly for the relief of evicted tenants, and he and his party were 'still occupied in the same profitable employment', and hence 'it must have been very provoking to have the real facts of the case exposed and the pockets of the sympathisers closed.' Responding to Dillon's reference to his 'dastardly' letters, he turned from Dillon's honesty to his courage. 'I would tell him', O'Dwyer stated, 'that if at any time I should find myself put into prison for a cause that I professed to believe just, I should rot there before I allowed my friends to send up a miserable whine for my release from every end of the country on the plea of health, and that if I sneaked out thus and then went off to the Antipodes on a twelve months' tour until the storm blew over, and my vows to defy the act of parliament under which I had been imprisoned were forgotten, he might call me a dastard without fear of contradiction.' 'But, Sir,' the bishop added, 'I am almost ashamed of myself to waste so many words – on personal offensiveness to myself, when I read the language which he dares to use towards the august and sacred person of the Vicar of Christ.' It was 'an honour for a poor, simple bishop to receive a few spatters of the dirt that is flung at the representative of his Divine Master.' 'If only I could get it all', he commented unctuously, so as 'to spare out Catholic nation the shame before the world of one of the foulest charges ever levelled against the successor of St Peter … amidst the cheers of English Protestants and English unbelievers, by one who professes to be a member of the Church' and uses 'the privileges of the faith in order to get near the Father of the Faithful and stab him in the back'. 'This gentleman', he then observed, 'has often boasted of his intimacy with bishops and archbishops … It will be interesting to observe how many of them now will be anxious to identify themselves with him publicly until this insulting slander is withdrawn.'

'The question for the public now is', O'Dwyer continued relentlessly, 'am I, or am I not, within my rights in thinking as a man, and teaching as a bishop, that the Plan of Campaign and boycotting are against the law of God?' 'And this suggests another question', he added acutely, 'which I beg to submit to the consideration of thoughtful statesmen, such as Mr Parnell, Mr Justin McCarthy, Mr Sexton, and Mr Arthur O'Connor. If Mr Dillon, whether he has the right or not, has the power, without check or remonstrance from any one of his party, to denounce an Irish bishop, as he has denounced me simply and solely for my action in the exercise of my spiritual jurisdiction, what guarantee is there, should Home Rule come, that all of us bishops shall not find our authority crippled, not by words, but by force?' 'Are there not interests enough arrayed to the death against Home Rule', he asked shrewdly, 'to make it at least a matter of common tactical prudence not to force the bishops of Ireland to review their position in relation to it?' 'I commend that view of things', he then advised, 'to the consideration of serious Home Rulers, and beg of them not to drive us to compare the religious liberty we enjoy at present with the prospect of things under Mr Dillon as Minister of Worship. Again and again I have said I am a Home Ruler. At home and abroad I have maintained the right of my country to self-government. In so far as the agitation legitimately advances that cause, I am with it. I would join it tomorrow if I had any assurance that the movement was to be purged from sinful methods, but while Mr Dillon and men like him, in defiance of their own leader, are the practical leaders, I must only stand aloof.'[41]

It was bruising, bare-knuckle fighting, all the more discreditable and arresting of attention because written by a bishop. It was far more of a calculated exercise than Dillon's hot-headed, vindictive outburst; reflecting, it would seem, his advice to Aubrey de Vere in 1881 that 'the only expedient that would reconcile newspaper readers to so long a letter is hard hitting personality'.[42]

The letter was widely read and, for the most part, widely criticised. It attracted attention outside of Britain and Ireland, notably in Rome and France. Croke was approached on 15 July by the editor of *L'Univers*, a French Catholic paper, a M. Godre, for his opinion on the merits of the case. Noted himself for bristling letters to the press, part of him admired O'Dwyer's skilful polemics. His judgment was more even handed than most commentators. 'Dillon's language in the House of Commons in reference to Dr O'Dwyer, besides being quite uncalled for, was most offensive and reprehensible. But on the other hand, Dr O'Dwyer's letter was unjust as far as Dillon was concerned, and most undignified as coming from a bishop.'[43] Several days later, in a letter to Kirby, Croke commented briefly: 'Both parties were in fault: but the bishop erred ever so much more grievously than did the layman.'[44]

Archbishop Walsh was far less objective. On 30 July he complained to Kirby that O'Dwyer's letter was offensive 'to all the archbishops and bishops of Ireland' in maintaining that the only reason the nationalists were attacking him was that he alone in Ireland was 'maintaining the authority of the Holy See'. Walsh, who tended to accept Dillon's version of events, was annoyed at reports that the pope had sent a message of congratulations to O'Dwyer for defending the papacy against Dillon.[45] Kirby, however, viewed matters differently. Although the pope had not sent a letter to O'Dwyer, he had asked the Irish bishops' representative to send a consoling message in his name. This Kirby did. He also gave O'Dwyer the benefit of some paternal criticism and advice on replying to provocation. On 5 August, a much encouraged O'Dwyer replied that he had just received the letter 'in which your Grace conveyed to me in terms so consoling the precious message which our Holy Father deigned to send me'. 'I cannot tell you, your Grace,' he confessed, 'what a comfort this has been to me in the midst of much obloquy. I thank your Grace most heartily for the wise and holy suggestions of your letter just received.' 'If some one else, the primate, or one of the archbishops, would speak out,' he concluded smoothly, 'it would be much better: but if I have to write again I shall take care that no provocation induces me to go beyond the high and strong ground of principle.'[46]

The 'obloquy' to which O'Dwyer referred was largely orchestrated by the National League, which had representatives or supporters in the main local bodies. Thus, in Limerick, the Sarsfield branch of the National League met on 20 July to register its solidarity with Dillon and to accuse the bishop of abusing his position. Similar censures on O'Dwyer and support for Dillon followed at the Kilrush Board of Guardians, the board of the Ennis Union,[47] and many other bodies. On 25 July, at a public meeting in the Town Hall, Limerick, which was attended by representatives from Glensharrold and from Herbertstown, purporting to speak for the tenants of the Delmege and the O'Grady estates, a proposal was passed expressing confidence in Dillon and disappointment with the bishop, who had 'separated himself from the great pillars of our Irish church'.[48] An effort, however, to orchestrate support for Dillon and censure of the bishop at a meeting of Limerick corporation, on 31 July, proved unsuccessful. The moving spirit of the proposal was Alderman Stephen O'Mara, who described himself as a friend of the bishop. Following this failure, an 'indignation meeting' was called to express disapproval of the members of the corporation who had voted against O'Meara's proposal. The latter launched a patchwork attack on the bishop at the public meeting. 'John Dillon was head and shoulders, aye, a tower in front of Bishop O'Dwyer', he declared. The bishop had never done anything for the suffering Irish people and as a politician 'he had always been wrong'. Then moving to class distinction, he declared that those who supported O'Dwyer in Limerick, whether in the Poor Law Unions or in any other public body, were 'all the shoneens of the landlord Protestant class', and in Limerick, according to this member of a wealthy and prominent business family, it was not just a case of Catholics competing against Protestants but of Catholics versus 'aristocracy with landlordism behind it'. Finally, he charged that, ever since his consecration, Bishop O'Dwyer had done nothing to forward their movement, and he had canvassed the members of the corporation against Dillon and had intimidated the mayor.[49]

On 7 August, the Limerick branch of the League followed up the indignation meeting by expelling from the League those who had voted against O'Meara's proposal on 31 July. They were alleged to have betrayed 'the trust reposed in them by the nationalists in Limerick'. These included the mayor, William J. O'Donnell, five councillors, and Alderman Dundon. It was also arranged to invite Dillon and O'Brien to a monster meeting in Limerick on 24 August to protest at the lack of support from Limerick corporation, and, of course, to demonstrate the strength of the party and their approval of the Plan of Campaign.[50]

Dillon, meanwhile, took little note of the protests, merely jotting in his diary with reference to O'Dwyer, 'I think that gentleman is finished'.[51] He was warned, however, by a Franciscan friend, Fr David Fleming, not to push the dispute against O'Dwyer.[52] Voices were heard also within the party counselling caution. One such was W.J. Lane, a prominent party member from Cork, who wrote to William O' Brien on 5 August to warn against carrying 'this miserable business too far'. Dillon could 'small afford', he added, to ignore the charges O'Dwyer had brought against him. His references to the bishop had been infelicitous and would have been better left unsaid. He added that he had consulted with many priests, and his view, and that of many others, was that O'Brien and Dillon should not attend any rally in Limerick unless the clergy were present on the platform. Perceptively, he pointed out that the price for resisting 'one cranky bishop' would eventually be the alienation of the rest of the hierarchy from the movement.[53] Dillon, for his part, consulted anxiously with O'Brien, who was on honeymoon in Switzerland, about the Limerick meeting. O'Brien, in reply, urged that they had to go ahead, and that priests should be brought in from Cashel and from Clare. 'If the thing is properly organised', he assured Dillon on 16 August, 'I believe the feeling against O'D. will sweep all before it.'[54]

THE LIMERICK MEETING

O'Dwyer issued no public statement forbidding his clergy to attend, but their bishop being defied in his own city was sufficient to decide even the most fervent supporters of the National League against attending. The meeting, on Sunday 24 August, was attended by some 30,000 from all parts of Munster. Banners carried slogans proclaiming – 'Religion from Rome, Politics from Home', and 'Religion is one thing, Politics another'. Alderman Francis A. O'Keefe, MP, acted as chairman, and shared the platform with Dillon, O'Brien, Harrington, three other MPs, two aldermen and fourteen other members of Limerick corporation. A resolution in support of 'the character of honest John Dillon' and in condemnation of the bishop for 'vilifying and maligning' him, was carried with acclamation.

In his address, John Dillon denied the charge of misappropriating the money collected from the tenant farmers, and announced that he had come to Limerick 'to ask the people of Munster whether in politics – I speak not of religion – but whether in politics they are prepared to follow our leadership (cheers) and cries, 'We are', or the leadership of the Bishop of Limerick ('No' and cheers). 'The great significance of this meeting', he insisted, 'is this, that you are here in your tens of thousands (cheers) to tell the Irish nation, and the scattered Irish race in millions all over the world who will read of this meeting tomorrow, that your confidence in the Irish party is unshaken (loud cheers).' On the issue of nationality and religion, he assured the audience that there was no opposition between them, and that they were bound by stronger bonds than ever before and that 'no power, whether it be a Catholic bishop or a coercion government,' would ever sunder them (cheers). 'I wish to say a few words now', he observed, on 'an old friend in this country, and that is the practice of boycotting.' It could be 'grossly abused' and had been, but it was 'the war of unarmed people' and when 'wisely used and wisely controlled' it was 'a most effective weapon in the service of the Irish people (cheers)', and what had been achieved over the past ten years had been due to this weapon. 'I ask the people', then, he went on, 'are they going to part with this good and old tried weapon (cries of 'No' and cheers).'

With a direct reference to O'Dwyer, he admitted that he had used strong language, which it might have been better for him not to have used. But he had not come to Limerick 'to withdraw or to explain anything whatever'. Such criticism as he had made of the bishop's action had been occasioned by Dr O'Dwyer's attempt to justify the eviction of the Glensharrold tenants. In conclusion, he added further fuel to the fire. He expressed his 'disgust and contempt' for men 'who had never made one sacrifice for the national cause, ... who stayed at their fires while we were facing the elements and the batons of Balfour's policemen, 'and yet 'ound nothing better to do than criticise and abuse us.' 'If they found fault with our motives', he challenged, 'let them come down and propose something better.' Let Bishop O'Dwyer rise up from his comfortable surroundings among 'the Clarinas, the Delmeges and Gaston Monsells of this country'[55] and devise some positive and workable scheme that would benefit the farmers of Ireland.

William O'Brien, sensing the mood of the meeting, was even more blatantly hostile to the bishop. It was ludicrous to ask people to choose between John Dillon and Bishop O'Dwyer, as the latter had lost all credibility when he sided with Delmege against the tenants of Glensharrold 'amidst the jubilations of the landlords of the county club and the benedictions of Mr Balfour and *The Times* newspaper'. From 'within the heart of his own diocese', O'Brien proclaimed, the bishop had now received a rebuke, which, although moderate, was 'most solemn and irresistible'. He had doubts initially whether it was worth the inconvenience to come to Limerick to 'crush so insignificant an obstacle' as Dr O'Dwyer, but the honour of his colleague, and of his country, demanded that he be present. As a politician, the bishop was 'cranky and cross-grained', and it was always safe to have him on the opposite side, since his friendship was likely to be an absolute harbinger of failure. Then, recalling the election of 1874, he proclaimed that O'Dwyer had begun his career in politics 'as the champion of the exterminator, Kelly' and he was now about to end it as a supporter of a rack-renter. The diatribe concluded by associating the bishop once more with the establishment, and with 'every Orange newspaper which cursed the pope'. The Irish people, however, would never need the help of men like the bishop of Limerick so long as they had champions like Archbishop Croke and Walsh 'shining in the forefront of battle' for them.[56]

Once again the bishop's name made headlines in almost all the important journals in Britain and Ireland. Unionist papers like *The Times* and the local *Limerick Chronicle* played down the meeting. The *Chronicle* remarked that many, who for years had been regarded as the leaders and pillars of the nationalist cause in Limerick, were conspicuously absent. It accused the speakers of side-stepping the real issues, and of harping instead on 'the personal matter' between Dillon and the bishop, but admitted that 'the bishop had incautiously laid himself open to attack'.[57] The *Standard*, however, focussed attention on some pertinent issues. It suggested that 'indignation meetings' were a device invented by politicians to suppress free speech. It defended O'Dwyer's right to answer Dillon's attack on him in the Commons, and questioned the wisdom of granting an independent parliament to men like Dillon and O'Brien who used such high-handed methods against their critics.[58] The nationalist press, on the other hand, praised the meeting as a great success and echoed the sentiments critical of O'Dwyer. What annoyed the latter particularly was the account of the meeting, and the editorial, in the *Freeman's Journal* of 25 August 1890.

The editorial conceded that some of the language Dillon used in the House of Commons, and elsewhere, was unwarranted, but also observed that O'Dwyer 'returned him the compliment with interest'. He was not beyond hitting his opponent 'below the belt' in vindicating his 'wounded self-esteem'. He had no grounds for the allegations made against Dillon, which, if they had not been made by a prelate would have been treated as 'the frothings of an impotent malignity'. The editorial endorsed the view that O'Dwyer had never put himself out to alleviate the lot of the tenant farmers. He had, in mixed metaphors, 'never moved from his palace, never came down from his high horse'. Moreover, his 'most grandiloquent protestations of patriotism' were for a patriotism fashioned to his own taste, which allowed no room for any other variation. In conclusion, the editorial found fault with Dillon for not apologising for his intemperate words and not retracting them, and informed the bishop that he would have done better to have left the work of abusing and blackening the character of the Irish representative to Balfour and *The Times*.

The same day as the editorial appeared, O'Dwyer replied at length. Notwithstanding the editor's criticism that day, he began, 'I venture to think that a good body of Catholic opinion in Ireland will not endorse your judgment on yesterday's meeting or regard it in any other light than as an attempt by popular intimidation to silence everyone who presumes to disobey the present leaders of politics in Ireland. Whatever be the merits of the controversy between Mr Dillon and myself, I should like to know how far does the shouting of a multitude go to settle them.' 'Whether I am a dastard', O'Dwyer stated, 'and an unfaithful bishop to the people … I maintain it is an improper thing to come into a bishop's cathedral city and there by denunciation of him to rouse the passions of his people against him as a mercenary and a traitor, and that if it be allowed to go without protest it will become a fatal precedent.' 'But what particularly I object to', he maintained, 'in yesterday's proceedings and in your article of today' was the clever plan of concentrating attention on the merest fringe of the whole controversy generated by Mr Dillon's speech in parliament, namely, the scouting of papal authority and the insult offered to the pope. 'I take it', however, he observed righteously, 'that whatever explanation may be forthcoming consistent with Mr Dillon's veracity we may assume now, after yesterday's silence, that the line is drawn at Rome, and for the future the sacred person of the vicar of Christ will be held above all attacks. That alone is something gained, and although you may think very lowly of me as a bishop, I assure you in all honesty that I regard it as a result worth all the annoyance of achieving it.'

Towards the end of the editor's article, O'Dwyer observed, he was asked if he had a plan for the regeneration of his country. 'I am not a politician,' he answered. 'I have another profession. My mission is to teach to the people of the Christian religion the duties that it imparts.' Soon after his consecration, he was confronted with the practices of boycotting and the Plan of Campaign, and after the best consideration he could give he became convinced 'of their utterly sinful character'. When the pope spoke, there was no shadow of doubt about the matter. 'With me, then,' he declared, repeating the argument used at the synod the previous year, 'it is not a question whether the Plan of Campaign and boycotting are effectual means for any man, but whether they are lawful means; and I tell you plainly that if the use of them freed Ireland from political thraldom tomorrow, and established a parliament in Dublin, and diffused wealth and prosperity throughout the length and breadth of the land, I should say – I should have to say as a Catholic – we must not do evil that good may come. It is not a question that admits of compromise. It is one of right or wrong ... ' If he were a simple priest in a parish, he could stand aside and abstain from all interference in the politics of men who persistsd in defying the head of the Church and bringing his authority into contempt, but being a bishop, he could not without cowardice shirk the obligation of teaching his clergy and his people the course which they were bound to follow. 'Furthermore,' he observed, adjusting the perspective, 'I am distinctly of opinion that the persistence of the Irish people in disobedience to the Holy See, and worse, in the impugning of its authority, will, like a canker, eat into the heart of their faith, and leave it without vitality for the hour of trial that may come. Loyalty to Rome is the foundation of the Catholic system, and whoever impairs that is undermining the people's faith.' 'I hold my authority', he declared firmly, 'not from politicians, not from the people, and, while God spares me to govern this diocese, I shall maintain to the best of my poor ability, my own personal independence and the rights and prerogatives of the Vicar of Christ.'[59]

Following the Limerick meeting, the immediate reaction in the Glensharrold area appeared unfavourable to the bishop. Dillon visited there and received a warm welcome. At Newcastle West, the local committee of the National League, chaired by a Mr John Condon, declared that the eight families that were evicted were made to suffer because of the bishop's 'infelicitous letter'. It had precipitated the doom of the unfortunate tenants.[60] Various town councils and governing bodies continued to pass motions in support of Dillon and critical of Bishop O'Dwyer, but not the Limerick Corporation, which held out against the efforts of Stephen O'Mara.[61] Shortly after the Limerick meeting, Dillon went to Clonmel to receive the freedom of the town. There, he commented on O'Dwyer's most recent letter to the *Freeman*. He respected the church as much as any man, he claimed, but he would resist any attempt politically to interfere with the interests of the Irish tenantry. He also availed of the occasion to deny having attacked the pope in his 'Common's speech. His remarks, he claimed, not very convincingly, had been aimed solely and directly at Balfour, Salisbury, and the intrigues of the Tory government at Rome.[62]

REACTION AMONGST THE IRISH BISHOPS

A significant pendant to the most recent O'Dwyer and Dillon clash was the response among the Irish hierarchy. Dr Walsh, about to go on his holidays, washed his hands of the conflict in a less than impressive manner. On 27 August, in the *Freeman's Journal*, he requested that 'if this unhappy wrangle' was to be continued, his name should not be dragged into it. It was a dispute with which, 'in any of its aspects – political, personal, or otherwise controversial' – he had 'nothing whatever to do.'[63] Croke, however, was prepared to go further to cement the clerical-nationalist alliance. He went to the train station to meet Dillon, only to find he was not on the train. Dillon and O'Brien had gone to Clonmel. From there on 28 August, O'Brien, at whose wedding Croke had officiated, wrote to thank him for the compliment of going to the train to meet Dillon. 'The bare announcement of your Grace's happy thought … would have been worth a dozen Limerick meetings.'[64] Regarding Walsh's letter, which had appeared that day, he expressed disappointment. 'A right word rightly spoken' would have completed 'the chastening effect visible in every line of his Lordship of Limerick's letter'. Of O'Dwyer, he added, with a flash of partial insight, 'it is his impression that the bishops dread him that alone emboldens him. He is a most dangerous man to run away from. I don't think one word more is necessary on our side.'[65] He and Dillon accepted Croke's invitation to visit him the following Sunday.

But among a number of members of the hierarchy a different view was being taken of the behaviour of Dillon, O'Brien, and their followers. Already, before the Limerick meeting, but after the speech in the House of Commons and O'Dwyer's response, the primate, Archbishop Logue, expressed his concern to Dr Walsh. On 31 July 1890 he maintained that the only way to deal with the bishop of Limerick was 'to leave him alone'. 'If they continued to attack him', he noted shrewdly, 'he will cut up very rough and the further things go, the worse they will become.' He feared that O'Dwyer's view that he was the only bishop doing his duty was likely to be the view taken at Rome. 'A few of the nationalists were compromising the bishops', he added, by claiming that their silence to avoid dissension amounted to approval of the Plan of Campaign. 'No one regrets more than I do the course taken by the Bishop of Limerick', Logue pointed out, but 'the worst of it is that however intemperate he may be, he is right at bottom. He believes he was right in advising the Glensharrold tenants to accept terms which any other tenants in Ireland would be glad to jump at, but his manner of conveying his advice was very unfortunate.' 'Again', the primate conceded, 'he was right in defending himself against the attack made by John Dillon if he could do it like another person, but here again his unfortunate temper carried into extremes which no one can justify.' 'The only authority he would acknowledge,' Logue judged, 'is that of Propaganda, and I fear as matters stand that Propaganda would be rather for than against him.'

In the same letter, this perceptive and cautious prelate reminded Walsh that the Irish party had 'climbed to their present influential positions on the shoulders of Irish priests and Irish bishops', and now they 'think they are secure enough to kick away the ladder by which they mounted'. They now 'have got the priests in their hands, and in a little while they will be able to attack the bishops, priests, and the Pope himself with impunity'.[66]

Following this significant attempt at a sober analysis, Logue wrote to Walsh again over a fortnight later with some further reflections. Once more he expressed his concern that Limerick would be seen as the only defender of the honour of the Holy See, pointing out that he had just learned from Monsignor Kirby that the pope had instructed him to thank Dr O'Dwyer for his defence of the papacy against Dillon. Logue warned that priests would grow cold in the national cause if Dillon's 'unjust and unwarrantable charges are to have full indemnity, while the Bishop of Limerick is called to retract', and he commented on the Limerick branch of the National League expelling Catholic members of Limerick corporation because they refused to condemn their bishop, while in the north of the country the National League were sacrificing their principles to win over a few Protestants.[67]

As if this were not enough for Walsh, and his efforts to preserve the clerical-nationalist alliance, he received a letter from Laurence Gillooly, the redoubtable bishop of Elphin, some ten days before the Limerick meeting, which stated that he had consulted a number of colleagues and all were agreed that the meeting should either be prevented or else publicly condemned by the episcopal body. 'We regard it', he declared, 'as the first act of a system of outrage and intimidation against the clergy who may dare to differ in opinion or action from the parliamentary party or self-constituted leaders thereof.' 'No bishop or priest', he added, 'can without self-compromise maintain friendly and confidential relations with such proud, misguided men or submit to their tyrannical dictation...'[68]

After the Limerick meeting, Dr Coffey, of Kerry, complained to Kirby that it was 'deplorable to see men calling themselves leaders of our people and Catholics using language in and out of parliament calculated to subvert ecclesiastical authority'. 'Last Sunday,' he pointed out, 'a great meeting in Limerick was wholly taken up with the abuse of the bishop. Speakers pledged themselves to prosecute the Plan of Campaign more vigorously than ever, asserting they had the support of nine-tenths of the bishops and priests of Ireland.' 'A recent letter from Dr Walsh in the *Freeman*,' Coffey added, was 'so indecisive that many clergy and laity interpret it as a condemnation of O'Dwyer'.[69]

Of more significance from Dr Walsh's point of view, was a letter from Dr Woodlock, bishop of Ardagh, dated 2 September, which awaited him on his return from his holiday, stating that the stoutly nationalist bishop, Thomas Nulty, of Meath, felt 'intensely' the insult offered to O'Dwyer in his cathedral city, and considered the politicians to have been exceedingly guilty in the way they set about raising an outcry against him.[70]

Thus, a definite change had come about in the attitude of many bishops because of the belligerent and disparaging behaviour towards O'Dwyer of Dillon, O'Brien, and a number of other members of the Irish Parliamentary party. None of the hierarchy, however, in the absence of leadership from Walsh and Croke, was prepared to speak out in public. O'Dwyer was left, therefore, subject to public censure and abuse, and seemingly deserted by his fellow bishops. How did he cope with such pressure and contumely?

COPING WITH DEFAMATION AND PRESSURE?

To outward appearances, the bishop of Limerick seemed unperturbed. Before the August meeting, indeed, he seemed debonair and even scornful of his opponents. Writing to a priest of the diocese on sick leave in London, Michael Donor, he remarked almost facetiously:

> The marionettes having danced and sung in various places, the owners of the show are to come before the public here to prove I suppose by the ribaldries and blackguardism of the mob that Dillon never used those words and that Hansard was wrong.

Referring to Francis O'Keefe, the member of parliament for the city, who supported Dillon, he added: 'O'Keefe is the hero of the hour', and then admitted unashamedly, 'I tried to intimidate him but failed.'[71]

After the bishop's reply to Dillon at the end of July, and the subsequent excited attacks on him, Lord Emly had informed Capt. Ross, who passed on the letter to Balfour, 'that the agitation against Dr O'Dwyer on account of his letter is very fierce, but he does not mind it.'[72] Even in mid-September, Balfour received a similar message, this time from a confidant of his, J. Parker Smith, who had interviewed the bishop. He was impressed by his *sang-froid*. 'I found him very firm and confident', he informed the Chief Secretary, 'in his power of maintaining his ground against Dillon and O'Brien.' 'I have spoken,' O'Dwyer said. 'My strength is to sit still. They come and hold a meeting and then go on. I stay here and in a month or two the effect of the meeting is over and I can move.'[73] Yet, despite the apparent stiff upper lip, eleven days earlier the bishop had requested a sick man to go to Rome to enlist aid on his behalf.

On 5 September 1890, O'Dwyer asked Michael Donor, then recuperating in Switzerland, if he would go to Rome to put before the authorities there 'the real facts of the case' and 'to impress upon them in particular ... the danger to the people's faith in allowing things to drift further.' Walsh and Croke ('W & C') make believe at Rome', he continued, 'that they wish to do right but they dare not on account of the public feeling, whereas in reality it is they themselves by their action are sustaining the opposition to the Holy See. If any good is to be done, the Holy See should require every man of our body to inform the people explicitly that the Plan etc are condemned, and if that were done there would be little difficulty in the future.' 'My own position now against the whole force of the League with W & C', O'Dwyer concluded frankly, 'is well nigh untenable.'[74]

Donor, conscious of his bishop's kindness to him during his recurring illnesses, agreed. Hence, five days later O'Dwyer informed him that he had written to Cardinal Mario Rampolla del Tindaro about his coming,[75] and that Donor should impress upon him in particular that 'our people up to this moment believe in perfect good faith that the Plan etc are not really condemned and that Walsh and Croke are with the politicians in these things.' 'My position is very difficult', O'Dwyer explained.

> Personally I have no trouble with my people, but if the whole force of the League, with the archbishops' approval, is to be concentrated on victimising this diocese I shall find it hard to continue to defend the Holy See. If you are asked for a suggestion, I think the very best thing would be *an explicit command to the bishops*, who meet on Oct. 15th next, to make a *distinct announcement to the people that boycotting and the Plan are forbidden.*

In case Donor had not seen recent Irish newspapers, O'Dwyer enclosed issues that included an account of 'Dr W's miserable letter and Dr Croke's ostentatious entertainment of Dillon and O'Brien immediately after their meeting here'. 'I wish the Holy See to understand', he explained, 'the significance of these things and to know that the authority of these archbishops, as alleged anyhow without contradiction on their part – is the real cause of the people adhering to these forbidden things.' He advised him to go as soon as possible to Rome and to meet with Cardinals Rampolla and Simeoni, but to let no one know his mission.[76]

Two days later, the bishop wrote to Donor to assure him that the primate, Dr Logue, was thoroughly with him and had a letter ready for the newspapers, but had been induced to withhold it. If asked privately by Propaganda 'he would come out'. 'I enclose a short letter', he added, 'which puts the case very well. D.Ds W & C have treated the decree as waste paper and even in private amongst their priests have not spread the opinion that it binds all consciences.'[77]

Meanwhile, O'Dwyer had suggested to Fr J.S. Flanagan, then in London, to call on Cardinal Manning to discuss the matter. Flanagan had doubts about the advisability of that course of action and asked for confirmation on 12 September, adding frankly:

> It seems to me that having done your duty and acted up to the dictates of your conscience, you will have to undergo a certain amount of humiliation, for a time, owing to your isolated position, and your rejection by Croke & Walsh, if not indeed all the bishops – but the day will come when your conduct will be justified before the world – Rome must speak sooner or later. I suppose no bishop has written you a word of sympathy.[78]

With renewed earnestness, O'Dwyer, on 20 September, wrote again to Donor. 'The arrest of Dillon and O'Brien was very unfortunate', he reported. It came 'just as the reaction was setting in against them'. The arrests had led to 'various boards of guardians and town councils' passing resolutions in favour of the Plan of Campaign. It was a great scandal, O'Dwyer insisted, and would continue if the bishops did not stop it. 'It seems to me', he reiterated, 'that the episcopal meeting of 15 Oct. would be an excellent occasion for a pronouncement, and the recent resolutions of public bodies and articles in newspapers are sufficient reason for it, but it will not be done unless the authorities in Rome require it.' Once again he mentioned – 'the primate is so well disposed that a word would bring him out'.[79]

On 24 September Donor made his first report. He had an interview with Rampolla, who was pleased with O'Dwyer's stand and thought that the bishops' meeting at Maynooth would be an appropriate occasion for an intervention, but the matter would have to be cleared with the pope, and he suggested that Donor have an audience with the Holy Father.[80] Next day Donor met with Cardinal Giovanni Simeoni, who again spoke favourably of O'Dwyer, but stated 'it would be necessary to act with great caution for fear things would go from bad to worse'.[81] He also suggested that Donor see the pope. On 26 September the busy Donor wrote once more. He had failed to get an audience with the pope, but he met with Archbishop Domenico Jacobini, the secretary of the Congregation of Propaganda, who was well informed about the Irish scene. He gave him newspaper cuttings and brought him up to date. He tried to get the prelate to approve of a public declaration by the Irish bishops, to be read in all the churches, condemning the Plan of Campaign. Jacobini was evasive, but he expressed his sympathy with O'Dwyer 'in the pain that all this must have brought to him', and said that he had done his duty.

On 28 September, the pressure felt by O'Dwyer was reflected in a message to Donor stating, 'So far so good' and then announcing that he was heading for Rome and hoped to be at the Irish College, Paris, in a few days.[82] Donor replied urgently on 8 October. He had failed so far to get an audience with the pope but he had met Cardinal Simeoni, whom he told O'Dwyer was on his way to Rome. 'He seemed much surprised and looked quite displeased', Donor reported. 'Several times he said, "Why does he come now so inopportunely?"' After some minutes of silence, the cardinal informed him 'under the strictest reserve', Donor explained, that

> On the previous day he had written a letter to Dr Logue to be read at the (bishops) meeting, and it was most necessary that you should be present when action was taken on it. There should be union amongst the bishops, and you and those who thought with you should be present to support Dr Logue. If concerted measures were not taken now his action was useless.

'That is the substance of what he said', Donor added. 'In reply, I told him that I would write to you immediately … I am afraid, whatever it costs, you must try to go to the meeting.' He concluded by noting that Bishop Nulty, of Meath, was in Rome with two of his priests.[83]

From Donor's letters it was evident that a number of bishops had written to Rome expressing their dissatisfaction with the Plan of Campaign and boycotting and with the attitude of the leaders of the Campaign, and also with the way in which the papal decree had been handled. Moreover, the *Freeman* for 17 September carried news of the bishop of Cork, T. A. O'Callaghan, reminding his people of the papal condemnation of the Plan of Campaign and boycotting, while the *Daily News* of 29 September had a similar reminder from Bishop James Lynch of Kildare and Leighlin.[84] On 24 October, indeed, Sir George Errington was to write to Abbot Bernard Smith, OSB, at Rome, that he understood that at the bishops' meeting on 15 October a considerable minority sided with O'Dwyer, among them Dr McRedmond of Killaloe, and Dr Donnelly, auxiliary of Dublin, and he had heard '6 or 7 names and others alluded to'.[85]

At the episcopal meeting of 15 October, Dr Walsh had come prepared for change, all the more so in that Archbishop Croke was not present. A number of resolutions were adopted that were published in a pastoral letter, as Donor had recommended at Rome. These reiterated the application of the papal decree to the moral rather than the political domain, and that as regards 'moral lawfulness' the methods known as the Plan of Campaign and boycotting could not be lawfully employed. The people were also to be reminded of their lordship's warning two years ago against 'any hasty or irreverent language with reference to the Sovereign Pontiff'.[86] It was also agreed that collections for the tenants' defence fund were not to be made at the doors or gates of churches, and that clergy contributing individually should do so 'for distressed tenants *generally*, (and not *exclusively* for those evicted under the Plan of Campaign')'.[87]

As a result of the meeting a letter was drafted to Parnell drawing his attention to certain 'disquieting abuses' that could lead to open division in their ranks as regards supporting the national parliamentary party. The abuses were:

1. 'The independent action of individual members of the party in originating and sustaining movements involving the gravest consequences political, social and moral, without the sanction of the party as such.' This sanction was required before priests and people were invited to give their cooperation.

2. 'The want of supervision, even in matters of gravest importance, over *United Ireland*.' It was the organ of the national party, and the clergy who cooperated with the party were, as a result, held responsible by many for its editorial comments, and 'even its vituperative attacks on individuals'.[88]

Not surprisingly, O'Dwyer felt justified and pleased. Writing of the meeting to Kirby, on 10 November 1890, he expressed pleasure at the outcome, adding sanguinely that if what was done at the meeting 'had been done when the decree was first issued Ireland would have been saved a good deal of sin' and the people 'would have done their duty if it had been put to them plainly'.[89] Despite the expression of pleasure at the outcome, he was still genuinely concerned for the future of the church. Three days later, he informed Cardinal Rampolla 'that the greatest firmness on the part of the Holy See' was 'necessary to safeguard the faith in Ireland'. All the political parties had their own ends in view. The governing party as well as the radicals 'would exploit the church'. It was necessary, he advised delicately, 'to keep away every suspicion of a political end but at the same time not to tolerate the least diminution of the doctrinal authority of the church'.[90]

Dillon's attack on O'Dwyer in the House of Commons, the form and vigour of O'Dwyer's response, and the subsequent behaviour of Dillon and O'Brien at Limerick, brought home to the Irish Catholic bishops, as Professor Emmet Larkin has observed, that the interests of nationalism were being asserted as paramount, and that the wrath of the people was being stirred up to assert that supremacy first against Rome and the papal decree, and now against the bishop of Limerick. The prospects of such arrogation of power did not augur well for the future, as O'Dwyer had publicly warned. After Limerick, as a result, there was a hardening of episcopal opinion, as indicated above, against the agrarian wing of the party, as represented by Dillon and O'Brien, 'and an attempt by the bishops to turn the national movement in a political and constitutional rather than a social and agrarian direction'.[91] To this end, *rapprochement* with Rome was essential.

O'Dwyer, of course, had no need for a *rapprochement*. His name was well and favourably known. Even to the present day there remains in the archives of Propaganda a remarkable quantity of newspaper reports and letters, and even some pamphlets, dealing with his defence of the papacy against Dillon! Apart from his own communication by letter and through Michael Donor, there was his *entrée* to Persico, and the assistance of prominent English Catholics and the *Tablet*, and of such as Lord Emly and John Ross of Bladensburg. 'It may interest you to know', Ross had informed Balfour on 10 September 1890, 'that I sent full details of the recent scandalous proceedings at Limerick and elsewhere. I think the Roman authorities have now pretty well everything before them.' Not content with information to Rome, he informed the first secretary that he also had got 'the Bp of L's first letter in a French paper'. 'It is being circulated, (and) a pamphlet in French dealing with the whole matter will follow shortly.'[92] Praise of O'Dwyer marched step by step with criticism of Walsh, in Ross's versions. On 4 October, moreover, the duke of Norfolk wrote to Cardinal Rampolla, stating that he had just heard that Dr O'Dwyer had gone to Rome. 'We all feel most deeply', he declared, 'that the Bishop of Limerick is the Champion in Ireland of the cause of the Holy See and of the Church and that the hopes of that cause in Ireland are centred in him'.[93] Rampolla assured him on 10 October that O'Dwyer would have from the Holy See 'a good an encouraging welcome' and would have 'the special benevolence of the Pope'.[94]

DECLINE OF THE PLAN

Five months after the Limerick meeting the parliamentary party was in disarray over the O'Shea divorce case, and on 6 December 1890 Parnell was deposed from leadership by a majority of the members. The Plan of Campaign began to unravel. Funds were no longer available to support evicted tenants. On the Delmege estate, the collapse of agitation in April 1891 heralded the end of the Plan.[95] A deputation from the tenant farmers called on O'Dwyer to express their regret 'for not having accepted the advice he gave them a year previously'. They requested him to act on their behalf. He approached the court of chancery. Originally the tenants had demanded an all round abatement of 57 percent, later they spoke of 40 percent, but on several occasions, as has been noted, they had rejected the court's proposals to reduce their rents by 30 percent. Now, in response to O'Dwyer's advocacy, the court agreed to repeat the offer, and the tenants gratefully accepted it. Subsequently, their representatives, John O'Connor, John O'Connell and James Downey, denied a report in the *Limerick Leader* that the evicted tenants on the Delmege estate had been well cared for, that they had been in receipt of grants from the time of their eviction and that such grants had been paid promptly. They stated that, when they were originally 'induced' to adopt the Plan of Campaign, they were promised that they would 'want for nothing,' and if they were evicted they would 'be gentlemen going back' to their homes and farms. Instead of which, they maintained, 'our houses are ruined, our farms are like a wilderness, and our pockets are empty'. In conclusion, they tendered their heartfelt thanks to Bishop O'Dwyer and to Fr Walsh for interceding on their behalf and recorded their 'everlasting hatred' for Edward Fitzgerald, the man responsible for the Plan of Campaign in the Glensharrold district.[96]

The bishop of Limerick, as a result, wrote to Monsignor Kirby on 21 April 1891 with a feeling of justification and fulfilment: 'All goes wonderfully well at present in my diocese. A few days ago I saw the end of the only case of the Plan of Campaign, and got all the poor people of Glensharrold reinstated in their holdings. We have perfect peace now.'[97]

This 'landlord bishop', however, had also been concerned for tenants outside his diocese. Moved by the plight of those caught up in the long drawn out dispute at the Ponsonby estate, Co. Cork, and those involved in the bitter struggle in Tipperary town, in both of which contests William O'Brien was ranged against Arthur Hugh Smith-Barry, the leader of the federation of landlords, O'Dwyer had written earlier to Smith-Barry with some proposals. The latter, replying on 19 January 1890, assured him that he shared to the full 'the pity which you have expressed for the unfortunate people, who, as you say, are the victims of a movement which they did not originate and cannot control'.[98] With regard to his lordship's proposals, he needed to discuss them first with Mr Ponsonby. On 28 January he reported that Ponsonby agreed with his lordship's thinking that 'the solution may in all probability be found in the purchase by the tenants of their holdings'. It had been one of the possibilities he had offered back in April 1889 in what was, in Smith-Barry's view, an offer 'generous to the tenants', but it had been rejected. Thos who contrived and supported the Plan of Campaign on the Ponsonby estate, Smith-Barry observed, had objects outside and beyond 'any immediately connected with the property or the ruin of the tenants who act under their advice'. They sought 'a victory for the Plan' and viewed negotiation on the part of the landlord as a sign of weakness.[99] A letter from Smith-Barry on 25 February 1890 made it clear that efforts at settlement had failed, and that Ponsonby felt 'driven by the authors of the conspiracy to evict practically the whole of the tenantry with whom for so many years he lived on terms of friendly relationship'. Smith-Barry concluded by assuring O'Dwyer that Ponsonby and his advisers would under no circumstances desire to fix rents 'at a rate above which the tenant could be equitably expected to pay'.[100] The final settlement did not take place until 1905–7, when the estate was sold to the tenants.[101]

With respect to Smith-Barry's Tipperary tenants, O'Dwyer commented wryly to Dr Donnelly on 31 January 1891 that '134 of Smith-Barry's tenants have paid the November '90 rent, and in a few weeks more the rest will follow'. In conclusion, he could not resist an expression of spiteful gloating, yet another example of what Archbishop Logue termed euphemistically his 'unfortunate manner': 'What a blessed coincidence it is that the ruin of the whole vile thing should be brought about by the blackguardism of the one Irish politician [Parnell] whom the Holy See ever condemned by name, and that they [the party] are finally borne down under the dead weight of the Plan, with the Church's malediction upon it.'[102]

One other agrarian area had occupied his special concern, as has been noticed, the O'Grady estate. By mid-May 1891 it was reported that the evicted tenants had not received any grants for more than two months. the Plan of Campaign organiser, J.F.X. O'Brien, advised them to settle, as there were no funds to pay them.[103] O'Dwyer's intercession was sought at the beginning of 1892 as the acceptable mediator between the tenants and The O'Grady.[104] This, though the estate was not in the Limerick diocese. It was a fitting response to Scawen Blunt's comments four years earlier.

O'Dwyer's successful intervention on behalf of the tenants of Glensharrold in April 1890 was hailed warmly by the *Nation* newspaper. It was due to the efforts of 'the kind-hearted bishop' that the tenants had been able to go back to their holdings. The paper expressed the hope that the imputation of bad and improper motives to him would be at an end.[105] From this time forward, O'Dwyer's popularity began to grow, assisted by the disillusionment experienced with politicians as a result of the bitter divisions following the O'Shea divorce case and the deposition of Parnell by a majority of the party.

In the autumn of 1891, O'Dwyer paid his first *ad limina* visit to the Vatican. 'Only today I have got my audience', he wrote Bishop Donnelly on 3 November, 'but it was worth waiting for. His Holiness was kindness itself and kept me a full hour with him, and directed me to come to see him again the evening before I leave here.' 'We talked of many things', he continued, 'and I was greatly impressed at the singular power which he has of putting one entirely at ease.'[106] Overjoyed and cheered at his reception, O'Dwyer wrote freely of it and word spread quickly at home. Consequently, on his return he experienced the fickleness of people and how easily public feeling is swayed. He was presented by an address of welcome by the mayor, Patrick Riordan, who, with a large gathering of clergy and people, met him at the railway station. The address was signed by 11,000 people, who wished to be united with their bishop in homage to the supreme pontiff.[107] It also referred to the many acts of 'benevolence and charity' which O'Dwyer had performed before and since his consecration and expressed admiration for the zeal that he had brought to his role as bishop. In many ways it was an act of reparation. Appreciating this, yet manifestly pleased with the welcome, O'Dwyer responded that he was glad to be reassured that 'the Catholic bishop in the city of Limerick had a home, a warm, a bright, a happy home'.

Over a fortnight later, settled back into pastoral considerations after months of turmoil, he happily wrote to Monsignor Kirby that he was sure his grace would hear 'with great pleasure that nothing could be more hearty and cordial than my people have been towards me since my return, and what is more important that we have going on at this moment in all the parochial churches of the city the most magnificently attended mission that I have ever seen.'[108]

It was a setting in sharp contrast to the scenes of bitterness and disillusion-ment occasioned by the Parnell split and by the shock of the former leader's unexpected death two months earlier. The political world had changed. Time would tell that not for another thirty years would a monolithic national party wield a *comparable* dominating influence over priests and people. On this last, Aubrey de Vere was to recall the many clergy who refused to join in the land agitation and were boycotted, and how he himself had been bitterly denounced for his outspoken criticism of the excesses of the land struggle, and how he had answered that

> There is an Ireland larger than that of the Tenant League ... the Ireland that did not confound licence with liberty, that reverenced law, and therefore made no man judge in his own cause. That Ireland survives. She is my Ireland and I have a right to remain faithful to what I have loved long ...[109]

An idealistic paean, perhaps, but it reflected an honourable position which O'Dwyer respected, and which many contemporaries too easily dismissed.

In concluding the hectic early years of Dr O'Dwyer's episcopacy, it remains to explore his distinctive response to the Parnell split.

10

An individual approach to the Parnell split

When Mrs O'Shea and Parnell did not enter a defence against Captain O'Shea's suit for divorce, and the verdict went against them on 17 November 1890, the vast majority of people and clergy in Ireland were surprised and shocked.[1] 'Nothing in my time has more deeply affected the clergy,' John Egan, bishop of Waterford, wrote to Monsignor Kirby. 'They are stunned by the blow. No one or at least very few believed that the charges would be proved, hence the event had the effect of a sudden and unforeseen calamity.'[2] Even the well-informed Archbishop Walsh was taken aback, particularly as Michael Davitt had told him that he had Parnell's assurance that there was no truth in the charges.[3]

O'Dwyer, from his own past experience, was less disposed to accept Parnell's word or, indeed, to have great personal respect for him, but he had known of the truth of the charges for some time, and had been made aware of Parnell's readiness to lie. On 3 November 1888, while the case was in progress between Parnell and *The Times* over the letters produced by the paper which seemed to implicate Parnell in the murder in the Phoenix Park in May 1882 of Lord Frederick Cavendish, the chief secretary, and T.H. Burke, the under secretary, O'Dwyer received a letter from Captain William O'Shea which revealed his sad situation. He explained:

> Mrs O'Shea is under a written engagement never to communicate directly or indirectly with Mr Parnell, and Mr Parnell is under a written order of mine never to communicate directly or indirectly with Mrs O'Shea. I know this engagement and this order have been violated. Under Parnell's hand I have a written lie about this great social wrong.

'My religion prevents me taking an action for divorce,' O'Shea explained. 'I have been separated from my wife for nearly two years. Her engagement described above was entered into because my son left her house and refused to return there unless he [Parnell] did so.' 'Every effort of my life', he concluded, 'is directed to saving the children, who are Catholics, from the scandal.'[4] Four days later, O'Shea responded gratefully to a 'kind letter' from O'Dwyer, and to the word 'pity' which he used. It would represent also, he observed, the feelings of his other friends.[5] Despite his religion allegedly preventing him taking an action for divorce, however, he moved for divorce on 24 December 1889.

In the aftermath of the trial, Gladstone and his Non-Conformist supporters made it clear that there was no prospect of Home Rule while Parnell continued as leader of the Irish party. Parnell refused to resign, even temporarily. The Irish bishops, meanwhile, were under pressure from Rome, Cardinal Manning, and many lay Catholics, to come out against Parnell. Archbishop Walsh, wisely, refused to move until the Irish party had themselves faced the problem. Monsignor Kirby took it on himself to write to the bishop of Limerick suggesting that Rome might intervene. If he was expecting in this way to put pressure on Walsh and the more political bishops, he was disappointed. O'Dwyer was conscious of the strength of feeling across the country and, indeed, of a strong initial support for Parnell in Limerick. The city branch of the National League had come out vigorously in the Chief's favour.[6] Consequently, he wrote carefully on 28 November 1890: 'Your Grace must feel with us all not only the disgrace of recent events but the anxiety as to the future that must weigh upon all Irishmen.' The *Freeman's Journal* had come to the point of teaching the people that private morality had nothing to do with public affairs, and to that end was going so far as to blacken the moral character of Daniel O'Connell. It was impossible, he added, to forecast the course of events, and if Parnell and the *Freeman* succeeded at the meeting of the parliamentary party next Monday there would be 'a period of great unsettlement and confusion'. If, however, Parnell agreed to retire, a great deal would depend on the character of his successor, and his power to keep the party together. In either case, it would take at least six months to estimate the consequences of the present disruption. For this reason, he believed that 'the attitude of those who are responsible for the spiritual interests of our people – should be one of caution.' 'In myself,' he added firmly, 'I should very much regret to see any move made by the Holy See beyond whatever suggestions it may be found necessary to make confidentially through individual bishops. Men are so excited now, that in their anger they will turn fiercely on *any one* who may be suspected of interfering with their projects.'[7]

Controversy continued to rage among members of the parliamentary party beyond the Monday date. As the discussions continued without resolution in Committee Room 15 in the House of Commons, the standing committee of the bishops issued an address to hasten political decision. The address, released to the press, declared Parnell unfit for leadership on moral grounds, and from a social and personal viewpoint as a result of divorce court proceedings, and also because his continuance would cause an 'inevitable disruption, with defeat at elections, wreck of Home Rule hopes, and sacrifice of tenants' interests.'[8] All ten members present agreed with the address, though three bishops refused to sign it. These were O'Dwyer, Healy, and Coffey. Coffey voiced the unease of the other two in objecting to the political reference in the address. It was 'an abomination', he informed Archbishop Walsh on 5 December, to have the destinies of a Catholic country confided to such as Parnell, but the alternative, consisting of men like Healy, O'Brien, and Dillon, was 'fraught with equal' and, to his mind, 'greater danger'. They had denounced and calumniated bishops and had gone 'the length and breadth of the country preaching disobedience to the Holy See' – two things sure to result 'in the demoralisation of our people and the destruction of the church in this country.'[9] Bishop Donnelly of Canea, Walsh's auxiliary, conveyed similar sentiments to Kirby five days later.[10]

On 6 December, O'Dwyer reported to Kirby that the controversy still raged and he reflected how strange it was in so Catholic a country that people were prepared 'to support so disgraceful a character' as Parnell. 'My explanation of it is', he observed, 'that for several years the moral sense of the people has been growing dull, and they have learned to put expediency before principle.' Then, forestalling any reports to Rome from his colleagues, he explained adroitly: 'With the bishops' manifesto I entirely agree, but I have not signed it, as I have never been either a follower or an ally or Mr Parnell, whom the true instinct of our Holy Father condemned years ago.'[11]

On the day O'Dwyer wrote, the meeting concluded in committee room fifteen. By majority vote Parnell was deposed. Forty-five members withdrew, leaving Parnell in the chair with a rump of twenty-eight. Three days later he returned to Ireland to continue the struggle for power by appealing over the heads of the majority of the party and the bishops to the Irish people.[12] The country was riven. Already on 6 December, Bishop T.A. O'Callaghan, returning to Cork after the bishops' meeting, remarked: 'The people seem to have gone mad and lost their reason. What is most singular is that even good pious people who frequent the sacraments are in some instances carried away by the fury.'[13] To the magic of his name – 'Parnell', 'The Chief' – and his political skill, was allied, as O'Dwyer indicated, the power of Ireland's main newspaper, the *Freeman's Journal*. All now became focussed on a by-election in North Kilkenny scheduled for Monday, 22 December. In Limerick, meanwhile, the city member of parliament, Francis A. O'Keefe, had voted with the anti-Parnellites, and on 16 December Limerick corporation came out against Parnell.[14]

Amidst the mounting turmoil and abuse, O'Dwyer wrote almost detachedly to Donnelly on 13 December:

> I think that the hand of God is in the whole thing. None of us knew what a set we were dealing with, and if they had gone on without a break until Home Rule was got, we should have found ourselves, helpless, in the hands of as bad a gang of ruffians as any in France or Italy.

'I do not see much to choose between the parties', he observed. 'Parnell committed, and they gladly condoned, the adultery, and for my part I cannot see the great gain of getting rid of one blackguard to replace him with the gentlemen who boast that they 'stood up against the bulls of the pope of Rome for him!' 'They have met now in a most appropriate place,' he added waspishly, referring to Kilkenny, 'and my fervent prayer is that as little of them may survive as of the cats.'[15]

The election was marked by bitterness and absence of charity on both sides. The clergy engaged in a virtual crusade against Parnell. Those who had been the strongest in his support when leader, such as Archbishop Croke, now became his fiercest opponents. On 22 December the Parnellites were heavily defeated.

At the beginning of the New Year, O'Dwyer remarked to Kirby on the support Parnell was receiving 'in defiance of common decency', and indulged in a variation of a familiar theme. It was all, he observed, evidence of the demoralisation that had gone on for the last ten years, during which crime had been 'connived at for political purposes', and the authority of the Holy See, 'even within its own sphere of moral teacher', had been repudiated by that very section of the politicians to whom the people now look for an alternative to Parnell. 'If we had less politics', he concluded, echoing Persico, 'and more religion, the church in Ireland would do better.'[16]

At a large public meeting at Limerick on 11 January, Parnell put the bishops on the defensive by proclaiming that their opposition to him was not on moral but on political grounds, in support of which he pointed to their delay of two weeks after the divorce action was granted before intervening. O'Dwyer claimed not to have been impressed. 'Parnell will be no cause for anxiety, though he may give trouble for a while', he informed Kirby on 25 January. 'The meeting here was a complete fiasco, and most who went did so out of curiosity.'[17] No priests attended this meeting, or a later one in March. A few days later, in a letter to Donnelly, to whom he wrote more freely, O'Dwyer's independent, challenging mind was questioning the moral issues involved in opposing Parnell. 'I should like to know if it is seriously held by our politico-theologians', he mused, 'that it is sinful to sustain Parnell's leadership.' There was 'so much insistence on its being a *moral* question', but in his view it was 'entirely a political question without sin on either side'. 'No one can pretend', he judged, 'that voting to keep Parnell … is formal co-operation with his adultery or approval of it.'[18]

On 13 February he sent word to Kirby of the breakdown of negotiations at Boulogne between Parnell and the representatives of the majority of the party. The politicians' failure to agree may, he observed, in the light of the 'evil tendencies' shown by many of them, be 'a merciful providence that delays Home Rule'.[19] Two weeks later, however, he gave vent to frustration and disgruntlement in a letter to Bishop Donnelly. 'The one safeguard between us and the deep sea at present', he commented, reflecting the prevailing intimidation and upheaval, 'is the government of our friend Balfour: … if we had an Irish executive, under an Irish parliament, I am convinced that you would have an Irish 'terror'.'[20] The exaggeration reflected the disenchantment with politics being experienced by many.

He returned, on 4 March, to the theme that the disruption of the Irish party before Home Rule was granted was 'a mercy from God', and that the bitterness and extent of the support for Parnell were 'the fruits of the demoralisation of the last ten years'. A further unwelcome feature, he confided to Kirby, was 'the excessive devotion of the clergy, young and old, to politics'. This was a new feature. The younger priests, in particular, were as a body more extreme in their views and more excited than the people.'[21]

During that month he produced two very different yet distinctive letters, one on 9 March, the other on the 18th. On 9 March he conveyed to Donnelly that he was still much concerned about the theology of 'the preposterous claim' being imposed on the conscience of the country by 'two ecclesiastical politicians', evidently Croke and Walsh. He insisted:

> It is no sin to support Parnell. If a man repudiates sympathy with his offence, ... and on merely political grounds supports him as the ablest political leader, he may be, and in my opinion is mistaken, and has certainly loose views on decency, but he acts within his rights.

'The illustration of the professor is trash', he asserted, 'unless it is established that a political leader of bad character has a power of evil influence like that of a professor on his pupils.' 'The other day,' O'Dwyer added, 'the priests of Cashel were free to take sides. Now it is a sin to take one side.' In his view, referring to Parnell's seat in Cork, Cork, 'there is nothing wrong in Cork re-electing him, but he must not be put on a pinnacle. But if a man thinks that on the pinnacle is the place where Parnell will be most useful, like Nelson on the quarter-deck, why may he not vote for him?' 'The worst of it all', he observed, 'is that they will ruin the religious belief of the country by their absurdities. When there was a clear case, with the authority of Rome at their back, they were afraid or unwilling to vindicate the moral law, and the rights of the church, but now we have a claim almost for infallibility from Cashel and Dublin,[22] and enforced in Down & Conor almost by excommunication, in a case in which, in my humble opinion, the church is entirely outside its jurisdiction.'

Then, lest perhaps he might be thought to be about to speak out publicly on the matter, O'Dwyer rounded off his letter on a relaxed and detached note. 'Excuse me, my Lord,' he declared, 'for allowing myself to run on like this, but it is a relief to blow off some steam,' adding, 'the serious interests of religion aside, is it not all a most amusing exhibition. Sitting on the ditch is after all a pleasant place to watch from.'[23]

Had Croke and Walsh known of this letter, they would have been even more disapproving than they already were. As it was, Croke complained to Kirby on 10 March about O'Dwyer not signing the bishops' manifesto. He enclosed a letter from one of the Limerick members of parliament, William Abraham, which indicated that O'Dwyer was lukewarm in his opposition to Parnell. Croke urged Kirby to press O'Dwyer to sign: impressing on him 'how P. is looked on in Rome, especially by the Holy Father'.[24] Walsh had already written on 5 March to complain of the danger to solid union among the bishops occasioned by the bishop of Limerick's refusal 'to sign our episcopal document'. It was now 'openly stated among the Parnellites', he declared, that because O'Dwyer was keeping studiously aloof from his brethren it was 'all nonsense' for the bishops to say that a question of morality was involved in the party retaining a leader who had been publicly discredited. The persistent action of the three bishops who did not sign was, in Walsh's view, 'the direct result of the encouragement given them from Rome' on more than one occasion. They now take up at the bishops' meetings 'the attitude and tone of people fighting for the authority of the Holy See in the face of an all but schismatic episcopacy'.[25]

Kirby, impressed by the letters of the archbishops, took it upon himself to write to O'Dwyer: presenting Walsh's views as his own, and requesting him to make common cause with the other bishops. The bishop of Limerick replied on 18 March with another masterly response, artfully disarming in its reasonableness and politely devastating in its criticism.

His letter opened with some requests regarding members of his diocese going to Rome, and then, having disposed of these matters of business, he addressed the matter raised by the influential and elderly prelate with fitting deference. 'Allow me to thank your Grace most heartily for the frank and even paternal manner in which you have given me your views upon my action or rather inaction in the present political crisis. It is of great importance for one placed so near events as I am to learn the impartial and deliberate judgment of one whose very remoteness from the scene of action enables him to study it with more calmness and accuracy; and I am sure that I need not say that I shall study yr Grace's views with the utmost care and give them the full consideration which on every ground they deserve.' He then went on introduce Monsignor Kirby to his almost impregnable position. 'As to Mr Parnell there can be no room for doubt or room for hesitation as to his utter unfitness for the position of leader of a Catholic nation, and you need not have the least apprehension that at any time one word will be spoken in his favour by any priest in Limerick or any countenance given to his supporters. But there are circumstances of a local character in which perhaps yr Grace may be able to give us some assistance that would simplify matters.' He explained:

> The anti-Parnellite member for this city [Francis A. O'Keefe] transgressed all bounds of decency last year in his attacks upon Monsignor Persico, and the Holy See, and in his personal insults to me. So bad was his conduct that we never can support him unless he withdraws these outrages and apologises for them.
>
> One of our county members, Mr William Abraham, is even worse. He is one of the worst libertines whom I have ever known, and it is a matter of common rumour, and I believe true, that he returned himself an atheist in the last census paper. Surely such a man is not the fit representative for so Catholic a constituency as ours, and it is rather an excessive demand on the cooperation of a bishop and his priests to ask them in the name of morality to take an active part in supporting such a fellow, yet that is the position in which I am placed; and if unsatisfactory consequences follow, Mr McCarthy and his friends have only themselves to blame. It is not too

much to require as the condition of our support that we get as our candidates men of good moral character whom Catholics may trust.

'It is very painful to find also in the national press and other anti-Parnellite organs', O'Dwyer added pointedly, 'constant references to the Plan of Campaign as if the pope had never condemned it. Parnell's crime is bad enough; but in my opinion this continuous sapping of the people's faith in the Holy See is worse, and the present resistance to the authority of the bishops is the fruit that it is bearing already. ... If your Grace could bring your great personal influence to bear on those who have the direction of Irish affairs so as to have these things remedied you would, I presume to think, render a great service to our country and its people. 'Begging your Grace to excuse the inordinate length of this letter', he concluded dutifully, 'and the entire freedom with which it is written.'[26]

Two days later, the first meeting of the anti-Parnellite National Federation, which had been approved by seventeen prelates, took place in Limerick. The day after the meeting, the *Munster News*, of 21 March 1891, published a letter from a 'Limerick priest' explaining why none of the Limerick clergy attended the meeting. The priests of Limerick, it declared, had opted for a policy of non-interference 'in the present grave crisis'. This even applied to meetings called 'in resistance to Mr Parnell's dictatorship', as otherwise they might seem to be identifying themselves with men like Francis A. O'Keefe. If he were to retire from political life, however, things could be different. But so long as he continued to represent the city in parliament the priests would be compelled to refrain from taking an active part in the political life of the community.

In style and views expressed, the letter read like a composition of the bishop. There would be other times when his lordship was believed to have written anonymously. O'Keefe replied to the letter in the belief that it came from the bishop.[27] He described the 'cowardly criticism' of himself as a retaliation for his part in the Limerick demonstration, and stated that he had been assured that the priests of the diocese were in perfect accord with their colleagues in other dioceses and that the 'anonymous libeller' in the *Munster News* spoke for nobody but 'his own nonentity'. Putting someone like O'Keefe on the spot was likely to amuse the bishop of Limerick. Certainly on the day the letter appeared, O'Dwyer was in high spirits in a communication to his friend Donnelly, and apparently quite detached from political pressures and animosities.

'It will be a great pleasure when you come', he assured Donnelly on 20 March, 'and we shall then "talk of what hath been and might have been, of who is changed and who is dead" politically, and I think by that time the corpses will be pretty numerous.' The Parnellites were in for a lively time in Sligo, he pointed out, referring to the by-election there. If defeated, Parnell would be discredited fatally. The appearance of some of the bishops on election platforms, however, was a mistake that must ultimately weaken episcopal influence. The *Freeman's Journal*, he admitted, was influencing his judgment. 'At first I had a kind of sneaking partiality for Parnell as I thought the opposition to him on *moral grounds* was *not honest*, but now I cannot stomach the open attacks upon the bishops of that wretched paper.'[28]

A month later, after the ending of the Plan of Campaign at Glensharrold and the reinstatement of the tenants in their holdings, he was telling Kirby 'that everything goes wonderfully well in my diocese', and that there was perfect peace, which he hoped would last for many a day.[29] At Newcastle West on Easter Monday, nevertheless, he returned to the excesses of the *Freeman* that had made him 'an anti-Parnellite'. It was now, he announced, 'becoming a stand up fight between the Church and Parnell, and at that stage we must all stand by the ship, however we may deplore the management that brought things to that pass'.[30]

On 23 May, still conducting his visitation of the parishes and in relaxed mood, he informed Donnelly that he hoped to be finished in two weeks and that then, after the bishops' meeting at Maynooth, he looked forward to Donnelly revisiting him at Corbally, by the banks of the river Shannon. 'This place is looking lovely just now', he enthused. 'It is a positive pain to go away again as I shall this afternoon.' He sympathised with the persistence of his friend's 'Limerick cold' from his last visit, but suggested that the remedy might lie in 'a hair of the dog that bit you'.[31]

Matters took a more serious turn, where O'Dwyer was concerned, during June. At their general meeting, the bishops approved a common statement recording their 'judgment as pastors of the Irish people', that Mr Parnell, by his public misconduct had utterly disqualified himself to be their political leader, and they called on the people to repudiate his leadership.[32] The statement, drawn up by Walsh and Croke, was circulated to all the bishops on 25 June for their signature. The fact that the pope had requested a common statement led all to sign the document, except O'Dwyer. Sending him the printed statement, Bishop John Healy added the written note – 'I have no doubt that it is the wish of the Holy Father that we should sign this.'[33] O'Dwyer had not been at the meeting, and had asked Donnelly to convey his views on Parnell to the other bishops. He had received Donnelly's letter on his return home from visitation. He was not happy that the statement allowed no alteration. 'Cover it as they will, it is all a Gladstone *cum* Healy move against Parnell', he observed to Donnelly on 26 June, 'and much as I abhor the latter I do not despise him as I do the other gang. It is all very well to condemn adultery, but when I am told that in a month, when the coast is clear, that the political bishops are to install John Dillon in the leadership, I must confess that I am inclined to allow them to clear their own hay, and to wait until there's a body in Dublin life with whom I can as a Christian bishop decently unite.'[34] Dr Coffey also conveyed to Donnelly that 'in talking up Dillon', the archbishop of Dublin would get no support from him, and he told him that he could show his letter to his friend, Dr O'Dwyer.[35]

Despite their opposition to being politically involved, and to any support for Dillon as leader, Coffey, Donnelly, and Healy signed the bishops' statement. O'Dwyer continued to refuse. He viewed the document as political at bottom, he informed Donnelly, as an example of 'Gladstonian morality' from which he was delighted to have held aloof. And once again he emphasised the danger to religion from Dillon.[36] Writing to Coffey, on 30 June 1891, he mentioned a further ground for grievance. Like him, he had left the bishops' meeting when the question of the new condemnation of Parnell was raised. 'Since I became bishop', he complained, 'it has always been the same plan of springing political resolutions on us without notice at the end of our meeting. On my part, even if I stand alone, I do not intend to sign this document.' Several bishops at that very moment were negotiating to give the leadership to Mr Dillon. He was 'not prepared to accept him'. He regarded such a man 'as infinitely more injurious to the religious and moral interests of our people than Mr Parnell'. As to the argument that the Holy Father desired that all should join in the condemnation of Parnell. He did not believe it. 'The Holy Father himself, as well as every bishop in Ireland, has found in the split among the rogues a revival of our former liberty of action'.[37] On 1 July, Walsh put his point of view to Dr Kirby once more. There was no reason why O'Dwyer did not sign. All the political references to Home Rule, and the other matters objected to in a previous form had been removed, and the Holy Father had requested a common front. All these factors 'would overcome the most obstinate tendency to opposition, except that of opposition for opposition's sake'. 'That, in fact,' Walsh observed, 'is what it would seem we have to deal with in this unhappy case.' Dr O'Dwyer seemed to think that his general attitude of 'independent opposition' to all joint episcopal action was 'in some way favoured at Rome!'[38] On the same date, the bishop of Limerick covered his reputation with his own constituents by means of a letter in the *Munster News* which, according to his friend and mentor, Fr Flanagan, was both happy and opportune, 'a deadly arrow shot into Parnell's vitals' in which 'while you pronounce upon *him* you keep yourself free of all complications with regard to his successor.'[39]

On 2 July the episcopal statement was published, just five days before the critical Carlow by-election. The same day, O'Dwyer claimed to be relieved that the statement did not carry his signature. 'Perhaps when next month Mr John Dillon gets into the saddle again, and gives the episcopal ribs a dig of his heels, their lordships may find themselves under as tight a rein as ever Parnell held.' 'Parnell never was mine', he added. 'Let those who owned him, disown him.'[40] Two days later, Donnelly commented that O'Dwyer 'got off pretty easy from the press' with respect to the document;[41] while Coffey, explaining to the bishop of Limerick, as to a 'most affectionate friend', why he had signed, declared significantly that 'there should be some strong and effective protest against the custom of springing resolutions of a political character on the meeting. Nothing should be discussed which is not on the agenda paper.'[42]

By 9 July, however, in the wake of the resounding defeat of Parnell's candidate, O'Dwyer was having second thoughts. 'I cannot make up my mind', he observed to Donnelly, 'whether I did well or ill in not signing.' He went on, however, with the rhetorical question – 'Did they not do it well in Carlow?' and added wonderingly, in the same vein: 'Is not the determination of Parnell under such a blow almost worthy of admiration'.[43] After Carlow, Parnellites, grasping at straws, claimed at a convention in Limerick that O'Dwyer, in not following the example of the other bishops, was supporting them. Thus challenged, the bishop of Limerick 'reluctantly' intervened in 'the quarrel agitating the country'. He made his reluctance clear in a public letter addressed to his vicar-general, Dr Moloney, and then stated that his sense of national decency would not permit him to support Parnell, and that he concurred most heartily in the bishops' resolution at Maynooth, though he did not explain why he had not signed it.[44]

Although Parnell struggled on for some months more, his cause was finished after Carlow. The Irish party remained deeply split, seemingly irreconcilable. The Parnellites, not surprisingly, were bitterly anti-bishops and anti-clerical. The clerical church found itself increasingly identified with the anti-Parnellite majority, which was itself tenuously held together externally by Justin McCarthy as leader, while internally rival groups gathered around old rivals, John Dillon and Tim Healy. Archbishop Croke favoured Dillon as the future leader. Walsh was more circumspect but his inclination was in the same direction. O'Dwyer sensed this and it drew him further and further away from Walsh. It seemed, indeed, as if their old friendship only deepened their growing apart. Wilfrid Blunt recalled being told by Prior Glynn, an Augustinian, that O'Dwyer was jealous of Walsh and sought to head a rival party in the episcopacy.[45] Whatever might be said for that insight, and the evidence is not compelling, O'Dwyer's letters to his friend Donnelly were marked, as already seen, by sniping remarks about Walsh, whom he frequently termed 'Your Man'. The letters to Donnelly were important in that they were one of the few places where he felt free to give expression to passing moods and to convey the paradoxes and contradictions that are part of the human condition. When Dillon and William O'Brien were involved, the critical remarks had an added edge. Thus, on 17 July 1891 he commenced with the observation:

> It would be all very well with us in the Irish church if we had at our head in Dublin a man like Cardinal Cullen, who went straight, and *was a churchman first of all.* As it is we have been led by a ... of *political gadfly into our present wretched position,* and I see no sign that our body, as a body, has learned anything. They are plotting away for Dillon's leadership as hotly as if nothing happened.

He went on to relay the prevailing gossip that 'St William O'Brien' was to be arrested for bigamy, adding maliciously – 'if our little idols are knocked down at this rate, we shall soon be without one on the shelf'. Concluding on a lighter note, he invited Donnelly to join him in Limerick where there was glorious summer weather, adding happily, 'the country is looking simply superb. With average weather we shall [have] a fine harvest, and that, curiously enough, as with other blessings for the country, will be another trouble for our patriots.'[46]

A month later he again mixed social, personal and political comment. Providence did not wish him to go to horse shows, it seemed. 'Having missed our own in June,' he observed regretfully to Donnelly, 'I find I cannot get away from here next week, and must lose that in Dublin and with it the pleasure of your hospitality with the pastor of Little Bray thrown in.'[47] 'I am extremely sorry', he added gracefully, 'but all the same as thankful to you for your kind invitation as if I accepted it.' Then, as if unable to resist it, he commented regarding 'Honest John' (Dillon) that next Sunday would be the anniversary of 'his blackguardism' in Limerick, but he did not think Dillon would celebrate the event, and referring to O'Brien he observed that 'the "other buffer" is in his cottage by the sea engaged on his novel'. Finally, he rejoiced in the waning sales of the *Freeman* with the decline of Parnell.[48]

On 15 September, as his first *ad limina* visit to Rome drew near, the bishop of Limerick wrote to Monsignor Kirby in the deferential manner and somewhat unctuous style he had adopted in writing to the old man. He requested certain dispensations, and then expressed his appreciation of the success achieved by Fr Kelly, the new rector of the Irish College Rome, remarking pointedly that 'every day is showing the increasing necessity of a well trained and holy priesthood who will in all things "seek first the kingdom of God"'. Referring to the anti-episcopal attitude of the Parnellites, he emphasised once more that the bishops would be in a more convincing position if a better stand had been made when the attack was directed against the pope, adding that it was disheartening after all that had occurred to learn that ecclesiastics were engaged 'planning another collection to keep up the Plan of Campaign scandal'. He closed with guileful flattery: 'I trust your Grace does not object to the freedom with which I express my views to you. I know your long tried devotion to the Church, and our poor country, and feeling profoundly anxious at seeing our Irish church departing from the old safe courses of our predecessors, I think it right to express my views to one in your Grace's position.'[49]

O'Dwyer's standing in Rome continued to be bolstered by the support of the duke of Norfolk and influential English Catholics. The Duke had written to Rome on 21 March 1891 suggesting that on O'Dwyer's visit he should receive 'some distinguished mark of the favour and approbation of the Holy See', which 'would be an immense encouragement to those Catholics in Ireland, and among the clergy especially, who are struggling in the midst of trials and difficulties to maintain the cause of morality and the authority of the Pope'. He reminded the cardinal that the bishop of Limerick had 'received insult, contumely and misrepresentation in his own country' because he had chosen 'the path of duty'.[50] Rome responded on the occasion of O'Dwyer's visit. On 1 December 1891, Walsh protested to Kirby about an item on the previous day's paper about 'the special compliment' paid to O'Dwyer on his recent visit to the Vatican. This was yet another indication, he stated, 'of the animus of *some* very influential persons immediately surrounding the Holy Father'. It was important to counter the ill-effects of such an honour, he went on, by conferring 'a similar compliment' on Dr Brownrigg, bishop of Ossory, who was then in Rome and 'was the first bishop on whom the brunt of an election in the Parnell dispute fell'. He added cuttingly:

> It is notorious to everyone in Ireland that Dr O'Dwyer has been singled out in this way because of his unvarying course of opposition to his brethren in the episcopacy. It is no less notorious that if the Irish bishops had been guilty of acting with the incredible folly displayed by him since his appointment, Ireland would have been helpless in the hands of Parnell.[51]

Clearly, the two former friends had drifted far apart. In the first five years of O'Dwyer's episcopate he had opposed Walsh and the majority of the bishops on three major issues – university education, the Plan of Campaign, and a united policy towards Parnell, in all of which nationalist politics were involved. He had acquired, as a result, a maverick reputation, but at the end of the five years he indicated no signs of wishing to have done anything otherwise. He was now well known and highly regarded in Rome, he was popular once more in his native city, and was generally respected for his intellect and polemical skill, and he had a few good episcopal friends notably Donnelly, Healy, Coffey and McRedmond, and many of the others remained open to his charm, his gifts of conversation, and his readiness to be of assistance, and, while his deafness was a limiting factor it enabled others make allowances for him. Moreover, some reflection on his attitude to Parnell suggests that he was not as unreasonable and capricious as his episcopal critics painted him. There was a logic to his actions. Unlike Croke and Walsh, he had never been enthusiastic about Parnell. He had been made aware, through Captain O'Shea, as early as 1888, that Parnell was an adulterer and liar. When the adultery was exposed, however, he discouraged Rome from intervening because of the delicacy of the situation. Subsequently, when the party split, he judged the alternative leaders, John Dillon and William O'Brien, more unwelcome than Parnell. Dillon and O'Brien, who had ridiculed him in his own city and had spurned his appeal to moral arguments in respect of the papal teaching on boycotting, were now hypocritically appealing to moral arguments to suit their own purposes against Parnell. Besides, if he publicly condemned the former leader, he would be seen as tacitly approving not only Dillon and O'Brien, but their colleagues in Limerick, Francis A. O'Keefe, who had openly defied his bishop and criticised Persico and the Holy See, and William Abraham 'one of the worst of libertines'. Consequently, he felt he had justifiable, indeed compelling reasons for not adding his name to his colleagues' document of condemnation.

The years from 1886 to 1891 had been tumultuous, embattled, and exciting. The return of relative peace and daily routine, however, did not signal rest for the bishop's combative spirit and great energy. He was already engaged in disputes of a denominational and educational nature in his diocese which would expand and keep him immersed in one conflict or another for the next sixteen years.

PART THREE

Educational strife within the diocese, 1887–1907

The first disputes. Leamy's School and Roxborough School

The educational disputes took place over a twenty-year period from 1886 to 1907. The opponents were the Protestant community in Limerick, the Jesuits, and the Christian Brothers. The Protestants were involved in respect of Leamy's School, 1886 to 1894, and Roxborough School, between 1887 and 1897; the Jesuits with regard to Mungret College, largely from 1895 to 1904; and the Christian Brothers and the local population in the bitterest of the disputes, often known as the Bruff 'scandal', from 1897 to 1907. It is necessary to consider each issue at some length without an excess of detail. This chapter will be devoted to the disputes with the Protestant community.

LEAMY'S SCHOOL

The school took its name from William Leamy, a native of Limerick, who spent most of his life at sea, and died on the island of Madeira, off the coast of North Africa, on 24 March 1814. During his life he amassed a large fortune and in his will, after various donations, he left the residue of his estate to his executors 'to be by them applied to the education of the poor in Ireland, principally those in and about Limerick city; or as they, my executors, in their better judgement, shall deem meet to give this bequest the most extensive efficacy'.[1] Unfortunately, his executors proved unreliable. One of them used up a considerable part of the money for his own purposes. Legal processes and costs led to further delay and expenditure, with the result that it was not until 1839 that the endowment remaining, now reduced to a total of £10,000, could be applied to educational purposes. The Irish master of chancery, a Mr Townsend, drew up a scheme for a school in 1842. Leamy, in his will, made no distinction between poor children on the grounds of religion. Townsend recognised that the majority of the poorer children were Catholic, but found himself bound by the court of chancery in England to ensure that in religion instruction the bible was read 'without note or comment'. This requirement was objected to by the Catholic clergy. Hence, when the school opened at Hartstonge Street in 1844 it faced immediate difficulties. It was well attended by Protestant children, but the number of

Catholics did not exceed twenty-five. In 1865 the school closed for some years. In 1874 a modified scheme was introduced, but the number of Catholics remained few. By the 1880s, despite the preponderance of the poor children being Catholic, Leamy's was a school providing intermediate education almost entirely for the children of affluent Protestants. In 1885, as a consequence, Bishop Butler forbade Catholic children to attend.[2]

There appears to have been much criticism in Limerick as to how public funds were being used in Leamy's School. The new bishop, with his concern for justice and for education, decided to intervene personally to secure the benefits of the endowment for the children of the Catholic poor. He expressed the belief that Leamy had died a Catholic and, therefore, could be presumed to have been particularly concerned that poorer Catholic children should have the benefit of his estate. He appealed to the Educational Endowments Ireland Commission, which had been set up in 1885 and was empowered to deal with endowments deemed to be non-denominational in nature. The Leamy, Roxborough, and Mungret endowments came under this heading, and, as all were contested, all were examined by the Commission. The Commission was chaired by Lord Justice Fitzgibbon, with Lord Justice Nash as the other judicial commissioner. The commissioners were aided by three assistant commissioners: Revd Dr Gerald Molloy, Dr Anthony Traill, Trinity College, Dublin, and a Professor Dougherty, MA. The final decisions, however, rested with the two commissioners. The Commission held its first session in Limerick in 1887.

The protagonists were, Bishop Edward Thomas O'Dwyer, on one side, and on the other, the Revd Mr Bunbury, Church of Ireland dean of Limerick and chairman of the current board of governors of Leamy's School. He also acted as spokesman for the Non-Conformists, which included Presbyterians, Wesleyans, Congregationalists and Methodists. The Protestant argument focussed on the second part of Leamy's instruction. They realised that if the emphasis were placed on the 'education of the poor in Ireland, principally those in and about Limerick city', they would be placed at a disadvantage as their children were outnumbered among the poor by about twenty to one. Hence, they emphasised that Leamy was a Protestant, who entrusted his wishes to Protestant executors and left it to them to give his bequest 'the most extensive efficacy'. These instructions, Bunbury argued, could be interpreted to include the provision of education at a higher level than primary education, which, in Limerick, was otherwise catered for by the non-denominational Model School – if the Catholics wished to avail of it.[3] A sharper edge was added to the Protestant case by an English clergyman of the Congregational church, the Revd Walter Baxdale. His children were attending Leamy's School, and, as there was, he declared in October 1887, 'a great want of middle-class and intermediate education in the area', his children and others like them would be left with nothing if Leamy's were closed.[4] Continuing his evidence on 26 October 1889, he described Dr O'Dwyer as 'a cantankerous individual', and criticised the Commission and Catholics for the 'perversion of public funds' in permitting Mungret College to fall into the possession of a private Catholic body, the Jesuits.[5] He would wish to send his children to university in the area, but the only university college was at Mungret, in Jesuit hands. He then moved from the particular to the general, pretending that Mungret was open to all Catholic students, and so he argued: 'The Roman Catholics have a larger thing in Mungret than we have, and they should let our ewe lamb alone'. In effect, let the Catholics have Mungret, the Protestants Leamy's.[6] It was a clever, disingenuous argument. He suspected, as his evidence indicates, that there were splits among the Catholics as there were among the Protestants.

Dr O'Dwyer, for his part, continued to devote his ability and some of his endless energy to building up facts and figures to convey the needs of Catholic children. Comparisons were provided between Dublin, Cork and Limerick that demonstrated that in terms of the percentage of poverty in each city, Limerick had a 19 percentage compared to about 7 percentage in Dublin and Cork. In terms of educational provision in Limerick, the bishop demonstrated that over 5,000 Catholic pupils, the greater part of them poor, were enrolled in schools run by religious sisters and the Christian Brothers, schools receiving no state assistance.[7] He then outlined to the Commission, in characteristic style, the contrasts between the Protestant and Catholic populations in Limerick in terms of their social position and their attitudes to education.

> You have in Limerick a Protestant body about 5,000 strong, including all the landed gentry, like Lord Clarina and Lord Monteagle and Lord Limerick, and all the great wealthy merchants and the principal shopkeepers of the town, so that practically you have the wealth of Limerick in the hands of the Protestants. And you have 35, 000 Catholics who range through every grade,from what you call the upper middle class down to the very poorest of the poor. You have but this one endowment of a neutral character in the whole city to deal with, and these 5,000 wealthy gentlemen come to you and say – 'Give us that for ourselves, we want it for this, or we want it for that, we are badly off in that way.' And you say – 'What about the 35,000 Catholics?' 'Oh, they have the National Board or the Intermediate Examinations, and one thing and another.' But have not the Protestants the same State and in every way? Are we not on all fours with regard to any aid from the State? And furthermore, you have seen the educational establishments now in Limerick. Did you ever see in Limerick an educational establishment built by Protestant money?

Then, continuing the comparison, he pointed to the Christian Brothers' and religious sisters' schools that had been built, and added: 'Within the last twenty-five years the poor Catholics of Limerick have spent £40,000 to £50,000 on educational establishments for the education of their children; there is not a single school standing in Limerick, at this moment, in which the Protestants of Limerick have put a £5 note.'[8]

O'Dwyer was determined that he would not be faced with a solution on undenominational lines. 'I will never allow the Catholics of Limerick, while I am bishop, to attend a mixed school', he told the Commission on 10 October 1887.[9] Knowing, however, that there was no chance of obtaining a purely Catholic school as matters stood, he aimed to bring about a division of the spoils by presenting a very powerful case for the children of the Catholic poor and by weakening his opponents' case as much as possible. An opportunity to effect this last was presented by Revd Bunbury in his evidence to the Commission on 26 October 1889. He expressed the opinion that one of the reasons for the failure of Leamy's School was because 'it is a godless institution – there is no religious education'. But when Lord Justice Fitzgibbon pointed to the waste of educational resources, to the fact that the Protestant population provided only 100 children in Leamy's School, which could hold 400, Bunbury agreed that the school should remain non-denominational.[10] 'One day have it undenominational', O'Dwyer taunted, 'another day have it denominational, for the simple and sole purpose, it is obvious, of securing the endowment for the party which the Dean represents. But if ever it is true, it is true here that a minister of religion cannot serve God and Mammon.'[11]

The eventual solution took place in April 1894, largely to O'Dwyer's satisfaction. Leamy's current assets were calculated at £6,000 invested in securities, and the school buildings at £2,000. The Protestant side received a quarter of the total, that is, £2,000; the Catholics obtained the school buildings and the remainder of the money. Twelve days later, on 25 April, the first meeting of the Leamy's Catholic Board of Education was held under the chairmanship of Bishop O'Dwyer. Thereafter, he attended every monthly meeting, except for three, up to the year he died. He devoted enthusiasm and time to the school and brought the numbers up to 600 pupils within a year. The premises were improved, pupils were encouraged to take up science, arts, and practical subjects, and to enter the trades, and his relations with the teachers were marked by respect and an effort to promote both efficiency and contentment. Inspectors' reports were uniformly complimentary during his years as chairman.[12]

The bishop's efforts before the Commission and in the press coincided for a number of years with the other public issues in which he was involved in relation to the land struggle, the papal condemnation, and political developments. The Leamy's School dispute added to his reputation in the field of primary and intermediate education, and earned acknowledgement of his concern for the less well off in his city, and of his political skill and toughness in achieving his aims. In the case of the Roxborough School his political skill became a casualty to impatience, and to assertive emotional involvement.

ROXBOROUGH SCHOOL

The dispute over Leamy's School was largely a local issue. The Roxborough School controversy was reported in British and Irish papers, involved debates in the House of Commons, and implicated able parliamentarians like T.M. Healy and W.H. Lecky, the celebrated historian, as also the chief secretary for Ireland, Gerald Balfour, the lord lieutenant, Lord Cadogan, and the educational commissioners, Lords Justice Fitzgibbon and Naish, and, after the latter's death in 1889, Lord Justice O'Brien.

The main protagonists were James Fitzgerald Gregg, canon of St Patrick's cathedral, Dublin, and occupant of the Roxborough School, and Edward Thomas O'Dwyer, bishop of Limerick. The former proved a doughty and resilient opponent. The Leamy's dispute occasioned sharp disagreement between members of the Catholic and Protestant communities, but this was mild compared to the rancorous sectarian squabble associated with the Roxborough premises, in which the Revd Gregg was accused of fraud and proselytism. In the long-drawn-out contest from 1887 to 1897, in the early part of which he was under a variety of heavy pressures, Dr O'Dwyer manifested some of his least attractive characteristics: giving way to intemperate, hectoring language, and to blustering outbursts when not getting his way.

The history of the Roxborough School went back to Queen Elizabeth's efforts in the sixteenth century to promote the Protestant religion and the English language in Ireland by means of diocesan schools. In 1570 she decreed 'there shall be from henceforth a free school in every diocese'. The Limerick school came into being only in 1611 and little is known of its subsequent history. In 1812 it came under the Commissioners for Education, who arranged for the sale of the old schoolhouse and had a new one built on Roxborough Road. The school was founded as a free school, but successive headmasters in the nineteenth century collected fees from their small number of pupils and lived on the premises. Thus, out of taxes raised on the community at large, lodgings intended free of charge for poor children were used by the headmaster and his family and by the children of well-off Protestants, who paid so much to the headmaster.

In 1874, when the schoolmaster, the Revd Mr Hall, died, the Revd Gregg approached Mrs Hall with an offer of £20 to give him first option on the tenancy of the premises to which, in fact, she had no legal right apart from current occupancy. Out of religious sympathy and friendship she agreed. The recent disestablishment of the Church of Ireland had occasioned anxiety lest the buildings of the diocesan schools might fall into Catholic hands. Gregg sought validation of his occupancy through the Commissioners of Education. The secretary, Dr Kyle, appears to have encouraged him to occupy the buildings and to have assured him that his title would not be questioned by the Commissioners. Gregg occupied the buildings and set up a school for Protestant girls. His manner of running the school caused embarrassment to a number of Protestant clergymen, and laid him open to charges of proselytism by the Catholic community.[13]

Shortly after O'Dwyer became bishop, he determined to deprive Gregg of his entitlement to the Roxborough School. The sittings of the Educational Commissioners in Limerick between 1887 and 1890 gave him the opportunity to bring forward charges against the occupant of the school. The charges were mainly four:

1. Gregg gained possession of the school by means of 'an underhand and discreditable transaction'.[14]
2. The school was built with public money, raised by the Grand Juries of Limerick county and city, and should not be in the hands of a private individual.
3. Gregg was practically a free tenant, paying no rent and expending little on the upkeep of the building.
4. Gregg's school was a proselytising institution, 'a standing insult to the Catholics of Limerick'.[15]

Gregg in reply declared:

1. He did not gain possession by underhand means; every step he took was 'in strict honesty and openness'.[16]
2. Even if the school were built with public money, so too was Mungret College now under the control of the Jesuits. Why victimise him, and not them?
3. He paid £20 a year to the Commissioners in rent, and, moreover, he had spent large sums to keep the buildings habitable.
4. His pupils were educated in strict accord with the Protestant faith, but it was not a proselytising school. He did take a special interest, however, in educating the children of mixed marriages 'as it was necessary to protect them in this city'.[17]

Roxborough School was a primary school offering free education, even free clothes and food, to young girls mostly from Protestant families, and from mixed marriages, and to girls who were illegitimate. The establishment appears to have been well run, and Gregg admitted that he sought to preserve the property for the Limerick Protestant community. Lord Justice Fitzgibbon, to the bishop's annoyance, exonerated him from the charge of fraudulence. O'Dwyer protested vigorously that Gregg having been advised to take possession through Mr Kyle of the Commission, then went to Mrs Hall, paid £20 for possession, and then wrote 'an innocent letter' to Mr Kyle, who then wrote 'an innocent letter' to Mr Gregg as if he had heard of him for the first time. 'I affirm that this was an underhand and discreditable transaction', O'Dwyer continued, 'and I say possession taken in such a way establishes no moral right whatever, and entitles the man who has it to no consideration at the hands of such a Commission as this.'[18]

This argument, which the bishop continued up to the end of the dispute, was one of a number that backfired on him. In the final year of the controversy, one of the assistant commissioners, Dr Anthony Traill, of Trinity College, drew attention in the *Irish Times*, 20 March 1897, to the fact that Dr O'Dwyer must have known that Mrs Hall had first been approached by a Roman Catholic magistrate, Mr Ambrose Hall, for the sale of her interest and possession of the premises and that she had agreed to a purchase price of £100, but subsequently, out of conscience, obtained permission from Mr Hall to be released from her bargain and took £20 from Mr Gregg instead. If the building had been obtained by a Roman Catholic, Traill asked, 'would the bishop have raised this outcry?' He went on to reverse the kind of argument O'Dwyer had used against John Dillon and some other members of the Irish party.

> Bishop O'Dwyer seems to me to have got Canon Gregg and proselytising on the brain, and if his views are allowed to predominate, the case will become one of persecution, pure and simple, and it will afford a good object lesson in advance of what Protestants may expect, in the south of Ireland, at least, from a Home Rule parliament under the thumb of the Roman Catholic hierarchy.[19]

The question of proselytising was a very live one for O'Dwyer. Grounds for it were indirectly acknowledged by Gregg when he admitted to the Commission that he specialised in the education of illegitimate children and the children of mixed marriages.[20] He expressed himself unsure as to how many children in his school had been Catholic before they came to his school. Gregg's practices, as indicated earlier, were an embarrassment to Dean Bunbury and many other Protestant clergy. O'Dwyer knew this, and tried to isolate Gregg from his *confrères*, but he over did it and, instead, united them behind him. Thus, Dean Bunbury went so far as to say 'candidly' that both Protestants and Catholics 'look upon the children of mixed marriages as fair game'. 'I think it is a common sense view of it', he added, 'and I really do not think that this institution of Canon Gregg is such a terrible thing after all.'[21] To O'Dwyer, such an attitude on the part of Protestants promoted 'a slave market in Catholic souls'; [22] and when Dr Traill pointedly queried if there was not proselytism on both sides, his lordship replied heatedly – 'I don't admit that, and I don't understand your object in putting such a question to me.' To which, Traill responded smoothly: 'Well, I am sorry if I have annoyed your lordship.'[23]

Hours of the Commissioners' time were spent on the proselytising issue, and also on the easy financial terms under which Gregg occupied the school. Gregg emphasised that he had spent a good deal of his own money on the upkeep of the building, hoping that this would encourage the Commissioners to grant him a right of pre-emption in their scheme of settlement. The bishop was determined to prevent this and gave vent to his determination and anger in a dismissive manner.

> We have no objection to pay Canon Gregg fairly for any outlay he has made, and let him take his money elsewhere, and have a Ragged School in one of the back lanes, where he had it before, but we object to public money being used by him in this school. Pay him liberally. I would subscribe out of my own pocket to get rid of him.[24]

The Commisioners and Assistant Commissioners became divided on the issues of proselytism and the use of public money. On this last, Limerick corporation began to side with Dr O'Dwyer and to claim that the school belonged to the people of Limerick. Gregg, and prominent members of the Protestant community, on the other hand, persisted in pointing to the use of public money in the Catholic interest in the case of Mungret College.

Eventually, after the case had gone before the privy council, it was ruled that Gregg had a pre-emptive right valued at £831, and this was placed before the House of Commons as part of the settlement. By now, this small school of 71 pupils had become a *cause célèbre*. In the House, T.M. Healy, MP, a friend of O'Dwyer, successfully presented his case in the early hours of the morning of 20 May 1895, with the reputed connivance of John Morley, chief secretary for Ireland. In consultation, presumably, with the bishop, he went so far as to persuade the House to excise the pre-emption clause from the scheme, without substituting any compensation clause in favour of Gregg. Thus, the affair appeared to have ended completely in O'Dwyer's favour. All that was required was the signature of the lord lieutenant. But he delayed in signing his approval. Meanwhile, the government fell in June 1895, and a Conservative government was returned in July. This led to a reconsideration of the matter.[25] A key figure in arguing against the original decision was a new member of parliament, William E.H. Lecky, of Trinity College, who had won wide acclaim, between 1878 and 1890, for his eight-volume *History of England in the eighteenth century*, and his subsequent *History of Ireland in the eighteenth century*.

O'Dwyer, upset by the delay and the prospect of a change in the decision, pressed his case with the lord lieutenant and the Conservative chief secretary, Gerald Balfour. The latter informed him that the government had referred the issue back to the Judicial Commissioners and that he would get an opportunity to press his case before the matter was finalised. In fact, the Commissioners gave no one a chance to remake their case. When this happened, the bishop, bitterly disappointed, accused Balfour, in February 1896, of having 'distinctly and deliberately' broken his pledged word and seriously deceived him.[26] Next, O'Dwyer turned his anger on the Commissioners, going over the case in detail, and issuing, on 2 March 1896, the futile threat: 'Before I am done with it, the parties in the Castle, who have attempted by underhand means to defeat the rights of the people of the City of Limerick under the action of the House of Commons, will be as well pleased that they had not soiled their hands with so nefarious a business.'[27] This letter and threat of 2 March, addressed to the secretary of the Commission, did not reach the Commission until 10 March. The bishop had first had it published in the *Freeman's Journal* of 3 March 1896. Not surprisingly, the Judicial Commissioners did not think it necessary to reply to the bishop's letter.[28] By November, Fr Flanagan of Adare, the bishop's firm supporter, was concerned for O'Dwyer 'because of all the labour and anxiety' he had gone through about the Roxborough School and because the bishop viewed an amendment to the decision as intrinsically unjust.[29]

On 9 March 1897, a motion proposed by Lecky, rectifying the injustice to Gregg by restoring to him the right of pre-emption, was passed in the House of Commons by a majority of nearly three to one.[30] O'Dwyer had appealed to him the previous day in the *Daily Independent* not to proceed with the motion. He argued in support of the deliberations and the scheme of the privy council, and urged Lecky not to be 'the mouthpiece of the very lowest of religious bigots in Ireland'. On 9 March, the day of his motion, Lecky assured the bishop by letter that he was tolerably well acquainted with all the relevant facts, and declared himself astonished that his lordship, 'in the face of the emphatic language in which the Judicial Commissioners of Education (two of the most competent judges in Ireland and one of them a fervent Catholic)' had 'recently protested against the extreme injustice of taking from Canon Gregg the pre-emption which 3 Privy Councils assigned him, without granting him the compensation which the Commissioners, after careful investigation, pronounced to be his due.'[31]

After the passage of the motion in the House of Commons, O'Dwyer continued to argue the case in the press, but met two formidable opponents in Lecky and Traill. In the *Daily Express*, 26 March 1897, Lecky concluded his interchange on the subject in a quietly devastating manner:

> These, Sir, he stated, are the 'inaccuracies' and 'misrepresentations' upon which Bishop O'Dwyer dilates. I shall certainly not follow him in importing into controversy such terms as 'fraud', 'falsehood', 'deliberate misrepresentation', 'dishonesty', 'low blackguards' which he profusely employs. In the case of a layman such language would appear vindictive, intemperate and singularly wanting in self-respect. Whether it is less becoming in a Roman Catholic bishop is not for me to say.[32]

Six days previously, Anthony Traill had been no less pointed in his letter, noted earlier, which demonstrated that there had been no outcry when Mrs Hall had agreed to sell the school, built out of public funds, to a Catholic individual.

Traill's letter undermined the charge of 'fraud' in obtaining possession that the bishop had persistently levelled against Gregg. O'Dwyer remained convinced, however, that the Gregg case was a great wrong, and that only one who got 'a glimpse behind the scenes of such transactions' could understand how 'utterly corrupt' was the government of the country.[33]

Canon Gregg remained in possession of the Roxborough Road School, and continued on much as before until his death in 1905, when the property passed to his daughter. O'Dwyer, who had come so near victory, bitterly resented his defeat, and still smarted in regard to it until the end of his life. Even in 1916, the year before his death, he was in correspondence with T.M. Healy about the possibility of challenging the currant occupant of the school.[34]

The issue of public money, which he had raised so frequently against the Protestant communities, had been turned around by them in relation to

Mungret College. They had as much right to benefit from the use of public money for the Protestant community, as the Jesuits at Mungret College had for the Catholic community! The position of Mungret weakened his lordship's case and sharpened his resentment against that institution.

12

The controversy between Dr O'Dwyer and Mungret College

The criticisms of the Limerick Protestants regarding the abuse of public money in relation to Mungret College were, however, far from being the sole grounds of Dr O'Dwyer's clash with the Jesuits at Mungret. An examination of the main extant sources[1] indicates that the bishop's differences with the Jesuits went back, at least, to his years as a curate, when, as noted in chapter two, he was leader of the critics of the Limerick Jesuits at the time of the 1868 election in the city, and later when, as headmaster of St Munchin's diocesan college at Hartstonge Street, Limerick, his school was closed and his pupils sent to Mungret College. To understand the clash with the Jesuits at Mungret it is necessary to return to that last event.

It will be recalled that Mungret College had failed as an agricultural school and had been taken over as part of the diocesan college by Fr Bourke, subject to certain specifications laid down for the original foundation. When Fr Bourke's venture failed, he retired, and the headmastership of the Hartstonge Street part of the college passed to Fr O'Dwyer. Meanwhile, Fr William Ronan, rector of the Jesuit community at the Crescent and director of an expanding Apostolic School there, was encouraged by the Bishop Butler to raise with Lord Emly, chairman of the board of Mungret College, the possibility of moving the Apostolic School to Mungret. On 29 December 1881, Ronan informed his provincial superior, Fr James Tuite, that the bishop expressed the wish 'that we should get Mungret College and should educate there our apostolics and his diocesan students'.[2] A fortnight later, he reported that Dr Butler said to him at his last interview 'that he could not hand over his students to us before midsummer as he had engaged Fr O'Dwyer to conduct the school (at the corner of Hartstonge Street and the Crescent) for a year, when he hoped to make other arrangements'. The bishop gave him to understand that the school at the corner house was 'not paying its expenses' and when its surviving students left at midsummer it would close down.[3]

Lord Emly, welcomed Ronan's proposal, and assured him that the lease requirements that the school must be non-denominational, must teach agricultural science, and must cater mainly for boys from Limerick city and county, were largely a formality and not a real obstacle. Agreements regarding the Limerick seminary students were exchanged between Bishop Butler and the

Jesuit general, Fr Pieter Beckx. Because of the stipulation in the original lease of the agricultural school that the college must cater for boys from the city and county of Limerick, it was understood that there would be some lay boys from there at the school. Again, because of the lease requirements, the college was advertised as a normal secondary college preparing young men of different religious denominations for various professions. At the same time, however, Ronan sent a copy of the prospectus to the clergy of the diocese with a note stating that the bishop wished to inform them that candidates for the secular priesthood must spend at least one year at Mungret College.

It is relevant to note that the Jesuit general took a particular interest in the Apostolic School. The Irish provincial and his consultors had opposed the movement to Mungret, mainly because the province was already over stretched. Ronan appealed to the general of the order. The latter, having made enquiries, instructed the province to accept the offer of the college.[4] When the provincial and his advisers were hesitant in carrying out his instructions, he reminded them of two considerations. First, that their founder, St Ignatius Loyola, held it of great importance that the Society carry out the wishes of the prelates of the Church. Consequently, as the bishop of Limerick wished them to undertake the work at Mungret as soon as possible, it was their duty to find out how that could be done 'most expeditiously'. In the second place, they should keep in mind that the need for Catholic education was greatest among 'the children of the poor' and should be pursued even if it meant some deflection from their 'accustomed way of acting'.[5] Furthermore, without consulting the provincial and his consultors, the general appointed Ronan rector of the new college.[6]

Because of the shortage of manpower, however, Ronan, in the early years, had to rely to a considerable extent on French Jesuits, who were available because some of their foreign missions were closed down because of war or persecution. A French Jesuit, Jean Baptiste Réné, was the first director of the apostolic students, Ronan taking charge of the seminarists. The college started well.

Bishop Butler, as noted in chapter three, did not inform O'Dwyer about his negotiations to transfer his seminary students to Mungret. It was only when arrangements were being made final that he was told. Thus, while he was head-master, the diocesan college was closed, and Mungret was the cause. To someone as able, ambitious, and sensitive of his position as O'Dwyer, the hurt and sense of slight must have been intense.

The success of Ronan's college at Mungret made additional building neces-sary. As friends of Lord Dunraven, Dr Butler and Lord Emly were left £2,500 in his lordship's will, which they decided to devote to additional buildings at the college if Ronan could supplement it with additional money for both school buildings and for a large chapel. They encouraged him to go on a fund-raising tour of North America. He set out in 1884, and in two years covered more than 20,000 miles and collected some £12,000. When he returned, in May 1886, the buildings were virtually complete. The following month, Edward Thomas O'Dwyer was consecrated bishop.

On the death of Bishop Butler, concern for the future was felt at Mungret. It seems to have been felt that there was opposition in the diocese to the seminary being run by the Jesuits. Réné indicated this in a letter to Lord Emly, on 3 February 1886, conveying the sad news of the bishop's death that day. 'You may well imagine', he added, 'in what state of consternation we feel ourselves now in Mungret deprived of the support of that devoted and holy apostolic bishop ... I have written to poor Fr Ronan.' 'We have now', he concluded, 'to abandon the future of Mungret, as concerns the seminary, to God. For in respect of the Apostolic School, whatever may be the new bishop, I think we are pretty safe.'[7]

Ronan responded to Réné from Portland, Maine, on 20 March 1886.

> In the spirit of faith I believe with you that God's representative in the diocese will not injure God's work. ... Fr Dwyer [*sic*] knows from his own experience the difficulties of working a seminary with secular priests and he would I think be the last man to do it. He was glad that we got Mungret, but he was hurt because Dr Butler told him nothing of the transfer of the seminary to us until it was accomplished.

'Besides', he added, 'a *contract* with all the conditions clearly laid down has been made regarding the diocesan students between Dr Butler and Fr General and is signed by both. There are two copies. One is in our safe, the other must be among the bishop's papers. Now as long as we keep to the conditions of the contract it will not be easy to break it up.'[8]

Within months of his return home, Ronan received an indication of a less sanguine future. Years later, he recalled that 'shortly after his consecration, Dr O'Dwyer called on me and asked ... for the conditions on which the seminary was given to us by his predecessor'. Ronan showed him a copy of the conditions. 'There were 2 copies', he explained, 'one signed by the General and given to Dr Butler, the other signed by Dr Butler and given to us. Dr O'Dwyer asked to have our copy to look over it.' 'I could never succeed in getting it from him', Ronan added. 'He insulted me the last time I asked for it.'[9] There soon emerged, also, signs that the bishop wished to determine the college's policy on student entry.

FIRST SIGNS OF DISAGREEMENT

Fr Réné went out of his way to please the new bishop. They had many discussions, and, as he later put it, Dr O'Dwyer gave him two years to come to a decision regarding the future of Mungret. The bishop viewed his own position as one which entitled him to exercise control over all Catholic education in his diocese. Where Mungret College was concerned, he asked Réné to put forward on his behalf to the provincial, and even to the general, three requirements. He put these in writing on 27 October 1887. They were:

1. The main work of Mungret College to be always the education of the students of the Apostolic School.
2. Students, other than apostolics, to a number not exceeding twenty at any time, may be taught at the college.
3. But none but apostolics may be received from the diocese of Limerick.

Although drawn up in October 1887, these formal requirements were not entrusted to Réné until early January 1888. He forwarded them, with a covering letter, to the provincial, Thomas Browne, on 7 January.[10] In retrospect, it seems evident, as indicated already, that Dr O'Dwyer, with the withdrawal of his seminarians and the reestablishment of St Munchin's College in mind, sought to limit Mungret to the Apostolic School and to remove rivalry to a revived diocesan institution.

On 11 January, Réné, whose interest almost exclusively was in the Apostolic School, assured the provincial that he need not be worried about the second clause in Dr O'Dwyer's requirements, because it 'means simply one thing in the mind of the bishop', namely, 'as he declared expressly to me, viz. that the number of students other than apostolics must never be so large as to prevent the main work of Mungret College from being always the education of students of the Apostolic School. Provided the first clause be carried out into practice by our Society in a 'bona fide' way ... his lordship does not care at all about the second clause.'[11] After writing this letter, Réné contacted Fr Robert Fulton, an official representative of the general then visiting the Irish province, about the second clause. It had occurred to him that, as it stood, it might exclude young Jesuit students, whom superiors might wish to send to Mungret for the completion of their classical or philosophical studies. Fulton wrote to him that he approved of the clause if it did not exclude young Jesuits. Réné then went to Galway on retreat, and thence, on 13 January, acquainted Dr O'Dwyer of Fulton's views.[12] His lordship declared himself happy to accept the proposed arrangement. Meantime, on 12 January, the provincial had replied to Réné, addressing his letter, most probably, to Mungret. Réné, unfortunately for future relations, had not received his reply before writing to the bishop the next day. Fr Browne replied cogently to Réné's comments.

> If, as you say, 'his lordship does not care at all about the second clause', he shall not object to having it expunged. As it stands it would effectually shut the doors *in aeternum* against student no. 21 ... *I shall not approve of, or consent, to any guarantee in which this clause is found.*

'You advert, of course,' the provincial added, 'to the fact that we cannot go against the government scheme, one of the articles of which prescribes that we shall admit Protestant or Catholic boys.'[13] The conflicting messages sent to the bishop gave him grounds for feeling that he was not being dealt with in 'a *bona fide*' manner.

There was a further complication, this time arising from the sitting in Limerick of the Educational Endowments Commission in October 1887. Before the Commission, the trustees of Mungret College, with the approval of the Jesuits, sought a change in the trust governing the college that was unwelcome to Dr O'Dwyer. The change was felt to be necessary because the college, under the terms of the act of parliament establishing it, was meant to be, as noted previously, non-denominational, and was to teach agricultural science and to enter its students for the Intermediate examinations, whereas under the Jesuits it was effectively a Catholic college, teaching little agricultural science, and entering its students for the Royal University examinations. Legal advice made it clear that the Society of Jesus was vulnerable to challenge as regards its lease, and that it was advisable to seek from the Commission a settlement which would give the members of the order undisturbed possession. The Commission sought to determine the price of the public interest in the property, while taking account of the more than £12,000 already put into the property by the Jesuits. They required the order to pay £2,500, to which would be added £2,000 in the keeping of the trustees from the original endowment, the full sum to go towards agricultural and technical education in Limerick. Although the arrangement did not receive the formal confirmation of the lord lieutenant until 1892, it was clear to the bishop from the beginning that what was being sought, in effect, was a virtually independent Catholic college in the diocese of Limerick, which would benefit from the privileged exemptions enjoyed by the Jesuit order in those years. Bishop O'Dwyer, therefore, it would appear, turned in a new direction to ensure his control.

On 28 January 1888, a disappointed Réné reported to the Irish provincial: 'You need not trouble yourself any more, I am sorry to say, about the agreement proposal by the bishop. His lordship has rejected altogether the scheme proposed by the trustees with our approval and is thinking of a new settlement. I told his lordship that my opinion on the matter had no value until sanctioned by my superiors in the Society.'[14] What Dr O'Dwyer had in mind in terms of 'a new settlement' was suggested in a letter to him from Revd Dr Gerald Molloy, one of the Assistant Commissioners of the Educational Commission, who wrote from St Moritz, Switzerland, on 21 January 1888, in response to a letter from O'Dwyer that had just reached him. He entirely agreed with his lordship, he stated, 'that all the undenominational endowments with which we deal in Limerick should be distributed between Protestants and Catholics according to their numbers and educational wants' and, he added, 'I will endeavour to get this principle adopted by the Commission'. He then continued, with more direct reference to Mungret:

> You speak of the possibility of getting an act of parliament to incorporate a small body to take charge of Catholic educational endowments in the diocese of Limerick. It is quite in the power of the Commission to incorporate such a body; and I think I may say the Commission will be

quite ready to incorporate a body that will be satisfactory to your lordship. This may be done either in connection with Mungret and Leamy endowments, or it may be done independently as may be found most convenient.

In conclusion, he observed that on his return, when Dr O'Dwyer was in Dublin, he could explain everything more fully, 'and there would be no difficulty in fixing a day on which you could meet the Commission and confer with them about the incorporation of a Catholic educational body for your diocese. I dare say it will be also considered desirable to hold a further inquiry into the question of the Mungret endowment, at which your lordship and other parties interested may be able to supplement the evidence we have already received on the subject.'[15]

Nothing further, however, seems to have come of this interchange. Other events in close succession filled the horizon, seriously threatened the future of Mungret College, and occupied the attention of his lordship.

Already in September 1887, William Ronan had left Limerick for Dublin, and, a straw in the wind, some seminarians were sent on to Maynooth without completing their course at Mungret. Two months later, at a synod of priests, Bishop O'Dwyer announced that he had decided to withdraw the remainder of his students from Mungret and to reopen St Munchin's College, after Christmas, in the former residence of the earl of Limerick at Henry Street. The reasons that he gave to his surprised priests were that he wished to have his seminarians under his personal supervision and wanted them to participate in the life of the cathedral, in keeping with the thinking of the Council of Trent. At the same time, he was careful to let it be known publicly that his decision was in no way a reflection on the Jesuits, who had done their duty 'conscientiously and efficiently'.[16]

In July 1888, Réné, and two other French Jesuits, Aubier and Daniel, were recalled by their provincial. In the autumn, the remainder of the French Jesuits, and the seminarians, left the college. The seminarians had been fully fee-paying. The college buildings were completed in the autumn as the seminarians left. The premises were now capable of catering for 100 pupils but had only 45 apostolics. The financial blow to Mungret was immense. It looked as if once again the college would prove a failure.

The college, however, as noted, had originally advertised as a school for lay boys, in accordance with its lease, and it always had had some lay pupils, neither seminarists nor apostolics, including a nephew of the former bishop. Now, the new rector, Fr Thomas Head, advertised for lay pupils, and the lay school opened in September 1888. The following year, at the Educational Endowments Commission, he was able to announce that 'We have 35 lay boys and are confident that we should have 50 or 60 next year, the numbers are increasing rapidly.'[17] Thus, the withdrawal of the seminarians had led to what Dr O'Dwyer had feared, a greater number of lay students than of apostolics.

A further irony in the situation was that his lordship could not complain about this because the new rector was an old friend and capable of speaking up to him and reminding him that the difficulties he, Head, was trying to cope with it were due to his lordship. Head's appointment was both appropriate and adroit. He managed well, and he was a Limerick man, with numerous links with people in the city and the county. He had been a curate in the diocese for fourteen years, serving in Cratloe, Croom, and St John's parish, Limerick. He had been at school with Edward Thomas O'Dwyer, was senior to him in ordination by two years,[18] and they had made their first visit to Rome together. Their friendship and shared background, and Head's readiness to speak frankly to the bishop, something the latter claimed to appreciate, made a major contribution to good relations between Dr O'Dwyer and the Jesuits. Head was rector at Mungret from 1888 until July 1891, when he was made rector at the Crescent, Limerick. He had guided the college through a critical phase. The year after his departure, the order acquired outright ownership of the college. The new rector, Fr Vincent Byrne, however, was not the best choice in that new situation. He was, perhaps, too much like the bishop in temperament to establish an easy rapport with him. Tension returned to the relationship.

It grew in a climate of expanding rivalry between schools, a rivalry fostered by the prevailing system of payment by results. A school's reputation might be made or marred by results. In Limerick city, three schools vied for the same limited Catholic middle-class population, St Munchin's and the two Jesuit schools, the Crescent and Mungret. The bishop had spent a great deal of money expanding St Munchin's, was concerned for its future, wished it to excel, and to ensure this had placed the very able Fr Andrew Murphy as its headmaster. He was upset by the many lay students attending Mungret, and lost to St Munchin's, despite the assurances he had had from Fr Réné and from the general's representative, Fr Fulton. 'He determined to solve the problem by a two-pronged initiative: by advertising St Munchin's more effectively, and by appealing more vigorously to the Jesuit general to restrict numbers at Mungret.'

A new aggressive promotion of St Munchin's took the form of a large advertisement in the *Munster News* during 1897. The college at this stage had three divisions: a day school which prepared boys for the Intermediate examinations, for the Royal University, and for various professions; a boarding school for lay boys under 15 years of age, and a seminary for ecclesiastical students. The *Munster News* in August 1897 reminded parents of the 'many advantages of having their sons prepared for the Matriculation and First Arts examinations of the Royal University, at a nominal cost, and without withdrawing them from the influence of their homes'. The Crescent, however, also found mention in the *Munster News*, while Mungret advertised in a quieter way,[19] as most of its students came from outside Limerick.

Dr O'Dwyer's renewed negotiations about Mungret had been going on from at least the beginning of 1896, and probably from the previous year. He had raised the matter with Vincent Byrne, and then verbally with the provincial, Fr Patrick Kenny, but without success. By March 1896 he had become thoroughly disillusioned with the whole body of Jesuits, and gave vent to his animus in a remarkable communication to Archbishop Walsh on 2 March. The immediate occasion was a public letter by Dr Walsh critical of two articles by William Magennis in the *New Ireland Review*, which had expressed disagreement with the idea of a Catholic college in the University of Dublin, the archbishop's preferred solution to the university question. As Magennis was on the teaching staff of University College Dublin, under Jesuit management, and the editor of the magazine was a very well-known Jesuit professor, Fr Tom Finlay, the archbishop detected an ulterior Jesuit purpose at work, namely, to obtain the solution of the university question by an ample endowment of University College, removed to a new site and fully independent of the bishops. In the event, there was no plot on the part of Magennis or the Jesuits, though a temporary mutual misunderstanding had arisen between Dr Delany, the president of the college, and the archbishop.[20]

Dr O'Dwyer, having read his grace's letter, wrote approvingly:

> Your letter today seems to me one of the best you have written, and to go just far enough to discredit the *N. I. Review* without committing us to anything. Certainly they are a mischievous and selfish lot who are at the bottom of the whole thing. But you see that is the policy of the Jesuit body everywhere. They seem to postpone every interest of religion and duty of ecclesiastical propriety to their own ends and interests.

He went on: 'Manning and Wiseman had that experience in Westminister, Vaughan in Salford, and here now you have the body that one would think would put their power, and influence at the disposal of the bishops, systematically undermining us.'[21] Walsh knew his volatile correspondent too well to take him literally, and could not but be aware of the historical difference in relationship between Irish bishops and Irish Jesuits, marked by good will and mutual support, and that of the English clergy and English Jesuits, which had been bedevilled by instances of difference and criticism going back to the sixteenth century and the continental seminary colleges run by the English Jesuits.

Dr O'Dwyer's concerns evidently reached the Jesuit general, Fr Louis Martin, during 1896. He sought clarification from the provincial regarding the original entry policy of Mungret College and the promises said to have been made to the bishop by Frs René and Fulton. The provincial turned to Fr Ronan then in France for his views. Ronan responded on 12 September 1896, taking in turn the issues raised for the general by Dr O'Dwyer.

> 1. The conditions on which Mungret College was made a diocesan seminary were settled by the late Bishop and our Fr General Beckx. The Bishop asked us to make the college his seminary and to prepare students

to take degrees in philosophy in the Royal University; so that they should
enter Maynooth for their theology; those who did not take degrees were
to be sent out to some of the foreign colleges. The Bishop said, of his own
free will, that all students of his diocese should pass through Mungret
College before they went to their theology; *he made no stipulation that lay
boys should not be received and prescribed no limits*; nor was any promise made
to the present Bishop by me or any superior except Fr Réné. Whether he
made a promise or not is of little consequence as he had no authority. He
worked very hard to get into Dr O'Dwyer's good graces and he might
have said something of what was imputed.

    2. There was no contract (with the present Bishop) as the Bishop did
nothing for us, but was hostile to us.

    3. The Bishop, Dr Butler, gave the seminary to us and enabled us to
build the chapel for the proper training of the students. On the faith of his
promise we expended £12 or 14,000 on building. When Dr O'Dwyer
took the seminary from us I told him this; I asked our people to lay the
case before Propaganda but they would not fight. Excuse haste.[22]

The bishop had not received a satisfactory answer by the summer of 1898. This
circumstance, joined to a blunder by Fr Byrne of Mungret College, which his
lordship chose to take in a personal manner, brought the strained relations
between the bishop and the Jesuits in Mungret to a new intensity. The 'blunder'
was the failure of the Jesuits at Mungret to attend a diocesan synod meeting on
13 June 1898. It was only on the day before, according to Fr Byrne, that he had
received notification to attend the synod. That evening he supplied, as requested,
a list of the names of the Mungret community to the bishop's secretary,
Fr Andrew Murphy, but did no more. A tradition had grown, it was stated, which
exempted the community from attending diocesan synods and meetings;[23]
though this was not the way in Ronan's time as rector.[24] When no Mungret
Jesuit turned up at the June 1898 synod, Dr O'Dwyer is reported to have
adverted pointedly: 'One college, Mungret, has not sent even one representative.
This is improper, insulting to myself personally, against canon law and the
custom of the diocese and I will not tolerate it.'[25] Vincent Byrne, with suitable
apologies, explained what had happened, but his lordship was not appeased.

    On 14 September 1898, Dr O'Dwyer wrote formally to the Jesuit provincial,
Fr Patrick Kenny, in the course of which he stated that he had sent word a
number of times, and had once spoken verbally on the matter to the provincial,
but had received no reply. Fr Kenny, in fact, was no longer provincial. Fr Patrick
Keating had been in the position for some time. 'My complaint is', the bishop
stated clearly, 'that Mungret College, having been formed by the alms of the
faithful as an Apostolic College, has largely been transformed into an ordinary
lay college for paying students, who, in number, largely predominate over the
ecclesiastics. Whether you have the privilege of opening such a college in a
diocese against the will of the Bishop I do not know, but I am sure you will not

allow that at any rate such a thing should be done in violation of a distinct agreement with a bishop.' He then moved to the kernel of his argument:

> Fr Réné when rector asked my assent to his taking some lay boarders to supplement the ecclesiastics, and, as an inducement to me to assent, when doing so stipulated that he should not take more than 20 lay boarders, none of whom were to be from this diocese. Fr Fulton, the Visitor from the General, sanctioned this agreement and on those terms I agreed to his taking some ordinary paying boarders. You know that this agreement has been broken and I now appeal to you to restore it. In doing so I am confident you will act in the spirit of the benefactors who endowed the Apostolic College, but had no intention of founding an ordinary boarding school in my diocese and interfering with my diocesan college in supplying priests to the home mission.[26]

As is evident, the bishop's presentation differed considerably from that of Réné and Ronan already outlined. Fr Keating's reply on 17 September contained, unfortunately, a number of inaccuracies that exacerbated an already tense situation.[27] He had been on the Australian mission for a number of years, which may partly explain the mistakes. He claimed that the Jesuits had taken over Mungret and its debts at Bishop Butler's request, and had opened it as a college with his full approval both for apostolics and lay students. As to Réné's promises and the approval given by Fr Fulton, Keating stated he could find no account of them anywhere and, besides, Réné had no right to make promises as he was not superior of the house. In fact, although the Jesuits had bought some of the furniture that Fr Bourke had in the diocesan college at Mungret, they did not take over the college and its debts from the bishop. The place was vacant for a year, before Ronan approached Dr Butler. The college was not formally opened for apostolics and lay students. Ronan, because of the nature of the lease, announced the college as for 'boys without religious distinction, but inhabitants of the city and county of Limerick', but, as indicated earlier, in a prospectus sent to the clergy he explained that 'By the express desire of our venerable Bishop I have made no allusion to the diocesan seminary, in order to save the Trustees from all embarrassment. However, I am directed by his lordship to inform your Reverence that the candidates for the secular priesthood of the diocese must spend at least one year in Mungret College.'[28] Again, Keating was at fault with respect to Réné, who *had been superior* of the house. In the remainder of his letter, the provincial emphasised that while he would be happy to run Mungret without lay boys, the college could not now survive without them because his lordship had taken away the seminarians for which the college had been extended. Of lay boys, besides, the rector had informed him that he never had more than ten from Limerick, and that they would have gone to Rockwell or Castleknock if they had not come to Mungret, and as for the other lay boarders, he could not see how they could be said to interfere with the interests of the Limerick diocese.

Dr O'Dwyer replied on 19 September, latching on to Keating's mistakes and adding some of his own. He pointed out that the Jesuits did not take over directly from Fr Bourke, nor take over debts, and that Fr Réné was superior. He then claimed that at no time was Mungret a diocesan seminary. Fr Bourke was headmaster under a board of trustees, bound to conduct the college as an agricultural school, and the only connection with the diocese was that Dr Butler, for his own convenience, sent his students there for one year to study classics. 'At that time Fr Ronan was carrying on his Apostolic School at the Crescent. He got into communication with Lord Emly, who was one of the trustees of Mungret, persuaded him that it would be a good thing to get it for the Apostolic School and finally got it for this purpose.' The bishop pointedly made no reference to his predecessor's involvement in the process. Instead, he added: 'Then, Dr Butler said to me that he did not wish to have his ecclesiastical students at a mere day school, such as mine, and he arranged to send them, and them only, to Mungret the next year. But, as far as I know, he never gave your body leave to open a general boarding school in the diocese nor did the trustees of Mungret ever contemplate such a thing ...' As to Keating's response regarding Réné's agreement and the approval of it by the Visitor from the General, the bishop declared himself astonished. 'Fr Réné at the time', he observed, 'was supposed to be the superior of the house, and if your view is right, both he and Fr Fulton were guilty of deception. Whether your General will now take the same view I rather doubt, but I would ask you in the first instance, if you do not accede to the request I made in my last letter, to submit the correspondence to him.'[29]

At this, Keating did what he should have done much earlier. He contacted those who had connections with the college in its early years. Fr Fulton was dead, but Fr Réné wrote from Alaska and Ronan from France. Réné's and Ronan's accounts were as given earlier. Fr William Sutton reported on 20 September 1898 that he had been at Mungret from the start in 1882 to 1884 and again from 1887 to 1890. 'There was no restriction at all about taking anyone. In fact, we had to take all who applied, the preference to be given to natives of the County of Limerick.' 'I remember in the autumn, I think it was 1887,' Sutton continued, 'Monsignor Persico and Dr O'Dwyer came to visit us at Mungret. Mons. Persico delivered a discourse to the community and boys in which he insisted very emphatically on the important duty we had in training the future priests of the diocese of Limerick, since Mungret was the diocesan seminary.' 'I could not swear Dr O'Dwyer was present,' Sutton added, 'I can that Monsignor Persico spoke to us as having charge of the diocesan seminary.'[30] Fr Charles McKenna, also in the first community, testified that Dr Butler wished it to be his seminary and 'a general school, no limitations. His own nephew was there'.[31] A key witness, however, was Thomas Head, who was not only one of those who started with the school but, as noted, was an old friend of Edward Thomas O'Dwyer. His letter to the provincial on 23 September 1898 stated firmly: *'With regard to Dr Butler's sanction for the lay school, there is not the slightest doubt about it. Indeed, I never heard Dr O'Dwyer's throwing doubt about it before. We had lay boys from the very first year, and among them Dr Butler's own nephew.* Dr Butler had, I believe, a principal part in getting Lord Emly and through him the other trustees to get this Act (of parliament) passed in order that the college might be given to Fr Bourke. He certainly knew all about it. By virtue of this Act … we were bound to carry on an Intermediate school properly so called and to which boys of all religions should be admitted, Limerick boys having preference. It is quite clear, therefore, we were bound to carry on a lay school just as Fr Bourke had done before us. Surely this is very different from Dr O'Dwyer's assertion that the trustees only required us to teach agriculture. Dr Butler knew all.' Head added an interesting personal note:

> Shortly after I became rector (in 1888) he (the bishop) complained to Fr McKenna about our not carrying out Fr Réné's promise. *I wrote to him at once an explanation of our obligations* (under our lease). He wrote no answer, but a few weeks after he said the reason he did not was that he *could not answer my arguments. He did not,* I think, renew the matter *till after we had bought out Mungret*, which was at least six years after the promise.

'During the three years I was rector', Head continued, 'he never once complained to me that I was violating any contract though he must have known that I was taking as many lay boys and Limerick boys as I could get. This indeed was a public fact and he met me frequently during the time and we were intimate friends at the time.' Then, warning the provincial, whose persistence, perhaps, he doubted, Head reminded him with respect to his lordship: 'It is the experience of all who have to deal with him that it is folly to yield unless there is real necessity. The more one yields the more he tramples on his rights, at least the more he tries to extend his own authority.'[32]

Fr Vincent Byrne, who succeeded Head as rector in 1891 and continued until 1900, pointed out that at the Educational Endowments Commission Fr Head had publicly testified that the number of lay boarders exceeded that of the apostolic students, that there were 54 out of a total of 96. This was given in the bishop's hearing, Byrne declared, two years after the alleged understanding with Réné. Why did his lordship not protest or take exception then? Nothing was said until seven years after Réné's departure from Ireland. Byrne was determined not to be dominated by Dr O'Dwyer, whom he distrusted as much as the bishop distrusted him. He feared that Keating might yield. On 11 September he warned him: 'I do not doubt his lordship's hostility or his eagerness to strike if he can find a vulnerable point in our armour … His game at present is a game of bluff. He strove to intimidate Fr Head when rector. He strove to intimidate me. He now strives to intimidate your Reverence.'[33] On 21 September, Byrne insisted that all the evidence of the Jesuits involved in Mungret supported his interpretation of events.[34] Two days later, he wrote again. He was clearly concerned about his provincial's resoluteness. 'His lordship's memory is at fault and many of his assertions are incorrect … I implore you to stand firm and not allow his lordship to starve us out of Mungret. He will not always be bishop.' Byrne frequently referred to Dr O'Dwyer's hostility to the Society of Jesus, which he ascribed to his experience at the time Mungret was set up and his college closed. Again he warned Fr Keating: 'His lordship is subtle as well as bold in assertion. If we give him an opportunity he will shift the controversy from the firm ground on which we stand to confusion of the issue.'[35]

He had reason for his concern about the provincial. Even before Fr Keating had received Fr Byrne's last letter, or that of Fr Head, and against the advice of most of his own consultors, he had written to Dr O'Dwyer with a compliant proposal. Like the vast majority of religious superiors, whatever privileges their order enjoys, the last thing he wanted was a condition of hostility with a local bishop. He suggested the possibility of interchanging Mungret College with the Jesuit novitiate at Tullabeg, near Tullamore. It was a well-meaning gesture, not adequately thought through, that brought even greater suspicion and misunderstanding. On 22 September the bishop replied that the proposal 'would meet all the needs of the case' from his point of view. 'I should be ready', he stated carefully, 'to give my formal sanction to the opening of the novitiate.'[36] The general, however, refused to approve the scheme for a number of reasons, including financial considerations and the interests of so many bishops invested in Mungret College. This reaction, however, was not reported to the bishop. Almost a year later, not having heard anything further, he wrote to know what was happening. The injury to his diocese occasioned by Mungret, he claimed, had brought things to such a pass this year that he had no student to send to Maynooth, and to fill his place at the Irish College Rome he had to withdraw one of his subjects from Maynooth. 'I do not know what is to become of the priesthood of the diocese', he proclaimed, 'and therefore I feel bound to press the demand which I have already made for the discontinuance of the boarding school at Mungret.'[37] A discomfited Keating replied on 7 September 1899, explaining that he had called to see his lordship two or three times when he was last in Limerick but did not find him at home, and then outlined the difficulties he had encountered as regards the interchange with Tullabeg. He continued, on now familiar lines: 'I regret very much that your lordship should think that Mungret is interfering with your lordship's seminary. By far the greater number of boys at Mungret are from other dioceses, and we are most anxious to encourage any boy who should show a vocation for the diocese to persevere in his vocation. We could not do away with the boarding school without completely crippling the Apostolic School.'[38]

The following spring the bishop was in Rome for his quinquennial visit and while there raised the matter of Mungret College. He informed the Congregation of Propaganda that he could not get enough priests for his diocese because Mungret, contrary to agreement, took lay students from the diocese. He was advised by the cardinal prefect of Propaganda to raise the matter with the Jesuit general. When he called on the general, Louis Martin (1892–1906), the latter was ill and could not see him. He explained his case to the assistant-general, and on his return to Ireland sent a forceful letter to the general. 'My complaint is this', he wrote, 'that your Fathers, without any permission from me, and in distinct violation of an agreement made with me, have carried on for some years a boarding school for secular students within two miles of this city where I have my seminary.' He went on to give his account of the nature of the Apostolic School, saying little about the role of his predecessor, and stated that Fr Réné came to him 'and represented that it would be a great help to him if I allowed him to take in a few boarders so as to fill up his classes and supplement his income. He asked me to be allowed to receive as many as 20 such pupils, and stipulated that none of them should be from my diocese'. His lordship then mentioned the approval of Fr Fulton to the agreement, and added that 'unfortunately I cannot put my hand on any written evidence of this agreement, and Fr Réné can inform you about it and there must be some other members of your Society who know of it.' He also explained that because he had no room for boarders at his ecclesiastical college, Dr Butler, on a temporary basis, sent his pupils as boarders to Mungret. He continued: 'As far as I know, this temporary provision of my predecessor is the only circumstance which can be twisted into an assent to Mungret College being used for any purposes but its own. But even that was all past when Fr Réné made his agreement with me.' Last year, O'Dwyer stated, 'your Provincial proposed ... to meet my complaints by substituting your novitiate for the school at Mungret, but after I gave my assent to the suggestion, abandoned it on account of difficulties which he said arose in connection with it'. He concluded assertively:

> I trust that you will see your way to reinstate that agreement. If not, I should ask by what authority your Fathers conduct a secular college in my diocese. It is not with Episcopal consent. I do not know whether or not your privileges enable you to put aside my authority, but I feel it my duty to contest the point. But I should much prefer to any litigation that you should satisfy yourself as to the accuracy of my statement of the agreement made by Fr Réné and Fr Fulton, and then give directions to your Fathers in accordance with the simple principle of good faith and honour between man and man.[39]

The general replied on 19 June 1900 expressing his regret that any member of the Society should have caused distress to his lordship. He then gave Dr O'Dwyer the accounts he had already received from Réné and the Irish Jesuits who were present in the early years at Mungret, and assured him he would send on further information when he received it and would endeavour to respond to any questions his lordship wished to ask.[40] Fr Martin sent a copy of his reply to the provincial. On 30 July 1900, he further emphasised to the provincial the importance of the charge that the Society had broken faith with the diocese of Limerick in not honouring the agreements made with both Bishop Butler and Dr O'Dwyer, and that he had received a letter from Propaganda containing the queries sent to them by the bishop which corresponded to the one sent him. He required from the provincial a report setting out clearly and quietly the issue of the agreements as soon as possible, and he urged that the task be entrusted to a man of special ability such as Fr James Murphy or Fr Peter Finlay.[41]

Meantime, the bishop and Fr Keating made a further attempt to find a solution. Anxious, like his lordship, 'to come to a friendly understanding regarding Mungret College, without further reference to Propaganda,' he made a further proposal. It was to the effect that if his lordship agreed in writing that the Jesuits might admit as many lay boarders as they wished, without any limit to their number, they would agree not to receive any lay-boarders from the diocese of Limerick without his lordship's consent. They required, however, to be allowed, when refusing lay boys from the diocese, to mention that it was because of an arrangement with his lordship. If Dr O'Dwyer agreed to this proposal, Keating would send a copy to the general for his approval.[42] The bishop, evidently as eager as Keating to avoid a trial before Propaganda, replied compliantly the next day, accepting the proposal but adding to 'without the consent of the Bishop of Limerick' the words 'for the time being'.[43] The last four words changed an arrangement with the present bishop into a perpetual commitment, thereby undermining one of the order's privileges. The general and his advisers took a month to consider the matter and then decided against it. Keating, on 17 October 1900, explained that the general had pointed out that the order had a 'full right to take lay boys from any diocese', but because he was 'anxious to show his regard for your lordship' he made the concession 'during your lordship's reign in Limerick'. 'He could not consent to yielding up the Society's right in *perpetuum*'. He asked his lordship to reconsider his response.[44] On 3 November, Dr O'Dwyer replied to the provincial, refusing to make any change.[45] He made one more effort, however, to resolve matters locally.

A new Jesuit provincial, Fr James Murphy, was appointed on 13 November 1900. In December 1900 he was in Limerick and called to Corbally to pay his respects. After an initial friendly chat, the bishop raised the issue of Mungret and brought to him all the letters he had on the matter and asked him to read them there and then. Murphy did so, and assured Dr O'Dwyer that he would give the matter full consideration and consult his own superior and let his lordship know as soon as he could. He impressed on him that anything he said 'was only conversation and that any agreement would be in writing' and that it was on that understanding that he spoke. 'Well now, that is honest I like that,' was the bishop's reply. He then related his version of the story in full, admitted that he had no writing to confirm it, and explained how he had gone to Propaganda.[46]

About March 1901, Bishop O'Dwyer wrote to Fr Murphy asking if he had heard from the general. He replied that he had not, and immediately wrote to Rome saying he had to have a reply. The general replied that as his lordship had placed the matter with Propaganda, Murphy should not interfere. When the latter was in Limerick after Easter for his visitation of the Jesuit houses he called on Dr O'Dwyer. The bishop asked him if he had a reply from the general.

Murphy replied: 'Yes, my Lord. Fr General wrote that as your lordship has placed the matter in the hands of Propaganda, he thinks it more prudent that I do not interfere.' 'He was very indignant at this,' Murphy noted. 'When I could get in a word I added the rest of Fr General's letter.' At the general's words that he would 'receive with all due respect any proposal your lordship might make', Dr O'Dwyer got very angry and 'declared he had no proposal, that there was no use in dealing with us; that we cheated him, that that was the history of the order in Limerick'. 'I quietly withdrew', Murphy concluded, 'being shown most politely out. In form all most polite but war to the knife.'[47] A final breakdown in communication between the two sides had taken place. The conflict took three more years before Propaganda came up with a solution.

The course of the deliberations has been succinctly summarised by the authors of *St Munchin's College Limerick, 1796–1996*, following a detailed examination of the relevant section in the Archives of Propaganda Fide.

BEFORE PROPAGANDA

The full hearing was held at the Congregation of Propaganda Fide in December 1903, with His Eminence, Sebastiano Cardinal Martinelli, as Presiding Judge.[48] The presentation ... summarised the objections of Edward Thomas under three headings, that Mungret College had changed from its original purpose, that it threatened the existence of his diocesan seminary and thirdly that the Jesuits broke a pact which they made to limit the number of lay students at the College. It reminded O'Dwyer the Jesuits believed that his predecessor had approved the foundation of the College, that he allowed lay pupils to attend it and that the agreement proposed by O'Dwyer was never approved by them. The sentence then defined the issues at stake as (a) the characteristics of the foundation of Mungret College and (b) the effect which the alleged agreement had on the purpose of the College.

On the question of the foundation of the College, the Judge found in favour of the Jesuits on the grounds that Bishop Butler had approved it and supported the education of lay students by sending his own nephew to Mungret. ... His Eminence put on record that both sides had engaged in a fervent debate (*fervido dibattito*) on the issue.

On the issue of the agreement between the Jesuits and the Bishop, the Cardinal noted that the issue was an intricate and subtle one. ... He was of the opinion that in 1888 Edward Thomas did not make it clear that the sole purpose of Mungret was the work of the Apostolic School and therefore, by implication, it appeared that he accepted that Mungret College could have a role in educating lay pupils as well as apostolics. He summarised the opinion of the Consultor in the case, Monsignor Sebastianelli, who recommended that Mungret College had a right to educate lay pupils and that the Congregation could determine the number of these, if it wished.

The decision was given at a Congregation on January 18th 1904 and it found in favour of the Jesuits, who were now entitled to have both an Apostolic School and a school for other pupils at Mungret.[49] 'In accordance with the nature and purpose of the Apostolic School, the Fathers of the Society of Jesus, are within their rights to establish the School and the College and to determine the number of students in both'.

It seems clear that from the beginning of his episcopate, Dr O'Dwyer planned the revival of St Munchin's College, the diocesan college of which he had been the last headmaster, and this led him to withdraw his seminarians from Mungret College, and subsequently to take steps to ensure that Mungret would not be in a position to attract students likely to attend St Munchin's College. The Jesuits viewed this as contrary to their agreement with Bishop Butler, and as not only an attempt to control their institution but as a process that would effectively close it. Trepidation for their respective colleges led the bishop to bring the matter to Rome and induced the Jesuits to accept his challenge. The failure of the Agricultural College at Mungret and the subsequent failure of Fr Bourke's college there and in Hartstonge Street, touched both parties deeply and made them equally sensitive to the possibility of failure. Edward Thomas's undefined previous relations with Limerick Jesuits appear to have played a part, too, as did personality clashes, and the general social, political and religious climate of the time.[50]

AFTERMATH: CONFLICT AND CALM

Unfortunately, the tension concerning Mungret spilled over into relations between the Dr O'Dwyer and the Jesuits in Limerick city. From 1901 Dr O'Dwyer made it more difficult for Jesuits to obtain faculties to hear confessions and preach in the diocese. Collection of money at the Jesuit church was not permitted, and to ease pressure on the very extended St Michael's parish a new church was built within 150 yards of the Crescent church, and modelled on it in style. It was opened on 24 April 1904 and was soon labelled, in unkind local comment, 'the church of spite'.

The Jesuit provincial from 1901 was James Murphy, as noted above. He, like the bishop, was an unyielding man, and seemed to bring out the worst in his lordship. Because of Dr O'Dwyer's insistence that every Jesuit had to be examined by him personally before he was granted faculties in the diocese, irrespective of his qualifications and his being deemed worthy of having faculties in other dioceses, Murphy refused to allow Jesuits give retreats in the diocese. The tit-for-tat approach deepened the sense of hostility already felt by his lordship towards the Society of Jesus, and Fr Murphy received the brunt of it. On 25 November 1904 he sent an indignant letter to Dr O'Dwyer.

Your lordship expressed a wish that I should always speak freely to you, and said you 'liked a man to be honest and open'. May I avail myself of that expression of wish on your lordship's part to say that on these occasions I think I was *very badly* received. Calling merely through etiquette and politeness and to pay my respects to your lordship, I found I had to sit for some half hour or more and to hear all that I most respect and love insulted and abused, being told that 'the history of our Society is one of fraud and deceit, that that was beginning to be realised and that soon we would not have a friend in any diocese in Ireland, that beginning with the chapel at the time of the Kellys we had broken every pledge we had ever given, and again that 'all the infidelity and immorality and spirit of revolution in France was the fruit of the teaching in the schools of the Society'; and not a little more of the same kind ...[51]

Edward Thomas O'Dwyer's spites and dislikes, however, often appeared to be more personalised and volatile than deep-seated. Relations with the Jesuits eased considerably the following year, when James Murphy came out of office as provincial and was succeeded by Fr John Conmee, destined to serve as the model of the benign and cultured Jesuit in James Joyce's *Ulysses*. Of even greater relevance was the wise appointment as rector of the Crescent of Father Michael Browne. A burly man of striking appearance, with a long ascetic face, Browne was an efficient administrator, and was reputed to combine a selfless humility with a determined will. Previously he had been novice-master, and he had so impressed his best-known novice, the Venerable John Sullivan, that he modelled his life on that of Michael Browne. The latter's spirituality was on the traditional lines of fasting, prayer, preaching, and the service of the poor, and by the time he came to Limerick he was already widely referred to as 'Father Browne the saint'.[52]

So far as the bishop was concerned, however, it was probably of more practical importance that Browne was a Limerick man, born in William Street into a well-known family with which Dr O'Dwyer was probably acquainted. His father was a prominent flour merchant, his brother James was an architect and engineer and had worked for Limerick corporation, and his other brother, Daniel, was county court judge for Kerry. His three sisters, moreover, Elizabeth, Margaret, and Kate, were religious in the Faithful Companions of Jesus, a congregation that Dr O'Dwyer held in affection and high regard.[53] Michael Browne's combination of fondness for his native city, a lively sense of humour, and a powerful penetrating voice known to have shattered glass, overcame both the prejudice and the deafness of the bishop. Some of his letters to his provincial are as illuminating on the personality of Edward Thomas as they are on Browne himself.

'I have just come back from seeing the bishop at the Palace Corbally', he commenced on 2 September 1905, and continued:

He received me with all the marks of real friendship, beginning with 'So, you have come to take charge of us'. I told him how sudden the change had been. From that we went on to all manner of questions. I shouted as your Reverence knows I can, for the Bishop is deaf and conversational success in such circumstances depends largely on clear shouting. After we had discussed Irish snobbery, temperance, dogmatic preaching, preaching 'over people's heads', teaching of Christian doctrine, winding up with the university question, I said to him: 'Well my Lord, what about faculties?' 'Are your ready to be examined?' 'Certainly, but I don't know what your lordship will find on examination.' 'That's right, that's a good fellow.' Then he continued, 'Well now, I give you *durante officio* [during your term of office] all the faculties of the diocese.'

'Of course I thanked him warmly', Browne went on, 'and promised to do all the work I was capable of doing, especially to do all in my power to make the (pupils) know the Christian doctrine. On this last subject he had much to say: that our own boys did not know the Christian doctrine and that they, especially, were to be the professional men of Limerick. While on the university question, I said that I had often heard Fr Delany say that we Catholics were not prepared for a university, that we had no prepared professors. 'Delany is right; he has been working education, the bishops know nothing of it.' One great initial difficulty seems thus removed', Browne concluded. 'By great trust in God and lots of prayer I hope I shall gird my laggard spirit to face the rest of them. All this, I am sure, will give your Reverence very great pleasure.'[54]

On the vexed issue of faculties for retreats, Browne called on the bishop on 19 September 1905. The superior of the Reparation Convent had asked the Jesuit provincial for a Jesuit to give a retreat. Browne told the bishop that the provincial had left the matter in his hands and that he 'had come to ask what his lordship wished in the matter. 'What am I to do?' he said. 'If your lordship allows me to give the retreat I will give it.' 'Of course I allow you to give it.' 'There is also another retreat', I said, 'at the Good Shepherds.' 'They had a retreat some time ago.' 'Yes, but not a community retreat, this is the community retreat, and if your lordship allows me I will give that also.' 'Certainly give it, you will do them no harm at any rate.' 'Now, Father, tell me did it do you any harm to ask these things.' 'No, my Lord.' 'Tell me then why your Fathers are forbidden to ask me for faculties to give retreats; but that is not a fair question to ask.' 'I will give your lordship any explanation I can.' And then, without touching the past at all, I said: 'The provincial is quite ready to carry out any arrangement your lordship may make as he is convinced that your lordship will ask for nothing that is inconsistent with our rule.' 'Not only would I ask for nothing inconsistent with your rule but I would ask for nothing inconsistent with the respect due to your community, I would ask for nothing unreasonable.' 'Then he went on', Browne observed, 'to the obligation of a bishop towards the communities of nuns under his charge. After that I reminded him of the public retreat in our church in November for which he gave me faculties for any of 'ours' who gives it.'

'My own impression', Browne added, 'is that he could not have done much more to make things easy considering the past. His strong objection was that arrangements for retreats had been made by Reverend Mothers with the provincial and that he was asked to approve of a man whom he did not know. 'I ought', he said, 'to have something to say in the appointment.' 'I have gone through this matter with tedious prolixity', Browne concluded, 'in the hope that you may be able to see the trend of affairs.'[55] By 2 June 1906, Browne was able to report that for the feast of the Holy Name the bishop had agreed to preside at the mass and come to dinner with the community that evening.[56]

In Mungret also, from 1905, another new rector, of a different style, but of a genial disposition, considerable presence, diplomacy, and width of vision, Fr T.V. Nolan, also experienced a welcoming reception from Dr O'Dwyer. He expanded the buildings, and in 1907 held prominent silver jubilee celebrations at Mungret,[57] without any friction with the bishop. At the Crescent, meantime, under a new rector, Fr Charles Doyle, friendly relations continued. In 1913 he was able to report to Fr Nolan: 'I was with the Bishop the other day getting a number of permissions. He was very amiable and gave me all I asked for, even faculties for Fr Tighe, who is to give a retreat here after Lent – which his lordship has of late years refused, I believe, unless the man had faculties formerly in the diocese.[58]

Despite the outer harmony, however, the Limerick Jesuits continued to walk warily. They sensed, it would seem, that though his lordship had buried the hatchet, he kept the location in mind. Fr Doyle received evidence of this the following year. On 12 May 1914, he observed in a letter to the provincial that he was loath to go to the bishop for faculties just then 'after what has just occurred'. A public meeting had been held to raise funds for the Sacred Heart church, the Jesuit church in his care. A past student of the Crescent, Mr Stephen O'Mara, without consulting Fr Doyle, had gone to the mayor to call a public meeting to aid the church. 'Neither directly or indirectly', Doyle insisted, had he or anyone in the Crescent community approached Mr O'Mara. After the meeting, a Mr Roche and Mr Moran, called on the rector to say that it was the wish of the meeting that an appeal in the press should be made, and they asked for his approval. 'I told them', Doyle explained, 'that, since I had been brought into the matter, I could not sanction such an appeal without the Bishop's permission, and I asked them to see that no such appeal appeared. They promised to do so. Yet to my surprise and annoyance it did appear, by whom inserted I know not.' As the church was in poor condition, and had not been permitted to have the usual public collections, it seems likely that some past students decided to press ahead, fearing perhaps that permission would not be granted by Dr O'Dwyer. In the event they placed Fr Doyle in an awkward position.

When he explained to the bishop what had happened, the answer he got was:

> I don't wish to be offensive. You have doubtless something in your mind that to yourself justifies this statement, but, on the face of it, it is perfectly incredible that all this should have happened without your sanction and authority. There should be a paragraph in the papers expressing regret that such an appeal was made and such a meeting held without my authority.

'I pointed out', Doyle continued, 'that such a paragraph would be an admission that the meeting and appeal had my sanction, which would be untrue. Moreover, it would be a public censure on those who had acted very kindly towards us, and who, at least, in the matter of the meeting, were, I supposed, quite within their rights. He did not press the point. A few days after this interview I had to go to him again on business, and I brought him the facts concerning the meeting and appeal written out, as it is extremely difficult owing to his deafness to carry on a conversation. He said he would read them over, and was altogether more gracious than at the first interview, and, perhaps, the matter has ended.' 'Of course, the appeal in the press was a mistake', Doyle concluded, 'and the Bishop had a right to feel aggrieved, but he might have accepted my explanation. However, he may do so in the end, though once he gets an idea into his head it is very hard to change him.'[59] Doyle continued as rector until 1918, that is until after his lordship's death, and no further instance of disagreement was chronicled. The bishop had other matters of greater import in those final years. He was once again a prominent figure on the national stage.

The disagreement over Mungret College gave rise to mutual feelings of hurt, some bitterness, and a sense of being hard done by, but it remained a matter between the two main contestants. The conflict at Bruff, on the other hand, took on a public character, was regularly discussed in the local newspapers, and led to the bishop being jeered in the streets of Limerick.

13

The bishop, the Christian Brothers, and 'the Bruff scandal'

In a celebrated sermon on 'The Office of the Bishop', delivered at the conse-cration of Robert Browne, bishop of Cloyne, on 19 August 1894,[1] Edward Thomas O'Dwyer observed that the bishop, as a successor of the apostles in a particular diocese, 'gathers into his hands' the 'threads of all the activities' of the many agencies in the diocese and 'not only presides over it as its head' but 'truly governs and directs it'. 'He has full legislative and authoritative power' for 'he is placed by the Holy Spirit "to rule the Church of God"'.[2] In his diocese he is the guardian of the faith, obliged to protect it, irrespective of human applause or criticism. 'In his decisions', O'Dwyer acknowledged, 'the bishop is not infallible', but, nevertheless, his decisions remain 'authoritative and binding on the con-sciences of his people'. If they disagree with his decisions, their duty is to obey, and 'to appeal within the Church to the higher authorities that can overrule his decisions', but 'as loyal Church members they should not make the matter a public issue in newspapers and other publications'.[3]

The foregoing might be seen as, in part, an apologia for his independent stand in the land struggle, but it also laid out the ground rules he wished opponents to follow, and mirrored the magisterial, paternalistic attitude assumed by many of the Catholic hierarchy in the years after the first Vatican Council, particularly in the politically divided Ireland of the 1890s. At the same time, Irish prelates had to bear in mind that they were dealing with an increasingly better educated and more critical public, which was not unfamiliar with open defiance of their bishops on political and social issues. Episcopal moral hegemony, therefore, required sensitive expression if it were not to drift into intimidation and bullying on the one hand, or to provoke strong protest, on the other. Sensitivity in verbal expres-sion was not one of O'Dwyer's attributes, as Archbishop Logue had noted.[4]

Given O'Dwyer's views on 'the office of bishop', and his particular person-ality, it is not surprising that he sought to re-establish St Munchin's as a seminary college under his own control, or that he endeavoured to assert his authority over Mungret College, which he associated with the closure of the diocesan establishment during his leadership, and which was sheltered by privileged immunity from his 'reasonable' demands as bishop. There was a similarity in his dealings with the Christian Brothers in Bruff, Co. Limerick. Again, there was a perceived rivalry with a local diocesan establishment, and the Brothers appealed to privileged rights against the 'reasonable' demands of their parish priest and bishop. A further similarity is suggested by the fact that the conflict in both places had its beginnings in the same year, 1892, not long after Dr O'Dwyer's first visit to Rome, an event marked by a warm welcome there and by popular exultation on his return home. His stormy years seemed past, all was peaceful, and there was opportunity to give more attention to diocesan affairs. Confrontation with the Christian Brothers, however, brought him up against the most influential and most popular religious body in Ireland, which had instructed the greater part of the Catholic male population and which had identified with the popular spirit of nationalism and with the struggle for justice on land issues.

The following account of events is indebted to the detailed information preserved in the archives of the Fratelli Christiani, Rome (AFCR), to reports in various newspapers and other material gathered by John Rushe, MA, to papers in the Limerick Diocesan Archives, and to articles in the *Old Limerick Journal*. Bishop O'Dwyer and the parish priest of Bruff, Charles McNamara, left relatively little material on the issue apart from some public letters and a small number of letters to the local superior and to the superior-general of the Christian Brothers. There are no diaries or other sources of private comment or explanation. As a result, one is frequently constrained to seek behind the thorough accounts preserved by the Christian Brothers for a reasonable explanation of the parish priest's and bishop's actions and statements.

THE BROTHERS AND BRUFF

In 1859 Fr Robert Cussen, VG, PP, with the assistance of William Monsell, later Lord Emly, obtained, from the earl of Limerick's estate, a portion of land adjoining the town of Bruff, Co. Limerick, in order to establish some schools. Cussen was both a man of means and a dedicated and popular priest. The parish under his control contained the town of Bruff and the districts of Grange and Meanus, an area of generally good land, embracing the ancient pre-historic site of Lough Gur. From early times it appears to have been well populated. In the second half of the nineteenth century, it contained a considerable number of cottiers, as well as many strong farmers – having fifty or so acres – who had good sized families, and employed farm workers and domestic help. The town of Bruff was centrally situated: some 15 miles from Limerick city, 6 miles from Kilmallock, 5 or 6 miles from Hospital, and less than 8 miles from Bruree. It contained a number of shops, a hotel, and a very large police station – signifying the town's central location and the strong nationalist feeling in the region. Fr Cussen, during his time as parish priest, built churches at Grange and Meanus, improved the church at Bruff, and at the far end of the town from the church, beyond the Morning Star river, on the land from the Earl of Limerick's estate, he built a convent and school for the religious sisters of the Faithful Companions of Jesus, a large house for himself and other clergy, and a community house and school for members of the Irish Christian Brothers.[5]

In 1859 the Brothers agreed to accept Cussen's invitation to Bruff, subject to certain conditions laid down by their superior-general, Br M.P. Riordan. These later became a focus for discussion, and need to be noted. They required: that there would not be less than three Brothers in the establishment 'viz.: two school Brothers and one lay Brother'; that they would be permanently provided with a suitable furnished residence; that there would be suitable classrooms, together with the furniture and stationery necessary to begin with. The Brothers were to have the control and internal management of the school. The education was to be gratuitous, and the admission of pupils free. The payment of one penny a week, from those who could afford it, was to be applied by the Brothers at their discretion for the benefit of the children solely (as in supplying school requisites, repairing or improving the school). Thirty pounds per annum for the maintenance of each Brother was to be provided locally, and where sufficient funds were not available for this purpose the required sum was to be made up by means of a charity sermon or of an annual collection in the parish church on a fixed day announced beforehand by the pastor. Brothers, moreover, were to be allowed accept voluntary contributions for the benefit of the establishment. Finally, the Brothers were to be allowed free exercise of their religious rules.

The terms were 'cheerfully' accepted and signed by Robert Cussen.[6]

The first community arrived on 24 April 1860, and was composed of two teaching Brothers and a lay Brother.[7] The school opened on 30 April. The numbers seeking admission were so large that a third classroom, an adjunct to the building, was put up by the parish priest. By June 1860, the Bruff establishment was said to consist of four Brothers, three school-rooms, and three hundred pupils.[8] Two years later, the third classroom was closed and became an outhouse, because of insufficient support from the local community and because the taste for learning of many of the grown students was said to have 'been sated'. The additional Brother was withdrawn.[9] Thereafter, the school continued to function smoothly, and there were good relations with the parish priest and the local population.[10] In May 1865, Dean Cussen died in London. He was succeeded by Dr Denis Cregan, a good friend of Bishop George Butler. He raised the question of the Brothers teaching Latin to their older pupils. In this, it is likely that he reflected the views of his bishop, who had observed to Archbishop Cullen: 'I see no remedy for our lack of clerical aspirants unless the Christian Brothers take on Latin in their schools – nearly all the bishops are of the same opinion.'[11] The superior-general, however, refused the request. The Brothers' resources were overstrained.[12] Dr Cregan employed a classics teacher and obtained the use of the Brothers' parlour as a classroom. The demand was slight and the venture failed. After the introduction of the Intermediate Education Act, 1878, with its payment to schools on the basis of results, Dr Cregan made a further attempt. To secure permanency he obtained from Bishop Butler a diocesan priest, John Sheehan, to teach Latin. The classical lessons, as before, were given in the parlour, but the pupils received their English and Mathematical lessons from the Brothers in the classrooms. The arrangement was fraught with strain, but the priest teaching Latin was popular and, with support from neighbouring priests, the number of his pupils grew. Fr Cregan obtained the use of the outhouse from the Brothers, and in 1879 had it fitted up and furnished. Thereafter the classical school was known as 'St Patrick's Seminary'.[13] It began to draw pupils away from the Brothers' school. Clever boys, it is alleged, were offered free places.[14]

Two years later an important report on the Bruff school and the Bruff area was made for the superior-general of the Christian Brothers, Richard A. Maxwell, a former lawyer with the Dublin legal firm of Maxwell and Weldon. The report was made by Br Philip Slattery on 17 September 1881. The farming class were the backbone of the area, he observed. Many of them were wealthy and proud and had large families. The daughters of these respectable farmers were 'employed as teachers and monitoresses', and these positions were 'entirely in the gift of the parish priest'. The only opening for the farmers' sons, not remaining on the land, was 'as priests, doctors or solicitors', and hence they had to be provided with a classical education. 'You see then', Slattery explained, 'how the seminary next door has dealt a heavy blow at the school here, directly by taking away the elite of their pupils and indirectly, at the collection.' He believed, however, that the once flourishing academy would not survive much longer because of its want of proper management and discipline, and when it became defunct the Brothers would have to undertake to teach the classics, and then they would have 'plenty of means to hand'.

Turning to the condition of the Brothers' school at Bruff, Slattery was unsparing in his criticism. 'The character of the schools (classes) have decidedly suffered, and very few respectable boys attend them.' A 'sober-and-easy style of doing business is the order of the day'. It would not be wise, however, to close the Bruff school, he concluded, it is the most lovely and delightful spot in Ireland, and will yet by proper attention become a great success.'[15]

The situation as regards Latin instruction had become clear, therefore, by 1881. It was necessary to meet the ambitions of the well-to-do farmers, and well-to-do shopkeepers, for their children, especially for their sons. It was becoming attractive to the Brothers as a means towards financial survival. The regulation remained, nevertheless, against their teaching Latin. In the 1880s the town population decreased and the 'whole country around … had financial difficulties'.[16] It was the era of the land struggles and, besides, the town suffered from being by-passed by the railway. By 1888 the number of Brothers was down to two, but from the annals for that year it seems clear that they were comfortably situated. Shopkeepers and the young men of the town had combined to provide financial support. Young people organised plays and concerts for the Brothers, and a considerable sum was realised. Pupils, moreover, were returning to the school from the classical establishment, and in the collection the parish priest increased his contribution to £8. The Brothers, as a result, were able to have their two front parlours papered and painted, and their chapel painted and varnished. The happy situation was enhanced at Confirmation during June, when the bishop confirmed eighty pupils from the school and 'expressed himself well pleased with their answering'.[17] In 1890 the Brother presented pupils for the Intermediate examinations. Three boys passed. The Brothers and the Academy were now presenting boys for the Intermediate. Rivalry was inevitable. In January 1891 a new director was appointed, Br Florence Kelly. At this stage, it would seem 'that one of the two Brothers was preparing a dozen or so boys for the Intermediate examinations, the other, … with the aid of monitors, taught the primary section of the school,' comprising 80 to 100 pupils.[18] Following Br Kelly's arrival, matters continued smoothly much as before. Then, on 22 January 1892, Dr Cregan died.[19] He was succeeded by Fr Charles McNamara, VG, PP, a tall slight man, who made his first visit to the Christian Brothers' school in March 1892, and by July had made his first exertion of authority in their regard.

THE BEGINNING OF PROBLEMS

On 29 June he asked the director by what authority the Brothers had the Blessed Sacrament in their oratory. Br Kelly told him they had a rescript from Rome. McNamara asked him to write to the superior-general about it and said he would like to see a copy of the rescript. The superior, in reply, announced that he had the rescript in his possession. Br Kelly showed the letter to the parish priest, who was far from satisfied. He had asked to see a copy of the rescript, and felt slighted. He promised to report the matter to the bishop, who would not be pleased.[20] On 4 August 1892 the bishop was in Bruff, and the Brothers were on their holidays at Kilkee, except for the lay Brother, Francis Kinsella. Dr O'Dwyer, it appears, ordered the curate, Fr Reeves, to remove the Blessed Sacrament from the Brothers' oratory, and left instructions with the parish priest not to restore it until he (the bishop) would have seen the rescript, and, if satisfied with it, he would have the Blessed Sacrament returned.[21] Fr McNamara and the bishop were concerned that the obligations of the canon law with regard to the reservation of the Blessed Sacrament in a private oratory were not being fulfilled, namely, that there should be a community of four people and that mass was said in the oratory once a week. The Brothers had not had a community of four, nor had they had a mass said in the oratory for years. Hence, the annoyance of the parish priest and of the bishop at their request for a copy of the rescript being seemingly ignored. It was as if the superior-general was seeking to conceal the conditions under which the Brothers were permitted to retain the Blessed Sacrament, and was not treating them with appropriate respect. His lordship, predictably, reacted impulsively, and a cycle commenced. The Brothers original agreement, it will be recalled, spoke of a community of three Brothers, and over the years no problem had been raised about their having the Blessed Sacrament in their chapel. Not surprisingly, they viewed the new parish priest as hostile to them, while he considered them to be uncooperative and unyielding.

The superior-general hurriedly sent a fourth Brother to the community on 11 August. The Brothers, meanwhile, had obtained permission from the superior of the religious sisters to make their evening prayer before the Blessed Sacrament in the convent chapel. After the fourth Brother arrived, Br Kelly approached the parish priest to have the Blessed Sacrament restored to them now that they had the required number of Brothers. Fr McNamara, on 18 August, refused on the grounds that there should be a weekly mass in the oratory and he could not provide it. He objected, besides, to the Brothers going to the convent for their evening prayer, and stated that they should go to the parish church, almost a half-mile distant. Dr O'Dwyer , after a long delay, was sent the rescript, and, when visited by Br Philip Slattery on 8 September, he advised that the superior-general should arrange with the parish priest that a stipend be paid to the curate to say mass in the Brothers' oratory once a week. Subsequently, Br Maxwell observed that he offered a stipend, but Dr McNamara would not undertake to have a weekly mass provided.[22]

Despite this impasse, the bishop seems to have remained reasonably detached in his relations with the Brothers. The annals for 20 May 1893 noted that on 'the feast of the Most Holy Trinity, forty-one boys were confirmed, most of them working boys. The bishop, Dr O'Dwyer, was very well pleased with their answering and expressed himself so.' The Brothers, during the year, undertook extensive repairs to the school and had the external walls of school and community house repainted. They continued their work of refurbishment and painting the following year. Their success, influence, and seemingly comfortable way of life, appear to have presented a problem for the parish priest. Money was scarce, and the Brothers' collection left less for the parish. Its continuance, given that they also had a new source of income from the Intermediate examinations, seemed excessive. The fact that there were two schools competing for a small number of pupils in a relatively small area was an inevitable irritant. On 1 July 1894 he proposed a compromise solution to the Brother Visitor on his arrival at Bruff. Br O'Brien reported to the assistant-general the following day. His letter pin-pointed the main issue.

'The vicar here, Fr McNamara, saw me yesterday', O'Brien wrote, 'about the question of amalgamating the classical school here with ours.' He had told him that he would lay the matter before his superior and let him know the result. 'He proposes', O'Brien continued,

> that the boys come to the Brothers in the morning, that they be sent over at certain times in three classes, one class at a time, to the priest for the Classics, that the Brothers get a certain proportion of the fees and results, that the amount would be a considerable help to the Brothers' slender income, which at present is so scanty that he does not understand how the Brothers manage to live on it !!!

In the evening, O'Brien went on, he met the curate in charge of the classical school, Fr O'Driscoll, who told him he had up to 30 pupils during the past year and that the average was about 26. He entered 'eight boys for the Intermediate in the preparatory, junior and middle grades' and 'his income from fees for the past twelve months, not including bad debts, was about £120'. 'He would propose that the Brothers should get three-fifths of the fees and results – that this would probably leave the Brothers a net income of about £100 a year.' Fr O'Driscoll urged that the superior of the Brothers give the arrangement a trial for a year, and if it did not work they could withdraw. 'When I asked him', O'Brien observed, 'who would be the recognised head of the concern, he said that the parish priest was the manager of the classical school … but does not interfere with Fr O'Driscoll' and 'would not interfere' with the amalgamated arrangement. O'Brien added, however, that when he was speaking with the parish priest earlier in the day, the latter informed him that he was manager of the classical school and Fr O'Driscoll 'would have to abide by any how he would arrange with the Brothers for letting the boys over to the classical department'. 'This looks ominous', O'Brien concluded.[23] Significantly, Fr O'Driscoll mentioned to another Brother shortly afterwards, 'if it is not to their advantage let the Brothers not take it, but there shall not be but one Intermediate school here'.[24]

The issue was clearly one of control, leavened with funding. It was part of the on-going tension between bishops and some parish priests and the Christian Brothers Congregation. At an earlier stage, the then bishop of Ossory, Dr Patrick F. Moran, had challenged the Brothers' control of their schools in the light of the Maynooth statutes. The matter had gone to Rome and the Brothers had preserved their independence. Now in the 1890s the issue was to the fore once more. The national schools were becoming virtually denominational. The Patrician and Presentation Brothers were happy to work in them under the management of the local parish priest, and at Hospital, a few miles from Bruff, the De La Salle Brothers had commenced in 1893 to run a national school under the parish priest and with no cost to the parish. In the light of this, the Christian Brothers' insistence on keeping independent of the national system, on the grounds that they wished to use religious emblems in their schools and to have moments of prayer during the day, while also requiring that they be independent of the clergy and supported by the local population, rendered them less attractive to bishops and parish pastors. Already there had been open conflict with parish priests at Mallow and Tullamore, where, allegedly, the pastor had them removed 'as too heavy a tax on the town'.[25]

O'Dwyer, when in Rome in December 1895, corresponded with Cardinal Logue about control of their primary schools and how to bring about clerical management in Christian Brothers institutions.[26] Like many bishops, neither man could see how the Brothers could reasonably object, seeing that the De La Salle Brothers experienced no difficulty in having the parish priest as manager.[27] Logue, in Rome in January 1896, informed Archbishop Walsh that he was preparing a statement about the Christian Brothers and the management of their schools 'at the request of Cardinal Mazzell and the Secretary of Propaganda', and that he did not foresee 'any trouble in coming to a satisfactory arrangement'. The Holy Father had assured him that he took 'the same view on the matter as the Bishops'.[28]

In February 1897, when there was question of an education bill which would provide support for the Christian Brothers schools, Logue conveyed to Archbishop Walsh, who was supporting the measure, his belief that the bishops should oppose any provision for the Brothers which would leave them still a charge on Catholics who contributed so largely to the public educational tax.[29] O'Dwyer was also critical, in private, of the bishops giving time and effort to fighting the Brothers' battles with the government, especially 'after their declaration to Propaganda that they would leave Ireland *en masse* rather than accept the Bishops as managers under the N. Board'. His policy would be to concentrate on the university question and to allow the Christian Brothers 'to slide'. He believed that such a policy would command the approval of a majority of bishops.[30]

Dr O'Dwyer's raising of management issues at Rome and in personal letters with respect to the Christian Brothers, was also influenced by a project he had undertaken on behalf of children living in the unwholesome atmosphere of workhouses. His concern for the children led him in 1894 to plan a special establishment for them in a salubrious setting near the river Shannon in Glin, Co. Limerick, where they would be well looked after and educated. He negotiated with the Local Government Board, and his intention was that the Christian Brothers would take charge of the boys, and that the girls would be cared for by the Sisters of Mercy.

The superior general of the Brothers, Richard A. Maxwell, who had the reputation of being a tough and shrewd negotiator, was not adverse to the project but was determined that the Brothers would not be controlled by the bishop. Consequently, he dealt directly with the Local Government Board prior to sending four Brothers to Glin.

In August 1895, Dr O'Dwyer made it clear to Br J.B. Welsh, the popular director of Sexton Street School, Limerick, that he resented Maxwell's independent dealings with the Local Government Board without consulting him. The schools, he remarked, had been set up in a way he had not wanted. Subsequently, he instructed that church collections for the Brothers in Limerick were to stop, and also that the weekly contributions paid directly to the Brothers from the workers in the local industries were to cease. When this last was announced in January 1896 there was considerable public resentment expressed at the bishop's action, many contributors continued to provide the Brothers with financial assistance.[31]

These various developments were the prelude to events in Bruff later in 1896. The subsequent conflict brought to light a deep-seated clerical grievance over the Brothers' involvement in intermediate, or secondary, education in Bruff – a branch of education in which the diocesan clergy had been the pioneers in the locality and which they had viewed as a source of vocations to the priesthood. Fr McNamara, as a result, could be sure of much clerical sympathy, and of the bishop's support in dealing firmly with the Brothers. It is possible, indeed, that he was acting in conjunction with his lordship.

On 12 September 1896, he sent a brief, almost peremptory message to Br Maxwell.

> Dear Mr Maxwell,
> I have long since considered that a change in the management of the schools taught by your Brothers here is necessary. It would be my wish that the intermediate class should be discontinued, and that the two teachers should devote all their time and energy to primary education for which the school was originally intended. Should any parents desire to have their children prepared for the intermediate examinations, I have a school conducted for that purpose by Fr O'Driscoll, one of my curates. I hope you will see your way to fall in with my views in this matter for otherwise you will put me to unnecessary trouble.[32]

Maxwell, who, as superior-general, presided over numerous schools and thousands of pupils across the English-speaking world, was not well at this time, but also, it would appear, was in no hurry to respond to the self-important parish priest of a small country town and its hinterland. More than a month later, on 15 October, he apologised for his delay in replying, explaining that he had been 'under the doctor's treatment for a troublesome attack of rheumatism'. He then sent a carefully prepared response. 'When the Brothers were introduced into Bruff by the late Dean Cussen', he commenced, 'there were certain conditions agreed upon by him and the then superior of the Bros., and amongst them was one that the Bros should have the control and internal management of the schools in their own hands. Under this condition the Bros., with the sanction of the Superior General, arrange the course of studies to be followed in their schools.' 'Prior to the establishment of the intermediate system in Ireland', Maxwell continued,

> many of the subjects on the intermediate programme were taught to the more advanced pupils in our schools. The examinations of the Board have afforded a healthy stimulus to work to the pupils competing, and this stimulus extends its influence to those even who are yet too young to (take) part in them, while the results supplement the means of the community which would otherwise, in many cases and certainly in Bruff be inadequate for their support.

'For I am bound to say', he added pointedly, 'that the Bros. establishment in Bruff in years past has had much to suffer from insufficiency of funds and the

Brothers complained to me, and indeed with reason, of the difficulty of realising by collection and subscription what was absolutely necessary for the maintenance of the community.' He also felt bound to say that the children attending the Brothers' schools, but not engaged in intermediate work, were 'as carefully attended to now as they' had 'been in the past', and the reports of the school examiners appointed by him to inspect the various classes of schools of the institute throughout Ireland fully justified him in his remark.[33]

The response defended the Brothers' position without adverting to the diocesan Latin school or acknowledging that it had come into existence because the Brothers in the past had not found it worth their while to teach Latin. The parish priest, besides, because of the delay in Maxwell's reply and its tone, considered that he was not treated with sufficient respect. On 27 October, when visiting the school to examine the children's Christian doctrine, he informed the superior, Florence Kelly, that his request of the superior-general to have the intermediate classes discontinued had been refused. He seemed 'very displeased about it', Kelly observed. 'He also said that the superior did not know who he had to deal with when he had to deal with him'(the parish priest).[34] A further account noted that on that occasion Fr McNamara asked to see a copy of 'the conditions'– which, it appears, had not been kept in the parochial files – 'and said he could not understand how any parish priest could renounce his right to the managership of his schools.'[35] Less than a fortnight later, on 8 November 1896, he prohibited the Brothers from attending Mass at the neighbouring convent, obliging them to journey to the parish church where Mass was at a later, less convenient time. This act of seemingly petty tyranny seems to have had the backing of Dr O'Dwyer, or been at his behest. The bishop later justified it in a rash manner in a public letter.

On 18 November 1899, O'Dwyer defended himself against criticism on a variety of fronts by means of a letter published in a number of Dublin and provincial papers. Referring to the prohibition against hearing Mass in the convent, he explained:

> I was about celebrating Holy Mass in the convent chapel, and when making my preparation I looked up, and saw a Christian Brother and one of the Nuns engaged at the same time in arranging the altar. I never saw anything more unbecoming in my life. After Mass I enquired of the curate who assisted me how such a thing could be and I then learned that the Christian Brothers heard Mass daily, and frequently answered Mass in the nun's chapel, which was situated in the centre of the house, and that there was no separation whatever between them and the Nuns and the young lady boarders. I then said, 'All this is improper and must cease, but do nothing until I come again'. In the meantime I thought it all over, and, feeling my responsibility in such a case, I directed the parish priest to say to the superior of the Christian Brothers that in future they could not continue to hear Mass in the convent. Against this decision the superior of

the Christian Brothers appealed to Rome, and again my decision was upheld.[36]

This assertion, when linked to the Brothers' secret departure from Bruff two years later, gave rise to what the local historian, Pius J.A. Browne, has termed 'an adamant element in local tradition' which still insists that the departure of the order was in consequence of some misdemeanours between the Brothers and Nuns.[37] It must be said that there is no known evidence for the suspicion, as Mr Browne admits, and it is possible that Dr O'Dwyer was thinking in terms of canon law, and of his measuring rod – how the matter would be viewed if brought to the attention of Propaganda. At that time, altar rails prevented access to the sanctuary except for very specific purposes, and to have a Christian Brother and a Sister preparing the altar together would not be usual. It is interesting to note that the Brothers' successors, the De La Salle Brothers, were permitted to hear Mass in the convent, but they did so from the sacristy and entered by an external door and hence did not go through the house.

It never entered Br Maxwell's head, it seems, that there was any question of misdemeanour, and he clearly gave little credence to the bishop's explanation for the prohibition, which, he pointed out, came on 8 November 1896, three weeks after the parish priest 'had received a letter from me in which I expressed my unwillingness to discontinue the intermediate classes in Bruff'. His riposte to his lordship was robust.

> From the date of our establishment in Bruff in 1860, the Brothers had heard Mass daily in the convent by *direction* and *arrangement* of the Venerable Dean Cussen. Dr O'Dwyer acted as curate for some time in Bruff, and must have celebrated Mass at the convent for the Nuns, Boarders, and Brothers. Moreover, as Bishop, his Mass was often served by one of the Brothers in the convent chapel in the midst of all the surroundings now described by his lordship as so 'unbecoming' and 'improper'; and yet there was no question of the impropriety of the arrangement until November 1896.[38]

Maxwell explained that he had not 'appealed to Rome' on this issue, as the Bishop had said, he had mentioned it as just one of a number of matters in a letter to Propaganda on 15 January 1897. That letter had followed further interchanges between the parish priest and the Brothers. On 26 November 1896, Fr McNamara, accompanied by the curate, Fr Reeves, had called to the Brothers' house and asked to see them. He then proceeded to read a document he had received from the Brother Superior-General giving the terms of the agreement at the time of the Brothers' arrival in Bruff. He wished to inform them 'that for the future he would stick rigidly to the terms of the agreement'. This meant that the Brothers would not have a collection. He, the parish priest would hold it, and from the proceeds pay them £30 each. This, however,

Br Kelly reported, 'was on condition we had no intermediate as that was not in the agreement, and, in reply to a remark, he said that if we teach intermediate we must support ourselves by it. Likewise, he then forbade our questing.' 'He also announced', Kelly stated, 'that he was going to take the lower school and some of the rooms of the house as class rooms for his classical school, the little shanty being, as he said, a miserable place for a priest to teach in, while his house (meaning the Brothers' place) was made an hospital for the sick and super-annuated. All our boys, he said, could go to the top room.'[39]

The details of that meeting on 26 November are not available, but Fr McNamara's manner and language were such as to cause a strong reaction. It was the behaviour of a man acting under strong emotional feeling, or under severe pressure. It seems out of character, so far as other indications go, and raises questions about other possible factors not directly mentioned in correspondence or the public press. The bishop would later mention that strident opposition came from Parnellites and from some others whom the parish priest had publicly challenged because of their violation of the ninth commandment and the scandal, presumably, it occasioned. Were these elements already siding with the Christian Brothers? Did the parish priest suspect, indeed, that the Brothers were stirring up such elements against him?

In any event, the Brothers complained about him to Br Maxwell. On 27 November, 1896, Maxwell wrote of the matter to the bishop. Dr O'Dwyer acknowledged his letter and stated he would communicate the contents to Fr McNamara. On 1 December, his lordship enclosed the statement made by the parish priest and asked Maxwell's views. As this statement differed considerably from the account sent him by Br Kelly, the superior-general required the three Brothers to send an account to him. These agreed with what Kelly had said. On 7 December, Br Maxwell addressed the bishop once more, giving the substance of the individual statements made by the three Brothers and appealing to his lordship to enable the Brothers to carry on their work at Bruff. On 9 December, O'Dwyer replied through his secretary that it was useless trying to carry out an investigation given the conflict of statements between the Brothers and his vicar-general. He could not accept the accusations against the latter. He then asked a number of questions concerning the teaching of the intermediate, the stipend gained and other matters. Br Maxwell responded, in turn, 'giving his reasons for thinking Dr McNamara hostile to the Brothers and replying to the other points in the bishop's letter.'[40]

On 15 January 1897, feeling that he was making no headway with Dr O'Dwyer, Br Maxwell sent his letter to the prefect of Propaganda, Cardinal Ledochowski, containing 'a full statement of the Bruff case with copies of all correspondence'.[41] It covered the various incidents from the removal of the Blessed Sacrament in 1892, soon after Fr McNamara's arrival, up to the time of writing. Rome contacted O'Dwyer and made him aware of the Brothers' complaints, and he, in turn, forwarded the parish priest's case, which included – according to a letter to Maxwell from Cardinal Ledochowski in March 1897 – a denial by Fr McNamara that he had 'forbidden the intermediate in the school in Bruff'.[42] Taken aback, it seems, by the complaint to Rome, and knowing how much he depended on the Christian Brothers in his diocese, O'Dwyer distanced himself from some of McNamara's demands. It was one thing to try to assert control in Bruff on the grounds of canon law or on those linked to the duties of parish or episcopal office, it was another to support the virtual eviction of the Brothers from part of their house. As well as the likelihood of it raising problems in Rome, there was a need for him to preserve overall good relations with the Brothers for he could not manage without them. They had 24 schools in his diocese, and some 2,210 pupils.[43] Consequently, he pressed the parish priest to withdraw his demand for a room (rooms) in the Brothers' house, and Fr McNamara 'acquiesced'.[44]

A chastened parish priest, it would seem, called to the Brothers' residence on 5 April 1897, his first visit since 26 November 1896. He is represented as coming grudgingly and with truculence to make a partial retraction of his previous demands, while still endeavouring to save face. For an account of the meeting, the only report once again is that of Br Kelly, told somewhat disjointedly, in the Annals of the house. He has McNamara declaring:

> You may continue the intermediate, but out of the results the two teaching Brothers are to get £30 each. All monies, from whatever source received, above the £60, or, should there be a lay Brother, £90, are to be handed over to me. Your superior may supplement it if he wishes. I shall not do anything at present about taking part of the building for Fr O'Driscoll. Your communities are not suited for small places. What an advantage you would have in large communities … Were you under the Board (of Education for National Schools) you would have £200 a year … National schools in rural districts do very well as the priests are on the spot. Whilst you had the Blessed Sacrament the house was left without a Brother – all going out to Mass and sometimes all were away for a day: this could not be allowed.

Moving from this argument, he stated, according to Kelly: 'The representations made to Propaganda were not fair: "The parish priest of Bruff sent the Brothers from a church door that was near them to one far off". The convent is not a church.' He went on: 'The Bishop feels that he has not been treated with that deference due to him; and I have been treated – as regards letters – by your superior, as if I were a mere curate. He (the superior-general) quoted to the Bishop, in confirmation of what occurred in November last, the testimony of a superior sent from Limerick to investigate it among you. I may have dropped some expression on that occasion which should not have been used – as persons when riled are not always guarded in their expressions. However, what I now state as to terms is final. You can apprise your superior thereof, but be careful to report it correctly.'[45] The final words signified his lack of trust. It was mutual.

The Brothers' reports, besides, managed to present him in a pathetic light, as a boorish, vain and greedy man, which the bishop refused to accept as a fair portrait.

In his public letter of 18 November 1899, Dr O'Dwyer stated that he had been directed by Cardinal Ledochowski (probably in early May 1897, as a result of Maxwell's January letter) to inquire into the financial arrangements of the Brothers in Bruff 'and to re-adjust them equitably according to the times'. 'In obedience to these instructions', the bishop continued, 'and to put an end forever, as I hoped, to the sole remaining cause of difference, I wrote to the superior of the Brothers and asked him to send down, as he was infirm himself, one of his assistants to sit with me and the local superior and the parish priest around a table.'[46] O'Dwyer's reference 'to the sole remaining cause of difference' is instructive. Earlier in his 1899 letter, he mentioned that Cardinal Ledocowski had written to the superior of the Christian Brothers 'that having regard to the proper spirit of his institute, it would be better for him to abstain from teaching the intermediate classes'. This, in fact, was not written by the cardinal until June 1897, so that O'Dwyer, recalling two years later, telescoped events in memory and confused their order. In the process, however, he indicated that there were two key factors in the whole Bruff dispute: the Brothers teaching intermediate classes, and thereby presenting a problem for the diocesan school, and the financial income of the Brothers and how that was impacting on the local clergy. The financial factor, of course, also infiltrated the discussions on the intermediate and its payment by results, and rendered attractive a national school system, which would not be a drain on the parish and which would be under the management of the parish priest. The issue of management was the central underlying issue. If that lay in clerical hands, it was felt, everything could be managed harmoniously!

What held in Bruff, however, did not necessarily apply in Limeick, at least not in the same way. The bishop still had the need to control, and to be seen to control, within his diocese, but he did not apply the control in the same way or in the same areas. Thus, where the Brothers and intermediate classes were concerned, he was on record at the beginning of his episcopate as stating at Sexton Street, Limerick, that he did not regard the Brothers entering students for the intermediate 'as going outside their province nor the scope of their mission', as he believed their work was 'to give justice to the children under them – to give them some opportunity of advancing themselves according to the abilities with which Almighty God had blessed them'. Why, he asked, 'should not the best prizes in life be thrown open' to the clever sons of the poor man and of the working man.[47]

The letter which O'Dwyer stated publicly, on 18 November 1899, he had sent to Br Maxwell, the latter declared he had not received.[48] Both parties, meanwhile, had recourse to Bishop T.A. O'Callaghan of Cork, whom they trusted. On 14 May, O'Callaghan informed his Limerick colleague that the superior-general would send one of his assistants as O'Dwyer had desired.'[49]

The meeting of O'Dwyer and the parish priest with the Brother Assistant and the local director, Br Kelly, on 20 May 1897, was a key event. Unfortunately, there are conflicting accounts of what took place. Once again, the bishop is at a disadvantage as he appears to have taken no notes and his account was written two years later. The Brother Assistant, Br W.S. O'Brien, on the other hand, sat down immediately after the meeting and wrote a detailed report for the superior general.

As the bishop recalled the occasion, he 'asked the Brothers how much they thought each Brother ought to be paid by the parish. They said £50 a year. The parish priest said that was excessive, that the people could not afford it, and that it was hard enough to get £30 each at the time'. After considerable discussion, O'Dwyer said to the Brothers: 'I really am puzzled by these statements and counter-statements. I see only one way of determining the matter. You keep accounts. Show me what it actually is costing you to live here on an average of, say, five years past, and I will assign that with an addition for contingencies, as the 'amount to be paid'. 'No', said the Brothers. 'We cannot show you our books.' I asked why, and they said 'We cannot allow any investigation by any bishop into our affairs'. I replied that I had quite enough of episcopal visitations on my hands already without taking on theirs, but that I wanted merely authentic information on one specific point. They then changed their answer, and said they could not let me see their books without consulting their superior-general, and to this I said they were right and I would adjourn the matter until I heard from them again.' The bishop added: 'They never as much as showed me the courtesy of communicating with me about it, and the next letter I got was from the superior, stating that he would withdraw the Brothers from Bruff.'[50]

The Brothers' account came from two sources, from Br Maxwell's reply to Dr O'Dwyer's description, and from Br O'Brien's own version forwarded to Bishop O'Callaghan on 23 May 1897. Both versions are virtually identical, except that Maxwell adds that there was a brief meeting prior to 20 May. It occurred following a confirmation carried out by his lordship, and was terminated at his request because he was fatigued. In the course of the brief meeting, however, he made the unexpected statement: 'Ah you know it is all a bit of jealousy on the part of the curate who keeps the Academy!' 'I presume,' Maxwell observed, 'he referred to the Classical School taught by one of the curates in Bruff.'[51]

Br W.S. O'Brien's account was sent on 22 May to Br Dominic Burke in Cork, who forwarded it the following day to Dr O'Callaghan. It is revealing on many aspects of the controversy. He began his 'detailed account':

> Dr McNamara, PP, VG, was present, and also Br Director of Bruff at the wish of the Bishop. His lordship began by stating that the only point he had to settle was that referring to the stipend of the Brothers, and then asked me what I had to say as to it. I replied that we were satisfied to allow things go on as in the past, that is to have an annual collection, and the

Intermediate in the schools, but as the PP wished to return to the original terms of agreement, the Br Superior was satisfied to accept £30 a year, and to have the Intermediate carried on.

'The PP then spoke of the Brothers' support being a burden on the parish, that he and his curates had to be supported by the people, and that he felt having to make so many appeals to them that he was going to ask his lordship to allow national schools be got up in town.' 'He then complained', O'Brien noted, 'of the teaching staff in Bruff having only two (Brothers), and one of these taught the Intermediate; that the Brothers were introduced to Bruff for primary education, that when he asked the Brothers to give up the Intermediate he was refused, and told that he had no right to interfere in the internal management of the schools. He then complained of the want of respect shown to him in his correspondence with the superior, in allowing his letters to remains some time unanswered.' 'I had the superior's letter referred to with me', O'Brien explained, 'and produced it, saying it contained the best statement of our reasons for having the Intermediate in Bruff, and that anyone who read it should admit that it was most respectful to the PP. The Bishop asked me for it, and read aloud a passage in which the superior feelingly apologised to the PP for the unavoidable delay in replying, caused by his illness. The Bishop said that was fair, and there was no cause to complain.'

Dr O'Dwyer, it would appear, then sought to familiarise himself with the internal working of the school. 'By a series of questions to the Director' he 'elicited the following points – That the Director taught the junior boys, another Brother taught the Intermediate, and that he was assisted by another Brother for four hours a day – that there were 19 boys in the Intermediate class – that the subjects taught in it were English, French, Algebra, Arithmetic, Euclid, Drawing – that the old Brother was about 68 years of age – that he was paid for by the superior, but was expected to help in school as far as his strength would allow – that there was a monitor in each school, over 16 years of age, that each had passed in the Intermediate Junior (Examination), that each was paid 2s. a week – about the amount paid monitors in national schools, the Bishop said.'

'The PP then charged the Brothers in Bruff with trying to excite the people against him for removing the Bl. Sacrament and excluding them from the convent Mass.' 'I never heard the breath of such a charge before', O'Brien stated, 'and told the Bishop if our superior knew it to be the case, he would come down with a heavy hand on the director. The director positively denied the charge, and said that a few persons asked him to get a deputation of two of the principal men of the town to wait on the parish priest and try to induce him to restore the Bl. Sacrament and allow the Brothers to hear Mass in the convent, but the director would have nothing to say to it.' O'Dwyer appears to have had his suspicions. 'The Bishop put a series of pointed and minute questions to the director about this, but only learned what I state, and that on the first morning of their exclusion, when returning from Mass, a person on the street asked the director "What had the Brothers done that they were turned out of the convent?"'

Then the Bishop asked the amount of last year's collection,' O'Brien continued, 'and the amount of Intermediate results. He then asked the expenditure and to have the accounts showing the Brothers' expenditure submitted to him there and then. I said this was a serious matter, that I had received no instructions to allow this, and asked his lordship not to press the matter. He said shortly, 'I will press it'. I said I could not allow it, that I should consult the superior, that it belonged to episcopal visitation to examine the accounts, that this question was settled by Rome at the time of the controversy about the Maynooth decree.' O'Dwyer, it would appear, sensing a denial of his authority and that he was being deliberately obstructed, became assertive. 'He said he wanted no episcopal visitation, that he was there appointed by Rome to settle this question, that he was the representative of the Pope in the matter, and that he could not settle it without seeing their accounts, that if they were not produced there was no use in his remaining there, and he then stood up. I again asked him to allow me to consult the superior. He said he could not be coming every day to Bruff, and then added I will now ask you formally, to the director, 'Do you refuse to show me the accounts?' The director said he would not. He then asked me – I said 'I have already asked your lordship to allow me to consult my superior, and I ask you again, but I cannot allow the account to be shown as I have no commission for this. The Bishop said he would have to report to Rome that he would not be shown the accounts. He and Fr McNamara then left the house.'

The Br Assistant added:

> It was for me a very painful interview, but surely his lordship, after hearing from me that we were satisfied to accept £30 and have the Intermediate, did not need more to say what was his proposed settlement, but he did not say one word as to it.

He concluded, nevertheless, with the informative comment: '*I must say that Doctor McNamara's overbearing and unkind manner was in striking contrast to that of the Bishop's.*[52]

It seems evident that O'Dwyer, prompted from Rome, was anxious to have the matter cleared up at that meeting, and that the Brothers' secrecy about the accounts completely upset his plans, and appeared to confirm the PP's suspicions that they were much better off than they let on to be. In the event, it would have made little difference if his lordship had curbed his impatience and allowed Br O'Brien to consult the superior general. The latter made this clear in a letter to Monsignor Antonini, Rome, just over a fortnight later. On 5 June 1897 he stated categorically:

> Our accounts are never submitted to parish priests or Bishops. From the foundation of the Institute, over ninety years ago, they have never been

shown to anyone except to the Superior or his Assistants at the visitation of the houses; and I could not as guardian of the rights of the Institute, and, as such, accountable to the Holy See for their preservation, grant to the Bishop what he asked; to do so would be to admit interference with our internal discipline and with the internal management of our houses.

He added that there was 'no change for the better for the Brothers in Bruff'. There was 'still the same hostile attitude on the part of the parish priest towards the Brothers'.[53]

Br. Kelly provided a further instance of the parish priest's harassment in a letter to the Brother Assistant on 30 May 1897. The Brothers now occupied 'the first seat near the altar rails' in 'the respectable portion of the parish church of Bruff' with the permission of Mrs Fogarty of the Hotel, who owned the seat. She told Kelly the previous day 'that the PP spoke to her about six weeks ago and wanted to know if the Brothers caused her any inconvenience by being in her seat, as he would speak to us and put us out of it. She told him that they were very welcome to the seat, and that Mr Kelly had spoken to her about it, and that there was always a good understanding between this house and the Christian Brothers. So he left it there.' Kelly then went on to reveal something of his own mind: 'The poor dear man still wanted to harass and annoy us by putting us out of the seat. *God bless him.* He is very bitter and be assured we will never get any of our privileges back again that he has deprived us of except through Rome and the great power of St Joseph. But that should not discourage us in the least. He will not be always PP of Bruff. Never show him nor his Bishop the accounts, nor never give the place up to him. If he refuses me the collection next October at the church door, if the superior gives me permission I will make it myself through the town.'[54]

The mixture of condescension and defiance, when linked with Fr McNamara's accusation, on 20 May, that he had been working up public opinion against him, suggests that Kelly may have been a far more subtle and political person than the parish priest, and that, as at Mungret, the situation was exacerbated by a clash of personalities. In his letter, Kelly added a footnote that Dr O'Dwyer was to be in Bruff on Sunday 13 June 'making visitation and will have Confirmation'. He was apprehensive as to what might occur. On the evening of 13 June he wrote with palpable relief to the Brother Assistant. His letter underlined O'Dwyer's pastoral concern and his human touch.

> The Confirmation came off today and I am glad to inform you was a great success. The Bishop (was) very nice and well pleased. After last Mass he went to the pulpit and explained the object of the visitation, said a great deal about drunkenness etc and then touched on education, said a great deal to the parents on the obligation of sending their children to school and told them that they had good schools in the parish, that they had the Christian Brothers, the Nuns, and the national schools under the care of the clergy etc.

'After his long sermon', Kelly continued, 'he made a very searching examination with the children in every part of the catechism, nearly all the questions outside the catechism.' The children answered well. The bishop praised them and told them they ought to be thankful to their teachers who had instructed them so well and that they ought to pray for them. 'On the whole', Kelly observed, 'the Bishop was very nice, and when he saw me outside the sanctuary rail when examining the children inside, he told me to come inside, which I thought was very nice of him. I was a bit nervous in the morning, thinking he might have said something public about our business or that he does not want us here or something like it. Thanks to St Joseph, everything came off splendidly.' 'It's a pity', Kelly added in a footnote, 'we haven't a fair PP.'[55]

The bishop, then, had managed to preserve good external relations with the Brothers in Bruff, unlike his parish priest, while at the same time he had quietly presented an eloquent and plausible case to Rome in favour of the Brothers withdrawing from intermediate education. The first Br Maxwell learned of its effectiveness was in a letter from Rome, dated 14 June 1897. The extant copy, a translation into English, is not signed, but from subsequent references it is clear that the author was Cardinal Ledocowski. After receiving Br Maxwell's letter of 30 March, the cardinal explained, he had contacted Bishop O'Dwyer concerning 'having an annual collection for the Brothers, and the carrying on of inter-mediate education by them, ... without loss of mutual harmony between the Brothers and the parish priest of the place'. To his 'incitements', the bishop had answered that he had 'made public his inclination and wish to fully carry out my desires', but he added 'several observations ... which I think it well to make known to you.'

> The Bishop writes that the teaching of the Intermediate on the part of the Christian Brothers is not without detriment to elementary instruction; since even out of two Religious Brothers given to teaching one must be entirely devoted to the Intermediate, for the elementary instruction of about eighty boys there remains only one teacher whose work, indeed, seems to be unequal to this burden. On which account, if the Intermediate is to be retained in the school of the Brothers, it is necessary to send there another Brother, that there may be at least two Brothers for giving elementary instruction; the matter to be arranged with the parish priest for a sufficient maintenance.

A reasonable educational case for the more effective teaching of the pupils – though the difficult issue of 'sufficient maintenance' remained. The bishop's over all presentation is not available, but it is likely to have urged Ledocowski to a further more radical step: for he went on to state that he considered 'that it would be wiser for the Brothers to abstain from intermediate education, not only on account of the particular circumstances of Bruff, where there is another intermediate school directed by a secular priest, but chiefly on account of the principal end of their Institute, which is for the instruction and Christian education of the poor and of the children of the lower orders'. 'A most noble end', he added, 'from which you are not suffered to depart even in the least; in this is your highest praise, and principal fountain of heavenly blessings. Let others have the glory of letters, do you imitate Jesus Christ, who said suffer the little ones to come to me.'

'Moreover, I say all this,' the cardinal observed, 'because while there are not wanting many other Institutes which devote themselves to the higher instruction of boys, I think that it is more pleasing to God that you devote all your powers to the most holy end of your Institute.' 'For the rest', he concluded, 'I will again ask the Bishop to deal liberally with you that the Brothers may be able to be sustained altogether suitably in the school of Bruff.'[56]

Propaganda evidently informed Dr O'Dwyer of the advice given to the superior of the Brothers, because two months later, on 18 August 1897, Fr McNamara sent a brief, almost curt note from Kilkee to Br Kelly:

> As the Bishop has informed me that the Propaganda advised your superior to discontinue the intermediate classes, I will trouble you to let me know what you intend to do as to Bruff school. An answer will find me here.[57]

Ten days later, still at Kilkee, the parish priest expressed his surprise that Kelly's superior 'should disregard the express wish of the Cardinal, founded on the spirit of your Institute, (and) that you should continue teaching intermediate classes at Bruff' and should ignore the parish priest in making 'these arrangements', not consulting or informing him before hand. Such proceedings were 'derogatory' to his position as parish priest.[58] The nature of 'these arrangements' was explained by Br Maxwell in a letter to Ledocowski on 14 October 1897. He had sent an additional Brother to Bruff to teach the primary classes, as the Cardinal had suggested, and had written to Fr McNamara offering to give up the teaching of the intermediate in Bruff if he 'would give two Brothers one hundred pounds a year for their support, and twenty-five pounds a year for the support of a servant'. This was 'the lowest sum' he 'could ask for their expenses'.[59]

The parish priest's reaction had been negative and indignant. He had felt he had won the contest when Ledochowski had advised the Brothers withdrawal from intermediate education. On 1 September 1897, he informed Maxwell that as he 'did not think it necessary' to consult him 'before making the recent arrangements in Bruff school', he 'must decline to have anything further to say or do regarding either the management of the school or the support of the Brothers'. This was in violation of the original contract with the Brothers! He then went on accusingly:

> I should say that it appears strange that having disregarded the wish of the Cardinal, and ignored Most Revd Dr O'Dwyer as Bishop, and me as parish priest, you can state that your desire is to live and act in harmony with ecclesiastical authorities.

Turning to the vexed question of funding, he bared his designs as well as his teeth:

> When you ask me to undertake to give each Brother £50 per year you evidently little know how unwilling parents are at the present time to contribute to the education of their children. My parishioners know that the French Brothers have a national school in this neighbourhood [Hospital], and they can't see why your Brothers should not submit to the rules of the National Board of Education also, and thus free them from the annual collection, and other expenses necessary for the keeping of the Bruff school.[60]

Thus, the lines seemed drawn finally, where Br Maxwell was concerned. The parish priest did not want the Brothers teaching intermediate classes, and was not prepared to pay them sufficient funds to teach the primary classes or to allow them to conduct a public collection.[61] In short, he did not want them in Bruff, and the bishop either could not, or would not, intervene on the Brothers' behalf. Maxwell decided to withdraw his men from Bruff.

On 20 September 1897 he informed Bishop O'Dwyer of his intention to withdraw at the commencement of the Christmas holidays, or sooner if the parish priest had made arrangements for the school. The bishop replied on 23 September stating that he had communicated Maxwell's decision to the parish priest and had requested him to inform Br Maxwell when he would be ready 'to relieve the Brothers of their charge'. He added:

> With reference to the immediate reasons which have determined you to withdraw the Brothers, I do not think that, as stated in your letter, they fairly represent the attitude of the parish priest, and for myself, I am entirely at a loss to understand the reason of the treatment which I have received in the matter.

That was all. There was no mention of regret at the departure of the Brothers after nearly forty years of service in Bruff. His focus was rather on aggrievement at the treatment *he* (not the Brothers) had received.[62]

The following day, the parish priest wrote to Maxwell that he would be 'in a position by the first of November to provide new teachers for the school' and would be ready at that date 'to take over the schools from your Brothers'. The tone made it clear that Fr McNamara was well prepared for the Brothers departure, and welcomed it. His parting gesture of magnanimity served only to reflect insensitivity and unconscious irony. 'In the meantime', he declared, 'a collection will be announced which they can make in the usual way on next Sunday fortnight; for it is only right that the Brothers should be paid for the work of the past year. Trusting this arrangement will suit.'[63]

Anticipating, from past experience with some of the inhabitants of Bruff and its hinterland, that there might be trouble over their departure, Br Maxwell wrote to Br Kelly that same day. Not having yet received McNamara's letter, he informed Kelly that the Brothers would be leaving at the commencement of the Christmas vacation, and that he was not to 'speak to any individual in the locality on the subject'. 'We have reason to fear much trouble', he warned, 'if we mention the matter in the town, hence absolute silence is necessary.' Kelly was not to tell the other Brothers anything, for the present, and to disclaim any knowledge if asked by anyone. 'In fine', the superior concluded, 'silence is now our great safeguard. We need all our prudence to preserve the Institute from grave trouble.'[64]

A little over a month later, Kelly was able to report that by the following day, 29 October, all books and furniture would have been sent away, without any one in the locality, so far as he knew, being aware of their going. He had paid all their debts, had the house washed, and the place looked very well. He would leave 'tomorrow night to Limerick', he declared, 'and bid goodbye to Bruff and our *good* PP that has always been so kind to me'.[65] Meanwhile, during these days, the bishop was exploring with his friend, Bishop Richard A. Sheehan of Waterford, the possibility of the De La Salle Brothers coming to Bruff.[66]

AGITATION AT BRUFF. PROTEST IN LIMERICK

If the parish priest expected a smooth transition to alternative teachers at the school, he was soon disillusioned. Almost immediately, word reached employees of the *Limerick Leader* that there were suspicious circumstances surrounding the Brothers' departure. As early as 3 November, one of them, Edward T. Moran, wrote to the superior general for an explanation of the Brothers' withdrawal. Br Maxwell replied two days later that he wished, in the first place, to assure him 'that the Brothers were always kindly treated by the good people of the town and neighbourhood of Bruff', and that they always 'felt it a pleasure to labour for the education of the boys attending their schools in Bruff.' 'In the second place', he added vaguely but adroitly, 'I feel bound to say that I myself gave notice to the Bishop of the diocese, Most Revd Dr O'Dwyer, that I was obliged to withdraw the Brothers from Bruff in consequence of circumstances which caused the Brothers much trouble, circumstances, too, over which they had no control, and which rendered it impossible for them to remain any longer in Bruff.' In conclusion, he thanked the writer for his kind words about the Brothers 'during their many years – close on forty in Bruff'.[67]

It was a clever letter, which gave no explanation beyond the vague 'circumstances over which they had no control' but which caused them 'much trouble', and which, by implication, were caused by someone else, thereby directing the blame elsewhere without directly naming the parish priest. On 8 and 10 November 1897, the *Limerick Leader* reported that public concern had led to a meeting of 1,000 people, that a member of a prominent family in the area, Mr J. Carroll, JP, chairman of the Kilmallock Board of Guardians, had presided, and that the meeting had been called to consider the steps to be taken to bring the Brothers back. The reply from Br Maxwell was read to the meeting. It was noted that the circumstances of their departure were known to the bishop. A deputation waited on the parish priest who declared that there was no chance of the Brothers being brought back, but assured them that he would write to Dr O'Dwyer asking him to bring in the French Brothers. This seemed to satisfy the deputation. Fr McNamara was reported to have denied all knowledge of the reasons for the Brothers' departure. He held no antagonism towards them. The superior of the Christian Brothers in Limerick was prepared to say only that the Brothers 'found it necessary to leave Bruff, and the people of Bruff knew three-quarters of the reasons'. At this stage, the editor of the struggling *Limerick Leader*, Andrew McEvoy, sensed a promising story. He visited Bruff to interview individuals, and unearthed details about the Brothers relations with the parish priest going back to the removal of the Blessed Sacrament in 1892, and about 'the prolonged petty persecution' to which they 'were subjected', which indicated that people who were privy to the history, perhaps even a Christian Brother, were providing information.

On 12 November the *Leader* referred to the rivalry between the Christian Brothers, who charged nothing or very moderate fees, and the diocesan seminary over the Intermediate, and judged that there could be 'no room for doubt where the present trouble originated'. The paper displayed itself increasingly partisan. On 15 November the clergy were criticised for a treatment of the Brothers that was 'the reverse of what one would expect from those whose duty it is to preach Christian charity'. Two days later the paper carried the heading – 'Brothers' Tale of Tyranny in Bruff', and urged the public to uphold the Brothers' cause.

Meantime, the French congregation of Brothers, sought by the bishop and the parish priest, had declined to come to Bruff. Fr McNamara now planned to bring in national school teachers. On 19 November the *Leader* carried a heading which became standard – 'The Bruff Scandal'. The *Weekly Independent* now took up the question – 'Why do the Brothers have to Leave?' Letters on the issue began to appear in newspapers. By 22 November the *Leader* had drawn attention to the 'Silence of Most Revd Dr O'Dwyer', and commented that he should not allow such injustice and cruelty to be practised in his diocese. It asked him to recall the Brothers, and urged 'the sturdy men of Bruff', if the Brothers were not recalled, 'to make the life of the grabbers, whoever they may be, an intolerant burden for them to bear'. This irresponsible application of a Land League form of denunciation to national teachers or other teachers replacing the Brothers, was calculated to inflame feeling and to make it difficult for local clergy and people who might wish to speak up for the parish priest.

Fr McNamara criticised from the altar the hostile attitude of some of the parishioners, and the rather precipitous curate, Fr Reeves, caused offence by calling those who were protesting, 'Moonlighters'. The parish priest also protested to Mr McEvoy that the *Limerick Leader* was endeavouring to create friction between priests and people.[68]

The paper, however, continued its campaign. Columns of new letters appeared. The parish priest was depicted as endeavouring to grab all sources of income for himself.

By this, O'Dwyer judged that the situation had become such as to require special remedies. At what must have been considerable cost to his personal pride and self-sufficiency, he requested Bishop O'Callaghan to ask the assistance of Br Maxwell. 'The withdrawal of the Christian Brothers from Bruff', O'Dwyer explained on 30 November 1897, 'has led to considerable unpleasantness between the PP and a section of the people, and may easily develop into a great scandal. A large deputation waited on me today to request me to bring the Bros. back. This, I told them I would not do, nor did I think the Bros. desired to come; but I said if Mr Maxwell wrote to me expressing a desire for the Bros. to return and submitted conditions which I though reasonable, that I would favourably entertain the proposition. They, on their side, promising that if Mr Maxwell declined to take that step, they would withdraw all opposition to the parish priest.' 'Now I venture to write to your lordship to ask you

> to telegraph in the morning to Mr Maxwell, and get him to telegraph tomorrow, in answer to the letter which he will get from Bruff, distinctly saying that he thinks it better *not* to send his Brothers back to Bruff.

'Whatever may be thought of the circumstances that led up to his withdrawal,' O'Dwyer continued, acknowledging, it seems, unease about past happenings, 'there can be no doubt that harmony could never be restored between the Bros. and the priests there, nor any good ensue to religion, and on the other hand if he encourages the people now with the hope that under any conditions he will come back, it will be impossible to deal with them, and we may have an outbreak of irreligion which would do much harm.'

He concluded with the warning: 'Already the Parnellites here and in the country are trying to fan the flame, and unless the thing is stopped at once they will succeed.' 'But,' he added, 'one single word from Mr Maxwell tomorrow, to say that it is too late now, puts an end to it all; and I shall thank you very much if you get him for religion's sake to say it.'[69]

Dr O'Callaghan, in a quandary, sent a telegram to Br Maxwell on 1 December, and then sat down to give further information. He enclosed the letter to him from the bishop of Limerick. 'I found it hard to intervene in the matter', he explained, 'and I was perplexed as to what I should do', but, 'on consideration' thought it not a mistake to send the telegram.[70] As a result of this intercession, Maxwell wrote to Mr John Carroll, JP, that he had 'come to the resolution, though with great regret, that it has now become most undesirable, if not impossible, for me to send the Brothers back to Bruff.'[71]

In subsequent days, Br Maxwell's generous gesture brought embarrassment to the Brothers. On 10 December, Michael O'Shaughnessy, one of the leaders of the protestors, informed Br Redmond, a former director of the Bruff school, that a deputation to the parish priest seeking a return of the Brothers had been informed that Br Maxwell had sent a telegram to the Bishop stating that he would not send back the Brothers to Bruff. O'Shaughnessy wanted to know if this was a fact, or 'one of the many lies' to which they had 'been treated since the inception of this business?' If it was a fact, was 'it not a shame to have led the Bruff deputation, the true, tried and fighting friends of the Christian Brothers' cause, into a fool's paradise in allowing them the faintest hope of the return of their friends'. When he heard of it, he had 'put it down as a lie or, at least, the telegram' had 'been put through a process of wriggling and equivocation'. He asked for a quick response, as a deputation was leaving for Limerick on Monday to see the Bishop. In a postscript, he added: 'Of course any information will be treated as strictly confidential'.[72]

The protestors' distrust of the local clergy, and perhaps even of the bishop, was evident, as was the implication that they had been given to understand that the Brothers approved of the demands for their return. On 12 December, in response to a letter from Mr Carroll, JP, sent on the same day as that of O'Shaughnessy, Br Maxwell confirmed that he had sent the telegram to the Bishop 'in the interests of religion and peace', and consequently he had informed a deputation to him that he 'could hold no hope of the Brothers return'.[73]

Despite the finality of this, the agitation in Bruff increased, spurred on by fighting language in the *Limerick Leader*, now enjoying greatly increased sales. The focus of the trouble was the arrival of a national school teacher, appointed by the parish priest. Thomas Bowman had taught previously in the village of Capamore, Co. Limerick. On 1 December 1897, Andrew McEvoy, editor and leader writer of the *Limerick Leader*, described the arrival of the new teacher in Bruff in inflated and inflammatory language which subsequently merited a charge of libel.

> It was Father McNamara's intention to open the evicted schools on yesterday, a brand new teacher named Bowman, or No-man, having been somehow or other secured to take the place of the pious Christian Brothers. But the sterling men and women of brave and sterling Bruff trooped in their hundreds to the spot and put … the kibaush on the Very Revd gentleman's little plan, and the schools did not open. The house, we understand, in which 'No-man' has taken up his temporary abode is guarded by a posse of Royal Irish Constabulary, who, it would appear, are the only class upon whom the Parish Priest can now look for support in his unjustifiable and reprehensible work of eviction and grabbing. Hostilities at the scene of the conflict are at present suspended, and the schools closed by order of the Bishop, awaiting the result of the negotiations which, it is understood, will at once take place between his lordship and the Superior General of the Christian Brothers.

'Until that result is made known', the writer advised, 'we have only to counsel the people of Bruff to rest steadily on their oars, to bide their time patiently, to act respectfully, as they have ever done, towards their priests, to bear themselves in every way as the strong, trusty, and self-respecting men we take them for … Stand together, brothers all, and if it should happen that, as a consequence of the pending negotiations, your old beloved friends, the Christian Brothers, are not recalled, then we ask you', he declared menacingly,

> to do that duty, which as honourable, upright, and God-fearing men, it will become your part to perform, namely, to boycott the evicted schools and the emergencyman imported into your midst as never exterminator or landgrabber was boycotted, and never permit it to be said that your children were taught by a grabber, or that in a critical hour, when all Ireland looked to you, your heroic resolve and brave deed in a noble cause, you failed to uphold your good name and to honour your county and country.[74]

No pupil turned up at the school. The teacher was obliged to leave the town on 2 December under police protection. His position at Capamore was no longer available. Dr O'Dwyer appealed to Bishop H. Henry, Down and Connor, to find a position for him.[75] The parish priest continued to be presented as the required target by the *Leader*, which spoke of him as 'the clerical Napoleon of East Limerick', noted for his 'despotic and autocratic rule'.[76]

Despite the clear indications from the bishop and from Br Maxwell that the Brothers would not return, which the *Leader* had chosen virtually to ignore, a memorial signed by numerous members of 'the parishes of Bruff, Meanus and Grange, with reference to the school at Bruff' was sent to O'Dwyer. He replied on 31 December 1897 in a letter written by his secretary, Fr Andrew Murphy, and addressed to John Carroll, JP, chairman of the protesting group and the leading signatory. It was a combative response. He was instructed, his secretary stated, to direct their attention to the fact 'that the Bishop had already given his decision upon the matter'. He went on:

> I am also to state that, seeing the gross and most unworthy libels and insultsthat have been heaped upon your worthy parish priest, the Very Rev. Dr Mc Namara, it is a source of surprise and great regret to the Bishop to see your name, and those of several other parishioners of Bruff, attached to this memorial without one word of respect or apology for the misconduct with which this movement has been conducted.
>
> After this, the Bishop hopes that the respectable people of the parish will withdraw from this agitation, which can do no good and is fomented by persons whose whole aim and purpose seem to be to seize every opportunity of driving a wedge between the clergy and people. They began with politics, but now they are carrying the war into religion. It is

for a Catholic people, such as you are, to consider whether you will accept the decision of your Bishop on a question of this kind, or try to carry your own way by mob violence, and the writings of an anti-clerical press.

'It has been stated', the letter continued,

> that your clergy, by a system of petty persecution, carried on for vile and sordid motives, drove the Christian Brothers out of Bruff. It ought not be necessary for the Bishop to assure you, Mr Carroll, and other men like you, that Dr Mc Namara is incapable of such conduct, and one would think that with your experience of him and his fellow priests, you your-selves, instead of associating with those who thus insult him, would be the first to defend his honour. But it would seem that times are changed.

In a letter from the superior of the Christian Brothers, 'which appeared in a local anti-clerical newspaper', his lordship added, people were referred to the Bishop for the reasons that impelled the Brothers to leave. 'The Bishop desires me to state', Murphy declared, 'that he cannot tell what determined them to take that course. He only knows that the Christian Brothers made a number of serious charges against the parish priest last summer to the Holy See, that every single one of these charges was dismissed by Propaganda as unfounded and the conduct of the parish priest vindicated in every respect.'

Murphy concluded:

> Whether the agitation which is now fomented in Bruff is a schismatical attempt to prevent him by violence and insult from giving effect to the decision of the Holy See, the Bishop cannot say, but whether it is or not, he thinks that the experience of other people of greater pretensions who tried that course in the diocese before [referring presumably to Dillon and O'Brien] ought not to lend much encouragement to the people who mean to lead the parish of Bruff astray.[77]

Once again, Dr O'Dwyer took shelter behind 'the decisions of the Holy See'. His exaggerated statement, moreover, about the Holy See dismissing all the charges against the parish priest, as if there had been a formal examination by Propaganda of formal charges, only weakened his credibility. The exaggeration was subsequently highlighted by informed protestors, and shown up by Br Maxwell. At the start of the New Year, on 18 January 1898, O'Dwyer once more endeavoured to play the papal card, appealing to people's respect for the papacy by representing the opposition as defying 'the decisions of the Holy See'. The occasion was the interest being generated in Limerick regarding the Bruff dispute. The bishop felt it necessary to pen a public letter to the mayor, Michael Cusack, concerning the Brothers departure. 'They left Bruff of their own accord,' he insisted. 'They did not even pay me the courtesy of asking my opinion, but simply notified their decision to me. I consider it, then, rather unreasonable to be asked now to invite them back. I was extremely sorry that they left Bruff ... but ... if this agitation is being fomented as an attempt to intimidate the parish priest and punish him, or to prevent me from giving effect to *the decisions of the Holy See,* I think the parties concerned will find that they are mistaken.' He added: 'If the Brothers had consulted me before they left, I should have advised them to remain. Things have now gone so far that I do not think the good of the people or the interests of religion would be served by their return.'[78]

Dr O'Dwyer's entire career had been marked by defiance in the face of any attempt to intimidate him. Fr McNamara had already warned his parishioners of this at Sunday Mass on 7 January 1898. Were it not for his intercession, he claimed, the chapel would have been closed and the people excommunicated. He advised them to cease the agitation, adding: 'Your actions will not change his lordship's determination – You do not know with whom you have to deal.'[79] By 1 February, the bishop was under the impression that the Brothers were involved in encouraging the opposition. On that day he wrote to his good friend, Bishop Donnelly of Dublin: 'I have a great lot of evidence that the Bros. are actually fomenting the resistance there, I dare say *pour encourager les autres eveques,* but before I have done with them I hope to bring them to their senses.'[80]

As the agitation and the criticism of the clergy continued, the bishop responded with his ultimate weapon. On Sunday, 20 February 1898, as the Lenten season approached, Fr McNamara read to the congregation a letter from Dr O'Dwyer: 'The Bishop directs me to announce to you that I am to hold no stations as he considers it would only be a mockery to administer sacraments to you owing to the sinful conduct of which you have been guilty within the past few months.' The letter went on to announce that no ashes would be blessed [for Ash Wednesday], and that morning Masses and evening devotions would not be allowed in the church.[81] The action did little to quieten the protestors. The *Limerick Leader* led the defiance: 'Whatever threats his lordship may make or carry out will not in the least shake the determination of the people of Bruff. They are conscious that they have done nothing that they need to be ashamed or sorry for. It is the first time they have been denied the right of having blessed ashes placed on their foreheads – a sacred function of our Church which should recall to his lordship's mind that he, as well as the people, will some day have to appear before a just and merciful judge.' The article concluded with the question: 'What crime did the Christian Brothers commit that has prejudiced his lordship so much against them that he will not accede to the wish of his people by directing the return of the Brothers.'[82]

Early in March, the Limerick Board of Guardians passed a resolution concerning the withdrawal of the Brothers from Bruff that induced Dr O'Dwyer to indulge in public remarks which further inflamed the situation, but which also revealed the standpoint from which he viewed criticism. His concept of the role and function of the bishop, noted at the beginning of this chapter, was involved.

He considered their resolution, he declared, 'most improper and even irreligious'. In his public letter to the mayor he had made clear 'that the Bruff affair was one of a purely spiritual and ecclesiastical character' on which the ecclesiastical authorities had spoken. Did the Poor Law Guardians think 'that because they have been elected to manage a workhouse, they are competent to rule the Church?' He went on to comment critically on the reported remarks of certain members of the Board, and observed severely that other members were 'following out the principles of the anti-clerical party in the country'. He had seen 'this evil growing' over the years, and he had warned the people in pastoral letters 'that the inevitable result would carry them far beyond the political issues, and possibly land them outside the Church'. 'To that it is coming fast', he declared. 'A resolution such as your Board, breaking away from all its Catholic traditions, passed on Wednesday is the worst symptom we have had yet. And it is because of the seed of infidelity which is in it that I thus openly denounce it.'[83]

His excessive reaction provided a further opening to the Bruff party, which, in turn, sent a public letter to the chairman of the Poor Law Board of Governors. They insisted that the issues leading to the withdrawal of the Brothers from Bruff had never been submitted to the Holy See, despite the Bishop's statement, and they pointed out that the alleged 'irreligious and immoral' people opposing the Bishop were the same people whose faith and practice were highly praised by his parish priest just six months previously, and whose subscription to the 'Propagation of the Faith' was the highest of any parish in the diocese.[84]

In the face of 'the gratuitous annoyance' Dr O'Dwyer was receiving, Bishop Thomas McRedmond, of Killaloe, expressed his sympathy on 10 March, and added that he understood from his priests 'that the Christian Brothers' were 'secretly fanning the flame', that in Ennis and Kilrush the Brothers received the *Limerick Leader* regularly, 'and read and *comment* on those infamous articles and correspondence for their grown boys during school hours'. 'This, however,' he added, 'it would be hard to prove, as they have the boys entirely in their hands.'[85]

On 25 March, the bishop agreed to meet at Kilmallock with a deputation of parishioners from Bruff.[86] The meeting produced little practical improvement, though the optimistic Fr McNamara was of the view by 7 May that 'the agitators are looking for some pretext to submit.'[87] Whatever vague signs of improvement there may have been were firmly put aside the following month when a libel action brought against the *Limerick Leader* by the teacher, Thomas Bowman, came to court. He complained of the language used against him by the paper, particularly its description of him as 'an exterminator and grabber', terms which in Bruff, as John Carroll, JP, admitted under questioning, 'would put him in danger of unpleasant consequences'.[88]

The *Leader's* counsel, Mr O'Shaughnessy, QC, claimed that Mr Bowman was but a pawn in the hands of others. The parish priest wished to turn out of the school the Christian Brothers who had been there for forty years, and to establish a school 'in which the State would pay the teachers and of which he would be manager'. 'The Bruff school had been founded by the people', he stated, and 'not a single parishioner was on the side of the Bishop and priest in this dispute'. The *Leader's* articles were not really directed against the plaintiff, but against the Bishop and the parish priest, the counsel claimed, and he asked, 'Was a newspaper to be run to earth because the Bishop did not like the way it commented on a public matter?' He added emphatically: 'If the jury thought that the priest and Bishop had a right to walk over people, let them find it so; but if they thought that the people in Bruff and every other district in Ireland had a right to have a word in the education of their children they should find for the defendant.' In support of his case, he sought to establish that there had been a campaign of hostility and discrimination against the Brothers by the parish priest. Three Brothers, who had been in Bruff for a number of years, gave testimony of interference in their lives from shortly after the arrival of the parish priest in 1892: the removal of the Blessed Sacrament and the instruction not to attend Mass at the convent received particular mention. Dr O'Dwyer, called by Mr MacDermott, QC, and cross-examined on the part of the defendants, represented these events not as part of a pattern of interference as they appeared to the Brothers but as isolated happenings unrelated to the school issue in 1896.[89]

Mr Burke, QC, for the plaintiff, addressing the jury on 10 June, said that

> he was as strongly opposed to clerical despotism as his learned friend, who had just addressed the jury, but people should be protected from the despotism of the newspaper Press, which spoke with a thousand voices, and although anonymous, was sufficient to damn a man for life. That was what the jury had to deal with, and not with any question of ecclesiastical policy. This was a civil court, in which an editor of a paper had been called upon to explain singularly atrocious language, in which he held up an individual to a fate which only pursued those who in this country were branded as grabbers. The man who penned these shameful articles had not been put into the box, but an attempt had been made instead to draw across the real issue the question of a dispute between ecclesiastical personages ... as to whether in 1892 the Bishop of Limerick was right or wrong in withdrawing the Blessed Sacrament from the oratory of the Christian Brothers.

Concluding, he 'asked the jury to put their foot down on the dishonest defence which had been attempted here, and which never arose so frequently as when a truculent leader writer, who would not face the witness box, pretended that he was the champion of religion against his Bishop and the Pope.'[90]

The jury found for the plaintiff, but he was awarded only £40 instead of the £500 he had sought. The *Irish Independent*, in its comments on 11 June, supported the *Limerick Leader* in its defence of the Christian Brothers, while acknowledging that more moderate language would have achieved the purpose in view without legal risks. The real issues in the case, it proclaimed, were wider than Bruff. These were the continuing efforts of the bishops and clergy to obtain and retain managerial control of schools and teachers, and the need for security of tenure for teachers. In the diocese of Limerick, the paper commented, there was the anomaly that in the city children were prevented from attending national schools, while in Bruff and elsewhere they were encouraged to attend such schools under clerical management.

The dispute continued unabated into 1889. In February 1898 members of the Congregated Trades and other worker societies had met with Br J.B. Welsh, a popular figure in Limerick, at Sexton Street School to discuss how they could help the Brothers' schools financially and with maintenance, and on 20 June they held a large public meeting in which they extended their sympathy and support to the people of Bruff and pledged support to the *Limerick Leader* and its proprietor. The bishop was not pleased. Consequently, when Br Walsh requested, in April 1899, to be allowed to collect for repairs to St Mary's primary school, described as in dangerous condition, his request was turned down.[91] On 16 April, Walsh was informed by the bishop's secretary that all the heads of religious communities had been asked by his lordship 'to abstain from making special collections while the parish clergy' were 'engaged in raising the large sum ... necessary for building the new church of St Michael's', and then was pointedly advised that the Brothers

> might well apply to the purpose you mention some portion of the very large sums received from the intermediate in addition to the ordinary income from several years past in this city, amounting to from £800 to £1100 a year, and in all Ireland to £15,000.[92]

If the bishop, however, allowed frustration over the Brothers and Bruff spill over into his relations with the Brothers in Limerick, the protestors in Bruff, later in the year, brought their exasperation with the bishop onto the streets of his city. A group of them journeyed to Limerick in November, and as Dr O'Dwyer and a Mr Guinane walked the streets they followed them hooting and shouting. At William Street, an outraged member of the Pork Butchers Society, a Mr Nash, strode into the middle of the street, took off his hat, and gave three cheers for the bishop which, he subsequently reported, 'was eagerly responded to'.[93] The response was indicative of a widespread reaction in the city. The Pork Butchers Society came out strongly in favour of 'the prelate who fought hard on behalf of the Pork Butchers when they were struggling for their existence against capitalists'. They pledged not to buy the *Limerick Leader* in future.[94] St Michael's Temperance Society, at a meeting of 'hundreds of angry young men', denounced the disgraceful affair, and the Rathkeale Temperance Society and the Limerick Stonecutters Society also protested. Various letters to the *Limerick Echo* attacked the Bruff agitation. A letter from Bruff, signed 'Truth', told of 'terrorism and intimidation' being used to get a meeting together, and that only a small number of parents attended. A letter signed 'Observor', from a

Limerick address, maintained that clergy in Bruff 'have been almost continually submitted to mob violence, that one of them, even when carrying the Blessed Sacrament to a dying person, was hooted and yelled at', and Mr Wall, a deacon of the Church, was struck with a cow's liver.[95] A sermon in Bruff, by Fr Tierney, CSsR, which appealed to the people to end the agitation and obey the pope's decision, was interrupted by one or two people, while other men entered and left the church as if by arrangement. Yet, when the priest concluded his sermon, all who were present went on their knees for his blessing.[96] The leading article in the *Limerick Echo* of 28 November 1899 proclaimed that 'from one end of the diocese to the other the insults to the Bishop and priest have aroused the feelings of Catholics', and quoted a letter from 'Truth' that said that 'a certain limited number of laymen have set themselves up as a kind of lay tribunal whose decisions must control all ecclesiastical questions as far as the same relate to their parish'. The Brothers themselves came in for criticism. A sermon by Dr Hallinan, PP, VG, Newcastlewest, noted the extraordinary silence of the superior-general of the Christian Brothers in the dispute, and observed that it surely cannot be that he wished his 'illustrious order' to 'be used as a reason for continued opposition to the Bishop and clergy of the diocese';[97] and 'Truth', on 27 November, made further comment that

> the priests and Christian Brothers, working together, could not make the contribution of the Catholic laity of Bruff more than £112–9–6, yet, strange to relate, having a knowledge of this fact, the representative of the Christian Brothers school, at the conference around the table, called the PP to undertake the payment of £50 per year to each Brother ... In making this demand, the representative of the Brothers knew well he was requiring what was utterly impossible for any PP to grant.[98]

On 4 December, the same 'Truth' claimed that the Christian Brothers 'deliberately sought to provoke a revolt of the laity against the authority of the Church' and for so doing had now 'received from the shocked consciences of the horrified laity a stinging rebuke'.[99] The evidence offered for the Brothers involvement was circumstantial, but that a reaction against the Bruff protesters had taken place because of the insults offered to the bishop in his own city is very evident. Limerick corporation gave formal witness to it when it denounced 'the conduct of certain residents of Bruff, who, while in this city lately, insulted his lordship, the Most Revd Dr O'Dwyer,' and they assured his lordship that this conduct aroused 'the indignation of all classes and creeds in the city'. They wished to convey to him, they continued, the expression of their 'deep attachment, respect, and veneration for His lordship's sacred person and office'.[100]

The bishop, much heartened and strengthened in his resolve and judgment, remarked, in a letter of thanks to the members of St Mary's Temperance Society, that 'popular indignation' had 'made short work of such proceedings here', and he was confident that the effects would soon be felt in Bruff, where there were plenty of good Catholics but 'as generally happens to decent, quiet people, they shrink from contact with rowdies'. Hence, he asserted, 'a gang of reckless men, who are only puppets in the hands of a few designing people, are allowed to speak for the whole place'. Yet, he thought the 'tyranny' was near its end. 'A great improvement has set in', he explained, 'since the scandal in our city three weeks ago let the light in on these champions of religious education', and he was confident that it would extend 'until no Catholic in Bruff' would 'be afraid or ashamed to salute his priest, and even until it' would 'be possible for parents to send their children to school without danger of life or limb to themselves or to their children'.[101] Once again, like his parish priest, he proved unduly optimistic.

With revived confidence, he wrote a public letter, on 18 November 1899, to the Dublin and provincial papers in which he gave 'the essential facts of this deplorable case', from 1892 to 1899, so that public opinion, 'rightly informed', would 'draw its own conclusions as to the merits of the irreligious agitation which is now being carried on, and as to the responsibilities of its authors'.[102] As noted earlier, he wrote mainly from memory, and Br R. A. Maxwell, who replied in detail, in a printed letter sent to every prelate, highlighted a number of mistakes in the bishop's presentation and, in consequence, stated 'most respectfully' that he could not accept 'what his lordship has written as "the essential facts of the case",' and, he added, 'I emphatically disclaim any responsibility for the unhappy occurrences in Bruff.' 'The real question at issue', he claimed, 'had been confused and lost sight of by the introduction of side issues. The Christian Brothers left Bruff because the PP refused them the means of support.'[103]

The masterly reply did little to improve relations in the Limerick diocese between the local clergy and the Brothers. Some months later, the ill feeling over Bruff appeared to have been passed on to Christian Brothers' pupils in Limerick, even as it was reputed to have been at Ennis and Kilrush. On 14 April 1900, Fr Andrew Murphy complained to Br Welsh that at a recent match between St Munchin's College and Sexton Street Christian Brothers' School stones and mud were thrown at the clergy, allegedly by Christian Brothers' boys, and that the previous year, when Sexton Street won the cup, the team went to St Munchin's College, Henry Street, and cheered non-stop and cries of 'Bruff, Bruff', were heard. Br Welsh was advised to see the bishop about the matter. When he did so, his lordship made it clear that he also believed that the Brothers had incited the boys 'to make hostile demonstration towards the clergy'. He had in his possession, he said, letters written by Brothers in connection with the Bruff dispute which he was taking with him to Rome. Proof of the boys' misconduct at the match could be confirmed by a number of witnesses. He gave the names to Br Welsh. None of these, however, proved able to identify any Christian Brothers' boy as involved in misconduct. It was an indication of the prevailing tension that Br Welsh felt it necessary to go to Dublin to consult with his superiors as to what to do next. The situation was discussed in detail and suitable responses were worked out to possible questions or comments from the bishop. On Tuesday, 17 April, Br Welsh met with Dr O'Dwyer and, after a brief conversation, forgot all his planned responses. He allowed his bottled up hurt and resentment to boil over, and he told his lordship that he 'was shocked and alarmed the other day at the statements made implicating me and my Brothers and I believe it unworthy of you, Bishop, and all that you are'. Edward Thomas O'Dwyer, unused to such treatment, rose from his chair and shouted indignantly: 'How dare you! How dare you!' and ordered Welsh to leave the house and never to set foot there again.[104]

On his return to his monastery, a more chastened Welsh wrote to the Brothers' headquarters at Marino in Dublin explaining what had happened despite their earlier preparations. On 19 April he received instructions to write an apology to the bishop. The text was included in the letter. Straightway, he assured his lordship as instructed:

> I regret extremely having allowed my excited feelings to overcome me so far as to forget the respect due to your exalted position, and to speak in a manner quite unbecoming. For both my words and manner on the occasion I earnestly beg your lordship to accept my very humble and sincere apology.[105]

That same day, O'Dwyer replied:

> I read your letter with great satisfaction and accept it. You may have your collections as usual.[106]

The response appears to indicate that what his lordship needed was a token of submission to him as prelate, as having 'full legislative and authoritative power' in matters pertaining to the diocese, and that once that was conceded he would be quite supportive. If this is a correct interpretation, it follows that a sensitive diplomatic approach, with the trappings of concession, might have avoided much controversy. That is also suggested by the bishop's response to the pliant approach of Fr Michael Browne, SJ with regard to faculties. The problem was that Dr O'Dwyer's domineering manner made it difficult for people to respond in a pliant, diplomatic way. One wonders what difference it would have made had the Jesuit provincial, Fr Murphy, and the Brothers' superior-general, R.A. Maxwell, dealt in a less defensive manner with his lordship, while yet preserving their basic rights and privileges.

In the event, the Bruff conflict continued. The opponents in Bruff of the parish priest and to the establishment of a national school, set up their own evening classes in 1903 and applied to the National Board of Education for recognition and financial subsidy. This evoked a sharp protest to the Board from Dr O'Dwyer on 16 October 1903, pointing out that the proposal had been made 'by the very parties who, by organised intimidation' had 'persistently endeavoured to ruin the national school established in Bruff under the parish priest as manager, avowedly because it is a national school'. They sought recognition from the Board as a means of helping to pay a teacher's salary, and if their evening school was recognised it would be used as a means of preventing children from attending the national school during the day.[107]

The sorry disagreement dragged on for another four years, a cause of deprivation and inconvenience to a whole generation of children. In 1907 a request from Propaganda for an end to the conflict, and that a religious congregation be permitted to take over the school, was the occasion of *rapprochement* between the war-weary combatants. In his visit to Rome that year, O'Dwyer was able to report that a reconciliation had been reached and a solution satisfactory to both sides.[108] The De La Salle Brothers agreed to take over the school. Their manner of doing so promised well for the future.

A Brother Anthony responded to the bishop's letter on 8 July 1907. He had obviously studied the situation, and his lordship, with considerable care. His letter could hardly have been more welcome to the bishop. In content and flexibility it differed greatly from what he had experienced with the Christian Brothers. Br Anthony thanked him 'for inviting the children of St De La Salle to take up the work', assured him of his 'sincere desire of seconding' his lordship's views, and that pending the return from New York of the assistant superior general he would hold 'three thoroughly well trained and qualified Brothers in readiness for the work' with a view to their taking up duty on 2 September, subject 'to details being arranged between the Revd. Manager and our Superior General'. He took the liberty, he added, 'of submitting items to form the basis of an agreement between the Revd. Manager and the Superior General'. There followed what must have seemed an answer to prayer from the parish priest's perspective.

> I most respectfully suggest the local parish priest as manager of the school. Your lordship's approval would be sought for the agreement. Having the parish priest as manager would, I think, secure his interest in visiting the the school and in encouraging both teachers and pupils. I purpose taking an early opportunity of calling on the parish priest of Bruff with the view of making his acquaintance, and also to see the house designed for the Brothers and the school.

He concluded with equal astuteness: 'I shall defer doing so, however, for a week, so that I may have your lordship's permission.'[109]

The new arrangement worked well, and, in time, as noted earlier, the new Brothers were allowed to hear Mass in the convent, but from within the sacristy. The conflict had enabled Dr O'Dwyer to demonstrate once again that, while he might try to intimidate others, he would not allow himself to give way to threats and intimidation from anyone. Evidence of this was already plain to see, as both he and the parish priest had warned the Bruff congregation, but there was a certain section of the Bruff population, accustomed to dominating others by threats of violence, who were also determined to have their way. In the past this form of expression found outlet in the land struggle, and also, ironically,

1 Bishop O'Dwyer, shortly after his ordination as bishop

2 Archbishop William J. Walsh of Dublin, Bishop O'Dwyer's contemporary

3 Isaac Butt: a drawing by John Butler Yeats

4 Lord Emly

5 T.M. Healy

6 John Dillon

7 A view of Kilkee, Co. Clare, *c.*1900

8 St John's Cathedral, Limerick, *c.*1910

9 Garryowen, Limerick: a photograph taken around the end of the nineteenth century

George's Street, Limerick.

10 George's Street, Limerick, c.1900

11 General Sir John Maxwell

12 Eamon de Valera in Volunteer uniform, *c.*1917

The Crescent, Limerick

13 Sacred Heart Church and Crescent College, Limerick, *c.*1900

"Ireland will never be content as a province God made her a nation, and while grass grows and water runs there will be men in Ireland to dare and die for her."

(Extract from speech of the Most Rev Dr. O'Dwyer when the freedom of Limerick City was conferred on him, Sept. 14th, 1916).

14 Postcard of Bishop O'Dwyer and quotations from his speech to Limerick Corporation, 1916

15 Leamy's School, at a later period

urel Hill Convent Limerick.

16 Laurel Hill Convent, Limerick

according to 'Truth' in the *Limerick Evening Echo* of 12 December 1899, against the Christian Brothers. This anonymous writer alleged that when Br Redmond was changed from Bruff to Westland Row in 1890 there was an outcry against Br Maxwell, and Christian Brothers were pelted with mud and clods; and a number of young men 'with sticks and ash plants' stood on the bridge and stopped boys attending catechism class on Sunday after the last Mass. Br Kelly, as replacement for Br Redmond, was greeted with groans and mud and the pupils went on strike. The clergy settled the dispute with great difficulty.[110] The tragedy was that the clergy and the bishop were the target from 1897, there were no mediators, and the majority of the parents and their children were the victims.

A postscript to the long drawn out Bruff story. Fr Charles McNamara lived on until 18 February 1926. In July 1915 he learned from Monsignor O'Riordan, rector of the Irish College Rome, that he was to be appointed dean of the diocese. Writing to thank him, he remarked: 'Scarcely had I received your letter when I had a telegram from the Bishop announcing the appointment. The old relations are evidently reviving. The Bishop is very kind, but he is too impulsive.'[111] Andrew McEvoy of the *Limerick Leader*, would not have been happy with such a mild comment on Dr O'Dwyer. The paper's readership expanded because of the controversy and held up thereafter, but McEvoy is said to have lost his job because of pressure from the bishop and, it is alleged, he had to leave Limerick to secure employment.[112]

This section has been concerned with the bishop in conflict with educational institutions. To some extent these overlapped, so that the bishop was engaged in more than one dispute at a time. All this was in addition to the daily work of the diocese over which he maintained a close eye, and to involvement in a variety of other activities. Among these last were positive contributions in the areas of technical and third level education. It is time to turn to these, and to some other constructive happenings, to balance the more negative aspects that have emerged in considering his conflicts.

PART FOUR

The prelate, the man, the educationalist

The prelate and the man

On Dr O'Dwyer's return from his 'ad limina' visit to Rome in 1895, he was met by a large gathering of the clergy of his diocese, both secular and regular, with an address to welcome him and to hope that as St Paul took courage, when met by the brethren on the way to Rome, so his lordship might take courage from this 'affectionate greeting' from his brethren in the priesthood and fellow workers in the ministry and be helped to face all the difficulties he might encounter 'in the administration of his important diocese'. The address, carefully prepared by his old friend, Dean John Flanagan of Adare, went on to praise his achievements, carefully avoiding any reference to disputes or to politics. The matters chosen provide convenient headings under which to examine Edward Thomas O'Dwyer as prelate and human being. But before doing so, it is appropriate to turn again to the one person who knew him best of all and who loved and respected him whatever his failings, his sister, Annie. Confident in her devotion to him, he wrote freely to her and, in turn, readily accepted her mild sisterly criticism. His letters are not extant, but her letters indirectly reveal him. They had much in common. She shared the family humour and forthrightness, if in a gentler vein.

In November 1887, with reference to a photograph of his recent portrait, she quoted some of the nuns as remarking that he was 'getting a presence', and they 'wouldn't care to vex him'. She added that the features were perfect but there was 'a slight expression, a *soupçon* of disdain, that I don't like.'[1] His attendance at the Royal Limerick Horse Show in 1890 had been chronicled and had evoked comment. She understood and was supportive. 'I am glad you enjoyed the Horse Show. They could hardly believe it here, but they don't know the elasticity (is that the right term?) of your nature.'[2] She could hardly explain to Sisters from a very different background that her episcopal brother owned brood mares and had horses for racing,[3] and that the horse show, attended by all classes, was celebrated in a local ballad, to the air of 'The Last Rose of Summer':

> The Royal Show was the place to go
> For fun and fashion of every sort;
> Sure the Lord Lieutenant himself was in it
> And the Countess with him to see the sport.[4]

It would have required Dean John Flanagan, with his many contacts with British and Irish gentry, to explain further that it was in order for him to inform Bishop O'Dwyer that a gentleman called Clifford had asked him to find out whether his lordship 'could get his colt, Prador, into W. Blake's training stables'. He was 'entered for some of the classical Irish 2 year old races at the Curragh, and he would like to give him a fair trial by having him properly handled and ridden.'[5]

The bishop was aware that his sister found it difficult at times in the English atmosphere of her convent, consequently he wrote regularly to her, corresponded with the Revd Mother, and provided her and the community with gifts from time to time. In June 1892, he sent her Père Dudon's two volume *Life of Christ*, which she had requested. He, in turn, was presumably amused by a number of her frank, independent comments. Thus, later in 1892, she remarked:

> I hear his Grace of Westminster is going for the 'Red Hat'. Everyone here says he is a very nice as well as a very holy man, but curiously, I don't care for him at all, nor, if there is no harm in saying it, for the Holy Father himself. They will probably outlive my prejudice; there it is firm enough too.[6]

After the relief of Kimberley, she wrote on 25 February 1900, "'Tis a great pity the poor Boers are lost. You never in all your life saw anything to equal the bloated swagger of the people here.' And at the beginning of 1901, she praised a letter of his which, she thought, would render the *Tablet* furious, and added: 'The Boers must be a grand people – fifteen months stand against this colossal Empire'.[7] Views, which she dared not air in her convent!

In January and February 1893, she joined with him in lamenting the cruel wrongs being experienced by Christians in Uganda, and for whom he was endeavouring to enlist support;[8] and on 14 February, praising his pastoral letter, she remarked justly that no other bishop wrote as he did and that it sounded 'more like an Epistle to the Irish than a letter to the Limerick diocese'![9] With the news of his forthcoming *ad limina* visit in 1895, she looked forward to seeing him twice, going to and from Rome.[10] In November, he wrote from Lourdes, and she, rejoicing at his visit there, hoped his hearing would be cured, adding consolingly that at his recent visit 'all here noticed how well you heard'. She reflected, 'God has permitted this drawback as a sort of counter-poise to the great gifts he has bestowed on you'.[11] It was the effect of some of these gifts that the clergy of the diocese celebrated when they welcomed him home later that month.

The first of the gifts to which they witnessed was his 'constant, unflagging, daily and fatherly vigilance over the Holy Religious Sisterhood, both of the city and the country, and the charitable institutions and schools which are under their care and guidance.'[12]

THE RELIGIOUS SISTERHOOD

Dr O'Dwyer inherited a large body of nuns or religious sisters working in schools, and nursing, caring for the elderly, and for unmarried mothers and others requiring residential care. These included the Sisters of Mercy, the Presentation Sisters, the Irish Sisters of Charity, the Good Shepherd Sisters, and the Faithful Companions of Jesus, engaged in secondary education for girls at Laurel Hill, Limerick, and at Bruff. During his episcopacy he added two other congregations: in his first years the English Nursing Sisters of the Little Company of Mary to run St John's hospital, Limerick,[13] and much later members of his sister Annie's congregation, the Sisters of Charity of St Paul, to open a school at Kilfinane, Co. Limerick, in 1903.[14]

He took his pastoral care of the convents in his diocese very seriously, and generally manifested a human, caring face towards women religious. His annual visitation of the convents commenced in the first days of the New Year, and few other calls were allowed to interfere with this commitment. To country areas he travelled by horseback until late in life: covering at times, going and returning, over 100 miles.[15] Writing to Dr Donnelly from Newcastle West on 23 January 1895, he announced that he was doing so after a smart ride from Abbeyfeale, adding that 'as soon as we have fortified the inner man, and horse, we shall set out for Limerick and by the time we get there we shall have done over thirty Irish miles.'[16] Travelling across country, he had some unexpected encounters. The previous January he had informed Donnelly: 'I was in the saddle all last week, and one day between this (Limerick) and Bruff rode right into the middle of the fox hounds to the great delight of the whole field, who welcomed me as if I had come by intentionally'.[17] In his travels he took in some of the local parishes, and at times the priests along the route turned out on horse to join him and form a cavalcade.[18]

Many years later, on 3 February 1917, because of poor health, he asked Monsignor Denis Hallinan to take on the visitation of the convents for him. He made little of what was involved to ease the task for his substitute. 'The visitation is almost entirely formal. You say a prayer in the chapel, then receive each sister in the parlour, hear anything she may have to say, give her your blessing, and that's all. You will finally see the accounts and, if they are correct, sign them, as you will see that I have done in previous years.'[19]

Apart from formal visitation, the bishop also called in an informal way on a number of convents. Fortunately, the author Kate O'Brien, who had vivid memories of Dr O'Dwyer in the first decade of the twentieth century, has captured two such examples. They occur in her 'Christmas in the Presentation Parlour', which tells of her family's visit to her aunt, Mary Thornhill, Reverend Mother of the Presentation Convent, on Christmas Day. Beforehand, the family attended Mass in St John's Cathedral. Reflecting on the experience, the author commented that she had heard bad sermons all over the world, 'but for sheer agonising badness, flatness, inexcusable platitudinous fatuity those Christmas sermons from the various head priests of St John's Cathedral over my years of childhood and girlhood – and I was an attentive listener – take all the cakes and every imaginable biscuit. They were agonising.'[20] From noon until three o'clock the family visited the convent where there was food, piano playing and singing in the parlour. After a while, 'the Bishop of Limerick … was shown brilliantly in and brilliant he was and looked, Edward Thomas O'Dwyer'. Her father, who kept horses, and 'who loved Bishops and Princes of the Church – only imaginatively and with no experience of them – was delighted to have Aunt Mary place the deaf prelate beside him. He knew him well, and mounted him. Bishop O'Dwyer, who would allow none of his priests to hunt, was a great horseman. So there they sat, shouting at each other. Bishop O'Dwyer shouted high and shrill anyway, and Father's only attack on the deaf – in this case useless – was to bellow. And as they bellowed my sister Clara, persuaded by some gentle nuns near the piano, began to sing … ' After some time, 'the Bishop rose and we with him, dropping all on one knee for his blessing – and a minute later one could watch him pacing down the garden, silky, silver hair blowing, pink hand cupping his good ear as he conversed with Aunt Mary, this Reverend Mother whom he admired extremely. His carriage horses champing, and even if the wind was cold he would linger with this nun – and hear what she said. An autocrat mostly disliked by his priests, a man of iron principle and courage as he was to prove in political troubles yet ahead, and one who expected to be listened to and obeyed, he often listened and often, I think, without knowing it obeyed when this young nun, his mere subaltern, spoke … But he was a man with an unexpected regard for the brains of women.'[21]

'He proved that', Kate O'Brien observed, 'in his long liking for the society of two unusually brainy nuns of Laurel Hill Convent, in Limerick. I was educated there, and I know how rarely intelligent were these two Latinists, Mother Lelia and Mother Thecla – and I know too how he liked to visit them, to tackle them about Latin, about the revival of Irish, about Irish history and Ireland's future.' 'His twanging, unpleasantly pitched voice was nevertheless clear and cultivated,' the writer insisted,

> and we could hear him from far off if it pleased him to walk into our garden classroom of an afternoon. Then he would take Horace out of Mother Thecla's hand, and singing out the ode would turn mockingly on me or on Nellie Dundon or whomsoever, for a lightening scan. No use being scared; the thing was to make a stab at the lines – and he never mocked, always bent his good ear down attentively. Then after a few minutes he would slam the book shut, wave dismissal at us, and take Mother Thecla off into the garden in loud, learned argument, often talking Latin to her, to our deep edification.[22]

Bishop O'Dwyer had a special fondness for Laurel Hill, even though the Sisters were members of an independent religious congregation frustratingly removed from his control. He brought Cardinal Logue and other dignitaries to visit the school and convent, he made many of his publicised speeches at prize-giving there, and 'he was not satisfied', as the convent annals proclaimed at length after his death, 'with testifying on public occasions only, his regard for the community, his interest in our work, and his pride in our success, he entered into our daily life, he helped us in our difficulties, and was, on all occasions, our father and friend … He kept us in touch with all educational movements of impor-tance, and when it was decided that Latin was to be introduced into the curriculum, he himself condescended to teach that subject' to some of the Sisters. Later on he prepared two of them for the BA degree, teaching them Logic and Psychology. 'He was always anxious that we should be abreast of the times', the account asserted eulogistically, 'and took a genuine pride in any success achieved by our pupils: at the same time he insisted strongly on the importance of the religious spirit, and was most watchful that no risk to that should be incurred under any pretext of meeting the requirements of the times. His kindness to the sick was proverbial. No one ever died here without receiving his last blessing, and he always insisted on giving nuns what he called 'the honours of war' – a solemn office and requiem Mass, at which he himself was present. He loved children and delighted being with them, and they loved him in return. Many of our old pupils owe him a debt of gratitude, which they will not easily forget, for by timely aid, he helped them to prepare for careers, to which it would be otherwise impossible for them to aspire. His charities were countless. We often received large sums from him for the needy, but always on the condition that the money should be given in (Reverend) Mother's name, and not in his.'[23]

O'Dwyer's care for the convent was put fiercely to the test in the summer of 1895, when the community and some of the students were laid low by a particularly pernicious form of food poisoning, which took the lives of three sisters and one 17-year-old student. For days many others were on the danger list. O'Dwyer called in the ablest doctors, and the Sister of Mercy to nurse – 'for', as the chronicle for the year noted, 'not one of seventy three could do a thing for herself'. Laurel Hill became a hospital. The bishop was in constant attendance on the sick and dying. He stayed by the dying in their intense suffering right to the end, and then presided at their solemn office and burial. One of the sisters who died was only 28. The bishop, 'who had given her the habit and received her vows, gave her the last absolution,' and stayed with her to the end. The parents of the seventeen years old, Josephine O'Flynn, were deeply touched by 'the Bishop's sincere grief'. 'He scarcely left her for a moment, his was the last voice she recognised, and on him her eyes rested as she breathed her last sigh.' Not surprisingly, then, the chronicle for the year, after praising the devotedness of priests, nuns and doctors, judged that 'foremost among these angels of mercy was our Bishop, he remained with us from morning till night'.[24]

At last, on 10 July, O'Dwyer informed his friend, Donnelly, 'We are over, or nearly over it. All are better today, and if they hold their own until night we may hope that the terrible affliction has passed. It would break your heart to see this house in the last week. If I lived for ever I should not forget it.'[25] In the tragedy, support and help came from far and near, and Bishop O'Dwyer's personal sense of pain and loss was widely recognised. Not surprisingly, then, the clergy who came to meet him on his return from Rome in November 1895 added to their address words of deep sympathy with him in his 'anxiety and anguish of mind' over the affliction at Laurel Hill, and expressed their intense admiration at how he laboured almost day and night in those days – ministering to the sick, giving the sacraments with his own hand, burying the dead, and 'providing for the large temporal assistance required in such a calamity'.

Continuing in a pastoral vein of thorough-going commitment, the clergy also informed their bishop – 'We are all of us, in our turn, spectators of the toils you impose upon yourself at your parochial visitations, and we have heard with delight those truly apostolic addresses you make to our parishioners; and are as often astonished at the drudgery of hours, and day after day, you go through in the catechetical examination of the children before administering to them the Sacrament of Confirmation.'

VISITING THE PARISHES. CONFIRMATIONS AND INNOVATIONS

Richard Canon O'Kennedy, in his articles in the *Irish Monthly* after the bishop's death, recalled that during his visitation of the parishes, O'Dwyer was accustomed to address the people after the celebration of Mass in a simple, informal, and warm style. He usually began with something from the people's daily lives, something he had noticed coming to the church, the state of the crops, the tidiness and cleanliness of their houses, and then led them on to think of and give praise to God the creator and caring Father. 'His intimate knowledge of domestic things, cattle and horses, and the devout use he made of them in his sermons, like the simple parables of the Scripture, was', O'Kennedy explained, 'what especially amazed and delighted the people.'How aisy it all came to him, Glory be to God!' you would hear them say when leaving the church.'[26]

What he liked to hear at visitation was that there was no drunkenness and no case of scandal. He usually asked for the number of communicants, compared that with the number of Catholics in the parish, and at once formed an estimate of the spiritual state of the parish from those two sets of numbers. 'On the whole', O'Kennedy judged, 'a pretty fair estimate may be formed from them.'[27] Despite his fondness for discussion with intelligent people, he also had 'the common touch' as indicated above, and he had a remarkable way with children. Fortunately, O'Kennedy left examples of this.'I don't think I ever met so many-sided a man,' he observed. 'You were for temperance, we will suppose. He had a talk with you. Parting with him, you were convinced that he had an interest in nothing else under the sun. You had a good eye for a horse, so had the bishop ... but you should see him with children.

'He sat within the rails at Confirmation to examine, and because of his deafness the children were brought up in a little group of five or six. He put out his hand and drew them near him. "Well, now, young gentlemen," he would cry to a body of little boys, "you know I am a deaf old man, and holler to me as if you were frightening crows. And now the first thing I want to know is [visitations were during May], How many birds' nests had *you*? How many had *you*?" And so on round the group. The ease of mind and the joy which the opening gave the whole body of children need not be told.

'A group of little girls came next.

> 'Well, young ladies, come near me now', and he drew them familiarly with his hand. 'Oh, thank you child; God bless you, these are lovely flowers … But now I want you to baptise a child for me. Suppose my cap is the head of a little baby. Look at me baptising that baby, and tell me am I right or wrong?'
>
> He lifts his hand as if pouring water, and says: 'In the name of the Father and of the Son and of the Holy Ghost, Amen. Is that right or wrong now? Well, young lady?' to the first child.
>
> 'Wrong, my Lord!'
>
> 'Wrong! Do you mean to say that I am not able to baptise a baby?'
>
> The child laughs. He laughs.
>
> 'Well, now, tell me what was wrong?'
>
> 'You left out – I baptise thee – my Lord.'
>
> 'Ah! That's good. You are right!'
>
> 'Say the whole of it, now, for me, do *you*', he would say to the next.
>
> 'I baptise thee in the name etc.'
>
> 'And tell me, now, if there were no priest there, and you poured the water on the head of the little baby that was dying, and said the words rightly, would the baby go to heaven?'
>
> 'Yes, my Lord.'
>
> 'Then we ought to learn it, and to be sure we know it rightly, for we may send a soul to heaven.'

'After that there would follow a dozen or so questions on the sacrament of baptism …'

'To watch him when a poor, neglected adult was brought up', O'Kennedy emphasised, 'was a lesson in tenderness and piety.' O'Kennedy went on to tell of Maurice, 'a gentle giant of twenty-two or twenty-three', who was simple and had a habit of swearing. He was afraid to go forward for Confirmation, but eventually agreed if a certain priest prepared him. The priest agreed and taught him his prayers and the simplest rudiments. The morning of the Confirmation Maurice's mother warned him not to give a swear, and he was brought up to the bishop after the other children had been examined. 'Seeing his towering figure, the bishop, who had picked up Maurice's name, stood up, and taking his hand, said:

"Now, Maurice, you will bless yourself with my hand," and he offered it to him. Maurice was delighted. The bishop had not 'shook hands with any of the lads' but him. He made a great cross with the bishop's hand, and was easily heard all over the church – "In the name of the Father, and of the Son, and of the Holy Ghost. Amen."
"Now, Maurice, how many persons in God?"
"Three; the Father, the Son, and the Holy Ghost."
"But, Maurice, isn't the Father older than the Son?"
Maurice moved back
"He's not elder than the Son, whatever you say. They are all equal alike; Father X told me so, however they managed it."[28]

O'Dwyer's interest in and concern for children found particular expression in his preoccupation with providing opportunities for education. 'School atten-dance he took as another criterion of the working of the parish. The number of children on the school roll was examined, and he insisted that the average of attendances, and the percentage of attendance be kept. His reasoning was clear. The early years were the morning of a person's life. 'If children are neglected in those early years they can never make it up.' Those years provided the oppor-tunity for the future. He exhorted both teachers and parents on these lines. The requirements of teachers received a ready hearing from him, and deputations were usually greeted warmly, encouraged and assisted.[29]

INNOVATIVE ADMINISTRATOR

In his role as pastor, O'Dwyer also changed some practices surviving from penal times and did so with courage and devotional purpose. In the past, the Blessed Sacrament was kept only in churches where, as a rule, the parish priest resided close by. O'Dwyer ruled that it should be kept in every church for the devotion of the people who, when passing, might wish to enter and say a prayer. Marriages used be performed at any hour of the day, and the church often rang with noise and chatter. He brought in a regulation that all marriages were to be performed with a nuptial Mass, thereby giving a solemnity and dignity to the occasion. It also helped to emphasise that marriage was a sacrament, bestowing grace, and carrying obligations and responsibilities for the married couple. Again, with respect to ceremonies for the dead, he sought to wean people from wakes, with their drain on the funds of those already overstretched financially, and their not infrequent drunken irreverence. He exhorted the bereaved to bring the dead to the church on the evening before the funeral, and subsequently to have Mass celebrated in the church for the deceased. If the parties were poor, the Mass was to be offered without charge, and if the burial took place in the parish the priest was to attend the funeral.[30]

He also introduced modifications in the sensitive area of family pews. The custom had grown that certain prominent members of the parish, who had come up in the world, paid so much for a pew, which only they and their family could occupy. It was an obvious mark of division, of class distinction in God's house. O'Dwyer, after careful discussion with eminent legal counsel, announced that 'the right to occupy a pew in church is a licence from the parish priest to the occupier to use it for himself and his family', and this licence, he declared, was 'revocable' at the will of the parish priest or his successor. The parish priest, though not owner of the pews, was the administrator for the parish, the diocese. Any pew-occupier who thought he was unfairly treated could appeal to the bishop![31]

A further innovation was in relation to the renovation of St John's Cathedral, expressly mentioned in the address by the clergy in 1895, and the manner in which it was celebrated by the entire city. 'I am on visitation getting as much work out of the way as possible before 'the event', which will be, D.V., on *21st June*,' O'Dwyer informed Donnelly on 15 May 1894.[32] The build up to 'the event' was staged with skill. Already on 10 February he sent a public letter to Father Quain, administrator of St John's Cathedral, announcing that it was time to begin preparations for having the cathedral in proper condition for its consecration. 'His Eminence Cardinal Logue and his Grace the Archbishop of Cashel would attend and, it was hoped, a large gathering of the bishops of Ireland and the clergy.' The renovation and the occasion would require a considerable financial outlay. He instructed Quain to establish weekly collections throughout the parishes of the city, and assured him he would receive every help and sympathy from the parochial clergy in these first steps towards a great event in the diocese.[33]

Following this preparation of the ground, the bishop summoned a meeting of clergy and laity to St Munchin's College on 11 May to concert measures between them so that they might work unitedly for their common purpose. For the cathedral was theirs as well as his, he told his audience, including the mayor of the city. 'It was the possession of a cathedral in a town, being a Bishop's seat, that constituted it a city, and it was as holding that cathedral that this great city originally possessed the right and title of a city'. After this doubtful argument, O'Dwyer referred to the forthcoming attendance of Cardinal Logue at the cathedral. So far as he knew, it would be the first time they had ever a cardinal in Limerick. When Rinuccini was in the city he was papal legate, but he 'was only a Bishop, and not a Cardinal'.[34] A month later, following his request, the mayor of Limerick and the corporation agreed to attend High Mass at the cathedral on the day of consecration; and they decided, besides, to confer the freedom of the city on Cardinal Logue on the occasion of his visit.[35]

Not surprisingly, 'the event' on 21 June was described as 'a magnificent religious function, which was at the same time a great popular demonstration of the living Catholic spirit of the people'. The episcopacy was represented from Ross to Raphoe. The cardinal presided, and over 200 clergy, not just from Limerick and neighbouring dioceses, but from Dublin and other places, took part in the consecration ceremonies. 'As for the people', the report in the *Irish Catholic Directory* observed, they were there in their thousands. They came in by train from distant places, and from the neighbouring towns and districts they gathered, pouring in, in all sorts of vehicles, all through the morning; Limerick itself ceased business for the day. ... The streets presented a most picturesque appearance. They were literally covered with bunting ... and in the neighbourhood of the cathedral triumphal arches were erected ... Not a hundredth part of the people could, of course, find room within the walls of the spacious cathedral, and so the streets were thronged to witness the procession of the confraternities from the old town to St John's.

'The order with which the entire proceedings were conducted was most remarkable', the report continued. 'The people heartily accepted the regulations made for the proper conduct of the functions', and there was none of 'the crushing and confusion sometimes to be witnessed on occasions of popular demonstrations'.[36]

The success of the occasion added further to Dr O'Dwyer's reputation for organisation, administration, and skill in speech and presentation. His greatest act of innovative administration during his episcopate, in the view of Canon O'Kennedy, was, however, of a very different nature. It was *'what he did for the workhouse children'*[37] Already by 1895, O'Dwyer's involvement in workhouse reform was known to the government. It continued throughout the remainder of his life.

CHILDREN OF THE WORKHOUSE

The workhouse was a deprived area, seldom noted, which deeply concerned him in human terms, and in his concern for religious training and educational opportunity. He became, in fact, something of an authority in the work to improve conditions in these institutions, and in the provision of nursing for the sick within them. Thus, on 24 February 1895 Bishop John Clancy of Elphin, seeking to have some nuns trained as nurses in the workhouses, wrote: 'I find your Lordship set down as a pioneer in the Workhouse Reform Movement. Will you be good enough to enlighten me on a few points?'[38] Three years later he was able to report some progress, and spoke of O'Dwyer's high standing with the officials of the Local Government Board.[39] Negotiations on the training of nuns as nurses in the workhouse system, however, were still going on a year later when Dr Abraham Brownrigg of Ossory and O'Dwyer were deputed by the bishops to represent them on the matter in a meeting with Henry Robinson, vice-president of the Local Government Board. On 12 October 1899, after the meeting, Brownrigg requested O'Dwyer 'to use that mastery which your Lordship is known to have over the pen and the blarney and frame a few logical, nice, diplomatic sentences ... to the great gain of the nuns and of the poor'.[40] Reform was a slow process. County Boards of Guardians were hard to persuade and slow to move, and the Local Government Board and its inspectors, auditors and advisers, slower still.

Where the care and education of children was concerned, reform was particularly difficult. They lived in the crowded adult workhouses, amid squalor, quarrels, and foul language. The bishops expressed their opposition to the way the system treated young boys and girls, but as Brownrigg noted in letters to O'Dwyer on 8 and 14 November 1894, the obstacles to having a separation of the children from the rest were many and entrenched. Some indication of the squalor and inadequacy of the conditions in which the children lived has been provided by Canon O'Kennedy, who had the experience of working in the Limerick city workhouse or union.

There were workhouses, he observed, in Limerick, Rathkeale, Newcastle West, and Kilmallock. In each there was a colony of children exposed to human degradation. In the Limerick workhouse, where he worked at the time of O'Dwyer's consecration, there were 180 to 200 boys and a larger number of girls. There were three male teachers on the boys' side, and four nuns and two lay teachers on the girls' side. The entire buildings and population were crushed into a few acres of land, and everywhere there was a confined air. No matter how many windows were opened the tainted air remained. All the beds were straw and gave off a foul smell. The condition of the boys' dormitories were such that O'Kennedy had to complain to the senior master about the absence of detailed supervision of the filthy state of the beds in which some of the boys were sleeping. 'But "fowler than the fetid air", he added, was the overall "moral atmosphere" though everything "had been done by religion to purify it"'. In addition to all this, the children and men had to wear the pauper uniform. Those children of the Limerick workhouse who were boarded-out in country areas, had to wear their hated garb when going to school until, after many years, this mark of discrimination was abolished through the exertions of Lord Emly.[41]

Following this account, O'Kennedy continued: 'If there was one act of administration more than any other in his episcopate that I would extol Dr O'Dwyer for, it was what he did for these workhouse children.'[42] The four unions in Limerick city and county had between them about 400 boys, and a greater number of girls. In all there were 800 to 1,000 children. The bishop set about providing separate accommodation for them. Through the action of the Local Government Board, an auxiliary workhouse, built many years earlier, was made vacant at Glin, Co. Limerick, on a commanding height surveying the Shannon estuary. From the first seeds of the idea to its eventual fulfilment took a long time, vigorous negotiation, and O'Dwyer's almost magnetic influence in emphasising the justice of his cause. All the workhouses in the diocese had to agree to the project and contribute to the expense, and the project, if approved, involved the teachers in each union being 'disemployed' and being dependent on the voice and vote of their friends on the Board of Guardians to be elected on the new scheme. Tact as well as courage and persistence were required to bring the venture to fruition. It was accomplished, and O'Kennedy, writing in

1917, was of the view that 'the poor children are now in as healthy a home as could be desired, and under circumstances far happier than their natal stars could have promised them. The boys are under the Christian Brothers, the girls under the care of the Sisters of Mercy, where they are taught various trades, and no longer brought up as … apprentices to the workhouse life with its rottenness and degradation.' The numbers, as O'Kennedy was writing, were no longer as large as they had been because the boarding-out system had been a good deal resorted to.[43]

THE BISHOP AND HIS PRIESTS

Also in pastoral terms, but more concerned with the clergy themselves, was a further observation in their address to the bishop, namely, 'We know with what regularity you carry out the Canons of the Church with regard to Diocesan Synods, and we feel how the wise and prudent decrees you have passed have benefited the faithful of the diocese, and bettered in many respects our own condition as regards the administration of the Holy Sacraments and other matters'. O'Dwyer's regard for education and knowledge extended beyond the school room to the general body of the laity and to the clergy themselves.

His annual pastoral letters were part of the process of educating the laity, and also, to some extent, the clergy. They reflected first his response to the liturgical season and the needs of the diocese, and then moved to wider issues. Written in a readable style, they were at times eagerly bought and read by large numbers of the laity. As might be expected entering the Lenten season there was always a reference to aspects of prayer, to fasting, and other expressions of devotion, before the bishop drew his readers' attention to such matters as the country's educational needs, the issue of temperance, to aspects of proselytism, to the persecution of the church in foreign countries, to prayer for Christian unity, to the authority of the church and the role of the papacy, to pleas for peace in times of war, and to current political challenges. It was, however, on occasions such as synodal addresses that he directed himself expressly towards the improvement of his priests and, in the process, revealed a number of his own priorities and something of his personal spirituality. It is instructive in this regard to take his address to his priests at his final synod, that of 1916, even though the final part of the manuscript is missing.

In his visitation of the parishes, he declared on 5 June 1916, it had come home to him once again the people's special reverence for the office of priest – as one with the 'awful power' to raise his hand in absolution, and to use the words of Christ at the altar to consecrate bread and wine to the body and blood of Christ. But apart from this reverence for the priest's office, there was in Ireland, he insisted, a unique sense of identity between priests and people, forged perhaps in penal days and following the collapse of the native Irish lords. Whatever the reason, 'the Irish priest in all his thoughts and feeling is identified with the people: just as a sod which one might cut in a field is one with the land around it'. Some think that the priest's power had declined. He did not agree. True, 'with good sense and prudence the clergy have withdrawn largely from interference in and with those local interests which the laity are now quite capable of managing themselves', but their unity of belief remained a great bond between clergy and people.

That belief, however, the bishop warned, could become just routine, while underneath secularism was gnawing away. There was great need for the priests to provide an intellectual and personal presentation of the faith; not learned, abstruse discourses – but the elementary matters, which are the bases of religion, put 'in such a way as to make them a living influence in the lives of the people'. 'The fundamental truth of all religion is God,' O'Dwyer emphasised, and a solid foundation of a good Christian life is laid when a man feels he is answerable to God for all his actions. Then he could practice his religion out of a sense of duty and not simply do what his neighbours do. The religious habits of most people were as 'an empty shell of religion'. 'Observe most men at Mass: no prayer book or beads, no sign of prayer, they are just there.' The reason so many fell away when they left Ireland, he believed, was the absence of a clear conception of their relations to God. They need to be taught the principal mysteries of their religion, but before all it was necessary 'to bring the thought of God's love to their hearts and consciences'. That was the very first commandment – 'Thou shalt love the Lord thy God'. The psalms show how to speak to God as 'I and thou'. God, in turn, speaks to us in our consciences; hence, O'Dwyer remarked, 'we should speak to even the simplest people about the voice of conscience as God's voice'. The bishop went on to stress St Paul's teaching that God's invisible world, his eternal power and duty can be perceived from the things that have been made. 'If we could bring that pearl of truth home to the minds of the people with what Newman calls a real as contradistinguished from a notional assent, we would have infused into them a leaven which would change the whole tenor of their lives.' The earth, the flowers of the field, the animals, all would through their beauty raise hearts and minds to a beauty greater than all the world. The best route to a personal knowledge of God, however, O'Dwyer added, was the instruction of conscience. All have a sense of right and wrong. All experience the text – 'I see the better, and approve of it, but follow the worse' [Rom 7: 19, 22-23]. 'When we preach that, the people know its truth in their own lives, and appreciate the need of God's help which comes in Jesus Christ: 'Christ crucified … the power of God and the wisdom of God' [1 Corinthians 1:23–24]. 'That is the second great truth', O'Dwyer explained, 'which should be constantly the burden of your teaching. It is the whole Christian religion, and by the great love and mercy of God it is given to us in a way that draws to it the whole strength of our natural sympathies. 'The Word was made flesh, and dwelt amongst us', and by that very community of nature draws us to himself as to our own brother. From the crib of Bethlehem to the Cross of Calvary our Blessed Lord's life is one long appeal to our human feelings.'[44]

The rest of the text is missing. The address is instructive in its concern to bring home to his priests the need to preach the reality and love of God in clear simple terms, but also in encouraging them to develop an 'I-Thou' relationship with God, to find God in the world about them, and to be imbued with a deep sense of Christ's humanity and of his brotherhood with them. In the process, he reveals, perhaps, something of his own inner life. The address also indicates once more his sense of his responsibility as a bishop to care for the spiritual welfare of his people and the spiritual growth of his priests.

The foregoing accounts indicate that Edward Thomas O'Dwyer could be the most human and *simpático* of men, particularly in his dealings with children and women. Where his priests were concerned, however, the weight of the evidence indicates that, despite his eloquence and high ideals, most of them disliked him, largely, it seems, because they feared him. Some, like the fearless and dominant personality, Dean Punch, who, as a young man, looked on the elderly bishop with something akin to hero worship, still judged him fifty years later 'the ablest man I ever met in my life'.[45] He refused to consider him an autocrat. 'He had a great respect for honesty,' Punch declared, 'no respect for the slave mentality. He'd respect you if you talked up to him.'[46] This, however, was not everyone's experience; especially if the issue was one on which his Lordship's heart was set. What frightened many of those under him was his volatile, bullying temper.

Canon John Begley, author of *The diocese of Limerick*, mentioned, in unpublished notes, a number of instances where clergy 'fell foul' of the bishop. Daniel Curtin, PP of Colman's Well, was alleged to have been offered the parish of Ballygran by the bishop in an interview following the death in 1889 of Mortimer Fitzgerald, parish priest of that parish. Also, during the interview, he asked Fr Curtin to resign his own parish. When he resigned, Fr Quain, later of St John's Cathedral, was appointed instead to Ballygran, and Curtin was relegated to a curacy. George O'Connor, parish priest of Patrickswell, who died in 1896, was not granted a 'month's mind' because he did not leave his money to the diocese. Similarly with Timothy Halpin, PP of Donoughmore in 1900. A former professor in the diocesan college, Revd Patrick Carroll, who served as curate in the parish of Croagh, had a drink problem and was severely censured by the bishop at a diocesan conference in the presence of all the priests of the diocese. The problem continued. Another person with a grievance was Jeremiah O'Grady, said to have been a very brilliant man, who became parish priest of Killeedy but did not persevere there. He lived for many years in the city, retired, but claiming he had not received fair play. He expressed his grievance by writing a letter every day to the bishop – without a stamp![47]

The most interesting example, however, has to be Fr John S. Flanagan, parish priest of Adare, who revered O'Dwyer as both bishop and friend. The friendship was mutual. His lordship made him a dean of the diocese, and they exchanged gifts as well as theological queries and comments. In 1895, the bishop presented him with a set of Roman Mass vestments, which the overwhelmed Flanagan proposed selling so that he might be able to make a larger donation to the bishop's cathedral fund. He went on to thank God for O'Dwyer's 'laborious episcopal work'. 'It can with truth be said', he observed, 'that very few bishops, in Ireland or elsewhere, have fulfilled their duties with such exactness, vigour, and zeal.' He also thanked God, he said, with much feeling, 'for having given to me in you such a warm-hearted, affectionate friend'. He could not forget the bishop' solicitude following his serious operation.[48] In return, he offered devotion and an admiration that expanded further his lordship's self-esteem. 'You have the most astoundingly versatile genius,' he informed the self-assured bishop, on 15 January 1897,

> You are able in quick succession to take up a matter and pronounce upon the most disparate/if there is such a word/of subjects, passing from sanitary cottages to education primary and university – Pig buyers & dock labourers' disputes to complicated financial questions dovetailed in with historical knowledge & so on & so on. And now you write off … a learned essay on the nature of the Bull on Anglican orders.[49]

In August that year O'Dwyer invited him to join him at his lodge in Kilkee. The older man regretfully declined. Much as he would have liked to go, he was unable to leave home at all because of his illness of three years ago.[50]

The close friendship was to be undermined two years later, when Flanagan found himself caught between two allegiances – to the bishop and to Lord Dunraven. O'Dwyer was his bishop and friend, but the Dunravens treated him as confidant, as almost one of the family. Each of the three main participants told a somewhat different story to the public press, but the bones of the story are as follows.

The Irish Local Government Act was passed in 1898, and Flanagan headed a deputation asking Dunraven to stand for the first election for the Croom division of the county council in the spring of 1899. Dunraven consented.[51] At the end of January 1899, at a time when the Irish unionists' opposition to a university for Catholics was generating deep resentment, Dr O'Dwyer, riding back from his visitation in West Limerick, encountered Flanagan and a Fr McCarthy in Adare and, as they discussed the university question, he, allegedly, gave way to what Dunraven called his 'effervescing temper',[52] and told Flanagan to convey what he had said to Dunraven. Flanagan did so in some detail. He seemed to see in the Bishop's words an intent to rally support against Dunraven and Monteagle in the Local Government elections, and an implied criticism of himself. 'The Bishop rode by here today on his return from his visitation in the West', he informed Dunraven on 28 January. 'I saw him on the road for he did not alight,' Flanagan stated. 'I saw wrath on his countenance and he said, 'I intend to make it impossible for any Catholic to vote for a Liberal Unionist (or no doubt Conservative) if the Govt. they are supporting does not pledge itself at once to deal with the University question, so the men like Lord Dunraven and Monteagle may as well retire. He said with emphasis 'You may tell Lord D. this'.

I answered that I would certainly do so at once.' 'He spoke throughout hotly and almost passionately,' Flanagan added, 'and it was quite evident that he was very mad with Fr Mac. (McCarthy) and myself for the position we had taken up. I suppose sooner or later he will come down on us in some form or other and that he will take some occasion between this and the Election to express his displeasure with Catholics who vote for or in any way support L. U's or Conservatives. Fancy the absurdity of making you or any candidate responsible for the action of the Govt.' Flanagan, always so laudatory and even ingratiating in his communications with the bishop, went on censoriously:

> It annoys and irritates me excessively to be unduly interfered with in this way, the more so as I am Dean, and can't without scandal fight with the Bishop. Nor of course can Fr Mac. who is removable at his will. All that I can infer now is that he will in any way he can oppose your Election. *How* I know not. I have told no one but Lady D. & Rachel & Aileen & the Knight. We must keep the collision entirely to ourselves and not let it get abroad as it will damp the spirits of those who are working in the cause.

'Very few other words passed between us,' Flanagan concluded. 'I remained silent, and made no remark whatever. Fr Mac. was standing by speaking to the priest who was riding with the Bishop and he said he had told the Croagh priest to oppose you vehemently. There is a bit of clerical tyranny.'[53]

Apart from being taken aback by the bishop's outburst, Flanagan appears to have been undisturbed. He was used to O'Dwyer's storm clouds passing after an interval. On 3 February he explained that he had written to Lord Dunraven, as his Lordship wished, 'and told him what you said in your *ipsissima verba* so far as I could'.[54] Then on 9 February, The *Munster News* carried an account of an address by Dunraven in which he revealed the bishop's message to him. Flanagan, writing to O'Dwyer that day, expressed his 'amazement and horror' at finding the message published.[55] He did not fully envisage the effect on O'Dwyer. He was soon left in no doubt. The bishop's letter to him on that same date is not extant, but it was such as to reduce his former friend to an abject condition. He accused the old man of presenting a 'lying version'. Flanagan replied almost melodramatically in his effort to convey his distress.

> Your letter has given me the deadliest blow I have ever received in my life, & caused me the most intense grief I have ever suffered. I am almost unable to hold a pen, and my thoughts are paralysed. I have incurred your deepest displeasure, and strongest condemnation. I am willing to do any public act your Lordship may impose upon me to make amends for whatever I may have done in error to displease or to do wrong to your Lordship … Anything whatever you point out I am ready to comply with, except of course to admit that I knowingly gave a lying version of your words.[56]

O'Dwyer was mortified by the publicity, particularly at the mention of Lord Monteagle, with whom he was friendly and by whom he had been supported in his workhouse activities. He wrote to Monteagle, explaining the private nature of his remarks to the Dean, and that what he really said was: 'If Protestant bigotry is allowed to wrong us, I shall put it to the Catholics of this county, whether in honour or self-respect, they can support the followers of the Unionist Government, and you may tell Dunraven that I said that, in face of such an appeal, it would be impossible for Catholics to support him. Then your name was mentioned ... there was a lot more of the same kind, but I never dreamed the thing would go further, and did not weigh my words ... You can imagine my feelings at reading in the papers that I said that 'I would make it impossible for Catholics to support Unionists', suggesting that I would do so by some exercise of ecclesiastical authority as Bishop, a thing that never entered my head.' Monteagle obtained his permission to publish the letter. It appeared on the *Munster News* on 11 February, the original letter having been written post haste on 9 February, when the report of Dunraven's address appeared.

Subsequently, in the *Limerick Chronicle* of 11 February,[57] the distressed Flanagan sought to make amends by suggesting that Dunraven had not reported him accurately and by giving an alternative version of the bishop's words. A version which did not correspond with his lordship's account given Monteagle. On 23 February, he wrote to the bishop offering to write to all the newspapers stating that the reference to the Croagh priest was 'false from beginning to end'.[58]

On 17 February Dunraven sent a letter to the *Munster News* defending his position and enclosing the copy of the letter he received from Fr Flanagan, excluding, it seems, some of Flanagan's personal comments. On 25 February, however, the bishop commented on Flanagan's letter, as supplied to the newspaper offices, and remarked that it was 'inaccurate in almost every line'. 'Even the date is wrong', he stated. 'I passed through Adare on 27th, not 28th January.' Fr Flanagan wrote, 'that in my manner I showed anger towards him'. 'This, too,' O'Dwyer declared, 'was mere imagination. I never was in better humour in my life.' The explanation seemed to be, he suggested, that the dean took it into his head that he, the bishop, was opposed to Lord Dunraven's candidature for the county council election and that 'this feeling coloured in his mind everything I said and did that afternoon, and gave a meaning to my words and bearing that I never intended.' He then took up his pen to write to Dunraven 'with the freedom with which a man writes to his friend', chatting away upon paper. 'This is my sincere belief as to the origin of the whole thing,' the bishop observed, 'and I rather think it is the true explanation.' He added: 'I must say that the poor man in his 79th year, has been cruelly treated, such a letter should never have been made public...'[59] Whatever the 'truth' in the whole affair, it was Fr Flanagan who was made to look inept and unreliable, although both Dunraven and O'Dwyer made it clear that there could be no question of deliberate deception on his part.

The old man sank into decline. The bishop made no attempt to contact him. The year passed, and Christmas was approaching in yet another year before the coldness dissolved. The solvent was a monsignor, whose name is not mentioned. On 4 December 1900, O'Dwyer wrote to the monsignor: 'Your letter about the Dean touched me so much that I wrote to him on the spot to say that I intended going to see him today, and shaking hands, and putting the mis-understanding out of our minds.' 'I am sorry the poor man is so broken,' he added, 'and more sorry that the wretched occurrence that has caused him so much sorrow ever took place,'[60] The bishop was not able to make the intended visit that day because of bad weather. A curate in Adare, Fr J.K. Fitzgerald, wrote to the 'Mon Signore' on 6 December 1900, however, confirming that Dean Flanagan 'had a very nice letter from the Bishop yesterday morning'. He no sooner got the letter 'than he sent an equally nice reply by return of post'. 'This', Fitzgerald added, 'is a happy consummation to an unfortunate business.'[61] The following day, a much-relieved Flanagan wrote to the 'Mon Signore':

> I wish to tell you that his Lordship paid me a visit this afternoon and sat by (my) bedside for perhaps half-an-hour. Our reconciliation is happily most perfect and there is not a trace of bad feeling remaining on either side. So far as you have been instrumental in bringing this around I desire to express to you my most deep felt gratitude. 'Tis of course, a most signal grace shown to me by God and I may now sing my '*nunc dimittis*'.[62]

His expectations of death were premature. Flanagan lived on for another five years, dying in 1906 at the age of 86 years.

Despite the public confrontation with Dunraven, the bishop and he became good friends,[63] and Monteagle was only too ready to forgive. Years later he was to write of O'Dwyer – 'his transparent sincerity and fearless championship of the truth as he saw it in every relation of life won the respect even of his opponents, while the charm of his personality and the brilliance of his intellect endeared him to all who enjoyed the privilege'.[64]

The charm, generous hospitality, and kindness, of O'Dwyer the human being, which many experienced, often overcame obstacles presented by his deafness. Thus, Sir John Ross invited him many times to his house at Rostrevor, and a number of his letters convey a special message of good wishes from his wife; Edmund Dease pressed him to stay at his house in Portarlington, whenever he was travelling to Dublin; and he was always welcome to visit the Emly and Monteagele households. O'Dwyer, for his part, was a generous host. Bishops McRedmond and Fogarty of Killaloe stayed with him at Corbally, as did Bishops Sheehan of Waterford, McCormack of Galway, and Donnelly of Dublin.[65] He regularly invited people to visit and stay with him at Kilkee. There are a number of extant letters from bishops and clergy thanking him in this regard for his hospitality and kindness.[66] Numerous fellow bishops, in Britain and Ireland, and Archbishop Kirby in Rome, received letters of support, or congratulations, or sympathy from him; and for others he was ready to preach on special occasions as at Waterford, and as Bishop Browne of Cloyne acknowledged, he did so in a 'ready and friendly way'.[67] Others wrote to him for advice and help on educational matters, and social and other issues, and always he seemed to be ready to be of assistance. As a result, O'Dwyer's range of friends and contacts was wide. As a guest or host, part of his attraction, apart from his wide knowledge, and sparkling manner, seems to have been his wit and his capacity to tell an amusing story. Bishop Brownrigg, writing to him from Kilkenny, told of a visit from Archbishop Croke, who was very depressed but cheered up when he heard of O'Dwyer's story of the Limerick woman and went about telling it to others![68]

Such benign instances of this 'many-sided man', as Richard Canon O'Kennedy termed him, did not match the experience of many of his priests, as has been indicated. Even the devoted O'Kennedy, writing after O'Dwyer's death, when the bishop was being hailed as a national hero, gave some indication of difficulties under his lordship. The latter, he observed, took a point of view with 'lightning rapidity' and 'with an unconscious claim to infallibility he held that his own opinion could not be wrong, and 'all the king's horses and all the king's men' could not make him recede from it an inch. In fact opposition only made him cling to his views with greater tenacity.'[69]

In short, it is extremely difficult to present adequately this remarkable pastor in human terms. It was as if the contraries in most men were writ large in him, as if indeed he were two persons rather than one.

Finally, returning to the priests' address to their bishop in 1895, one notes a key factor, the one everyone was aware of and agreed on, namely, his 'Lordship's zeal in the cause of education both religious and secular,' and his 'increasing efforts to have justice done to us Catholics under this head'.[70] The remaining chapters in this part of the biography are concerned with his contribution to primary, technical, and university education.

15

Primary and technical education, adult instruction and teacher training

PRIMARY AND TECHNICAL EDUCATION

In the course of his parish visitations, O'Dwyer, as has been observed, paid particular attention to the local primary school. He enjoyed children, but he felt responsible for their future. He examined the roll with an eye to the average and percentage of attendance, and, depending on the result, bestowed 'lavish praise or unstinted blame' on the parish. Attend carefully to the child, he instructed, and you give that person an opportunity of preparing for a fruitful future life.[1]

Careful attendance to the needs of the children required not only sound teaching in literacy and numeration, but also a grounding in practical subjects likely to be useful in their future occupations. In Leamy's School, under his chairmanship, as noted earlier, training in practical skills, such as woodwork for the boys and needlework for the girls, was part of the curriculum. Such practice reflected a growing trend in the last decades of the nineteenth century. Already in 1886 Archbishop Walsh had publicly proclaimed that as the great bulk of the population must live by the labour of their hands, an education for the children of that population that was purely literary positively unfitted them for the work of their lives. He placed emphasis on the training of eyes, hands, and fingers.[2] Ten years later, as a Commissioner for National Education, he pressed for an organised and comprehensive scheme of manual instruction in the national education system, and, subsequently, he was a member of the Vice-Regal Commission that led to the introduction of a system of manual training in the National Schools.[3] O'Dwyer, however, was not content with merely promoting practical training in primary schools, he also advocated technical instruction and applied science at secondary or intermediate level, and amongst school leavers and adults. Many years later, in 1911, at a formal function in the new Limerick City Technical Institute, he endeavoured to establish a distinction between technical instruction and general education.

THE RELATIVE ROLES OF INSTRUCTION AND EDUCATION

Technical instruction, he explained, was concerned mainly with teaching people how to do things rather than to know theories about them. 'It concerns not children, but youths and adults, instructing them in the methods by which the actual work on which they are to be engaged for life may be efficiently performed.' Its scope was co-extensive with every form of industrial activity. It taught 'the true principles and methods of work to the ordinary tradesman or mechanic, to the builder, the engineer, the agriculturist', and 'there was no phase of industrial life into which it could not enter with authority'. In short, it was concerned with the verb 'to do' in all its forms. 'That is the essential difference', O'Dwyer claimed, which 'marks off technical instruction from education, at all stages.' 'The schools', by comparison, 'whether primary or secondary, or even university,' had 'for their scope and purpose to educate, that is to train and develop faculties of mind and body, to form character, and in comparison with these aims even the imparting of knowledge takes a secondary place. We see the evidence of this truth in our own experience. Many of us have forgotten for long years the most of the knowledge which we acquired so laboriously, and even painfully, at school, but it is to be hoped that we have retained our education.' Schools, O'Dwyer continued, were a time of growth for mind and body. Even in the university, the aim was to educate, to develop intelligence, to form character, not just to provide a training-ground for a profession.[4]

In a notable earlier address, entitled 'Technical Instruction', given at Limerick Catholic Institute, October 1900, and published as a pamphlet, the bishop had propounded a favoured insight, namely, that although the education of a country might be divided into various branches, it remained 'an organic whole', and one could 'no more provide vigorous or healthy primary or technical education, apart from university education, than' one could 'grow a sound trunk or healthy limbs on a tree that is cut off from its root.'[5] This led him to take issue with Michael Davitt, who had stressed the need of technical education rather than that provided by a university, and to emphasise the importance of university education to the prosperity of the country. Davitt had misread the educational situation, O'Dwyer claimed. There was 'no opposition between university education and technical'.[6] He returned to this theme in 1911, revealing in the process his almost exaggerated esteem for university education. The knowledge acquired and used in the technical institutes, he averred, depended on the scientific research and teaching of the universities. Such research and teaching had become more and more a requirement for industrial development. He wished to correct, therefore, the unenlightened view that the university served only a select minority. 'There is no mistake', he insisted, 'the university is the most national institution in any country. It is the foundation head from which we derive our teachers, and what is more, the intellectual energy that is the driving force of progress. In Germany, in England, in the United Sates of America, the universities are the ultimate source of all their prosperity, and if in

Ireland, agriculture or manufacture or trade is to prosper, we must look at the same source for success.' He hoped that in Ireland, the universities (mainly the colleges under the new National University and Queen's University), as well as seeking learning for its own sake, would 'remember their duties to the material interests of the country and maintain schools of research', which would study 'the special problems of our own industrial life, and give us in our technical institutions adequate knowledge for our needs and teachers capable of imparting it.'[7]

O'Dwyer's desire to develop prosperity and opportunities for people was an abiding feature of his episcopate. The shortage of teachers of applied science, to pass on the necessary knowledge and training, was a cause of concern. The surest way to provide a supply for the future, he suggested, was to introduce practical science in the schools; and he looked almost automatically to the Christian Brothers, as 'by far the ablest and most economical teachers', to effect this. They should take up science teaching, he proclaimed in 1900, and withdraw as much as possible from 'the barren Intermediate system' and 'direct their great teaching power into useful and practical lines for the working classes.'[8] He also impressed on local authorities the need 'to train a race of intelligent workmen', and indicated that a beginning should be made by having the study of science in the schools so that ultimately they might 'have the materials for scientific colleges and institutes of a high class'.[9]

ADULT INSTRUCTION AND THE WORK OF HORACE PLUNKETT

O'Dwyer's interest in science and the economy led him to welcome the methods being introduced in agriculture and dairying by Sir Horace Plunkett and also the latter's belief that the material conditions of the country 'could be indefinitely improved by the people themselves, even under the present conditions'.[10] Plunkett's dynamism and influence had led to the formation of the Irish Agricultural Organisation Society (IAOS) in 1894, the *Irish Homestead* newspaper in 1895, and the Recess Committee, which combined all shades of political opinion in an effort to produce a report that would lead to major progress in Irish agriculture and industry. The fruit of the Committee's work was reflected in the Agricultural and Technical Instruction (Ireland) Act of 1899, which established the department of Agriculture and Technical Instruction with Horace Plunkett at its head. The 1899 Act, in conjunction with the Local Government (Ireland) Act of 1898, provided considerable opportunities for education and the economy. The local authorities could now play a direct part in promoting agricultural and technical instruction at post school and adult level. These Acts, O'Dwyer observed, in his address on 'Technical Instruction', in 1900, heralded 'a great awakening throughout the country to the … practical importance of education'. He identified with Plunkett's desire to employ the resources of the Department of Agriculture and Technical Instruction to bring the benefits of modern science to the Irish farmer. Before long those benefits were applied to milk testing, and to animal and cereal breeding. Efforts to improve the quality of barley and flax were introduced, and Plunkett, moreover, set up a statistics and information branch to produce a complete picture of the country's agricultural resources.[11]

Not surprisingly, O'Dwyer displayed little patience with those politicians, including John Dillon, who criticised Plunkett's work for agricultural and technical advancement as 'killing Home Rule by kindness'. 'If Home Rule can be killed by kindness', he remarked astringently in his address on 'Technical Instruction', 'it has no right to live.' The true nationalist should be able to appreciate 'in every growing interest and prosperity the rise of a stronger and sturdier race to claim the rights of freemen'.[12] In that same address he asserted his belief that 'Mr Plunkett is a true Irishman; that he loves his country and his people; that his aim is to make them richer and more prosperous'.

The bishop and Plunkett appear to have met as early as 1889. The first extant reference to a meeting, however, is in Plunkett's diary for 1891. On Friday, 16 January 1891, he noted that he had spent that day in Limerick on cooperative dairying and in looking into the affairs of the Limerick clothing factory, which employed 'nearly 2000 men and women' and was 'in a hopeless trough'. 'Had a long and pleasant talk', he added, 'with R.C. Bishop O'Dwyer of Limerick, a very nice and not oily ecclesiastic.'[13] He had a number of satisfying encounters with the bishop during the year. On the 28 March, in the course of a visit to the region in regard to the union of cooperative creameries, he enjoyed 'a long talk' with O'Dwyer. 'He will back us up', Plunkett observed. 'He says the farmers are beginning to fear Home Rule and its probable taxation of land. He would have boldly reduced rents 30% to 50% and (placed) under this a *permanent* tax on land. Much like Davitt's plan, he says, but more honest.' A month later, Plunkett, back in Limerick, sought the bishop's advice. 'Called on Bishop O'Dwyer to sound him as to probable reception His Excellency (Viceroy) would get if he visited Limerick. He said if he came very quietly he would be respectfully received. The only difficulty was owing to any civility being interpreted by the *Times* and Tory papers as a brilliant reception – breakdown of the Nationalist sentiment etc etc.' By 20 August 1891 it was clear that Sir Horace looked forward to his exchanges with the Limerick prelate

> Had a delightful interval with Bishop O'Dwyer, a man who always interests me with his rugged independence of thought. He told me he had become tired of the agitation and sick of Home Rule and many of the clergy were the same. He thought that if the next election did not return Gladstone with a working majority – good-bye to Home Rule for many years.

By the beginning of the following year, Plunkett had decided to go forward for parliament. When he met his Limerick friend on 10 February 1892, however, O'Dwyer freely conveyed his views on this and on a variety of subjects. 'Met Bishop O'Dwyer who told me that he regretted my going into politics, that

Fr Finlay was the ablest man in Ireland, that Kerry girls employed by Limerick farmers went wrong – were considered fair game, that the creameries kept boys away from school but that he wished success to our organisation.' Four years later, Plunkett would describe the bishop to Gerald Balfour, chief secretary for Ireland, as 'a very old friend', and was disposed to 'positively assent' of him 'that he is incapable of any duplicity'.[14] A claim which, perhaps, said more about Plunkett than about the bishop!

Where O'Dwyer was concerned, the fact that Plunkett was a Protestant and a unionist presented no obstacle to their friendship. They had a common interest and a shared purpose. The bishop was pleased to have the first cooperative creamery at Drumcollogher, Co. Limerick, in 1889, and, also in his diocese, the first creamery society in 1891 at Ballyhahill, near Lord Monteagle's home.[15] It was a measure, indeed, of O'Dwyer's interest in Plunkett's work, and of his 'rugged independence of thought', that he strongly recommended to him the Jesuit, Tom Finlay, as 'the ablest man in Ireland', at a time when his relations were strained with Finlay's colleagues in Limerick. Plunkett, in fact, had already recruited Finlay and had no doubt of his importance to the work for cooperation. He was professor of philosophy at the Royal University, and was destined to become professor of political economy there and in the National University. He had studied agricultural cooperation in Germany and France, and was to prove Plunkett's abiding support in numerous ways – as editor of the *Irish Homestead*, as vice-chairman of the Irish Agricultural Organisation Society, as a public speaker and writer, as a link between northern and southern farmers, being a Cavan man himself, and as an *entrée* to many of the bishops by whom he was highly regarded.

Plunkett, wisely, sought to ensure good relations with the bishops, and, apart from O'Dwyer, he became friendly with Patrick O'Donnell of Raphoe, Denis Kelly of Ross, and, for a time, with Michael Cardinal Logue. The central role that O'Dwyer played in his plans, especially in the key Limerick area, is indicated by a letter to Lord Monteagle, three months after the report of the Recess Committee had been published. On 5 November 1896, C.W. Shaw, of Shaw's bacon factory, Limerick, strongly advised Monteagle 'not to hold any meeting in connection with the report of the Recess Committee until the matter with regard to the bishop has been satisfactorily arranged, because if once he puts his veto on it I am afraid it will be defunct here for evermore. However, if he can be got to view it favourably from the first, it will do a great deal towards making the matter a success.'[16]

Once 'the matter', such as it was, was handled carefully, there was never any doubt of O'Dwyer's support. On the contrary, his enthusiasm for what Plunkett was doing led him rather to an excess of support. He devoted his pastoral letter of 1909 to land purchase and agricultural education. It reads, at times, more like a production of the Department of Agricultural and Technical Instruction than a prelate's letter to his people. Thus, he reproduced the returns of 1908 on the areas of land in County Limerick, showing in parallel columns the number of acres devoted to different usages – e.g. to corn crops, green crops, fruit, hay, pasture, woods, barren mountain, turf, roads, town and building land etc. The table revealed a great preponderance of grassland over tillage, and this situation, to the bishop's mind, was a grave abuse of the land of Ireland and a menace to the moral fibre of the people.

It was 'a deplorable state of things', he declared, to have '95 percent of the land of the county under grass', and he drew a moral conclusion in a manner unlikely to win acceptance in the dairy lands of the Golden Vale. 'For what does it mean, if not universal idleness for the men with all its consequent demoralisation.' 'With the exception of a few districts, over all this county the men have absolutely nothing to do. There they are by thousands, eating and drinking and sleeping, and doing no kind of useful work whatsoever.' 'Can that by any possibility', he asked rhetorically, 'be a sound and healthy state of society?' He was overstating to make a point. When a nail was bent in one direction, it could only be straightened by hammering it in the opposite direction! He was advocating the greater cultivation of land, and the use of the research and services being provided by the Department of Agricultural and Technical Instruction. Plunkett had shunned advice to establish agricultural colleges, and instead had set up a team of mobile inspectors – a venture approved of by O'Dwyer. The latter urged farmers, in his pastoral, to give the Department 'a fair trial', and to follow the advice of the agricultural expert employed by the Limerick County Council, whom he understood to be 'an extremely capable and practical man'. Then, addressing the members of the county council, he bluntly informed them that it was not 'too much to expect' that they would be the first to give good example by obeying the expert's advice and ploughing some of their own land, taking maybe only a few acres at first to see how things went, but, he cautioned, 'do not stand in the path of progress' thinking 'that what your grandfather did must therefore be good enough for you'. Again and again, O'Dwyer had emphasised the importance of 'a programme of scientific study which would develop the mental faculties of the pupils and even gain the good will of their parents' because of its connection 'with the physical occupation of their lives'. This applied to agriculture would, he believed, have countrywide benefits, Ireland being an agricultural country.

The bishop's pastoral was written five years after Plunkett had become the target of extensive criticism and had forfeited the support of many priests and prelates, including the cardinal, because of an outspoken, rather ill-judged book, *Ireland in the new century*, which appeared in 1904. Among the many clerical voices raised in anger, the most polemical and cutting voice remained silent. O'Dwyer, indeed, shared much of Plunkett's critical view of the Irish character, of his thinking on the prevalence of intemperance and laziness, and, even, on the attitudes of many Irish Catholic churchmen. On 11 October 1903, four months before the book was published, Plunkett wrote to him stating that he would be going to Limerick shortly and wished to talk with him. He declared that he had decided to go ahead with the publication of the work, 'which', he acknowledged, would get him 'into great trouble'.[17] It did. Home truths, which involved sharp criticism of the Irish character and of Irish Catholic clergy were not likely to be well received, especially when coming from the head of a Department of State who was, besides, both a Protestant and a unionist! The anger generated against Plunkett weakened the work of his department, and greatly lessened recognition of his major achievements.

With more moral courage than political judgment, he had observed that the undoubted zeal of the Roman Catholic clergy had led them to 'excessive and extravagant church-building in the heart … of poor communities', when the best monument to their influence was rather to be found 'in the moral character and spiritual fibre of their flock'.[18] Indeed, the clergy, with 'their unquestioned authority in religion' and almost equally 'undisputed influence in education', had not done enough to counter intemperance, and moreover, could not be exonerated from some responsibility for the Irish character manifested amongst a majority of the people – with its 'striking absence of self-reliance and moral courage; an entire lack of serious thought on public questions; a listlessness and apathy in regard to economic improvement which amount to a form of fatalism; and, in backward districts, a survival of superstition, which saps all strength of will and purpose – and all this, too, amongst a people singularly gifted by nature with good qualities of mind and heart.'[19] 'Nor can the Roman Catholic clergy altogether console themselves', Plunkett added, 'with the thought that religious faith, even when free from superstition, is strong in the breasts of the people'. The test of that faith was not at home, where the social environment and public opinion worked in favour of religious observance, but abroad, where the extensive 'leakage' from Catholicism amongst Irish emigrants in Great Britain and the United States indicated 'how largely emotional and formal must be the religion of those who lapse so quickly in a non-Catholic atmosphere'. He further suggested that the Catholic Church's condemnation of relatively innocent amusements and its 'rigidly ascetic' approach to relations between the sexes, constituted an 'enforced asceticism', the 'evil of grafting upon secular life a quasi-monasticism which, not being voluntary, has no real effect upon the character … '[20]

The book rendered the author's days numbered as an effective promoter of cooperation in Ireland. To his regular censurers in the Irish party, were now added critics from other shades of nationalism, as well as the voices of many clergy. O'Dwyer, as mentioned, stayed silent in public, and contented himself in private with the mild rebuke that Plunkett's criticism of the Catholic Church's neglect of technical education was scarcely fair. After all, Jesus Christ did not include technical education in his discourses to the inhabitants of Palestine![21] Plunkett responded good-humouredly and effectively, on 8 March 1904, that it was as anachronistic to talk of a Department of Technical Instruction in Palestine as it would be to talk of a Marconi station or even a creamery, and that 'in the circumstances of the day Our Lord did give the highest possible sanction to technical instruction by his attendance and work in the best of all technical schools, St Joseph's workshop'.[22] His attitude towards the Catholic Church, he insisted, had been 'wholly misunderstood'. He did not argue, as many Protestants did, that there was 'an essential antagonism between economic progress and Roman Catholicism', rather was it his desire 'to get the Catholic Church recognised as a powerful auxiliary to economic progress'. This was all the more necessary because the world was 'getting more and more critical of clerical influence on secular life'. He did not wish to see clerical influence lessened, 'but rather given new worlds to conquer', and, at the present stage of human progress, what required attention was the economic factor, 'the most powerful factor in large national problems'.

He had been condemned by Cardinal Logue, he remarked sadly, not upon what his book contained but upon extracts in the letter of a parish priest of County Meath. Nevertheless, although there had been much hostile criticism, there also had been many letters of support. He hoped the balance would ultimately be on the side of good. He finished the letter on a relatively sanguine note.

> I have had letters from educated and thinking opponents who, like yourself, are liberal enough to credit me with pure, if misguided, motives. These have deeply impressed me with the hope that we may travel a good deal of the road together, if we may not be together all the way when our starting points are so different, before we reach what begins to look like a common goal.

'Surely, too,' he concluded, 'all recent history cries aloud for a broader view of the Irish question, and this I have laboured to open to seeing eyes.'[23] It was an aspect that appealed also to O'Dwyer.

In the event, he retained his friendship with Plunkett, while also being indirectly and fortuitously identified with a reasoned voice of opposition. The most exacting and detailed examination and criticism of *Ireland in the New Century* came from a priest of the Limerick diocese, Michael O'Riordan, in a series of articles in *the Leader*. These dealt with the book's criticisms and provided an extensive and positive picture of the Catholic Church in Ireland. The articles were expanded and published in a volume of 500 pages entitled *Catholicity and Progress in Ireland*, which won wide acclaim. O'Dwyer wrote to O'Riordan, in Rome, expressing his 'intense satisfaction' with his work, and adding that he felt proud to have among his priests a scholar of such calibre.[24]

SECULAR EDUCATION AND CLERICAL MANAGEMENT

Plunkett's reference to the growing criticism 'of clerical influence in secular life' seemed to be borne out later that year by a celebrated public controversy in the *Freeman's Journal*. The protagonists were O'Dwyer and Michael Davitt, the theme, secular education, which Davitt championed. Not content, however, with letters to the newspapers, the bishop was sufficiently concerned to devote most of his 1906 pastoral letter to an attack on secularism and a defence of clerical management in primary education. He drew attention to the British government's trend towards control of the Catholic schools in England, and warned that it might well be the prelude to a similar development in Ireland. The thinking behind these secular proposals in England, he declared, were

> that education belongs to the State: thence it is asserted that there can be no place in it for religion, for the State as such has none: further that the teachers are State officials, and cannot be subjected to any test more than the members of any other branch of the public service, and the ultimate consequence is that there cannot be any distinction by religion between schools, a school can be neither Catholic, nor Protestant, but simply secular, with as little reference to Christ, our Lord, and his Redemption, as there was in the schools of pagan Rome, and less than there was then to God our Father.[25]

The way the secular system goes to work, the bishop went on, 'is to ascribe education to the State as its function, and the next step to secularism is short and easy'. The sorry physical condition of the National Schools was used as a comment on their being run by clerical managers, but, in fact, he insisted, their physical neglect was due to the government's lack of adequate support, while the quality of education provided remained good. He, O'Dwyer, was for reform, not against it, but for a reform, however, that would not open 'the floodgates of party and religious strife'. He was for three immediate reforms: 1. Reform of the Commissioners. 'The domination of Trinity College over this and every part of Irish education should be overthrown', and be replaced by people really representative of the country; 2. Increase of the salaries of the teachers, particularly the initial salaries, and a shortening of the periods for earning increments; 3. Improvement of the condition of the school buildings.[26]

Religion, O'Dwyer insisted, had not proved a barrier to success in Ireland. 'In university education our poor unendowed Catholic college of St Stephen's Green, Dublin, in a fair competition, can beat any or all of the Queen's Colleges; in intermediate education, 74 percent of all the prizes are carried off year by year by Catholic schools'; and in the primary system, the report of the English school inspector, Mr F.H. Dale, had shown Irish convent schools equal to the best of English primary schools. Furthermore, he commented tellingly, in Germany – the country in the van in education, setting the standard for all other countries – education was 'religious and denominational'.[27] Nevertheless, the British government wanted to set up a Department of Education independent of Irish Catholic opinion, and 'at the same time place the management of the schools in the hands of the local authorities'. 'They imagine', he continued, 'that the little authority and patronage connected with the management of the schools would bribe our local authorities to turn round on their clergy, and take the schools out of their hands.' 'But they are mistaken', O'Dwyer stated rhetorically. 'This is not France; this is not England, this is Ireland, Catholic to the core and resolved to remain so.'[28]

Michael Davitt died that year, fortified with the last rites of the Catholic Church but adhering to his prophecy addressed to O'Dwyer in the *Freeman's Journal* of 21 January 1906: 'Make no mistake about it, my Lord Bishop of Limerick, Democracy is going to rule in these countries.'

MIXED EDUCATION

Commitment to denominational education, and to clerical management of Catholic primary schools, was a mark of the Catholic Church in Europe and the United States of America in the later decades of the nineteenth century and the first half of the twentieth century. A similar commitment was displayed to the separation of the sexes in education during the same period. It was an attitude shared by many people, irrespective of their religious persuasion.

In 1905, O'Dwyer, in another year of controversy for him, confronted the Commissioners of National Education on the issue. The latter, presumably on economic rather than educational grounds, had decided to amalgamate boys and girls schools on an extensive scale. O'Dwyer was sufficiently roused to produce another of his more formidable letters. To the amalgamation policy, he announced, 'we are vehemently opposed, and when I write 'we' I mean the Catholics of Ireland as a body'. He explained:

> You have seen, I presume, the published statement in·which the Catholic Bishops of Ireland, with absolute unanimity, declared their condemnation of the mixed education of boys and girls in the same school. The clerical managers of National Schools, in their diocesan, provincial, and national committees, have expressed the strongest and most vehement aversion to that system, and I may add that the Holy See has in most explicit terms condemned it as a source of moral corruption.

'You see, then,' he added, 'that our objection to the policy you have adopted is founded not in caprice, or a passing feeling, but has behind it the highest authority by which Catholics are guided in questions of the kind.' Because it was a matter of conscientious conviction for Catholics, to try to force them to amalgamate was 'to disregard the very elements of liberty'. Their views might seem like 'prejudices' to the Commissioners, O'Dwyer observed, but, even so, for the Commissioners to enforce their views seemed to him 'nothing less than bigotry', and, since the victims were the whole nation, it was 'gross tyranny'. He viewed with the greatest pain and sorrow, he said, the prospect which faced them in Limerick diocese. Peace was essential for primary schools, but the

Commissioners' policy had aroused angry passions. He went on to outline areas of grievance and hostility. At Borrigyone, in the parish of Shanagolden, under an able educationalist, Revd M. Doner, VF, mentioned in an earlier chapter, cooperation in sending the girls to the boys' school was refused. Now the girls had no school. At Kilmeedy the Commission had destroyed 'the separate existence of the two best schools in the diocese.' He gave two other examples, and then urged the Commissioners to change the two new rules that were causing distress and provoking opposition and disorder, or, at least, to get rid of the most objectionable rule and be ready to modify the other.[29]

The letter indicated, on the one hand, shortage of funds, and little real contact between the central headquarters and the remoter country areas, but, on the other hand, it demonstrated the bishops', and the Vatican's protective attitude towards the allegedly 'weaker sex', and their presumption and fear that mixed education must lead to moral corruption. In this, of course, they shared the views of a large, perhaps a major part of a population emerging from the protective Victorian world. Something of this protective attitude, joined to a chivalrous, idealised image of womanhood, found its way into Bishop O'Dwyer's thinking with respect to the education of girls; and, as by now one has come to expect, it led him into vigorous statements that gave an unbalanced impression of his thinking.

THE EDUCATION OF GIRLS

During his address on 'Technical Instruction', speaking of girls' education, he contended – 'What we want for them is to make them good housewive.' If they could cook, keep their houses and their families' clothes clean, and know how to mend and make, there would be 'more domestic happiness, less drunkenness, and each succeeding generation would advance in thrift and comfort and prosperity.'[30] Hence, he nominated cookery, laundry and needlework as the subjects 'clearly determined for us as the field of our labour for girls'[31] and he urged the provision of such on the Limerick City Technical Instruction Committee. In March 1901, with a particular care for country girls, he applied to the central office of the Department of Agricultural and Technical Instruction for 'the establishment at Newcastle West of a school partly literary and partly technical and industrial for farmers' daughters'.[32]

Such views on female education were commonplace at the period. 'The woman's place was in the home.' Women did not have votes, and degrees were still denied to women in Oxford, Cambridge, and Dublin University; though, significantly, women could take degrees in the Royal University, of which O'Dwyer was a senator. In the above remarks he was referring to the majority population, to the greater number of girls of working class and small farmers' families, and to the many who did not have the opportunity of secondary education. In his pastoral letter of 1912, also largely devoted to technical instruction, he sought to make it clear that remarks of his, such as the foregoing, did not mean 'that our Catholic girls should not get the fullest and best literary and general education, according to their means and position in life'. 'The two things harmonise with one another,' he insisted. 'The refinement which true education gives becomes every woman no matter what her social position.' His contacts with Laurel Hill School, noted earlier, and the mention in the school's chronicles for 1917 of how he had furthered the careers of a number of students, bore testimony to his 'respect for women's brains', in Kate O'Brien's phrase, and his desire to promote 'the best literary and general education' among those who could benefit from it. His foundation of a teacher training college for women teachers was, however, the crowning testimony.

THE LIMERICK TEACHER TRAINING COLLEGE

Background

When the idea for a system of National Schools was heralded in 1831, the training of teachers became a major consideration. In 1838 the government opened a central training college at Marlboro Street, Dublin, which was to be supplemented by model schools around the country under the direction of teachers of superior ability. The problem, from the point of view of Catholic churchmen, was that the venture was seen as an attempt to establish a national non-sectarian educational system. As religion was not provided for in such establishments, they were not considered acceptable for teacher training by both Church of Ireland and Catholic authorities, who set about establishing their own training colleges. The government, nevertheless, went on with the development of the model schools, though they came to be virtually boycotted by the Catholic population. O'Dwyer opposed them as a danger to the faith of Catholic children because of their 'mixed', undenominational character, and because, as he claimed in the light of the Report of the Commissioners of National Education, 1895, they were quite uneconomical, each costing on average as much as six ordinary National Schools.[33]

The opposition of the Catholic hierarchy to Marlboro College and the model schools meant that the situation regarding trained teachers steadily worsened. By 1866 the chief secretary, C. S. Fortescue, pointed out that the model school system was turning out about 400 teachers every year whereas the number of new teachers required each year was around 900.[34] Nevertheless, denominational training establishments remained unendowed in Ireland, even though they had been endowed in England and Scotland since 1839.[35] Eventually, in 1883, when two thirds of the teaching force was untrained, the chief secretary, G.O.Trevelyan, removed the ban on the recognition of denominational colleges and allowed them limited financial assistance.[36] Within months, through the impetus of Cardinal McCabe, archbishop of Dublin, two Catholic training colleges were opened in Dublin: St Patrick's Training College for men, at

Drumcondra, and Our Lady of Mercy Training College for women at Baggot Street. The following year, the Church of Ireland brought its Kildare Place Training College for men and women into connection with the Commissioners of National Education. That same year, Dr William Walsh succeeded Cardinal McCabe to the see of Dublin and straightway pressed for parity of treatment with the State-run college at Marlboro Street. The concession was granted in 1890. The following year, the De La Salle Brothers opened a training college for men in Waterford. The situation where women teachers were concerned, however, remained critical. Already in 1888 there were 264 female teacher vacancies and only 99 trained teachers available. Conscious of the large numbers of girls being deprived of the services of trained teachers, Dr O'Dwyer determined to establish a college in Limerick.

The Limerick development

On 18 October 1896 he sent a brief, business-like letter to the Commissioners of National Education:

> Gentlemen,
> I beg to apply for a licence for a Training College for Female National School Teachers for the Catholic Religion which I propose to establish in this city.
> I believe that the College of Our Lady of Mercy, Dublin, is not equal to the supply of our needs and on the other hand, this city which is the centre of railway lines running into counties of Clare, Tipperary, Kerry, Cork and Waterford is well situated for the purpose. Should you sanction this proposal, inform me as to the steps for obtaining a building loan for the College.[37]

Early the following year, his application gave rise to correspondence between the Commissioners of National Education, the chief secretary for Ireland, and the Treasury at Whitehall, London. Convinced by the representations of the National Board in Dublin that the supply of trained female teachers was inadequate, the lords commissioners of Her Majesty's Treasury informed the chief secretary, Gerald Balfour, on 26 July 1897, that they were 'pleased to approve of the grant of licences to two new training colleges at Belfast and Limerick to accommodate 80 and 75 students respectively'. Their lordships were 'prepared to make provision for capitation grants etc.'.[38] O'Dwyer, looking to the future, and with experience of the tardiness of government departments, had the architect draw up plans for a college of '100 Queen's scholars' rather than for the 75 mentioned in the licence. In weighted words, he informed the Commissioners:

Although my certificate at present is only for 75 students, I am morally certain that within a very few years, your Board will see the necessity of increasing it and consequently I have thought it better, dealing with an important public institution which will last a very long time, to anticipate future needs rather than have to spoil the whole thing by afterwards adding entirely different structures.[39]

Before the end of 1898, all legalities were completed, plans for a college to accommodate 100 students were approved, and all was ready for building to commence. On receiving official sanction for the setting up of the college, O'Dwyer had joined with the Sisters of Mercy in purchasing a suitable site on the southwest side of the city. He had entrusted the running and staffing of the college to the Sisters of Mercy, who were educating more than 2000 girls in four primary schools in the city, and who had previously embarked on an educational tour of schools in England to study organisation and teaching methods. Now, as the new college was being built, the principal and vice-principal designate – Sr Paul Quinlan, and Sr Veronica Cullinan – went for a year to the leading English Catholic Training College, at Mount Pleasant, Liverpool, to prepare for the Limerick venture.[40]

The construction of the college began in 1898 with William H. Byrne, Dublin, as architect, and a Mr Glynn, of Dublin, as building contractor.[41] The work was expected to take two years. His Lordship kept a close eye on developments. By April 1901, he was concerned that the building would not be ready on time and, through the architect, sent a sharp reminder to the contractor. On 7 April, Byrne, the architect, informed Dr O'Dwyer that he had read out his letter to Mr Glynn 'and informed him that on account of the way the work has been carried on' he 'could not see any prospect of its being completed in time, and that unless immediate steps' were 'taken to put on more hands your Lordship was determined to take the work from him and employ the men yourself so as to get the college ready on time'. The builder answered that he would come to Limerick forthwith and bring extra hands with him. As regards his lordship's offer of extra money, 'he said he would not take any except what he was entitled to'.[42] The additional pressure proved effective, and the college was able to open in autumn 1901.

The formal commencement of the construction and the formal opening of the college were major happenings for O'Dwyer. They underlined in his own eyes his standing as an educationalist, as well as being in themselves a tribute to his vision and persistence. The laying of the foundation stone on 8 December 1899, the annual feast day in the Catholic Church calendar of the Immaculate Conception of the Virgin Mary, reflected both his personal devotion and his decision to name the institution the College of Mary Immaculate. In his address, he made clear his values and his hopes for the new structure. This, he asserted, 'will be purely and thoroughly a Catholic institution in all its parts'. 'The atmosphere of religion', which he hoped would 'surround this college', would be important in the training of the teachers, and through them would influence the rising generation. He went on:

> With a good priest, I believe a good teacher is the greatest blessing God can send a parish: and by a good teacher, I mean, not a person of high intellectual power or of literary attainments only, but one who holds those gifts of God, united and informed by the Spirit of God's wisdom, that religion alone can give. So I am satisfied, I am confident, that this College will do great work yet.

'Even looking to education in its narrowest and technical sense', he added, any hope of progress in primary education 'has to begin not in the schools, not in the pupils, but in the training colleges … '.[43]

Before concluding his address, he did not miss the opportunity of drawing public attention to the anomaly in which the Limerick and Belfast Colleges found themselves. They, together with the Waterford College, were being excluded from the benefits granted the Dublin denominational colleges in 1890. Prior to that date, he reminded his listeners, the two private Catholic colleges in Dublin, and also the one Protestant Training College, had to provide for their building fund out of income, and thereby lessened the amount available for their educational work. This contrasted with the Marlboro Street College, which had been built and equipped by the government, and had its whole income available for its educational work. After long agitation, Mr Balfour in 1890 had acknowledged their case, and provided them with what he termed a 'free homes' grant, and also made an arrangement whereby they could obtain a building grant.[44] The three provincial colleges, the bishop pointed out, were as much part of the National Education system as their Dublin counterparts; all were sanctioned by government authority; all were doing the same work; and that work was measured by the same standards. It was a compelling argument.

He did not mention, however, that he and Bishop Henry Henry, of Down and Connor, had agreed to the precise financial conditions laid down by the Commissioners before their training colleges were sanctioned, and that it was only after approval was sanctioned that they sought equal terms with the Dublin colleges. Henry seems to have led the way in the demand for equal terms. As early as August 1897 he informed O'Dwyer that it would be very important to him to have his assistance 'in fighting for the privileges the Dublin Colleges enjoy'.[45] Thereafter, it was Limerick that was in the van of the agitation. On 10 December 1900, Henry was to request a copy of a letter O'Dwyer had drawn up, as it had put the Belfast case well.[46] What was granted once can be granted again, O'Dwyer argued. There was no inviolable principle involved. The government can change. For more that ten years, from 1898, he wrote on the matter in newspapers, and in the *Irish Educational Review*, October 1908, and he corresponded with successive key functionaries, M. Hicks Beach, James Bryce, H.H. Asquith, and with Sir Anthony Mac Donnell and other educationalists, as well as various Irish politicians.[47] It was not until 1911, nevertheless, that his eloquence and pertinacity prevailed. On 17 May 1911, at a time when he was not well, he was relieved to receive word from John Redmond: 'I have at last succeeded with regard to the 3 Training Colleges ... An announcement will speedily be made that our demand has been fully conceded.'[48]

The Limerick College opened to its first students on 21 September 1901. Of the 75 students who registered, 75 were classified as 'one-year' students: these were students who had previous experience of teaching, either as principals or assistants, and they were entitled to an exemption from the first year of the course. Most of them were older than the average student. The others were known as 'King's scholars'(the queen died early in 1901), and they entered for the two-year course of training. Of the 75 students, 41 came from Munster, 17 from the West of Ireland, 11 from across the counties of Leitrim, Monaghan, Meath, and Cavan, and 6 came from Wexford and Kildare.

The formal opening took place on 16 May 1902. The bishops of Waterford and Ross attended, together with many clergy and a range of dignitaries, which included the mayor of Limerick, the high sheriff, Sir Vincent Nash, and Lord Monteagle and the Knight of Glin together with a number of other Protestant guests. Following the official opening by Dr Richard A. Sheehan, of Waterford, there was an address by Dr O'Dwyer very much adapted to his mixed audience. He extended a special welcome to members of other religious persuasions, quoted the Protestant archbishop of Dublin, and linked the financial difficulties of the Kildare Place Training College with that of Limerick. He then confined his attention solely to educational issues. Once again he emphasised that the different sectors of education formed 'one great organism', and that the founding of a training college was of more than local importance. On its work, more than on any other single influence, would 'depend the efficiency and success of the schools in the future'. He went on to observe that teaching was an art and that, apart from rare exceptions, teachers, before they teach, 'must first learn the methods of their art, and acquire, besides knowledge, the ways of communicating knowledge, and, much more, developing the minds of their future pupils (applause)'. 'For this reason', he declared, 'it is desirable to build and equip these training colleges in a very complete and elaborate manner.' Also speaking on the occasion, was his Protestant friend, Lord Monteagle, who pointed out that 'of the twelve thousand national teachers in the country only half were trained' and that, consequently, he had no difficulty in supporting denominational training colleges, which, he remarked, were 'the only colleges on which they could rely to supply the needs'.[49]

O'Dwyer was manager of the new college, and, as one of the early students recalled, 'he visited us frequently and took a deep interest in our progress'.[50] The first year was very much a trial year. The subjects presented in the examinations of July 1902 were: Reading, Penmanship, Spelling and Punctuation, Grammar, Composition, Geography, English Literature, Arithmetic and Mensuration, Theory of Method, Practice of Teaching, Needlework, Music, Drawing,

Bookkeeping, Cookery, Science, Manual Instruction.[51] French and Irish also formed part of the curriculum.[52] The exam results at the end of the first year were considered satisfactory, and, following a favourable report from the chief inspector, Albert Pursur, the National Board granted its formal approval on 26 July 1902. This sanctioned the grants to the college and confirmed the officers who had been appointed. With this, Mary Immaculate College began to develop on various fronts. Additional rooms were added in 1902, followed by an assembly hall, and in 1906 a college chapel. The numbers grew to 100 in a very short time, as the bishop had foreseen. Various cultural activities were introduced from time to time to expand the horizons of the students: music recitals, poetry readings, guest speakers, and dramatic productions. New paintings and copies of Old Masters were acquired to adorn the walls and cultivate taste. These were mainly acquired as gifts from Bishop O'Dwyer and the Sisters of Mercy.[53]

The Sisters were a key factor in the development of O'Dwyer's college. The early staff was composed of the two sisters who were principal and vice-principal, and four other Sisters of Mercy. In addition, there were three priests, and four lay teachers. By 1909 the College was entitled to feel secure. That year, following an inspection by Dr William J. Starkie, Resident Commissioner of National Education, and four other Commissioners, Starkie wrote to express his colleagues' and his own gratitude for the kindness with which they had been received, adding, 'we were literally amazed at the beauty and excellence of all we saw'.[54]

In the extensive field of education, O'Dwyer's contribution had been considerable. At secondary level, he had re-established St Munchin's College and brought an outstanding educationalist, Fr Andrew Murphy, to head it; and among school leavers and adults he had promoted technical instruction and education and had urged local authorities to provide opportunities for such instruction and for the teaching of science. As regards primary education generally, he had not only actively promoted it throughout the diocese, and given encouragement and support to primary teachers, he had established a training college for primary school teachers. This last was, perhaps, the most significant and enduring of his educational contributions; and yet what caught public attention most of all, in Britain and Ireland, was his championing of university education and his efforts to make it available to the highest standard to the majority Irish population.

16

Struggling for equality in university education, 1889–1903

The issue

The university question arose from the demand by Catholics for equality of treatment in education with their Protestant fellow countrymen. Through the bishops, as spokesmen, the envisaged solution took the form of: a Catholic university as well endowed as Dublin University, or, perhaps, a Catholic college, well endowed and equipped, in a neutral university, such as the Royal University, or a Catholic college in Dublin University equally endowed and equipped as Trinity College. This last was the preferred choice of the leading figure in the hierarchy, Archbishop Walsh.

Part of the difficulty on the Catholic side was that many of the bishops had small interest in a university and did not see it as a priority. Under the guidance of a number of prelates they opted for the first or second options, and, under the leadership of Dr Walsh, they actually agreed to the third option while retaining a vague preference for one and two. The widespread lack of commitment and unity of policy amongst his episcopal colleagues infuriated Dr O'Dwyer. From the government side, the difficulty about the Catholic demands was that neither Conservatives nor Liberals wished to give control over university education, in a Catholic university or a Catholic college in another university, to the Catholic bishops. Where other groups were concerned: the Protestant majority, the Episcopalians, opposed concessions to Catholics in so far as they involved interference with Dublin University; the Presbyterians, generally, were not supportive of Catholic claims; and the Non-Conformists, mainly in north-east Ireland and in Britain, were totally opposed to any concessions to Catholics. Finally, the struggle was conducted amidst a rising tide of national feeling and of dissatisfaction with British rule.

This chapter is divided into two stages in the struggle for educational equality: the first from 1889 to 1900, the second from 1901 to 1902, in which the centrepiece is the Robertson Commission.

STAGE I, 1889–1900

Dr O'Dwyer and the bishops' statement, 1889

Following their experience of him on the university and land issues shortly after his consecration, Archbishop Walsh, and, under his leadership the other arch-bishops, tended to bypass O'Dwyer, and this had the effect of making him more assertive and independent than ever, while always being careful to stand well with Rome. With respect to the general statements of the hierarchy, however, he mostly expressed agreement. Thus, he enthusiastically supported the resolution forwarded to the government by the Irish Catholic bishops in July 1889. This pressed for a solution to the university question, and stated they would be satis-fied substantially by having 'one or more colleges conducted on purely Catholic principles' and enjoying the privileges of other colleges 'in an exclusively Catholic or in a common university', with their students, equally with others, being admitted to university honours, and with Catholics being assured of an adequate representation 'in the senate or other supreme university council'.[1]

At the end of June 1890, at the Jesuit college, the Crescent, Limerick, O'Dwyer spoke of the episcopal resolution as an earnest that the bishops did not mean 'to allow the question to drop out of sight'. There were differences of opinion among them on many points, he acknowledged, 'but in this question, which is a religious one affecting the aspirations of our flock … there is no disagreement'. He appealed to the authorities of Trinity College, Dublin, to be supportive, warning that Home Rule would come some day and implying that it would be wise not to be obstructive now. He concluded, for the benefit of members of the Irish party and of some of his episcopal colleagues, by denouncing those who were advocating the postponement of a solution of the university question to an Irish parliament. Such a body, he observed, would have enough problems to solve 'without artificially preserving for it the elements of a religious feud with all its proverbial bitterness'. He appealed to the government to solve the matter, assuring them that once the main principles were agreed Catholics would not be hard to satisfy in details.[2] O'Dwyer, still a junior member of the hierarchy, was putting himself forward as a voice of the bishops on university education.

In response to the bishops' statement, Arthur J. Balfour, chief secretary, showed himself sympathetic and indicated that the government hoped to present proposals to the House in relation to higher education.[3] Hopes were raised, and then were dashed in December 1889, at Partick, Glasgow, when he announced that no effort would be made to solve the Irish university question without the general consent of all major political and religious parties in England, Scotland, and Ireland. He was responding to the hard reality of anti-Catholic animosity amongst his political supporters, but to O'Dwyer it was yet another instance of English perfidy. In his speech at the Crescent at the end of June 1890, the bishop of Limerick, had exhibited a defiant, relatively optimistic front, but now, in effect, the university question had been placed in abeyance. It was to remain virtually dormant for the next five years.

The years between

Those years, it will be recalled, were of particular significance for O'Dwyer. They included his contest with Dillon and O'Brien, and his depiction of himself as champion of the Holy See. Ironically, his account of his stance, sent to Archbishop Kirby in Rome and forwarded by him to Propaganda, was returned by officials of that congregation as 'unintelligible'. Such letters were highly important, Kirby reminded him on 12 June 1890. He should get someone else to write his official letters and he just sign them![4] The following month, never-theless, he received the letter of approval from the pope that upset Archbishop Walsh.[5] The closing months of that year and all through 1891, brought distur-bance and pressure. There was the O'Shea divorce case, the split in the Irish party, and the pressure on himself from his fellow bishops to join with them in condemnation of Parnell, and his defiant refusal. Despite his independent stand, he was personally honoured by the pope on his visit to Rome in December 1891,[6] as has been seen.

That year witnessed the death of Parnell and a political hiatus in Ireland. Early the following year another major figure died, Cardinal Henry Edward Manning, who also left a hiatus, this time in the English Catholic Church so far as nation-alist Ireland was concerned. But O'Dwyer was not discommoded. Herbert Vaughan, Manning's successor as archbishop of Westminster, was a personal friend. Although he had been critical of Manning's support for Archbishops Croke and Walsh in their land and political policies, O'Dwyer, with a number of other Irish bishops, attended the cardinal's funeral, described as 'one of the most wonderful sights ever witnessed in London' – as members of both Houses of Parliament, of the Trades and Workingmen's Guilds of London, representatives of the Royal Family, and foreign ambassadors and statesmen, joined numerous other mourners to pay their respects to a great churchman and a national figure.[7]

Manning had been a friend of Archbishop Walsh, his successor, Vaughan, was to join with the duke of Norfolk in opposing Walsh's appointment as cardinal. Another conspiring to the same end was Persico, now secretary of Propaganda. On 28 November 1892, the bishop of Limerick was able to tell his friend, Bishop Donnelly, that Armagh was to be cardinal. 'In many personal gifts', he remarked, 'Your Man would be better, but for the substantial interests of religion I have no doubt of the greater safety and reliability of the other.'[8] He subse-quently told Dr Fogarty, of Killaloe, the significant story that when he was in Rome he had a meeting with Persico, who informed him that his Holiness was considering the appointment of an Irish cardinal and was sure to ask his opinion as between Walsh and Logue. Persico pressed him to oppose Walsh and vigor-ously to support Logue. At the audience, Pope Leo did ask O'Dwyer to state frankly which of the two ought to be appointed. He seemed favourably disposed towards Walsh. O'Dwyer reported that he had respectfully declined to express his preference.[9].

During the years 1892 to 1894 O'Dwyer, in addition to his administration of the diocese and to special sermons at the consecration of Richard Sheehan as bishop of Waterford and Robert Browne as bishop of Cloyne, was engaged in making life difficult for Protestants over Leamy's school and for the Jesuits over Mungret, was actively involved in a campaign with John Ross of Bladensburg and the Irish members of parliament, for the relief of Catholics suffering persecution in Uganda,[10] and was immersed in preparations for the consecration of his expanded cathedral. Then, early in 1895 there came a change that opened once more the prospect of university reform.

Renewed hopes of educational reform

On 11 February, in the *Freeman's Journal,* Archbishop Croke made the significant statement: 'The hope of obtaining a legislature for our country within measurable time is no longer entertained by reasoning men.' The general election in July 1895 bore out his prediction. The Conservatives gained a comfortable victory.[11]

It was evident to the episcopacy that Home Rule would not happen under a Conservative government, but concessions in education were a distinct possibility. It seemed an auspicious time to O'Dwyer, who distrusted Liberals, and had a number of Unionist friends, and felt that in the hiatus caused by the Parnell split the bishops had a unique opportunity to have their demands in regard to education taken seriously. He misjudged, perhaps, the depth of opposition.

Contending parties

In the aftermath of the fall of Parnell, a section of the population harboured a deep antagonism to the bishops and clergy, but among the majority of the people the standing and authority of the episcopacy had expanded. The absence of agreed political leadership left the bishops free to assume ascendancy on a number of issues, most notably education, which they perceived as an area vulnerable to attack by proselytising groups or undenominationalist Liberals. Part of their role, as the prelates envisaged it, was to preserve the 'religious freedom' of the majority population from educational policies likely to subvert their belief. In this they enjoyed the support of the majority population, and, generally speaking, of the nationalist politicians.

The main English political parties, for their part, as indicated earlier, were guarded where the bishops were concerned. The position of their lordships had to be respected, their support sought, if necessary, but their control in education was not welcome. The Liberals were opposed to denominational education. The Conservatives, although they traditionally favoured denominational education, had to reckon with the almost hysterical suspicions and unreal fears of their Irish 'loyalist minority' and, more significantly, with clamant Non-Conformist opposition in Britain. As might be expected, they did not wish to have any interference with Dublin University and Trinity College, and had great difficulty in understanding why Catholics could not be content to seek their education there.

Thus, even a Liberal Unionist like W.E.H. Lecky, M.P., who was favourably disposed towards providing university education for Catholics, and had a number of Catholic friends, maintained in the *Times*, 13 December 1895, that Dublin University was 'a national and unsectarian institution', eminently suitable to meet the needs of the Catholic population if it were not for 'strong sacerdotal pressure'.

Lecky's assertion was too much for the bishop of Limerick. He responded vigorously. The interchange of letters in the *Times* served to establish O'Dwyer as a formidable voice on the side of suitable university education for the Catholic majority. Recognising what was happening, Fr John Flanagan, on 22 and 23 December 1895, drew his attention to two cognate matters: one, that the educated laity in Ireland were quite out of sympathy with the bishops and the clerical body in general, that, with some rare exceptions, there was no social intercourse between them and the clergy, and that these were the Catholics whom Lecky met at the Athenaeum Club and from whom he took his views; that, in the second place, 'judging the bishops by the clergy', he suspected that O'Dwyer had no followers on the Episcopal Board. 'Scarcely any of the priests', he observed, 'have the slightest idea of what a university education means.' 'Would any of them,' he asked, 'were they bishops in your place, have written as you have done, or have gained admission to the *Times*?'[12] Flanagan's admiration for O'Dwyer blinded him temporarily to the contribution of other bishops, but he conveyed a reality, which both O'Dwyer and Archbishop Walsh acknowledged, namely, that few of the bishops had any real interest in university education, and, also, that O'Dwyer by being published by *The Times* had achieved something important: he had been acknowledged as a serious voice on the university question.

Following up the interest generated by his interchange with Lecky, O'Dwyer canvassed support among Catholic unionists for an equitable solution to the university question. On the last day of the year, one respondent, Major John Ross of Bladensburg, expressed agreement with O'Dwyer's desire that the university question be removed from party strife and be considered on its merits, but he pointed out that those seeking higher education must be agreed on their demands so that the government knows that if it responds its response will be accepted. He favoured modest demands, as these would have a greater chance of success. For guidelines, he suggested two objectives emphasised by the late Lord Emly: a well endowed and well equipped college linked to the Royal University, and having a satisfactory governing body in terms of organisation and composition. The first point, Ross noted, excluded the idea of interfering with Dublin University. Such interference, if seriously entertained, would create obstacles not easy to surmount.[13]

The guidelines coincided with O'Dwyer's thinking. He even went so as far as to reply extravagantly – 'that no party in Ireland' was 'likely to seriously urge that Dublin University should be interfered with'; and then proceeded to give his own tentative solutions to the higher education problem. The first was to leave the Royal University as it was, except for a Catholic college within it, based in Dublin, and properly endowed. The second proposal was more involved: convert the Royal into a Catholic University, with a new Catholic college within it; absorb Cork's college into the Catholic University, abolish Galway, and erect Queen's College Belfast into a Presbyterian University. Ross thought the first proposal a possibility, if it were clear what endowment was being sought for the Catholic college.[14] On a subsequent occasion, in response to a query from O'Dwyer for his preference between a Catholic college or Catholic university, Ross preferred the former as better calculated to improve learning and education, and he referred to the views of 'a devout Catholic', Mr Wilfrid Ward, who was well informed on the issue. He had commented that the current of public opinion was 'so shaping itself, that no matter how high may be the educational standard of a university, yet if it is known to be denominational its degrees will not be equal to those of a mixed university'. Hence, he favoured a number of colleges in a mixed university, in which youths of all denominations would compete together, and he laid it down as a principle, 'that in order to achieve the best educational results, and to maintain the interests of religion, the colleges should be strictly sectarian but the university should be non-sectarian'. In the same letter, Ross responded to another issue raised by O'Dwyer, namely his desire for a solution which would enable Catholic clergy to enjoy university teaching and obtain degrees, and in which there would be a chair of theology in the university. Ward thought such arrangements could be provided. Ross personally favoured a university education for Catholic clergy, but 'wondered that aspirants to the priesthood' did not already 'take degrees in the Royal (*faute de mieux!*)'.[15]

Despite O'Dwyer's expressed preference for a Catholic college in the Royal University or for an independent Catholic University, he was not closed to the option of a Catholic college in Dublin University. He appreciated the argument proposed to him by Edmund Dease, a Catholic gentleman and intellectual, that 'if we had a college on all fours with Trinity in the Dublin University our degrees would emanate from a common source with those of Episcopal Protestants, and this is the solution which seems to meet with the approval of all Catholics'[16] The assertive equality of such a college, challenging Trinity's hegemony, appealed to the bishop of Limerick, but he also realised that such an outcome was unlikely to be realised because of government reluctance and Protestant opposition. He was prepared, nevertheless, to argue for this as a possible solution in the years prior to 1897, thereafter he appears to have turned definitely against it.

His deep interest in university reform led him early in 1896 to write to the Universities of Aberdeen, St Andrews, and Glasgow for information on their history and structures,[17] and to interchange letters with the new chief secretary, Gerald Balfour. The latter expressed himself supportive of a university for Catholics. Then, once more, the government pulled back. O'Dwyer, feeling he had been misled, angrily informed Balfour that he was about to publish their correspondence. This caused confusion and upset. Horace Plunkett wrote on 19 February 1896 that Balfour had shown him their correspondence and that there must have been a misunderstanding. His friend Gerald Balfour was 'incapable of any such duplicity towards yourself as your interpretation of the undertaking, which he gave you, would seem to indicate'.[18] On 25 February, Edmund Dease expressed similar sentiments.[19] O'Dwyer had gone ahead, however, and published the letters. On 9 April, Ross referred to the matter again. He assured O'Dwyer that Gerald Balfour was really interested in solving the university issue and had been 'disconcerted by the publication of the correspondence', indeed, he seemed 'bewildered' by it. He had informed Ross that the university issue would be raised in the next session of parliament, hence, it was advisable that O'Dwyer should press on with university matters.[20]

The bishop's publication of the correspondence caused embarrassment to some influential Catholics in his own diocese. The publication occurred while Gerald Balfour was visiting Adare as a guest of Lord Dunraven. The latter, as the host and as a Catholic, was upset by the prelate's insult to his distinguished guest. He asked Elizabeth, Countess of Fingal, also a Catholic and a guest, to call on his lordship. Her account of what ensued was not without humour, while manifesting on O'Dwyer's part a gracious courtesy and a rueful acknowledgement that he had given way to hasty impulse.

> I went. And, of course, I found the Bishop, so fiery on paper, charming and gentle to meet. I said to him, 'My Lord, are you mad to write in such a way to a man who has it in his power to give you so much of what you want for your people?'
>
> 'Ah', he agreed, 'You're right, my Lady, you're right! If we were to put all the letters we write under our pillows till the morning and then read them again, the half of them would never be posted!'[21]

One suspects that had his lordship been reproached by a man, rather than by a highly esteemed and beautiful titled lady, his response might have been quite different.

Bishop O'Dwyer had previously written to the chief secretary's brother, Arthur J. Balfour, now first lord of the Treasury, in connection with a speech he had made. The latter's reply on 28 March 1895 got to the heart of the hierarchy's case. He pointed out that at the time of the speech there was no specific proposal before the government, but that he understood from Roman Catholic representatives in the House that if this most vexed and thorny question was ever to be settled it must be on the lines 'that Catholics were granted an adequately equipped university or college which should be Catholic in the same sense as Trinity College is Protestant', that is that it be practically, though not theoretically, a Catholic institution.[22] Correspondence continued with the Balfours. O'Dwyer, clearly, had become an acknowledged voice on university matters.

T.M. Healy restored

In terms of interest, competence, and profile, O'Dwyer and Archbishop Walsh stood out as the authorities on education among the hierarchy. Given their differences in policy, it was inevitable that differences between them would continue, but, meantime, in 1896, the bishop of Limerick was instrumental in healing a bitter falling out between Walsh and T.M. Healy, MP.[23] O'Dwyer considered Healy the most effective voice to press the university case in the House, a judgment not uninfluenced by their mutual distrust of John Dillon. On 24 October 1896, Healy responded to O'Dwyer's overtures relating to higher education reform and to Dr Walsh. He was most keen to promote the university question, he declared, but doubted his competence, having left school at thirteen and being surrounded currently by jealousies and criticisms and without a newspaper at his back. Still, he was ready to aid in any way he could, and he would 'respond cordially to any proposition made by his Grace, the Archbishop of Dublin, for whom' he had 'the highest respect and admiration'.[24] With further complimentary words about Dr Walsh – all of which were relayed by O'Dwyer – Healy was restored to his Grace's favour. He remained good friends with O'Dwyer. That same month, October 1896, the Irish Catholic bishops produced a strongly argued and significant statement on university education.

Important episcopal statement
They issued a detailed statement on the higher education question at this time, they explained, because there was reason to hope 'that at length the government may be induced to deal with it'. They referred to promising and realistic statements made by both Gerald and Arthur Balfour. The Catholic grievance had been set forth with great clarity by the present first lord of the Treasury, Arthur J. Balfour, seven years ago in his remarkable speech at Partick. Recently, in the closing days of the last session of parliament, the chief secretary admitted that through the want of university education he found it necessary at times to pass over Catholics for Protestants in public appointments which otherwise he would have thought it right to give to Catholics. 'We must say', their lordships commented pointedly, 'that much as we feel humiliated by the statement, we are not quite surprised by it. To be crushed by law into a position of inferiority, and then made to suffer in consequence, has for a long time been the lot of Irish Catholics.' At the present time there were but two university institutions deserving of the name, they continued, namely, 'Trinity College, Dublin, and the Queen's College, Belfast'. They did not think the other Queen's Colleges worthy of consideration, and the Catholic Colleges, despite their brilliant successes at various examinations were limited by the conditions under which they existed to very small fields of labour. In the two mentioned institutions there were 1,500 students. Of these, less than 100 were Catholics, the remainder Protestants of the Disestablished Church or Presbyterians. In the condition of things it was not surprising that educated Catholics were not numerous in Ireland.

The doors of higher knowledge were shut in the faces of the majority population, their Lordships emphasised, and this was detrimental to temporal welfare and progress in the country. In recent years the deficiencies in the educational system had become more obvious. Intermediate schools had multiplied. That year, 8,700 students, the great majority of them Catholics, presented themselves for examination. The number was likely to grow; yet the greater majority would not be able to go beyond the Intermediate, even though a university career was the reasonable completion to their studies. Lord Cairns, a distinguished Irishman and Conservative statesman, had described the education structure in apt metaphor when he spoke of primary education as the foundation, the intermediate as the walls, and the university as the roof. For Protestants and Presbyterians the edifice was complete, the Catholics were without a roof. It was now obvious, the bishops declared, that Irish Catholics would not accept a university education that was either Protestant or godless. Hence, the only alternative was to keep them in ignorance or give them opportunities of university education which their consciences could accept. They had not the means to endow a university for themselves; and even if they were richer they would not be able to provide comparable facilities to those that were richly endowed by public funds.

'What, then, do we claim?' their lordships asked, and then responded once again – 'Simply to be put on an equality with our Protestant fellow-countrymen.' They did not wish 'to impair the efficiency of any institution', they reiterated, to take one shilling from the endowment of Trinity College or Queen's College, Belfast, but they sought, as a matter of simple justice, that the Catholics of Ireland should be put on a footing of perfect equality with them. How that equality was to be reached was not for the bishops to define. They had stated on many occasions that they were not irrevocably committed to any one principle of settlement; and whether that settlement was carried out through a distinct Catholic University or through a College, they were prepared to consider any proposal with an open mind, and with a sincere desire to remove rather than to aggravate difficulties. They stood committed to denominationalism in education, as the government clearly understood, and their demand was in harmony with principles which the government had professed. It was time, therefore, for a positive decision. It was twenty-three years since this was made a cabinet question, and, in spite of protests and agitation in Ireland, little had been achieved. 'Violence and excess', the bishops went on trenchantly, 'obtain ready recognition, and lead to the redress of grievances; but the constitutionally expressed desires of the Irish people, through parliamentary elections and the action of their members in parliament, count unfortunately for very little. It is little wonder, then, that the minds of our people are alienated from their government, and every day lose confidence in constitutional methods.' Although our task is a weary one, the statement concluded, 'we would ask our countrymen still to urge their claim for freedom of education, which, in reality, is freedom of religion.'[25]

New hopes

The following year gave promise of a positive response. In the House of Commons, Mr Engledew proposed an amendment in favour of establishing a Roman Catholic University in Ireland. Another nationalist member of parliament, Tim Harrington, supported the proposal. He was followed by Prof. William E.H. Lecky, 'a tall, ungainly figure', who, as one correspondent noted, spoke 'plain sense, framed in literary form' with 'a quiet, quaint humour that now and again caused a ripple of laughter'. 'The House gradually filled up as he proceeded.'[26] Lecky declared that he could not support the amendment, but he hoped the government would be able to see their way to gratify the desire of Irish Catholics to have either a university of their own, or, at all events, an endowed college in connection with the existing university (Dublin University); for there could be no greater misfortune for Ireland than to have two sections of her people continually separated.'[27] Lecky's speech enabled Arthur Balfour to dismiss the opposition of Mr William Johnson, representing the northern Irish unionists; and he went on to pledge the government 'to the setting up of a Catholic University in Ireland, which, in the course of two or three generations,' would 'rival Trinity College Dublin.' John Morley, from the Liberal benches, praised the spirit of Mr Balfour's speech; and Engledew withdrew the amendment because of the sympathetic and conciliatory attitude taken by the government.

Balfour's statement was seen optimistically by the *Tablet* as a recognition at last that 'the essential condition of university education is that it shall be in harmony with the religious aspirations of the people'.[28] The *New Saturday*, in a long examination of the Irish University Question, also took a sanguine view. The writer, who favoured a solution by means of a Catholic college in Dublin University, pointed out that 'The Roman Catholic Bishop of Limerick, Dr O'Dwyer,' had, 'in several important letters to the *Times*, most fairly suggested the foundation and endowment of a new college to the University of Dublin'. The objection that the college would be under clerical control was unreal, the writer declared. 'If the Bishop of Limerick may rightly be regarded as their spokesman – and there is a suspicion that his independence in on a level with his ability – the Irish hierarchy indignantly repudiate the suggestion of ambition to rule the proposed new college.' Only simple fair play is asked for. The article concluded optimistically: 'Mr Balfour's sympathetic and hopeful speech last week clearly indicates that the government intend to put forward some practical solution of the Irish educational difficulty before their tenure of office expires.'[29] The *Newcastle Leader*, by comparison, was astutely sceptical, pointing out that there had been twelve declarations by responsible statesmen in favour of such a university in the last twenty-five years; that Mr Balfour's promise was in the vaguest possible manner; and that if the government were thought to be serious about the issue the lobby would have been in ferment. As it was, there was a philosophic calm, and the Irish members were almost pathetic in their gratitude.[30]

Early in February 1897, when there was no movement from the government, O'Dwyer wrote to Balfour asking if it would be of assistance to have a declaration of their views from the hierarchy. Balfour, replying on 19 February 1897, thanked him for his offer, 'on behalf of the Catholic Bishops of Ireland, to communicate their views' on the proposed Irish university, and then added carefully that he did not see any chance of a bill during the current session of parliament, and, consequently, 'any formal communication had probably better for the present be deferred'. He added, pointedly, that he had marked his letter 'not for publication', as he doubted the expediency of any public correspondence between his Lordship and himself for the present. He then issued a discrete warning, that this object on which for many years past he had set his heart was 'not likely to be accomplished without arousing much opposition and much controversial bitterness.'[31]

It was characteristic of O'Dwyer's temerity and impatience that he offered to speak on behalf of the hierarchy without consulting its members, and of his *penchant* for using publicity as a weapon that he actually contemplated publishing his correspondence with Balfour. In a letter to Dr Walsh on 22 February, Cardinal Logue reported:

> Dr O'Dwyer told me he had written to Mr Balfour after he had done it. I wrote that it was a risky step for an individual bishop to take such action. Today I had a letter asking whether I thought he should publish his letter to Mr Balfour, the latter's reply being barred. I am writing to dissuade him from such a step.[32]

The absence of urgency and unity among the bishops annoyed O'Dwyer. He decided to act as if the achievement of a new university was only a matter of time. He drew up a University Bill, with details on the role of its senate and governing bodies, which he submitted to T.M. Healy for comment. On 6 March, the latter cautioned: 'Unless and until the bishops agree as a body on a line, I don't see how we can start any plan which has not their corporate sanction.'[33] By 11 March, Healy judged the prospects of any university reform by the government to be virtually impossible. There was general anti-papal hostility in the House. A week later, he observed that the Balfours were now frightened of any idea of a university.[34]

Raising wider issues

At this point, O'Dwyer appears to have opted to draw attention to the education scene in Ireland in a wider context that might catch attention in Britain. On 20 March he addressed a long letter to *The Times* on 'The Proposed New Commission on the Financial Relations between Great Britain and Ireland'. An important feature in the Commission's inquiry was to be 'the amount of expenditure by the state on local services'. Under this heading it may be demonstrated, O'Dwyer observed, that expenditure in Ireland is greater than in England and Scotland, and this, in turn, may be used to offset the Irishman's claim that his country 'is taxed beyond her capacity by three millions a year'. If the expenditure is heavy in Ireland, he went on, then it is worth examining what the Irish are getting for the money being spent; 'and if it is found to be wastefully or mischievously expended it is hardly fair to ask the Irish to accept it as a set off against their excessive taxation'. Having thus set the scene, he provided a summary of, and commentary on, the main areas of expenditure on civil government in Ireland.

The total charges came to £ 4,192,000, the greater part of which, over three millions, was expended in three areas: 'the courts, especially the administration of the land acts; the constabulary; and education.' 'Let me deal with them *seriatim*', he said, 'but very briefly.'

(a) *The Land Laws.* On the character of these land laws, O'Dwyer commented, 'we are informed by no less an authority than the prime minister himself that they are bad in principle, and most pernicious in their operation'; that they are 'barbarous', and the courts that administer them 'licentious'. Why then, 'if the law is bad', he continued, 'should we pay for it'? 'Why should we be crushed by taxation to support the operation of laws that work ruin on us?'

(b) *The Constabulary.* They were 'an excellent and magnificent body of men. They would probably hold their own against the Imperial Guard of Germany'. But it was 'rather unreasonable to impose such a force on the poorest country in Europe, nominally for police purposes, and then to compel' its population 'to provide the enormous cost of it'.

(c) *Education.* This area was the main focus of his attention. The complaint against Ireland under this heading, he suggested, was 'that proportionately we do not contribute from local sources as much as Great Britain', and 'that the whole burden of the support of our educational system comes out of general revenue'. This was a fact. 'But the question arises "Why is this so?"' 'To anyone who thinks', he responded, an immediate difference was evident between education in England and Ireland. 'In England ... you have the system of education that the majority of the people's parliamentary representatives demand, and subsequently you enlist in support of that system the good will and sympathy of the nation. In Ireland you do just the reverse.' Some young Englishman comes over and 'devises some plan of education which he thinks ought to suit us'. 'We are not consulted, our wishes count for nothing; the more numerous we are ... the more carefully are our publicly expressed opinions marked as things to be avoided – as you put buoys over rocks – and then you turn round and say, 'Why do you not put your hands in your pockets, as Englishmen do, and contribute to the cost of your education?'' Just take as an illustration the actual position of the University Question,' he observed reasonably, as he prepared to give trenchant expression to the unuttered resentment of numerous Irish nationalists.

> Out of 103 Irish Members of Parliament I dare say all but about 10 would vote tomorrow for a Catholic University. Yet, in submission to the clamour of that residuum, who notoriously represent a curious survival into the 19th century of a species of fanatic that flourished in England in the 17th, the Government have to give engagements to keep the Catholics of Ireland, as far as may be, in ignorance for a longer period.

'Yet you vote annually £ 50,000 for university education,' he pressed on, 'and you ask Irish Catholics, from the peer to the peasant, who complain of this injustice, to accept the cost as an equivalent for their taxes.'

Then, after an examination of the national education system, a system 'invented in England and forced on us by secularist doctrinaires', which was anti-Catholic and anti-national, he queried how such a system could be seen as 'a fair equivalent for crushing taxes?' In short, he declared, 'no true account can be made out between the two countries unless the nature and value of that expenditure is ascertained'. 'Such an investigation must lead to strange revelations and dangerous consequences', but if Unionists insisted on the *prima-facie* aspect of the case being accepted, they were effectively promoting Home Rule arguments and making 'the position of Irish Unionists ridiculous and untenable'.

O'Dwyer's long letter appealed to Irish nationalists because of its reasoned criticism of the government, while his reputation was enhanced among more neutral or even unionist middle and upper class Irish people by his criticism of the taxation policy!

Occasions of frustration
Meantime, he had written to Cardinal Logue calling for a meeting of the hierarchy to discuss the university question, and had enclosed his draft of a university bill. The cardinal's firm, common sense reply on 23 March made the bishop of Limerick seem precipitous. 'Seeing that Mr Balfour has repeatedly declared that nothing will be done regarding the university question 'till after February 1898', Logue did not see 'what a meeting of the bishops could do at the present moment except beat the air'. 'The fact that the government have neither given a hint of what they intend to do', nor invited the bishops' views, rendered it more difficult for the bishops to do anything practical. This was also the reason, Logue added, why it was pointless applying to Rome for advice, as O'Dwyer had suggested. Rome would do nothing until they had a written programme placed before them. His lordship's further suggestion that the views of the bishops be collected by a circular letter had led to such inconvenience in the past that he would not think of being a party to such a plan. He explained frankly:

> The bishops require to consult together in order to give a reliable opinion. You must remember that very few, if any of them except yourself and the Archbishop of Dublin are giving a thought to the details of this question at present. Hence, the opinion they would give right off in response to a circular might not be the wisest.

Moreover, he did not see that it would be wise to come forward with a spontaneous declaration as to how far they were prepared to divest themselves of control in the government of the proposed university and to make extra liberal offers of placing it almost exclusively under lay government. 'We have three Queen's Colleges already and that should satisfy us', he added sardonically, 'without adding a fourth under the misnomer of a Catholic University'. Besides, if the bishops volunteered all kinds of concessions in the beginning, they might find themselves with very little left to concede in the end. In effect, he could see no point in being in a hurry to convene a meeting. The Standing Committee, at its meeting after Easter, could decide if a meeting should be called. 'I have read your draft carefully,' the Cardinal concluded, 'and I think it very good as an outline; but it would require a good deal of filling in as to details.' He intended going over it minutely and making notes on it, but so far could not find time.[35]

That bishops other than O'Dwyer were becoming frustrated at the lack of progress was indicated by letters from Bishop Sheehan of Waterford in February and[36] and from Dr Donnelly the following month.[37] O'Dwyer, conscious that he had not communicated with Donnelly for some time, responded frankly on the tortuous situation on 27 March:

> Your Man [Walsh] thinks we ought to have a meeting. The Cardinal thinks not. Some good laymen think that they are in a foolish position, not being able to express an opinion on anything connected with the subject without running the risk of being contradicted next day by the bishops. Some of these latter think that the solution is to be had in a number of provincial colleges, while others think we ought to concentrate our strength, at least at first, in one.

He sent with his letter a copy of his draft bill, which he asked Donnelly to look at as he travelled by train across Europe to Rome. He had put it together, he explained, 'mainly to give us a text to discuss, and to raise in concrete form the principal points on which we must come to some decision'. He thought it was mainly in some such shape a university bill could be got through parliament.[38]

On 5 April, T.M. Healy sent a further bleak message from the House of Commons. The government had no heart for Irish legislation. 'G. Balfour', he continued, 'is quite well disposed (as I am towards bumble-bees) but he has an 18 lb Orange shot shackled to each ankle.'[39]

The combination of pressures arising from the Roxboro, Mungret and Bruff disputes, and from the university question, might be expected to have strained Dr O'Dwyer's volatile temperament. Fr J.M. Harty, of Maynooth, in any event, found him difficult to deal with at this time. Writing to Monsignor Kelly, rector of the Irish College Rome, on 12 April 1897, he apologised for troubling him once more, and went on:

> It was with difficulty we could get Dr O'Dwyer to grant permission to Mr Hogan to apply for a dispensation. At last he gave it – gave his signature – but forgot to put his seal to the letter. I fear to send it on directly to Propaganda because of the want of the seal and it would not be well to write again to Dr O'Dwyer for seal. So to make certain of dispensation I must again appeal for your assistance.[40]

The next important step on the university issue was at the June meeting of the bishops. They issued a new statement, with clear concessions.[41]

Bishops' statement and concessions

Responding to questions raised in the House of Commons in the course of a debate on the university question, they announced: 1. They did not seek a preponderance of ecclesiastics on the governing body of the projected Catholic University, and were prepared to have a majority of lay people. 2. They did not seek an endowment for theological teaching. 3. As to what security should be given to professors and others against arbitrary dismissal, they noted Mr Lecky's acknowledgement in the House of Commons regarding the removal and appointment of professors that 'they would be chosen not merely on the grounds of competence but also to a great extent on the ground of creed', but, having been chosen, they would enjoy security of position. Their lordships observed, however, that the reasons of religion which might prevent a man's appointment might in given circumstances tell against his continuance in office; but they suggested that both absolute security for the interests of faith and morals in the university, and all reasonable protection for the position of the professor, might be met by submitting such questions to a strong and well-chosen Board of Visitors, in whose independence and competence all parties would have confidence. To the 4th and final question – 'Were they prepared to accept the application of the "University of Dublin Test Act" of 1873'? – the bishops responded that given some modifications in the Act, in the sense of the English Acts of 1871 and the Oxford and Cambridge Act of 1877, they had no objection to the opening up of degrees, honours, and emoluments of the university to all comers.

The hierarchy then added, 'That in putting forward these views we assume that, if the government deals with the question, it will be by the foundation, not of a college but of a university.' 'These are our views', they concluded, 'upon the fundamental principles, which, as far as we can gather, the leading statesmen on all sides regard as the governing factors in the problem.'

The document had all the magisterial marks of Archbishop William Walsh. The government was left without objections in terms of ecclesiastical control. But Walsh had also undermined those who sought a solution through a properly endowed college in the Royal University. What was now sought was a full Catholic University solution. If this failed, he hoped to revert to his first preference, a college in the University of Dublin on equal terms with Trinity College. It is not clear what part O'Dwyer played at the bishops' meeting. It was one inevitably overshadowed by Walsh's position and role. The archbishop of Dublin managed to control meetings by a blend of sheer ability, timing, and guile.[42] He had mastered impatience, unlike his former friend from Limerick. The bishops' statement was the final contribution on the higher education issue before the summer recess.

The summer for Dr O'Dwyer had its high point each year with three weeks of swimming and relaxation at Kilkee, Co. Clare. From there he wrote to Bishop

Donnelly on 7 August asking when he might expect him to arrive from Kerry. 'The new connection by steamer between Tarbert and Kilrush', he wrote, 'puts the place in direct communication with Kerry.' 'If the weather lasts', he went on 'we shall have an enjoyable time. Bathing is the main point, and we have it every day to perfection.' Dr McRedmond, of Killaloe, was at a near-by seaside town, and if Donnelly came they would look him up.[43]

Resuming the pressure

By September, he was ready to resume pressure on the government. He contacted Bishop Healy with a view to putting on the hierarchy's agenda the promotion of public meetings calling for a university. Two months later, his grace of Dublin led the way with a public letter to the Catholic Commercial Club, which was sponsoring a public lecture on 'Irish Catholic and University Education', in which he welcomed the agitation of the question, and declared – 'We have now to concentrate our energies upon forcing the question upon the attention of the government, and pursuing with vigour for a speedy settlement of it.' They did not want 'half-measures'. They sought 'for the Catholics of Ireland what our Protestant fellow-countrymen have so long had in Trinity College – a place of higher education, free of everything to which they could object on any religious ground, and enjoying every advantage at present enjoyed by Trinity College, whether in respect of endowment, or in respect of university status.'[44] This followed a meeting, which he had chaired two weeks previously at St Stephen's Green, 'to consider the most effective way to bring public opinion to bear upon the government in reference to the speedy settlement of the Irish university question'.[45]

O'Dwyer pressed forward on a parallel course. In December, he organised a public meeting in Limerick, and gave what the *Cork Daily Herald* described as a 'very striking address on the Irish University Question' that 'must command … even a large share of respectful consent from those who for one reason or another are arrayed against the proposal to grant this country its rightful demands in the matter of higher education.'[46] The archbishop of Dublin, indeed, was moved to mention to O'Dwyer on 31 December, 'Your last speech struck me as about the best you have made on the question'.[47] The comment was made in the course of a letter conveying his Grace's wish to arrange a meeting in Dublin of the six bishops who had been '*personally* engaged in the movement … Yourself, Clonfert, Waterford, Raphoe, and Kildare'.[48] The meeting resulted in more coordinated pressure on the government.

On 11 January 1898 a 'great national meeting' was held in Dublin by Catholic laity in support of perfect equality with their non-Catholic fellow-countrymen in all that regarded endowment and privilege of university institutions. On 14 January, a similar meeting was held in Limerick County Court House, representative of 'Catholics of the city and county of Limerick'. Dr O'Dwyer was elected chairman. The mayor, M. Cusack, proposed a motion similar to the Dublin one. Stephen B. Quin, JP, high sheriff of the city, called on the members of parliament for the city and county to press the claim for educational equality upon the House of Commons. Copies of the resolutions of the meeting were forwarded to the prime minister, the chief secretary for Ireland, and the parliamentary representatives of city and county.[49] O'Dwyer's speech on the occasion received extensive coverage in the *Freeman's Journal* of 15 January 1898. He had drawn attention to points he had mentioned more than once: that a system of higher education was close to the root and foundation of progress in the country, and that a university was not for the wealthy alone – it was for the benefit of all. 'The Bishop of Limerick', the *Freeman* observed, 'does not accept Professor Mahaffey's theory that education ought to be organised upon a class basis, the result of which would be a stereotyping of class until it hardened into a deadly caste. It is Dr O'Dwyer's contention that superior talent and genius shall have their opportunity into whatever conditions they are born, and that it is the duty of the state to give them the chance of a proper cultivation.' In reference to an article in *The Times* critical of the lack of university education among the Catholic clergy, O'Dwyer acknowledged 'that the Irish clergy as a class' were among the chief sufferers from the absence of a university.

'I saw an account of the excellent meeting held in Limerick', Major Ross wrote on 25 January, 'and am happy to tell you that on talking about it to a Protestant friend, a Fellow of T.C.D., he told me how much he agreed with and sympathised with what you said on that occasion.'[50] On 2 February, Ross reported that the public meeting at Belfast went well. As at Limerick, the audience were attentive and earnest. The meetings, he observed, were important in order to dispel the notion that the public don't care about university education.[51] On the same date, even the mild-mannered Bishop Donnelly was moved by events to unexpected signs of national feeling:

> Lord Emly made a capital speech in Belfast. He has set the Orangemen wild; but I think it is well to let them see clearly that people will not tamely submit to their cool assumption of ascendancy. If he and his Catholic confreres were to go in straight for Home Rule, it would do more to bring the government and the Orangemen to their senses on the university and every other Catholic question than all the meetings that could be held for a century.[52]

The pressure, however, evoked no perceptible signs of movement from the government. O'Dwyer's instinct was to increase the pressure. He requested Cardinal Logue to call a meeting of the Standing Committee. Once again, Logue refused. Interest in the university question, he pointed out reasonably, was overshadowed by the Local Government Bill, and it was better to wait until that bill had been dealt with. For himself, he made it clear once more that he did not approve of any further concessions on the part of the bishops. If there was question of further concessions, they would 'do better to go in honestly and try to swamp Trinity College and the Queen's Colleges'. 'If the Catholics stick to their guns', he proclaimed, 'they will carry the question, at the very least, on the lines laid down by the bishops.'[53]

O'Dwyer allowed the cardinal's comments pass him by, and he pressed on with his campaign. He contributed on the university case to the *Tablet*,[54] corresponded with Sir Michael Hicks Beach, former chief secretary,[55] and negotiated with Bishop Sheehan, of Waterford, and Bishop Henry, of Down and Connor, to join with him in promoting the cause by correspondence. On 8 June, Sheehan forwarded to him a copy of Balfour's reply to the bishop of Down and Connor. Again, O'Dwyer contemplated publishing the correspondence![56] By October, he was getting sufficiently frustrated at lack of evident progress that he wrote a trenchant letter to the *Nation* newspaper, which was copied into the Belfast *Irish News*, where it was read by Cardinal Logue, who, forthwith, informed him: 'I think it is the best letter ever you wrote on the university or any other question.' As a northern Catholic, he was taken by its aggressive tone. It had the right ring about it. 'As you say truly', Logue stated, 'it is intolerable that four-fifths of the Irish people should be put under the feet of a few ignorant Orange bigots here in the North.'[57] In that month, however, a significant move forward was made, though this was not immediately apparent to participants.

Haldane's arrival and report

A Liberal member of parliament, R. B. Haldane, came to Ireland, with the prime minister's approval, to examine how far a bill embodying Balfour's plans would find acceptance. In his time in Ireland, he received assurances from Archbishop Walsh and Cardinal Logue, and from the heads of the Presbyterian Assembly. He also met with William Delany, president of University College, St Stephen's Green. It is not clear that he met any other bishop. He was sufficiently satisfied, however, on his return to England, to draft, with Balfour's assistance, a university bill to be introduced at a favourable moment. For a while, prospects seemed bright. 'You delighted Haldane, and I really think something may be done,' John Morley wrote to Delany on 11 November 1898. Eight days later, however, when Delany visited him at his home in England, Morley reported that he had met Balfour at one of the Rothschild residences and the chancellor had stated that he feared great difficulty from the side of the Radicals. Moreover, where the Whigs were concerned, he had learned from the chief whip that seven members at the outside were prepared to vote for the measure.[58]

On 23 January 1899, Balfour ventured to sound public opinion in the form of a letter to a constituent in Manchester. He reviewed the condition of university education in Ireland, and then put forward what he considered the most feasible plan for a settlement of the Catholic demand. It adumbrated the eventual solution: Establish by a single Act two new teaching universities on similar lines – one in Dublin, and the other in Belfast. The one in Belfast would absorb the Queen's College there and continue its tradition. The new university in Dublin was to benefit Roman Catholics. Its governing body would be to their way of thinking, but both universities would be subject to the Test Acts. All scholarships and fellowships paid out of public funds would be open to competition irrespective of creed. No public endowment would be given to chairs in theology, philosophy, or modern history. Professors would have a right to appeal against unjust dismissal, and the number of clergy on the governing body would be strictly limited. 'A university so constituted', Balfour added, 'would, I believe, meet the needs of Roman Catholics, but it would not be a Roman Catholic University. The scheme did not advance the power of the Catholic priesthood, he assured his readers, but rather would mitigate it 'by broadening knowledge and a more thorough culture'; and the scheme was not unfair to Protestants, since it would result in two Protestant universities and only one Catholic one, even though there were nearly three Roman Catholics to one Protestant.[59] Despite the mollification, the Manchester Letter met a negative reaction in the doubtful constituencies. The London papers, apart from the *Morning Post*, were well disposed, but in the constituencies, as Haldane informed Walsh on 7 February 1899, 'the old spirit of intolerance is still abroad, and the government is timid'.[60]

As the reaction in the constituencies became apparent, O'Dwyer feared the worst and, in his anger, according to Dunraven's story, threatened, on 28 January 1899, that he would make it impossible for a Catholic to vote for a Liberal Unionist if the government did not pledge itself at once to deal with the university issue. Whatever about the accuracy of that account, there is little reason to doubt O'Dwyer's disappointment and anger at the way the university issue was being handled.

Meanwhile, further pressure had come on the government from an unexpected quarter. On 2 February 1899, following protests that the examining system in the Royal University was unfair, in that the Fellows from the Queen's Colleges, University College, and the Catholic Medical School, were also examiners in the examinations set for all colleges under the Royal University, a motion was proposed by the O'Conor Don, and passed, 'that in the opinion of the senate, the present provisions for university education in Ireland are not satisfactory, and we therefore recommend the matter to the early attention of the government'.[61] Thus, the Royal University was being condemned by its own governing body. Moreover, the motion was seconded by Dr Thomas Hamilton, president of Queen's College Belfast, who subsequently came out in favour of Balfour's university scheme. Catholics and Northern Protestants had come to share common ground for a while on the reorganisation of the university system. Still, the government held back, frightened by the vocal opposition in parts of England, and Scotland, especially as a general election was in prospect.

At this stage, prominent members of the Trinity College faculty availed of the government's hesitations to raise obstacles to Balfour's scheme. A senior Fellow, Dr Anthony Traill, in the *Contemporary Review*, opposed a Catholic University in Dublin as likely to take students from Trinity. Dr George Salmon, the provost, in the same publication, reproduced the old argument that a Catholic University was unnecessary because Dublin University was open to Catholics and the only reason they did not avail of it was because of their subservience to their bishops. Besides, to establish three universities in Ireland would lead to a lowering of standards and the undermining of higher education in the country. He had no objection, however, to endowing and equipping University College, if its students attended the lectures and took their degrees in Trinity or in the Royal University.[62]

As the government wavered and deferred commitment, the Irish Catholic bishops began to shift and waver in their stance on the university. Dr Walsh reverted to his dream of an equal college within Dublin University, and discouraged his colleagues from making proposals for settlement. O'Dwyer disapproved. He was now strongly in favour of an independent Catholic University – Catholic in practice, if non-denominational in theory – and deplored the indefiniteness of the bishops. 'The whole university business is heart breaking', he commented to Donnelly on 27 March 1899. 'It is well for the political and material interests of the country that they are not in the hands of the bishops.'[63] Six weeks later, he was even more distressed. 'As to our university question', he observed to his friend, 'I have almost come to despair. All we bishops have no definite policy. We do not even agree as to an aim.'[64] Dr Walsh, however, was contemplating a focussed, aggressive approach that might quieten objections from Dublin University and put further pressure on the government. On 21 June 1899, he suggested to Logue 'that we now raise the cry against Trinity' but 'that we raise it only as a *dernier* resort' and only 'if justice cannot otherwise be done'. He was conscious that a number of Trinity men, such as Lecky, Carson, Judge Webb, Lord Justice Fitzgibbon, and even Mahaffy, had declared for a Catholic University. Nevertheless, there was a value in raising the cry. 'It will do no harm, and it will undoubtedly frighten those Trinity men who are still holding back.'[65]

A fighting pamphlet

In January 1899, O'Dwyer had published a substantial article in *Nineteenth Century* on 'University Education for Irish Catholics', in which he affirmed as the episcopal policy the bishops' statement of assurances given in 1897, emphasising that there was no question of discrimination on religious grounds in a university for Catholics, that professors who were not Catholics could be appointed, and Protestant students could attend without any danger to their beliefs as witness the twenty to thirty Protestants at University College Dublin, which was the property of the Irish bishops and conducted by the Jesuits. The article was well received. Later, in the face of the general disarray following the government's withdrawal, the apparent apathy among the people and the bishops, he determined to write at greater length. In March 1900 he published a pamphlet, which sought to present the importance of the university question to the Irish people in considerable detail. Entitled *A university for Catholics in relation to the material interests of Ireland*, it offered reasoned argument fortified by passionate rhetoric.

To 'any interested observer', he began, it was remarkable 'how completely the agitation for university reform in Ireland had collapsed within the last year'. The great meetings in support of the claim, the debates in the House of Commons, the unity of Irish Catholic members of parliament on this one issue, the remarkable declaration of the laity, all were no more, as if the question had been forgotten. It raised misgivings as to the steadiness and earnestness of Irish political methods, and even of the national character. It was perhaps a matter of *déjà vu*, of apathy. When the present government, after feeding the hopes of the Catholics of Ireland for many a year, put up the duke of Devonshire last year to announce that they had no intention of dealing with the issue, it was another example, 'for the hundredth time', of English ministers playing upon Catholic feeling in the interests of their party and government and then reverting when they no longer needed them.[66] 'The history of every measure of justice which Irish Catholics have ever wrung from the English parliament', he asserted, was marked 'by the same cynical disregard of the merits of the case.' Eventually, when political expediency required it, concessions were grudgingly made, not as a tribute to justice, but as a surrender to popular power.[67] Why then should Irish Catholics throw up the question in despair? 'The duke of Devonshire has not been the first, nor will he be the last English minister whom the fixed determination of a nation has made to change his loud-mouthed "No" into faltering concession. The days of Protestant ascendancy are gone', O'Dwyer proclaimed, 'Catholics can no longer be kept in a position of permanent inferiority in relation to the master-power of the modern world – education.' As to when redress would come depended on Catholics themselves. Steadiness, earnestness, perseverance would hasten the issue. But it was also necessary to look at a contributory cause of the suddenness with which the university question had been allowed to drop. He feared it was because its importance was not sufficiently understood, as if 'the people looked on it as more or less of a sentimental grievance'.[68]

He then moved on to recapitulate in some detail his old arguments on the relevance of university education to every aspect of a nation's life, and then, pointing to educational development abroad, he lamented an educational state of affairs which placed Ireland behind every country in Europe and, without exaggeration, 'a century behind civilization'.[69] 'In our time', he added vigorously, 'no question has arisen which ... so tests, as a touch stone, the capacity of the Imperial Parliament to legislate for this country. If that parliament is so dominated by English bigotry that, in the great matter of education, it can take no account of the religious convictions of the great majority of the nation, then no one can deny that it has forfeited all right to legislate for us.' 'Such a government', he concluded, his barely submerged nationalism erupting, 'is a cruel tyranny. Not merely on religious and sentimental grounds, but on the grounds of our material interests, it stands condemned; and, for my part, I cannot see how any Irish Catholic, no matter to what political party he may belong, can regard it as anything but an usurpation.'[70]

The anger and rousing sentiments in the concluding paragraph, at the government's injustice to, and cavalier treatment of Catholics, were signposts on the road to his later defiance of representatives of British government in 1916 and his subsequent support for Sinn Fein. They also reflected something of the new spirit in the country following the revival of Irish language and culture and the centenary celebration of the 1898 rebellion.

On 26 March 1900 he was pleased to hear from Bishop Donnelly that he liked his pamphlet. 'I have always held', O'Dwyer stated, 'that the laity ought to be taken into our confidence, and a joint committee of them and us proceed on this question.'[71]

At their annual meeting in Maynooth in May the bishops devoted much time to the university question, with a practical eye on the impending general election. They passed resolutions encouraging Catholic electors not to support any candidate who did not expressly pledge himself 'to use his best exertions for the establishment of a university to which the Catholics of Ireland can repair without sacrifice of their religious convictions', and they appealed to all fair minded men in England and Ireland to counter the efforts of certain English politicians and religious bodies endeavouring to prevent the granting of the Catholics' just demand.[72]

A variety of happenings, 1900

The year 1900, however, was auspicious for more than O'Dwyer's pamphlet or the bishops' resolutions. It was also a formal Holy Year for the entire Catholic Church, with special emphasis on prayer, repentance, and spiritual renewal. For dioceses and parishes it involved a great deal of additional work and planning. On the political front, there was the long awaited reunion of the two sections of the Irish Parliamentary party on 30 January, with John Redmond elected leader on 5 February. Queen Victoria, the still living symbol of the empire, came on an extended visit to Ireland, from 3 to 26 April, and received a warm welcome. Then, in October, came the general election, the so-called 'khaki election', when the fervour occasioned by the Boer War brought the Conservatives back to power; and in November, George Wyndham became the new chief secretary, an important appointment for Irish land and university issues. To round off the variety of events, on 11 December O'Dwyer's friend, T.M. Healy, was expelled from the Irish Parliamentary party through the machinations of their mutual *bête noir*, John Dillon.

For O'Dwyer, all these happenings were of particular interest, but the Holy Year and the preparations for a national synod took up much of his attention. On 15 July, nevertheless, he found time to pay a rare visit to the northern part of the country. On that date, according to the official account of the occasion, he performed the opening of 'a bazaar on a colossal scale' in Armagh, accompanied by the cardinal and several bishops. The object of the occasion was to collect funds for the completion of St Patrick's Cathedral. On 22 July, the main day of the 'gigantic fete', vast crowds attended, including representatives from all over Ireland, and from Scotland, England, and the United States of America, to honour the national apostle. O'Dwyer contributed what was described as 'a beautiful discourse'[73]

On 28 August, the first solemn session of the national synod took place at Maynooth. All the dioceses had made extensive preparations that resulted in the forwarding of material for consideration. O'Dwyer attended, together with Fr Andrew Murphy as his theological adviser. Various committees were set up to focus on the matters before the general body of the synod. O'Dwyer was appointed to two committees: *De Episcopis* (concerning the bishops), a committee composed of the four archbishops and six other bishops, and *De Scholis* (concerning education) – a group dealing with centres of education, especially diocesan colleges, and which had as members, Archbishop Walsh, Bishop O'Dwyer and five other bishops and some fourteen clergy. The extensive and exhausting exercise was brought to a close between 28 August and 2 September 1900.[74]

STAGE II, 1901–1902

New proposals for university reform

In the New Year the university question took on a new momentum. In this O'Dwyer, Bishop Healy of Clonfert, and Dr William Delany of UCD played prominent roles. They sought educational equality but they were conscious that a college in Dublin University, and a Catholic University, would meet with intense resistance. They remained open to the Balfour scheme as something attainable. They decided to make their move from within the senate of the Royal University. To allay the dissatisfaction expressed with the system of examinations, it was considered necessary to employ external examiners. A proposal was placed on the agenda for a meeting of the senate on Thursday, 21 February 1901, requesting the government to allocate additional money to that end. O'Dwyer and Delany, feeling the moment was right, exchanged letters about the wording of an amendment that would 'induce the Royal University to make an attempt on it own life'.[75] After much persuasion, O'Dwyer agreed to appear personally at the senate meeting to press the amendment, which was in his name. The carefully worded statement proclaimed that the ultimate cause of any inequality in the conditions under which students were examined was to be found 'in the anomalous constitution of the university itself, and its unsatisfactory relations with its own colleges and students, and, that in the opinion of the senate, it is most desirable that a royal commission should be issued to enquire into the working of this university as an examining and teaching body in relation to the educational needs of the country at large and to report as to the means by which university education in Ireland might receive a greater extension and be more efficiently conducted than at present.'[76] The amendment, seconded by Dr Healy, was passed unanimously. It was in regard to this important occasion that

O'Dwyer sent the rather sad note to Delany:'I fear I was a great bother to you on Thursday on account of my deafness, and for myself it was most disagreeable not to be able to follow the discussion'.[77]

The senate appointed a committee to present its amendment to the Lord Lieutenant. The bishop of Limerick, fearing that the deputation might be 'put off with a Lord Lieutenant's commission' urged that the three members, Delany, Healy, and Dr Thomas Hamilton of Queen's College Belfast, should press for a royal commission. 'Nothing less than the report of a royal commission', he informed Delany on 26 February 1901, 'would carry so big a reform as what we seek. And I should say that the more Englishmen and Scotchmen on it the better'.[78] Irishmen, he thought, would be less likely to judge the question purely on its merits, and their report would carry less weight as seeming to reflect a partisan spirit. On 9 March a royal commission was conceded. The following day, Dr Healy informed Archbishop Walsh that the Lord Lieutenant 'intimated that he was entirely with us', but it was clear that 'he would not touch Trinity'.[79] By 26 March, O'Dwyer's concern was the composition of the body. 'If this commission reports against us we're done for', he observed to Delany, 'and unless we get a safe and strong chairman, with a competent body of men to sustain him, we should be terribly at the mercy of the Protestant elements.'[80]

The reception of the announcement of the commission ranged from negative to approving. In the debate in the House of Commons, John Dillon declined all responsibility for the initiative. The *Daily Chronicle* observed on 23 April that ministers could not agree on the merits of the question and so they agreed to a commission, not with a view to legislation, but to relieve the government of the necessity of coming to a decision. The paper recognised no need for a Catholic University. There was nothing to prevent Catholics attending Trinity College. Similar views were propounded by the *London Standard* of the same date. In the debate in the Commons, however, Balfour put the case for a Roman Catholic University vigorously, and, pointing to the anomaly in the Irish educational scene, he commented that undenominational education in Ireland meant the equal treatment of denominations.

Preparing for the commission

On 28 June the names of the members of the royal commission were published. They were: James P. Bannerman, Baron Robertson, chairman; Professor Samuel Henry Butcher, fellow of Trinity College, Cambridge, and University College, Oxford; Dr John Healy, bishop of Clonfert and senator of the Royal University; James A. Ewing and Richard C. Jebb, professors, respectively, of Mechanics and Greek at Cambridge; Justice Madden, high court judge, Ireland; Dodgson H, Matthew White, Viscount Ridley, late Home Secretary and fellow of All Souls College, Oxford; John Rhys, professor of Celtic, Oxford; Dr WJM Starkie, Commissioner of National Education; Henry F. Dickie, professor of Divinity, Magee College, Derry; Professor James Lorrain Smith, Queen's College Belfast; and Mr Wilfrid Ward, examiner in Mental and Moral Science, Royal University of Ireland.

On 14 July 1901, Dr Healy informed Dr Walsh that the Lord Lieutenant had spoken recently of 'Your Grace and Limerick as most desirable witnesses' to appear before the commission.[81] O'Dwyer agreed to appear, Walsh declined. To appear in connection with a venture initiated by the senate of the Royal University would not have been attractive to him, but the fact that Trinity College was excluded from consideration was probably the main factor in his decision not to testify.

The difficulty for Catholics appearing before the commission was to know where precisely the bishops stood on the university question. The majority still appeared to have no particular opinion. Dr Walsh and his immediate supporters were evasive. O'Dwyer, anxious that the Catholic witnesses, lay and clerical, should 'follow some common lines and not be pulling in different directions', wrote to Cardinal Logue calling for a meeting of the committee of bishops appointed to survey the question. Logue agreed with him on 5 September, but pointed out that the archbishop of Dublin was away and that a meeting could not be held until after his return. He hoped to have a meeting before the commission opened. The cardinal concluded on a cautious note, which, at this stage, must have infuriated O'Dwyer. 'As to any bishop who may give evidence, it strikes me it would be the best policy, if it could be managed, to let the opposite party show their hand first; and then the bishops could make their points.'[82]

In subsequent days, in preparation for the commission, O'Dwyer corresponded with Dr Foley of Kildare, who thought that the majority of the bishops would prefer a university to a college,[83] and with Dr Healy, who impressed on him the need to have the bishops' steering committee meet before the witnesses were examined so that they might follow a common line.[84] In this tentative, uncertain time, O'Dwyer also corresponded with the lay philosopher, theologian and author, Wilfrid Ward, whom he already knew quite well, and who prepared him for the commission with a series of probing questions.[85]

Witness before the commission
The commission spent ten months, from September 1901 to June 1902, in hearing witnesses, one hundred and forty-one in all, whose evidence was published in three instalments. The body's aim was set out as follows:

> To enquire in the present condition of the higher, general and technical education available in Ireland outside Trinity College, Dublin, and to report as to what reforms, if any, are desirable in order to render the education adequate to the needs of the Irish people.

Wilfrid Ward, commenting on his fellow commissioners' mode of acting during the depositions, was quite critical. The chairman, Lord Robertson, he considered vehemently anti-Catholic. He was convinced that the bishops were seeking control of education and were 'using their position and influence not in the interests of religion but as party politicians'. He was also bad-tempered, in Ward's view, and frequently tried to browbeat Catholic witnesses. The bishop of Clonfert, John Healy, though genial, tended, on the other hand, to be unpleasant towards Presbyterian and Episcopalian witnesses. Dr Starkie was embarrassing in his anti-clericalism, lectured witnesses, and was generally 'very tactless'. The members, whom Ward considered most earnest and detached in order to discover 'the existing state of things, with a view to furnishing the best form of university education to the people of Ireland', were Professor Henry Butcher, Sir Richard Jebb, Mr Justice Madden, and presumably Ward himself.[86]

O'Dwyer received his call as witness shortly after the commission opened in September 1901. Some months on, in response to Bishop Donnelly's congratulations on his performance before the commission, he explained that he 'had hardly time to put the most meagre summary of evidence together in time'. But there was 'one bit of good luck'. 'I so felt the responsibility of my position, and the strangeness of the bishops making no preparation for the commission, that I wrote a very strong and almost angry protest to the cardinal, who was thus induced to call a meeting of the (episcopal) committee, and there', he explained, 'I submitted a series of resolutions covering pretty well the whole case that I had to make. When this was accepted, I was able to give authoritative information to Dr Delany, Nixon, Ross, and so we were all on the same line.' He added perceptively: 'I hope Your Man won't upset the cart. One can never know.'[87]

At the commission, O'Dwyer's years of reading, discussion, and involvement in education paid dividends. His knowledge was matched by fluency of speech, an occasional striking turn of phrase, and a capacity to think and respond quickly, and, at times, unexpectedly. The synthesis shattered any stereotype presuppositions about Irish bishops that some commission members may have had. Writing to his wife on 21 September 1901, Wilfrid Ward remarked: 'The bishop finished his splendid performance this morning, six hours address and six hours cross-examination. It has been most memorable … Justice Madden said to me that he had heard many a fine opening of a case in courts but nothing to approach the bishop's performance.'[88] And the following day he added:

> As Butcher said to me 'Today we fell from the ideal to the real'. Dr Clancy, bishop of Elphin, was a very ordinary Irish ecclesiastic – that is all one can say. Fr Delany, who preceded him, though not equal to O'Dwyer – or nearly equal to him in eloquence, was extremely able and interesting. Butcher says that in the course of seven years commission work he has never heard anything equal to the evidence of those two.[89]

On the first day, O'Dwyer ranged over the history of university education in Ireland, with comparative references to developments in other countries. In the process, he praised the facilities available for Presbyterians at Queen's College Belfast and for Episcopalians at Trinity College, and made it clear, once again, that the Catholic bishops of Ireland had no desire 'to see any measure taken that would in the least degree either lower the status or impair the efficiency of these institutions'.[90] He then pointed to the inadequacies on the Catholic side. The Queen's Colleges at Cork and Galway, meant originally to cater for Catholics, stood for 'a downright waste and squandering of public money', and taking Cork, in particular, he outlined the attendance figures in different faculties and remarked that 'for anything in the nature of university education, in the ordinary sense of the word, Cork College might as well not exist'.[91] With reference to University College, Dublin, he continued in the same critical vein: describing it as 'a burlesque', 'a house on the side of the street', 'number something in St Stephen's Green' with 'neither libraries, laboratories, museums, nor any of the apparatus of a university college'. He conceded, however, that 'this little institution in Dublin', under the leadership of Fr Delany, had had, 'for its size and circumstances, considerable success'; but this, he went on, pressing his case, was 'infinitesimal in its effects on the general educational conditions of the country'.[92] In short, university education for Catholics was so thin over the country as to make scarcely any impression. 'Gentry, merchants, professional classes (except, to an extent, the barristers), clergy, have no education corresponding to their position', and the teachers in Catholic secondary schools had no opportunity of university education.[93]

On the second day he focussed on the secondary education system, pointing to the number of Protestant schools that benefited from having teachers who had university qualifications, unlike the bulk of the Catholic schools. The talent, nevertheless, that existed in the Catholic schools was demonstrated by their success in the Intermediate examinations, but, sadly, at the end of that process, 'nine-tenths' of those boys were 'lost', having but half-an-education, unable to proceed to a university. At the same time, he called attention to the fact that 'the political centre of gravity in Ireland' had 'shifted towards the Catholics'. 'In three provinces practically all political and municipal power, with the control of technical education in the latter, has passed into their hands. It is a dangerous thing to have them uneducated.' He illustrated this observation with a feeling comment about the borough council of Limerick – 'at the present time … the most democratic body in the world' –, not adverting, perhaps, to the fact that his every word would be published.

> It is practically composed of working men, labouring men … But that working class – it is neither unkind nor disrespectful to them to say it, but it is a fact – are an uneducated body of men; they are absolutely and entirely unfit for the duties they have to discharge. They have complete power in our town, not only over municipal affairs, but over technical education. Really, it seems to me to be a preposterous thing to have men who can hardly write their own names regulating the technical education of a city like ours.[94]

What was needed were the 'natural lay leaders', men equipped with the wisdom and trained reasoning power acquired in a proper university, who would sympathise with peoples' needs while also controlling them and keeping them within limits.[95] Coming to recommendations with regard to a university for Irish Catholics, he made it clear that he envisaged it in Dublin, residential, and adequately equipped and endowed – 'It would be better not to get a university at all than to get it crippled by poverty'.[96] He had previously in his deposition endeavoured to convey the ethos of this Catholic University. The policy of parliament in recent years, he observed, had led to the opening up of Oxford, Cambridge, and Trinity College. 'We think it reasonable to take account of that, and, in framing our demands, to make them in such a shape as we think parliament can agree to. Therefore, though we would make our university, if we had the making of it absolutely in our own hands, denominational and Catholic, yet we would not, even if we had the power, make it a medieval institution ... We want a modern institution; ... we want to give our people the highest literary and scientific education that is to be obtained in the present day.' He desired, he assured the commissioners, 'the full and free air' of the present world 'to play into that university'. 'What we want is this,' he summarised, 'that scientific and literary education shall be given under conditions that will not be hurtful to the religious faith of the students who go to the university. We want history, science, and other subjects to be taught absolutely truthfully and honestly by the professors, as they know them.'[97]

On lines of solution, he spoke to the three alternatives he had presented to the commission in his written submission:

1. A second college, a college for Catholics, in the University of Dublin.
2. An endowed college for Catholics in a reformed Royal University.
3. Two new universities, one in Belfast (instead of the Queen's College), and one in Dublin, which would comprise a new college (for Catholics) and Queen's College Cork.

As he was about to discuss the first alternative, the chairman asked if he was putting this scheme forward only to reject it? 'No, no, my Lord,' O'Dwyer replied. 'I put it forward not to reject it; but I put it forward for consideration, and I point out the *pros* and *cons* of it, as they occur to me. I see a good deal in favour of it and I see a good deal against it.'[98] Following this, he was asked to withdraw while the commissioners sat in private for ten minutes. On his return he was told that the first solution was 'not within the terms of their references'. O'Dwyer moved on to the second alternative.

He did not rule out entirely the prospect of an endowed college in the Royal University, but he was not happy with it. In an effort to capture its unsatisfactory character he used an image that caught the public imagination. It would lack, he thought, the element of finality: and Catholics would not be satisfied 'to be put off with a mere college in a second class university, in which we and the Dissenters like second class passengers travelled together, while the privileged body of Episcopalians had a first class institution to themselves'.[99]

The third alternative was his preferred choice. 'Give Belfast Queen's College a charter and an adequate endowment, and set it up as a university. Give the

Royal University, with its endowments, together with a fully equipped college in Dublin, and Queen's College Cork, to Catholics. Leave Trinity College and Dublin University untouched, and make Queen's College Galway a technical and agricultural institution.'[100] His choice, in effect, was for a university that was not formally Catholic, but which in its arrangement and personnel would be as acceptable to Catholics as was Trinity College to the Protestants. Substantially, it was the plan Balfour had suggested. The great thing about it, in O'Dwyer's view, was its 'finality'. It established basic equality between the different denominations. Each would have its own university, yet each would be subject to the Test Act, and each would be open to students of every denomination although each denomination would mainly attend their own university. 'My own personal opinion', he stated, is that 'if these three universities were so established, you would change the feelings of the different bodies in Ireland to one another, that they would be more largely used by each other and by individuals than they are at present.'[101]

Such vision, freedom of spirit, and openness to modernity, impressed the commissioners generally, and confused those who came with fixed prejudices.

> 'There's a question I would like to ask you, [Robertson said], although I know what the answer will be ... I suppose you believe a Catholic University, such as you propose, will strengthen Roman Catholicism in Ireland?'
>
> O'Dwyer: 'It's not easy to answer that; not so easy as it looks.'
>
> Robertson: 'But it won't weaken it, or you would not be here?'
>
> O'Dwyer: 'It would educate Catholics in Ireland very largely, and, of course, a religious denomination composed of a body of educated men is stronger than a religious denomination composed of a body of ignorant men. In that sense it would strengthen Roman Catholicism.' Robertson: 'Is there any sense in which it won't?'
>
> O'Dwyer: 'As far as religion is concerned, I really don't know how a university would work out. If you ask me now whether I think that university in a certain number of years would become a centre of thought, strengthening the Catholic faith in Ireland, I cannot tell you. It is a leap in the dark.'
>
> Robertson: 'But it is in the hope that it will strengthen your own Church that you support it?'
>
> O'Dwyer: 'No, it is not, by any means. We are bishops, but we are Irishmen also, and we want to serve our country.'[102]

Dr Starkie was equally nonplussed by his frankness, particularly with respect to the education he received at Maynooth and its inadequacy for him as a teacher, and his expressed hope that 'the best of our clergy', especially those to be engaged in teaching, would go through the university courses and experience the influence of university life,[103] something, indeed, already implied in the hierarchy's statement of 1896. Cross-examined by Starkie, O'Dwyer further asserted that it would be a most desirable thing that the laity and ecclesiastics should mix together in their student days.[104] He, himself, had sent one of his priests to the Royal College of Science, in a completely lay environment, to train as a science teacher, and he intended to send a second one when the first was trained. It was his opinion that probably 200 of the 600 students at Maynooth would follow the Arts course in the university.[105] A few days later, however, Bishop John Clancy of Elphin and Dr Thomas O'Dea, vice-president of Maynooth, informed the commission that they disagreed with him on this point. One of the important planks in O'Dwyer's platform, namely, the need of university experience to counteract the limited education of the clergy, had thereby been greatly weakened, as Starkie subsequently reminded him.

Nevertheless, his performance had been outstanding. It had educated the commissioners and even enthused them for their task. 'The Commission are pleased with themselves', George Wyndham wrote to Arthur Balfour on 19 September 1901. They are 'surprised at the reality of the grievance, and sanguine of finding a remedy embodied in a unanimous report. Bishop O'Dwyer astonished them by a consummate statement of the Catholic case, unshaken during 3 days cross-examination.'[106]

The published evidence
When the evidence was published in November, O'Dwyer's reputation was greatly enhanced, and above all among many of his fellow bishops. The perceptive and critical Dr Foley of Kildare wrote to him on 25 November:

> I have read your Lordship's evidence and I congratulate you most warmly upon the masterly manner in which you dealt with the whole subject. I do not believe that it could be surpassed or even approached by any member of the hierarchy in the kingdom. Some of the questions which you had to answer required a great deal of consideration but the manner in which you disposed of them proved that you had given your attention to every phase of the subject.[107]

There was, however, one major matter of disappointment and even anger. Dr Delany and O'Dwyer maintained a detailed interchange of views during the commission. In one such interchange, Delany warned that he had reason to know 'that though Trinity College, Dublin, is shut out from the purview of the commission, there are powerful persons anxious to bring it in and to resuscitate Gladstone's scheme, or rather to substitute that much more objectionable one of having a Catholic college in the University of Dublin'. Conscious of the strong contemporary ethos of Dublin University, and of its narrow horizons, and the likely impact on Catholic students, and also having little respect for the quality of its degrees, Delany added that after twenty years 'anxious thought over this university question', he was 'absolutely convinced that the *very worst* solution of the question for Irish Catholics, and for *education generally*, would be the establishment of a college for Catholics in the Dublin University'.[108] O'Dwyer largely concurred. In conversation with Wilfrid Ward, he made the point: 'An English Catholic boy grows up among Protestants and has been acclimatised from his earliest youth to mixed surroundings; an Irish boy going to Trinity would come from a Catholic atmosphere and be plunged at once into a hostile atmosphere.' 'Hostile' because, as the commissioners realised as their enquiry went forward, Trinity College, unlike Oxford and Cambridge, was not neutral in the matter of religion, but was, as represented by most of its professors, positively bitter against Catholicism.[109] The 'powerful persons', mentioned by Delany, included Archbishop Walsh, Chief Baron Palles, the O'Conor Don, and N.J. Synnott. Palles, O'Conor Don, and Synnott were permitted by Lord Robertson to argue for a Catholic college in a reorganised University of Dublin, even though this was excluded by the terms of enquiry, and he had earlier precluded O'Dwyer from addressing the question. The archbishop had refused to be interviewed by the commission, but he cleverly conveyed his views to them by means of a letter. He wished, he said, to associate himself with Dr O'Dwyer's evidence 'in so far as he had an opportunity of expressing himself', and then added that 'on one important aspect of the case', namely the matter of the Dublin University scheme, Chief Baron Palles had said everything he would wish to say.[110] The only effect of urging the Dublin University issue, O'Dwyer commented to Delany, would be to divide Catholic opinion and offer the commission an easy outlet from giving any solution.[111]

Interlude: awaiting the report

Dr Walsh, nevertheless, was determined to foil any alternative to the Dublin University scheme. In the *Freeman's Journal*, a year previously, he had acknowledge that the Irish bishops had always preferred the establishment of a separate university for Catholics, but that he had frequently made it clear that his personal preference was for a national university including Trinity College, or, alternatively, for a Catholic college within Dublin University.[112] In a private letter to O'Dwyer, on 26 November 1901, he made it clear, moreover, that he did not wish to be involved in any scheme changing the status of the Belfast college or reconstructing the Queen's Colleges of Cork and Galway. 'It is enough', he pronounced obliquely and querulously, 'for one Archbishop of Dublin to have burned his fingers over it. I am not going to be a second.'[113]

It must have been disheartening for O'Dwyer, after his careful preparation and his outstanding presentation of the Catholic position. An indication of the disarray in Catholic preferences became public knowledge with the publication of a series in the *Freeman's Journal* entitled 'Points from the Evidence', by 'Reviewer'. The articles, which appeared from 16 to 23 November, claimed that the Dublin University scheme was the one preferred by probably a majority of

Irish Catholics and was supported by the archbishop of Dublin and the bishops of Ireland. Delany replied in four strongly polemical letters on 17, 18, 20, 21 December. His blend of educational argument, patriotic fervour, and heady rhetoric obliged 'Reviewer' to concede that he had been arguing for Dublin University as a second-best solution, only to be sought if the bishops' prior choice of a separate Catholic University could not be had. Delany's open stand, however, seemed to his religious superiors to be placing himself in conflict with the archbishop, and he was instructed not to speak out in public on the matter in future.[114] He continued his opposition in a private manner.

The disarray, from the point of view of the commission, was added to by the fact that the Dublin University witnesses opposed any concessions to the Catholics, while the Presbyterian witnesses were reluctant to change from the *status quo*. Thus, there was a situation in which a majority of Catholics appeared to favour a separate Catholic university; a smaller, but influential group, preferred a Catholic college in a reorganised Dublin University; a majority of Protestant witnesses were prepared to support an endowed Catholic college within the Royal University; and the body of Presbyterian evidence opposed any concession to Catholics. In addition, among the commissioners themselves, apart from those who were patently anti-clerical, there were some, like Professor Butcher, who had been impressed by O'Dwyer's depiction of the Irish clergy as largely uneducated apart from their theological course, and had genuine reservations about a separate Catholic university because they feared 'that the bishops would be so eager to control the education given in a Catholic university in the interests of the students' faith that the university would become second-rate educationally'.[115] Hence, the prospect of a satisfactory settlement became more and more remote as the commission's enquiries proceeded.

O'Dwyer, meanwhile, set about responding to a request from Lord Robertson for a draft of the proposed constitution for the new university. He already had a draft, and he now consulted further with fellow prelates without much enthusiasm on their part. Some had difficulties with different parts of the draft, others, like Archbishop Walsh and the Cardinal were still opposed to presenting plans or drafts to the government or government representatives. Rather did they desire such plans to be drawn up by the government, and submitted to them for examination. O'Dwyer, however, adapted shrewdly to the situation. He approached Chief Baron Palles for advice, and then submitted the draft with his recommendations to the Bishops' Standing Committee, which then considered and approved the document.[116]

In the early months of 1902, in the interval awaiting the commission's report, support grew amongst educated lay Catholics in favour of a Catholic college in the University of Dublin. Many were graduates of that institution. A meeting was held at the Shelbourne Hotel. The main organiser was N.J. Synnott, who had given evidence before the commission. Inquiring about this meeting, O'Dwyer expressed to Donnelly his suspicions that Archbishop Walsh was with the group. 'Surely he must see', he said, 'that from a Catholic point of view there are grave objections to such a scheme, and what is more important that the only effect of urging it now will be to give the commission an easy outlet from giving any solution.' 'We were winning all along the way', he declared, but now the opportunity has been given to 'Cadogan, or Wyndham, or Balfour to say "you have raised the very issue we sought to avoid and in such a way as to increase the weight of Irish Protestant opposition".' That, he concluded, 'is the position towards which we are being driven: and very probably that is the result which is being desired in more quarters than one.'[117] Later in March, Archbishop Walsh published a pamphlet, which pressed for equality between Catholics and Protestants either within Dublin University or in a common university including Trinity College; and Synnott's committee forwarded a petition to the commission signed by a thousand lay Catholics. O'Dwyer attacked the petition in the *Freeman* on 20 March. It was not true, he insisted, as had been implied, that the authorities of Dublin University supported the scheme advocated by the petition, on the contrary, they were solidly opposed to it. What the signatories were asking, in effect, he reiterated, was for the commission to make no recommendation, and thereby they were destroying all chance of a settlement.

Almost a year more was to pass before the commission's report appeared. In the protracted interval various rumours circulated as to its likely recommendations. As the year drew to its close, O'Dwyer was informed that the commission was hesitating in its recommendations and, in a sarcastic letter to Wilfrid Ward, he concluded that an equitable solution would be shirked in the interest of the 'twenty six per cent of the population who are Protestant'.[118] Ward passed the letter to Professor Butcher, whom he considered objective and well disposed. Butcher remarked that he favoured a national, well endowed college, but he wondered 'that a man of such gifts and so much largeness of mind' as Bishop O'Dwyer 'does not perceive that the difficulty lies not so much in what Presbyterians or Protestant Episcopalians think or say in Ireland as in the fact that educated thought, no less than popular opinion, in every part of the world, has set itself against such a university as the Roman Catholics of Ireland demand. It is not mere insular *English* prejudice – still less mere *Irish* sectarianism – that has to be reckoned with. Opinion in England is only part of a great body of opinion, which has become consolidated during the last fifty years.'[119]

The Robertson report

The commission's report appeared on 28 February 1903. It was indecisive. Although all but one of the commissioners signed it,[120] they added reservations that in most cases were equivalent to withdrawals of signature. A Catholic University was declared inadvisable. It was agreed that it would establish equality, that it would be strongly supported by Catholics, and would raise up a strong academic class likely 'to exercise a liberalising influence and to compete in influence with the clerics', but there was an intrinsic objection to giving the right to confer degrees 'to an institution intended for one religious denomination and largely controlled by ecclesiastics', and there was the insoluble difficulty that its establishment entailed the opening of another university in Belfast, which would be unfavourably received because it would be seen as a consequence of the much disliked Roman Catholic University.

The suggested principal alternative was the reorganisation of the Royal University into a teaching university, having as constituent colleges the Queen's Colleges of Belfast, Cork, and Galway, and a new college for Catholics in Dublin. This compromise recommendation had a number of features likely to recommend it to Catholics. It granted considerable autonomy to each college, and proposed machinery likely both to remove former grounds for complaint against the system of examinations and to assure the bishops that nothing would be taught or published in the Catholic College contrary to the teaching of the Church. On the other hand, Maynooth and Magee College, Derry, were to be excluded from affiliation; and Queen's College Belfast – but not Cork and Galway – was to receive more money, a larger staff, and additional buildings. The result was a hotchpotch. Lord Robertson, in a rider that seemed to have Dr Walsh and his supporters in mind, considered that it would not satisfy 'those who determine Roman Catholic opinion', and that most authoritative opinions contrary to it had been expressed.[121]

Thus, Dr O'Dwyer's bold stroke had failed. It had had, in fact, little chance of success. However factual the allegations of Presbyterian intolerance and the ascendancy bigotry of the senior fellows of Dublin University, and however insensitive a number of the commissioners showed themselves to the Catholic nature of the country,[122] the reality was that the 'consolidated opinion' of the time, in Professor Butcher's phrase, considered such control as the bishops sought – limited though it had become – to be unacceptable, and felt itself committed, where Catholics were concerned, to a system of education that was expressly undenominational. Not for them the privileged form of undenominationalism in operation in Trinity College.

The bishop of Limerick had been prepared for disappointment, and hence received the report with equanimity. 'The report has been the event of the week', he wrote to Wilfrid Ward. 'The Catholic papers criticised it fairly, and on the whole much more sparingly than I expected. The *Irish Times* tried to weaken its force by dwelling on the divergent views in the 'riders'. But the Irish Protestants if they could would put us back in penal times.'[123]

He was aware that he had made a big impression. He suspected that much had been achieved despite the unsatisfactory result. The report, as he suggested, had 'force'. His instinct was right. The Royal Commission had brought forward the cause for university reform. It had conceded that outside Dublin University there were no higher education facilities worthy of the name, and that the Catholic majority, unable to attend Trinity College because of conscientious convictions, suffered, in consequence, severe disabilities that were a source of evil not only to Ireland, but even to the empire. Much valuable information, moreover, had been brought together and rendered accessible.

'I really hope', Wilfrid Ward told Balfour, 'that Dr O'Dwyer and others have forged weapons which you will be able to use with effect in parliament.'[124] Balfour did not use the weapons with effect, but five years later, under a different administration, on the occasion of a national university bill, Augustine Birrell and other speakers were to make considerable use of the information supplied to the Robertson Commission.[125] Finally, the idea of an autonomous, national university had been well aired by witnesses before the commission and in written submissions.[126]

Meantime, however, the commission's recommendations were an embarrassment to the government, and were received with disappointment and disillusionment by some of the bishops and interested laity, and with mixed feelings by others. Activity on the university question was virtually suspended for a number of months.

For Edward Thomas O'Dwyer the commission had provided a stage on which to shine, and he revelled in his starring role. Fittingly, some of the more perceptive remarks concerning him came from a commissioner, who was also a friend, Wilfrid Ward. About 1892, following an evening at Lord Emly's house, at Tervoe, Co. Limerick, he described the bishop of Limerick as 'a regular little fighting cock and very amusing';[127] but later, especially leading up to and during the commission, he came to view him as a most remarkable man, adding, however, 'I can see in a 'peppery nature' something which has prevented his having the full weight which his extraordinary ability would lead one otherwise to expect';[128] and, as if in illustration of the 'peppery nature', Wilfrid Ward's daughter, Maisie Ward, observed judiciously: 'My father developed an enormous admiration for him, yet it was difficult to maintain a *peaceful friendship over a long period*.'[129]

Even as he waited for the Robertson report, and subsequently continued to work for a university solution, Dr O'Dwyer's thoughts were raised to a different plane by the deaths of a number of his episcopal colleagues.

17

Towards a university solution – *manqué*, 1903–1908

SERIOUS REMINDERS: LIFE AND DEATH

From summer 1902 until late autumn 1904, Bishop O'Dwyer was encircled by intimations of mortality. On 26 July 1902, he attended the funeral of Thomas Croke, archbishop of Cashel, and in December that of John McEvilly, of Tuam, and Bartholomew Woodlock, formerly of Ardagh.[1] The following year, his strong supporter, Herbert Cardinal Vaughan, of Westminster, passed away in June; and, on the wider stage, Pope Leo XIII, the next month.[2] In 1904 he lost two close friends, Thomas McRedmond, of Killaloe, on 5 April, and little more than a week later John Coffey, bishop of Kerry. In November, an old friend and a landmark in his life, Sir Stephen de Vere, passed away at his home in Foynes Island on the Shannon.[3]

The appointment of new bishops lightened the burden of loss and mourning. In 1903, John Healy was made archbishop of Tuam, and in July 1904 John Mangan was appointed to Kerry and Michael Fogarty to Killaloe. The latter was to become one of O'Dwyer's strongest supporters and closest friends. He attended the respective consecrations at Killarney and Ennis during September 1904.

IN COMBATIVE MOOD

Despite the various solemn reminders of the fragility of life and of dedicated service of one's neighbour, Edward O'Dwyer's pen lost nothing of its vitriol. It was called into action in the early winter of 1903 as a counter to offensive public comments by Professor R.Y. Tyrrell of Trinity College. The latter accused the Catholic clergy of inculcating 'on their flocks cold acts of observation in lieu of sincere feelings of religion', and had expressed indignation against 'the ill-considered zeal of the rank and file of an unscrupulous priesthood practising on the ignorance and superstition of an illiterate peasantry', and the weakening of the substance of an impoverished people by the expenditure of large sums of money on grandiose churches, churches with 'spires like tall bullies' that 'lift their heads and lie'. The professor weakened his case by over-statement, a serious defect when faced with an experienced protagonist such as the bishop of Limerick.

O'Dwyer replied on 30 November 1903. He drew attention to the 'tone of insolence and contempt towards Catholics' in Tyrrell's remarks, which, he feared, also reflected the mind of many of his co-religionists. 'What a comment', he exclaimed, 'on the invitation to the Catholics of Ireland to accept this gentleman and his fellows as teachers of their sons!' He then required of the professor evidence for his accusations. From his own experience, O'Dwyer observed, he knew them to be untrue and unfounded and to be simply the projection from the Protestant prejudices and animosities in which Professor Tyrrell's mind seemed to move regarding the Catholic Church in Ireland, 'which he could only know on the surface, and from the outside'. O'Dwyer could not expect him to accept his testimony, but Professor Tyrrell would do well to study the appreciation of the religion of the Irish people, and the influence of the Catholic clergy upon it, by a professor of Trinity, whose words might 'induce him to modify the rancour, if not of his views, at least of his language'. The bishop went on to quote at length from Isaac Butt's *The Problem of Irish Education* (p. 117).

On the issue of church buildings, their size and cost, O'Dwyer, instead of facing the issue directly, drew the professor's attention to historical events and built his argument around them. In most of Ireland, he pointed out, the Catholics had to build places of worship because 'English domination … deprived the Catholic population of every church and house of worship they possessed'. Those, which the Protestant's wanted for their own use, they expropriated, broke down the altars, and turned them from Christian churches into 'Protestant meeting houses'. 'There was no waste of the people's substance here', he commented with heavy irony. Irish Protestants did not waste money on building the House of God, 'theirs was the truly worldly wisdom of the cuckoo.' They did not build; they expropriated the property of others, as they had done in Limerick with St Mary's Cathedral. Now, however, thanks to his efforts and those of his two predecessors, O'Dwyer boasted triumphally, Catholics had a larger and more beautiful cathedral, with a spire that out-tops St Mary's. After further consideration of the professor's criticisms, he informed him that he was evidently interfering in an area that he did not understand, and then concluded in an assertive, triumphalist vein, that would have annoyed opponents and overjoyed partisan supporters, but which reflected his cast of mind.

> Neither Professor Tyrrell nor Dr Mahaffey, nor all Trinity College, can stop 'the growth of Romanism'. That is the real trouble. Our churches are but the symbols of our resurrection. They are the evidences of that growth in strength, in self-reliance, in independence which has marked the advance of the Catholics of Ireland for the last fifty years. *Hinc illae lacrymae.*[4]

Despite such indications of denominational dissent, 1903 had been overall a year of hope and of new life for many, unionists and non-unionists.

Various signs of hope, and the Dunraven proposal

On 25 March, George Wyndham, chief secretary, introduced the Land Purchase Bill in the House of Commons, which brought to an end the long and bitter land struggle. In July, eleven miles of bunting and cheering crowds greeted King Edward VII and Queen Alexandra as they travelled in an open carriage from Kingstown (Dun Laoghaire) to the Phoenix Park. Too seldom, Wyndham exulted, had the Irish 'been given a channel for their loyalty'.[5] In the euphoria of the time, following on a successful land act and royal visit, he was carried away. 'They do believe in me', he exulted, 'and tremble towards a belief in the Empire because of belief in me. By 'they' I mean the whole lot – Unionist, Nationalist, Celtic, Norman, Elizabethan, Cromwellian, Williamite, agriculturalist and industrialist, educationist and folklorist … We must give the Irish something sensible to work for …'[6] His desire to give the Irish 'something sensible to work for' brought the university question to life once more.

Urged on by his Catholic under-secretary, Sir Anthony MacDonnell, he believed the time was ripe for a solution. The hierarchy was now 'in a mood to take what they can get'.[7] The *Times* reported in October 1903 that the chief secretary had plans for a national university consisting of three institutions on an equal footing: Trinity College, Queen's College Belfast, and a third college so constituted as to be acceptable to Catholics. Sir Anthony MacDonnell, who envisaged Dublin University as the 'national university', embracing the three colleges, had been in negotiation with Dr Walsh for some time. The body of bishops had entrusted negotiation on the university issue to the four arch-bishops. 'Everyone will (and must) stand by whatever we four do', Walsh told MacDonnell on 28 October 1903, adding, with reference to Archbishop Healy and himself, 'you may take it that whatever we two may say will be said by the four'.[8] Trinity College, however, in the person of the provost and senior fellows, expressed opposition to any such scheme, and the council of the college rejected an inducement of £10,000 per annum.[9] Wyndham and MacDonnell met with Archbishops Healy and Walsh, and Wyndham decided to press ahead with the scheme despite the opposition. O'Dwyer, meantime, feeling left out, and strongly critical of the proposed scheme, availed of an invitation to speak to the Literary and Historical Society, University College Dublin, to make his views known. The invitation had probably been arranged through Dr Delany. In his address to the Society, on 11 November 1903, he played on the current popular feeling against Trinity to move attention away from a college in Dublin University to the idea of an independent university for the Catholic population.

> If the Episcopalian body in Ireland and the authorities of Trinity College wrapped themselves up in their wealth and in their privileges and turned tail at the idea of uniting with a Romanist College, then why not leave them there? Why not do the simple and straight thing and give the people of Ireland what they wanted, what they would rally to, and what would draw their best enthusiasm – *a university according to their heart*.[10]

His call was ignored. Archbishop Walsh gave his approval to a well-publicised meeting of graduates in Dublin on 8 December 'to voice the claims of the Catholic body for equality in university education', and, thereby, to strengthen Wyndham's hand. The latter's scheme was launched as a sounding, through the agency of Lord Dunraven, on New Year's Day 1904. Dunraven, in a long letter to the press, advocated the establishment within the University of Dublin of two additional colleges – the Queen's College Belfast, and a King's College in Dublin – which colleges, like Trinity College, would be well endowed financially and be autonomous and residential, with governing bodies selected exclusively on academic grounds.[11]

Knowing that O'Dwyer was likely to prove an influential opponent of the proposal, and that a public meeting had been called by him and the mayor of Limerick, Michael Donnelly, for 13 January, MacDonnell wrote to him soliciting his support for Dunraven's scheme. O'Dwyer thanked him for his letter, but declared himself opposed to the proposal and was of the opinion that this would be the view of the majority of the bishops. They had waited and worked for a long time, and it seemed to him 'a poor result of it all to surrender every shred of denominational principle for which we strove'.[12] MacDonnell sent his reply to Archbishop Walsh, who commented that he 'quite took it for granted that the view indicated would be not only taken, but expressed'. This was why, he added, he had called for a general meeting of the bishops for 12 January, the day before the threatened danger.[13] In a postscript, he added regarding O'Dwyer: 'No personal influence could be used with effect. Besides, I have none in the case in question.'[14]

At the Maynooth meeting, the prelates, with the exception, it seems, of O'Dwyer, privately agreed to a carefully worded resolution that Walsh be authorised to intimate confidentially to Mr Wyndham that while they did not express any preference for the Dunraven scheme, they considered that 'a satisfactory settlement of the university question' could 'be arrived at on the lines indicated by his Lordship's letter'. 'But', the bishops added, 'if, from the attitude of Trinity College, or any other (cause), the government are not prepared to give legislation to the proposals of Lord Dunraven, we then call upon them to adopt the alternative scheme for the settlement of the question recommended in the Report of the Royal Commission.'[15] At the same meeting the bishops conceded that while they expected *ex officio* representation on the governing body of the proposed Catholic college, they would not insist on this claim if the measure proved otherwise satisfactory.[16]

Two years later a dejected MacDonnell was to complain bitterly: 'I regard the Bishop of Limerick as an irresponsible vituperative politician. He *alone* of all the Irish bishops held aloof from the agreement to accept an additional college in the Dublin University as a solution'.[17] Nevertheless, at the well-attended Limerick meeting on 13 January, O'Dwyer was on his best behaviour, so far as MacDonnell was concerned. The large representative gathering, of Protestants as well as Catholics, was addressed by Lords Monteagle and Emly,

Alderman Joyce, MP, Fr Andrew Murphy, Mr Lundon, MP, and Mr A. W. Shaw, JP, president of the Limerick chamber of commerce,[18] as well as by Bishop O'Dwyer. He contented himself with vigorously supporting the claims of the Irish people for a reform of the existing system of university education, and assuring the government that if it had a plan to propose it could be sure that it would find in Ireland, and from the representatives of Ireland, nothing 'but the heartiest co-operation'. He explained to the audience, however, that he was prepared to accept a college in either the Royal University or Dublin University, but that in regard to the latter he would have to see the scheme presented in black and white by 'responsible persons' before committing himself. Reading the political scene astutely, he counselled his audience not to despair of a solution if Wyndham should fail to persuade his cabinet colleagues, and concluded with a cautionary story of the young Abbé de Bernis who was told by the archbishop of Paris, 'an old man tottering to his grave', that he would never give him a benefice. 'Monsignor', said De Bernis, 'I can wait.'[19] O'Dwyer sensed that with a general election not far distant the government would not alienate their unionist support in Ireland, Scotland, and parts of England.

Wyndham was aware of this reality by the end of January 1904, but he continued, it would seem, to live in hope. On 22 January, Lord Londonderry, president of the Board of Education, made it clear at a meeting in Dublin that the government had no intention of acting on the question. Two days later, John Dillon informed Redmond that the bishops would not get their bill – 'the Belfastmen have knocked the bottom out of the whole business'.[20] Nevertheless, on 29 January, Dr Walsh, and a prominent member of the Irish Parliamentary party, the lord mayor, T. C. Harrington, MP, held a representative meeting at the Mansion House which called for 'the immediate settlement of the Irish university question as a matter of extreme urgency'.[21] The same day, Dr Sheehan was involved in a public meeting in Waterford,[22] and on 6 February there was a large meeting in Cork.[23] Evidently, there was a concerted attempt to put pressure on the government to keep to its original intent.

O'Dwyer, meanwhile, followed a bluntly independent line. During February he wrote a number of letters on the issue to the *Freeman*. 'In my opinion', he stated on 20 February, 'the scheme is an impossibility unless it has the unanimous and cordial support of Trinity College … I look about in every direction to try and discover what can be the purpose of these who are still pretending to think that Mr Wyndham is in earnest about it.' Referring to a previous editorial in the *Freeman*, which called for unity, in obvious reference to differences between himself and Dr Walsh, he now replied that he agreed 'that it would be good politics for us to avoid discussions which divide us'. 'But, on the other hand,' he insisted, 'I think it utter folly to waste our time and our energies following an *ignis fatuus* like the T.C.D. scheme at the present time.' He issued a warning, however, to Dublin University, in an oblique reference to what might happen under Home Rule: 'We may yet have to deal with Dublin University, but if so, it will be on deeper and more drastic lines than the little scheme that has just been put to rest.'[24]

A PLEA FOR THE ROBERTSON SCHEME

Two days later, he embarked on a long and significant letter that explained his objections to the Dunraven scheme, and indicated why the Robertson proposal was his preferred solution in the existing political circumstances. He also insisted that the body of bishops had not given their support to the Dunraven proposal. The occasion of this letter was an editorial note in the *Freeman*, which stated that the hierarchy had given approval in principle to Lord Dunraven's scheme of university settlement. When asked by the bishop to quote a declaration of the bishops that conveyed such assent, the *Freeman* reproduced a quotation from a pastoral letter of their lordships issued as far back as 1871. O'Dwyer, taking up the matter in earnest at this point, observed dryly that 'a pastoral letter published in the year 1871 is ... a rather remote and anticipatory approval of a scheme which first saw the light in 1900'. He then drew attention to the difference between what the bishops sought in that pastoral letter and what was being offered in the Dunraven scheme. The pastoral, he pointed out, declared for colleges conducted upon purely Catholic principles, but the essence of the Dunraven scheme was the exclusion of denominationalism from it in every part. If he could gather sufficient political strength, O'Dwyer admitted, he would carry a University for Catholics through the House of Commons, but it was not achievable. In the circumstances, he favoured the moderate scheme put forward by the Royal Commission. It had 'no vested interest either of a religious or a pecuniary kind, as in the Trinity College scheme, to overcome', and he was satisfied it could be got. He understood the point of the argument that Trinity College should not be allowed to stand in the way of reform. 'Yet', he observed realistically, 'if you interfere with it you arouse against you forces that are formidable, and it is not every day that you will have a giant like Gladstone who will grapple with them.' Besides, as an educationalist he did 'not think it well to condemn Ireland to one university, and that of the federal type'. There was no precedent, so far as he knew, for a successful institution of the kind.

The Royal Commission scheme had its drawbacks, he conceded, but he asked his opponent to take the following into consideration:

> All the recommendations of the Commission are positive ... from a mere examining body it makes the Royal University a teaching institution. It gives to the colleges of Cork and Belfast the freedom for which they have asked for many a year, and brings each of them into touch with the population amidst which they exist. It gives to us Catholics a real college in Dublin of the first rank, residential and autonomous. No one can deny

that these things would be great and most beneficial reforms, and would carry us on for many a year.

Like Fr Delany, he regarded the scheme as a stepping-stone to further development. 'What the ultimate issue might be', he added sagaciously, 'no one can tell. But it would be for Ireland and the different sections of Irishmen to determine the nature of further developments. It might be that, then, when we all stand as equals some form of federation might bring us all together, or some of the colleges might expand into independent universities. Our position, then, would be that of free men, with their destinies in their own hands, and not as now, mendicants who practically must take whatever is offered them.'

He concluded on a moderate, conciliatory note, often missing in other letters. 'In writing thus, I trust you will not think that I am activated by any spirit of contention, or desire to make any points against you. I recognise your full right to hold the views which you have expressed, and I hope to work with you in the future for the realisation of our common claim to equality with our Protestant fellow-countrymen in higher education.' By comparison, O'Dwyer's third letter in a week was marked by harsh, and sweeping invective.

CHARITY IN ABEYANCE

It was directed against the Catholic laymen who, supported by Dr Walsh, strongly supported the Dunraven scheme. Not having the authority of the Holy See to appeal to on this issue, he turned instead to the rising tide of nationalism, which he welded to Catholicism in support of his argument. Many of these men, he declared grossly, were 'that type of Catholic of whom the *Irish Times* wrote lately that very little provocation would make them renounce the Catholic faith', adding with brash censoriousness:

> I suspected, and do suspect, those men. They are anti-Irish and anti-clerical, if not anti-Catholic. They want a Catholic edition of Trinity College: respectable socially, unionist in politics, liberal in religion. I want, and you, Sir (the editor) want something very different – a broad, national, Catholic, Irish institution, which will be living with the life of Ireland, and throbbing with the same pulse.[25]

By 8 March, the bishop of Limerick had such little faith in Wyndham and the government that he remarked to Delany that the one thing to do was 'to turn him and his party out'.[26] In June, at a prize giving at Laurel Hill Convent School, he indulged in a personalised attack on Wyndham that was unbecoming a gentleman, let alone a bishop, and was quite inappropriate to the occasion and location. He had been incensed, it seems, by a remark of the chief secretary in the House of Commons that 'neither in this session of parliament or the next will there be any reform of university education'. In the course of a sustained attack, he compared Wyndham to 'oily Gammon', a character in Sam Warren's story of 'Ten Thousand a Year', and described the Chief Secretary's speech of 18 April as being 'in oleaginous humbug … one of his most successful efforts'.

Despite the mounting demand across the country for higher education reform, and despite Wyndham's genuine desire to achieve a solution, all succumbed, as O'Dwyer had feared they would, to the cabinet's fear of extreme unionist opinion in Ireland, Scotland, and Lancashire.

Rejection and bitter reaction
On 3 August 1904, in the course of a debate on grant-in-aid to the Queen's Colleges, the unhappy chief secretary declared frankly that the government was not going to do anything on the university question, and had not pledged itself to do anything. It was the turning point in his career. Six months later he resigned, distrusted by both sides in Ireland. The Orangemen viewed him as part of a conspiracy to force Protestants out of the country. Catholics were angry at being sacrificed once again to Orange prejudice, despite preliminary promises of a solution. Not surprisingly, the widespread feeling of betrayal and indignation found expression in a paper of O'Dwyer to the Annual Conference of the Catholic Truth Society, held in the Rotunda, Dublin, on 11 October. The title indicated its trend: 'The Present Condition of University Education in Ireland: a Wrong to the Country and an Insult to Catholics.'

The paper, later published as a pamphlet, surveyed the effects of English maladministration in Ireland, asserted the right to Home Rule, emphasised the enormous endowments of philanthropists such as Carnegie, Rhodes and Rockfeller towards higher education in their own countries, displayed learning accumulated from his reading and his study of science, and finally set sail on the rising tide of national feeling and identity which was founded on dissatisfaction with English government and on the revival of things Irish.

There was hardly a statesman of first rank, O'Dwyer thundered, who did not admit the justice of the Irish Catholic claims. But this was not enough for Messrs. Balfour, Londonderry, and Wyndham. Instead,

> We, Irish Catholics, must submit our claims to the judgment of the Orange opposition. They are a handful; we are the nation; you count them by thousands; we are millions; yet in the counsels of Mr Wyndham the clamour of this handful of fanatics counts for more than the claims and needs of the whole nation. Yet Englishmen cannot understand the implacable feeling of the Irish heart that will never soften to them nor to their government.[27]

He was giving voice to a growing sense among the majority population that the Irish unionists, especially in the north of the country, were alien, and his 'we are the nation' conveyed the increasing identification of the Catholic majority with the true Ireland. In the address he also provided additional evidence of the current trend towards self-help; on which Arthur Griffith was to construct the *Sinn Féin* (we ourselves) movement the following year. 'However we explain the absence of active and vigorous agitation of this (university question', O'Dwyer proclaimed, 'one thing seems to me absolutely certain, and that is that the first step towards reform must be taken by ourselves.'

Constant disappointment at government hands had driven him to reverse his earlier order of preference, and to now put Home Rule before university reform. Indeed, with hindsight, there might be seen in the conclusion of his address a further indication of that militant nationalism that was to surface with a major impact years later. Thomas Edward O'Dwyer, by temperament, tended to force issues, to storm citadels. He concluded the address with a quotation from the Irish poet and songwriter, Thomas Moore, which referred to a former guerrilla fighter. 'This is the twentieth century', he observed, 'yet you might apply to us now the words of Moore written a hundred years ago:'

> As long as millions shall kneel down
> To ask of thousands for their own,
> While thousands proudly turn away,
> And to the millions answer, 'Nay',
> So long the merry reign shall be
> Of Captain Rock and his family.

Delany, unlike his Limerick friend, appreciated the efforts Wyndham had made in bringing in Sir Anthony MacDonnell as his Under-Secretary, and in appointing another able Catholic, Professor Bertram Windle, president of Queen's College Cork. On 13 October, the chief secretary thanked him for 'words written in kindness and charity, of which there are not many', and remarked subsequently that until something effective could be done for higher education it was part of his plan to at least refute 'the alleged dearth of eligible Catholics by a series of practical demonstrations'.[28]

Scholarship initiatives
The impetus for the next movement in higher education came, unwittingly, from Trinity College. For a number of years its student numbers and its educational status had been declining while those of the Royal University, and particularly of University College, were steadily increasing.[29] To counter the fall in numbers, a wealthy admirer, Sir John Nutting, offered to endow for five years a number of scholarships to Trinity College for Catholic students who had distinguished themselves at either the senior or middle grade in the Intermediate examinations each year, and who undertook to pursue their education at Trinity. The scholarships consisted of twelve exhibitions of £40, and ten of £100, but carried no obligation of college residence or even of attendance at a single lecture. If the scheme proved successful, Nutting promised to build, after five years, a Catholic chapel on a site that the Board of Trinity had offered for that

purpose. The scheme was announced on 16 January 1905. The Catholic bishops' Standing Committee, outraged at what they considered a blatant bribe, condemned the venture four days later; and Dr O'Dwyer publicly declared Nutting's scheme to be 'as offensive as it is absurd'.[30]

Reaction soon took a more positive form. On 31 January, the Catholic School of Medicine, Cecilia Street, attached to University College, announced the inauguration of a fund to establish a scholarship tenable at that institution;[31] and on 7 February, O'Dwyer came forward with a proposal to fight money with money by establishing 'a burse or scholarship for Limerick students in the (Royal) University for the next five years'.[32] The assembly of bishops, on 14 June, not only condemned Nutting's scheme, they also took up with enthusiasm the idea of 'Catholic scholarships'. They proposed scholarships for boys to University College, and for girls to Loreto College, St Stephen's Green, Dublin, or to the Dominican college, Eccles Street, on the basis of the senior grade Intermediate examination results. The scholarships consisted of eight at £50 a year, and four at £25, tenable for three years. A broadly-based committee – including the lord mayor of Dublin, the president of the Gaelic League, and the chairman of the Dublin County Council – was set up to administer the scheme. Its leading spirits and workers, however, were Archbishop Walsh, as chairman, Fr William Delany, as secretary, and Fr Andrew Murphy, secretary of the Catholic Headmasters' Association and O'Dwyer's assistant and aide. The details were published in the press on 4 September 1905.

O'Dwyer and Delany awaited the outcome with some misgivings, but the former felt that at least one thing had been gained, namely, 'the killing of Nutting's scheme'.[33] On 5 October, he forwarded to Delany his payment to the year's scholarship fund, adding that the point had been made by calling 'mad-dog' after Nutting, and it was to be hoped that the name would 'have its proverbial efficacy and stop a rush to Trinity College'.[34]

The misgivings were soon dispelled by the extent of the response. The prevailing mood of self-help was heralded by Wexford county council founding a scholarship for that county. The general council of county councils commended the example to other counties. It was taken up with enthusiasm. In response to the additional demand for places, Delany petitioned the bishops for permission to erect a temporary structure in the grounds of University College, which would provide additional lecture rooms and two or more large rooms for scientific lectures. These last were now particularly required, he explained, because the county councils were 'establishing local scholarships for higher scientific and technical instruction tenable in university situations'. The approval was availed of so eagerly that by the following May the new buildings were ready.[35]

Meantime, Delany, conscious of the unease among the better-educated and more self-confident laity regarding 'clerical influence', had been endeavouring to secure a more representative governing body for University College. O'Dwyer encouraged the idea. On 5 March 1904, he suggested to Delany that its members might be drawn from the Catholic senators of the Royal University, the teaching staff of University College, and, perhaps, from the Cecilia Street Medical School. The important thing was to have a body to which no exception could be taken and 'into whose hands we might ask parliament to entrust public funds'.[36] The envisaged governing body was to have extensive powers and to include many influential lay people. Delany submitted a detailed scheme to the hierarchy in June 1904. The programme was warmly supported by some bishops but was turned down. In October 1905 he put it forward once more, but once again without success. The opposition of Cardinal Logue was said to have led to its rejection.[37]

Storming the citadel
By then, however, there had been developments that brought Trinity College centre-stage once more. Dr Walter McDonald, of Maynooth, proposed at a college debate that Irish Catholics should 'carry the war into the camp – into the very citadel – of the enemy' by attending Trinity College in large numbers and saturating it 'with the microbes of Irish nationality'. His views received sufficient publicity to merit a dismissive editorial in *The Times* of 26 June, but otherwise seemed to have little effect. They were close, as has been seen, to the views long cherished by Archbishop Walsh, and to some extent by Cardinal Logue. The month after McDonald's proposal, Dr Walsh set about storming the citadel in a different manner. The previous year he had expressed to John Redmond his doubts about the efficacy of parliamentary action in 'getting redress of our grievances in Ireland'.[38] Now he returned to the idea he had first mooted in 1899, namely, a concentrated campaign of criticism against Trinity College, that last stronghold of ascendancy, as a different way of 'getting redress'. From July 1905 until well into the following year he waged his campaign, making use of severe strictures passed by the Medical Council on the method of conducting examinations at Trinity. He also availed of the atmosphere generated by the expanding interest in things Irish – in Irish language, history, and culture. In that setting, Trinity College's opposition to university education for the majority population appeared quite contrary.

Walsh's ultimate aim of a Catholic College in Dublin University received a boost, moreover, by the appointment, in December 1905, of James Bryce as chief secretary, and the retention of Sir Anthony Mac Donnell as under-secretary. Bryce, a Belfast Presbyterian and author of noted historical works, *The Holy Roman Empire* and *The American Commonwealth*, favoured a university solution along the lines MacDonnell and the archbishop had in mind. He had been appointed by the new prime minister, Henry Campbell-Bannerman, a Liberal, and when there was a 'Liberal landslide' in the British general election in January 1906 the prospects looked bright for a university settlement close to the archbishop's wishes.

On 23 January 1906, the episcopal standing committee publicly supported Walsh's campaign. They called on the Irish Parliamentary party to bring to the attention of the government the anomalous position of Trinity College, which 'holds for a small minority of the population the funds that constitute the Irish national endowment for higher education'.[39] The wording bore the mark of Walsh's shrewd political judgment. The reforming instincts of the Liberal party had already been evinced in plans to deprive the denomination primary schools in England of their privileged position. Hence, they might be disposed, with some guidance from Sir Anthony MacDonnell, towards a dispersing of Trinity's endowments. Redmond forwarded a copy of the bishops' request to Bryce with a request for the government's immediate consideration of the university question.[40] The response of the government, under prompting from Bryce and MacDonnell, was to announce, in March 1906, the formation of a new commission – 'to inquire into and report upon the place which Trinity College and the University of Dublin now hold as organs of higher education in Ireland, and the steps proper to be taken to increase their usefulness to the country'.[41]

O'Dwyer sought to counter the new venture by putting forward a resolution in the senate of the Royal University, on 7 March 1906, that the university be reformed so as to make it 'a teaching university, with colleges adequately constituted and brought into organic connection with it' such as the Robertson Commission had recommended.[42] On 22 March his views received indirect and unexpected support from the Unionist MP, Edward Carson, who announced that he would oppose any scheme what would interfere with Trinity College, but he would support a Catholic University.[43] The bishop of Limerick followed up his efforts in the senate with an impressive article in the *Dublin Review* during April 1906. Entitled 'Irish University Education', it detailed how the Royal University could be reformed into a teaching institution, with episcopal representation on a governing body that would have a majority of lay people. Among those impressed by it was George Wyndham, who wrote in its praise to the editor, Wilfrid Ward. He commenced by comparing O'Dwyer's presentation to that of another author.

> Contrast O'Dwyer! How direct he is, and with what sober gallantry his sentences march. But perhaps I am influenced not only by his style but even more by his matter ... I agree with every word he has written. He has made me feel a fool and I am glad of it. He is right ... it is so obvious when stated. We were blinded by the true objections of an Examining University ... Aim at a Teaching University, but find your constituent assembly – ready to hand – in the senate of the existing Examining University. This is sound, conservative and constructive statesmanship.[44]

O'Dwyer's efforts, however, made little impact. Expectation was centred on the new commission. Its members were appointed on 1 June 1906, and it took its name from the chairman, Sir Edward Fry, Lord Justice of Appeal.

Among the many reactions to the new venture, most of them favourable on the nationalist side, was an interview in the *Freeman's Journal*, 31 July 1906, with the archbishop of Dublin. He sought to encompass the view of all his colleagues, and silence O'Dwyer, by stating that the bishops were willing to accept 'A new college as Catholic as Trinity College is Protestant in a reconstructed Royal University, as recommended by the late Robertson Commission, or a similar college in the University of Dublin, as proposed by Mr Wyndham and Lord Dunraven'. Meanwhile, as he knew, MacDonnell and Bryce were pressing ahead with plans for the enlargement of Dublin University, quite independently of the Fry Commission's deliberations.[45]

A POLITICAL GAFFE AND ENGLAND'S CATHOLIC PRIMARY SCHOOLS

During the year, an embarrassing precipitous intervention by the bishop of Limerick did not help his reputation as an educationalist. His aversion to Liberals led him to intrude into the English political scene, early in 1906, by calling on the Irish party and on all Irish Catholics in Britain to oppose the Liberals in the January general election. His concern was the Liberals' opposition to denominational education in the English Catholic elementary schools. 'Complete popular control is the watchword of the Liberals on the school question', he wrote in the *Freeman* on 12 January 1906. 'They make no secret about it. Every one of them is pledged to it. That means complete Protestant control of Catholic schools.' In 1902 an education act had brought the Catholic schools under state grant but not under local rate aid. Now, in 1906, Augustine Birrell, president of the Board of Education, aimed to bring the schools under rate aid and, as a result, under the jurisdiction of the local educational authorities. John Redmond and the Irish party had supported the Liberals in the election campaign. They found themselves in a delicate situation when, on 25 January, the Irish episcopal standing committee reminded the party of the pledges they had given 'to shield the religious education of Irish Catholic children in the schools in England'.[46]

Their position was eased when the archbishop of Westminster, Francis Bourne, asked to meet with Redmond. They worked out an arrangement whereby the party would support the bill, but would win as many concessions as possible for the Catholic schools. On 15 June 1906, Bourne assured the Irish leader – 'anything is better than the dilemma which Mr Birrell proposed to me last February: "Accept my bill or be starved out of existence".'[47]

O'Dwyer did not know of the understanding between the archbishop and Redmond, and in headlong fashion, without further inquiry, launched an attack on the Irish party. On 23 June, at prize giving at Laurel Hill Convent School, he expressed astonishment that Redmond intended to support a bill that would result in reducing English Catholic schools to a ruinous condition.[48] The bill gave rise to divisions among English Catholics. The bishop of Liverpool, contrary to Archbishop Bourne's policy, called for resistance to the measure in an active sense.[49] O'Dwyer, on 15 December, rashly praised Liverpool's stand and, with reference to a speech by John Dillon, he assailed the Irish party and savagely branded Dillon as 'the man, who with canine servility licks the hand of Mr Birrell'.[50]

On 4 December, Bourne had issued an agreed statement to the effect that the Irish party had acted with the approval of the English Catholic hierarchy. Now, on 17 December, following O'Dwyer's letter, he wrote to Redmond to convey his distress and to assure him that he would write to O'Dwyer to remonstrate with him and tell him substantially how matters stood.[51] In his letter to the bishop of Limerick, a surprisingly mild document considering the embarrassment caused by O'Dwyer's precipitous, ill-mannered intervention, he included, 'in fairness to Mr Redmond', a copy of the resolution passed by the English hierarchy on 4 December announcing that the Irish party had acted with their approval, and then added:

> Last Wednesday, Mr Birrell gave the required assurances, and to clinch the bargain and make it impossible for the government to withdraw without exposing themselves thereby to a charge of manifest breach of faith, Mr Redmond led his party into the government lobby. It may have been a tactical error: personally I think there was much to justify his action.

'To understand the position it must be remembered', Bourne concluded pointedly, '... the situation is one of extreme difficulty and delicacy.'[52] In the event, the bill was withdrawn by the government after the House of Lords sent it back 'with a cloud of amendments'.[53]

O'Dwyer, for his part, did not seem discomforted by his blunder, though, for once, he did admit that he may have been wrong! In a letter to Bishop Fogarty, of Killaloe, on 18 December, probably before he had heard from Archbishop Bourne but after he had had an explanatory letter from John Redmond, he observed: 'If Redmond is correct in what he writes about the English bishops then I have done him a wrong, but they would want a guardian'. And, with reference to his abusive letter of 15 December, he explained childishly, betraying once again a virtual obsession, – 'my letter was strong but I was angered by Dillon's speech'![54] Ten days later he had rationalised his action. Writing to Michael O'Riordan, rector of the Irish College Rome since 1905, he commented: 'There is a great deal of quiet satisfaction at the failure of the Education Bill ... The Irish party are very angry with me for my letter in the *Freeman*, but both as Catholics and Nationalists they will do no good if they subordinate their own principles to the party exigencies of the Liberals'. He went on with the ironical news:

> I fear there is some foundation for the rumours that we are going to get Birrell for our Chief Secretary. If this should be done, and with the assent of the Irish party, it will be no good for Irish education.

He concluded sombrely: 'I am told that the R. Commission will report in favour of a college for Catholics in the University of Dublin, a Catholic counterpart of T.C.D. I fear that there is a drift of opinion amongst us away from the old moorings.'[55] This concluding sentence acknowledged the movement of the majority of the bishops away from their earlier position.

THE FRY COMMISSION AND THE AFTERMATH

At the Fry Commission the only Catholic churchman to give evidence was Dr Delany of University College. He caused a stir by telling the commission that Archbishop Healy, in seconding the proposal in the senate of the Royal University in favour of a solution by reforming that university, had made it clear that in doing so he was representing 'the views of substantially the whole of the episcopate of Ireland with just one possible doubtful exception'.[56] This appeared to contradict Dr Walsh's assurance that all the bishops had agreed to a settlement along the lines of the Dunraven programme. Another ally of O'Dwyer, the new president of Queen's College Cork, Professor Bertram Windle, opposed the Dunraven proposals in his evidence. He and Delany kept the bishop of Limerick informed on developments. They both regretted the influence enjoyed by his Grace of Dublin. 'I do not think that the prospect is a very hopeful one', Windle informed O'Dwyer on 27 December 1906, 'and I profoundly distrust those who will be most carefully consulted as to the settlement of educational affairs.'[57] Clearly, Archbishop Walsh's influence had become hegemonic amongst the majority of the episcopate, and focal from the viewpoint of government negotiators.

On 12 January 1907, the Fry Commission published its report. Eight out of nine commissioners called for the establishment in Dublin of a college acceptable to Catholics, but they were divided as to whether it should be in Dublin University or in the Royal University. It was a bitter disappointment for Archbishop Walsh, but the clouds lifted when, on 25 January, Chief Secretary Bryce, despite the announcement of his replacement by Augustine Birrell, informed a deputation from the Presbyterian General Assembly and the Catholic laity that the government had decided to establish a new college in Dublin University. The new scheme envisaged the abolishment of the Royal University, and the turning of the University of Dublin into a national university which included Trinity College, the new college in Dublin, and the Queen's Colleges in Belfast and Cork.[58] It was a dramatic last word before his departure. 'He shouts 'No Surrender' at the top of his voice', Arthur Balfour remarked, 'and he nails his flag to someone else's mast.'[59]

His scheme met with widespread approval, except in the west of Ireland where concern was felt at the exclusion of Queen's College Galway. Even the senate of the Royal University, 'in the interests of an early settlement', waived its support for the Robertson recommendation and welcomed the new venture. Bertram Windle, too, wished Bryce's programme 'God speed'.[60] O'Dwyer was not present at the senate meeting. William Delany remained opposed. He had studied Bryce's proposal and noted that the role of the 'new college in Dublin' was confined to providing teaching in less advanced subjects, and that Bryce had declared that the scheme was acceptable to 'the heads of the Roman Catholic Church in Ireland'. Incensed, he protested at length to O'Dwyer. 'Here we have at once,' he maintained, '*mixed joint education* under professors in whose appointment Catholics will have little influence, and the Catholic College lowered to the status of a mere preparatory institution.' Could it be that any such scheme was laid before the bishops and they expressed their willingness to accept it? And if this were so, 'what becomes of all the protests and condemnations of pope and bishops for the past sixty years? And what becomes of the demand for equality which was the main burden of all Dr Walsh's many pronouncements?' He asked the bishop of Limerick to advise him for his own guidance on the senate of the Royal University. He added that he knew 'on excellent authority' that Bryce's speech had no authority from the cabinet, and he felt confident that were the bishops to inform the government that they would prefer the Royal University proposals, the government would give the fullest consideration to the suggestion that might be made. He had written to the cardinal, but it was not clear that his Eminence realised the urgency of the situation.[61]

John Ross of Bladensburg had a similar message for the bishop. Bryce's action could not be taken as binding on his successor. 'It looks like a *balloon d'essai* inflated by bluff.' He, Ross, could not see, besides, how the new proposals could be made acceptable. In the new university the Catholics would have but a fifth of the votes in the senate. If only the bishops had taken a definite stance with regard to the Robertson scheme, they would have avoided having forced on them a scheme that they did not like. He believed there was still time to act.[62]

The bishops, however, indicated no desire to commit themselves before the bill was drafted. They appeared to accept Bryce's assertion that his was the only scheme politically possible. This, too, was O'Dwyer's view, which was not surprising given his negative perception of the Liberals, and particularly of Birrell. 'The alternatives are this scheme or nothing', he replied to Ross on 27 January. He preferred the Robertson proposals, but he did not think there was sufficient difference of principle between them and those of Bryce to justify him saying to the government 'give me my plan or nothing'. He agreed with Ross about the domination of a clique in the entire proceedings, but the question had now passed beyond that stage. 'We have to accept or refuse a large and – for Liberals – generous proposal for a national settlement. We have to ask ourselves: if we refuse it what chance is there in our lifetime of getting better, indeed of getting anything at all?'[63]

Ross passed on to Delany this unexpected evidence of dispiritedness on the part of the bishop of Limerick. On 16 February, O'Dwyer explained his inaction in a letter to O'Riordan, in Rome.

> We are in a very tight corner about this university question. The whole country, practically, has declared in general terms for the government scheme, which in its external and political aspects, is fair enough. In myself I dread an alliance with T.C.D. in any shape or form, but *I dare not take a line of opposition now*, and I think the safest course is to assent to the government plan, and fight, and if necessary to a breach, for full equality and perfect autonomy for our college.

It was quite possible, he added, that Trinity would have sufficient influence to counter the government plan, and 'that then we should get a solution on other lines'. 'But if the bishops came out in opposition, the government would say, "Well, Gentlemen, we will drop it all for the present".'[64]

The bishop of Limerick's new, more politically nuanced stance was, perhaps, partly a reflection of tiredness and of caution occasioned by his English schools blunder. Soon, however, he was negotiating with Windle about reviving the Robertson scheme. It may be possible, Windle wrote on 9 April, 'that Trinity may be frightened enough to push a Robertson bill for all she is worth'.[65] On 2 May he wrote again to say that the negotiations he had initiated at O'Dwyer's suggestion had broken down.[66] Their joint tactic had been for O'Dwyer to add to the public warnings to the Trinity authorities about their fate under Home Rule if they continued intransigent, while Windle availed of his good relations with the provost of Trinity College, Anthony Traill, to suggest that the pressures on Trinity from the Bryce scheme and public criticism could be averted if they supported the implementation of the Robertson scheme. Meantime, there was an important parallel development.

THE IRISH COUNCIL BILL AND A NEW INITIATIVE

On 6 May, Birrell introduced the Irish Council Bill. The main architect of this measure, also, was Sir Anthony MacDonnell. The Irish bishops vigorously opposed the measure, seeing it as removing education from their authority, and nationalists condemned it as a meagre pittance in lieu of Home Rule. At the same time, Trinity College mobilised opposition to the Bryce university scheme. A printed sheet signed by 6,361 graduates, and by the vice-chancellor and vice-provost, was directed to the House of Commons, reminding members of the history of 'the University of Trinity College' and humbly petitioning – 'that in any legislation affecting university education in Ireland, the Protestant constitution of the University of Dublin may be preserved unimpaired, and that the Protestant people of Ireland may not be deprived of privileges which they have enjoyed without interruption for three hundred years'.[67] Trinity's appeal rallied Conservative and Non-Conformist members in opposition to the bill. The government, as a result, found itself under attack from different directions.

Against this background, Windle sent an enthusiastic letter to O'Dwyer on 23 May 1907. 'The moment has now arrived', he began, 'at which it may be possible to snatch a settlement of the university question.' He went on:

> The situation is this: – the Devolution Bill goes onto the scrap heap. Either Birrell will resign … or he will bring in a University Bill, for he must bag one fish if possible to show for his two years sport.

If, however, he brought in the Bryce scheme, Windle continued, 'it will have an angry, dangerous passage through the Commons and will be thrown out in the

Lords'. As an earnest of Trinity's aim to bring about such a result, he happened to know that Trinity had got up a fund of £10,000 to fight the bill if introduced. Windle then reported the striking effect of his protracted negotiations. He had 'a very important letter from Traill' that morning. In it, the provost stated 'that he has reason to know that if the hierarchy and Trinity – with or without Presbyterians – ask the government jointly for the Robertson (scheme), the request will be granted'. Traill, whom Windle described as 'a curious person ... blunt but honest', had informed him that he had fully discussed the matter with Bishop Foley, a fellow member on the National Education Board, and found him quite of one mind with him. It might be, Windle added, 'that both sides, weary of a long struggle, were willing to sink differences so far as to come to this compromise'.[68]

As so often happened, however, a hiatus occurred once more in the university question. Campbell-Bannerman, embarrassed by both prospective bills, seized the opportunity of the rejection of the Council measure by the national convention of the Irish party, to declare on 3 June that his cabinet had abandoned both the Council Bill and the proposed university measure. Sir Anthony MacDonnell became the convenient scapegoat. Across the country, the government's handling of both issues added to the growing mood of dissatisfaction and unrest.

On the positive side, the abandonment of Bryce's scheme, and the departure of MacDonnell, gave new opportunities to Birrell, as Windle had foreseen. Both Trinity and the bishops were weary of the issues and ready for compromise. The bishops could not fail to see that the government would not force Trinity to give way, while Trinity had been chastened and frightened by the combination of government and public pressure. Both were prepared to listen to any form of attractive package from the Chief Secretary, provided he was diplomatic in presenting it and genuine in carrying it out. In the light of past history, however, Birrell had to surmount obstacles of credibility. Thus, when, in the autumn of 1907, he accepted an invitation from William Delany to address a public meeting of the Literary and Historical Society of University College on his plans for university education in Ireland, and pledged himself to do all in his power to solve the question in the next session of parliament, he was scorned and ridiculed by his audience to Delany's embarrassment. It seemed but another instance of fair promises by an English politician.

Accounts of Birrell's success in providing an acceptable solution to the university question are readily available.[69] Here, the intention is to summarise his efforts and to record O'Dwyer's typically individual response.

BIRRELL'S DETERMINED AND PERSUASIVE APPROACH

The chief secretary prepared the way with astuteness. He decided to base his proposals on those of his Presbyterian cabinet colleague, Richard B. Haldane, which had been largely acceptable in 1898 to Tories and Liberals, and to the

Catholic hierarchy and the Presbyterian general assembly. This scheme envisaged two universities, one in Dublin and the other in Belfast, which, though officially non-denominational, would be respectively, in practice, predominantly Catholic and predominantly Presbyterian. The venture was a practical acknowledgement of the political and religious division within the island of Ireland. Birrell won over Provost Traill and the senior fellows to his scheme on the understanding that Trinity College would be left untouched; he successfully wooed Cardinal Logue and Dr Delany, and finally persuaded Dr Walsh that there was no other available solution. Having brought Haldane's programme up to date, the Chief Secretary introduced the Irish Universities Act on 31 March 1908.

The chief proposals of the bill were that in the Belfast University there would be one college, the existing Queen's College, and in the Dublin institution there would be three constituent colleges, the existing ones in Cork and Galway, and a new college in Dublin. The Royal University would be dissolved. In neither of the two universities would religious tests be allowed; nor was the public money to be spent in providing or maintaining any church or other place of religious worship, or in providing any theological or religious teaching. The universities were to be governed by their senates, which would be nominated to begin with but which would later be academically elected, the Crown reserving, however, the right to make some nominations. On the Belfast nominated senate of thirty-five there would be one Catholic, and on the Dublin nominated senate of thirty-six there would be seven Protestants. The governing bodies of both Cork and Galway were to be reconstructed. For three years the governing bodies of all the colleges were to be filled by nomination. Professors were to be appointed and dismissed by the Senate, but they would have the right of appeal to the Crown through the agency of a board of visitors. The first president of the new Dublin College, in Birrell's view, should be a layman. The charters of the universities allowed for affiliation, and for their constituent colleges to affiliate, in turn, institutions capable of giving university teaching. As regards financial provision, Belfast was to receive £28,000 a year; the Dublin college £32,000; Cork £18,000; and Galway £12,000. In addition, £60,000 was to be given to increase the size of the Belfast institution, and £150,000 was to be allocated for the building of the new college in Dublin.[70] On 11 May, the second reading of the Universities Bill was carried by 344 votes to 31. On 25 July, it passed its third reading by 207 votes to 19, and was sent to the Lords. On 1 August it received the royal assent. A major achievement by the Chief Secretary, yet the bishop of Limerick remained unrelentingly critical.

ONE BISHOP AGAINST THE UNIVERSITY BILL

In October 1907, O'Dwyer founded the *Irish Educational Review*, edited in Limerick by the much-talented Fr Andrew Murphy. In the first issue the bishop delivered a vigorous attack on the duplicity of the Liberals, concluding that they had no intention of bringing in a university bill. When he was proved wrong in this, he turned his critical eye on the content of the new university bill following its introduction on 31 March 1908. He provided a reasoned, if somewhat biased, examination of the proposed measure.

There was 'no denying', O'Dwyer commenced, that the Irish University Bill was 'a great disappointment in many respects'. Catholics had worked for years for an institution in accordance with their religious principles, now weary years of frustration had 'reduced them to an accommodating frame of mind, and, like the man going home with his horse from the fair,' they were 'disposed to take less than they would have been prepared to accept earlier in the day'. Then, regarding some of the salient features of the measure, he insisted that the first question to be asked was: 'What provision does this Bill make for religion?' And the answer, on the face of it, he said, was 'none whatever'. 'It proposes to set up a university and colleges on a constitution that would be as applicable to a Mohammedan as to a Catholic country.' How different what English Protestants impose on Irish Catholics and what they give themselves! In Trinity College, Dublin, and in Oxford and Cambridge, the interests of religion were expressly catered for. With respect to the government of the proposed national university, the total omission of the bishops had surprised the country: 'Two of them are to have places on the temporary senate, … but at the expiration of that time they disappear'. After this less than accurate presentation, O'Dwyer pointed out that as professors were to be appointed without a religious test, a man of any or no religion might 'be appointed to teach any subject, say philosophy or history'. In Mr Birrell's university, moreover, there was to be, it seemed, no protection for the religious beliefs of the students, beyond a general confidence that everything would 'work out all right through some inherent goodness in Irish human nature.'

An indication of this last, was the fact that the university, for lack of funds, was not to be residential. 'One shrinks from the idea', the bishop observed, 'of sending young, innocent boys from their homes in the country to live scattered about in cheap lodging in a city like Dublin, with practically no control or supervision.' 'They miss, as a result,' he added eloquently, 'the experience of real university life. For a university

> was meant to be an *alma mater*, taking the place of home, and not only teaching learning but educating the whole man, forming his habits, training him to self-restraint, giving him strength of character, and basing its entire work on his religious faith.

There was no excuse, he went on, for 'the paltry pettifogging spirit in which the government was approaching the financing of this question'. They were keeping the Catholics of Ireland forever in a position of inferiority and ensuring that there would be no fear of any rivalry from the new university to Trinity. The small sum of money made available made it impossible to have a proper university out of the city in its own grounds. Instead, it was proposed to fit up the old Exhibition Building at Earlsfort Terrace. If ample grounds could be secured at the rear of that premises well and good, but if not, it was important to look elsewhere, to 'get a noble plan of a fine college and university from the best architect in the country. You may not see it standing for twenty or thirty years, but keep it before you as your ultimate goal. This is a great work, a national work, not for a generation but for centuries'. The magnanimous vision was in keeping with his high ideal and expectation of a university, a vision shared by William Delany, and fifty years later a president of University College would appeal to that earlier vision in support of the college's move from Earlsfort Terrace to the ample acres of Belfield outside the city.[71]

Finally, O'Dwyer expressed dissatisfaction at the exclusion of headmasters from the governing bodies and at the exclusion of Maynooth as a constituent college, and the possibility of it not even enjoying affiliation. He had not helped Maynooth's cause by his criticism of its deficient education in his testimony before the Robertson Commission, but now, in a different situation, and, as it were to redress the balance, he was prepared to alter his argument and vigorously press its case. The ostracism of 'the great college of Maynooth', he pronounced, was based on the 'distrust and dislike of the Irish priesthood' which ran through the Act. Sadly, the effect would be to 'effectually shut out from the university the priesthood of Ireland, not only from all share in the formation of its tone, and government, but even from a participation in its educational advantages. Surely', he declared, 'this is carrying things too far.'

On 13 June 1908, in the *Freeman's Journal*, before the third reading of the University Bill had taken place, he returned to his depressing suspicion that there was a 'systematic and almost scientific exclusion of the priesthood of Ireland ... from any position of influence' in connection with the university, and dismissed signs to the contrary.

> Some bishops are, no doubt, put on the temporary governing bodies of the university and colleges; but that is only as contrivance to allay Catholic apprehensions at the start; but when, at the expiration of five years, their institutions are in full swing, they will put the pilots ashore, and dispense with the services of the clergy.

HIS VIEWS CHALLENGED

His suspicion of all government motives, and his readiness to attribute unworthy aims to opponents, frequently weakened O'Dwyer's case. In this instance, he was challenged straightway by Stephen Gwynn, MP, with regard to the bishops being 'put ashore' after five years, and to the further remark that at the end of their initial period Mr Birrell would 'send them about their business, and deprive them of every chance of free election'.

'With all submission to Dr O'Dwyer', Gwynn remarked, 'Mr Birrell's bill does nothing of the kind. It is possible – though, unlike his Lordship, I do not think it probable – that predominantly Catholic academic electors may 'dispense with the services of the clergy'. But if they do, it will not be the fault of Mr Birrell, or of the bill, or of the Irish party. Under the bill, all posts are open to all persons – lay or clerical; attempts to exclude the clergy have been repeatedly defeated in committee – a fact which his Lordship does not care to mention.' Gwynn went on to point out that far from the bishops being 'deprived of every chance of free election', they could be freely chosen to represent any one of several bodies. Any bishop had 'at least as good a chance as any other person'. He concluded in the same democratic, trenchant vein:

> Under the bill the degree of representation which the hierarchy and the clergy of the Catholic Church enjoy, must depend on the will of electors mainly laymen. Dr O'Dwyer is apparently not willing to accept this compact. I do not know how it will seem to Catholics, but to me it appears that Dr O'Dwyer would sooner refuse the bill than trust his own people.

PERSISTING IN OPPOSITION

At this stage, his Lordship of Limerick might be seen to have isolated himself from his colleagues once more in relation to education. Nevertheless, despite his criticism of the bill, he did not oppose the nomination to the senate of the new university of his secretary, Fr Andrew Murphy. The latter might be seen as his representative in recognition of his services to university education, but Murphy also merited nomination on his own contributions to education and as secretary to the Catholic Headmasters Association. Other clergy nominated to the senate on 24 April were Dr John Healy, archbishop of Tuam, William J. Walsh, archbishop of Dublin, Revd W. Delany, SJ, president of University College, and Monsignor Daniel Mannix, president of Maynooth. The following month, clergy and bishops gave further practical signs of their approval of the new measure. Delany and Mannix accepted nomination to the governing body of the Dublin college; a Revd M. Barrett and W.E. Meade, together with Bishop O'Callaghan, to the Cork college; and Archbishop Healy of Tuam, and Bishop Francis McCormick of Galway, along with five priests, to the Galway college.[71]

O'Dwyer's personal suspicion of Liberals, and especially of Birrell, was a factor influencing his stand, but it was further bolstered by the unpalatable fact that John Dillon supported the measure.[72] He refused to accept T.M. Healy's advice. This was 'a take it or leave it measure', Healy counselled. Real amendments would only be obtained by means of future bills. 'Let us', he said, 'get this little plant bedded out and trust to God for sunshine and rain in better years. Its appearance at all over ground is a miracle.'[73] How isolated Dwyer's position had become was indicated by the statement of the hierarchy at a special meeting on 16 June 1908, some six weeks before the final vote in parliament:

Having given our best and most anxious consideration to the Universities
Bill now before parliament, we are of opinion that in setting up of a new university in Belfast and another in Dublin, with constituent and affiliated
colleges, it has been constructed on a plan which is suited to the educational needs of the country and likely to lead to finality in the university
question.[74]

Having made this commitment, the bishops indirectly acknowledged the
relevance of O'Dwyer's objections by going on to express their regret at the
omissions and inadequacies in the measure that he had highlighted: that the
provisions of the bill were not in accordance with the religious convictions of
a Catholic nation, that headmasters of secondary schools were not represented
on governing bodies, that the Dublin College was not residential, and that
Maynooth was not recognised as a constituent college. Despite these failings,
they made it clear that they accepted the bill as the best that could be obtained.

O'Dwyer, however, remained adamant in his opposition. This, at least, is what
Birrell later indicated in his book, *Things Past Redress*, when referring to the
difficulties that his bill encountered up to the end:

> Yet these difficulties we got over, despite, perhaps in consequence of,
> the efforts of three or four Ulster members, and of the *more dangerous
> machinations in Rome of the late Catholic bishop, O'Dwyer*, who was honestly
> convinced that the Bill was a Nonconformist conspiracy to obtain control
> of the education of the Irish laity.[75]

He explained with unconscious irony, not knowing, perhaps, of O'Dwyer's other
bête noir, John Dillon:

> Mr John Dillon's brother, a Franciscan monk, held in high esteem in
> Rome, and indeed wherever he was known, was of great service in keeping
> the Vatican well informed both as to the actualities and potentialities of this
> theologically harmless measure. John Dillon himself, always a genuine
> enthusiast for secondary education in Ireland, was of immense assistance.[76]

That O'Dwyer had an almost obsessive suspicion of Liberals and Non-
conformists is well substantiated, but of his 'machinations in Rome' there appears
to be no evidence in the O'Riordan papers, where one would expect to find it,
but it is possible that he worked directly through friends in Propaganda. The
circumstantial nature of Birrell's recollection appears to indicate a factual
foundation. In the event, whatever efforts he may have made, the bill went
through and the National University, despite all the constraints, proved a success.
Fittingly, many years after O'Dwyer's death, his training college was to become
one of the university's recognised institutions.

POSTSCRIPT

Once the bill was passed, the bishop of Limerick appears to have accepted it as an accomplished fact, attending, perhaps, to T.M. Healy's advice to allow the little plant get 'bedded out'. The election of Archbishop Walsh as chancellor, by the members of the university, on 8 December 1908, may have encouraged him, as it did Cardinal Logue, a prelate equally suspicious of English government schemes, that even as the national schools, with their initial brand of slavery and proselytism, had been taken up by the people and made tolerable for the education of the young, so, too, 'under the guidance of the learned senate', they would 'be able to make the National University tolerable, and would, perhaps, improve it as they went along.'[77]

Edward Thomas O'Dwyer, indeed, came round sufficiently to accept an invitation to become 'permanent chairman' of the Limerick County University Scholarship Committee. Subsequently, he stoutly defended the County Councils' decision to confine the scholarships to the National University. Trinity was 'one of the richest colleges in the world' and did not need their help. The National University, although not a Catholic University, was a university in which there was 'nothing offensive to their faith' and which had but 'a scanty endowment'.[78] On another occasion, conferring the scholarships on two outstanding girl students, and commending women getting their share of the higher education now within reach, he urged the authorities of the National University to make suitable provision for its women students, who ought to have 'at least one university college in Ireland for themselves'. He pointed to the example of the separate colleges at Oxford and Cambridge. Then, emphasising a factor that influenced his desire for a Catholic University, he observed:

> I should wish to make a remark that, I think, becomes my office. It is that, important as it is for these scholars to advance in learning, yet for the true purpose of life, learning, however high, without conduct, and moral and religious principle, is simply a power of evil.

But he added significantly, 'The reports which we have received under this head so far are most satisfactory, and I trust that they will always continue so.' Nevertheless, his concern for country students facing the danger of great cities, led him to conclude his address with a regional plea. Those gaining the scholarships were quite free to go to any of the three colleges of the National University, but, he observed:

> I should wish to say a word on behalf of the University College Cork. It is a splendid institution; it belongs to our own province of Munster; our County Council is represented on its governing body, and a hostel for the residence of students is now being established under the patronage of the

bishops of Munster. These are great advantages, and parents may think them worth consideration when selecting a college to which to send their children.[79]

Edward Thomas O'Dwyer may have been side-lined in the final solution to the university question, but his eloquent participation over many years advanced his reputation as an educationalist in both Britain and Ireland, and the memory of his evidence before the Robertson Commission was to be remembered and celebrated as long as he lived. Besides, as just indicated, he continued to promote the value of university education to a new generation and encouraged them to take up the opportunities provided by their National University.

He was sixty-six years of age when the bill was passed in 1908, and intimations of mortality, as has been seen, had become more frequent as colleagues and close acquaintances passed away. For all that, like a juggler with a number of balls in the air at the same time, he continued to synchronise a range of diverse activities.

PART FIVE

Challenges in the new century, 1900–1917

18

A medley of events, 1900–1912: the bishop and temperance, the Jews, the Gaelic movement, Modernism, a silver jubilee, and other issues

Historical narratives tend to focus on happenings and events that caused a public stir. Too often the many-layered texture of ordinary life is neglected. Yet, not infrequently, it is the texture of ordinary life that sets the scene and forms opinion. Edward Thomas O'Dwyer's popularity as a priest and bishop came primarily from his feeling for the ordinary life of his people.

THE MANY-LAYERED LIMERICK SCENE

The population of Limerick city, in the late nineteenth and early twentieth century, found employment by the waterside, in the docks and the timber yards, and elsewhere in large stores and countless small shops, in numerous public houses, in trades and education, in the legal and medical professions, in a large clothing industry, in milling establishments and bakeries, and, above all, in bacon factories. The city, in the memory of one imaginative resident, was 'the city of pigs'. 'King pig ruled over this ancient city, providing employment for literally thousands of people, food for every table, and a symphony of tastes, sounds and aromas which gave Limerick something of the ambience of a bustling city of the East.'[1] Shaw's, Matterson's, O'Mara's, and Denny's factories provided the employment, and made the famous Limerick bacon and ham, which was exported to Britain and other countries and had a place on many Irish tables.

Presiding over the commercial side of the city was the Chamber of Commerce and the Port and Docks' Board, composed frequently of many of the same people. It was the Port and Docks Board that O'Dwyer had challenged as a curate in an effort to remedy the appalling housing conditions in the city. Ranged on the other side of commercial life was the Trades Council, which became increasingly influenced by an active trades union spirit in the early years of the twentieth century. It was indicative of the respect and standing in which the bishop was held at the beginning of the new century, that in 1902 the

Amalgamated Society of Pork Butchers brought to him the new rules governing their working hours for his advice and approval, and later asked him to devise a settlement for the Cork and Limerick pork butchers.[2] The same year he received a letter from Manchester, from the general secretary of the Amalgamated Society of Carpenters and Joiners, conveying the thanks of the executive council for his efforts in restoring peace and satisfactory relations between employers and employed in the Limerick area.[3] To the end of his life, his reputation for fair, firm dealing led to his being consulted on labour issues. As late as March 1917, he chaired a panel of arbitrators adjudicating on a claim by 'working painters' for an increase in wages.[4]

Beneath, and close to the centres of this commercial bustle, were shameful housing conditions. The houses in 'Irish town', near the bishop's cathedral, were 'filthy dens', according to the German traveller, Julius Rodenberg, writing of his 'Pilgrimage through Ireland' in the 1850s. They emitted 'the indescribable stench which the lowest misery is wont to produce'.[5] Fifty years later, in 1909, the future leader of the Irish Labour parliamentary party, Thomas Johnson, made similar comments at greater length. In many parts of the city he found houses huddled together in peculiar alleys and lanes, houses which were no more than 'kennels', in which workers lived and appeared content to live and even paid a weekly or monthly sum of money for the privilege of living there. What appalled Johnson was that, 'while scores of men, women and children every year suffered preventable disease and death, and while the causes of this were apparent to the simplest, no fuss was made about it'. 'High rates, water, gas, the Irish language, the mayor's trip to Belfast, these topics monopolised public interest.' Merchants, professional men, clergy, artisans, labourers, even tender-hearted women – all seemed too familiar with the sights that appalled him – 'a stranger from another world' – to feel any indignation.[6]

The extent of the problem, its long continuance, seemed to paralyse the city officials. Too readily, the government was blamed, and Home Rule made the panacea. Increasingly, however, towards the close of the nineteenth century, reformers sought to get at the causes of the poverty and degradation, and to overcome apathy and instil a spirit of self-help. O'Dwyer, from the beginning of his life as a priest, was one of those who followed that path. Like many others, including Labour leaders such as James Larkin and James Connolly, he considered the abuse of alcohol to be one of the main causes of poverty and of stunted families; an abuse that was fostered by the practice of paying workers in public houses and by the rounds system. Reform was made difficult, not only by the problems presented by custom and human frailty, but also by the political lobby of the publicans, which exercised considerable influence on the Irish Parliamentary party.

O'DWYER AND THE DRINK PROBLEM

From early in his time as bishop, O'Dwyer had tried to limit the availability of alcohol. On 14 March 1890, a meeting of the magistrates was held at Limerick city courthouse to hear a statement from him on the licensing system of the city. Availing of statistical detail, he pointed to an English city with a population of 120,000 people, which had 300 public houses, and compared this to Limerick which had about the same number of public houses for a population of under 40,000. Following discussion, the magistrates resolved 'not to grant any future new licences until the old ones shall lapse, and to continue until the total number is reduced to one hundred and fifty'.[7] Eight years later, at the same courthouse, the bishop was asked to take the chair at a meeting concerned with the issue of temperance and Sunday closing. He recalled that twenty years previously, he was one of those interested in the temperance movement who was chosen to put the case for the closing of public houses on Sunday. He hardly expected a hearing, but the meeting listened and an almost unanimous vote was passed in favour of Sunday closing. 'In that year, 1878, Sunday closing became law, complete closing in the counties, partial closing in five exempted cities.' Twenty years later, no one could deny the benefit to the county. No longer were men lingering in pubs after Mass on Sunday, drinking and then quarrelling and fighting. 'All that is changed. The people go home after Mass, and the sobriety of Sunday has told, and is telling, on the whole tenor of their lives.' In his visitation of the parishes in his diocese, O'Dwyer declared, he had found that in many parishes habitual drunkards were now unknown.

Although the cause of sobriety had made notable progress in the county, the improvement was not so evident in the city. In an urban population, he observed, 'the problem was complicated by a variety of conditions of work, of dwellings, of social habits, and other such things, and one does not find it so easy to form an opinion upon any one remedy'. In his view, however, the most practical solution was 'the regulation and restriction of the trade'.[8]

That did not prevent him making use of another course of action: one of powerful social effectiveness in a city of churches, where male religious observance was high, and where, besides, there was an arch-confraternity, drawn from all classes and embracing several thousand men. The bishop used the pulpit of his own church, and encouraged the Redemptorists to preach to the confraternity, on the abuses of alcohol and other vices that undermined social and moral responsibility and behaviour. In addition, he marked the new century by a pastoral letter that reminded his people that 1900 was a Holy Year, a time for reform and renewal, for prayer, penance, and piety, and then asked compellingly: 'Can nothing be done to abate, if we might not hope to abolish, the sin of drunkenness amongst us?' Despite all our churches, confraternities and piety, 'this vice thrives and flourishes like some prolific weed before our eyes, and baffles all our efforts to extirpate it'.[9]

The depth of his concern can be gauged from a number of his extant addresses to men on their dignity and duties as fathers of families. The addresses reflect his abhorrence of the abuse of drink, but also his desire to create a sense of self-worth, a spirit of self-help, and an ambition to break out of poverty and apathy and raise the standard of living for the men and their families. The same motivation was present in much of his advocacy of primary and intermediate education.

The worst means of beggaring a workman's family is drink, O'Dwyer argued. 'You know a drunkard's house the minute you are inside the door. It is comfortless, and more, it is degraded. The children are squalid, hungry, miserable, starved in soul and body.' But many men, who were far from being drunkards, he went on, 'still waste a great deal of their wages on drink, and, for the sake of it, deprive their families of many of the advantages of life'. He spoke it would seem, from personal experience:

> Take a working man who earns 16 or 17 shillings a week, with a wife, and say four children to support. How much can he afford to spend in the public houses? Suppose he takes two or three pints of porter in the day, see what a hole that, together with tobacco, makes in his income. At the very least something between 8 pence and a shilling a day. None of you workingmen can afford to waste so much, and, if you do waste it in this way you have to take it out of the food or clothing or housing of your families.

'Many of you live in wretched houses', he bluntly pointed out. 'Some of the lanes in this parish are a disgrace to civilization, and the children who are reared in them can never reach the standard that God intended for them. Foul surroundings lower the people that live in them. But why do you live in such houses? Simply because you cannot, at least you have not been able hitherto, to pay for better.'

In another sermon on a similar theme, O'Dwyer warned of another social evil. Betting, he declared, was like drink in that 'it creates a craving for itself. A drunkard, the more he drinks the thirstier he becomes. He never has enough. The passion is insatiable. So it is with betting. It creates a craving for itself,' and was likely to lead not only to poverty but also to theft and gaol. How far all this was from what a good father should be, he exclaimed, from the example a father should give his sons. 'As his boys grow up, a man ought to be a friend and companion to his sons; he should rule them more by influence than authority, and whatever he seems to give up in this way he wins back tenfold in affection and confidence.' A man was bound to see that his sons went to school regularly, avoided bad company, and attended to their religious duties; and in Limerick, the bishop concluded optimistically, 'any man may do all this with very little trouble'. 'If he sees that his sons join the Boys' Confraternity, and attend its meetings regularly, he will not need to do much more. Everything else will follow in due course. And if a man is a faithful member of the confraternity himself, when the time comes his son will be proud to go with him.'[10]

COPING WITH DESTITUTION

Not content, however, with preaching, and restrictions on the trade, O'Dwyer had taken a number of practical steps to cope with destitution and its effects. As curate he had set up the Limerick Labourers' Dwellings Co. Ltd, with share-holders, directors, and a secretary, to provide a certain number of houses,[11] and he had established the Temperance Club, with its extensive premises for library and relaxation, as a place for young people to frequent. He kept in close touch with these foundations as bishop. His efforts for the most destitute of all, the inmates of the workhouses, have been noted. Among them, and among a wide section of the poorer population, he endeavoured to grapple with one of the direst effects of penury and squalor, namely tuberculosis. In September 1906, he was recorded as contributing £2,500 towards the erection of a sanatorium, and arranging with a friend, Mr O'Brien, of Southill, Limerick, father of Kate O'Brien, to contribute a further £1,000.[12] Such involvement was supplemented, as has been seen, by his on-going promotion of education for poorer children, including those in orphanages, and his strong support of the Redemptorists' Holy Family Confraternity, which by 1903 had about 6,000 members. The numbers were so large that the Confraternity met in three separate divisions, each on its own night of the week. Its members were drawn from all sections of the community, but they came in the main from the working class and the lower middle class.

On 22 November 1903, the golden jubilee of the Redemptorists in Limerick was celebrated. The bishop, the city corporation, and the general population joined in praise of the work of the Fathers, especially in their great con-fraternity.[13] Yet, two months later the cycle of penury and apathy experienced by many of the city's labouring classes was to lead, through the agency of an over-zealous director of the confraternity, to adverse publicity and embarrassment for the corporation, and the Redemptorists, and Bishop O'Dwyer. The occasion was the sermons of Fr John Creagh, in January 1904, on the exploitation of the poorer section of the population by usurious Jewish traders.

THE JEWISH BOYCOTT

Fr Creagh, who took over as director of the confraternity at the age of thirty-two, in 1902, was the first Limerick-born priest to hold the office. An athletic, cheerful man, he was a powerful demagogic, revivalist style of preacher, who spared no one. The congregation relished his preaching and filled the church. Dealing with the abuse of alcohol, he had assailed certain publicans as being without conscience and living for 'blood money'. In 1904 he turned his skills against the Jewish traders in the city. It appears that he had been approached by shopkeepers, who complained of the competition to their trade from Jewish pedlars.[14] On 11 January 1904, Creagh proclaimed that it was madness for a people to allow an evil to grow in their midst that would eventually cause them ruin. 'They were allowing themselves to become the slaves of Jew usurers'. They knew who the Jews were. They crucified Jesus Christ. They had cried, 'His blood be upon us and upon our children', and that curse came upon them. 'Nowadays', he continued, 'they dare not kidnap and slay children, but they will not hesitate to expose them to a longer and even more cruel martyrdom by taking the clothes off their backs and the bit out of their mouths.' The Jews had come to Limerick in a miserable condition, now they were wealthy at the expense of the poor. They went about as pedlars from door to door 'pretending to offer articles at very cheap prices'. They forced themselves and their goods upon people by treachery, and when their customers were unable to make the weekly repayments, they brought them before the courts. The mayor's sergeants were forced to become collectors of money for them. The bailiffs were put in, and the little property was 'seized and sold by the rapacious Jews'. Claiming that he had an authentic document containing the list of the summonses issued by Jews during the past two years, he stated: 'In 1902 some 337 summonses were issued for £303. 1. 1d. In 1903, 226 summonses for £172. 11. 4d.' 'If so many people had to be sued for money week after week', he continued, 'and for sums under £1. 16. 8d, how many people, must we conclude, are constantly dealing with them.' It was a terrible state of things. Moreover, they made Limerick their headquarters from which they 'spread their rapacious nets over the country all round'.

And moving on to religion, Creagh did not hesitate to assert that there were 'no greater enemies of the Catholic Church than the Jews'; he implied that they were involved in the ritual murder of Christian children in earlier centuries, and more recently they conspired with the Freemasons in France in turning out of the country all the nuns and religious orders. 'The Redemptorist Fathers to the number of two hundred had been turned out of France, and this is what the Jews would do in this country if they were allowed into power.'[15] Creagh advised his congregation to have no commercial dealings with the Jewish pedlars. If they had any transactions with them they should get out of them as soon as possible, and then keep away from them. His message, probably repeated on the next two nights of confraternity meetings, was interpreted as a call for a boycott, and to some rowdier elements as an excuse for violence.

Most of the Jews lived in Colooney Street, near the Redemptorist church, and on the night of 11 January, as large numbers passed by after the sermon, the residents were subjected to jeers and threats of violence. The following day, the local Jewish minister, Rabbi Elias Bere Levin, wrote to Michael Davitt that the priest's allegations were 'devoid of any particle of truth', that previously the Jews had lived in perfect harmony with their Catholic neighbours, and that he left it to Davitt to conclude whether the anti-Semitic outbursts had their roots in religious prejudice or had been promoted by local traders. He sought Davitt's intervention to prevent a general boycott of Jewish traders, and to forestall an anti-Semitic riot. Already, he said, 'several of us have been insulted, assaulted, and threatened with the most menacing language'.[16] Levin also wrote to Irish political leaders and to Jewish organisations in England asking for their public support.

Davitt responded quickly. In the *Freeman's Journal* of 16 January he protested as an Irishman and a Catholic 'against the spirit of barbarous malignity being introduced into Ireland, under the pretended form of a material regard for the welfare of our workers'. He challenged Creagh on the allegation of ritual killing. There was not an atom of truth in this insinuation of ritual murder, Davitt insisted. 'The dissemination of this falsehood had led in past times to the slaughter of tens of thousands of innocent lives throughout Europe.' He concluded by expressing his confidence in the city of Limerick, and by praising Bishop O'Dwyer, with whom he urged the rabbi to seek a meeting. Limerick, he observed, had 'a bishop of splendid intellectual powers, who is a great churchman, whatever faults some of us occasionally find with him in relation to other questions'. A mind as clear as that of Bishop O'Dwyer, he added, 'will not allow the fair name of Catholic Ireland to be sullied through an anti-Jewish crusade, under his spiritual jurisdiction, to the injury and shame of a city of which every Irishman is historically proud'.[17]

Davitt was attacked in the letters columns of the *Limerick Echo* and the *Munster News*, but was defended in the London *Times*, on 23 January 1904. Fr Creagh, for his part, responded at the meeting of the arch-confraternity on Monday 18 January. His sermon attracted international notice. He was greeted with loud applause from the congregation. He deprecated any violence towards the Jews, and denied that he had insinuated ritual murder. He then went on, however, to make a number of other charges, quoting for evidence various historical sources. Thus, referring to 'one of the greatest historians of the Catholic Church – one who could not relate a falsehood – the Abbé Rohrbacher', he quoted alleged passages from the Talmud, which stated that God gave permission to the Jews to appropriate to themselves the goods of Christians as often as they could, and ordered them to look on Christians as brutes, and to 'strive by every means to kill the Christians'. After these and other criticisms, in the cause of Limerick's poor, Creagh urged his listeners to investigate for themselves, and if they found what he had said of the Jews' commercial dealings to be true, then he appealed to them not to prove false to their country and false to their religion by continuing to deal with the Jews. If they 'are allowed to go on as they have been doing', he declared, 'in a short time we will be their absolute slaves, and slavery to them is worse than the slavery to which Cromwell condemned the poor Irish who were shipped to the Barbados'. Brazenly, he concluded:

> Now leave the Jews alone. Remember I warn you to do them no bodily harm. Such a thing I could never approve of. It would not be Christian-like. But keep away from them, and let them go to whatever country they came from, and not add to the evils of our state. Let Mr Davitt write what he pleases. We know our own business here, and let this self-constituted advocate of the Jews injure his country by nurturing such an evil state of things.[18]

Not surprisingly, that evening there were anti-Semitic outbreaks in the city and a number of summonses were issued by the police. The following day, Rabbi Levin, and another prominent member of the Jewish community, waited on

Bishop O'Dwyer. They were received by the bishop's secretary, Fr Andrew Murphy. There is no extant record of what took place. The only evidence in the Limerick diocesan archives is a brief reference, in response to a long letter from the chief rabbi of London, Herman Adler. The latter enclosed correspondence from 1889 between himself and Cardinal Manning, which dealt with the type of 'literary resurrection ... of medieval prejudice' that Fr Creagh largely relied on. Adler pointed out that Manning, and a number of the popes, had condemned such allegations regarding ritual murder; and with respect to Rohrbacker, whom Creagh had described as 'one of the greatest historians of the Catholic Church', Adler explained that he had been assured by the learned English historian, Abbot Dr Gasquet, that Rohrbacker was not regarded by the Church as a trustworthy authority. He concluded with a request that Bishop O'Dwyer would 'deem it fit to direct Mr Creagh not to continue that agitation which has already caused such deplorable mischief'.[19]

O'Dwyer's reply, sent through his secretary, and almost illegible in its extant form, was brief, and without reference to 'Mr Creagh'. 'I am directed by the Bishop', it ran,

> to acknowledge receipt of your letter of 29th inst. and to inform you in reply that a deputation of the Jews in Limerick waited on me nearly two weeks ago, and expressed themselves fully satisfied with the answers (?) which I gave to them on behalf of the Bishop.[20]

The meeting with Fr Murphy, together with a response from John Redmond, assured Levin that, at least, no major public figure, no national politician or bishop, endorsed Creagh's anti-Semitic assault. The *Limerick Leader, Munster News*, and *Limerick Echo*, however, and also Arthur Griffith's *United Irishman*, expressed criticism of Jewish trading, praised Creagh, and supported the boycott; while the English press condemned Limerick's intolerance and racism.

O'Dwyer found himself in a difficult situation. He was concerned for the poor of the city, and the evidence of extortion on the part of Jewish traders and money-lenders seemed strong. Moreover, he had a deep respect for the Redemptorists and a warm regard for the confraternity. On the other hand, he was opposed to violence and boycotting, and probably resented such criticism of the Catholic religion being provoked by a Limerick priest. Creagh, however, was a member of an international religious order and that made the question of disciplining him awkward for a local bishop, especially when, apart from his strong local support, he appears to have had the support of a former consultor general of the Redemptorist congregation, Fr John Magnier, and of the provincial, Fr Boylan. The province journal of the Redemptorists related that both 'were with Fr Creagh in his attacks on the Jews, and consequently Fr Creagh continued his campaign ...'[21] The same source observed that 'Bishop O'Dwyer was certainly not defending the Jews, but he was offended because he was not asked beforehand about the sermons attacking the Jews'. It was further recorded that the bishop 'gave up coming to the house. He also declared that he would not come to the General Communion of the Holy Family'. This was an event that took place in the autumn at the conclusion of the annual retreat for the members of the arch-confraternity, an event which Dr O'Dwyer had always liked to attend. Thus, he appears to have exercised his displeasure by a boycott of his own from January until the autumn. The rebuke was evident, and all the sharper for his previous close links with the Redemptorist community.

A further indication of the bishop's disapproval of Creagh's approach was the attitude of the priests in his personal parishes of St John's and St Michael's. Rabbi Levin had sought constant police protection for the Jewish community in all parts of the city. The police, encouraged by the lord lieutenant and from London, cooperated fully. A key figure in the endeavour to prevent molestation was District Inspector C.H. O'Hara. In his report to Dublin Castle, on 18 January, he remarked that he had a meeting that day with Fr J. Cregan, administrator of St Michael's parish, his curate, Fr John Lee, and the priests of the neighbouring St John's parish. He was pleased to find that Cregan and Lee were hostile to Fr Creagh's actions.

> Both these gentlemen exercise a very large influence here and *they dis-approve of Fr Creagh's attack entirely*, and I gather from them that the latter – who is not one of the parochial clergy but belongs to the Redemptorist order, which has a church here – was not authorised by anyone to speak as he did.[22]

He also reported that Cregan and Lee would advise 'their people not to interfere with or molest the Jews and *I think after a while that the excitement will subside*'.[23]

The priests' attitude had to reflect that of their bishop, but that, and his quiet reprimand of the Redemptorists, were the only responses he made. The boycott of the Jewish traders continued, and their position was not improved by a public statement by the Church of Ireland bishop of Limerick, Dr Thomas Bunbury, at the general synod, in Dublin. The statement was highly critical of Fr Creagh and vigorously defended the Limerick Jews.[24] The synod passed a motion drawing 'the attention of his Majesty's government and all Protestant members of parliament to the persecution of Protestants and Jews in Ireland'.[25]

The views of the bishop and the synod were not welcomed in Limerick. The bishop 'had given offence locally', District Inspector O'Hara explained to his superiors, as it was considered 'that he interfered gratuitously in a matter not concerning him and that he relied on statements made to him by the Rabbi without investigating their accuracy'.[26] The members of Limerick corporation were outraged. They assembled in a special meeting on 20 April to forward a plea to the Lord Lieutenant to release a young 15-year-old, John Raleigh, who had been given a one-month prison sentence for throwing a stone that struck a Jew. But, having expressed their views on this, they went on to convey their concern at the criticism of the city by the Church of Ireland bishop. The mayor,

Michael Donnelly, pointed out that Limerick had never been as free of crime as at present, and that the bishop's comments were based entirely on the views of one side. Others pointed out the inaccuracy of a number of his lordship's statements.[27] The meeting asserted its opposition to violence, but expressed concern at Jewish trading practices, and some members wanted the traders out of the city. One of the most eloquent contributors, Thomas Donnellan, made this very clear. He observed that Dr Bunbury indulged in excessive hyperbole because of his information coming 'from a contaminated source, from those immediately concerned – the Jews themselves'. 'As far as the question of the Jews in Limerick went', Donnellan insisted,

> There is one point which we should consider, and that is usurious trading by Jews, which our people, and we, as citizens of Limerick, ought to and will resent (hear, hear). They are living in this city as a colony amongst themselves, trading and dealing amongst themselves, and we have our own people walking the streets in thousands, and going to America to seek a livelihood, and Jews come in here and make a living, and I hold they ought not be encouraged (hear, hear)

'Statements have been made', he added, 'as to the religious portion of the subject, and a Rev. Gentleman we all respect – Fr Creagh – has been dragged into it. I believe Fr Creagh's action was not prompted by religion, but merely from a commercial standpoint, and for the well being of the poor. I emphasise that these people should not be permitted to trade as they are, and I hope we have heard the last of the matter.'[28]

They had not heard 'the last of the matter'. The boycott continued. The Jewish board of deputies in London wrote to Dublin Castle urging that Fr Creagh be prosecuted. The lord lieutenant refused, stating that there was not sufficient evidence to justify instituting legal proceedings. A letter in the *Irish Times* on 1 April, by the director of the Irish Mission to Jews, claimed 'no Jew or Jewess could walk along the streets of Limerick without being insulted or assaulted'.[29] This contrasted with the report of O'Hara, which described Creagh as 'a very excitable man' but stated that there was 'no religious censure', nor was there a 'general boycott of the Jews'. What was operating was a rejection of the weekly payment scheme, and he added that, in time, the Jews' trade would return, as 'the poorer classes cannot pay ready money in shops'.[30] Next, the duke of Norfolk made his concern felt with a request to Cardinal Michael Logue to put an end to the boycott,[31] and David Alexander, president of the London-based board of deputies, also wrote to the cardinal asking him to intervene. In addition, he wrote to O'Dwyer, enclosing a copy of his letter to Logue.[32] Logue replied to Alexander in sympathetic terms, but pointed out that 'he had no jurisdiction to interfere in Limerick except by way of friendly suggestion'. He was expecting to meet O'Dwyer within a few days and would bring Alexander's communication to the bishop's attention.

In July, Rabbi Levin availed of the visit to Ireland of the Redemptorists' superior-general, Fr Mathias Raus, to address a letter to him. His people, Levin said, 'only twenty-four families', were being deprived 'from earning the bare necessities of life' because the Catholic people, who were their customers, would no longer deal with them, under the mistaken idea that they were forbidden by their religion to do so. He, therefore, asked his excellency to address such remarks on this subject to his people, during his stay in Limerick, 'as will remove from them the idea that we are under the ban of the Church, and will give them to understand that there is no objection from any religious grounds to them dealing with any honest trader, whether Christian or Jew'.[33]

There is no indication that Fr Raus met with, or responded to Rabbi Levin. He did meet, however, with Bishop O'Dwyer. Shortly after his arrival in Limerick, on 22 July 1904, he had a long talk with his lordship at the palace, Corbally.[34] Inevitably, their conversation turned on the Holy Family Confraternity, Fr Creagh and the Jews. It is not clear what was the outcome, but subsequent developments suggest that some arrangements were arrived at. The *Limerick Leader* reported on 24 August 1904 that Fr Collier, formerly of Dundalk, had been appointed sub-director of the arch-confraternity. That same autumn, Creagh opened a bank, a shop, and the Workmen's' Industrial Association in order to supply the 'poorer classes with clothing etc. on the instalment paying system'. The goods were supplied at ordinary retail prices, provided security was given for the weekly payments.[35] In the autumn, also, Bishop O'Dwyer indicated his readiness to be present for the General Communion on the Feast of the Holy Trinity.[36]

Fr Creagh continued as director of the arch-confraternity for another two years. His sermons and policy had been actively supported by members of the confraternity, and had been endorsed by a trades union group, meeting in the Mechanics' Institute on 20 January 1904. The same group condemned Michael Davitt for interfering in the affair.[37] All Creagh's supporters, however, followed his lead in condemning violence against the Jews, and in stating that their motivation was only against those Jews who were involved in ruinous trading to the detriment of workers and the poorer sections of the people. During the following two years Creagh directed his attacks against the abuse of alcohol, evil literature, and obscenity in the theatre. O'Dwyer welcomed these campaigns as he was concerned not only about alcohol but about evil literature[38] and about certain English productions in Limerick theatres. In November 1905 he issued a letter, which was careful to praise the role of theatre in society but went on to urge the Catholic men of Limerick to stay away from the 'abominable stuff' that came from England. He had directly in mind, it appears, a particular production in a Limerick theatre.[39] Creagh's eloquence enrolled the powerful influence of the confraternity and ensured the success of the campaigns. Early in 1906 he was assigned to the Redemptorists' new mission in the Philippines. It was in no way a demotion. The local press paid tribute to his campaign against the usury of the Jews, and to his foundation of the Workmen's Industrial Association to keep the poor 'independent of Jewish usurers'.[40] At his last meeting with the arch-confraternity, large numbers sought to shake his hand and the members, at his request, sang with vigour the rallying hymn of the confraternity – 'Confraternity Men to the Fight'. On 12 May 1906, he was seen off by a large crowd at Limerick station.[41]

By comparison, the departure of significant numbers of Jews from Limerick happened quietly from 1905. Approximately 81 people left the city, but there was not the wholesale exodus sometimes suggested. Indeed, some new Jewish families appear to have come to the city, as the census of 1911 indicated that there were 119 Jews in the city and three in the county. It is also seldom noted that there were sharp divisions in the Jewish community. This was signified by the opening of a second synagogue in 1901, well before the boycott, by a section of the Jewish community, who did not wish to associate themselves 'with money-lenders' and claimed that in doing so they were following 'the full wishes of our Chief Rabbi, Dr Adler'. It would appear that Rabbi Levin ministered to the other synagogue. In the event, he left Limerick in 1911 and went to Leeds, where he served until his death in 1936.[42]

The departure of the Jews was not universally welcomed in the city. People who lived in Colooney Street and Wolfe Tone Street valued many of them as good neighbours, and resented the violence used against them, but they had no effective voice. The climate of opinion and feeling that had been created made disagreement difficult. The one public voice that would probably have been heard, and which had frequently been raised on unpopular issues, remained silent. Bishop O'Dwyer, as mentioned previously, found himself in a conflicting situation. He abhorred injustice, boycotting and violence, but it is likely that he gave credit to many of the charges of usury against the Jewish traders, and to the detrimental effect the traders were said to have on the poorer sections of the population. He also, presumably, shared to some degree the common European prejudice against the Jews. Moreover, he could scarcely come out in public criticism of the popular director of the arch-confraternity of 6,000 men without causing upheaval in the diocese, and without appearing to be siding with the British press, and subsequently with the Church of Ireland bishop; and, besides, interference with the workings of an international religious order was likely to cause problems in Rome. In the circumstances, he quietly took steps behind the scenes to alleviate the situation, and otherwise, like the city corporation, insisted that the issue was a commercial, not a religious one.

Their experience remained in Jewish memory as the 'Limerick pogrom'; and the hurt and grievance was to be resurrected once more some fifty years on, when the persecution of the Jews in Nazi Europe had evoked universal sympathy for them. And once again, the issue became one of embarrassment for Limerick's corporation, clergy and people.

A LIVELY TOWN AND A NEW SPIRIT

The texture of life in the city, in the first decade or so of the twentieth century, had, nevertheless, its lighter side. There was a tradition of song and music, and all classes attended the opera house to hear visiting opera companies, including that of their own fellow citizen, Joseph O' Mara, the internationally known tenor. Concerts and bands were a feature of life. 'It was a gay town … when the troops were in', Kate O'Brien recalled. 'At least, that was one aspect of gaiety that Limerick wore, up to 1914. It was a garrison town, and did not deny itself the glitter and spangle of such.'[43] The officers rode to hounds and frequented social occasions and dances; the soldiers formed part of the military bands, which gave rise to local bands; and both soldiers and officers participated in the city's rugby teams, which, almost uniquely, embraced all classes, and served, in consequence, as vehicles for the ferocity and passion that became the hallmark of Munster rugby. But there was another beneficent factor. Tom Johnson, the future leader of the Irish Labour party, noted in 1909 that topics other than the city's dreadful housing conditions 'monopolised public interest'.[44] One of the topics was the 'Irish language', and it, at first sight perhaps unexpectedly, helped improve social and personal conditions.

The bishop of Killaloe, Dr Michael Fogarty, opening the Clare Feis in Ennis, on 7 July 1906, commented enthusiastically that the 'Gaelic movement' had exercised a powerful influence for good.

> It had broken the backbone of the great domestic enemy – intemperance. It had put a new spirit into the young men and women, making them self-reliant, self-respecting, and sober. It had taught them where to look for their happiness and showed them how to find it in their own land. It was gradually laying the foundations of a prosperous, happy, and united Irish Ireland.[45]

The bishop of Limerick had a similarly high esteem for the Gaelic movement, and had, besides, an important instrument for spreading its influence, namely, the Mary Immaculate Teacher Training College.

DR O'DWYER AND THE GAELIC MOVEMENT

The prelude
Edward Thomas O'Dwyer grew up in an era when the Young Ireland movement was reviving interest in Irish history, and exalting its patriotic figures in poetry and ballad. In his student years at Maynooth, there were classes in the Irish language, and a prize for the best essay in Irish. In the 1880s this appreciation of things Irish took a major step forward. One of the main agencies was University College, St Stephen's Green, Dublin, which had among its staff a number of men interested in Irish history and archaeology, in Irish and Anglo-Irish literature, and in the Irish language. A key figure was the scholarly Jesuit, Edmund Hogan, professor of the Irish language and of Irish history. He was a ready source of information for others. Among those who wrote to him for

guidance and advice, regarding ancient manuscripts or Irish derivations or in regard to the cause of the Irish martyrs, were William J. Walsh and Edward Thomas O'Dwyer. Hogan taught John (Eoin) MacNeill, and subsequently brought him on to the staff of the college. MacNeill was to be co-founder of the powerful popular movement known as the Gaelic League, which sought the promotion of all things Irish, but, above all, of the Irish language.

Linked to this assertion of national identity was a growing emphasis on de-anglicisation. Significantly, the movement for a concerted restoration of the language was mooted in a lecture entitled – 'The Necessity for De-Anglicising the Irish Nation', given in 1892. Of significance, too, the lecturer was Douglas Hyde, a Protestant. The following year, the Gaelic League was founded by Hyde and MacNeill, and soon attracted people from all religious and political persuasions throughout Ireland. During the expanding years of the movement, which reached its zenith around 1913, its popularity and influence were linked as much, or more, to its assertion of de-anglicisation as to a love of the Irish language and readiness to learn and speak it. It was a way of asserting 'We are not English', and many, especially among the clergy, claimed that the revival of the language as the spoken language of the country, and the revival of Gaelic traditions, and of native music and games, would bring about, as Bishop Fogarty indicated, an uplift in self-respect and in moral standards, the abandonment of intemperance, and of the materialist and secular values attributed to British influence. Much of O'Dwyer's adult life was spent in this ambience of revival and national assertiveness, and as a bishop he responded positively to it.

Promoter of things Gaelic
The Irish language was taught in his Limerick teacher training college from the beginning, at his desire.[46] In the college's second year, 1902–3, O'Dwyer brought a young Protestant girl to visit the college and encouraged her to offer a prize for Irish step dancing. She and the bishop were present at the first competition in July 1903. The young woman was the Honourable Mary Spring-Rice, daughter of the second Lord Monteagle, whose wife, Elizabeth Butcher, was a sister of the Henry Butcher, professor of Greek at Edinburgh University, who had been a prominent member of the Robertson Commission (1901–3). O'Dwyer, as remarked earlier, was friendly with the Monteagles, and from shortly after his elevation as bishop he used to call on them, in the course of his visitations, at their imposing house, Mount Trenchard, overlooking the river Shannon some thirty miles from Limerick.[47]

Mary Spring-Rice, born in 1890, became interested in the entire Irish-Ireland movement early in her life. She learned the language, promoted music and dance, and subsequently supported Home Rule, and then the Irish Volunteers. She was one of the crew of five on board the yacht, *Asgard*, which landed arms from Germany in Howth, Co. Dublin, in July 1914. Because he knew of her interest as a young girl in Gaelic and national matters, O'Dwyer introduced her to his special creation, the training college. His enthusiasm for the language also led to it being included in the subjects for the final examination of the second year students, in 1903; and it was among the languages orally examined at the end of the session 1903–4.[48] He also encouraged the development of the Irish language at intermediate and primary level. At prize giving at Laurel Hill, coming up to Christmas 1901, having listened to recitations in French and German, he expressed the hope 'that at the next distribution of prizes they would have recitations in Irish'. He would be glad, he said, to see all the schools in the diocese doing their part to further the revival of the language, and he concluded:

> In their schools the children ought to be taught the language of their own country, and then if the next generation are not Irish enough or patriotic enough to maintain and extend what was being done for them now, that would be their fault, as we had done our duty (hear, hear).[49]

Here, there was an implied doubt about the continuance of the contemporary zeal for the revival. He had little confidence in his people's capacity to persist after early enthusiasm. Nevertheless, at the same venue six years later he expressed his delight at the great progress which the language was making, and felt 'safe in saying that the future of the Irish language was assured'.[50] Soon, however, there were ominous signs of a clash between the educational interests of the official Catholic Church and the more militant wing of the Gaelic League.

Tension between churchmen and the Gaelic League
The League had pressed strongly for the introduction of Irish at primary, secondary (intermediate), and then university level. In 1900, Irish was approved as a subject for the Intermediate examinations. The next stage was to press for Irish as a compulsory or essential subject for matriculation to the new National University. Once it became a requirement for entry to the university, Irish would become a required subject at secondary, and increasingly at primary level. The argument was clear, and it was pushed with an evangelical intensity by the compelling oratory of Douglas Hyde, and the persistent efforts of John MacNeill and others. To oppose it, was to be branded unpatriotic. In its zeal, members of the League, and its organ, *An Claideamh Soluis* (The Sword of Light), expressed criticism of the church and the government and the National Board of Education as causes for the earlier decline of the language. Priests, moreover, were denounced who would not preach in Irish. Cardinal Logue, an Irish speaker, and a number of the bishops, considered the League's publication to be 'most anti-clerical'.[51] Increasingly, those who disagreed with Irish being a compulsory subject in the new university were accused of being 'West-British' and anti-Irish. William Delany, who had done much for the Irish language and Irish history at University College, found himself so treated. The climate was such that Archbishop Walsh, before his election as chancellor of the new university, made it clear to Dr Hyde and Professor Mac Neill that he had been alienated by 'the shocking vulgar abuse in which a number of them (Gaelic

Leaguers) seem to revel and the utterly irrelevant arguments they bring forward'. He discerned, he declared, 'a determined, and to judge by some of the language used, a vicious attempt to intimidate and terrorise'.[52]

The O'Hickey case

The bishops themselves came under fire from within their own college. The professor of Irish at Maynooth, Fr Michael O'Hickey, was vehement in his support of the language and in his criticism of those he considered its opponents. In public letters he termed such opponents 'West-Britons', or not genuinely Irish, and in a lecture to his students in Maynooth, on 13 December 1908, he dismissed four of the Catholic churchmen on the senate of the National University, one of whom was the president of Maynooth, Dr Daniel Mannix, as no friends of an Irish Ireland. He resorted, moreover, to intimidation against those who ventured to disagree with his position:

> The treachery of those who show themselves false to Ireland at this juncture must never be forgotten … A black list of the recreant Nationalist senators must be preserved, that in after times all men may know who were the false and the vile.[53]

In addition, he published a pamphlet, *The Irish Bishops and the Irish University* (Dublin 1909), which assailed the hierarchy in unmeasured language. At their June meeting, 1909, the bishops as trustees of Maynooth, called on O'Hickey to withdraw certain of his remarks on pain of loss of his professorship. He refused, was removed from his post, and spent the remaining years of his life in fruitless appeals to Rome.

In 1916, O'Dwyer was called to play a part. The chair of Irish became vacant at University College Cork. Professor Walter MacDonald, who acted as friend and adviser to O'Hickey, thought a way out of the imbroglio might be found by having O'Hickey appointed to Cork. To have a chance of being appointed, the bishops of the province would need to refrain from opposition. MacDonald wrote to O'Dwyer, from whom, he said, he had personally experienced more sympathy than from other bishops, to use his influence with his fellow prelates in support of O'Hickey. O'Dwyer responded, not without compassion, but with his customary directness:

> I must say that as things stand between Dr O'Hickey and the Bishops, I cannot interfere, and unless he puts himself right with them, I doubt very much if the Governing Body of Cork College will elect him.

'My idea', he counselled, 'is that even now Dr O'Hickey ought to offer an apology to the Bishops, not for his appeal to Rome – for that was within his right – but for the language which led to his removal from his chair.' He had not his exact words before him, O'Dwyer stated, but he remembered that when he read them he thought them 'wild and unmeasured'. He would be only too glad of a chance to help him, but O'Hickey would have to withdraw from the position he had taken up before the hierarchy. 'After all, for a priest there is no humility or indignity in a manly and humble submission to ecclesiastical authority'. When he appeared before the bishops, O'Dwyer recalled, he had thought 'his attitude unworthy of a gentleman and a priest'.[54]

MacDonald responded with an argument in support of O'Hickey and forwarded O'Hickey's 'incriminating passages in his public utterances'. O'Dwyer was impressed by MacDonald's argument, but the impression was cancelled when he read the enclosed document. The worst of O'Hickey's language was in addresses to the students in the college at a time of seething insubordination among them. In O'Dwyer's view, the bishops, in their obligation to the students – to train them in habits of obedience, humility, and respect for authority– were left with no option. O'Hickey's excessive language indicated that he was not a fit man to train ecclesiastics.[55]

MacDonald considered O'Dwyer's concern about O'Hickey's language somewhat bizarre, given his own record of strong language against opponents, language lacking at times the courtesy of 'a priest and gentleman', let alone a bishop. And, writing some years later, he asked:

> Why should other bishops, after dismissing Dr O'Hickey for using language unworthy of a priest, eulogise Dr O'Dwyer as if his pronouncements were worthy not only of a priest and gentleman, but of a Father of the Church.[56]

Challenging the Gaelic League's policy

The popular enthusiasm for the Gaelic League, and the pressure put on the county councils, brought the latter out in favour of essential Irish, and as the university depended on the county council scholarships, the senate felt obliged to yield. The League's use of abuse and of intimidatory pressure to secure its objectives, O'Dwyer considered not only unjustified, but unwise, and, in some respects, hypocritical. Many of those shouting loudest had far less genuine interest in the Irish language than many of those who were being branded 'West British'; and the leaders of the organisation moreover, were leading the movement along unwise paths from the point of view of Irish becoming a living language. He made his views clear in February 1914, when he refused to attend a public meeting in Limerick at which Douglas Hyde, president of the Gaelic League, was scheduled to speak. His letter was read to the large gathering, and was answered vigorously by Hyde to the delight of the crowd. The bishop's letter, however, was an important document for the organisation and the language, but, sadly, was ignored.

He recognised, he said, the importance of the movement for the preservation of the language in certain parts of the country and its revival in others, but he doubted the efficiency of the methods being employed for these purposes. The great obstacle to the progress of the language was the *vis inertiae* of the great mass of the people. His teachers told him that the main problem they experienced in teaching the language was 'the indifference or hostility to it in the children's homes'. In that condition of things, it seemed to him that the principal duty of the Gaelic League should be to influence public opinion, and to convince the parents of the advantage to their children of learning the language of their country. Instead of that, the most of their energies were directed to brow-beating the National Education Board and other public bodies charged with the care of education, and denouncing them for regulating their policy by the views and wishes of the parents of the children rather than by the dictation of the Gaelic League. Not content with that, the bishop added, some of the leaders of the movement had made it plain that regardless of the religious interests that are involved, and of the official position of the clergy in the schools, their real objective was the complete overthrow of the national system of education. 'With all respect', O'Dwyer concluded,

> I submit that they have no right to use the Gaelic League for such a purpose, *ne sutor ultra crepidam* (Let the cobbler stick to his last). But if they will go outside their own proper sphere to interfere with interests higher than their own, they must not be surprised if people doubt their singleness of purpose.[57]

Douglas Hyde responded that the 'precious National Board' was hostile to Irish in the past and was still so, and that Dr O'Dwyer's gloomy view about the apathy of the people was out of touch with the reality. The other speakers virtually ignored the bishop's intervention. The *Limerick Leader*, of 2 February 1914, devoted an editorial to the meeting without referring to Dr O'Dwyer. Instead, it praised the successes of the League, declared that the fact that people did not throw their hats in the air did not mean that they were opposed to the Irish language, and continued the attack on the National Board, which it accused of adopting 'an outrageously absurd, antiquated, and un-Irish attitude towards the National Language,' and observed that 'the Gaelic League, and all interested in the country's progress, would be fully justified in bringing about its complete abolition.' The Gaelic League had achieved an ascendancy that rendered criticism 'absurd and antiquated'. The bishop of Limerick's views were no longer significant. He was, it seemed, a man of the past. His criticism of the League's actions, however, did not prevent him continuing to support the use and development of the Irish language.

Peadar O'Laoghaire
Apart from his promotion of the language movement through the schools in his diocese and by means of the training college, which had an influence extending beyond Munster, he also made a contribution of a very different kind. He was friend and supporter of the Irish scholar and author, Fr Peter O'Leary, more

generally known as 'an tAthair Peadar O'Laoghaire', celebrated for numerous published works in Irish. Among these were his novel *Seadhna*, his autobiography *Mo Sceál Féin*, and especially his translation of the Bible into Irish. From letters between him and O'Dwyer, it is clear that, in his view, O'Dwyer, who had been a classmate in Maynooth, was instrumental in persuading him to undertake the monumental work of translation. On 25 September 1916, he mentioned that he expected 'to have the Old Testament translated … before Christmas'. When he began, he had been 'rather heavy-hearted', but now that he found himself approaching the end he felt in great spirits. He added: 'I am exceedingly glad now that your lordship urged me to undertake the work'.[58] He also confided to O'Dwyer his problems with the Gaelic League and others, and O'Dwyer helped financially towards publication and with encouragement. In his final letter to the bishop, on 22 November 1916, following the completion of his work, he observed once again:

> I have to thank your lordship most sincerely for having urged me to do it. I feel that it was God that made you do it. I certainly would not have undertaken the work but for your lordship. It frightened me. It is done now and I am glad, very glad.[59]

The probing intellectual
Walter MacDonald's interchange of letters with O'Dwyer concerning O'Hickey, was occasioned by the bond that had grown up between them as a result of correspondence over years on theological and philosophical matters. This probing, intellectual aspect of O'Dwyer's life deserves consideration. It was very much part of his *persona* as a churchman, and added to his reputation among intellectual Catholics in Britain and Ireland, as well as in Rome. This was very much the case in the first decade of the twentieth century, when new developments in the physical sciences and in historical and scriptural studies led to a questioning of old ways that seemed at variance with the official teaching of the Catholic Church. Some of the proponents of the new views came to be known as Modernists, and some among them sought to bolster their position by attributing to celebrated dead theologians views supportive of their own. One name used in this way was that of Cardinal John Henry Newman. When the pope condemned Modernism in 1907, O'Dwyer stepped into the breach with a short book in defence of Newman's orthodoxy. It met with wide acclaim.

O'Dwyer, Walter MacDonald, John Henry Newman, and Modernism
Walter MacDonald was one of the most controversial and creative of Irish theologians in the final years of the nineteenth century and the first quarter of the next. He sought, expressly, to enlarge the borders of theological science.[60] A book of his on 'Motion' was proscribed by the Sacred Congregation of the Index in 1899, and nearly cost him his professorship at Maynooth.[61] On 26 October 1899 he wrote to O'Dwyer:

> When one has been trying to hold a position alone, against the opinion of
> everyone around him, it is very encouraging to get a kind word. And I
> assure your lordship I am very grateful, indeed, for the friendly interest you
> have taken in me and my opinions.

'Thank you', he concluded, for the 'kindness shown me both by your letter and
always'.[62]

The following month he sent O'Dwyer a copy of the document he had sent
to Rome, and also the 'animadversions' from Propaganda, which he considered
'a very disgraceful document'.[63] O'Dwyer replied in a manner that was encouraging and, perhaps, in sympathy with MacDonald's views. The latter responded,
in turn: 'Thanks for your kind letter, which has been burned and consigned to
oblivion, except in so far as I shall be always grateful for the encouragement it
gave me.'[64]

In 1905, MacDonald, after much questioning, received permission from the
Irish hierarchy to launch the *Irish Theological Quarterly*. Before long, some of his
articles were being questioned in Rome, and by Cardinal Logue and some other
Irish prelates. Those singled out were on – 'The Proof of Infallibility', 'Idolatry',
and 'The Ethical Aspects of Boycotting'. MacDonald withdrew from the
Quarterly, and desisted almost entirely from writing.[65] O'Dwyer's enquiring,
penetrating mind, however, ensured that their correspondence continued. On
6 June 1905, MacDonald responded to O'Dwyer's request that he be 'fully open
as to a brother priest' on the issue of changes in the Church's doctrine. He did
not hold with the views of those who argued that the Church, being guided by
the Holy Spirit, could never make mistakes in doctrine. Conscious of the
developments in historical method and knowledge, he gave it as his view

> that, from a very early period in her history, the Church has been making
> herself free of errors that had become traditional, although her teaching all
> along was under the special protection of the H. Ghost. Doctrinal devel-
> opment was thus not merely drawing conclusions which were not known
> previously, it was also getting rid of doctrines which had been in vogue.

Applying this to the Church's teaching on the 'historical inerrancy of Scripture',
he observed that, at most, it was but 'provisional teaching' that 'may be proved
erroneous'.[66] With a similar freedom, which says much for O'Dwyer, the
Maynooth professor boldly explained his challenging of the traditional teaching
of Scholasticism because of new developments in physics.[67]

In 1911, they exchanged letters on the accurate translation into English of the
Biblical text,[68] and, on 16 October, MacDonald self-consciously hoped that he
was not boring his lordship, adding: 'It is pleasant to find one interested in such
things'.[69] The correspondence continued. In July 1915, O'Dwyer's queries were
on how MacDonald conceived 'the divine nature to be present in Christ and
the Eucharist';[70] and on 18 July, MacDonald thanked the bishop for his

invitation to stay in Kilkee, which he could not take up because of a prior arrangement, and then went on to discuss a further question from O'Dwyer, this time on bilocation.[71] In his two final years, O'Dwyer took to sending some of his sermons and addresses to MacDonald for comment, while also raising theological questions on their content. On 24 June 1917, the professor praised his sermon on 'The Seven Words' (spoken on the Cross) as 'beautiful and touching', and then dealt with his query on the continuance of 'the real presence' in the particles of the Eucharist. Two days previously, on receiving the manuscript, he had written: 'It will be a pleasure to read it; as it is to read whatever comes from your lordship's pen. It will do me good, too; as I need a spiritual lecture badly.' And he added a sentiment probably shared by O'Dwyer: 'How well for those who have the old simple faith!'[72]

O'Dwyer's papers contain a number of manuscripts of philosophical/ theological reflection that were not published. One on 'Natural Religion' lays emphasis on Newman's argument from conscience to the existence of God, and, despite the obscure handwriting, it is clear, almost limpid in its thought and expression. On 'Science and Philosophy' he treats of the agnostic philosophy, expounded by 'the most distinguished scientific men of our time', that had spread beyond questions of God and of morality and now questioned 'the objective reality of a material world outside of us'. Thus, he observed, 'Professors Huxley, Tyndal, Herbert Spencer, and almost all the leaders of thought in England, are agnostics in philosophy, however materialistic they are in science. In truth, they carry on a double life in their thought.' There are also notes of a liturgical-theological nature on Extreme Unction, which, in the practice of the time, related very much to a sacrament directed towards those in imminent danger of death rather than to a sacrament of the sick. In that context, the presentation is, once again, quite clear. He examines the various requirements for the reception of the sacrament, including degrees of illness. Consumption, not being immediately dangerous, did not qualify![73]

Widespread public recognition of O'Dwyer as a philosopher and theologian came, however, only after his defence of Cardinal Newman against the taint of Modernism. In the confusion of the time, many came under unjust suspicion. MacDonald was one of those. His articles in the *Irish Theological Quarterly* were viewed in Modernist terms. He conveyed the climate of mental confusion and suspicion in vigorous language in his *Reminiscences of a Maynooth Professor*, published in 1925.

> We were unfortunate in the time at which our project was commenced, as the Modernists not only lamed, but killed us. They aimed at progress, so did we; therefore we were Modernists. It was of no avail to disclaim Modernistic views: were not our whole aims Modernistic? ... Is it not a strange, sad thing, that I, who not only hate Modernism, but feel contempt for it, should be classed as a Modernist by so many, even high-placed ecclesiastics – as I know I am? The Modernists have set back the hands of

progress in the Church, dear knows how many years – far beyond my
time, I expect … Is it any wonder that I dislike them?

He added that he disliked them primarily for what they taught as well as for
what they had done. 'It was hypocritical and mean of Loisy and Tyrell to pretend
to remain within the Church.'[74]

Alfred Loisy (1857–1940), the leading exponent of Biblical Modernism,
especially with regard to the Gospels, stimulated discussion and raised questions
in O'Dwyer's mind. In 1903, however, he had five books placed on the Index,
and was excommunicated in 1908. He subsequently abandoned all Christian
belief. George Tyrell (1861–1909) was born in Dublin. He became a convert in
1879, jointed the English province of the Jesuits, wrote for the *Month*, and had
some of his writings censured by Rome. Thereafter, he wrote mostly under pseu-
donyms. On his refusal to retract some of his teaching, he was dismissed from the
Jesuits; and his public criticism of Pius X's condemnation of Modernism, 1907,
led to his excommunication. He died shortly afterwards at Storrington in England.
He and a number of other Modernists claimed Newman as a progenitor.

The encyclical Pascendi

On 8 September 1907 the papal encyclical *Pascendi Dominici Gregis* was issued. It
analysed the opinions held by Modernists in philosophy, theology, history,
criticism, and the reform of the Church, pronounced them dangerous from
every point of view, and declared that Modernism was the synthesis of all heresy,
and must logically lead to atheism.[75] To counteract Modernist propaganda,
scholastic philosophy and theology were to be taught in all seminaries,
Modernists were to be removed from all teaching positions in seminaries and
Catholic universities, a council of censors was to be established in each diocesan
curia for the revision of Catholic publications, and a vigilance council was to be
formed in each diocese to prevent the diffusion of Modern errors.[76] The
drawbridge was drawn up, and was to remain up for more than fifty years. To
many intellectual Catholics, including Wilfrid Ward, editor of the *Dublin Review*,
there was concern that the encyclical appeared to deny the doctrine of the
development of doctrine, preached by Newman, and to condemn the cardinal's
view as to the value of conscience as a proof of God's existence.[77] Tyrell, indeed,
'declared in the *Times* that the encyclical condemned Cardinal Newman'.[78] It
was necessary, therefore, to present and explain the encyclical in such a manner
as to make it clear that Newman, despite appearances, was not criticised by the
papal document. O'Dwyer offered to undertake this in an article in the *Dublin
Review*. Ward agreed, was impressed by the completed article, but required the
removal of the first eight pages, which he considered too harsh, not sufficiently
sensitive to the difficulties that some well intentioned Catholics and non-
Catholics had with the encyclical. O'Dwyer refused, and told Ward that it was
his duty 'to feel with the Church' and not water-down its teaching. To which
Ward replied vigorously:

> In your letters I see an identification of the duty of 'feeling with the
> Church' with a duty of agreement with the immediate policy of Rome,
> which would on occasion reduce a good Catholic's attitude to absurdity
> or dishonesty. Dupanloup was an Inopportunist to the end of his life, yet
> who that knew him would call him disloyal?
>
> This kind of bullying principle (I do not speak of your words to me but
> of your view of the case) is, I think, an extreme as alien to the great
> Catholic mind as intellectualism is.[79]

In a letter in December 1907, O'Dwyer had the grace 'to apologise for the form
of my last post-card, which was discourteous, and no matter under what
provocation, unjustifiable'. He then went on, however, to criticise Ward for not
allowing him, a bishop, in a Catholic review, to range himself 'unreservedly on
the side of the Pope'. He intended, he made clear, to publish the manuscript as
a pamphlet.[80] He modified it somewhat in the direction Ward had wished, and
concluded the work on 21 December 1907. It was published the following
month under the title *Cardinal Newman and the Encyclical Pascendi Dominici Gregis*
(London 1908).

The pamphlet juxtaposed the teaching of the Modernists and that of
Newman in some detail. In the course of his analysis, O'Dwyer pointed out
with respect to Newman's theory on the development of doctrine and to his
argument to God's existence from conscience, that they were entirely different
from Modernist teaching. Where the argument to God's existence was concerned, the Humanists, as presented in the encyclical, believed that human reason
could not pass beyond phenomena to a knowledge of God, whereas for Newman
God was the object of human science, his existence could be reasoned from the
existing universe, as well as from the voice of conscience. The development of
doctrine was also something very different as taught by Newman from what was
condemned by *Pascendi Dominici Gregis*. Development in the condemned
Modernist position was a natural process, an evolutionary process, without any
question of revelation or of a deposit of faith, whereas Newman started from a
deposit of faith, based on revelation, and envisaged a development in the
understanding of the content of the deposit of faith in the light of different
situations and advances in knowledge over the years, and that this was part of
God's plan.[81] Overall, O'Dwyer collated the views upheld by Newman in a
series of nine propositions, every one of them directly opposed to the statements
of the Modernists condemned in the encyclical.

The pamphlet received a warm welcome. The *Freeman*, on 1 February 1908,
noted the author's intimate and remarkable familiarity with Newman's
'voluminous writings', and celebrated 'the masterly exposition of the great
questions dealt with in the essay, and the triumphant and unanswerable vindication of Newman, and through Newman, of the Holy Father and the
Encyclical'. The *Cork Examiner*, in praising the work was taken by O'Dwyer's
personal assertion:

I have read the Encyclical again and again, and during all my life long I have been a student of Newman's writing, and in my opinion, given of course, under correction, there is not a page of them, written after his conversion, which is not conceived in the full spirit of this great Encyclical.[82]

In Rome, Monsignor O'Riordan had the work translated into Italian and presented to the pope.[83] Beyond all O'Dwyer's expectations, there came a letter of approval and congratulations from Pius X. Dated 10 March 1908, it assured him:

> We would have you know that we emphatically approve of your pamphlet, in which you show that the writings of Cardinal Newman, so far from being at variance with our Encyclical Letter *Pascendi*, are, in fact, entirely in conformity with it. You could not have rendered a better service to the truth and to human dignity.

Then, after commenting on those who proclaimed themselves Catholics but placed the authority of a private thinker before that of the teaching of the Apostolic See, the pope congratulated O'Dwyer on exposing 'their contumacy as well as the fallacy of their arguments', and added:

> It is well known that in the full light of day in England he (Cardinal Newman) constantly upheld the cause of the Catholic Faith by his writings, so that his services have proved most salutary for his fellow countrymen and were most highly esteemed by Our predecessors. Thus he was deemed worthy to be named Cardinal by Leo XIII, undoubtedly an acute judge of men and affairs, whose close friendship he retained ...
>
> Wherefore we congratulate you for having, through your great knowledge of all his writings, so splendidly vindicated the memory of this good and learned man, and for having done all in your power to ensure that among your countrymen, and especially among the English, those who have abused the name of Newman shall no longer deceive the unwary ...

In conclusion, the pontiff 'lovingly imparted' his apostolic blessing.[84]

Such praise coming from the pope himself was the greatest honour in O'Dwyer's eyes, and he must have dearly regretted that his sister Annie had not lived to share it. The papal letter was noted in newspapers and Catholic journals in Ireland and Britain. In England it was received with much relief. On 23 March, Fr William Barry, a respected theologian and author of a 'Literary Life of Newman', conveyed the views of many in a letter to the bishop of Limerick. 'Though personally unknown to your lordship', he began, 'may I venture to offer, as I do, most hearty thanks and congratulations for the service you have rendered to all English-speaking Catholics, and to the Church at large, first by your vindication of Cardinal Newman, and then by drawing forth from the Holy See that admirable letter which puts an end to controversy.' He was proud as an Irishman that it fell 'to the lot of an Irish bishop to scatter the last vestiges of a cloud from the memory of one who deserved well of our country ... Your act, my dear Lord, at length pays a debt which Ireland owed to the founder of the Catholic University.'[85]

O'Dwyer received numerous messages of congratulation, not least from fellow bishops. He was conscious, however, that he owed much to the diplomacy of Monsignor Michael O'Riordan, and he acknowledged it on 21 March 1908. He had received 'a grand letter from the Pope', he informed O'Riordan on that date, and he had sent it, with a translation, to the newspapers. He went on:

> Apart from my own personal feelings, which are those of considerable elation, the letter is sure to do immense good amongst the admirers and followers of Newman, and to be a sore blow to the Modernists and semi-Modernists of England.

'Its tone of calm strength and authority is splendid', O'Dwyer remarked with his customary reverence for the Holy See, 'and the quiet way in which it puts even Newman in his place as a simple but most loyal member of the Church will be a lesson to many in England.' He concluded:

> I have just sent a letter of thanks, through Cardinal Merry del Val, through whom the Pope's *autographed* letter was sent to me. But I know to whom I am indebted for this great honour.[86]

The following year, in keeping with O'Dwyer's new international standing, O'Riordan informed him that Dr Sheehan, rector of the Catholic University, Washington, would probably be approaching him to contribute an article on 'Infallibility' to the *Catholic Encyclopaedia*. He hoped O'Dwyer would undertake it.[87]

HAPPENINGS SAD AND OTHERWISE

The recognition and adulation came at a good time for O'Dwyer. In 1907 he had lost his sister Annie, his closest relative and friend, and he grieved deeply. Then in 1908 he found himself the sole episcopal voice opposing the National University Act, and in November of that year he shared the sorrow of the Sisters of Mercy and of the staff and children at the orphanage at Mount St Vincent, O'Connell Avenue, Limerick. Up to sixty children suffered from what the jury termed 'cholera nostra due to meat poisoning', and nine died over two days.[88] The city corporation and general populace rallied to the support of the nuns and children, and 'the jury returned a verdict at the inquest that exonerated all concerned'.[89] Once again, O'Dwyer was the recipient of many letters, this time of sympathy and commiseration. His compassion was called forth again in 1910, in connection with his friend, Monsignor O'Riordan. He had been hospitalised a number of times with haemorrhages. On 2 April the bishop hoped he was taking reasonable precautions against relapses,[90] and a year later he was pleased to hear that he was taking a break in London and urged him, while there, to see a specialist about his stomach.[91]

Meantime, as noted earlier, he had been concerned about the social and religious impact of periodicals and newpapers coming from England. In 1910 he determined to initiate concerted action against this literature which, he declared was 'at best … Protestant and bitterly anti-Catholic; at its worst … agnostic and impartial in its hostility to all religion.'[92] The *Irish Catholic Directory* noted on 22 October 1911 that a movement had been started, and was growing daily in vigour, 'to stop the circulation in Ireland of immoral English newspapers and other publications of an evil tendency'. 'Limerick is the first place', the account continued, 'where practical steps have been taken to combat the evil. Acting on the exhortations of the bishop and clergy, secular and regular, a number of citizens of Limerick have established a vigilance committee, under the chairmanship of Revd J. O'Connor, Adm. of St Michael's, to prevent the sale of English Sunday papers and immoral literature of any kind in the city.' Twenty-two newsagents pledged themselves to sell no paper which the committee found objectionable. The newsboys were also organised for the same purpose. The Redemptorist Fathers enlisted the powerful aid of the members of the Confraternity of the Holy Family in destroying the evil traffic. All were actively supported by the Gaelic League organisation in the city. 'Following the example of Limerick', the *Directory* added, 'other places throughout Ireland are establishing vigilance committees for the same purpose.'[93] On 11 November, Dr William Barry, who had spoken on the subject at the Mansion House in Dublin and who had previously written to O'Dwyer regarding his pamphlet on Newman, wrote from Leamington Spa to express his 'admiration for the prompt and effective measures taken by your flock in Limerick by way of checking the circulation of pernicious literature, and especially of Sunday newspapers, sent over from this country'. Vigilance committees were necessary, he insisted, if Ireland was 'not to be corrupted at the heart'.[94] A week later, the *Irish Catholic Directory* reported that 'the crusade' had extended to Dublin, Belfast, Cork, Donegal, Cavan, Waterford, Longford and other places.[95]

CARDINAL NEWMAN AGAIN

O'Dwyer had a further occasion to dwell on Cardinal Newman at the beginning of 1912. Wilfrid Ward had produced a biography of the cardinal. The bishop of Limerick was less than enthusiastic. While still reading it, he informed O'Riordan that it did not impress him very much. 'It seems rather a history than a biography, and is so crowded with persons, and minute details, that Newman's personality is not very distinct.' 'As a picture', it was not 'at all equal to Snead-

Cox's life of Vaughan.' The chapter on the Catholic University was taken 'almost bodily' from 'a long Ms. on the subject which Newman left'. 'Newman's visit to Dr Ryan (Bishop of Limerick) is ludicrous', O'Dwyer continued.

> The Bishop, after dinner made a speech, in which amid the vociferous cheers of the clergy, he announced he there made Newman a V.G. of the diocese, and then the clergy sang '98!![96]

A week later, having completed his reading, he remained critical. 'Newman's Life is not pleasant reading,' he observed. 'It goes to show him as always far-seeing in his devotion to the Church, and always thwarted by narrow and unenlightened ecclesiastics. Cardinal Cullen is dealt with unmercifully: Wiseman something better, the English bishops with scant respect.' 'Yet I fear', O'Dwyer declared,

> the net result will be to injure Newman's reputation, and exhibit in him an immense amount of sensitiveness, self-opinion, and an intolerance of control, or opposition, and often a very bad temper.

'Ward's own thesis,' he concluded, 'seems to be that science should be absolutely free to go its own way.' 'But this', he warned O'Riordan, 'is for yourself'.[97]

Before concluding this chapter on some of the many-layered aspects of O'Dwyer's city and of his ability and character, it is instructive to consider how his fellow prelates and many of his people viewed him as he attained the silver jubilee of his episcopate in 1911.

JUBILEE HONOURS

Knowing that his silver jubilee might be made a public occasion, O'Dwyer made it clear that he did not wish to have any celebrations. A priest from the parish of Rathkeale, Co. Limerick, writing to O'Riordan on 5 June 1911, reported the bishop's stance but, in passing, provided the kind of information seldom recorded. 'The Bishop had a very severe attack at Easter, the result, it seems, of *rigorous fasting* ... though it has left its marks upon him, yet he is regaining his old spirits. He is completely opposed to any public celebration of his jubilee: after much pressure he is accepting a chalice from (the) clergy but no address. The chalice is to be presented by one or two priests at most, and will be given back to the cathedral.'[98]

The bishop's opposition to any public recognition, and the disappointment of the people of Limerick, was reported three days later in the *Irish Catholic Directory*. It noted, nevertheless, that the corporation had paid a striking tribute to the bishop at a meeting held that day, 8 June. The mayor, claiming to speak for the citizens, noted that twenty-five years ago Dr O'Dwyer had moved from his post as curate to the 'very high and trying position' of bishop. How well he had filled the office, they all knew. He continued:

Every work for the advancement of Limerick and Ireland, educational and industrial, including the housing of workers, every work of charity, mercy, and temperance, had his powerful aid. Not only did he give his wisdom, he gave his money and his deep sympathy and help to the sick in hospital, the dying and their friends, and above all the religious life of the people in his care.

'They most lovingly congratulated Dr O'Dwyer on the attainment of his Silver Jubilee', the mayor concluded, and 'prayed that he would be spared for many years to rule over the diocese which he loved so well.'[99]

His lordship's efforts to avoid public display, did not prevent many others showing esteem. The four bishops who were his classmates in Maynooth marked the day of his jubilee, 29 June, by sending a gold chalice, individual letters, and an address, which they had published. The four were: John Healy, archbishop of Tuam, James Browne, bishop of Ferns, Robert Browne of Cloyne, and Joseph Hoare of Ardagh. They recalled that in Maynooth he 'gained the highest honours amongst the most distinguished rivals of a singularly brilliant class, and at the same time won the affection and esteem of all' by his 'kindly sympathies and manly straightforwardness'. 'Even then', the address continued expansively, 'we all predicted for your lordship a brilliant career in the Church; and now all know how amply verified have been those predictions. As a writer, a preacher, a scholar, and an administrator, your lordship has during the past twenty-five years rendered signal services not only to the diocese of Limerick, but to the whole church of Ireland. To your brilliant evidence before Lord Robertson's Commission was largely due the satisfactory settlement of the Irish University question. On that occasion your lordship expounded the authoritative views of the whole Irish church with singular power and eloquence; and on many other great occasions the same eloquent voice was heard and never passed unheeded by your countrymen.'[100]

Hyperbole tends to reign on such occasions. O'Dwyer was conscious of the inflated picture presented by his former fellow students, but he was moved by the goodwill it presented. At the same time, he learned from Dr Fogarty that the bishops of Munster wished to make a presentation to him but had to defer doing so as the gift was not ready. Feeling humbled by this expression of regard, O'Dwyer replied to Fogarty on 29 June 1911 thanking him for his 'most kind and brotherly letter' and adding:

> But why on earth, should the Bishops of the province go out of their way to do me an honour? It humiliates me to think of it. I like the personal congratulations of persons like yourself, but these public demonstrations make me ashamed, in my own heart and conscience before God.

He added that he had 'a heavy Confirmation' that day in St Michael's, 'some 450 all told'.[101]

The *Munster News*, meantime, had not spared his lordship's blushes. On 28 June, to mark the silver jubilee, the paper recounted the 'many monuments of his zeal and devotion to duty'. The founding of St Munchin's Diocesan College, and of St John's hospital, were the achievements of his earlier years. 'Next in order of time', came 'the opening of Leamy's school for the benefit of the classes for which it was originally intended.' The bishop's 'crowning educational achievement', however, 'was undoubtedly the founding of the Training College of Mary Immaculate'. In the educational struggle, he 'struck sledge-hammer blows for right and justice', and then there was 'his splendid evidence before the Robertson Commission'. Apart from education, his zeal for religion and temperance were indicated by the building of St Joseph's church and St Michael's temperance hall. 'His single aim in public life and in the administration of his diocese', the paper insisted, 'had been to show that a bishop must be first, last and all the time a churchman'. He combined the spiritual interests of his people with their temporal advancement and prosperity. He had at all times shown a deep interest in the workers of the diocese, and 'on several occasions trade disputes had been referred to him for settlement, with the happiest results'. He had shown himself, moreover, at all times, a good friend to the Arch-Confraternity of the Holy Family. Finally, it was remarked:

> For the poor he has on all occasions displayed a genuine affection, tinged with pity. This has been illustrated in many ways, amongst them being the nursing of the sick and the provision of decent dwellings for workers. Through the agency of St Vincent de Paul's Nursing Association a vast amount of good has been done for the humble dwellers in the city's laneways, and the founding of the Thomond Artisans Dwellings Company was another step in the direction of decency and cleanliness as contrasted with dirt and squalor.

In short, the account concluded, 'columns might be written on the many-sided activities of this faithful father of his flock who's Silver Jubilee occurs to-morrow'.[102]

The occasion was not one for criticism of failings, and past events tended to be exalted to meet the occasion, but the list of achievements, nevertheless, was impressive by any episcopal standards. There was nothing, however, about the bishop's spiritual life. A very public personage, he remained intensely private. One is forced to rely on crumbs collected from his sermons for some vague indication. Even the Munster bishops, when they eventually came to make their presentation in November, skirted this essential requirement for a churchman.

Bishop Fogarty informed O'Dwyer that the archbishop of Cashel and the other bishops of the province were coming to Limerick to call on him at his residence in Corbally, and he forwarded a copy of the address they had ready. On 27 November, O'Dwyer asked him 'to be merciful' and to make at least the few changes which he had made 'to bring it somewhat nearer to proportion'. He added: 'I suppose we must give it to the newspapers, and that is the reason why I should wish to tone it down a little. I had no expectation that so many of the bishops would come.'[103]

In the event, all the bishops came, and Thomas Fennelly, archbishop of Cashel, read the address. Having expressed the sentiments of esteem and affection that brought them to Corbally, the address stated – remarkably for a body of sober senior ecclesiastics: 'We feel that in your case we are celebrating the jubilee of a dear colleague who will live in history as one of the most brilliant Irishmen of his time'. It then went on to praise 'his eloquent and fearless proclamation of Catholic truth and defence of Catholic interests', especially in connection with the Department of Education, and to state that not only had the see of Limerick prospered under his apostolic care, the whole church in Ireland was indebted to him as a peerless champion of her rights. The bishops then became slightly more personal, while shying away from any reference to an inner life of prayer and devotion:

> To your Brother Bishops you have been an example by your blameless life, your high ideals, your fervid faith and tireless activities in the service of Christ to whose sacred cause you have surely dedicated the life long energies of your gifted mind.

They presented him with 'an Episcopal jug and basin' as a memorial of their devotion to his person, their admiration for his character, and their gratitude for the distinguished services he had rendered to the cause dearest to their hearts and his, 'the sacred cause of Jesus Christ'.[104]

O'Dwyer's response was grateful, but suitably modest and down to earth. He thanked them for their extraordinary kindness and for the 'unprecedented honour' of their coming as a body to manifest their empathy with him and their goodwill. He then went on:

> My Lord Archbishop, I have listened with a full heart to your Grace's eloquent and glowing words, and although it is perhaps foolish and vain to say so, I know that they have stirred in me some feelings of gratification and joy that my poor administration as Bishop, with all its failures and short-comings, should receive so high, and if I may say so, so authoritative an approbation.

'Yet, together with them', he said, 'I have heard another voice insistent and clear, speaking within my soul and conscience, and pronouncing a very different judgment on the episcopacy to which you have so generously referred. And I seem to hear yet another voice which, in solemn tones, warns me

> that after all it is a very small thing to be judged by one's fellows, or by man's day, for he that judgeth is the Lord, and which reminds me that these

25 years and all our other years, with their duties and responsibilities, will yet come for the supreme and final review before His tribunal.

Then, turning to a more comforting prospect, he concluded: 'Yet, in your Grace's words, even with all the exaggeration which your large heart allows them, there is a suggestion of a comfort and cheer which permits me to hope that the Great Judge of all, when He pronounces lastly on each deed, may perchance see in mine, by the power of His own grace, something on which to look with mercy and favour.'[105]

A week later, O'Dwyer received a letter from Bishop Thomas O'Dea of Galway, who seemed to identify himself with the Munster prelates and apologised for his absence at the presentation. He knew nothing about it, he explained, until he saw the announcement in the *Freeman*. 'Few, if any,' he continued, 'have a higher admiration for the Christian honesty (that has) been conspicuous in your career than I have. I single out these qualities because of their worth in comparison with the most brilliant in other orders.'[106]

What was most remarkable in the various jubilee tributes, was not just the acknowledgement of O'Dwyer's many achievements, and these were considerable, nor of his intellectual brilliance, but the fact that despite his tetchiness, impatience, and even hurtful words, he yet inspired affection in a way that his more elevated and equally brilliant colleague, Archbishop William Walsh, never did. His very failings, and what O'Dea termed his 'Christian honesty' – not always notably Christian, and his hearing difficulties, all rendered him 'human', one of the weak and wilful human family.

There was about the episcopal address a sense of life completed. O'Dwyer, after all, was seventy years of age, a good age in the early years of the twentieth century. His colleagues magniloquently and unrealistically projected that he would 'live in history as one of the most brilliant Irishmen of his time'. Neither they, nor O'Dwyer, could foresee that the reason he would 'live in history' was yet to come, nor that it would not be for intellectual brilliance but for interventions on the national political scene at a critical moment in the history of his country.

19

The bishop and nationalist politics at home and at Rome, 1900–1915

INTERLUDE

The opening of the new century was marked by many notable events, as observed earlier, but for O'Dwyer there was the particular significance that 1900 was a Holy Year, to be marked by many liturgical arrangements at home and by a visit to Rome, and there was the piquant fact that the split in the Irish Parliamentary party was healed – under a leader other than John Dillon. This last helped to modify for a time the bishop's attitude to the party.

The reunification of the Irish party, with John Redmond as leader, took place in January 1900, the bishop's pilgrimage to Rome in May. On 21 May, he wrote to Fr Andrew Murphy: 'Nothing could be more loving than the poor old pope's manner. I have blessings for all of you'.[1] His high standing at Rome was to continue throughout the pontificate of the next pope, Pius X, thanks to his public support for the papal document condemning Modernism and his defence of Newman, and into the reign of Benedict XV, because of his championing of the papal quest for peace during the world war. His credentials at the Vatican were promoted by the diplomacy of Monsignor Michael O'Riordan. Both men had much in common. Both were from the same city, both deplored the influence in Ireland of the English press, and the spread of secularist values, and, as a counter to anglicisation, both promoted the sense of Irish identity, and the revival of the Irish language and Irish culture. Like many of their contemporaries, they also tended to identify 'Irish' and 'Catholic'. From O'Riordan's appointment as rector of the Irish College Rome in 1905 until the bishop's death in 1917, and particularly from about 1909, their correspondence casts light on O'Dwyer's influence and on his views on politics at home and at Rome.

RELIGION AND THE QUEST FOR HOME RULE

It was the bishop of Limerick's proud boast that he kept apart from politics except where the interests of religion were involved. Education, as 'the handmaiden of religion', was included in those interests. He viewed political parties, by and large, in terms of their attitude to the Catholic Church's religious concerns. Where the Irish Parliamentary party was concerned, as has been seen, he favoured its support of Home Rule, but was critical of its departure from Parnell's policy of independence towards the two major English parties. By its alliance with the Liberal party, it had become subservient, in his view, to that party, and there was a danger that in the interests of a Home Rule that might never come Irish party leaders, such as T.P. O'Connor and John Dillon, would bow to secularist Liberal pressure and sacrifice the Church's control in education. Meanwhile, like the other bishops, he remained supportive of the parliamentary party as a means of representing the needs of Irish Catholics at Westminster.

With the reunification in 1900 there was a renewed focus on national interests. O'Dwyer's old enthusiasm was stirred. He allowed himself become involved in the general election, albeit moderately, in a manner must unusual for him. He was approached for support by two candidates in the Limerick area. One, F.E. Kennedy, a Catholic, was backed by unionists. He stated publicly that his policy in higher education was modelled on that formulated by Dr O'Dwyer in his article in the *Nineteenth Century* the previous year.[2] The other candidate, Alderman Michael Joyce, a nationalist, called on the bishop and apologised for an insult offered him in 1888, admitting publicly that he had acted 'through ignorance'. The bishop accepted his explanation, and wished him every success in the contest. He added that he shared Joyce's views on national policy, and was also pleased that he was standing for 'the labour element' in the city.[3] Joyce made full use of his lordship's approval to win the votes of the clergy and laity, and later admitted that the bishop's mark of favour had played a large part in his success.[4]

Apart from this episode, O'Dwyer refrained from giving any commitment to the party itself, or to William O'Brien's United Irish League, though he did not hinder any of his priests from supporting either movement.[5] He continued to criticise the party, however, for not doing enough for education. At the silver jubilee of the Catholic Literary Institute, in October 1900, he re-emphasised the party's obligation towards higher education, and commented on the uniform half-heartedness of some Irish politicians and on their readiness to abandon Catholic claims in exchange for Lloyd George's support for Home Rule. Certain members of the party were, in effect, 'mere creatures of the English Radicals'.[6] Again, with the secularist philosophy of the Liberals in mind, he insisted before the Royal Commission in 1901 that secularism was not the true way to educate young men, and that it could not be introduced without 'touching on religious issues'.[7] In this, he was voicing not only the sentiments of the Irish hierarchy, but those of his political mentor, Isaac Butt, for whom, it will be remembered, religious education was essential for a healthy and prosperous society.[8]

In January 1904, Archbishop Walsh bluntly informed John Redmond that the ineffectiveness of Irish politicians had almost driven him to abandon 'the little faith that he still had in the efficacy of parliamentary action as a means of getting redress of our grievances'.[9] O'Dwyer, by comparison, was compliant at that stage. He had reason to be beholden to Redmond for his support of the

Catholic training colleges.[10] Consequently, when requested early in 1905 to make a contribution to the party fund, he informed Alderman Joyce that he would do so with the greatest pleasure.

Characteristically, however, he also contributed his views on how the party should be performing. He supported it, he stated, because it provided the only means for achieving any measure of political freedom with any reasonable hope of success. It was rendering no small service by 'keeping the flag flying'. He then made it clear that as a Catholic bishop it was natural that the interests closest to his heart were those of religion. He was confident, he said diplomatically, that such interests were safe in the hands of the members of the Irish Parliamentary party. Regardless of who was in power at Westminster, he expected Irish members to 'press our claims … persistently and honestly'. Alluding to the alliance between the party and the Liberals, he expressed the hope that Irish politicians would never subordinate the interests of their religion to the political intrigues of the English Non-Conformists.[11]

Later that year, in a very different context, he extended practical advice to the new rector of the Irish College Rome. On 8 November, he counselled that the first thing O'Riordan had to do was to increase his numbers and reduce the pension at the Irish College. As matters stood, no one would choose Rome before Maynooth, which was cheaper and had the reputation of being 'the *ne plus ultra*[12] of ecclesiastical colleges'. He added that if O'Riordan had not yet had his audience with the pope, 'the enclosed cheque' would be 'a good introduction'. With it he was to assure the Holy Father of the homage of all his children in the Limerick diocese.[13]

In 1906, O'Dwyer produced one of his most powerful pastoral letters. It was largely a defence of denominational education against the encroachment of the state. He pointed to the adverse effect of state control in France and in the United States, and warned that the effort to 'de-Catholicise' Catholic primary schools in England was likely to carry over to Ireland before long, and had to be stoutly resisted. He maintained that Irish primary education, despite poor facilities, was second only to that of Germany, and that German education, too, was religious and denominational. Irish education at other levels was also doing well. In university education, the unendowed Catholic College at St Stephen's Green had beaten all three Queen's Colleges in fair competition, while in intermediate education 74 percent of all prizes were carried off by Catholic schools. There was, therefore, no case for state control of education, but there was a case for reform at several levels. Reform was necessary at commissioner level. And at school level, two basic things were required. First, an increase in teachers' salaries, especially in initial salaries, with shorter periods for earning increments; if this did not happen male teachers as a class might die out, as they had done in the United States. In the second place, a moderate annual sum was essential for the improvement of school buildings.

His rapprochement with the Irish party foundered on the issue of state control of education. The pastoral letter's warning about the effort to 'de-

Catholicise' primary schools in England was aimed at the Liberal government's attempt to modify the Education Act of 1902 and thereby weaken Catholic control in the primary schools in England. His attack on the government's policy in the pastoral and in newspapers,[14] and his subsequent savage reference to the 'canine servility' of John Dillon and the slavishness of the Irish party in supporting the government, were made, as noted earlier, without consulting the English hierarchy and, as a result, without knowing of Cardinal Bourne's arrangement with John Redmond.

O'Dwyer's resultant discomfiture was relished, as might be expected, by Dillon. On the day the bishop's attack was published he had, indeed, the political discernment to assure Redmond that an outburst 'in such an outrageous manner' was fortunate in that it would make the other bishops 'unwilling to follow such a lead'.[15] Writing to his friend, Fr David Fleming, OFM, on 17 December, he explained that if the Irish members had crossed the Liberals just then they would have 'assassinated the parliamentary movement for Irish freedom'. He felt it difficult, he continued, to keep patience with the bishop of Limerick, who, in utter ignorance of the facts, had rushed into print solely 'to blackguard and abuse his own countrymen'.[16] A fortnight later, he felt able to inform Fleming that O'Dwyer's assault on the party had done nothing but good.[17] The bishop's stance, however, had not been as impulsive and politically mindless as Dillon suggested. In a letter to O'Riordan in Rome he outlined the political objective directing his actions:

> Unless the Irish party made a strong fight, the English schools are lost, but with a good fight the Lords would throw out the Bill and force an election on it – a contingency that the Nonconformists will not like.[18]

In the event, as seen earlier, the Lords made so many amendments to the government's bill, that the Liberals withdrew the measure rather than face an election on the issue.

O'Dwyer remained outwardly unmoved by his embarrassing mistake, and unchanged in his judgment of the Liberal party and of the unwisdom of the Irish party in identifying with it.

Despite his criticism of the Irish party, and his fear of Liberal intrigue, the bishop of Limerick was conscious of the great improvements that had taken place in Ireland. Reviewing Fr John Begley's *The diocese of Limerick, ancient and medieval* (Dublin 1906), his lordship hailed what had been achieved already: religious equality in law, if not in administration; freedom of election secured through the ballot; the drastic reform of the Land Laws which effected a revolution in the condition of the agricultural population; the Labourers' Dwellings Acts which provided something of a home for working men in place of the squalid hovels of former times; and the placing of local government under popular control. These, he observed, were great and wonderful changes. 'If O'Connell, or even Isaac Butt, were to come back now he would hardly recognise the country as that of the down-trodden unlettered half-slaves for whose freedom he had striven.' Yet simultaneously with these reforms, there was not, he observed, a corresponding advance in intellectual activity and material prosperity. The incessant stream of emigration went on: the emigrants being squeezed out of the country by poverty, and by want of true patriotism. Up to the time of the Irish revival, indeed, the country was on the road of intellectual decay. For 'between the intellectual life in Ireland, and her political and material life, the connection is closer and more real than many people think'.

Early in the following year, he returned to his fears of government encroachment in education. In May he publicly condemned Birrell's Councils Bill, deeming its plans for a Department of Education in Ireland as a Liberal plot to bring secularism into the country.[19] Five months later he availed of the *Irish Educational Review* to criticise yet again the party's alliance with the Liberals, and to appeal to Redmond to capture 'the genuine tone and drift of the mind of the nation' during the tour of the country he was about to make.[20] The following summer he was the sole episcopal voice inveighing against the party for its support of the University of Ireland Act.[21]

In the autumn of 1908 he found further occasion for criticism. Again, Dillon provided the ammunition. The Eucharistic Congress was being held in London. The Eucharistic procession was cancelled at the intimation of the government. Resentment among Catholics was intense, and the bishop in the Newcastle area, where a by-election was in progress, called on Catholics to vote against the Liberal candidate. In the face of Catholic indignation, the Irish party instructed its supporters in the area to do likewise. The Liberals lost the seat. John Dillon, to mollify the government, declared that Asquith had not forbidden the procession, but only suggested to Archbishop Bourne that it would not be wise to go through with it. As a result, he drew upon himself the hostile comments of many Catholics. Among his critics was the Limerick Board of Guardians. This last provided O'Dwyer with an opportunity to launch a righteously bitter assault. He thanked the Board for expressing displeasure at Dillon's action in defending the English prime minister, and then went on to accuse Dillon, along with some other members of the parliamentary party, of interfering in matters of religion. 'For the sake of his Liberal friends he had sunk so low as to befoul the sanctuary.' In the light of such an action, it was no wonder, he maintained, that Home Rule, in the hands of the Irish party, was 'steadily sinking into the grave'. He warned both Dillon and T.P. O'Connor that though the movement for self-government would manage to survive in some form, those who bartered it away for the Liberal alliance would eventually suffer total eclipse. Asquith, he continued, had no difficulty in 'squaring' the two or three political 'bosses' who were leading the Irish cause. As a result, he had managed to put the entire Irish party in his pocket. Irish political life had never descended so low. O'Dwyer concluded his exaggerated denunciation with a slighting reference to a recent lecture by Dillon on Home Rule, which he had given at a Nonconformist meeting house in London. That a leader of the Irish people should go as 'part time curate to a Nonconformist parson' was the last straw.[22]

When Dillon replied to O'Dwyer's charges three days later, he confined his remarks to explaining that he had given the London lecture at the request of a Nonconformist minister. He did not respond to the other issues raised by the bishop.[23]

By 1909, the party leaders were out of favour with at least four of the more prominent prelates in the Irish hierarchy.[24] Archbishop Walsh, as noted, had been critical for a number of years. Dillon, although aware of the situation, yet claimed in October 1909 that the general body of the Church was more solid behind the party 'than at any period that I can remember'.[25] O'Dwyer, while becoming increasingly alienated from the Irish party, remained, as a nationalist, seriously committed to Home Rule, all the more so because of the 'secularist drift in England'.[26] In his pastoral letter for 1910 he laid emphasis again on the danger of close links between English politicians and 'our Catholic members of parliament'. They must inevitably prove harmful to the interests of religion and nationality. The growing anglicisation disturbed him and O'Riordan. The latter, who thought the pastoral among the best O'Dwyer had written,[27] was struck during his visit to Ireland that summer by the impact of the death of king Edward VII and the coronation of his successor, George V. On 24 June he commented with a self-deprecatory but strong national feeling, which, it would appear, corresponded to that of his bishop: 'The portentous epidemic of loyalty' that had recently 'swept over the country', he observed, was likely to evoke 'an epidemic of hill-siding very soon as an anti-dote, and to show that we are rebels still; and when we have shown ourselves as rebel-loyalists we appear in our real national character – consistently inconsistent'. 'For myself', he added,

> I think I prove my loyalty quite enough when I have obeyed the laws. To wear crape, to shed tears and wear a long face for the loss of the old king, or to throw up my hat in the air for the coming of the new king, is an *exuberance* of loyalty, an enthusiasm which I do not think I owe to England, and which I shall never show etc. We owe England thanks for nothing we have received. All the rights which have been restored have been victories won; they are not *gifts*, nor even rights freely yielded.[28]

In the autumn, when John Redmond, Joseph Devlin and John Dillon attended a Home Rule demonstration in Limerick, none of the clergy appeared on the platform with them.[29] Yet, before the year was out, after Redmond and his party forced the government to agree to bring about the capitulation of the main obstacle to Home Rule, the House of Lords, the bishop publicly praised the party. He informed his audience at prize giving in Laurel Hill school, just before Christmas, 1910, that Ireland was on the threshold of great political changes that would place her destiny in the hands of her own children, and that the Irish party had made an important contribution over the years and possessed 'a good many capable men' anxious to serve their country in parliament to the best of their ability![30]

O'Dwyer's change of heart and language was strengthened by Redmond's declaration on Home Rule some weeks later. The Irish party, he proclaimed, was standing where Parnell stood, and Parnell had stood where Isaac Butt had stood before him.[31] The bishop's favourable opinion of Redmond just then found expression in a letter to Bishop Fogarty, whom he thanked for the help he had received from him and Redmond in obtaining a remittance from the government of the outstanding debt on the Limerick Training College. Redmond, he observed, must have brought 'great pressure to bear on Nonconformists like Lloyd George and Birrell, to whom it must have been like swallowing a horse-ball to admit such a claim'.[32] When, later in the year, Fogarty issued a condemnation of all secret societies, O'Dwyer advised him to seek the support of Redmond and of the other Irish leaders.[33]

The bishop of Limerick was still favourably disposed to Redmond and his party, as the debates on the Home Rule Bill got under way in 1912. The prospect of Home Rule, however, had accentuated certain demands that he considered harmful to society.

THE ISSUE OF WOMEN'S SUFFRAGE

In his Lenten pastoral for that year, which was centred on marriage and education, he devoted attention to the agitation 'to draw women into the turmoil of politics'. He made it clear that was not referring to women in administration and in works of a charitable nature, but to 'their claim to get the parliamentary suffrage and to vote, and … to act equally with men in parliamentary elections'. It was well, he counselled, to weigh the consequences 'of so profound a change in our social conditions'. Most women did not seek it. Yet, it could become law. He specified the grounds of his objection.

> The objection to giving votes to women is not that they would exercise the franchise with less judgment or honesty than men. In intelligence, in conscientiousness, in genuine desire for public good, they are not inferior to men. That is not the objection. But it is the total change it would work in their whole domestic and social position. From the peace of their homes they would be drawn into the angry and often squalid strife of political parties. Now they stand outside all such contentions.

O'Dwyer's own experience of politics, with its jockeying for power, its 'squalid strife' and corruption, made him desire to keep it apart from the home. It would not be possible if the woman of the house were actively involved.

His pastoral met with a response that did credit to the women's movement. At this stage there were branches of three women's organisations in Limerick:

the Irish Women's Suffrage and Local Government Association, the Munster Women's Franchise League, and the Irish Women's Franchise League. The last named was founded by Hanna Sheehy-Skeffington, whose uncle, Fr Eugene Sheehy, was one of O'Dwyer's more militant priests, and by Margaret Cousins. In a letter to the Irish Times, Cousins observed that 'the whole of Dr O'Dwyer's diatribe against votes for women' was 'based upon misrepresentation not facts'. She was concerned for women who did not have men to represent them, 'widows and women who have to work for a living'. The bishop was also wrong in stating that there was no demand for the vote. 'The two most representative bodies in his diocese, the Limerick County Council and the Limerick cor-poration', had 'passed resolutions in favour of women's suffrage', and in Limerick city there were three strong and active branches of suffrage societies. 'Belief in the justice and common sense of votes for women had been expressed similarly all over Ireland', and they were cheered by hearing from the Bishop that the movement was so near to victory. 'If politics are so bad and corrupt as the Bishop thinks them', the letter concluded, 'then the sooner the women who have public welfare at heart get an entry to them and start spring cleaning the better.'[34]

O'Dwyer was encouraged, however, by O'Riordan's approval. The latter announced on 23 February that he was having the pastoral read in the college refectory. He feared, nevertheless, that it would not succeed in its purpose. 'We ape whatever we see in England' and the suffrage movement 'is the latest we have borrowed'.[35]

STANDING BY REDMOND

Also during that month, Dr Fogarty encouraged his Limerick colleague to come out formally in support of the party. On 26 February 1912, O'Dwyer gently declined, pointing out that it would mean a departure from his long-standing policy of remaining clear of all purely political movements. His interventions, he claimed, had always been 'where religion was an issue'. His difficulties with the party, he added, were, among others, associated with Joe Devlin, who was bidding fair to become a dictator through the spread of his Ancient Order of Hibernians (AOH), a society that was being promoted without reference to either priest or prelate. He had other misgivings, but he would not voice them publicly lest he should 'damage the prospects of Home Rule'. He was not averse to giving his public support to the movement for self-government, but for him to do so at this stage, he remarked dryly, would be considered as 'a change before death, or senile decay in some form or another'.[36]

Redmond, doubtless briefed by Fogarty, wrote seeking a contribution to the party fund, and assured O'Dwyer that the Home Rule bill would meet with his approval 'in finance, and in every aspect'.[37] The bishop responded immediately. His feelings were very strongly with the Irish leader on the Home Rule question. But he needed to clarify a number of matters before committing

himself to supporting the party. He went on to repeat the points made to
Fogarty. He was reluctant to be involved in a 'purely political movement'; and he
was concerned at the growth of the AOH, which was supported by the party,
and which he believed could easily become a hotbed for anti-clerical, and even
anti-Catholic opinion.[38]

Before long, however, O'Dwyer's improved attitude towards the party suffered
a setback. Once again, John Dillon was the occasion. On 20 December, his
lordship expressed disapproval of statements made by Dillon concerning education. He viewed them as indicating that Dillon and some of his colleagues
were determined 'to recast the whole system of Irish education in all its branches
from top to bottom' as soon as Home Rule was granted. He, O'Dwyer, felt very
deeply that this was a time when all were gravely obliged to say or do nothing
that might 'embarrass' the leader of the Irish party in the great task that he was
shouldering with 'such conspicuous ability and statesmanship'. Dillon's remarks
at such a juncture, therefore, not only sent a cold shiver down his back, they
undermined unity by introducing a scheme likely to rouse amongst Catholics
and Protestants the 'angriest religious and political passions'. He had no doubt
that the intention was to deprive both churches of the management of their own
schools, and that it was motivated by Liberal policies towards education. Having
said all this, he declared himself confident that Dillon would not get his way
under Home rule.[39] Interestingly, Fr Michael J. Curran, secretary to Archbishop
Walsh and a strong nationalist, commenting to O'Riordan on O'Dwyer's
'characteristically able onslaught', agreed with the bishop's assessment. 'Dillon',
he wrote, 'is at the back of all the difficulties that have arisen about the Birrell
secondary school grant and makes no disguise of his intention to uproot the
managerial system on the first opportunity.'[40]

Despite his doubts about Dillon, and about the AOH, O'Dwyer remained
committed to not upsetting in any way Redmond's quest for Home Rule, then
facing serious opposition from Irish unionists and the British Conservatives. The
appointment of Edward Carson as leader in 1910 had given new verve to Ulster
unionists, a verve bolstered by the determination and organising ability of James
Craig. Most important of all, Balfour was succeeded as head of the English
Conservative party by Andrew Bonar Law in November 1911, and the latter was
prepared to go to extraordinary lengths to prevent Irish self-government. In
April 1912, before the Home Rule Bill was introduced, he reminded 100,000
Ulster men, marshalled outside Belfast, that, like the defenders of Derry in the
past, they held the pass for the empire, they were a besieged city. 'The government ... have erected a boom against you, a boom to cut you off from the
help of the British people. You will burst that boom.'[41] In July, he went so far as
to describe the government as unlawful, and to pronounce – 'I can imagine no
length of resistance to which Ulster can go in which I should not be prepared
to support them'.[42] Towards the end of the following year, the persistent pressure
induced the Liberals to urge the Irish leaders to accept a temporary partition.
Redmond indignantly refused, and informed the prime minister, H.H. Asquith,

that he and the majority of the Irish people considered the Ulster unionists to be bluffing.

The said majority were themselves far from happy with the meagre Home Rule Bill unveiled by Asquith. It proposed to give Ireland a separate parliament with jurisdiction over internal affairs, but it withheld from the parliament not only large issues of policy, such as defence, peace or war, relations with the crown, even, initially, the control of the police, but also effective control of revenue which, including the customs and excise department. Partly for this reason, and for future contributions in return for the 'imperial services' which Ireland shared (e.g. defence), Asquith proposed that a certain proportion of Irish members should continue to represent their country in the House of Commons. The offer of self-government was so limited that the only grounds on which Redmond was prepared to accept it was that it was just a provisional settlement. Carson also perceived it as provisional, and likely to be a stepping – stone to complete separation, and, hence, determined to oppose it, and to play the partition card, not as the solution he desired, but as a means of preventing Home Rule. He believed that an English government would withdraw Home Rule rather than approve partition. Many of his followers in the northeast of the country, however, thought otherwise.

PREPARING FOR HOME RULE

O'Dwyer, meantime, cultivated a positive stance. His Lenten pastoral for 1913 addressed the forthcoming political changes with hope and measured enthusiasm. 'Forces, the nature and strength of which none can foresee', were about to be let loose, and God alone could 'tell their ultimate issue'. Yet, 'while it was an anxious, it was also a hopeful time'. He went on to speak of the appropriateness and challenge of Home Rule with moving and reflective eloquence:

> It is only natural that a country, on which God has stamped the individual features of a nation, and in which through centuries the feelings and aspirations of nationhood have never died, should get into its own hands the management of some part, at least, of its own domestic concerns, and the shaping of its own fortunes.

'But', he added soberly, 'people must not expect that any sudden or miraculous transformation will come with self-government. There will be no immediate change in the material resources of the country, nor any extraordinary outburst of commercial or industrial prosperity, nor any rapid increase of wealth. Things will go on from day to day much in the same grooves in which they have moved hitherto. The essential change will be in the people themselves. With the advent of some measure, however limited, of freedom we may hope that they will develop a stronger manhood, a spirit of self-reliance, a fuller sense of responsibility, not only as individuals, but as a nation, and, it is out of that spirit that we must expect the true progress and regeneration of our country. But that is a harvest that will mature slowly.' The present generation would sow the seed; it was for their children and grandchildren to reap the fruit of their labours. He reminded his listeners and readers that what they would build rested on the past.

> While we look forward eagerly and hopefully to the future, we must not forget that we have behind us a history; we are not a new people settling in a strange land. We live where our fathers lived, and worked, and died before us, and, whatever success the future may bring will be measured by our fidelity to our own race, and its instincts and traditions.[43]

He went on to refer to education, and to speak of the three institutions mainly concerned in the full education of the people: 'the Home, the School, and the Church', each of which exerted its influence to the full for the well being of the country. Having treated of the role of each, and reiterated a favourite theme – that priest, religious, and lay teacher, were all united as 'members of the mystical body of Christ' – he criticised once again those who asserted 'that the schools of a country lie outside the Church's sphere and belong to the state, and then conclude by an easy inference that they must be purely secular'. This meant, he warned, that if education belonged of right 'to a non-religious, secular state'; it followed 'that religion' was 'as much an intruder there as it would be if it claimed recognition in the customs, or the excise, or the post office'.[44]

The following October, he openly supported a political demonstration in Limerick: a break with tradition that marked his concern for political unity. In the *Limerick Leader* it was made clear that he had informed the administrator of St John's parish that no permission would be required for the priests of the diocese to attend the meeting.[45] He followed this a week later with another public letter, which acknowledged his invitation to the public meeting, stated that he was unable to attend but wished it to be known that the demonstration had his fullest sympathy and best wishes for success. He had always held that self-government was 'an inalienable right' and an essential condition for the country's prosperity. It was only when the people would be compelled to carry the common burden and responsibility of nationhood that the various sections of the population would come together in 'a true bond of union'. He concluded by congratulating Redmond for the 'great power and dignity' with which he had led the national movement to its present position.[46]

Where Dillon was concerned, however, distrust ran too deep for understanding. In December, the bishop once more complained of his allying himself with the Liberals to introduce their education policies into Ireland. Dillon, he judged, had breathed 'more of the air of the Liberal clubs of London' than had been good for him. He warned Birrell, and all who sided with him, to leave the Irish education system as it was. In the Catholic view education was the 'handmaid of religion', and the school was the 'best pupil' of the Church, hence any policy that attempted to inculcate that there could be education without religion was both false and pernicious, and unacceptable to the Irish Catholic population.[47]

The following June, to his great distress, O'Dwyer's strongest ally and best adviser on educational matters, and his friend in daily life, Fr Andrew Murphy, died unexpectedly from a blood clot. Sending the news to O'Riordan, Archbishop Harty of Cashel described his death as 'a great shock to all of us. He is a loss to the country. Dr O'Dwyer feels his death intensely'.[48]

Meantime, there had occurred in Dublin a prolonged series of events, which disrupted the commercial life of the city, occasioned anger and abuse, and became one of the most publicised happenings in the country. Even at a considerable remove from the capital, O'Dwyer inevitably formed opinions about the great strike and lock-out. It is well to identify his views. Opinions and attitudes have been attributed to him relating to the strike that have little foundation.

THE DUBLIN STRIKE AND LOCK-OUT

The Dublin conflict came to a head after two years of industrial disputes and turmoil as James Larkin sought recognition for his new Irish Transport and General Workers' Union. He forced recognition by means of sudden strikes that received sympathetic support from workers in other enterprises. His most resolute opponent, William Martin Murphy, was a major employer who publicly made it clear that he did not recognise Larkin's organisation as a proper union and refused to have any member of the ITGWU in his businesses – the Dublin Tramway system, and the Independent Newspapers, which included the *Irish Independent*, the *Evening Herald*, and the *Irish Catholic*. Larkin decided to force concession by strike-action. Murphy organised a counter-union among employers, which shut-out workers and sought to bring about a quick end to the dispute. The contest, which lasted from August 1913 to January 1914, was kept going by means of material support and encouragement from English trade unions. Dr Walsh, as the archbishop of Dublin, found himself under intense pressure from press, business, and politicians, to condemn what was being termed a socialist, irreligious strike. He refused. He sympathised with the workers' demand for better wages and conditions, if not with Larkin's tactics and his instability in negotiations, and he refused to respond to warnings of international socialist conspiracy. He was later to mention to fellow bishops that he attributed much of the blame for the harrowing struggle to Murphy's obstinacy in refusing to recognise the union[49] and to his subsequent refusal to negotiate, but, at the same time, he considered Larkin reckless, unreliable, and self-willed, and he deplored his embarking on and continuing a strike which had no hope of success, and which could only lead, as it did, to destitution for families and emigration for numerous workers. Larkin's hasty scheme to send children to England eventually obliged the archbishop to intervene.

A few of Walsh's colleagues indicated in their letters to him that they accepted the extravagant charges of anarchy and red communism levelled at the strikers by Murphy's newspapers. Where did O'Dwyer stand?

Professor Patrick O'Farrell in his well-known *Ireland's English Question*, pp. 269–70, quoted O'Dwyer, without giving a source, as stating that syndicalism was 'one of the most un-Irish programmes ever tried on Irish people', and then moved from that to an article in the *Catholic Bulletin* of November 1913 in a manner that indicated O'Dwyer was the author. At least one Irish historian subsequently understood O'Dwyer to be the author and drew conclusions similar to O'Farrell.[50] In point of fact there was no article by O'Dwyer in the *Catholic Bulletin*, and the article which O'Farrell quoted was by a Jesuit named Michael Phelan, who had no links with O'Dwyer. Phelan's article was entitled 'A Gaelicised or a Socialist Ireland?' It indulged in a bitter, unbalanced attack on socialism and pointed to the Irish language and the values of Gaelic culture as the best safeguard for the Irish people. It's outburst against socialism indicated, in O'Farrell's view, that O'Dwyer and the Irish bishops and clergy were terrified that Larkin's socialist strike would separate the Irish workers from clerical influence, that they were shamed and humiliated by Irish workers seeking aid from England, and that O'Dwyer even considered that the workers, like their ancestors of old, should have been prepared to starve rather than accept a crust from English socialists. To bolster these sentiments, foisted on O'Dwyer, an extract was given from a letter of Bishop Nicholas Donnelly of Dublin to O'Dwyer. This stated: 'Larkin has got our entire working population in his hands, and *out of our hands*, and he is working hard to accentuate the separation of priest from people.' Donnelly's apprehension was presented as reflecting the fears of the great body of the hierarchy, as a result of which, allegedly, they were disposed favourably towards nationalism as a counter to socialism. Again, the information provided was misleading. A fuller quotation from Donnelly's letter suggested a more cautious conclusion.

O'Dwyer, it was evident, had written to Donnelly and made reference to the serious economic consequences of the Dublin conflict and that it was becoming 'a fight to the finish'. Donnelly's reply ran:

> The fight to the finish here in Dublin may be all very well, but there is much more at stake than the mere economic question. Larkin has got our entire working population in his hands & *out of our hands* and he is working hard to accentuate the separation of priests from people.

But Donnelly did not stop there. He continued:

> His Grace is not apprehensive. He says it was the same at the time of the Parnell row. I fear it is not quite so harmless. There was no socialism and anarchy preached then.[51]

Walsh, it need hardly be said, was the churchman at the centre of the storm and the most influential prelate in the Irish church, and far more likely to be representative of the body of bishops, so far as anyone could be so representative, than Donnelly and the real author of the article in the *Catholic Bulletin* of November 1913.

O'Dwyer's point of view was likely to have been close to that of Walsh. Both had a deep sense of social justice, both had acted as arbitrators in industrial disputes, both were highly regarded by the working population. True, O'Dwyer had been at loggerheads with labour representatives twice in the past. In the 1890s they had supported the Christian Brothers financially after the bishop had forbidden collections for their schools. During the mayoralty of John Daly (1899–1902), a former Fenian convict and a member of a secret society, there had been a dramatic act of defiance. When the mayor and the labour dominated corporation attended a religious service at St John's cathedral, at which the bishop presided, the mayor was requested politely to leave the church. He did so, but was followed, in protest, by the majority of the corporation.[52] Such brushes, however, were well in the past by 1913, and the Limerick Trades and Labour Council acknowledged O'Dwyer as 'their benefactor in the settlement of disputes' and 'as a champion of the workman',[53] and the Limerick Federated Labour Council, 'representing the entire labour element', would pay tribute to 'his untiring and painstaking interest' in their cause.[54]

The bishop of Limerick was very conscious, of course, of the growing strength of socialism across Europe, but there is no evidence that he saw it as a major factor in the Dublin strike and there is little evidence that fear of socialism disposed the bishops and clergy towards nationalism. There were a number of more obvious factors to dispose them towards nationalism in those years, and some were already committed nationalists.

O'Dwyer's attitude to the Dublin strike and lock-out was determined by Larkin's actions and abusive rhetoric. The latter's sympathetic strikes, his violation of contracts, and what O'Dwyer saw as his generally irresponsible leadership, were what influenced the bishop's views, not the distortions of the public press. He was a long standing critic of newspaper bias, and the absence of objectivity with regard to the troubles in society was already so marked by January 1913 that the *Catholic Bulletin* observed that they were 'fomented and multiplied by an unscrupulous press, anxious for 'sensations' and perfectly reckless as to their truth or falsity'. The article, entitled 'Social Unrest and its Remedy', went on to give a number of examples of contradictory reporting.

O'Dwyer, besides, had evidence nearer home of the effects of what was being termed 'Larkinism'. Limerick's dockers and carters had gone on sudden strike in January 1913, and were obliged to capitulate after three weeks with no change in their wages or conditions, but with a guarantee that they would not strike thereafter without a week's notice.[55]

O'Dwyer's sole extant statement on the Dublin conflict was brief, bald, and pragmatic. It was not made until 11 January 1914, and then, in passing, in a letter

to Monsignor O'Riordan in Rome. At that stage it appeared to him that all
attempts at conciliation had failed and that the only hope for industrial peace
and future industrial relations was for Larkin to be completely defeated.

> Larkin seems to be coming to the end of his tether, and it is of great
> importance that there has been no compromise, but that the men must
> return to work on the master's terms. There never was a more wanton
> strike, or an emptier-headed leader. And yet thousands of working men
> have followed him blindly. But I should hope that their fellows throughout
> the country have learned a lesson.[56]

Fortunately, the bishops' joint response to the disastrous conflict showed
greater compassion. In a pastoral read in all churches on 22 February 1914, they
exhibited profound feeling for the plight of the poor and the struggling workers
and sought to indicate a remedy to the prevailing unrest. Advocating the
establishment of conciliation boards for the prevention and settlement of labour
disputes, they ventured that had such been in existence it was more than likely
'that the recent strikes and lock-outs, with all their degrading consequences,
would not have taken place'. 'A paralysis of employment that was altogether
avoidable', the bishops continued pointedly, 'has left us the humiliating memory
that in a year of plenty many thousands of the toiling masses in the capital city
of our country were left for months in idle dependence on rations and strike pay
from England, and that large numbers of children had to be fed by charity away
from their homes when not deported into strange fosterage across the Channel.'
And conveying the idealised nationalist feeling of the period, their lordships added:

> Had the healing influence of native rule been felt for even a few years, we
> cannot believe that the bitter privation, the enormous waste, the loss, the
> shame, the sin of this insensate conflict, would have been entailed on a city
> in which commerce and manufacture need to be fostered with tender
> care, instead of being recklessly endangered in a senseless war between
> workers and employers.[57]

The joint document had given rise to much discussion at the bishops' standing
committee. O'Dwyer does not seem to have been immediately involved in
contributing to the pastoral, though Bishop Foley kept him informed on con-
tentious issues that had arisen.[58] He, necessarily, however, approved the document and made it his own.

The national feeling evident in the bishops' pastoral reflected the new edge
given to nationalism in the early months of 1913, quite unrelated to socialist fears.

National excitement and anger
In January 1913, unionist opposition to Home Rule prepared to express itself in
arms. An Ulster Volunteer force was formed. Rather than 'coerce' this private

army, British army officers at the Curragh proffered their resignations. In April, arms were landed in Ulster without intervention by police or army. The nationalists in the rest of Ireland reacted by forming an Irish Volunteer force. This body, which grew rapidly, contained members of the Irish Republican Brotherhood in key positions and determined to use the new force to launch a rebellion. In July of the following year, arms for the Irish Volunteers were landed in broad daylight at Howth, Co. Dublin, from the yacht, Asgard. One of its intrepid crew was Dr O'Dwyer's young friend, Mary Spring Rice, daughter of Lord Monteagle. That evening, troops fired on an excited crowd in the streets of Dublin, killing three people and injuring thirty-eight others. Anger and tension in the capital neared explosion point. Meantime, differences in the executive of the Irish Volunteers led to Redmond packing it with his own supporters and effectively taking control. Then, on 3 August 1914, the scene underwent a fundamental change with the outbreak of a world war.

THE POLITICS OF NATIONALISM AND INTERNATIONAL WAR

That same day, John Redmond publicly pledged Irish support for England in the event of the United Kingdom entering the war, and proposed that the Irish and Ulster Volunteers should be employed in defence of Ireland's coastline. It seemed like a sound unifying proposal. There was disillusion among many of his supporters, nevertheless, because two provisos had been added to the already very limited Home Rule Act, namely, that it would not come into operation until the end of the war, and then not until parliament had the opportunity of making provision for the northern unionists by special amending legislation. The disillusionment had reached the point with some nationalists that a group of them, including many IRB members, met in Dublin on 9 September to discuss using the opportunity of a European war to organise insurrection in Ireland. Then, on 20 September, in a surprise move, Redmond made a speech at Woodenbridge, Co. Wicklow, in which he called on the Irish Volunteers not just to defend Ireland, but to go 'wherever the firing line extends, in defence of right, of freedom, and religion in this war'. The precise reason for the sudden change has not been established, but in the background was the fact that Carson had called on his Volunteers to fight overseas, and the circumstance that Redmond was a man who thought imperially as well as nationally,[59] and who believed that the might of the British empire would ensure that the war would be a short one and that, as a consequence, it was important for Ireland's future that it take, and be seen to take, an active part in the victorious campaign. The Woodenbridge speech, however, proved the too much for that section of the Volunteers who had no desire to fight 'England's war', or to fight 'for small nations', while their own small nation was being deprived of freedom. Distrust of English promises about Home Rule ran deep. The organisation split in two. The larger section, some 170,000, stood by Redmond and took the name, National Volunteers, the remainder, perhaps 11,000, representing the more radical section, kept the name, Irish Volunteers.

In the early days of the war, the majority of the population, including the majority of the hierarchy, seemed to support Redmond's attitude. Most of the bishops, however, did so passively. Those who came out in support of England most notably were Dr McHugh of Derry, Archbishop Healy of Tuam, and Dr Gilmartin of Clonfert, each of whom condemned the German cause as unjust in their Lenten pastorals.[60] They, together with Cardinal Logue, expressed opinions about Germany and Belgium that were to be quoted subsequently in Irish recruiting posters. It was very much otherwise with the Archbishop of Dublin, who refused to become associated with support for either side in the conflict.[61] Some priests spoke at recruiting meetings, but by and large the clergy were not prepared to back Redmond fully in his pro-war, pro-recruiting policy.[62] In Dillon's view, indeed, there were, already in 1914, a very considerable number of the younger clergy who were 'openly pro-German'. He was sure, however, that the majority of the people were against Germany.[63] The *Spark*, an anti-Redmond newspaper, was to claim that, up to May 1915, only three bishops and fifteen priests had spoken out in favour of recruiting.[64]

O'Dwyer was slow in voicing his views. His friend, Dr Michael Fogarty, a staunch supporter of the Irish party, turned against the Irish leadership before he did. When a coalition government was formed at Westminster that included Edward Carson in a cabinet position, Fogarty wrote vigorously to Redmond to express his deep concern. This, he said, was 'a horrible scandal' and 'an intolerable outrage on Irish sentiment'. The party had taken the whole matter lying down, and, worse still, 'indulged in the usual nonsense about England's solicitude for small nations. Little she cares for small nations'. 'As far as Ireland is concerned,' he declared, 'there is nothing to choose between Carsonism and Kaiserism. Of the two, the latter is a lesser evil; and it almost makes me cry to think of the Irish brigade fighting, not for Ireland, but for Carson and what he stands for, Orange ascendancy here.' He was now convinced, the bishop stated, that Home Rule was dead and buried, and that Ireland had neither a national party nor a national press, and that the future probably held conscription and 'a bloody feud between people and soldiers ... There is a great revulsion of feeling in Ireland'. The beleaguered Redmond, who had been offered, and refused a cabinet position, forwarded the letter to Asquith, describing the author as 'one of the most able and broadminded Irish Catholic Bishops, and a man who has always been a strong supporter of the Irish party'. The letter, he assured the prime minister, was indicative of the mood in Ireland not only of the unthinking crowd but of intelligent men as well.[65]

It may be assumed that O'Dwyer was aware of his friend's views, but he refused to criticise Redmond. His pastoral letter of 1915 made no reference to Home Rule, and he gave no recognition to a Home Rule demonstration in Limerick in July 1915, which was attended by Redmond and Dillon,[66] but that was chiefly because his concern then was with world peace, and supporting the pope's call for peace. His first breach with Redmond, indeed, was to arise in connection with the papal plea for peace. As always, he was highly sensitive to guidance from Rome, and, through Michael O'Riordan, he was more attuned than other Irish prelates to developments at the Vatican, and, the Vatican, in turn, was probably more aware of him than of any other Irish bishop.

NATIONALIST DIPLOMACY IN ROME

O'Riordan, as has been noted, was consciously nationalist, and he availed of every opportunity to impress on cardinals that Ireland's political subordination to England did not mean that the Irish Catholic church was subordinate to the Catholic church in England. In 1910, indeed, on the occasion of the Eucharistic Congress in England, he had had the contributions of Archbishop Healy of Tuam and Archbishop Carr of Melbourne translated into Italian in order to make it clear 'that the Catholic Church in the British empire is the *Irish Catholic Church* and that the Eucharistic Congress was chiefly Irish'.[67] With the outbreak of war, and given the Vatican's neutrality, he was determined that the Irish Church be seen to be neutral. In this, he and O'Dwyer influenced each other.

Two of O'Riordan's future diplomatic opponents were mentioned by him to O'Dwyer in April 1914, almost four months before the outbreak of war. Referring to the papal consistory, he spoke of the surprise choice as cardinal of the Benedictine monk, Francis Neil Gasquet, and remarked, 'possibly some influence in England helped in his nomination'. He also suggested that Cardinal Merry del Val helped. The latter, he observed, 'certainly used his opportunity in helping to the front the country of his birth'.[68] Gasquet had been resident in Rome since 1908 as president of a commission for the revision of the Vulgate. With the outbreak of war, he was availed of by the British foreign office to press England's interests at the Vatican. He was convinced that the Italian Church, generally, supported Germany and was influenced by the efforts of the Austrian and Bavarian ministers.[69] He almost certainly did not know that the Vatican, from the end of 1914 to at least 1917, was saved from bankruptcy by German financial aid through the medium of Swiss banks. A further ground for papal distance from the allies was to be provided at the end of 1915, when it was learned that Britain and Italy had signed a secret treaty, in March 1915, which excluded the papacy from the future peace conference.[70]

Gasquet was benign in his attitude towards Ireland and Irish people. To O'Riordan, however, he was part of a powerful public relations apparatus, including Italian newspapers such as *Corriere d'Italia*, that helped confirm the supposition in the Vatican that Ireland was not important from an ecclesiastical point of view and that its interests were similar to those of England.[71] O'Riordan's vice-rector, Fr John Hagan, moreover, directly accused Gasquet of endeavouring 'to influence the Holy See and the Cardinal Secretary of State (Merry del Val) against Home Rule, on the ground that it was inimical to the church in Ireland',[72] and also charged him with persistently representing 'the Archbishop of Dublin as an opponent of Home Rule'.[73]

In the circumstances, both men were at pains to assert Ireland's distinctive identity. Thus, when an English special envoy, Sir Henry Howard, arrived in Rome, towards the end of 1914, at the head of a diplomatic mission, O'Riordan assured O'Dwyer that the Irish College would 'not be identified with him in any public occasion'. He believed that Cardinal Gasquet and Fr David Fleming, OSF, were organising a large reception 'at which all the *British* are to be invited'. He went on:

> I don't know what the other Irish in Rome will do, but this College shall not be represented! To anyone who asked me what was said about the special envoy in Ireland, I replied that nothing was said – that it does not concern them; he represents England, but not Ireland.[74]

A week later, he brought his bishop up to date. 'Sir Henry Howard is here', he reported sardonically, 'to counteract German falsehood by English truth! I hope he will not think it within his official competence to extend his services to Ireland; but of course he will.' O'Riordan then told of the reception that Cardinal Gasquet gave in Howard's honour the previous Thursday. He wanted at it 'the members of the Vatican court, the cardinals, prelates etc to meet him'. 'I was invited: but I happened to be taken up with other occupations!' The Cardinal 'held another reception last evening', O'Riordan added, 'to which all the British in Rome were invited. I was invited; also the students. As I am not a Britisher, I did not go. The Irish Dominicans did go, I believe. But that has always been their way ...'[75] Three days later, on 6 June 1915, he informed an Irish friend that his non-attendance 'had been much talked of – also at the Vatican: the very thing I wanted; for it will segregate Ireland and England in the minds of these good folk. I want them to be apart: separate entities.'[76]

In July 1915 he availed of a visit to the pope to venture the simplistic instruction that Cardinal Bourne of Westminster and the English hierarchy had very little influence on the English government, whereas the Irish bishops had 'much influence, not because they' were 'Catholic bishops or Irish, but because they' had 'the Irish Parliamentary party to enforce their view in parliament'.[77]

A favourite means of his, as noted already, was to translate into Italian for papal and curial consideration statements or writings of Irish churchmen. O'Dwyer was an ideal subject. In 1915, his pastoral on peace was sure to be well received. Following a papal instruction that 7 February 1915 should be a day of expiation and prayer for peace, O'Dwyer had devoted an eloquent Lenten pastoral to the cause of peace.

All the nations, he declared, were responsible for the present conflict, which should never have commenced. The past century had seen extensive scientific discoveries, and a multiplicity of mechanical inventions, all of which could have led to a new golden age, benefiting the poor and raising the whole human family to a new level, instead the most enlightened nations were 'driven by a mad hatred and rivalry into a disastrous war', which is said to be a fight to the finish. If it is, he continued, it must result in the deaths of millions, 'and human misery such as men have never known'. Yet, God is not absent. In the midst of the carnage, people immersed in materialism were turning to religion, and it was quite possible 'that God, in his mercy, may make this war the beginning of a new epoch of religion', and that, in some way, He will hear the prayers of both sides, each of which believes its cause is just. The bishop urged his people to pray for peace, Christ's sacred gift, and that God might strengthen 'all movements that make for peace'.[78]

O'Riordan had the pastoral translated and arranged to have it distributed to the pope and the curia. On 20 March 1915, he was able to report to O'Dwyer that it had been read by his holiness, and much praised.[79] Three months later he was still reporting favourable comments. Cardinal Prisco, archbishop of Naples, was particularly 'struck by the fact that the pastoral was thought out on a plane above the atmosphere of powder and shot, and explosives, and diplomatic quarrelling and duplicity'.[80]

PRESSING REDMOND TOWARDS PEACE

O'Dwyer's silent support for Redmond began to waver in the autumn of 1915, when Pope Benedict XV made his impassioned plea for peace to the warring powers, asking them to pull back from the 'revolting human slaughter' in which they were engaged. Moved by the plea, and seeing the lack of positive response from the British leaders, O'Dwyer decided to write to Redmond to ask him to raise the issue of peace in the House of Commons. The pope, he pointed out, did not ask the combatants to make any concession, to undergo any humiliation, but simply asked them to confer directly with one another, or through some neutral body, to seek terms to put an end to the war. He had personally been appalled, O'Dwyer stated, by the heartless untruth already uttered [by Carson[81]] 'that to talk of peace at the present moment is immoral'. On the contrary, it was immoral not to. The world was running red with blood. There was no wisdom in repeating like a parrot 'that no proposals can be entertained until Germany is beaten to her knees'. Was there, indeed, 'a competent man in England at this moment confident of crushing Germany?' The Russian 'steamroller', the accession of the Balkan states to the side of the Allies, as also the state of things at the Dardanelles, had raised great expectations in vain. 'It is time', he insisted, 'to look facts in the face … The prolongation of this war for one hour beyond what is absolutely necessary, is a crime against God and humanity.'

Over and above these considerations, O'Dwyer insisted, there were the vital interests of Ireland. Every day of the war was piling up a load of debt that would 'impoverish and cripple this poor country for generations'. The moment the war ceases, he cautioned, 'there will be a sudden collapse of prices'. 'Strong men will be hard set to keep their heads over water, but the ordinary farmers will find it enough to do to pay their annuities much less to meet an unheard-of load of taxation'. England would survive, whatever way the war went, because of her great resources. But if the war continued for another year, it would sink Ireland in irretrievable ruin, and 'condemn Home Rule, if we get it, to hopeless poverty and impotence'. 'Therefore, we may hope,' he concluded, 'that you will use your influence to get a fair hearing for the noble and Christ like proposal of the pope.' In England, some people had complained of his Holiness's silence, now that he had spoken it was to be hoped they would show deference to his words. But whatever about England, Irish Catholics had no excuse for disregarding the appeal of the pontiff. 'Our duty and our highest interests are on his side in this movement for peace', O'Dwyer concluded, 'and therefore I should hope that you will bring great influence to bear on the English government and press it to give his proposal a fair and reasonable consideration.'[82]

Redmond was placed in a very difficult position. Compliance with O'Dwyer's request would endanger his alliance with the Liberals, and emphasise for the Ulster unionists that the Catholic Church and the pope were dominant in Irish public life. He decided to answer briefly and negatively, ignoring the bishop's economic arguments. On 9 August, he sent a polite but firm refusal. The course of action his lordship suggested 'would not be calculated to promote the cause of peace', and he would not be justified in bringing pressure on the government to enter into negotiations for peace 'at a time when the German powers, who have been the aggressors in this war, show no sign of any disposition to repair the wrongs they have inflicted upon Belgium and our other allies.'[83]

Four days later, O'Dwyer informed O'Riordan: 'I have had a simple refusal from [Redmond] to bring any pressure to bear on the government, but I rather think that the popular fear of taxation and poverty will soon bring pressure to bear on himself. He and the Irish party are afraid to do anything. The Home Rule carrot keeps the Irish donkey moving, without even the smell of the vegetable for its pains.'[84] On 14 August, he wrote to Fogarty to thank him for his backing in face of the criticism he, O'Dwyer, had received over his appeal for peace. 'If you know how much I value your opinion', he observed, clearly moved, 'and what a comfort your sympathy and support are to me, you would understand how grateful I am to you. I don't care 'three tons of pins' for the mob, or the newspapers, or what they may say, but the approval of a brother bishop, who does his own thinking, and is a true friend, is worth a good deal.' 'Did you notice', he asked, 'that John Redmond in his answer did not mention the pope. And like a true imperialist talks of 'our allies'. Well, if they want more fighting, I think the Germans will give them a belly full of it, and perhaps in six months time they will wish they had listened to the pope. But all the time, the slaughter is going on, and the Gospel of Christ is almost as if it were not.'[85] The bishop of Killaloe agreed with his appraisal and observed that the party had sunk very low when they were afraid to mention the name of their own country or the pope, 'lest they should offend 'our allies'!'[86]

Public support for O'Dwyer's letter came from minority, interested groups. Eoin MacNeill in the *Irish Volunteer*, of 21 August, noted that Redmond had not contradicted O'Dwyer's forecast of 20 million pounds to be levied on Ireland – if Ireland submitted. He 'avoided the disagreeable subject, and blinked the bishop's questions'.[87] By that date, however, O'Dwyer had had time to reflect on Redmond's dilemma. Writing to Fogarty on 22 August, and enclosing a venomous postcard as an indication of the critical mail he was receiving, he observed that the Irish leader was caught in a 'cleft-stick'. If he had mentioned the pope, 'his English allies would, or might think that he was a genuine Catholic who could not be trusted with Home Rule'.[88]

The issue, however, continued to evoke response. On 7 September, O'Dwyer informed O'Riordan:

> There is a good deal in the papers about peace. The English don't seem to like the idea, and the Irish patriots boil over with indignation at the mention of it, but I think they are getting a belly full of fighting, particularly at the Dardanelles.[89]

The strong opposition of the 'Irish patriots' was necessarily linked to the fact that Ireland's agricultural economy was booming because of the war. Five months after the conflict commenced, O'Riordan, in a visit home, remarked on the prosperity and on 'a lowered sense of national identity, which had fallen more since the war began than in 30 years before'.[90]

The issue also evoked interest further afield. On 18 September, O'Riordan informed his bishop that he had translated his letter into Italian and sent it to the pope, who was pleased with it and spoke of having it published in *Observatore Romana*.[91] Subsequently, he arranged for an article by O'Dwyer in the *American Ecclesiastical Review* on 'The Pope and Peace'. The bishop, on 3 November, was able to report that he had sent on the article, adding in semi-jest, 'if it appears, I shall be ordered out of Ireland under the Defence of the Realm Act'.[92] In his contribution, he dealt with his letter to Redmond, and, addressing an American audience, spoke far more critically, and unfairly, of the Irish leader than previously. He found it sad that Redmond, because of the exigencies of politics, had felt compelled to 'simulate feelings' that he could not have entertained. He had convinced himself that if he showed any independence as an Irishman, or any spirit as a Catholic, his English masters would have found an excuse for throwing him over and for reneging on their promise to grant Home Rule. The prize of Home Rule was dangled before him 'to keep him draughting for the English government'. It was 'a pitiable position' for him to take, the bishop declared, and it was doubtful 'whether the game' was 'worth the candle'.[93]

O'Dwyer received a number of letters of approval and support, some of them militantly anti-English, from Irish-American clergy. On 24 December, O'Riordan wrote in praise of the article. It had been reproduced in the New York issue of the *Freeman's Journal*. He was having it, too, translated into Italian, but with an explanatory comment![94] By then, however, O'Dwyer had written a letter on another topic, which evoked a stormier response in both England and Ireland, and further weakened Redmond's position as leader.

THE EMIGRANTS AND 'THIS SNARLING PRELATE'

The indirect occasion of this other letter was a renewed recruiting campaign in Ireland by the British War Council, and renewed fears that conscription would be imposed. A number of Irish country people, mainly from the west of Ireland, decided it was a good time to follow the well beaten path of emigration to the United States. At Liverpool, they were mobbed by a crowd of English civilians, and jeered at as shirkers and deserters, and the crew refused to man the ship on which they were to depart. The English popular press made much of the event. John Redmond, embarrassed, wrote to the newspapers and explained that the attempt to leave for America was 'due entirely to a misapprehension' on the part of 'a number of fellows'. They had believed that conscription was about to be introduced and had decided to flee their country. He condemned their action as 'very cowardly', and guaranteed that such behaviour would not be repeated and that it was even then being dealt with in such a manner that it could not possibly spread.[95]

It was another instance of the pressure Redmond was under in an England in the grip of war hysteria. His letter evoked strong protests from several quarters in Ireland, and from the bishop of Limerick it brought forth the first of a new batch of formidable and celebrated public letters. Although the Dublin papers refused to publish his protest, it appeared in the local press and was widely circulated in leaflet form by the Sinn Fein organisation. It was written with a burning intensity that asserted independence of England and resentment at the treatment of fellow Irishmen.

'The treatment which the poor Irish emigrant lads have received at Liverpool', he began,

> is enough to make any Irishman's blood boil with anger and indignation. What wrong have they done to deserve insults and outrage at the hands of a brutal English mob? They do not want to be forced into the English army, and sent to fight English battles in some part of the world. Is not this within their right? They are supposed to be freemen, but they are made to feel that they are prisoners, who may be compelled to lay down their lives for a cause that is not worth 'three rows of pins' to them.

After this gripping paragraph, he pointed out that it was quite probable that 'these poor Connacht peasants' knew little or nothing about the war. 'Small nationalities and the wrongs of Belgium and Rheims cathedral, and all the other cosmopolitan considerations that rouse the enthusiasm of the Irish party, but do not get enough recruits in England, are far too high-flying for uneducated peasants, and it seems a cruel wrong to attack them because they cannot rise to the level of the disinterested Imperialism of Mr T.P. O'Connor, and the rest of the New Brigade.'

'But in all the shame and humiliation of this disgraceful episode', O'Dwyer protested piercingly, 'what angers one most is that there is no one, not even one of their own countrymen, to stand up and defend them. Their crime is that they are not ready to die for England. Why should they? What have they or their forebears ever got from England that they should die for her? Mr Redmond will say a Home Rule Act on the Statute Book. But any intelligent Irishman will say a simulacrum of Home Rule, with an express notice that it is never to come into operation.' This war 'may be just or unjust', he went on, but it was 'England's war, not Ireland's'. After it, if England won, she would hold a dominant power in the world, politically and commercially. But, 'win or lose, Ireland will go on in her old round of misgovernment, intensified by a grinding poverty which will make life intolerable. Yet the poor fellows who do not see the advantage of dying for such a cause are to be insulted as 'shirkers' and 'cowards', and the men whom they have raised to power and influence have not one word to say on their behalf.'

In conclusion, he turned the spotlight on England, something likely to further inflame the British press. 'If there is to be conscription', he pronounced, 'let it be enforced all round, but it seems to be the very intensity of injustice to leave English shirkers by the million go free and coerce the small remnant of the Irish race into a war which they do not understand, and which, whether it is right or wrong, has, but a secondary and indirect interest for them.'[96]

Reaction from the English press was immediate. The *Guardian* dubbed him 'this snarling prelate',[97] the *Daily Sketch*, after criticising him, expressed confidence that the Catholic clergy, who had already done magnificent work in informing the Irish people of the justice of the allied cause, would be O'Dwyer's 'severest critics'.[98] A letter from the celebrated lawyer, Sergeant A. M. Sullivan, criticised the bishop for using the Liverpool incident to attack the Irish party. He had attacked the Irish party over the past thirty years, and was now angry because the party did not share his pro-German views. This criticism, which appeared in the *Limerick Leader* on 3 December 1915, evoked letters defending the bishop, and Limerick corporation and the Glin Board of Guardians expressed their approval of his intervention on behalf of the Irish emigrants. The volume of support, indeed, greatly outweighed the criticism. Missives of support came from the United States of America, from people who had read both the *Ecclesiastical Review* and the letter on the emigrants, and letters poured in from all over Ireland praising his 'defence of his fellow countrymen'. Many favourable letters also came from England. One such was from a Michael O'Mahony, of the Liverpool Press Club. He thanked the bishop 'for the moving protest you made against the treatment of the emigrants here on the 6th inst, a protest, which, I am pleased to say, is now being largely copied by several newspapers in Great

Britain'. Matters, in fact, were worse than reported. The restraint of the emigrants had been wonderful. 'One youth merely smiled', O'Mahony observed, 'when an English recruiting sergeant violently struck him on the mouth for refusing to come to a café close to and have "a good tea".' 'Even amongst Lancashire Irishmen who still believe that Home Rule is won', his lordship's letter was causing deep satisfaction.[99]

O'Riordan was stirred by the power of O'Dwyer's intervention. 'That was a blizzard of a letter from the bishop on the characteristic conduct of the British bullies of Liverpool', he informed a Limerick friend on 29 November 1915. 'If they were not cowards and slackers they would not be there to call names: they would be *fighting in the trenches for their country*.'[100] Bishop Fogarty, with more restraint, described O'Dwyer's American article as a powerful plea for peace, marked by a strong attack on Redmond, and added: 'the whole body of the people have rallied to you and your letter on the emigrants. It has opened their eyes.'[101]

O'Dwyer's letter, in its defence of the emigrants and the sentiments it expressed, clearly had struck a chord across the country. He had become a new voice for nationalism, a voice for the many who could not be heard in the censorship and hysteria of war.

MAJORITY SUPPORT CONTINUES FOR THE PARTY

His dissatisfaction with the party does not appear to have been reflected in local opinion in his diocese. The *Limerick Leader* was to claim, in February 1916, despite the immense losses in the war, 'the heart of Limerick remains thoroughly sound and inflexible in its fealty to the leadership of Mr Redmond'. He was entitled to the fullest support of all those in the country who wanted to make Ireland 'a strong, self-centred (*sic*) and self-reliant nation'. The paper, pointedly, challenged 'all his critics' to indicate where Redmond, in advocating that Ireland should remain within the empire, was departing 'an iota' from the principles and policy of Parnell. Redmond was well fitted to putting 'the finishing touch' to what he and his party had already gained.[102]

Limerick, despite radical manifestations, remained a garrison town. This was made very evident in May 1915, when the Irish Volunteers decided to hold a demonstration of strength in the city. Some 1,000 Volunteers and boy scouts, drawn from Cork, Dublin and Limerick, marched through the city in uniform to the music of two bands. Among their leaders was P.H. Pearse. Not content with parading through the newer parts of the city, they marched through the old town, where a large number of homes had men serving in the war. They were jeered at, and had bottles thrown at them. Some had to seek police protection. That evening, as they gathered at the railway station to await trains for Dublin and Cork, large crowds accosted them, shots were discharged, and in the scrimmage seven rifles were wrested from Volunteers. Fifty police and a number of Catholic clergy were brought in to restrain the crowd.[103]

Less than a year later, the Irish Volunteers rose in rebellion. Their venture was no more welcome than had been their parade in Limerick. The subsequent change in public opinion was largely due to the actions of the English commander-in-chief and the public protest against his actions by the bishop of Limerick.

20

1916: Challenging carnage abroad and oppression at home

In the course of his hasty criticism of the Irish party over the English education bill in 1906, O'Dwyer foreshadowed happenings ten years later, and drew attention to the main socio-political forces at work in the country. The party, he asserted, were 'loosing touch with the healthy opinion of their own country'. They needed 'to return home and inquire' why 'a fine generation of young Irishmen' was 'turning away from them *en masse* for the Gaelic League, or Sinn Fein, or some other policy …'[1]

Under the titles 'Gaelic League' and 'Sinn Féin' was encompassed the wide-ranging movement that from about 1900 embraced Irish language and culture, the sense of Irish identity, various programmes for promoting Irish goods and the development of Irish industry. The assertion of Irish identity generated, almost inevitably, hostility towards the perceived opponent. Thus, Arthur Griffith's Sinn Féin political party adopted the pointed slogan – 'Burn everything English except its coal'. Other manifestations of what was called, loosely, the Irish Ireland movement, were the Irish Cooperative Agricultural Society, the foundation of the Irish General Workers' Union, and, in a way, the Anglo-Irish literary revival. The common factor among these various manifestations was the presence of idealism, the sense of national identity, and hostility to the dominance of English power and culture. The leaders of the 1916 insurrection were all associated with aspects of this pervasive climate, so much so that when the Irish Volunteers broke away from the main body they were popularly, if confusingly, called the 'Sinn Féin Volunteers', and the rising itself, the 'Sinn Féin Rebellion'.

O'Dwyer, with his life-long interest in young people, and his dislike of the Irish party, was drawn to the Gaelic League and other bodies manifesting idealism, energy, and pride in country. He found in them hope for the future as compared to a party that had become complacent and even arrogant, discredited by jobbery, and seemingly dominated by the policies and values of the English Liberals and, hence, associated with Anglicisation.

The party, nevertheless, remained the most highly organised body in the country. It reached into every parish in Ireland, apart from heavily dominated unionist areas, and it provided its version of 'the news' through the *Freeman's*

Journal. With the live prospect of Home Rule, from 1910 to 1913, its influence and popularity expanded; and when Home Rule ran into difficulties, and the party into criticism, the war came and solidified support behind Redmond. The party became part of the apparatus controlling information. On 8 September 1915, O'Dwyer exclaimed disgustedly to O'Riordan: 'The helplessness of our people is deplorable. They have given up the habit of thinking. That is done them by the "Machine".'[2] At the start of 1916, four months later, he grieved that 'Redmond and the *Freeman* speak and write like British gringos, and any fellow who has a coat on his back talks of "our army".' He conceded, however, that all national pride was not lost. 'There is still a good survival of nationality. The Gaelic League has done good work and deserves well of the country. The party are contemptible.'[3] Despite the conflicting situation, the possibility of an armed insurrection was far from the thoughts of all but a few in the early months of 1916.

THE EARLY MONTHS OF 1916

The year opened, ironically, in the light of subsequent events, with a letter from O'Riordan stating that Cardinals Gasquet and Bourne were endeavouring to convince those in authority in Rome 'that as between Ireland and England the past is past, and that the war has unified them in the 'cause of civilisation' and 'common interests'.[4] On 12 January, O'Dwyer informed him that it was very hard to gauge opinion in Ireland just then. He went on to make the remarks about Redmond and the Freeman behaving like 'British gringos', adding that 'there was a genuine feeling against Germany, on account of Belgium, and the Catholics were specially roused by the alleged outrages on nuns and priests'. Nevertheless, 'there was still a good survival of nationality', and he attributed this, as noted, to the Gaelic League.[5] Ten days later, a tired rector of the Irish College wished that all 'kings, superiors and cabinet ministers' of the belligerent nations be packed off 'to the front and the trenches'. 'It is a great thing', he commented, 'to play at patriotic heroism by proxy. The campaign of lying is quite equal in atrocity to the campaign in the trenches.' He feared, however, that 'the blundering' was 'all on the side of those who controlled "our army".'[6]

The horrors of the war and the need for peace became the topic of O'Dwyer's Lenten letter. 'I have read your Pastoral with absorbing interest and with the greatest admiration', Bishop Fogarty wrote him on 22 March. 'How you maintained such an impartial note all through it, surprises me. There is not a word ... that an Englishman could honestly object to, any more than a German.'[7]

THE 1916 PASTORAL LETTER

The letter commenced with a prayer that God 'would stay the calamitous war that was turning Europe into a human slaughter house', and went on to make

independent and, for the time, courageous comments on the conflict. As in his
other communications on peace, he referred a number of times to the statements
and appeals of the pope, and noted, by contrast, the attitude of the newspapers,
which were recorders of the 'abominable butchery' and acted as 'an agency for
intensifying and exasperating the national hatreds which have led to this war'.
Turning to the belligerents, he maintained, 'they planned and schemed, solely for
the sake of power and material gain. All the talk about righteousness' was 'simply
the cloak for ambition'. 'Truth and right and justice', he insisted, 'have had very
little to say to this war, which is an outbreak of materialism and irreligion. The
peoples did not want this war; there is no hatred of one another amongst them;
but the governing cliques in each country have led or driven them like sheep to
the slaughter.' The Holy Father had proclaimed the Gospel of Christ throughout
the conflict. 'Does any Christian man believe', O'Dwyer queried. 'The Prince
of Peace would say "Fight it out", "There can be no peace until your enemy is
crushed", "Force alone can settle this issue"'.[8]

Directing his gaze on Ireland, he observed that the hope for the future that
was there before the war had now changed for the worst. Land purchase, 'that
great measure of pacification', was arrested; the great problem of housing for
working people in the towns would remain unsolved; all schemes for the
development of the country would be impossible, and every day that the war
continued meant a deeper poverty, and a heavier burden of taxation, which
would 'drown the country and squeeze the people out of it in emigration'.[9]

The religious spirit, the felicity of language, and the hard realism could not
fail to make an impact. The letter was praised at home and overseas. Translated
by O'Riordan, it further deepened regard for the bishop of Limerick in the
Vatican. When the bishop was mentioned to Benedict XV in July 1916, he
comment was '*ha scrito della bellisimi Pastorala*'.[10]

Few noted, however, one of O'Dwyer's most perceptive observations, namely,
that if war ceased immediately Europe would be impoverished, but poverty
would probably be the least of its evils. There would be 'the paralysis of industry,
the restriction of commerce, unemployment on a scale … never known before',
and it was 'an anxious question how a hitherto powerful, well-paid, well
organised population of workers' would 'submit to the altered state of things'.
'We have had, from time to time,' he acknowledged, 'some ugly threatenings of
socialism, but we may fear that they are no more than the first mutterings of the
storm which will burst upon European society as soon as this war is over.' He
added prophetically, more than a year before the Russian socialist revolution:

> This terrible danger, which may be on us within the next three or four
> years may well be worse than the war itself, and deluge Europe again in
> blood. If anyone thinks that millions of working men, trained in arms, in
> every country in Europe, will settle down peaceably to starvation, in order
> to help to re-amass fortunes for their 'betters', he may have a rude
> awakening.[11]

Among extant references to the pastoral, one, from a gentleman who signed himself 'O'Donnell of O'Donnell', and claimed to be 'a senior foreign editor', formerly of the *Post* and the *Spectator*, praised the bishop's letter and declared his views on the war and a socialist revolution 'the best informed … in the English language'.[12]

OTHER PASTORAL/SPIRITUAL CONSIDERATIONS

Dr Fogarty, in the letter of 22 March which praised O'Dwyer's pastoral, paid tribute also to his 'brilliant discourse' at the consecration of Bernard Hackett as bishop of Waterford on 19 March. The discourse was largely a eulogy of the Church in all its vastness and unity, in its survival of centuries of persecution, and in the sustaining strength of the See of Peter. As O'Dwyer liked to do, he provided a broad historical sweep of events to illustrate his message. On this occasion, the choice of events was highly selective, the picture, at least to modern eyes, over-simplified and triumphant, and the language tired and conventional, unlike his pastoral. About the same time he gave the spiritual address to his clergy that was considered when treating of him as 'Pastor': in which he urged his priests to provide 'an intellectual and personal presentation of the faith' so as to make it a living influence in people's lives, speaking to them of the love of God manifested in creation and in the humanity and death of Jesus Christ, and encouraging them to pray in a familiar, 'I–Thou' manner.

In his seventy-fifth year, then, O'Dwyer's writings and sermons, in the early months of 1916, portray a man of peace and vision, an apologist for the universal church and the papacy, and a pastor with a positive perception of God and of the teaching and humanity of Christ. It was a picture that gave no indication of how he would be viewed nationally before the year was out.

THE EASTER RISING AND ITS AFTERMATH

On Easter Monday, 24 April 1916, the Dublin insurrection commenced. It concluded six days later with unconditional surrender. During that period much of central Dublin was destroyed, and some 1,306 people, between combatants and civilians, were killed or wounded.[13] On 27 April, while the conflict still raged, Prime Minister Asquith announced in the House of Commons that martial law had been proclaimed over the whole of Ireland, and that General Sir John Maxwell had gone to Ireland with 'plenary power'. The Irish executive was to place itself at his disposal.[14] Determined to teach all Irish rebels a stern lesson, Maxwell exercised his plenary power with precision, and scant wisdom. Almost daily from 3 May to 12 May the main leaders were executed. The relentless process of killing, the behaviour of some of the troops, and the imprisonment, without trial, of hundreds of people, turned popular hostility to the rising into sympathy for the dead insurgents. Their struggle, and their courage in the face of death, won them reluctant praise. As news spread of the spiritual quality of the lives of the executed, the sympathy deepened, and they began to find a place in the martyrology of Irish heroes. John Dillon both warned against this development and contributed to it in an emotional speech in the House of Commons on 11 May, when he demanded that the execution of the rebels be halted, and declared that the life work of the Nationalist Party was being washed out in a sea of blood. It was not murderers who were being executed, he pointed out, but insurgents who had 'fought a clean fight, a brave fight, however misguided', and he told interrupting unionists 'it would be a damned good thing for you if your soldiers were able to put up as good a fight as did these men in Dublin – three thousand men against twenty thousand with machine guns and artillery'.[15]

Information on events in Dublin was slow to reach the rest of the country. On 1 May the commandant of the Limerick district, Irish Volunteers, Michael P. Colivet, formally informed the mayor and the bishop that he had been requested to hand over arms, but that he had no authority to hand over arms or property without direct orders from his superior officer, Eoin MacNeill. 'It ought to be possible now', he explained, 'in view of the reported Dublin surrender', for MacNeill to contact the Volunteers.[16] MacNeill, however, had been imprisoned. The bishop, it appears, played a part, probably in conjunction with the mayor, in getting the Volunteers peacefully to 'lay down or give up their arms'.[17] Within a few days the plenary authority of General Maxwell reached into the bishop's immediate realm.

On 3 May, the day Pearse, MacDonagh and Clarke were shot, Maxwell had called on Archbishop Walsh with a list of the names of priests whom he accused of being linked to the insurrection. 'Maxwell wanted to deport them straightway', M.J. Curran, Dr Walsh's secretary, reported, 'and was apparently under the impression that the archbishop could do this himself. On learning the names of the priests concerned, the archbishop pointed out that he had no jurisdiction in the matter, as no Dublin priests' names appeared on his list. He advised Maxwell to consult their bishops and, noting the presence of 2 Limerick priests' names, had a little malicious pleasure in anticipating the reply he would receive from Dr O'Dwyer.'[18] Maxwell confounded matters by a business-like, rather peremptory letter to the bishop of Limerick. On 6 May he requested his lordship's co-operation with regard to two priests in his diocese, the Revd Thomas Wall and Revd Michael Hayes, both of Co. Limerick, 'whose presence in the neighbourhood' he considered to be 'a dangerous menace to the peace and safety of the realm'. Had they been laymen 'they would have already been placed under arrest'. He would be pleased, Maxwell concluded, if his lordship 'could obviate the necessity of such action by moving these priests to such employment as will deny their having intercourse with the people, and inform me of your decision'.[19]

On 9 May, from Kilmallock, O'Dwyer dictated a reply through James Canon O'Shea. He had no right to inflict 'the very severe punishment' that the General suggested 'except on a definite charge supported by evidence'. He requested, therefore, the grounds on which the priests might be considered 'a dangerous menace to the peace and safety of the realm'. O'Dwyer added pointedly: 'Whatever may be the rights of the military under martial law, a bishop in the exercise of his authority has to follow the rules of ecclesiastical procedure'.[20] Maxwell supplied the grounds three days later. Fr Wall had spoken against conscription in his church at Dromcollogher, had attended a lecture by P.H. Pearse, and had blessed the colours of the Irish Volunteers on 2 January 1916. Fr Hayes had been active with Ernest Blythe in organising Irish Volunteers, had had leaflets printed urging young men of the Gaelic Athletic Association (GAA) to join the Volunteers, and had been president of the Volunteers at Killoughton and Newcastle West. In what was meant to be a conciliatory note, Maxwell added: 'It should not be difficult for your lordship, under such disciplinary power as you possess, to prevent, at any rate, priests from mixing up with and inciting their flock to join an organisation such as the Irish Volunteers have proved themselves to be.'[21] Maxwell's evidence against the two priests was well founded, but when O'Dwyer contacted the two men, Wall, certainly, and, it would seem, Hayes, denied the accusations. They were not sure where the bishop stood on the issues involved and, doubtless, were fearful of his reaction. There is extant a letter from Wall, on the day after his lordship's celebrated final letter to Maxwell, admitting that he had misled him.[22] Believing, therefore, it would seem, that his two priests were unfairly charged, O'Dwyer opted for attack as the best method of defence. On 17 May his response to a commander-in-chief bedecked with plenary power, at a time of martial law, proved an act of defiance that stirred the feelings of young and old across the country.

As was his wont, he prepared the text carefully. He researched, or knew already, of an incident in Maxwell's career that might be used tellingly against him in a riposte. Maxwell had participated in the illegal and unsuccessful 'Jameson Raid' in December 1895 when Dr L. Storr Jameson led 470 mounted men from Bechuanaland into Transvaal intending to advance to Johannesburg and effect a rising to overthrow the government of Paul Kruger. Nobody was executed for the attempted insurrection. Maxwell was imprisoned for a while by the Boers. The leader, Jameson, was imprisoned in England, and subsequently became premier of Cape Colony, and was made a baronet in 1911.[23] Conscious of the scandal and the irony, O'Dwyer determined to use it to Maxwell's discomfiture; and although the correspondence between them had been private, he decided, not for the first time, to violate implied confidentiality and to go public without informing his correspondent. Conceivably, it may have been intended as a form of self-defence, but it was certainly in keeping with his stand-alone way of acting against what he viewed as injustice or oppression, especially British injustice or oppression. He was clearly angry, besides, at the treatment of the leaders of the Volunteers, and he sensed that he was giving voice to a widespread grievance. He stated:

Sir,

    … I have read carefully your allegations against ——— and ———, but do not see in them any justification for disciplinary action on my part. They are both excellent priests who hold strong nationalist views, but I do not know that they have violated any law, civil or ecclesiastical.

    In your letter of 6th inst. you appeal to me to help you in the further-ance of your work as military dictator of Ireland. Even if action of that kind were not outside my province, the events of the past few weeks would make it impossible for me to have any part in proceedings which I regard as wantonly cruel and oppressive. You remember the Jameson Raid, when a number of buccaneers invaded a friendly state and fought the forces of the lawful government. If ever men deserved the supreme punishment it was they. But officially and unofficially the influence of the British government was used to save them, and it succeeded. You took care that no plea for mercy should interpose on behalf of the young fellows who surrendered to you in Dublin. The first information which we got of their fate was the announcement that they had been shot in cold blood. Personally I regard your action with horror, and I believe that it has outraged the conscience of the country. Then the deporting by hundreds and even thousands of poor fellows without a trial of any kind seems to me an abuse of power as fatuous as it is arbitrary, and altogether your regime has been one of the worst and blackest chapters in the history of the misgovernment of this country.[24]

The context in which O'Dwyer wrote, and his attitude to Maxwell's letters, was conveyed to O'Riordan on the day after his response. 'There is hardly a *second opinion* in Ireland', he reported, 'as to the savagery with which the government has been acting. But it will *do good*. The country was being *hypnotised* by the politicians, but it is *being revivified* these days.' 'Imagine', he suggested, 'Sir. J.G. Maxwell had the impudence to write to me, asking me in rather peremptory terms to remove the Revs. Mick Hayes and Thomas Wall as being a serious danger to the peace of the realm. I told him to specify his charges against them, and the evidence which he had to support them, and then I would investigate the matter. He then wrote more civilly that he thought I could deal with the case by disciplinary methods.' O'Dwyer concluded with waspish vanity: 'I don't think he will forget the answer which I sent him yesterday.'[25]

    The bishop's letter was not published by the main newspapers. It appeared, however, in the *Cork Examiner* and the Dublin *Evening Mail* despite the warnings of the authorities.[26] The issues were sold out. The letter was also widely circulated in leaflet form. O'Riordan on 27 May expressed his 'great joy' at the reply made to 'that military autocrat', and observed that O'Dwyer's reputation had reached the point at Rome that those supporting the Allies asked if Mr Asquith's visit to His Holiness was intended –'amongst other things, to get the Bishop of Limerick to keep silent'. 'The wish had been father to the thought',

O'Riordan observed, for if these people had not been so distracted they would have seen that for the pope to be displeased with O'Dwyer's pastorals 'would be to feel displeasure with himself' since O'Dwyer had 'simply followed the line he had traced for peace'.[27] Two days later, Fr Curran reported from Dublin that the effects of the insurrection were 'indescribable and incalculable'. 'The national soul', he declared, 'is roused, scoffers of Sinn Fein are now sympathisers'. 'Dr O'Dwyer's latest had been suppressed.'[28] Nevertheless, the letter found its way overseas. Some 50,000 copies were said to have been distributed in San Francisco alone.[29] From South Australia, a Limerick girl wrote proudly to O'Dwyer that his letter to Maxwell had come by cable and had appeared in all the morning papers.[30]

At the beginning of June, the bishop was presented with a further opportunity to stir the pot, and increase the attention he evidently enjoyed. The Limerick Board of Guardians forwarded to him a resolution in support of his letters 'in reply to the commander's impertinent request'.[31] The following day, O'Dwyer sent a public response that, in O'Riordan's view, nicely supplemented his reply to the commander-in-chief.[32] He proclaimed:

> It would be a sorry day for the church in Ireland if her bishops took their orders from agents of the British government. As to the poor fellows who have given their lives for Ireland, no one will venture to question the purity and nobility of their motives or the splendour of their courage. But many blame them for attempting a hopeless enterprise. Yet we cannot help noticing that since Easter Monday Home Rule has come with a bound into the sphere of practical politics ...[33]

O'Dwyer's stance had grown increasingly belligerent for a man associated with peace and with opposition to violence. A few days later, he informed Andre Geraud, an agent of the French government investigating public opinion in Ireland: 'The English only give in to coercion. They will only give in to our demands when constrained and forced to do so'.[34]

Something of the complexity of the developing situation was illustrated in two letters received by O'Riordan. The first came from PJ Roughan, who had arrived in Dublin from Rome two days previously. 'Dublin's attitude towards the military', he wrote on 9 June, 'could hardly be equalled by that of the Belgians towards the Germans: it's a case of 'hands off' now; before the rebellion the tune was ' join the army'. Stepping off the boat at Kingstown, a street urchin came buzzing along with the *Evening Herald* calmly announcing 'the butcher's drowned, Father'. I thought he referred to ... some of the local victuallers [*sic*] but I learned the drowned man to be Kitchener of Khartoum!' Roughan added that 'though everyone seems to be in a revolutionary humour, the street arabs are the only persons anxious to express their opinions in public. Last evening about 30 in number sailed down O'Connell Street singing "A Nation Once Again" as loud as their little lungs would permit'. 'Dr O'Dwyer of Limerick', Roughan added, 'is the hero of the hour.'[35] O'Dwyer, it would appear, was becoming the voice of all those 'in a revolutionary humour' but afraid 'to express their opinions in public'. On 6 June, Asquith informed his cabinet that there was a complete revulsion of opinion in Ireland generated by some five factors, of which one was a letter of Bishop O'Dwyer of Limerick.[36]

The second letter came from Bishop Fogarty on 16 June in response to understandable confusion on O'Riordan's part regarding the use of the word 'Sinn Féin'. 'There are Sinn Féin and sinn féin', he explained. 'Those on for rebellion' and 'those short of that, in pursuit of the preservation of Irish ideals, religious, mental, social etc.' Those for rebellion were few. The great body belonged to the other class, which had been joined 'by practically all Irish Ireland' since the rebellion. 'They don't want rebellion, but the brutal shooting and deportation of their young insurgents after surrender has filled the country with indignation and raised such an anti-English feeling as I never saw before.' As regards the priests, to Fogarty's knowledge there was only one priest in all Ireland who actively supported the rebels. A great many, especially among the younger men, were in sympathy with the Volunteers, Sinn Féin etc 'but not for rebellion. No one knew rebellion was in the air until thunder broke. They were in these movements because they aid Irish ideals as opposed to English, American, sensualistic materialism, and as a defence against the threat of attack from Carson's Orangemen!' 'They were merely exponents of a general sentiment which washed all round them.' In conclusion, the bishop noted three things: the *Freeman* had become 'rotten'; 'the Irish party, Dillon excepted, had fallen into disrepute'; and 'the chances of Home Rule being accepted with part of Ulster cut off' were 'very problematical'.[37]

O'Dwyer, during the same month, rejoiced that 'the old spirit' was 'bubbling up again' and would 'probably end by squelching Redmond and his gang'. The immediate issue, however, was 'the division of the country to conciliate the Orangemen, or rather to please the Nonconformists'. The *Freeman*, he complained, was using every dodge and falsehood possible 'to deceive the country'.[38] Nine days later, he conveyed his annoyance at the startling decision the nationalists of Ulster had come to. They had yielded to Redmond's and Devlin's assurances about partition being temporary, and 'patriotically … agreed to cut their own throats in the interest of Ireland'. 'We shall have two countries', he added, 'the Orange Free State, and the Three Provinces.'[39] Subsequently, he observed that in spite of the opposition by the bishops a majority had been obtained through the influence of Devlin and the AOH in Belfast and County Down. He feared that the national convention of the organisation would follow suit and trust the party leadership. ''Tis a queer country', he remarked ruefully, 'but the 'Machine' now-a-days is universal.'[40] This despite the swing in popular feeling against the party.

The build-up of popular feeling continued to be noted by outside observers. A former student of the Irish College informed O'Riordan on 25 June that former opponents of Sinn Féin were now moving to it in large numbers because of the government's repressive measures. 'On every side', he noted, 'The letters of Bishop O'Dwyer are accepted as exactly the right word in the right place and time.' Moreover, at the recent meeting of the hierarchy at Maynooth, 'he was frantically cheered' by the students, 'singled out above all the other bishops'.[41] His was a confident assertive voice amidst uncertainty, and in the absence of credible leadership. His standing was further acknowledged by the accolade of a ballad in his honour. The title told the theme: 'Correspondence between Bishop O'Dwyer and the Tyrant Maxwell'. The two final stanzas of eight convey the ballad's flavour, and something of the mounting popular emotion.

> Descendant of a noble clan
> May you be left us long,
> Fearless and true to uphold our cause,
> 'Gainst tyrants cruel and strong.
> They thought that every voice was stilled,
> That our hearts were cold with fear,
> No swords nor threats our hearts could chill,
> Or make our voice less clear.
>
> And Oh! Thank God that there are men
> To speak with love and pride,
> Of those who lie in prison cells
> And those who nobly died.
> And when the glorious tale is told
> Of Ireland's latest fight,
> In letters golden shall be writ,
> 'O'Dwyer upheld the right'.[42]

'If the bishop were censured', Thomas Carey wrote to O'Riordan from London, 'there would be an awful uproar in Ireland. Even here now amongst Irishmen, his name is one to conjure with, and they are framing his recent letters.'[43]

In the midst of all the adulation, there was at least one critical voice from an old friend. In the course of a long letter to O'Riordan, on 23 July, Richard O'Shaughnessy, the former member of parliament for Limerick, remarked that he had heard that Dr O'Dwyer had got the Limerick Sinn Féiners to lay down their arms, and then went on: 'I can't say I am in harmony with his choice of language, but be it remarked that it came *after* the rebellion and when it came it could do no harm; but it did not justify the rebellion. Remark, too, that *all* his policy, and for a long time, has been directed against what he regards as the errors of the National party, which are the errors of J. Dillon, and that he was attacking the party and the man named, when he replied to Sir J. Maxwell.' After this last illogical inference, O'Shaughnessy returned to reality with the query: 'But why, oh why, did Maxwell write to him?' Anybody could have told him, 'Whatever you do, don't write to Dr O'Dwyer'. As to O'Dwyer's letter, he had misgivings on the grounds 'of taste and judgment'. 'I should like to have read a plain, solemn enunciation of the boundaries of right and wrong, and I have no doubt it would have saved many a life and strengthened the power and dignity of the Church.' In his view O'Dwyer was not acting as a bishop should, but, not knowing where exactly O'Riordan stood, he continued obliquely and carefully: 'I wonder which was more admirable, Dr O'D's letters or the advice given by a prelate as prelate to his flock – "Keep out of the streets".'[44]

At the end of June, a tired bishop of Limerick looked forward to his holiday in Kilkee. Writing to Sr Catherine, at the Mercy Convent, Rathkeale, obviously a friend, he spoke in a musing, relaxed manner very different from his trenchant public letters. He thanked her for her letter, and went on: 'The years are passing very fast, and one does not know when the score will be full. But it is one of the blessings of old age that it gives full notice, and ample time to prepare for the end. And yet how little we do to turn it to that purpose.' 'I hope to go to Kilkee on Monday next', he confided, 'and to luxuriate in a month of heavenly idleness. That is my idea of supreme happiness. As the old cook said, "Oh to do nothing for ever and ever".' Turning to the rising in Dublin, he added, quite sure of his reader's sympathy: 'It is very pleasant to see how the hearts of the people are turning towards the poor fellows who fell in Dublin. Their deaths have touched a cord [*sic*] of religion and nationality that were hardly ever more beautifully united.'[45] Three weeks later, in a brief response to O'Riordan, he sympathised with his 'perplexity in the present welter of Irish affairs' but assured him that no one knew where they were, and then almost immediately went on, 'I am enjoying glorious weather and the *dolce far niente* in this most delightful of sea side places'.[46]

On his return to Limerick, there was a letter from a Samuel F. Darwin Fox, Fribourg, Switzerland, informing him that his letter to General Maxwell had 'appeared (more or less complete) in several foreign newspapers' and that his article in the *Ecclesiastical Review* was appearing in pamphlet form in French and German.[47] There was also a cheerful note from Dr Michael Fogarty informing him that he had received an Australian paper the previous week and it contained 'a big and good portrait of "the famous Bishop of Limerick".'[48]

O'Dwyer, in response, expressed his belief that the position of the Irish party now was 'hopeless'.[49] As if in confirmation of this, he received a letter from Laurence Ginnell, MP, signifying his intention to form a new party and suggesting, 'the best place to launch it would be at a public meeting in Limerick'.[50] He also wrote to Archbishop Walsh for support. Neither prelate displayed enthusiasm. By the end of August, O'Dwyer was musing: 'If O'Brien and Healy had not discredited themselves, we should have an alternative, but as it is, I do not see who are to displace the "party", unless, as is not improbable, the Sinn Fein men gather strength enough to rout them.'[51] Again, it was an instance of envisaging a possibility that few would have contemplated at the time. 'He seemed to see through things almost by intuition', one of his priests was to write of him after his death.[52]

At this point, there came an opportunity for a further important public statement. He was invited to accept the Freedom of Limerick. He was proud of the honour being offered, but he determined to avail of the occasion to remind the corporation of a past time when they derided him as anti-national and pro-British. He also intended, however, to make a speech that would give voice to the mood of the nation. He prepared carefully. A copy of the address was sent to Fogarty for his perusal and comment. 'When I am over this ordeal', he declared unconvincingly, 'I will shut up, and bid good-bye to politics. They are too engrossing, and with them, and the war, I can hardly say my prayers properly the last few months.'[53] Two days later, he responded to Fogarty who had thought parts of his speech too inciteful to rebellion. 'Your criticisms are just, and very valuable, and I have made the changes that they require. But I try not to throw over the rebels who have all my sympathy.' Then, turning to the moral requirements for a just rebellion that were currently being discussed, he observed: 'I do not know whether you have gone thoroughly into the theological bearings of the question of rebellion, but, for myself, who am a mere amateur, I think a good deal of the old arguments are obsolete. Nationality is a comparatively modern idea, and the rights of a nation against another are different from those of an individual against his sovereign.'[54]

O'Dwyer's address before Limerick corporation merits consideration at some length, not only because of its power and influence but also because of its self-revelatory aspects. It is, in part, a form of *apologia pro vita sua*, a justification of certain past actions and stances in his episcopal career.

THE FREEDOM OF LIMERICK

The special meeting of the corporation in the council chamber of the town hall on 14 September was attended by some members of the public. The chamber was filled to capacity, and a large crowd, unable to find a place within, assembled outside the building. At his lordship's arrival at the entrance, 'cheer after cheer was raised, and the bishop repeatedly bowed his acknowledgements'. As he and the mayor, Councillor A.B. Quin, and the sergeants bearing the corporation mace, and the town clerk, made their way to the dais, 'every member of the Corporation and general public rose' with loud and prolonged cheering. The reporter for the *Cork Examiner* noted, 'great enthusiasm prevailed throughout the proceedings'. The minutes were read. They paid tribute to Bishop O'Dwyer's for his work for the city, and especially for the working class, for the services he had rendered to education and temperance, for his care of the sick and the poor, for his work of arbitration, but above all for the fact that in his people's 'hour of sorrow and trouble' he proved himself 'their valiant champion against tyranny and wrong'.

The mayor presented the scroll enrolling Edward Thomas O'Dwyer a Freeman of Limerick, the city's highest honour. 'Amidst a scene of great enthusiasm, his lordship, who was visibly affected, signed the roll of freedom, and then thanked them very heartily for the great honour they had conferred upon him but confessed that he felt somewhat strange in these surroundings of public favour'.[55] 'Popularity is a novel experience for me (laughter)', the bishop suggested, 'and I must be on my guard against its fascination, not indeed that I ever attached much importance to it, or sought it (hear, hear).' They were all familiar with the fickleness of popularity, he stated, thereby providing an opening for a pointed introduction to his address.

'Some of you will remember the early years of my episcopate', he observed mordantly, 'when the correct thing politically was to treat me as an enemy of my country, because I had the audacity to think and to say that the methods of the political agitation were not amenable to God's law.' 'He was heartily in sympathy with the farmers in their movement to emancipate themselves from the yoke of an intolerable landlordism', he asserted, endeavouring to overcome residual misunderstandings, 'but he condemned as immoral the methods of the Plan of Campaign and boycotting as intrinsically unjust, and the latter as essentially unchristian, and for that, and that alone, an attempt was made to hound me down and silence me (hisses).' 'A meeting was held here in my own city', he proceeded relentlessly, 'under the shadow of my own cathedral, and the full strength of a powerful organisation was exerted to discredit and defame me. Some men prominent in the agitation took part in that meeting and seemed to be borne along on a full tide of popular enthusiasm, yet within six months I saw these mighty leaders hooted and pelted in the streets of Limerick (laughter), and guarded by their enemies, the police, from the fury of their own friends (laughter with applause). It was a lesson, as well as my own experience, of the unsteadiness with which the wind of popular favour blows. And, therefore, Mr Mayor and Gentlemen, I trust you will not imagine that I am the less grateful for the signal mark of your favour, which I have received today, if I remind myself that the weather may change at any moment, and the wind blow from another quarter (laughter).'

Not content to mention past events and move on, he justified himself further: indicating thereby that the humiliation and hurt of the past still rankled and left him with the need to vindicate his stance of years ago. 'At the time to which I refer', he explained, 'I was drawn into controversies by my sense of duty as a bishop. I did not interfere for the sake of politics (applause). I spoke in defence of the moral law of which I am, however unworthy, the guardian. But that did not save me from abuse and misrepresentation.' 'At other times', he added, 'particularly in connection with education, which is closely related to religion, I have had to interfere and incur the displeasure of some politicians, who think they can deal with ecclesiastics after the manner of continental infidels. But I was right all the time (applause). I knew I was right, and that testimony of my own conscience was more to me than the cheers of any multitude (applause).'

After this classic example of protesting too much, he directed his words to a wider audience, knowing what he had to say would be read avidly.

Now, again, Gentlemen, I have been drawn into collision with politicians in the discharge of my ecclesiastical duties. General Maxwell (hisses) had the effrontery to give me directions for the government of my diocese but I hardly think he will repeat the experiment (laughter and applause). He was trained in Egypt and South Africa and was brought back. He thought because he had the military power of England at his back that I would not dare to disobey him. He did not know much about Irish ecclesiastics, who have a proud tradition and who have been shown by our predecessors to stand up to English brutality (applause).

From this personal and corporate expression of hubris and bravado, he moved on to point out that apart from the protection of two priests, there was also the question of his attitude to the young men who had been 'murdered' by Maxwell in Dublin. Was he to condemn them? 'Even if their rebellion was not justified theologically,' he said carefully but rhetorically, 'was I to join in the condemnation of Pearse, MacDonagh and Colbert, who were shot without trial, and of the men and women who, without trial, were deported from this country in thousands (applause).'

He then proceded with a virtual defence of the rebellion, and an incitement against Britain, that left a number of his colleagues uneasy.

The British government and their friends ring their charges on the hopelessness of the rising, and the folly of a couple of thousand badly armed Volunteers attempting to overthrow the British power in Ireland. The Irish Volunteers were too few for the enterprise, but that, perhaps, is the worst that can be said against them (applause). Rebellion to be lawful must be the act of a nation as a whole, but while that is true, see the case of the Irish Volunteers against England ... I should like to ask Mr Asquith if the destruction of the Irish parliament was not an atrocious crime against this country (applause), and if as a nation we have ever condoned or forfeited our right to redress. If he were an Irishman, would he submit tamely to the perpetration of the present misgovernment of the country? Would he patiently look on at the deceit and chicanery with which this supreme interest of Ireland had been treated and never more scandalously than for the last ten years?

'Does he imagine', O'Dwyer persisted, 'that the young men of any nation would have the patience to bear with the tantalising perfidy, which, after years of strenuous agitation, pretended to concede their claim and pass into law a measure of Home Rule, and then hang it up and announce that before it could be put into execution it had to be amended.'

In the midst of all 'this juggling', he went on, the war broke out 'and the political leaders of Ireland took up their cry from their masters in England that this was war for small nationalities (laughter) – to protect them from oppression, and to allow them to live and develop on their own national lines'. The Volunteers, not surprisingly, asked, if this was true for Belgium, Serbia and Poland, why not for Ireland? 'These Irish Volunteers imagined that Ireland had an inalienable right to govern herself (applause); that the deprivation of it was worse for every interest of their country ... that it was an usurpation, and that resistance to it was a duty (applause). Of course they were wrong (laughter). These reasons might hold good against any other country, but not against England, the home of freedom, the chivalrous and disinterested friend everywhere of small nationalities that take her side (laughter and applause).'

O'Dwyer had the audience totally with him, responding to every nuance, virtually cheering him on as he became more daring and provocative in his speech. Truly, no bishop had spoken as this man. 'The Irish rebels', he proclaimed, 'only carried into practice their rulers' principles, and must be judged by the same standards that were applied to the Belgians in revolt against Germany, or the Serbians in revolt against Austria.' When Mr Asquith came to Ireland after the Rising, what did he find? 'That the Castle government had failed (applause). That is the recorded judgment of the prime minister of England and will stand for ever as the vindication of the victims of the rebellion (applause).' Continuing with the spurious reasoning, the bishop drew powerfully emotive conclusions.

> What frightened him? It was not the number of rebels nor the strength of their armaments, but the knowledge that they were the true representatives of Ireland and the exponents of her nationality (loud applause).

'He knows that English government in Ireland is indefensible', he pressed on outrageously, 'that no people in the world that could help it would stand being governed by strangers, men like Wimborne and Birrell and Nathan, a gang of carpet-baggers who came here for their personal interests at the behest of their party. But he has not the manliness to concede what he knows is our absolute right. Does he think that partitioning a country by religions is the way to emancipate it?' If Germany were to offer corresponding proposals to Belgium, with what burning indignation he would denounce them as an outrage on national rights, 'and if some young Belgians, with more courage and patriotism in their hearts than worldly wisdom, faced the German soldiers and fought like men until their resources were exhausted, and when they surrendered were shot in cold blood in twos and threes for days after, how England would appeal to heaven for vengeance on their murderers (applause), and some day or other when the light of freedom broke again over their land the monument to these young heroes would be set up in the *Place des Martyres* in Brussels.'

There had been much about the Empire and Ireland's place in it, since the war began, he went on. An empire in any true sense consisted of a number of self-governed kingdoms that came together for their mutual support and benefit. Canada and Australia were such. Ireland was not. 'We are a subject province,' ruled 'not by ourselves, but by some English barrister from Bristol or

Manchester or some Jew from Shoreditch (applause). That is our share in the Empire and I for one avow that it does not fire my enthusiasm for the Union Jack (loud applause). Ireland is a nation and never will be at rest until the centre of gravity is within herself (applause).' That last sentence and the subsequent paragraph were to be quoted again and again by young revolutionaries in the months and years ahead. 'Clever and plausible English ministers', he went on, 'may do a good deal by way of corruption; they may buy the national press; they may mislead the members of parliament, they may demoralise individuals, and even large classes, by an insidious system of bribery, but in my humble judgment there is deep down in the heart of Ireland the sacred fire of nationality which such influences can never reach, much less extinguish, and which will yet burn on the altar of freedom.

> They may think that prosperity will wean our people from the old cause, that education will turn their thoughts into other channels. It is the flattering unction which tyrants are always laying to their souls, but the history of the world is against them. *Ireland will never be content as a province, God made her a nation, and while grass grows and water runs there will be men in Ireland to dare and die for her* (applause). It is that national spirit that will yet vindicate our glorious country and not the petty intrigues of parliamentary chicane. And if our representatives in parliament had relied on it, instead of putting their faith in Asquith and Lloyd George and the Liberals, they would not be where they are today.

The Irish party in self-defence had recently asked for an alternative policy to theirs, 'as if the captain of a ship, after running her on the rocks, invited the passengers to give their views of how the vessel should have been navigated (laughter)'. 'I have no responsibility for the present deplorable condition of things', O'Dwyer declared, 'yet I will state my alternative to trusting the party, who trust the Liberals, and are now reduced to the statesmanship of Micawber – waiting for something to turn up.'

His 'alternative', as put in his vigorous, resounding prose, lingered in the public memory.

> When war was being declared I would have said to the English government 'Give us our national rights; set up a genuine parliament in Dublin, and we are with you'. Again this very year, when the English government played false, I would have said to the Irish members of parliament 'Come home, shake the dust of the English House of Commons off your feet, and throw yourselves on the Irish nation'.

'These are my alternatives. I think they would have been effective, but I fear they would not be in favour with our present parliamentarians.' 'O'Connell used to say that England's difficulty was Ireland's opportunity', but the modern axiom was 'stand by England in her difficulties and trust to her generosity when you have got her out of them … The gratitude of conquerors is not worth much. *Sinn Féin is, in my judgment, the true principle* (loud and prolonged applause). An alliance with English politicians was the alliance of the lamb with the wolf; and it is at this point precisely that I differ from the present political leaders, and believe that they have led, and are leading, the national cause to disaster.'

Winding down, his lordship sought to avert any accusation of animus on his part. 'Some people imagine that because I condemn the policy of certain politicians I am their enemy, and even a bitter enemy. In this they are wrong. I entertain no enmity to any living person, but if I am to speak at all on public questions, I must say the truth and if I put my views strongly, it is not for the purpose of offence, but because the matters at issue are of vital importance and touch my deepest feelings.' With this hollow excuse, a porous bandage aid for the wounds inflicted on John Dillon and other leaders of the Irish party, Dr O'Dwyer turned graciously to the mayor, aldermen and councillors, to thank them and to pray that God might bless them, and all belonging to them, 'and have our city in His keeping until we shall take our place once again as freemen in our own country (loud applause)'.[56]

Dr Fogarty's comments on the text submitted to him prior to the occasion had been friendly but penetrating. Few bishops in the Church would have the courage to make that speech, he observed. 'It is studded with thoughts and phrases of the finest colour, and is bound to trouble the mind of John Bull and his family.' Although O'Dwyer did not personally approve of rebellion, and could be seen as giving just the Volunteers' point of view, to the cursory reader it might well seem an approval on his part of the right of revolt until the Irish parliament was regained. Some high ecclesiastics might view it thus, Fogarty continued, and the English government was sure to delate it to Rome. He counselled his friend, without success, that the clause 'but that is the *worst* thing to be said against them' was 'too comprehensive' and implied 'indifference to the moral aspect of the rebellion'. He warned that the retort might be made to him – 'Why condemn the land agitation because of boycotting, if the Dublin rebellion is not to be condemned because of the objective morality attached to the whole enterprise?' Strangely, Fogarty thought the Irish party were treated fairly and 'it might do them some good'; and he judged the address would 'bring joy and consolation to many a troubled Irish conscience'. He hoped, however, he would not be visiting his friend 'as a prisoner in Kilmainham' as a result of the address.[57]

The following day he added the reflection that while the sweeping views of the old theologians need to be much modified in the light of later historical examples, especially that of the United States of America, 'at the same time, as regards the poor Dublin fellows, it has to be remembered, even from the point of view of nation against nation, that their effort had not the approval of the Irish nation as a whole but only a very small minority'. He admired the motives and the bravery of the insurgents, but 'their action was objectively indefensible from a moral point of view'. It would, therefore, Fogarty concluded sagely, 'be

a very risky thing for a bishop to openly approve of this rebellion. Its consequences on the future peace of this country would be very dangerous. The
ardent spirits of each generation ... would appeal to his authority in warrant of
their extremist action'.[58]

Writing to Fogarty on 16 September, O'Dwyer reported that the censor had
forbidden the Limerick newspapers to publish more of the speech than the
abridged account that appeared in the Dublin papers the previous day. 'I dare say
they will make complaint to Rome', he added, 'but, if they do, they will gain
nothing.'[59] A degree of confidence that neither Walsh nor Croke were able to
experience in the 1880s or early 1890s.

Responding, in turn, the bishop of Killaloe noted that the changes O'Dwyer
had made in the text had safeguarded his position, which was an advanced and
brave one. 'I feel', he said, 'that it is a great blessing that someone with your
prestige has had the courage to stand over the dead bodies of Maxwell's victims
and vindicate their memory. One of the most disgusting thing in our recent
public life is the way our public bodies, Co. Councils, Urban Councils etc have
all rushed out with sickening resolutions condemning the rebellion.' 'You have
your critics among "the sober brows",' Fogarty concluded, 'but the great body of
the people, especially the young, male and female, are in boundless admiration
of you.'[60]

Despite the censorship, numerous copies of the address were circulated in
leaflet form and messages of congratulation poured in from many sides. The
Limerick City regiment of the Irish Volunteers sent their appreciation on
14 September, three days later praise and congratulations came from a Mr
Wheeler Doyle, of Cheshire, and among other extant messages of praise were
ones from W. Grattan Flood, Wexford, a Mr A. Newman, editor of the *Irishman*,
Belfast, and D.J. Lawton, a parish priest in New South Wales, who was moved to
write, 'This most fearless speech ... will be among the most cherished possessions of my life'.[61]

By 24 September, O'Dwyer was measuring the opposition to his address. He
thanked O'Riordan for speaking up for him, and suggested that he would now
need to supplement the *apologia*. He was conscious 'that many of a certain class'
resented his speech, 'but', he insisted, 'I spoke, honestly, *ex abundantia cordis*. The
Irish Volunteers were wrong, and I have said so explicitly, but while my
judgment condemns them, all my sympathy is with them, as strongly as I condemn the government and despise the party.' 'It's the old story', he added perceptively, 'time wears away all the circumstances of our rebels except the fact
which survives in the heart of the country, that they died for Ireland.'[62] At the
end of the month he was sufficiently relaxed to counsel O'Riordan, half in jest
and half in earnest, with regard to his contacts with a 'sound Catholic Englishman',
that he should have only 'a non-committal kind' of friendly relationship with
him because 'the English are Catholics only so far as the interests of their
country will allow, but, if I were Pope!!! I would not go tiger hunting with
them'.[63]

As well as to Bishop Fogarty, O'Dwyer sent a copy of his speech to Dr Foley, of Kildare and Leighlin, who had a reputation as a theologian. This gave rise to a correspondence, which has been published elsewhere, with an introduction and commentary.[64] The discussion was on the right to rebel. Foley held to the more traditional position that only justified a rebellion when certain requirements were present: a just cause, all other means of solution had been tried, the oppression was so intolerable that rebellion was the only means of getting rid of it, there was a reasonable chance of success. None of these, except perhaps the first, had been present in the Dublin venture. At the close of their interchange, from 9 November to 28 December 1916, during which both quoted authorities in their support, O'Dwyer remained unmoved. Pointing to the Act of Union, he insisted: 'The English parliament in Ireland is an usurpation, and, having regard to the modern development of the ideal of nationality and its rights', he would hold that there was sufficient ground to justify revolt.[65]

His thinking in these final months of the year seems to have become increasingly belligerent with regard to Ireland, while remaining strongly for peace and harmony in the rest of the world. He declared to a bemused Archbishop Walsh, partly perhaps in rodomontade: 'When did we ever get anything by constitutional means? We won the land laws by shooting landlords. We won Emancipation by the threat of civil war.'[66]

A different exchange of letters took place in the *Catholic Times*, of Liverpool, between the well-known Anglo-Irish priest and scholar, William Barry, and a Limerick priest, J.A. O'Connor, alias Edward Thomas O'Dwyer. Once again, O'Dwyer's strong nationalist views on the party and the rebellion were made evident. To Barry's assertion that the Irish Parliamentary party was in duty bound to honour Redmond's pledge of support for England's cause in the war, O'Dwyer responded that Redmond had been elected to secure Home Rule, he had no authority 'to pledge the lives of the young men of Ireland to a continental war' on England's behalf. His pledge had been 'the blunder of his life', it marked 'the parting of the ways between him and his countrymen'. Nobody could speak on such a momentous issue except the Irish people through a plebiscite or through a parliament of their own in Dublin. Since the Rising, he added, a 'total revolution' had taken place in Ireland. Although he was not defending their actions, any more than those of previous rebellions, the fact was that those who gave their lives for the cause were an inspiration to the young men of later generations, and hence the men of Easter Week were deemed worthy successors to Wolfe Tone, Robert Emmet, and the Fenians.[67] The bishop relished the freedom of anonymity in his exchanges with a distinguished opponent. Responding to a comment from Fogarty that 'Dr Barry had met more than five times his match',[68] he remarked mischievously: 'I quite agree with your verdict on the encounter between Dr Barry and Dr O'Connor. It was real fun. I would give anything to see Barry when he got one of Dr O'C's punches in his solar plexus ...'[69] Part of O'Dwyer's power as a controversialist was that there appeared to be nothing he would not say to win his case, whereas his opponents were frequently hampered by the code of 'gentlemanly behaviour', the more so as he was a man of 'the cloth'.

Meantime, there had been developments at the hierarchical level. In October, at their annual meeting at Maynooth, the bishops set out 'to consolidate a position on the current state of the country'.[70] Proposals were made to condemn conscription in Ireland, to oppose the continuance of martial law, and to endorse the constitutional as opposed to the physical force movement. On the first two, agreement was reached easily. The third proposal, however, was dropped after some prominent members of the hierarchy pointed out that if it were endorsed it might be interpreted as implying satisfaction with the policy and course of action being pursued by the Irish party. T.M. Healy was able to inform William O'Brien that the opposition had come from Dr McHugh of Derry, and was backed by Cardinal Logue, Archbishop Walsh, and Dr O'Dwyer.[71]

A further episcopal issue concerned the arrival in Ireland of a number of French bishops seeking to encourage support for the war effort. Fogarty told O'Dwyer on 14 November that the bishops had been warned in London against contacting him, and that his fearsome reputation had deterred a Dr Clune, a pleasant army chaplain, from calling to Corbally because he was dressed in khaki![72] O'Dwyer, once more evading easy categorisation, replied on 16 November: 'I am sorry the poor French bishops were misinformed. Although I detest the French government, I have the greatest admiration and even love the church there. The bishops and priests are splendid fellows, and I never admired them more than in their magnificent patriotism during the present war.'[73]

As might be expected, a sense of uncertainty and unsettlement pervaded the country as the year drew to a close. 'The party is going down the hill daily', M.J. Curran informed O'Riordan in September, 'but there is nobody to replace them.'[74] 'The state of unsettlement is depressing', Richard O'Shaughnessy observed on 23 November, 'and I see less hope of rescue than ever. The mere look of Sackville Street, without a stone yet laid towards restoration, is miserable. But still we live and joke and eat and drink as of old, though our food is going to be cut down one of these days.'[75] In December, Curran remarked that the organising of opposition to the party was improving, but was still poor and confused and 'at sixes and sevens';[76] and six days later he reported, 'They tell us things are quieter here in Ireland. They are in a sense, but all the same we are living on a live volcano, if a quietening one. Half a dozen things would cause a new eruption – conscription, partition or injudicious application of legislation framed for England.' He feared that public opinion in England would force the government to apply 'the so-called 'equal privileges equal service' nonsense', and he observed how 'the treatment of the interned men at Frongoch, and of those imprisoned at Dartmoor and elsewhere' caused 'intense exasperation'. There were small attendances at party meetings, and he thought there might be a schism before long. Dillon was 'assuming the leadership to himself'.[77]

The sense of change and unsettlement was emphasised by the recall of General Maxwell early in November, the resignation of Asquith as prime minister and his replacement by Lloyd George on 6 December, while Sir Edward Carson retained his position as first lord of the admiralty, and Bonar Law became chancellor of the exchequer as well as leader of the House of Commons. Then, on 22 December, 600 untried prisoners were set free from Frongoch, and the next day others were released from Reading Jail. On arrival home, they were welcomed, to their surprise, by bonfires and torchlight processions. Among them was an aggressive young man of vast energy and ability named Michael Collins. More than was realised, a new era was in birth. Yeats had wondered if some words of his had sent men out to die in 1916, O'Dwyer, had he lived, might well have wondered if his emotive, fighting words might not have sent men to their death in subsequent years. Certainly, his words had much wider currency among the young than those of the poet.

21

1917: *Nunc dimittus* – 'in harness and in a blaze of glory'

As the New Year opened, Dr O'Dwyer appeared as vigorous and trenchant as ever, and his name was now so widely known that he featured in popular fantasy humour, and was so highly regarded that he was placed already in the pantheon of national martyrs. 'A funny story, an invention, of course, came to us from Newcastle West,' Richard O'Shaughnessy wrote to O'Riordan on 12 January 1917. 'A sailing vessel was near to Foynes, from Limerick. A Hun submarine rose and a man at the prow asked 'How is O'Dwyer?' Answer: 'Very well, thank you'. The German: 'That's right. Say I was inquiring. Pass on.' The submarine dives, the ship proceeds.'[1]

The new nationalist movement took on new strength and purpose with Michael Collins's appointment as secretary to the Irish National Aid Fund for the dependents of those killed or imprisoned as a result of the rising. His vast energy and organisational ability was also turned to reorganising the Volunteers, the IRB and Sinn Féin, and to building up contacts in Britain and the United States.[2] The names of those who were executed in 1916 were publicly exalted to promote the new movement. A ready link to Church approval was acquired through O'Dwyer, and it was a remarkable testimony to his standing that he was named in a popular ballad among the honoured heroes of 1916. The ballad, 'Easter 1916', ran to 16 stanzas, of which 15 were devoted to the dead leaders of the insurrection, and the final one, to a living witness. The first and last convey the message.

> Who shall write the Easter story
> Who is worthy to relate
> All its romance, hopes, and glory
> How our leaders met their fate.
>
> God has left us yet one hero,
> His pen is like a sword of fire,
> Ireland loves him, Ireland thanks him,
> God watch o'er you, Bishop O'Dwyer.[3]

Despite his apparent energy, O'Dwyer, on 20 January, afforded O'Riordan an oblique indication that his health was seriously impaired. Having asked O'Riordan to obtain a renewal of faculties for him, he observed, 'It will be the last time for me. Yourself or some other good man will probably soon, but not if I can help it, take my place.' He added: 'I have had a very sharp cold for the last week, but am now, thank God, mending.'⁴ O'Riordan took the remarks as a passing mood due to the cold. The bishop felt sufficiently low, however, to request Monsignor Denis Hallinan to undertake his cherished convent visitations.⁵

Within a short time, nevertheless, he was in the limelight once more with a Lenten pastoral letter. On 17 February he sent the text to Bishop Fogarty for his comment on it 'as a plea for peace'. 'Britishers will say that it is pro-German, but they say that of everyone who is not a partisan of theirs. But it is not my intention', he explained, 'to make out a case for the Germans, but to argue against the people whom the French call ... "fight-to a finish-men".' The amount of debt that was being piled on Ireland, he reiterated, would mean 'dire poverty for generations' and would 'condemn Home Rule to failure'. 'But', he concluded, 'I suppose I might as well hold my tongue. *Myself*, and the *Pope*, and a *few others* are in a hopeless minority!!'⁶ Two days later, Fogarty assured him it was a treat to read everything he wrote and that he agreed 'with every line and word in it, admiring also its ability and courage'. 'I heard you were sick some time ago', Fogarty concluded, 'the Pastoral is a proof that you are now as vigorous as ever.'⁷

O'Dwyer's reputation for vigorous, daring, un-episcopal writing was now such that his new publications were read avidly. Young people queued to buy the pastoral, and it also made an impact in Rome.

PASTORAL LETTER, 1917

He commenced with the observation that prayers for peace appeared to have gone unanswered for two years. He urged people, nevertheless, not to give up hope; and he criticised the Allies for their refusal even to discuss terms of peace in response to overtures from the German emperor. This seemed so 'arrogant and unreasonable' as to indicate a determination 'to fight the war out to the finish'.⁸ The refusal would only bring the German people closer together and prolong the struggle. At the beginning of the war, the bishop observed, there was some trace of Christian feeling among the belligerents, but that had all disappeared, and in its stead the evil work of statesmen and newspaper writers had 'produced a coarse, black, brutal hatred of Germany and Germans' that made the war 'more like the deadly struggle of wild beasts than a contest among men'. Among English people, and many Irish, 'no falsehood' was 'too gross to hurl at the Germans'. There was no consideration of the truth of their claim that they were fighting a war of self-defence, that for 44 years, from 1870 to 1914, they had never done any act of aggression against any country, a claim which neither

England nor France nor Russia could make for itself. 'Common sense dictates', O'Dwyer went on, that on moral issues there were two sides, yet 'we are not allowed to hear a word or a hint to suggest that there may be something to be said for Germany'. People were asked to believe that a nation that had devoted itself to the works of peace for forty years, and occupied 'the foremost place in all the intellectual achievements of the human race', had 'suddenly lost all moral sense, and sunk to the lowest depths of degradation by the mere fact of going to war with England. It is too great a demand on our credulity.'[9] Indeed, after looking at the different factors that contributed to the outbreak of war, he concluded that 'Russian ambition, coinciding with English fear of Germany', was 'the real root of all the trouble'. It was not his purpose, O'Dwyer insisted, to offer a justification for Germany, but just to show that the morality of the war was 'not altogether the one-sided affair that the British government and its political allies represent it to be.'[10]

The Irish people, therefore, had to think and speak for themselves, and not be taken in by propaganda and economic benefits. 'We have for the moment', he declared, 'a fictitious prosperity. War prices have made the farmers and others imagine that they are accumulating wealth', but, in fact, 'they are accumulating paper, which, in circumstances that are quite conceivable, might be as valuable as old newspapers.' Bank notes without gold behind them were worthless. When the war was over the crash would come. 'The national debt of England is now more than three thousand millions of pounds. That is the money that at present, in the shape of paper, is in circulation.' 'If the war goes on for another year', he said, repeating his previous warnings, 'I do not see how this country can escape bitter, and irretrievable ruin.' That was a reason 'for the people to pray, and to press their representatives in parliament to have some regard for the interests of their own country.'[11] On the wider scene, if peace was ever to come, people had to rise above 'the bitterness and anger of recriminations and catch some of the spirit of Christ's 'Peace I leave with you, my peace I give you'. He asked, finally, that prayers for peace arise from generous hearts of charity, mirroring the charity of Christ.[12]

Before the end of the month, Fogarty reported to him – 'Your Pastoral has created a furore of delight and pacification amongst the people. They are all scrambling, especially the young, to get a copy of it. It echoes their hearts. They are sick of the falsehood, hypocrisy and cowardice with which the papers drench them.' 'By the way', he added, 'the priests tell me that a favourite name in Baptism now is "Edward Thomas".'[13]

By March the pamphlet had reached Rome. O'Riordan had made out a typed translation and sent copies to the pope and several cardinals. On 25 March he was happy to tell O'Dwyer that all the cardinals were pleased with it, and the pope was enthusiastic. 'I had an audience with His Holiness on Saturday', he explained. 'Whilst I approached him after my genuflection, he stood up, and with a joyful smile told me at once that he thanked me for sending him the letter. He then began to launch out in its praise as he sat down, and spoke of it for quite four or five minutes. He commissioned me to thank you for it, and to tell you what he thought of it.' The pontiff mentioned that Cardinal Gaspari had come to him about it and stated: 'It contains everything; the very things we have been saying for the last three years; it is a pity it cannot be published'. The pope said, O'Riordan added: 'What the Pastoral says is all true; and the truth said with great accuracy and power – "Quell'uomo ha una testa".'[14]

In the same informative letter, Cardinal Guistini was represented as asking several questions about Bishop O'Dwyer. 'He asked your age', O'Riordan reported. 'I said 'in years he is 74: in energy about 40.' 'I am very glad', O'Riordan went on, 'I have translated all those. They help to raise the prestige of the Irish church. Since Cardinal Cullen's time, nothing of that tendency has been done.' He added poignantly:

> I think I sent you my congratulations on your 50th anniversary or jubilee of priesthood. If not, do accept my congratulations now, with a hope that several years are to follow 'till you reach your diamond jubilee. I spent my silver jubilee in hospital throwing up blood by the pint, 'till I was in the throes. I have no hope of seeing my golden jubilee.[15]

SOMBRE NEWS

That sombre jubilee note was matched by O'Dwyer in public announcement and private letter. On 2 March, thanking the people of the diocese for their congratulations on his fiftieth anniversary, which he did not wish to celebrate publicly, he announced: 'I pray God to bless them and theirs abundantly. And I would ask one favour at their hands. My time must be short now; it would be a comfort and support if I felt that the people of the diocese would pray that God, through the merits of his only Son, and the intercession of his holy mother, would grant me the grace, for the remainder of my days, to prepare for the great account which I shall have to render of myself and the souls that have been committed to my care.'[16]

In retrospect, it reads like an awareness that time was running out very quickly. His people and priests, however, had no more insight than O'Riordan when he described him as 74 in years, but aged 40 in energy. On 3 April, however, the bishop shocked his friend in Rome, now happily out of hospital once more. He first thanked him for his efforts and his news concerning the pastoral, and acknowledged that 'in the state of opinion in Ireland, amongst ecclesiastics as well as laymen, a man wants some confidence in himself to take an un-English line in the war'. 'As to your account of my years', he continued, 'I fear you were a little roseate. I am 75, and my energies would hardly do for 40.' 'I may tell you, in *strict confidence*,' he added,

> That my health is not at all well. Some few weeks ago, I was secreting albumin in large quantities, but that has ceased, and now my condition is

nearly normal, in the sense that for the last six years I have had valvular disease of the heart, but, as it was doing me no harm, I saw no good in speaking about it, and setting fellows speculating on the succession.

He finished off with a practical, run-of-the-mill query. 'I wonder what will the U. States do: declare war, and not fight? Or lend dollars to the Allies? In either way, it will go hard with Germany.'[17] Three days later, the United States declared war on Germany.

Meantime, the bishop had continued to live from day to day with no outward concession to his state of health, and with his interests in home and world affairs as lively as ever. O'Riordan remained a regular correspondent. On 11 March, his lordship asked his assistance in obtaining special permission to erect and delegate to others the Way of the Cross, and added, voicing an on-going concern, in the wake of Germany's new unrestricted submarine warfare, 'food is growing scarce and dear, and the poor are suffering'.[18] Two weeks later, O'Riordan shared with him some of the vexations caused by the war. He had attended the funeral of the duke of Norfolk 'as a mark of respect, and a sign of Catholic union'. His attendance was given 'a political twist'. 'Persons of sense have lost their senses in this war', he pointed out. 'They cannot let their respective armies fight it out; they must quarrel in private life, as if those personal bickerings could help one side or the other. A lady sent some time ago from England to a friend here for (rosary) beads, with a request that they were to be blessed by Cardinal Gasquet, not by the Pope!'[19]

VOCAL ON HOME AFFAIRS ONCE MORE

On the Irish scene, in the wake of the victory in the North Roscommon by-election of George Noble, Count Plunkett, and his adherence to the Sinn Féin policy of abstaining from parliament, O'Dwyer, in a letter to Monsignor Hallinan, agreed that 'the party' was 'a nuisance'. 'If it were out of the way', he observed, 'it would be possible to organise a broad national movement that would have strength and be able to do something for the country. But these fellows, by the 'machine' and the resistance of the masses, and the influence of the government, are able to defeat any independent political action.' 'We must wait', he added with his usual perception, 'until some strong man, like Parnell, arises and gives the country a lead.'[20]

By 1 May, his lordship was once again in the public eye. The occasion this time was a public letter, signed by Niamh ni Pluingeid and Maire ni Rian, on the treatment of Irish prisoners in Lewes jail. O'Dwyer's letter evolved into one of his fiercest, most ignominious attacks on the Irish party. 'We are a mean nation', he declared, 'if we take the benefit of the sacrifice of our fellow-countrymen and allow them to linger and rot in English jails, without at least a protest which the world will hear.' What had brought Home Rule to the front

and given it a chance of becoming law? Was it 'the droning of the English
'friendlies' that they call the Irish party?' 'They are the "patriots", he announced
savagely, 'that allowed the wretched measure which has been passed by
parliament to be hung up during the war, and having suspended the liberties of
their country, turned to recruiting in Ireland for the British government. He
continued in the same unrelieved strain:

> These are not the seed of the men by whom salvation is wrought in Israel.
> They are British parliamentarians; and when they lost touch with their
> own country, and were absorbed in their dealings with the Liberal Whigs,
> a new Ireland was growing up, reviving the language of their fathers,
> reading the history of their country, and breathing a spirit of manhood and
> independence. If we had a leader who was an Irishman, they would have
> followed him to the death, but they never would be content with the
> servility to England and English parties that has been called nationality.

'That', he concluded, 'is the explanation of the rebellion of 1916. It was a
reaction against weakness, and stupidity, and corruption.' 'But hopeless as it was',
he added trenchantly, 'it has not been fruitless. It has galvanised the dead bones
in Ireland and breathed into them the spirit with which England has had to
reckon', and the treatment of the brave young men in Lewes jail would do little
to lessen it. Such methods would not subdue the people of Ireland, but it was
remarkable 'that astute politicians as the English unquestionably are' did not see
the inconsistency of promising a measure of government while 'imprisoning and
deporting the very men who … convinced them of the righteousness and
necessity of it.'[21] It never seemed to have occurred to his lordship that he was
not getting the truth about conditions at Lewes, and that dissatisfaction with the
regime there was organised by a minority of prisoners led by de Valera.[22]

O'Dwyer's letter was refused publication, but it was taken up by the Sinn
Féin organisation with a view to the coming trial of strength in a by-election in
County Longford. 'The enclosed may be of interest to you', O'Dwyer wrote to
Fogarty on 4 May. 'The Sinn Féin men have had it printed in great quantities
and have already sent it to Longford. It is a little strong in language but
substantially sound, and, I think, unanswerable.' He then shifted to a lighter key
without any sense of incongruity. With regard to the regular visit they were to
make to Rome that year, he intended, he said, to beg off for reasons of health
unless a general dispensation were given on account of the war; adding with a
wry touch, which indicated his awareness of the stories about him,

> I am told that the submarines are busy in the Irish Sea. If they knew I was
> travelling I'm sure they'd give me a safe conduct.[23]

Just four days later, on 8 May, O'Dwyer was one of the sixteen Catholic and
three Protestant bishops, and many prominent laymen, whose names were

attached to a declaration against the partition of the country. The same day, a letter was published by Archbishop Walsh stressing the urgency of the declaration and adding, in one of his celebrated postscripts, that he understood the mischief was already done, and that the country was practically sold. Sinn Fein rushed the archbishop's letter to Longford for the morning of the election. It was reputed to have swung the election.[24] The Sinn Féin candidate, Joseph P. McGuinness, still interned, defeated the strong Irish party representative, Patrick McKenna, by just 32 votes. O'Dwyer's letter may also be said to have played a part, though its clearly partisan nature may have limited its effect. The party was enraged at the interference by the two churchmen, and its organisational machine criticised and ridiculed Walsh 'up and down through the country'.[25] Where O'Dwyer was concerned, a formidable public letter critical of him appeared in the *Freeman* on 25 May. Indicative, perhaps, of the power of his lordship's pen, the author did not put his name to the missive. He signed it, 'Faith and Fatherland'.

UNDER DETERMINED ATTACK

The writer, in his long contribution, focussed on as many weak points as possible in O'Dwyer's career. Unfortunately for his case, he was more zealous than accurate in some instances, and this enabled the bishop to discredit much of his powerful argument.

O'Dwyer, the author declared, had inaugurated an uncharitable, almost scurrilous campaign against men whose only offence had been that for a generation – most of them for thirty, some of them for forty, years – they had 'served their country fearlessly and unselfishly, unshaken in their cause by the blandishments of the Whigs or Tories, and undeterred in their fight by jail or coercion'. To direct attention to the shortcomings of a bishop was to be accused of attacking 'the cloth', but Bishop O'Dwyer had 'gone beyond the beyonds' and taken up such a posture in the forefront of public life, that the time had come to ask

> What his political history is, by what title he can claim to lecture as from an eminence, men better than himself? And who has accorded to him the predominance in the Home Rule movement that entitles him, singling himself out from all the bishops of Ireland, to stigmatise the Irish Parliamentary Party with the *bitterness* and *malice* of which he has recently given evidence?[26]

O'Dwyer, the author conceded, was a man of great intellectual power and ability, and also 'a great ecclesiastic', but there had been ' great ecclesiastics' in the past who were not the 'wisest of politicians or the best patriots'. Curates had been the backbone of the national movement, except for one at Rathkeale who opposed W.H. O'Sullivan in 1874, thereby siding with Whig supporters against Home Rule. O'Sullivan won, and 'thus as a Whig curate did Most Revd Dr

O'Dwyer begin his political career'. 'The general course of mental development' was 'from impetuous democracy in youth to cautious conservatism in maturity', the writer observed, but in Dr O'Dwyer's case 'progress was all the other way'. Parnell had to fight against him. O'Dwyer met with Mr Balfour, at the height of his coercion career, at Lord Emly's table. And from that time on, the writer stated misleadingly, Balfour's campaign of evictions, clearances, imprisonments and murders followed. Then, quoting many of O'Dwyer's utterances in recent times, including the letter to Maxwell, in support of people who were suffering under English oppression, he raised the question – Where were such utterances and support in previous years when 'the homes of his diocese resounded to the sounds of the battering-ram' and 'when British bullets and bayonets were slaying the people', and 'when the gaols were full of priests, members of parliament and peasants'? 'He alone of all the Irish bishops declared that the conduct of the people was sinful;' and 'forbade a meeting in his diocese.'

The author went on to give a long extract from William O'Brien's address at that meeting, and an extract from O'Dwyer's response in the *Freeman's Journal* in which he opposed 'violent agitation' as likely to lead to a collision with the armed forces of the government. How could his lordship explain, the writer asked, why he applied the letter of the law to the oppressed campaigners but had 'nothing but words of palliation for the authors of the proceedings on Easter Monday'. He had made every effort 'to ascribe the rising to disgust against the Irish party' on the part of the youth of Ireland. But where was the evidence for this? The insurgents' own proclamation made no reference to the Irish party, instead it was clear from it that the rising was the work of a secret society and of syndicalists combined with a body of young men of sentiment and poetry. There was nothing spontaneous about it, it was 'a carefully prepared affair' in which was sought 'a theologically unjustifiable' alliance with Germany. The bishop talked of betrayal by the party over many years, the writer pressed on inexorably, yet at the end of 1913 he expressed his 'admiration of the great power and dignity with which Mr Redmond' had 'led the national movement to the present position'. He praised Redmond once again in his letter seeking support for the peace proposal on 4 August 1915. This was written less than nine months before the rebellion. What changed his view of Mr Redmond and the Home Rule Act? Was it due to the fact 'that the Irish leader refused to echo the bishop's cry for peace where there was no peace, and remained unmoved over the unlucky Hapsburgs?' Was this 'the explanation of his somersault on Home Rule and the Home Rule Act?' The bishop was then writing in favour of peace. Could he not have some thought for the peace of Ireland now? 'Can he not', the author queried sardonically, give up his patronage of the organisation which is 'inviting the country to the pastime of calling republics from the vasty deep, and trying to hasten Home rule by alliances with 'gallant allies' who are in deadly grips with the British Empire and the United States? Apparently the bishop is unable to declare himself for peace in Ireland.' 'Doubtless, it is not because he has turned Fenian in his old age', the writer concluded. 'It is inevitable to suppose that it is some feeling of malice, which, I regret to say, is not unknown even in bishops.'[27]

If 'Faith and Fatherland' thought that his powerful and telling polemic might silence the bishop, or curb his uncharitable vitriolic expressions, he was soon disappointed. Because so many of the comments struck home, O'Dwyer's reaction was all the fiercer. His reply appeared the following day in the *Cork Examiner,* and was reprinted later that day in the *Evening Herald.*

There was 'a *prima facie* case', he commenced, that any statement which the *Freeman* made about a political opponent was 'a falsehood'. It was so in its reference to his meeting with Mr Balfour and, by implication, his being involved in Balfour's crimes. He had never met Mr Balfour. Again, he was termed 'a Whig curate', which was 'a deliberate lie'. He began his career as a supporter of Isaac Butt, and, far from being an opponent of Home Rule, he was the only priest who stood on the hustings with him when the standard of Home Rule was raised, and furthermore he 'was honoured by the friendship of that great man up to his death'. Then, avoiding much of the strength of his critic's argument about his inconsistency in opposing violence against the government in the past and praising it in the present, he focussed on certain points and went on the attack.

He was accused of opposing the Plan of Campaign and boycotting. He had done so, but he was in good company. Pope Leo XIII 'confirmed' his judgment on these matters,

> and although the *Freeman's Journal's* master, Mr John Dillon, was not ashamed to denounce that great and illustrious Pontiff to the English House of Commons as a corrupt and dishonest Pope (God forgive me for writing it!), I think history will know how to judge between one of the great successors of the Fisherman and this poor drivelling bottle holder of the English Liberals.

After words which bore the marks of 'malice' mentioned by his critic, O'Dwyer moved on to face the alleged inconsistency in his attitude towards Redmond. Even more than in his reaction to Dillon, he spewed unpardonable defamation against the party leader. As to 'the few complimentary words' he used in the past about Mr Redmond, 'I admit they were a mistake', he said. 'I beg to withdraw them. I thought at the time that he was an Irishman. I have learned since that he is not even a man. He is a mere figurehead, painted green; but I thought, at that time, that he had some strength of character, and some national feeling, and I believed we were on the point of getting Home Rule. But the war has showed what he is made of, and the partition of Ireland, which he attempted to smuggle through, is the best indication of his ability and his patriotism.' 'I admit that I did not see through him in time', the bishop concluded, 'and when I praised him for powers and dignity, he had neither the one nor the other, but was the worthy fellow or follower of T.P. O'Connor and Dillon.'[28]

A week later, his lordship sent a brazen letter of thanks to the Limerick Board of Guardians for their criticism of the conduct of the *Freeman* towards himself.

'The letter signed 'Faith and Fatherland' was of such a character', he wrote, 'that no respectable paper would publish it, except over the name of its writer. It was an entirely personal and bitter attack which no man of honour would make anonymously, and any reputable paper would not allow be made from behind itself, as an assassin fires from the cover of a hedge.' He suspected that 'Faith and Fatherland' was an alias for the *Freeman's Journal*. A full week had passed since he 'demonstrated that the whole letter from first to last was a tissue of falsehoods and misrepresentation', yet 'no line of defence or withdrawal of its scandalous statements had been made by the *Freeman* or its correspondent – if there was such a person.'

The editor in a footnote to the published letter was brief and to the point.

> There is no foundation for the Bishop's suggestion that the letter of 'Faith and Fatherland' was not the letter of a *bona fide* correspondent uncon-
> nected with the *Freeman's Journal*. The Bishop's dislike of personal attacks is a new statement.[29]

O'Dwyer's behaviour in this interchange indicates how he, a self-proclaimed lover of truth, could temporise and be deliberately misleading. To attack his critic for hiding behind an alias came strangely from a man who had hidden behind the name of a non-existent priest in his public controversy with Dr Barry. It was not true to say, moreover, that he had 'demonstrated that the whole letter from first to last was a tissue of falsehoods and misrepresentations'.

The letter of the '*bona fide* correspondent' was part of an outspoken campaign by the party's 'machine', the United Irish League, following the defeat of the party's candidate in South Longford. It paid particular attention to the clergy, particularly the younger clergy, whom it accused of using 'falehood and calumny' against party leaders.[30] There was patent anxiety at the party's loss of ground, and at the attention being paid to the new movement by the English government.

NEW DEVELOPMENTS

Already on 16 May, a week after the Longford election, Lloyd George had proposed fresh alternatives: a bill for the immediate application of the Home Rule Act, but with exclusion for five years of six Ulster counties, or, the establishment of a convention of all interested parties, from all over the country, for the purpose of producing an agreed self-government scheme. The immediate application of the Act was seen as a concession to militant Sinn Féin, but the exclusion of six counties was viewed with suspicion and hostility by all except some extreme Unionists. There were solid grounds for suspicion. Unknown to the nationalist interests, the prime minister had assured the Unionist leadership that exclusion was not just for five years but permanent, and that their secured position would not be affected by the deliberations of the convention. Many viewed the convention as offering a last opportunity. On 21 May, Lloyd George announced formally 'A Convention of Irishmen of all parties for the purpose of producing a scheme of Irish self-government'. It was generally recognised as a pacifying gesture to public opinion in the United States.

A little more than a fortnight on, O'Dwyer advised O'Riordan – 'The convention is all the talk now'. The government wanted to win the Irish in Ireland and America very badly. The 'small nationality' cry was being re-echoed on all sides. It was possible that something might be done. 'My idea is', he declared, 'to let them hold their convention, and make their proposals, and then let nationalist Ireland give its answer, but take no responsibility at this stage.'[31]

A day later, on 7 June, Major Willie Redmond, the popular brother of the Irish party leader, was killed in action on the Western Front. His funeral drew large crowds to Dublin; but, within days, interest shifted to his vacant seat in East Clare. That soon became associated with the release from English prisons, on 16 June, of 120 Irish prisoners serving sentence for their part in the Easter rebellion. They included Eamon de Valera, and Joseph P. McGuinness. The latter had been elected for South Longford while still in prison, de Valera's name was put forward for East Clare shortly after the prisoners tumultuous welcome home.

The prisoners had been released to create a more favourable climate for the convention. Within a week, O'Dwyer informed O'Riordan that the bishops at their summer meeting had nominated four of their number for the convention: 'Cashel, Ross, Raphoe, and Down and Connor, all staunch *party* men.' 'I agreed,' he explained, 'on the ground that, if we refused, the government might drop the whole thing, and then say that the Catholic bishops killed H. Rule.' 'It's a pity', O'Dwyer added, 'that as a body we are not more independent. Cullen, in politics, was a Britisher, but in religion, a Catholic. I don't know what we are. In every part of our ecclesiastical system we are continually surrendering, … if we don't mind ourselves, we shall lose our hold of the young men.' The party had 'a severe contest in Clare', he concluded, 'with, I think, slight odds in favour of de Valera, a good Catholic and a clever fellow'.[32]

On 3 July, he provided further information about the convention and the bishops. He agreed with what O'Riordan had written about the convention being 'only the latest English fudge to amuse the Irish and please the world'. Many of the bishops understood that as plainly as he did, 'but several of them, perhaps a clear majority,' were 'political party men who look to John Dillon as the Israelites did to Moses. He's for the convention and that is enough for them.' 'Yet', he added, 'it was I proposed that we should send representatives, for the very reason that we knew it was a fraud and that we might not give the government a chance of throwing the blame for its failure on us.' The four bishops elected, he confided, were appointed on the private understanding 'that they were not to agree to partition in any shape or form'.[33]

O'Dwyer, as usual, went to Kilkee early in July. Before he went, he was visited by a tall, angular man, with a County Limerick accent, staring eyes, and a prison-pale complexion. De Valera, dressed in Volunteer uniform, which he was to wear all during the election campaign in Clare, took care to call on him to gain his support. He received what he later described as 'a reception of the warmest description'.[34] O'Dwyer told him, he reported, 'There will be no advance in Ireland until you sweep the rubbish out of the land,' to which de Valera replied that the party would die of its own accord. O'Dwyer rejoined: 'If you want to have a real Irish nation, such as you desire, you, first of all, must clean out the rubbish and build from a decent foundation.'[35]

The East Clare election stirred the hearts of the younger generation as never before. Clare was the 'Banner County', which concluded the case for Catholic Emancipation by electing Daniel O'Connell in 1828. Now it had the oppor-tunity of another historic advance by electing the only living signatory of the 1916 Proclamation, dressed symbolically in his Volunteer uniform. Young people poured into Clare to walk and cycle its roads and by-ways in his support. De Valera, ever conscious of Church influence, and of the exalted popularity of O'Dwyer, identified himself with the latter's sentiments, quoting the bishop's emotive lines at Limerick town hall, which had caught the public imagination – 'Ireland will never be content as a province. God made her a nation. And while grass grows and water runs there will be men in Ireland to dare and die for her.'

The result of the East Clare by-election on 10 July declared Eamon de Valera (Sinn Fein) elected with 5,010 votes against Patrick Lynch (Nationalist) with 2,035. The news of the result and of the margin of victory swept rapidly throughout the country and evoked widespread rejoicing.

De Valera's confident reply to O'Dwyer that the party would die of its own accord was virtually fulfilled after the Clare election. The party's newspaper, the *Freeman's Journal*, was on the verge of bankruptcy, as was the party itself. John Redmond was fatally ill. Dillon, after Longford, no longer trusted the news from the constituencies with their over-confident predictions of favourable election outcomes, and he expected little from the convention. Worst of all, was the awareness that the government had abandoned them, and seemed ready to pass them by.[36]

THE DARKENING OF THE LIGHT

Where O'Dwyer was concerned, however, more immediate concerns occupied his attention. 'I thought it was all up on Tuesday night', he wrote to Fogarty from Kilkee on 13 July. 'For five or six years, I have had valvular disease of the heart in a rather bad form, and that frightened me when, for the first time, I got a most extraordinary heaving of the chest, with a sensation of smothering. Fortunately, Fr Fenton was in the next room and gave me absolution, and when the attack grew worse, we sent for the curate, a nice quiet man, Fr Dinan, who anointed me.' 'The whole thing passed off in half an hour, and I fell into a lovely sleep, and am now, thank God, in *statu quo*.'

Having conveyed this rather dramatic news of what had happened in Fogarty's own diocese, O'Dwyer observed that de Valera's victory was 'grand',

and that the whole course of the election justified Fogarty's policy 'in leaving political liberty to the clergy'. 'There was not an incident', as far as O'Dwyer could learn, 'that was unworthy of their calling.'[37]

A fortnight later he thought it well to inform O'Riordan, as it were in passing.

> You will be surprised to hear that I was anointed some three weeks ago. I got an extraordinary heart spasm, which was so severe, and so strange, that I thought my end was come. Thank God, it passed away quickly, and has left me little the worse except for a certain apprehension that it may occur at any moment.[38]

On the same day that he wrote to O'Riordan, his lordship sent a letter to Walter McDonald concerning the principles of moral science in which he again made reference to his state of health. He received a rather detached, but down-to-earth reply from the Maynooth professor. The latter regretted to learn that he had been unwell, and he would pray God to spare him for many years. 'It takes courage and patience to live a threatened life', he went on, 'but, then, all lives are threatened, and to any man the summons may come at any time. It is, moreover, easy for one who is blessed with your lordship's great and simple faith, to look out for the Judge; but for a critic – or worse – like me, it takes some courage to face the music. God grant that it may not fail – nor yet the fear – when the time comes, that, in any case, cannot be far distant.'[39]

Still preoccupied by his unsettled condition, he informed O'Riordan, on 4 August, of his return from Kilkee and his fear that the attack might recur. 'It was in God's hands', he said, and it was a good 'to get notice and time to prepare'. He remained concerned about world peace. 'If the present offensive fails', he commented, 'we may hear of peace before Xmas.'[40]

O'Riordan had been so often near to death that he was good person to whom to write. 'The news you give that you have been anointed does surprise me', he replied on 5 August, 'although I take getting anointed myself, by this time, as a matter of course. One gets used to it; and it never kills; rather cures, even physically.' He recommended that the bishop approach a good specialist, who 'should be able to apply preventatives to keep another attack away'. 'The heart cannot be bad', he observed, 'else you would have lost your activity long since.' He suggested that the bishop remove the work of visitations, confirmations, and examinations by getting an auxiliary bishop. Later in the letter, O'Riordan thoughtfully tried to offer further assistance by referring to his own experience.

> I would say for your encouragement, that when you are as often going to die as I have been, you will come to take little notice of it. It will appear the most natural thing in the world. More than once during the the past ten years have I, during the night, got up from bed in hospital, sat down and wrote out instructions to leave the vice-rector, not knowing that I should ever see the college again.[41]

The next news he heard of his friend, the bishop, was that he was 'very seriously ill', that his recovery was 'very doubtful', and that a sympathetic letter, 'accompanied with the Pope's blessing', would be very grateful to him.[42] By the time the telegram arrived, Edward Thomas O'Dwyer was dead.

THE DEATH AND ITS IMPACT

Writing on 22 August to, presumably, Monsignor Hallinan, O'Riordan explained about the communications he had from Dr O'Dwyer about his heart condition, and then added a striking assessment:

> He has, after many strifes, gone out in the end in a blaze of glory. He has been, beyond question, *the first bishop in Ireland these last years, and I have good reason for saying that in the mind of the highest ecclesiastics here he is one of the first bishops in Europe.* His pastorals on peace made a real impression; but the frenzy of those who don't want peace 'till absolute victory brings it, prevents one from telling of the impressions which his pastorals have made.

Speaking out of a full heart, yet keen, as ever, to seize an apostolic opportunity, O'Riordan continued: 'I hope you will secure a fit person to preach at the month's mind. Don't commit it to a platitudinous duffer … It is a great opportunity for a pronouncement of lasting effect. His action at the time of the Plan of Campaign (although *in detail* perhaps not always wise), and his defiance of Sir J. Maxwell last year, would suggest a glorious idea – that the Church speaks independently of demagogues or kings … that the bishop's action is a concrete illustration of that spirit which condemns Erastianism in religion. Imagine an Anglican bishop writing such a letter as he sent to Sir John Maxwell! Said St Basil to the Emperor of his time, who expressed astonishment at the bishop's straight talk to him – 'I am not used to such talk', said the Emperor, 'You are not used to speaking with Catholic bishops', said St Basil. Then there is the occasion for setting forth a good lesson of warning (if skilfully done) against the possible attempts of some of our leading patriots with Erastian tendencies'. Finally, O'Riordan warned that he was not available as a successor to Bishop O'Dwyer.[43] Subsequently, he had to withstand numerous efforts to get him to agree to allow his name go forward.

Newspaper reports filled in the gap in public knowledge about the bishop's unexpected death. He fell ill on Monday, 13 August. Dr Malone, who attended him, called in a second local opinion, Dr Devane, and, in turn, they called on a Dr Dempsey of Dublin. The latter, having examined the patient, confirmed the diagnosis, which pointed not to an immediate heart condition but to an internal growth, the removal of which might prolong life for a short time. O'Dwyer, in the circumstances, decided against an operation,[44] thanked the specialist for his forthrightness, and instructed that there should be no public announcement of his condition.[45] He remained conscious almost to the end. On Friday evening, when Fr Michael O'Donnell went to see him, the bishop remarked: 'I have been suffering extreme pain. I fear I shall not get over this, pray for me.'[46] He died the next day, Saturday, 19 August. The city was completely unprepared. The following Wednesday, the *Munster News* still wrote of 'a stricken city' where 'the very air seems grief-laden'.[47] The *Limerick Leader* of 22 August wrote in solemn tones how at the appointed time for the removal of the remains from the palace at Corbally every vantage point to view the funeral procession was occupied. 'The windows were crowded, the footpaths and doorsteps were thronged.' Every street 'swarmed with moody and silent men, women and children. On all sides … the reality of the sorrow felt for the death of Bishop O'Dwyer was unmistakeably evidenced. As the hearse passed the heads of all were reverently uncovered and bowed.'

As might be expected, various letters concerning the dead prelate were sent to O'Riordan in the days following the death. Fr Pat Lee, parish priest of Kilfinane, Co. Limerick, commented that Dr O'Dwyer had 'found a big place in some of our hearts, and it was growing as time went on'. Although he was going around much as usual, the attack in Kilkee had taken a great deal out of him. Yesterday, Lee had a visit from an Australian army chaplain, who conveyed his sympathies and those of fellow Australians and remarked that O'Dwyer 'was all but adored by the Irish out there'. 'No man, I dare say,' Lee went on, 'was so fervently popular with Irish people all over the world as Dr O'Dwyer. And he must have done great service in moderating the Sinn Fein people.'[48] A Mr H.W. Cleary, a friend of O'Riordan, wrote from Howard Hotel, the Strand, London, to convey his sympathies, and to state with respect to the late bishop: 'He is a loss to all Ireland: an able man, a strong man, for Ireland an *unusual man*, who struck out his own line, followed it boldly, and had the supreme grace – when a great occasion befell – to say just the right thing, at the right time, and in the right way. And, therein, he stood alone. R.I.P.'[49]

Other letters told of both the funeral and peoples' impressions. A regular comment was that no one realised Dr O'Dwyer's fragile health. One writer, whose signature is undecipherable, declared, 'He was so active and energetic one could never think that he was suffering from heart disease.' The correspondent acknowledged:

> He certainly died in harness and in a blaze of glory. There were twelve Bishops – including the Cardinal – at the funeral and about four hundred priests and a great concourse of people. His advocacy of Sinn Feinism, or quasi advocacy, swelled the crowd immensely.[50]

Another correspondent, in the holiday atmosphere of Lisdoonvarna, also had some significant comments to report about the late bishop. He had been talking with many of the clergy who frequented the resort from all parts of Ireland. 'Nearly all the priests we talked to stated that never was nationality and

Catholicity so identified in Ireland before, and that this was largely and chiefly owing to the action of the dead bishop – that he saved the situation, and that it needed a man of his courage, position and ability to do it.'[51]

This stated reaction was at variance with another significant letter, from Michael O'Donnell, parish priest at Rathkeale, who had visited the bishop the night before his death. He confided to O'Riordan, with respect to Dr O'Dwyer:

> I could not agree with his policy of the last twelve months or so, nor could I understand it. True, he did not go in for physical force, but 'the man in the street', I fear, would think that he did – that was my difficulty. Had he lived I was inclined to think that sooner or later he would have let the man in the street know plainly that he did not go in for physical force.

'That is why', O'Donnell explained, 'I consider his loss so great. No one else can teach that lesson as well as he could have taught it, especially under the circumstances. Now the danger is that he may be cited as a teacher of the opposite. We are in very unsettled times.'[52]

Both insights on the bishop's influence were valid. The empathy between the new popular movement, widely called Sinn Féin, and the Catholic Church owed much to numerous young priests and two prelates, Archbishop Walsh of Dublin and Dr O'Dwyer of Limerick. Walsh was a revered national figure. He had associated himself with the popular struggle in Land League times, consciously seeking to keep the Church in touch with the people, even though it might lead to misunderstanding with Rome. In 1916 he significantly remained silent in the face of a rebellion in his own city that was condemned on all sides. As a result, his stature rose even higher in the minds of the leaders of Sinn Féin, and to the end of his life they respected his judgment and regarded him with deference and almost awe. O'Dwyer was very different. In Walsh's view he endangered the Church's links with the ordinary people in Land League days, and did so in the name of the pope. As a result of his opposition to the policy of the League, he was seen for many years as an establishment figure, though to those who knew him well it was clear that he was a far more complex personality than the caricature allowed, and that he was deeply nationalist. In 1916, through a confluence of circumstances, he was placed in a position where his nationalist feeling and his sense of episcopal authority were jointly disturbed by the manner of General Sir John Maxwell, and he deliberately defied him in a public way. His action had an almost electric effect on a subdued, uncertain, yet angry majority population. From then on, O'Dwyer, as has been seen, entered into the pantheon of national heroes. Thanks primarily, therefore, to the leadership of Archbishop Walsh and Bishop O'Dwyer, the new nationalist movement, in the years of violence and outrage from 1918 to 1921, remained in contact with the Catholic Church. De Valera's comment at a meeting in Tipperary, following O'Dwyer's death, was significant and indicative. 'As long as there are bishops such as Dr O'Dwyer there will never be anti-clericalism in this land. A man like Dr O'Dwyer was a model Irish bishop.'[53]

A further matter to be specifically noted on the positive side is that, thanks to the work of Michael O'Riordan and the writings of Bishop O'Dwyer, the Pope and the Roman curia had been instructed on the special role of the Irish church, and became favourably disposed to the legitimacy of Irish independence.

On the other hand, there were grounds for Fr O'Donnell's fears. Archbishop Walsh remained honoured above the fray. O'Dwyer, on the other hand, had clearly taken sides. He had spoken of the Easter Rising as 'theologically unjustifiable', yet he had praised the insurgents and used emotive patriotic language which challenged young men and stirred their blood. Hence, he was viewed as a champion of their cause, as, in some way, one of themselves, and after his death he was not only linked in ballad with the dead leaders of the epic insurrection, a postcard was circulated in thousands that carried a portrait of himself and his words about God making Ireland a nation, and how 'while grass grows and water runs' there would 'be men in Ireland to dare and die for her'. As Fr O'Donnell feared, the bishop's sudden death allowed him to be cited as a supporter of a struggle for freedom in which physical force became a means to the end. This was implicitly forecast by the naming of a Limerick Sinn Féin club after him during his lifetime, and by the condolences from Sinn Féin clubs all over the country following his death. It was also significant that the leading members of the Irish party did not attend the funeral, whereas the new leadership was represented by such as Arthur Griffith, Eamon de Valera, William Cosgrave and Count Plunkett.[54] Griffith, moreover, paid a distinctively patriotic tribute to the former prelate in *New Ireland,* 25 August 1917. Dr O'Dwyer, he alleged, hated everything associated with English domination, believed firmly 'in the ultimate triumph of the Irish nation' and worked consistently to bring it about. His was the voice that halted and dismayed the 'march of armed tyranny', when it seemed that it was in the process of effecting the last conquest of Ireland. He had rallied 'a distracted and leaderless Irish nation' and had helped to give it cohesion and inspiration.

O'Riordan's desire that the month's mind should not be entrusted to 'a platitudinous duffer' was fulfilled. The panegyric was entrusted to O'Dwyer's friend, Michael Fogarty, himself an orator of note and with similar nationalist feelings. He was to carry on, in effect, O'Dwyer's practice of forceful political commentary. His sermon or address, however, was an exaggerated eulogy rather than the more profound presentation O'Riordan had desired.

In his paean of praise, Fogarty paid tribute to his friend's fearlessness and to other qualities that made him a fascinating personality – 'the priest adored by his people, the ardent apostle, the vehement churchman, and the dauntless champion of his country's freedom'. Maynooth College, said his lordship, had nurtured many distinguished churchmen, but never one more brilliant than this great prelate. Reference was made to O'Dwyer's work as a curate, to his energetic episcopal career, to the various monuments to his zeal and piety, and to his devotedness to the care of the sick and the poor. His pride in the largest men's confraternity in the world, at the Redemptorist church, was noted, as also his work in relation to the National University and the Mary Immaculate teacher training college, his confutation of Modernism and the resultant personal appreciation bestowed on him by Pope Pius X.

Turning, with particular emphasis, to O'Dwyer as a nationalist, Fogarty declared: 'He was an Irishman to the very fountains of his life. But this burning Irish heart was doomed for a time to the saddest of destinies – to see itself cruelly misunderstood in the minds of its own countrymen, as it was in the days of the land agitation.' He hated the unjust system of Irish land laws and desired their abolition, 'but, unfortunately, the movements got mixed up with methods like the Plan of Campaign, which he considered was opposed to the moral law, and which, with characteristic and holy courage, he publicly denounced as such.' 'The consequences', Fogarty declared, 'were most tragic and mortifying.' He was 'denounced for years from every platform in the country as anti-Irish and a landlord's man.' 'The after-developments were as dramatic as they were signifi-cant and full of warning. The great bishop, the victim of so much suffering for conscience's sake, became the object of enthusiasm in recent days. When brave and heroic Irishmen were being shot in Dublin, Irish emigrants kicked and spat upon in the streets of Liverpool, the whole country raided of its manhood and dragooned into terror, the one man who had the courage to raise his voice in Christian protest and challenge the march of tyranny was the 'anti-Irish' Bishop of Limerick!'[55]

In the mounting national feeling of those years, Edward Thomas O'Dwyer was on the way to occupying a permanent place in the gallery of nation builders. One suspects that he would have been both honoured and wryly amused at the prospect.

Conclusion. A retrospective assessment

'Speak of me as I am. Nothing extenuate,
Nor set down aught in malice.'

(Julius Caesar)

Time is the master of perspective. That is very evident in a perusal of Edward
Thomas O'Dwyer as a political figure. For long, as has been seen, he was decried
as a 'Castle-bishop' who, for one reason or another, discovered nationality in the
last years of his life. Now it is clear that his was a strongly nationalist spirit from
early on, and that the only reason for calling him a 'Castle-bishop' was his refusal
to equate national spirit, or patriotism, with support for the aggressive activities
of the Land League. In this attitude, he was in line with another noted patriot,
Isaac Butt, whom he regarded as mentor and friend. Again, O'Dwyer has been
described, in more recent times, as not very interested in the issue of partition
and, perhaps, as being disposed to see the loss of the predominantly Protestant
counties as good riddance.[1] In fact, it is evident from his letters that he, even
more than many of the bishops, abhorred partition. The *Irish Independent,* indeed,
whose proprietor, William Martin Murphy, worked ceaselessly to prevent
partition,[2] acknowledged, prematurely, on 20 August 1917 that 'last year he
(O'Dwyer) fought against the proposal to partition Ireland with a degree of zeal
that played an important part in the destruction of that unfortunate scheme'. The
passage of time, and further research, has also unveiled Dr O'Dwyer as not just a
national figure, but as a bishop who took an active interest in educational matters
in Britain, and who, as a writer and publicist exercised influence in the United
States and in Australia, and, even more significantly at the time, helped to
increase understanding of, and empathy for the Irish church, and for Irish
national aspirations, at the Vatican.

A feature of obituary references is that they sometimes disclose information
not generally known about the deceased. In O'Dwyer's case, one learns from ' A
Priest of the Diocese', writing in the *Irish Independent* of 21 August 1917, that, in
addition to his numerous other attainments, he 'loved the classics, spoke French
fluently, Italian tolerably well, translated it with ease, and was a close student of
Dante, many portions of which he could quote at any moment. He was a
botanist and scientist'… and 'he shone as a raconteur.' These provide further
examples of the depth and range of the talents and activities already indicated in

the preceding pages. All of them, conjoined with his complex personality and conspicuous inconsistencies, added to the colour, richness, and contrariness of his life. The instances of the inconsistencies are sufficiently numerous to stand out and require mention.

Bishop O'Dwyer claimed that his over-riding concern in his career was to fulfil, as well as he could, the duties of his office. It was this, he alleged, that led to his defiance of the Land League and to his prohibition of the giant public meeting in his city. This concern for episcopal duty, and the dignity of his office, was also in evidence in his clash with Sir John Maxwell. Yet, despite his exalted view of his episcopal office, displayed in actions and in sermons at episcopal consecrations, he frequently indulged in invective unworthy of that position, even allowing for the fact that it was an age marked by harsh invective, as witness Arthur Griffith's papers and Jim Larkin's *Irish Worker*. Even his good friend James G. Barry acknowledged that

> In his public utterances he was simply Edward Thomas O'Dwyer, forgetting for the moment his dignity as a bishop; having no respect for rank or position or public applause, he spoke strongly, criticised openly without reserve and often in language neither select or dignified, without a thought of its effects on others as coming from a bishop.[3]

A prime example of this was the occasion when he took a man to court who sold him a defective horse. He attended the court and interrupted the witness a number of times from the body of the court in a most unseemly manner![4] In his ordinary exchanges he not infrequently carried Anglo-Irish cutting directness to an extreme, and even his humour is recollected as having a sharp edge.[5]

Where John Dillon was concerned, he conducted what amounted to a vendetta, and his words about him, about T.P. O'Connor and John Redmond, were at different times not just un-episcopal but un-Christian. In general, he took an almost malicious delight in an opponent's discomfort; and those who had experienced prolonged differences with him must have smiled sardonically at his assertion at the conferring of the Freedom of Limerick, 'I entertain no enmity to any living person'. Although his lordship may have believed that he held no grudges against past opponents, not a few of the latter felt that when his lordship buried the hatchet he carefully marked the spot, and they walked warily in his vicinity.

Apart from such instances of discordant behaviour, there were other features incompatible with the standard image of a good shepherd. He sought to control situations and people, even to dominate, and brought to bear his position, his strong personality, and his sharp and waspish tongue to achieve his ends. As a result, although some of his clergy revered and liked him, the general body of priests feared him and a small section of these actively disliked him. One man, indeed, destined to become a vicar forane in the diocese, spoke of him as 'a dirty little tyrant', and Bishop Patrick O'Neill summarised him as 'a terrible little man'.[6] The desire to dominate and control was also evident in his long campaigns over the schools in Limerick, in relation to the Christian Brothers at Bruff and to the Jesuits at Mungret College. Fr Thomas Head, SJ, a former friend and contemporary of Edward Thomas as a diocesan priest, and later rector of Mungret College, observed forthrightly 'It is the experience of all who have to deal with him that it is folly to yield unless there is real necessity. The more one yields the more he tramples on "one's" rights, at least the more he tries to extend his own authority'.[7] Fr Michael O'Donnell, of Rathkeale, indicated the lengths to which the bishop was prepared to go in his passion for control. He had not yet accepted the tender for the decoration of the church, O'Donnell informed his lordship on 17 July 1917, because 'Your lordship once told me not to decorate the church without consulting you as to the nature of the decorations'.[8] A further aspect of this need to be in charge, to control events in his domain, was reflected in his attitude to his former friend, Archbishop William Walsh. Once O'Dwyer became bishop, he seemed to feel the need to assert his independence where Walsh was concerned. The elderly Archdeacon Ryan, interviewed in the 1970s, had the impression that O'Dwyer was envious of Walsh's ability and authority, and hence sought to assert himself against him. Instances of this were: his defiance of the Archbishop of Dublin with respect to the senate of the Royal University, his pursuit of the university question when Walsh and Croke viewed it as a distraction from the central quest of Home Rule, his stand against the Land League and his proclamation of himself as loyal to Rome, to the seeming detriment of Walsh and most of the other prelates, and his campaign for an independent Catholic University as distinct from Walsh's preference for a Catholic College in Dublin University. His letters to Bishop Donnelly add some weight to this interpretation in their frequent comments critical of the archbishop.

Accentuating this tendency to regulate and dominate, was the habit of authority, and the loud voice of a deaf man who considered himself the last word on an almost endless range of matters. Kate O'Brien, novelist and playwright, captured something of these aspects in a passing portrayal of his lordship in relaxed moments in Laurel Hill.

> Very deaf, with the piercing, tiring voice of a deaf man, he used to yell at Reverend Mother that she must cut down the Elm trees that shaded the Visitors' Walk. It was clear from her courteous acknowledgements of these shouts, clear even to him, that she would never do so.[9]

In the view of friends, he was also 'often dogmatic', and 'stern and unbending when his mind was made up on any subject'.[10] He frequently took a point of view hastily, and, as Canon O'Kennedy recalled, 'with an unconscious claim to infallibility he held that his own opinion could not be wrong, and … opposition only made him cling to his views with greater tenacity'.[11]

And yet, and yet, 'he was great company',[12] and 'the charm of his personality and the brilliance of his intellect endeared him to all who enjoyed the privilege of his friendship'.[13] 'On Holy Thursday', Dean Punch still recalled sixty years later, 'he took us all out to his house for dinner. He was deaf, but he kept the whole of us laughing the whole time – he had a power of humour. Then, he stood at the door and shook hands with everyone as they left.'[14]

Part of his undoubted appeal was his simplicity and ease of manner, the absence of all 'side' and affectation, and a self-assurance, probably fostered by an admiring mother and sisters, that enabled him to be equally at ease in the stately homes of gentry and in the cottages of the poor; though his 'half-joke whole-earnest' form of conversation led to misunderstandings at times![15] In addition, there was what Lord Monteagle termed his 'transparent sincerity and fearless championship of the truth';[16] and his concern for justice and the development of the faith of the people entrusted to him. His special concern for the poor, the defenceless, and workers in difficulty, together with his efforts to further his people's material future by means of improved educational facilities, inevitably earned public respect and admiration. The people of the diocese came to feel pride, too, in their prelate's many gifts, his dignity and style, and the competence of his administration; and across the country he became a familiar name because of his prominent stand against the Land League, his persistence in the quest for university education, his outstanding performance before the Robertson Commission, his work for teacher training, and above all for his courageous championing of the emigrants, and his censuring of the commander-in-chief for his injustice and cruelty towards the insurgents of Easter Week. In his final years, his identification with national feeling gained him widespread popularity. A popularity and appreciation, which was increased by the fact that despite deafness he carried on without fuss or self-pity and with remarkable buoyancy.

This last was probably the greatest testimony to the mettle and spiritual strength of the man. Through the long years of his episcopate, 'this very handsome, aristocratic-looking man',[17] every inch a bishop, with a brilliant mind stored with information, and with a rare ability to communicate and be the life of a gathering, was afflicted with deafness. It was a defect and burden that he viewed as 'a cross' to be borne with patience, but which probably exacerbated his at times volatile outbursts. In his later life, the affliction virtually debarred all conversation, and rendered him largely isolated except for a small circle of mainly clerical friends. Yet, his deep and simple faith enabled him retain an inner peace, and in his last days he assured his doctors that he had had 'a long life, and not an unhappy day'.[18] The same faith, it may be said, kept him from being carried away by the adulation and influence he enjoyed.

Surveying his long career, his range of abilities and activities, his striking personality, with its asperities and singularities as well as its charm, one seems, more than in most cases, to be viewing two persons rather than one. The amalgam that was Edward Thomas O'Dwyer was certainly 'for Ireland an unusual man',[19] or as a puzzled Augustine Birrell described him before the Commission of Enquiry into the Easter Rising, 'a very queer man',[20] a figure undoubtedly unique among prelates in Britain and Ireland, and appreciated as such in Rome. He had a magnetic, star quality which, at best, exuded an optimistic vitality and a liberty of spirit and courage that lifted hearts and challenged listeners and readers, and which, given his political prominence at a key moment in his country's history, has made and is likely to make his name and career remembered after successive successors, of more caring and gentle disposition, are long forgotten. Although feared by many of his priests, to whom he seemed something of a tyrant, he knew his people in their weaknesses and their strengths, their joys and their sorrows, and, like a benevolent despot, he instructed them on matters of religion and morality, championed them in their distress, and worked for them upon four great measures of social reform – Housing, Nursing, Temperance, and Education. They, in turn, came to look on him with respect, affection and pride for his work, interest, and achievements and also for the very human frailties, of body and temperament, which brought him closer to them; and when he died they mourned his loss as a personal grief.

Notes

LRTV   *Limerick Reporter and Tipperary Vindicator*
LDA   Limerick Diocesan Archives
DDA   Dublin Diocesan Archives
CDA   Cashel Diocesan Archives
IM   *Irish Monthly*
IJA   Irish Jesuit Archives

I BOYHOOD TO EARLY PRIESTHOOD, 1842–1868

1 *LRTV*, 19 Mar. 1886. Edward was baptised on 30 January – parish records, Holy Cross, cit. John Rushe in 'Bishop O'Dwyer of Limerick 1886–1917 & the educational issues of his time', MA thesis, National University of Ireland, 1980, sect. 2, p. 63 (= 2.63).
2 Martin Callanan, *Records of four Tipperary septs*, Galway 1938, pp. 112ff, 137–41. See Sir Michael O'Dwyer. *The O'Dwyers of Kilnamanagh. The history of an Irish sept* (London, 1933); and Colmcille O'Conbhuidhe, OCSO, *The Cistercian abbeys of Tipperary*, ed. F. Donovan (Dublin 1999).
3 A. Young i, p. 388, ed. A.W. Hutton (2 vols 1892).
4 *LRTV*, 14 June 1887, obit. Roger Keatinge-O'Dwyer, cit. Rushe, op. cit., 2.63.
5 Idem, 9 Mar. 1886, reprint from *Cashel Gazette*, cit. Rushe, 2. 63.
6 John Begley., *The diocese of Limerick from 1691 to the present Time* (Dublin, 1938), p. 563.
7 *LRTV*, 9 March 1886.
8 T.F. O'Sullivan, *The Young Irelanders* (Tralee, 1944), pp. 249, 253. His songs include the popular 'Eileen a Ruan'.
9 *LRTV*, 9 Mar. 1886.   10 Idem.   11 LDA, O'Dwyer papers, folder 3.
12 *LRTV*, 20 Feb. 1872. Obituary.
13 E.H. Bennis, *Reminiscences of Old Limerick* (1937), cit. Rushe, 2.1, 2.63.
14 *Irish Catholic Directory*, various issues, cit. Rushe, idem.
15 Monsignor Michael Moloney, PP, an historian of Limerick diocese, in a 'Muintir na Tire Fireside Chat' reported in *Limerick Leader*, 21 Nov. 1942, cit. Rushe 2.3 and 64.
16 Born 1840, died 1907. Information to John Rushe from Sr Alexine, Secretary General, based on Selly Park archives: Rushe 2.63.
17 LDA, folder B, Annie's letters 1872–1907.
18 Idem. Letter of 29 Aug. 1888.   19 Idem. Letter of 27 Aug. 1891.
20 See Letter of 8 Jan. 1886.   21 Idem.
22 *LRTV*, 20 Feb. 1872. Obituary.
23 *Limerick Chronicle,* 27 Oct. 1870, cit. Rushe, 2.63
24 LDA, folder Q, O'Dwyer papers.
25 DDA, Archbishop Walsh papers, O'Dwyer to Walsh, 18 Oct. & 2 Nov. 1886, in Rushe, 2.63. Dr McCormack, bishop of Achonry, was translated to Galway the following year, 1887. The training college is presumably St Patrick's Teacher Training College, Drumcondra, Dublin.
26 Begley, op. cit., pp. 564–5.
27 CDA, biographical note on O'Dwyer. See Rushe, 2.64.   28 Idem.

29 Francis Finnegan, SJ, *Limerick Jesuit Centenary Record, 1859–1959*, p. 9; also *LRTV*, 21 Dec. 1888, quotes O'Dwyer at prize giving in the Crescent College referring to himself 'as an old pupil of this same college'.
30 Finnegan, op. cit., idem.
31 Francis Finnegan, former archivist at Irish Jesuit Archives, recalls a reference in the archives, not found by the present author, to O'Dwyer's fees not having been paid while a student at the Jesuit College, a circumstance which might well have occasioned upset for someone as proud and self-centred as Edward Thomas.
32 P.J. Joyce, *John Healy, archbishop of Tuam* (Dublin, 1931), pp. 80–1.
33 Fogarty's panegyric after O'Dwyer's death. LDA.
34 See Joyce, pp. 10–1; & the Maynooth College Calendar, courtesy of Prof. P.J. Corish, Maynooth, in a letter to author.
35 Murphy after some years quarrelled with his archbishop and went to the United States where he died in a hotel fire – Joyce, op. cit., pp. 10–11.
36 Monsignor Moloney in his 'Fireside Chat', *Limerick Leader*, 21 Nov. 1942.
37 IJA. Sc/Cres/2 (4)–(8). Province Consultors' book, 4 Jan. 1864.
38 IJA. Sc/Cres/2 (4)–(8). Copy in Fr Finnegan's hand.
39 Idem. Decision of 6 Jan. 1865.
40 Finnegan. *Limerick Jesuit Cent. Record*, p. 17.
41 Idem, p. 77.
42 Thomas Kelly, 30 Nov. 1868. IJA. Sc/Cres/2 (4)–(8).
43 Idem. 3 Aug. 1870, IJA. Idem.
44 John Fleming and Sean O'Grady, *St Munchin's College Limerick, 1796–1996* (Limerick, 1996), pp. 56–7.

2 THE CURATE: A DIFFICULT APPRENTICESHIP, 1867–74

1 Monsignor Ml. Moloney to Fr Sean Hughes, SJ, during the 1960s. Retailed to author by Fr Hughes.
2 M.M. (Ml. Moloney). 'Park House' in *Our Catholic Life*, summer 1962.
3 For these other references to his locations see Begley, *Diocese of Limerick*, p. 566, also *Irish Catholic Directory*, 1873.
4 Implied in Kate O'Brien, *Land of Spices* (London, 1941; 1988 ed.), p. 209. Kate O'Brien was from Limerick and something of an admirer of the bishop.
5 Begley, op. cit., p. 566.
6 Rushe, 2.10, citing *Letters and diaries of John Henry Newman*, LDXXII, p. 544.
7 Begley, p. 567.
8 Kate O'Brien. 'Christmas in the Presentation Parlour' reprinted in J. Kemmy (ed.), *The Limerick anthology* (Dublin, 1996).
9 Edward P. O'Callaghan, O.F.M. 'Bishop Edward Thomas O'Dwyer and the course of Irish politics, 1870–1917', MA thesis, NUI, 1976, n. 17, p. 410.
10 Begley, p. 564.
11 *Munster News*, 20 Jan. 1874.
12 *Limerick Chronicle*, 10 Jan. 1874.
13 Idem, 3 Jan. 1874.
14 All those mentioned were articulate and well educated. William Shaw was MP for County Cork, John Martin, an MP for Meath, was the first member elected to parliament by the Home Rule Association, and Rowland Ponsonby Blennerhasset was a Protestant Home-Ruler, elected for Kerry in 1872.
15 O'Callaghan, op. cit., pp. 52–3.
16 *Cork Examiner*, 3 Jan. 1874, cit. O'Callaghan, pp. 53–4.
17 *Munster News*, 7 Jan. 1874.

18 Idem, 14 Jan. 1874, cit. O'Callaghan, p. 55.
19 See *Limerick Chronicle*, 6 Jan. 1874, where Kelly remarked at a meeting in Limerick that his opponent would not cut an impressive figure with 'Disraeli and Co.'.
20 L.J. McCaffrey. 'Home Rule and the General Election of 1874 in Ireland' in *Irish Historical Studies*, ix, no. 34 (Sept. 1954), p. 202; cit. O'Callaghan, p. 56.
21 F. Finnegan. *Limerick Jesuit Centenary Record*, p. 80.
22 *Munster News*, 7 Feb. 1874.
23 David Thornley. *Isaac Butt and Home Rule* (London, 1964), p. 194.
24 O'Callaghan, op. cit., p. 58.   25 *Munster News*, 14 Feb. 1874.
26 *Limerick Leader*, 20 Aug. 1917, cit. O'Callaghan, pp. 59–60.
27 *Limerick Chronicle*, 18 April 1874.
28 Idem, 29 May 1888.
29 Butler–O'Dwyer, 3 June 1874, LDA, File A – '45 Miscel. Letters'.

3 ST MICHAEL'S PARISH: MEETING NEEDS, 1874–1886

1 F. Prendergast *St Michael's Parish, Limerick. Its life and times* (Limerick, 2000), p. 3.
2 James Canon O'Shea, PP Kilmallock, replying to queries about O'Dwyer's early life from Monsignor Denis Hallinan, 30 Oct. 1917. LDA, file on the University Question.
3 His enthusiasm for temperance, and the relative absence of reference to his father, encouraged some to think that Edward's father may have had an alcohol problem.
4 *Limerick Reporter and Tipperary Vindicator*, 14 Nov. 1877. See John Rushe 'Edward Thomas O'Dwyer and the Temperance Movement' in *Old Limerick Journal*, 8 (Autumn 1981), pp. 12–13.
5 In interview with S. Rushe.
6 Canon O'Shea's response to Monsignor Hallinan, 30 Oct. 1917.
7 Printed pamphlet in file on Limerick Catholic Institute, LDA.
8 Minute Book of the Institute, 1887–1905, cit. Rushe 3. 41.
9 *LRTV,* 3 Aug. 1886. Bishop O'Dwyer's address to the Institute's council.
10 LDA, Limerick Catholic Institute file, doc. No. 2; also see Rushe, 3.42.
11 Kate O'Brien 'Christmas in the Presentation Parlour', op. cit., p. 21.
12 *LRTV,* 25 Feb. 1876.   13 Minute Book. 25 May 1894, Rushe 3.43.
14 For details of authors and books in the library, and the extensive list of papers and magazines in the reading room, see appendices 2 to 4 in Rushe Ms.
15 Rushe 3.21, & see Appendix 4, pp. 3. 37ff.
16 LDA, printed pamphlet *Technical Instruction*, Dublin 1900, by Bp. O'Dwyer.
17 Finnegan, *Limerick Jesuit Centenary Record*, Limerick 1959, p. 10
18 *Archivium Hibernicum*, 30, Kirby Papers, Irish College Rome, ed. P.J. Corish, Cullen–Kirby, 18 April 1875, no. 209, p. 78.
19 Fleming & O'Grady, *St Munchin's College*, p. 58.
20 Printed privately, Limerick 1881. Copy in LDA.   21 *St Munchin's College*, p. 60.
22 LDA, Canon O'Shea responding to Monsignor Hallinan.
23 LDA and National Library Ireland, pamphlet by Fr Bourke, 1 Sept. 1881.
24 IJA, Ronan–Réné, 20 March 1886. See also typed summary entitled 'The Apostolic School' by Redmond Roche, the last director, pp. 8–9.
25 Royal Commission on University Education, *First report. Appendix. Minutes of evidence*, 1901, RC 459, p. 20, Q. 324; and pp. 120f. Q. 325.
26 *Limerick Chronicle*, 5 April 1881; also John Rushe, 'Rev. Edward Thomas O'Dwyer and the Artisans' Dwelling Company' in *Old Limerick Journal*, Winter 1981.
27 *Limerick Chronicle*, 16 Dec. 1980.   28 *Old Limerick Journal*, art. cit.
29 *Encycl. Brit.*, 1911, vol. 13, N. 820, cit. Rushe.
30 O'Shaughnessy–O'Dwyer, 1 Jan. 1877, LDA, file D.

4 HOME RULE ENTHUSIAST AND LAND LEAGUE CRITIC, 1870–1886

1   Pages 17–18, 25, 53, cit. Edward P. O'Callaghan, 'Bishop Edward Thomas O'Dwyer', pp. 33–4.
2   Terence de Vere White, *The road of excess* (Dublin, 1946), p. 259 in O'Callaghan, op. cit., p. 36.
3   *Cork Examiner*, 25 May 1917, in O'Callaghan, p. 20.
4   *Limerick Chronicle*, 21 Sept. 1871.
5   *Limerick Reporter & Tipp. Vindicator*, 21 Sept. 1871, cit. Rushe 2.18.
6   Idem and see O'Callaghan, p. 38.
7   *The Nation*, 23 Sept. 1871, cit. O'Callaghan idem.
8   Butt–O'Dwyer, 18 Sept., no year given but clearly 1877, in LDA, file S 'Unfinished Letters'.
9   Emmet Larkin. *The Roman Catholic Church and the emergence of the modern Irish political system, 1874–1878* (Dublin 1996), p. 486.
10   Idem., p. 479.
11   Butt–O'Dwyer, 25 Dec. 1877, LDA, file C.   12 Butt–O'Dwyer, 13 Jan. 1878, idem. O'Regan was parish priest of Mallow and a respected member of the League.
13   *Freeman's Journal*, 15 Jan. 1878; Larkin, p. 487.
14   Idem. 16 Jan. 1878; Larkin, idem.   15 Idem.
16   *Limerick Chronicle*, 17 Jan. 1878, cit. Rushe, 2.66.   17 Larkin, pp. 494–5.
18   Idem. p. 497.   19 Idem. p. 498.
20   *Limerick Chronicle*, 27 April 1878, cit. O'Callaghan, p. 76.
21   Idem.   22 Larkin, pp. 505–6.   23 *Cork Examiner*, 9 Nov. 1878.
24   *Freeman's Journal*, 30 Nov. 1878.   25 Idem. 2 Dec. 1878.   26 Idem. 6 Dec. 1878.
27   Butt–O'Dwyer, 14 Dec. 1878, LDA, file C.
28   *Hansard*. 243: 1265, cit. Larkin, p. 544.   29 Larkin, p. 545.
30   *Freeman's Journal*, 13 May 1879.   31 Idem.
32   *Limerick Chronicle*, 24 May 1879.
33   Gabbett–O'Dwyer, no date except 1897. LDA, file A.
34   Meldon–O'Dwyer, no date. LDA, file A.
35   *Nation*, 5 March 1881, cit. O'Callaghan, p. 88.
36   Casey–O'Dwyer, 22 Aug. 1882. LDA, file A.
37   *Limerick Chronicle*, 30 Oct. 1880.   38 Idem. See O'Callaghan, pp. 94–5.
39   Idem, 2 Nov. 1880.   40 Idem. 15 March 1881.
41   O'Dwyer–A. de Vere, 17 Jan. 1881, 24 March 1881, de Vere Papers, NLI. Ms. 13,126(1).
42   Idem. 24 March 1881.
43   *Limerick Chronicle*, 20 Oct. 1881.
44   F.S.L. Lyons. *Ireland since the Famine* (Glasgow, 1976 edition), p. 175.
45   *Limerick Chronicle*, 3 April 1883.

5 SCHOLAR AND PUBLIC COMMUNICATOR

1   The *Irish Ecclesiastical Record* (*IER*), a monthly periodical, was first established in 1864 by Cardinal Cullen 'as a link between Ireland and Rome' and to act 'as a medium of communication within the church in theology, history, and the natural and philosophical sciences' and be 'a bond between the priests of Ireland themselves'. It lapsed in 1876, but was successfully revived by William J. Walsh in 1880.
2   Flanagan's own description of himself in a letter to O'Dwyer, undated, but *c.*1885. LDA, file E.
3   Flanagan–O'Dwyer, 24 April 1880. LDA, file E.
4   Flanagan–O'Dwyer, 14 May 1880. Idem.   5 *IER*, Aug. 1880, p. 472.
6   Walsh–O'Dwyer, 24 March 1884. LDA, file A.
7   Idem, 29 March 1884. LDA, file A. 'Trevelyan' was G.O. Trevelyan, Chief Secretary for Ireland.

8 *IER*, Sept. 1883, pp. 558ff.   9 Idem. Nov. 1883, pp. 700–6.
10 Healy–O'Dwyer, 4 Oct. 1884. LDA.   11 *IER*, Jan. 1883, pp. 168–72.
12 Idem. Feb.1883, pp. 88 ff.
13 Idem. Jan.1886, pp. 54ff.
14 O'Dwyer–de Vere, 1 Apr. 1881. NLI. Aubrey de Vere Papers, Ms.13,126(1).
15 I. Murphy, *The diocese of Killaloe* (Dublin, 1995), p. 175.
16 George Sheehy–O'Dwyer, 20 April 1884. LDA, file A.

6 THE ARRIVAL OF THE NEW BISHOP. ASSURED BEGINNINGS, 1886–1888

1 Croke–Kirby, 14 Feb. 1886. Kirby papers. Irish College Rome. Copy in Glenstal Abbey archives.
2 *Irish Monthly*, 1917, pp. 632–3.
3 John Begley, *The diocese of Limerick* (Dublin, 1938), p. 561
4 *Month's Mind*, 4 March 1886, sermon/pamphlet by Fr Edward Thomas O'Dwyer, p. 9
5 Idem, pp. 14–15.
6 Begley, op. cit., pp. 561–2.
7 C.P. Kenny–Kirby, 30 March 1886, Kirby papers, no. 164, Irish College Rome (ICR)
8 April 1886. *Archivio Storico Congregazione per l'Evangelizzazione dei Populi. Acta S.C. de Prop. Fide. Anno 1886*, n. 11, f. 228, Proposals for the vacant see of Limerick.
9 Dr Hallinan's Diaries 1883–88. LDA.
10 Begley, op. cit. p. 562
11 ODwyer–Kirby, 14 May 1886, Kirby papers, no. 227, ICR.
12 Bp. James McCarthy–O'Dwyer, 13 June 1886, LDA. yellow file 33.
13 The family motto was conveyed to the author by Mr Sean Rushe, already mentioned.
14 Hallinan Diaries, LDA.
15 Idem.
16 *Irish Catholic Directory* 1887, covering 1886, pp. 183–6.
17 Michael Fogarty, *The great bishop of Limerick*, panegyric/pamphlet, 18 Sept. 1917.
18 Begley, p. 505.
19 Croke–Walsh, 12 Jan. 1887, DDA. Copy in Glenstal archives.
20 *Munster News and Limerick and Clare Advocate*, 3 July 1886, in LDA.
21 Anecdote related to author by a distinguished member of Limerick diocese, 2001.
22 Croke–Walsh, 22 Jan. 1887, DDA Copy in Glenstal archives.
23 *Irish Monthly*, 1918, vol. 46, p. 27
24 Annie–O'Dwyer, 17 July 1886. LDA, Annie's letters in Folder B in envelopes.
25 Monsignor Hallinan's Diary, Sept. 1886. LDA.
26 Interview on tape in LDA made by Fr Tim Culhane in 1970s, copy courtesy of Fr O'Callaghan, OFM.
27 He used as textbook the work of Augustin Lehmkuhl, S.J. instead of that of Jean Pierre Gury, SJ.
28 *IM*, 1917, pp. 632ff.
29 Idem. p. 636.
30 Idem, pp. 636–7.
31 Annie's letters in Folder B in LDA.
32 *Munster News* 3 July 1886. *IM* Nov. 1917, p. 699.
33 LDA, 44 letters from priests, file E; and 82 miscel. letters, file F; and parish priest's letter, 13 Nov., no year; his death in Begley, p. 629.
34 Dr T. Woulfe Flanagan–Dear Father, 21 Oct. 1886, recommending specialists for Dr O'Dwyer's eye complaint ('a detached retina', it seems). LDA, file V.
35 Annie–O'Dwyer, 15 Aug. 1887. LDA, Annie's letters, folder B.
36 Bp. Carr–O'Dwyer, 2 Oct. 1886. LDA.

7 UNIVERSITY EDUCATION AND THE SENATE APPOINTMENT: DEFYING THE EPISCOPAL
   STANDING COMMITTEE, 1886–1888

1 DDA. Dr McCabe papers, f 215/9. Dr Henry Neville's memo for bishops, Oct. 1882. See
   Morrissey. *Towards a National University* …, p. 60.
2 IJA. Delany–Browne, Jesuit Provincial, Oct. 1883. See Morrissey, op. cit., p. 73.
3 See Morrissey, idem. pp. 75–97; also Morrissey, *William J. Walsh, archbishop of Dublin,
   1841–1921*, pp. 34–46.
4 IJA. Croke–Delany. 19 Feb. 1882; see Morrissey *Towards a Nat. Univ.*, p. 84.
5 Butler–Walsh, undated but end of June or early July following Walsh's resignation. DDA,
   Box 357, 1, f. 350/5.
6 Cruise's letter in IJA. Cit. Morrissey, idem, pp. 92–5; and 7 Dec. 1884, cit. idem, p. 97.
7 Delany–Emly, 12 Dec. 1884. NLI, William Monsell (Lord Emly) Ms. 8318 (14), henceforth
   cited as Emly Ms or Emly papers.
8 IJA. See Morrissey, op. cit., p. 85.
9 Idem. Butler–Delany, 24 Nov. 1884; also Morrissey, p. 91.
10 Royal Commission on University Education in Ireland. *First Report*, 1902, continuing
   O'Dwyer's evidence, pp. 117, 19. Rushe 7.27.
11 *Limerick Chronicle*, 19 Oct. 1886. Ref. in O'Callaghan MA thesis, p. 111.
12 DDA. Walsh papers. O'Dwyer–Walsh, 18 Oct. 1886.
13 Idem. 2 Nov. 1886. Ref. O'Callaghan thesis.
14 *Limerick Chronicle*, 19 Oct. 1886, cit. O'Callaghan, p. 112.
15 LDA. File N. Walsh–O'Dwyer, 20 Oct. 1886.
16 Idem. File O (Letters of various bishops). Bp. Healy–O'Dwyer, 25 Oct. 1886.
17 *Munster News*, 21 and 25 April 1894: 'The panegyric of Most Rev. Dr O'Dwyer at
   obsequies of Rt. Hon. Lord Emly, 25 April 1894'. In pamphlet, pp. 15–16, 19, in LDA.
18 Pamphlet, idem. p. 20.
19 LDA. File 76. Emly–O'Dwyer, 14 June. No year given, but internal references suggest 1886.
20 DDA. Croke–Walsh, 14 Jan. 1887. Copy also in Croke papers, Glenstal archives. Italics in
   text.
21 LDA. Walsh–O'Dwyer 1 Nov. 1886.
22 Idem. File S. Unsigned letter to O'Dwyer, 1 Nov. 1886, but clearly by Keating.
23 LDA. File N. Walsh's letters. Walsh–O'Dwyer, 6 Nov 1886.
24 LDA. File Q. Keating–O'Dwyer, 7 Nov. 1886.
25 Idem. File H. Capt. O'Shea–O'Dwyer 20 Nov. 1886. On O'Shea's links with Limerick
   see *Munster News*, 31 March 1880, cit. Ignatius Murphy *Diocese of Killaloe*, p. 226.
26 LDA. [2nd Brown folder] O'Shea–O'Dwyer, 22 Nov. 1886.
27 Idem. File S [Unfinished letters]. Italics in text. The original letter, which was translated
   into Italian and sent to Rome, ran to 32 pages and made its case under four headings –
   Religious, Educational, National, Political. See Archives Prop. Fide, *Scritture Referite nei
   Congressi (Sc)*, vol. 1886–7: docs. referring to weekly meetings of Sacred Congregation.
   For a fuller treatment in English of this long letter, see Morrissey op. cit., pp. 118–23. By
   the time Kavanagh read the letter to the archbishops, Dr Walsh had already undermined
   its argument by a public attack on Trinity College in an address at Thurles.
28 DDA. O'Dwyer–Walsh, 24 Nov. 1886
29 LDA. File 77. O'Dwyer–Londonderry, 25 Nov. 1886.
30 DDA. O'Dwyer–Walsh, 24 Nov. 1886.
31 Literally 'We cannot do, we are unable' so, a refusal to act, plea of inability.
32 DDA. O'Dwyer–Walsh, 24 Nov. 1886.
33 Walsh–O'Dwyer, 26 Nov. 1886; LDA. Folder N, and see Rushe, MA thesis, pp. 7.35, 7.193.
34 DDA. O'Dwyer–Walsh, 27 Nov. 1886.
35 LDA. O'Shea–O'Dwyer, 29 Nov. 1886.
36 LDA. Folder on Univ. Question. O'Dwyer–Hicks–Beach, Dec. 1886, no precise date.

37 LDA. O file [Various Bishops]. Healy–O'Dwyer, from Royal Univ., no date.
38 Croke–Walsh, 13 Dec. 1886. Croke papers, Cashel archives, copy in Glenstal.
39 LDA. File N [Logue's Letters], Logue–O'Dwyer, 13 Dec.1886
40 Idem. Logue–O'Dwyer, 21 Dec. 1886.
41 Walsh–Kirby, 19 Dec. '86, cit. E. Larkin. *The Roman Catholic Church and the Plan of Campaign* (Cork, 1978), p. 30.
42 Larkin, p. 31.
43 Croke–Walsh, 23 Dec. 1886, from copy of Croke papers in Glenstal archives.
44 LDA. File N. Walsh's letters. Walsh–O'Dwyer, 30 Dec. 1886.
45 LDA. File 77. Dwyer Gray–Fr Murphy, 5 Jan 1887.
46 Idem. 7 Jan. 1887.   47 Idem. 9 Jan. 1887.
48 Croke–Walsh, 11 Jan. '87, cit. Larkin, op. cit., pp. 33–4.   49 Larkin, idem, p. 34 fn.
50 Idem, p. 34.   51 DDA. Croke–Walsh, 13 Jan 1887, cit. Larkin p. 34.
52 Archives Irish College Rome (ICR). Walsh–Kirby, 22 Jan. 1887
53 DDA. Croke–Walsh, 22 Jan. 1887.
54 ICR. Kirby papers, 1886–9, no. 113. O'Dwyer–Kirby, 22 Feb. 1887.
55 LDA. File on Univ. Question. Walsh–O'Dwyer, 20 Feb. 1887.
56 ICR. Kirby papers. O'Dwyer–Kirby, 9 March 1857.
57 Idem 13 March 1887, cit. Larkin, op. cit., pp. 46–7.
58 ICR. Kirby Papers in *Archivium Hibernicum*, 32, p. 12
59 Walsh–Kirby, 9 June 1887, idem. pp. 12–13.   60 IJA. O'Dwyer–Delany, 26 Feb. 1901.
61 For the analysis of his attendances see Rushe, 7.41.

8 THE PLAN OF CAMPAIGN, 1886–1888: THE BISHOP AND THE PAPAL CONDEMNATION

1 Laurence M. Geary, *The Plan of Campaign, 1886–1891* (Cork, 1986), p. 16.
2 Idem, pp. 19–20.
3 See Emmet Larkin. *The Roman Catholic Church and the Plan of Campaign, 1886–1888*, p. 4; F.S.L. Lyons, *John Dillon* (Chicago, 1968), p. 84.
4 Geary, op. cit., pp. 26–7.
5 Wm. O'Brien, MP, *Irish ideas* (London, 1893), p. 21, based on public lecture given in Dublin, 8 Sept. 1887.
6 *Freeman's Journal*, 8 Nov. 1886, & 4 Jan. 1887.
7 *United Irishman*, 11 Dec. 1886, q. Geary, p. 25.
8 F.S.L. Lyons. 'John Dillon and the Plan of Campaign', *Irish Historical Studies*, xiv (1965), p. 346.
9 Fr Donnellan at Finnegan's Cross, Co. Armagh, 18 Sept. 1887, State Paper Office, CSORP 1888/26521, q. Geary, p. 28.
10 Fr Ryan at Herbertstown, 1 Nov. 1887, idem, q. Geary, p. 29.
11 SPO. CSORP 1891/28047, q. Geary, p. 29.
12 Public Record Office, CO 903/1, Irish Crime Records 1885–1892, Intelligence notes iv, meeting at Herbertstown, end of April 1888, q. Geary, p. 30.
13 Geary, p. 44.   14 Ignatius Murphy. *The diocese of Killaloe, 1850–1904* (Dublin, 1995), p. 229.
15 *The Times*, 5 Nov. 1885, account by Richard Bagwell, a Co. Tipperary landowner, q. Geary, p. 37.
16 *Limerick Chronicle*, 19 Oct. 1886, q. Edward O. O'Callaghan in 'Bishop Edward Thomas O'Dwyer', op. cit., p. 112.
17 *Limerick Chronicle*, 21 Dec. 1886.
18 T.J. Morrissey. *William J. Walsh, archbishop of Dublin,* pp. 80–1.
19 *Tablet*, 5 Dec. 1886, & 12 Dec., q. Larkin, op. cit., pp. 6–9.
20 P.J. Joyce, *John Healy, archbishop of Tuam* (Dublin, 1931), pp. 138–9.
21 Larkin, op. cit., pp. 13–14.   22 Italics mine.
23 O'Dwyer–Aubrey de Vere, 12 Jan. 1887, de Vere Papers, NLI, Ms. 13126 (1)
24 Idem, 31 March 1887, idem.   25 Italics in text.

26 Croke–Walsh, 9 March '87. DDA. Copy in Glenstal Abbey archives. Italics in text.
27 Letters of Lord Emly to O'Dwyer, LDA. File 76. Friedrick von Hugel, 1852–1925, theologian and philosopher. Alfred Loisy (1859–1940) biblical scholar and modernist, who left the Catholic Church and gave up all belief in Christianity. Albert de Broglie (1821–1901), statesman, writer on morals, history, and Catholic education.
28 Panegyric at obsequies, 25 April 1894. Pamphlet, p. 19, LDA
29 Emly Papers. Ms. 8317(8), and 3 Sept. 1892, Ms.8317(15).
30 Idem Ms.83178(8). Italics in text.
31 O'Dwyer–Emly 3 Sept. 1892, Emly Papers NLI, Ms. 8318(15). Leamy's school, and a school at Roxboro, Limerick.
32 S. de Vere–O'Dwyer, 27 April 1887, LDA. File F.
33 Italics in text. Heinrich F. Stein (1757–1831), a reforming German statesman, sought to sweep away all class distinctions regarding callings and all distinctions arising from land tenure, and to foster local government. Hardenburg (*sic*): Hardenberg, Karl August von, 1750–1822, Prussian statesman who carried out Stein's far-reaching schemes of social and political reorganisation: serfdom abolished, civil service thrown open to all, much attention devoted to education.
34 Stephen de Vere–Emly, 11 April 1882, from Monare, Foynes. Emly papers, Ms.8317(8), NLI.   35 Idem.
36 See Emly–O'Dwyer, 9 Dec., no year, Letters of Lord Emly, LDA. 'You, Ross, and I seem to be the only Irishmen who bestow a thought on Uganda'.
37 Larkin, op. cit., pp. 50–2.
38 Ross–Norfolk, 15 Sept. 1885. Arundel papers, cit. O'Callaghan, op. cit., p. 129.
39 Sir Redvers Buller–Balfour, 24 July 1887: 'So far as I can make out, Lord Emly has been the inspirer of the visit of his Ex.[Excellency]', Balfour papers 29807, q. Larkin, p. 117.
40 Verdon–Walsh, 18 June 1887, q. Larkin, p. 98.   41 Morrissey, *William J. Walsh*, pp. 92–3.
42 Errington–Gladstone, 10 Sept. 1887. Gladstone papers. Brit. Museum, Add. Ms. 44501, q. Larkin p. 124.
43 Turner–Buller, 25 July 1887, who forwarded the letter to Balfour. B. Papers, 29807, q. Larkin p. 117.
44 DDA. Walsh papers. Book of 'Extracts', vol. 2, for 26 July. See Morrissey, pp. 94–5
45 DDA. Walsh papers. Croke–Walsh, 31 July.   46 Idem. 4 August. Also Larkin, p. 118.
47 W.S. Blunt, *The land war in Ireland*, p. 320.
48 Papers of Archbishop Thomas William Croke, *Collectanea Hibernica*, 16, p. 103, no. 25.
49 Idem, no. 26.   50 Blunt, op. cit., p. 429.
51 PRO. CO 903/2 Irish Crime Records 1887–1892, Miscel. Notes, Series XII June 1891, q. Geary op. cit., p. 47.
52 LDA. Letter of Jas. W. O'Grady, Kilballyowen, Bruff, 13 Aug. 1887; also NLI. The O'Grady papers, Ms. 22461, cit. Geary, p. 47.
53 George Pellew, *In castle and cabin, or talks in Ireland, 1887* (New York & London, 1888), p. 151, cit. Geary, pp. 47–8.
54 Blunt. *The land war*, pp. 320–21.
55 Croke–Walsh, 19 March 1887: 'The great difficulty is to keep the 'Campaigner', who is a dreadful enthusiast, within becoming bounds'. Croke papers in Glenstal Abbey archives. See, too, Croke papers, no. 31, in *Collect. Hib.*, 31, no.16, p. 104. Also Glenstal archives, from Chief Secretary's Office, copy of 'Prosecution of the Rev. Matthew Ryan of Herbertstown, Co. Limerick', 21 Dec.1887.
56 *Coll. Hib.*, 33, no. 16, Matt. Ryan–Croke, 3 Nov. 1887; & no. 36, O'Dwyer–Croke, 7 Nov. 1887, p. 105.
57 Blunt op. cit., p. 429.   58 *Limerick Chronicle*, 3 Sept. 1887, cit. O'Callaghan, op. cit., p. 130.
59 Larkin, op. cit., pp. 138–9. 60 Cit. O'Callaghan, pp. 133–4.
61 Croke–Walsh, 5 Nov. 1887. DDA.
62 *Limerick Chronicle*, 15 Nov. 1887; cit. O'Callaghan, p. 135.

63 Persico–O'Dwyer, 21 Nov. 1887. LDA. File 48.

64 Persico–Walsh, 25 Dec. 1887. DDA. Walsh papers.

65 Persico–O'Dwyer, 28 Nov. 1887. LDA. File 48. The source appears to have been Walsh, see Persico–Walsh, 28 Nov. 1887; also O'Callaghan thesis, p. 146.

66 Persico–O'Dwyer, 10 Dec. 1887, LDA. File 48.

67 Persico–O'Dwyer, 15 Dec. 1887, idem.   68 Persico–O'Dwyer, 19 Dec., idem.

69 *Freeman* 20 Dec. 1887, and O'Callaghan, pp. 138–41.

70 Persico–O'Dwyer, 21 Dec. 1887. LDA. File 48.   71 *Freeman*, 26 & 30 Dec. 1887.

72 Idem, 26 Dec. 1887.   73 O'Callaghan, pp. 147–8.

74 *Limerick Chronicle*, 3, 17 Nov. 1887.

75 Idem, 31 Jan. 1888.

76 Amongst the main judgments were the following: 'A rent fixed by mutual consent cannot, without violation of contract, be reduced at the arbitrary will of the tenant alone'. This was all the more so because courts were available for settling such disputes. Again, it was not lawful 'that rent should be extorted from tenants and deposited with unknown persons, no account being taken of the landlord'. 'It was altogether foreign to natural justice and Christian charity' to put ruthlessly in force 'a new form of persecution and prescription' against persons who agreed to pay 'the rent agreed with the landlord' or against those 'who in the exercise of their right take vacant farms'. See Morrissey. *William J. Walsh*, pp. 109–10.

77 Morrissey, idem, p. 110.

78 *Irish Catholic* (Dublin), 5 May 1888, cit. Larkin, p. 204.

79 Larkin, p. 277.   80 *Limerick Chronicle*, 22 May 1888.   81 Larkin, p. 226

82 *Limerick Chronicle*, 28 May 1888.

83 Walsh–Kirby, 28 May 1888; Archives Irish College Rome, Kirby papers; and in *Archiv. Hib.* vol. 32 (1974).

84 *Limerick Chronicle*, 29 May 1888.

85 FSL Lyons. 'John Dillon and the Plan of Campaign 1886–90', *IHS*, op. cit., p. 329; and O'Callaghan, p. 165.

86 *Limerick Chronicle*, 29 May 1888, and Larkin, p. 228.   87 *Chronicle*, idem.

88 Vaughan–O'Dwyer, 21 May 1888. LDA. File 49.

89 Donnelly–O'Dwyer, 26 May 1888. LDA. File N.

90 Healy–O'Dwyer, 28 May 1888. LDA. File O. 91 Cit. Larkin, p. 229.

92 *Irish Catholic*, 2 June 1888, cit. Larkin, p. 234. 93 Larkin, p. 258.

94 Dr O'Callaghan–Kirby, 2 June 1888. ICR. Kirby papers; Larkin, pp. 235–6.

95 Croke–Kirby, 6 June 1888. ICR. Kirby papers; Larkin, pp. 236–7.

96 Larkin, p. 237.

97 *Freeman*, 12 June 1888. LDA. Partial copy in O'Dwyer's hand.

98 O'Dwyer–Donnelly, 12 June 1888. DDA. Walsh/Donnelly papers.

99 Croke–Walsh, 14 June 1888. DDA. Larkin, pp. 256–9.

100 *Irish Catholic*, 16 June 1888.

101 O'Shea–O'Dwyer, 14 June 1888. LDA. Among other correspondents were Edwin de Lisle, 13 June 1888 (LDA. File F), and the Bishop of Shrewsbury, 17 June 1888 (brown folder, LDA).

102 O'Dwyer–Donnelly, 16 June 1888. DDA. Walsh/Donnelly papers.

103 Ross papers, cit. Larkin, p. 287.

104 Larkin, p. 277.   105 Idem, pp. 290–91.

106 O'Dwyer–Donnelly, 11 July 1888. DDA. Walsh/Donnelly papers, File 373/4–9.

107 O'Shea–O'Dwyer, 14 June 1888. LDA.

108 *Irish Monthly*, vol. 46, 1918: 'The Most Rev. E. T. O'Dwyer, D.D.', p. 28.

109 Archivo Vaticano. Segretaria Di Stato. Anno 1888, Rubica 278, fasc.2, ff. 83r–144v; ff. 128r. p. 192; and see p. 93ff. f. 29.: The full document in translation – 'A Report on the Religious and Civil Conditions of Ireland' by Archbishop Persico to Cardinal Rampolla, Secretary of State, at the Vatican. It's a lengthy document, some 123 pages (A 4 size).

110 See Letters of Persico to Rampolla in *Collect. Hib.*, vols. 24–25, 34–35, ed. Edward P. O'Callaghan, O.F.M.

111 Persico Report, p. 59, f. 112.

112 Idem, p. 38, ff. 101r   113 Idem, p. 40, ff. 102r.   114 Idem, p. 105, ff. 135r.

115 Idem, p. 110, ff. 138.

116 Idem, p. 114, ff. 140.

117 Persico–O'Dwyer, 1 Aug. 1888. LDA. File 48.

118 Walsh–Kirby, 23 Aug. 1888. ICR. Kirby papers; *Archiv. Hib.*, vol. 12, p. 17.

119 Walsh to fellow Bishops, 15 Sept. Croke papers. Larkin, pp. 304–5.

120 O'Dwyer–Donnelly, 15 Nov. 1888. DDA. Walsh/Donnelly papers.

121 Woodlock–O'Dwyer, 9 Nov. 1888. LDA. File 31; Bp.Power–O'Dwyer, 17 Nov. LDA. File 49; Bp.Higgins–O'Dwyer, 21 Nov. 1888. LDA. File O.

122 MacEvilly–Kirby, 22 Nov. 1888. ICR. And *Archiv. Hib.*, vol. 32, p. 18.

123 O'Dwyer–Donnelly, 20 Nov. 1888. DDA. Walsh/Donnelly papers.

124 Idem, 17 Nov.   125 Idem, 24 Nov.

126 Walsh–Kirby, 7 Dec. 1888; James Lynch (Kildare)–Kirby, 15 Dec. 1888. ICR. Kirby papers. See also Larkin, pp. 308–12.

127 O'Dwyer–Donnelly, 3 Dec. 1888. DDA. Walsh/D. papers.

128 Idem, 9 Dec.

129 Idem, 23 Dec. Italics in text.

130 H.Vaughan (Salford)–O'Dwyer, 19 July, 1888. LDA. File O. 'English Bishops'.

9   CONFRONTING THE PLAN OF CAMPAIGN: FROM ITS ZENITH TO ITS DECLINE, 1889–1891

1   Croke–O'Dwyer, 6 Jan., no year. LDA, N file, Croke's letters.

2   Croke–Walsh, 9 Jan. 1889. DDA. Walsh papers. Copy in Glenstal Archives.

3   T.S. Flanagan–Emly, 8 Jan. 1889. NLI, Emly papers, Ms. 8317 (9).

4   Idem, 7 Jan. 1889.

5   ICR, Kirby papers, 1886–1889, no. 56; O'Dwyer–Kirby, 18 Feb. 1889.

6   ICR, Kirby papers, no. 411. O'Dwyer–Kirby, 1 Dec. 1888.

7   *Tipperary Vindicator*, 21 June 1889.

8   Flanagan–Emly, 21 June 1889. NLI, Emly Ms. 8317 (9)

9   *Limerick Chronicle*, 22 Oct. 1889; cit. O'Callaghan, p. 175.

10 O'Dwyer–Emly, 19 Oct. 1888. NLI, Emly Ms.8318 (15)

11 Geary, *The Plan of Campaign*, pp. 122–25.

12 Geary, op. cit., pp. 126–7; F.S.L.Lyons, 'John Dillon and the Plan of Campaign', *IHS* p. 338.

13 MacEvilly–Kirby, 29 Dec. 1889. ICR, Kirby papers; also *Archiv. Hib.*, Vol. 32, p. 23.

14 A. Murphy–Jn.Redmond, 29 Nov. 1889. LDA.

15 Redmond–Andrew Murphy, 30 Nov. 1889. LDA, folder on Land Issues.

16 Telegram, Redmond–Murphy, 2 Dec. (?). LDA.

17 *Limerick Chronicle* 3 Dec 1889, cit. O'Callaghan p. 176.

18 Bp. Mac Redmond–O'Dwyer, 3 Oct. 1889, He hopes O'Dwyer has recovered enough to be able to ride, his favourite exercise.

19 Croke–O'Dwyer, Nov. date difficult to decipher. LDA, file N, Croke letters.

20 O'Dwyer–Simeoni, 3 July 1889, replying to his of 26 June. Arch. Propaganda Fide, SOCG 1033, PIIIa, ff 516r–517r.

21 Walsh–Kirby, 5 Aug.1889. ICR, Kirby papers in *Archiv. Hib.*, 32, p. 22; see Larkin. *R.C. Church in Ireland and fall of Parnell*, p. 78.

22 Ignatius Murphy, *Diocese of Killaloe*, p. 93.

23 Larkin, op. cit., pp. 85–6, 98.

24 John Ross–Dean Griffin, 16 Sept. 1889. Kerry Diocesan Archives. Copy in Glenstal Archives.

25 Hansard Parliamentary Debates, 3rd series, cols. 743–54, cit. Larkin, p. 110.
26 Larkin, pp. 113, 116.
27 LDA. Cit. in *Daily News*, 21 Dec. 1889.
28 *Limerick Chronicle*, 4 Feb. 1890.
29 Idem.
30 Idem, 8 March 1890.
31 Account in LDA, file 74.
32 *Limerick Chronicle*, 18 March 1890, cit. O'Callaghan, p. 180.
33 Idem, 31 May 1890; *Annual Register*, 1890, p. 227; *Freeman's Journal*, 30 May 1890; and see O'Callaghan, p. 181, and Geary, p. 129.
34 *Annual Register*, idem and O'Callaghan idem.
35 *Freeman's Journal*, 4 June 1890, in O'Callaghan, p. 182.
36 *Limerick Chronicle*, 7 June 1890.
37 Idem, 17 June.
38 O'Callaghan, pp. 183–4.
39 Hansard series 3, cccxlvi, 1497–8. *IHS*, xiv, (1968), Lyons, 'John Dillon and Plan of Campaign', p. 340.
40 *FJ.*, 14 July 1890.
41 Idem, and Larkin, op. cit., pp. 164–7.
42 O'Dwyer–A. de Vere, 1 April 1881. NLI, de Vere papers Ms. 13,126 (1).
43 Croke–M. Godre, 18 July 1890. Croke papers, cit. Larkin, p. 168.
44 Croke–Kirby, 3 Aug., ICR, Kirby papers; also Larkin, p. 169.
45 Walsh–Kirby, 30 July 1890, idem, and in *Archiv. Hib.*, vol. 32, p. 24.
46 O'Dwyer–Kirby, 5 Aug. 1890, idem.
47 *Limerick Chronicle*, 22,24 July 1890.
48 Idem, 26 July 1890.
49 Idem, 2 Aug. 1890
50 Idem.
51 Lyons, art. cit. *IHS*, p. 340, from Diary of John Dillon in Dillon papers, TCD.
52 Fleming–Dillon, 14 July, in Dillon papers in Glenstal Archives.
53 Lane–O'Brien, 5 Aug. 1890, in Dillon papers NLI.
54 Larkin, op. cit., p. 171.
55 'Clarinas' refers to Lord Clarina, whose estate was at Clarina, Co. Limerick. 'Monsell' is family name of Lord Emly, Tervoe, Co. Limerick.
56 *FJ.* 25 Aug. 1890.
57 *Limerick Chronicle*, 26 Aug. 1890.
58 *Standard*, 25 Aug. cit. O'Callaghan, p. 204.
59 *FJ.*, 26 Aug. 1890, in Larkin, pp. 177–8.
60 *Limerick Chronicle*, 30 Aug. 1890 in O'Callaghan, pp. 207–8.
61 *Limerick Chronicle*, 4 Sept.
62 *FJ.*, 28 Aug. 1890.
63 Cit. Larkin, p. 179.
64 Idem.
65 Idem, pp. 179–80.
66 Logue–Walsh, 31 July 1890, Armagh Diocesan Archives (ADA), Logue correspondence, Toner type-scripts.
67 Idem, 16 Aug.
68 Gillooley to Rome, 16 Aug., DDA, cit. in Lyons, *Charles Stewart Parnell* (London 1977), pp. 470–71.
69 Coffey–Kirby, 30 Aug. 1890. ICR, Kirby papers. *Archiv. Hib.*, vol. 32, p. 25.
70 Bp. Woodlock–Walsh, 2 Sept. 1890, DDA, Walsh papers.
71 O'Dwyer–Donor, 8 Aug. 1890, in LDA, Michael Donor Letters.
72 Ross–Balfour, 29 July 1890, Balfour papers 49821, cit. Larkin, p. 183.

73 Parker Smith–Balfour, 16 Sept. 1890, Balfour papers 49847, cit. Larkin, p. 184.

74 O'Dwyer–Donor, 8 Aug., LDA, file 51: Letters of Ml. Donor & Dr O'Dwyer, 8 Aug–28 Sept.

75 O'Dwyer–Rampolla, 10 Sept. 1890. Vatican Archives: ASV, Segr. Stato, Ep. Moderna, an. 1893, rubr. 18, fasc. 4, ff 41r–42r. When he proposed the obligation on all to obey the decree of the Holy Office, O'Dwyer explained, the reply is given by the clergy and people that the other bishops do not agree and that the decree is invalid. The only remedy, it seemed to him, was that the Holy See compel the bishops finally to pronounce clearly and distinctly against the injustice of the methods of the Plan of Campaign and boycotting. N.B. The references in this chapter to letters to Rampola, I owe to Ambrose Macauley who kindly furnished me with copies from Vatican archives and Arundel Castle archives. The extensive role of Cardinal Rampola in Irish affairs may be perceived in Macauley's *The Holy See, British policy and the Plan of Campaign in Ireland, 1885–93* (Dublin 2002).

76 O'Dwyer–Donor, 10 Sept., idem. Italics mine.

77 Idem, 12 Sept.

78 Flanagan–O'Dwyer, 12 Sept. 1890, LDA, file L.

79 O'Dwyer–Donor, 20 Sept.

80 Donor–O'Dwyer, 24 Sept.

81 Idem, 25 Sept.

82 O'Dwyer–Donor, 28 Sept.

83 Donor–O'Dwyer, 8 Oct.

84 Cit. Geary, op. cit., p. 131.

85 Abbot Smith papers cit. Larkin, p. 203.

86 Cit. Larkin, p. 200.

87 Idem, p. 199. Italics in text.

88 Draft letter cit. Larkin, p. 199.

89 O'Dwyer–Kirby, 10 Nov. 1890. ICR, Kirby papers, *Archiv. Hib.*, vol. 32, p. 25.

90 O'Dwyer–Rampolla [in French], 13 Nov. 1890. ASV, Segr. Stato, Ep. Moderna, an 1893, rubr. 18, fasc. 4, ff 43r–44v.

91 Larkin, op. cit., p. 183.

92 Balfour papers, 49821 f. 62v in Glenstal Archives, also see Larkin, p. 195.

93 Duke of Norfolk–Card. Rampola, 4 Oct. 1890. ASV, Segr. Stato, Ep. Moderna, an. 1893, rubr. 18, fasc. 4, ff 27r–28r.

94 Rampolla–Norfolk, 10 Oct. 1890. ASV, Segr. Stato, Ep. Moderna, an 1893, rubr. 18, fasc. 4, ff 29r–30r.

95 *Limerick Chronicle*, 21 April 1891.

96 PRO, CO. 903/2, Irish Crime Records 1887–92, Miscel. Notes, series xiii, June 1891, cit. Geary, p. 137.

97 O'Dwyer–Kirby, 21 April 1891, ICR, Kirby papers, and *Archiv Hib.*, p. 32.

98 Smith–Barry–O'Dwyer, 19 Jan. 1890, LDA, file 59.

99 Idem, 28 Jan. 1890.

100 Idem, 25 Feb. 1890.

101 Geary, p. 173.

102 O'Dwyer–Donnelly, 31 Jan. 1891, DDA, Walsh/Donnelly papers.

103 SPO. CSORP. 1893/3904, cit. Geary, p. 137.

104 Letters of Geo. D. Fottrell & Sons, Solicitors–O'Dwyer, 22, 29 Jan. & 1 Feb. 1892. LDA, file 62.

105 *The Nation*, 25 April, 1890, cit. O'Callaghan, p. 211.

106 O'Dwyer–Donnelly, 3 Nov. 1891. DDA. Walsh/Donnelly papers.

107 *Limerick Chronicle*, 26 Nov. 1891.

108 O'Dwyer–Kirby, 12 Dec. 1891. ICR, Kirby papers.

109 *The recollections of Aubrey de Vere* (London, 1897), pp. 346–50.

10 AN INDIVIDUAL APPROACH TO THE PARNELL SPLIT

1 *Irish Catholic* 4 Jan. 1890.
2 Egan–Kirby 30 Nov. 1890. ICR. Kirby papers.
3 Thomas J. Morrissey, *William J. Walsh* p. 125
4 O'Shea–O'Dwyer, 3 Nov. 1888. LDA.
5 Idem, 7 Nov. 1888   6 *Limerick Chronicle* 22 Nov. 1890.
7 O'Dwyer–Kirby, 28 Nov. 1890. ICR.
8 Morrissey, op. cit., p. 130.
9 Coffey–Walsh, 5 Dec. 1890. DDA.
10 Donnelly–Kirby, 10 Dec. 1890. ICR. Kirby papers.
11 O'Dwyer–Kirby, 6 Dec. 1890. ICR. Kirby papers.
12 Larkin, op. cit., p. 232
13 T.A. O'Callaghan–Kirby, 6 Dec. 1890. ICR. Idem.
14 *Limerick Chronicle* 16 Dec. 1890.
15 O'Dwyer–Donnelly, 13 Dec. 1890. DDA. Walsh/Donnelly papers.
16 O'Dwyer–Kirby, 4 Jan. 1891. ICR. Kirby papers.
17 O'Dwyer–Kirby, 25 Jan. 1891. ICR. Kirby papers in *Archiv. Hib.*, 32, pp. 28–9
18 O'Dwyer–Donnelly, 31 Jan. 1891. DDA. Walsh/Donnelly papers.
19 Idem, 13 Feb. 1891.   20 Idem, 25 Feb. 1891. An incomplete letter.
21 O'Dwyer–Kirby, 4 March 1891. ICR. Kirby papers.
22 Donnelly–O'Dwyer, 11 March 1891. LDA – (brown box with ribbon). Donnelly was careful to point out that Walsh felt 'great indignation' at Croke's theological views.
23 O'Dwyer–Donnelly, 9 March 1891. DDA. Walsh/Donnelly papers.
24 Croke–Kirby, 10 March 1891. ICR. Kirby papers. Copy at Glenstal.
25 Walsh–Kirby, 5 March 1891. ICR. Kirby papers. *Archiv. Hib.*, 32.
26 O'Dwyer–Kirby, 18 March 1891. ICR. Kirby papers.
27 *Freeman's Journal* 23 March 1891.
28 O'Dwyer–Donnelly, 20 March 1891. DDA. Walsh/Donnelly papers. Italics in text.
29 O'Dwyer–Kirby, 21 April 1891. ICR. Kirby papers.
30 O'Dwyer–Donnelly, Easter Monday (1 April) 1891. DDA. Walsh/Donnelly papers.
31 Idem, 23 May 1891.
32 Printed form, 25 June 1891, in letter from Bp. John Healy to O'Dwyer. LDA. File H.
33 Idem.
34 O'Dwyer–Donnelly, 26 June 1891. DDA. Walsh/Donnelly papers.
35 Coffey–Donnelly, 28 June 1891. DDA. Idem. File 373/4–9.
36 O'Dwyer–Donnelly, 30 June 1891. DDA. Walsh/Donnelly papers.
37 O'Dwyer–Bp. Of Kerry, 30 June 1891. Kerry Diocesan Archives.
38 Walsh–Kirby, 1 July 1891. ICR. Kirby papers.
39 Flanagan–O'Dwyer, 1 July 1891. LDA. Flanagan papers, file 6.
40 O'Dwyer–Donnelly, 2 July 1891. DDA. Walsh/Donnelly papers.
41 Donnelly–O'Dwyer, 4 July 1891. LDA.
42 Coffey–O'Dwyer, 7 July 1891, LDA. File 49.
43 O'Dwyer–Donnelly, 9 July 1891. DDA. Walsh/Donnelly papers.
44 *Limerick Chronicle* 16 July 1891.
45 W. Blunt, *The land war in Ireland*, p. 332.
46 O'Dwyer–Donnelly, 17 July 1891. DDA. Walsh/Donnelly papers.
47 Pastor of Little Bray was Fr John Healy, noted for his wit and entertaining conversation.
48 O'Dwyer–Donnelly, 19 Aug. 1891. DDA. Walsh/Donnelly papers.
49 O'Dwyer–Kirby, 15 Sept. 1891. ICR. Kirby papers.
50 Norfolk–Card. Rampolla, 21 March 1891. Arundel Castle Archives.
51 Walsh–Kirby, 1 Dec. 1891. Idem.

11 THE FIRST DISPUTES. LEAMY'S SCHOOL AND ROXBOROUGH SCHOOL

1   LDA. Original will of William Leamy.
2   J. Rushe, 'Bishop O'Dwyer of Limerick 1886–1917 & the Educational Issues of His Time', MA thesis, NUI, ch.4, pp. 4,6,7.
3   Rushe, idem, 4. pp. 7,8.
4   Report of Educational Endowments (Ireland) Commission, 1887–88, for 11 Oct. 1887, p. 40.
5   Idem, 1889–1890, 26 Oct. 1889, p. 25.
6   Idem, 25 Oct. 1889, also cit. J.Fleming and S.O'Grady in *St Munchin's College Limerick 1796–1996*, p. 65.
7   Idem (Report …), 11 Oct. 1887, p. 37.
8   Idem, 1889–1890, 26 Oct. 1889, p. 27.
9   Idem, 10 Oct. 1887, p. 38.
10   Idem, 26 Oct., p. 26.
11   Idem, pp. 26–7.
12   Rushe, op. cit., 4.15.
13   Idem, pp. 24–33.
14   Commission's Report 1889–1890, 10 Oct. 1890, p. 44. Cit. Rushe, ch. 4, p. 34.
15   Idem, 26 Oct. 1889, p. 32.
16   Idem, p. 49.
17   Idem.
18   Idem, 10 Oct. 1890, p. 44.
19   Rushe, 4.36–7.
20   Commission, 26 Oct. 1889, p. 32.
21   Idem, p. 38.
22   Idem, pp. 32–3.
23   Educational Commissioners, 1889–1890, 26 Oct., p. 37
24   Idem, p. 35. Rushe, 4, p. 39.
25   Rushe, idem pp. 39–41.
26   LDA. O'Dwyer–Balfour, 13 Feb. 1896. Printed copy of 'Roxborough School Limerick (Correspondence). Return to an Order of the Honourable House of Commons dated 5 May 1896' which contains correspondence from/to O'Dwyer, to/from Chief Secretary, Judicial Commissioners, and Lord Lieutenant. Also Rushe, 4, p. 53.
27   Idem. O'Dwyer–Judicial Commisasioners, 2 Mar. 1896.
28   Idem. Secretary of Commission, N.D. Murphy–O'Dwyer, 10 March 1896
29   LDA. O'Dwyer Papers. Fr Flanagan's letters: to O'Dwyer, 14 Nov. 1896.
30   *Freeman's Journal*, 9 March 1897.
31   LDA. Folder K. Lecky–O'Dwyer, 9 March 1897.
32   Cit. Rushe, 4, p. 47
33   LDA. folder 33 (yellow): O'Dwyer–John Conrick PP, Kilfinane, 14 April 1897.
34   LDA. T.M. Healy–O'Dwyer, 14/11/1916.

12 THE CONTROVERSY BETWEEN DR O'DWYER AND MUNGRET COLLEGE

1   The chief sources consulted were: The O'Dwyer papers in the Limerick Diocesan Archives; the Irish Jesuit Archives – particularly the papers relating to the Mungret Apostolic School; the papers of William Monsell, Lord Emly, in the National Library of Ireland; the Archives of Propaganda Fide in Rome. Of considerable assistance was the typed, carefully researched history of the Apostolic School by Redmond Roche, SJ, the final director of the Mungret Apostolic School, which is in the Irish Jesuit Archives, Dublin; and the history of *St Munchin's College Limerick 1796–1996* by John Fleming and Sean

O'Grady, which contains an account of the Mungret College dispute based on detailed research by John Fleming in Propaganda Archives and the Jesuit Archives in Rome.

2   Ronan–Tuite, 29 Dec. 1881, in papers of Mungret Apostolic School, IJA.
3   Idem, 12 Jan. 1882.
4   P. Beckx–Provincial, 16 Jan. 1882. Idem.
5   Beckx–Tuite, 23 July 1882. Idem.
6   Idem, 1 June 1882. Also in Roche ms. p. 17.
7   Réné–Emly, 3 Feb. 1886. Idem.
8   Idem. Ronan–Réné, 20 March 1886. Italics in text.
9   Ronan's letter, written 1901, no other date, in Roche's typed account of 'Apostolic School', p. 7, and in his 'The controversy between Dr O'Dwyer and Mungret College', p. 2. IJA
10 Réné–Provincial (Thomas Browne), 7 Jan. 1888, papers Mgt. Ap. School, IJA.
11 Idem, 11 Jan. 1888.
12 Congregation of Propaganda–Jesuit General, Fr Martin, 12 June 1901, with a copy of a letter of Réné–O'Dwyer, 13 Jan. 1888. Copy IJA idem.
13 Browne–Réné, 12 Jan. 1887. I.J.A idem. Italics in text.
14 Réné–Provincial, 28 Jan. 1888. Idem.
15 Molloy–O'Dwyer, 21 Jan 1888, found among Ronan's letters to Réné. Idem.
16 *Mungret Annual*, 1907, p. 10; and 'Annual Report of Mungret College' 1895. Also Fleming & O'Grady, *St Munchin's College*, p. 72.
17 Report of Educational Endowments Commission for 15 Oct. 1889.
18 Fleming & O'Grady, op. cit., p. 75.
19 Idem, p. 76.
20 T.J. Morrissey, *William J. Walsh* pp. 165–6.
21 O'Dwyer–Walsh, 2 March 1896. DDA. Bishops' file, box 368, f. 370/1–7.
22 Ronan–Provincial, 12 Sept. 1896. IJA Italics in text.
23 Fleming & O'Grady, op. cit., p. 77.
24 Dr Butler–Ronan, 11 Nov. 1882, reprimanding him and the community for not attending the diocesan conference, even though they were fully involved in setting up the new college at Mungret. They attended thereafter, at least while Ronan was rector. Papers Mgt. Apost. School, I.J.A
25 Byrne–Provincial, 22 June 1898. Idem.
26 O'Dwyer–Provincial, 14 Sept. 1898. Idem.
27 Keating–O'Dwyer, 17 Sept. 1898. Idem.
28 Prospectus 1882, comment attached. Transcript in Roche mss. August-Sept. 1882, p. 19.
29 O'Dwyer–Keating, 19 Sept. 1887. IJA
30 Sutton–Keating, 20 Sept. 1898. IJA Also in Roche transcripts.
31 Charles McKenna–Keating. Idem.
32 Head–Keating, 22 Sept. 1898. IJA Mgt. Ap. School papers, and Roche transcripts. Italics in text.
33 Byrne–Provincial, 11 Sept. 1898. Idem.
34 Idem, 21 Sept.
35 Idem, 23 Sept. 1898.
36 O'Dwyer–Provincial, 22 Sept. 1898. Idem.
37 Idem, 4 Sept. 1899.
38 Keating–O'Dwyer, 17 Sept. 1899. Idem.
39 O'Dwyer–Jesuit General, 4 Jan. 1900. Idem.
40 General–O'Dwyer, 19 June 1900. Idem.
41 Fr Martin, General, –Provincial, 30 July 1900. Idem.
42 Keating–O'Dwyer, 14 Sept. 1900. Idem.
43 O'Dwyer–Keating, 15 Sept. 1900. Idem.
44 Keating–O'Dwyer, 17 Oct. 1900. Idem.

45 O'Dwyer–Keating, 3 Nov. 1900. Idem.
46 James Murphy's 'Statement of Mungret Question during my Provincialate', for Dec. 1900, in Roche's typed account of 'The Controversy between Dr O'Dwyer and Mungret College', pp. 13–14, IJA
47 Murphy, idem. 1901.
48 Archives Propaganda Fide, Rome. Prot. no. 57901. Acta. Vol. 275, f. 128–30.
49 Idem. Acta. Vol. 275, f. 131.
50 *St Munchin's College*, pp. 83–5.
51 Murphy–O'Dwyer, 25 Nov. 1904, IJA Sc/Cres/2 (8). Italics in text. 'The Kellys' refers to Edward Kelly, rector of the Crescent from March 1859 and his brother, Thomas, who succeeded him from Aug. 1864–1872. The reference to the chapel remains obscure. No other mention of it has been found by the author.
52 Thomas Hurley. *Father Michael Browne, SJ* (Dublin, 1949), pp. 214, 143.
53 Idem, pp. 14–24.
54 Browne–Provincial, 2 Sept. 1905. IJA Sc/Cres/55 (1)–(15)
55 Idem, 19 Sept. 1905.
56 Idem, 2 Jan 1906.
57 'Annals of Mungret College' in *Mungret Annual*, 1907, p. 82.
58 Charles Doyle–Provincial, 3 Feb. 1913. IJA Sc/Cres/56 (1)–(22).
59 Idem, 12 May 1914.

13 THE BISHOP, THE CHRISTIAN BROTHERS, AND 'THE BRUFF SCANDAL'

1   *The office of the bishop* (Dublin, 1894).
2   Idem, p. 11.
3   Idem, pp. 14–15.
4   Logue–Abp. Walsh, 31 July 1890; Armagh Diocesan Archives, Toner Transcripts.
5   Begley. *Diocese of Limerick*, pp. 350–1.
6   AFCR, folder 2058. Terms for Bruff.
7   Idem, brief yearly annals of Bruff school & the Brothers (1859) in hardcover notebook.
8   *The Christian Brothers Educational Record*, 1914 (Dublin 1914), AFCR.
9   AFCR, f.2058. Hardcover notebook with annals and a letter of Br Redmond to Br T. Innocent O'Neill, 22 Jan. 1913, which gives an account of the Brs. in Bruff.
10 Idem, the annals for each year.
11 *Christian Brothers Educational Record*, 1952 (Dublin, 1952), in section on 'Our Lost Foundations in Ireland', p. 27. AFCR.
12 Idem.
13 Amalgam of 'Christian Brothers School Bruff' in *C.B. Educational Record*, 1914, pp. 25–6, and article on Bruff in *Educ. Record*, 1952, pp. 27–8. AFCR.
14 AFCR, f.2058: Letter of Br J.B. Redmond, 29 Jan. 1891, in hardcover notebook.
15 AFCR. f.2058, lxiv–14: Br P. Slattery–Br Superior, 17 Sept. 1881.
16 Idem, Br Redmond–Br J.I. O'Neill, 22 Jan. 1913.
17 AFCR, f. 2058, annals for 1888.
18 Idem. Typed ms. by Br Laurence O'Toole, De La Salle, 1984.
19 Idem, annals 1888–91.   20 Idem.
21 Idem, and 'Bruff Case', 4 Aug. 1892, in AFCR, f. 2059.
22 'Bruff Case' in AFCR, f. 2059.
23 W.S. O'Brien–Br Assistant, 2 July 1894, in AFCR, f. 2058.
24 'Bruff Case' AFCR, f. 2059.
25 *Limerick Leader*, 22 Nov. 1897, Letters.
26 LDA. Card. Logue–O'Dwyer, 8 Nov. 1895.
27 Idem, 14 Nov. 1895.

28 Idem, 17 Jan. 1896.
29 DDA. Logue–Dr Walsh, 22 Feb. 1897.
30 DDA. In Walsh/Donnelly papers, O'Dwyer–Donnelly, 17 Dec. 1895.
31 Richard Ahern. 'A History of the Christian Brothers in Limerick', Part Two, in *Old Limerick Journal* 22 (1987), pp. 20–21.
32 AFCR, f. 2058. Chas McNamara–Br Maxwell, 12 Sept. 1896.
33 Idem, Maxwell–McNamara, 15 Oct. 1896.
34 AFCR, f. 2058, annals for 27 Oct. 1896.
35 'The Bruff Case', 27 Oct. 1896, AFCR, f. 2059.
36 AFCR, f. 2059. In Br R.A. Maxwell's printed reply, 23 Nov. 1899, to O'Dwyer's public letter.
37 Pius J. A. Browne. 'The Bruff Agitation. A Brief History, 1897–1907' in *Old Limerick Journal*, 11, p. 16.
38 AFCR, f. 2059, Maxwell's printed reply, 23 Nov. 1899, to O'Dwyer.
39 AFCR, f. 2058, annals for 26 Nov. 1896.
40 'The Bruff Case' in AFCR, f. 2059.
41 Idem.
42 AFCR, f. 2059. Br Maxwell's printed reply to O'Dwyer, 23 Nov. 1899, p. 2.
43 S. Rushe. Notes entitled 'Dr O'Dwyer and the C.Bs in Bruff'.
44 In Maxwell's printed reply, which gives extracts from O'Dwyer's letter of 18 Nov. 1899.
45 AFCR, f. 2058, annals for 5 April 1897.
46 In Maxwell's reply of 23 Nov.
47 *Limerick Reporter & Tipperary Vindicator*, 12 Oct. 1886.
48 Maxwell's letter.
49 O'Callaghan–O'Dwyer, 14 May 1897. LDA, file 49.
50 Maxwell's letter.   51 Idem.
52 Br J.D. Burke–O'Callaghan, 23 May, enclosing O'Brien's letter of 22 May 1897. AFCR, f. 2058. Italics mine.
53 Maxwell–Monsignor Antonini, 5 June 1897. AFCR, f. 2058.
54 Kelly–Br Assistant, 30 May 1897. Idem.
55 Idem, 13 June 1897. Idem.
56 Rome, 14 June 1897. No names, begins 'Dear Honoured Brother', addressed, from context, to Br Maxwell. AFCR, f. 2058.
57 McNamara–Br Kelly, 18 Aug. 1897. Idem.
58 Idem, 26 August. Idem.
59 Maxwell–Ledocowski, 14 Oct. 1897. AFCR, f. 2058.
60 McNamara–Maxwell, 1 Sept. 1897. Idem.
61 Maxwell–Ledocowski, 14 Oct. 1897. Idem.
62 O'Dwyer–Maxwell, 23 Sept. 1897. Idem.
63 McNamara–Maxwell, 24 Sept. 1897. Idem.
64 Maxwell–Br Florence Kelly, 24 Sept. 1897. Idem.
65 Kelly–Maxwell, 25 Oct. 1897. Idem. Italics in text.
66 Dr Richard Sheahan–O'Dwyer, 8 Nov. 1897. LDA, file 38.
67 Pius J.A. Browne. 'The Bruff Agitation …' in *Old Limerick Journal*, 11, p. 13.
68 The account of the campaign in the press is indebted to the detailed notes of S. Rushe compiled in working for his major MA thesis, during which he had the opportunity of inspecting material left by Andrew McEvoy.
69 O'Dwyer–O'Callaghan, 30 Nov. 1897. AFCR, f. 2059.
70 O'Callaghan–Maxwell, 1 Dec. 1897. Idem.
71 Maxwell–Jn. Carroll, 3 Dec. '97. Idem.
72 O'Shaughnessy–Br Redmond, 10 Dec. 1897. Idem.
73 Maxwell–Jn. Carroll, 12 Dec. 1897. Idem.
74 *Daily Express* report, 10 June 1897.

75 Bp. Henry–O'Dwyer, 29 June 1898. LDA, O'Dwyer papers.

76 *L. Leader*, 1 Dec. 1897.

77 Andrew Murphy–Jn. Carroll, 31 Dec. 1897. AFCR, f. 2059.

78 Cit. in *Limerick Chronicle*, 18 Jan. 1898, and in Pius J.B. Browne in 'The Bruff Agitation ...' in *O.L.J.*, 11. Italics mine.

79 R. Ahern. 'A History of the Christian Brothers in Limerick' in *Old Limerick Journal*, 22, p. 21.

80 O'Dwyer–Dr Donnelly, 1 Feb. 1898. DDA, Walsh/Donnelly papers.

81 R. Ahern. Art. cit. p. 22.

82 Cit. Dermot McEvoy in 'Scandal at Bruff', part three, in *Old Limerick Journal*, 6 (Spring 1981).

83 O'Dwyer–Board of Guardians, 5 March 1898. LDA, file 74.

84 Residents of Bruff – Chairman of Board of Guardians, 8 March 1898. Idem.

85 McRedmond–O'Dwyer, 10 March 1898. LDA, file 39.

86 A. Murphy–John Carroll. LDA, file 74.

87 McNamara–Fr A. Murphy, 7 May 1898. LDA, Fr Murphy's Letters.

88 *Daily Express*, 10,11 June 1898.

89 Idem, in Rushe notes.

90 Idem, 11 June 1898.

91 R. Ahern. 'A History of the Christian Brothers in Limerick' in *Old Limerick Journal*, 22, (1987), p. 22.

92 Br Welsh–O'Dwyer, 5 April 1899. Response, 8 April. Welsh–Murphy, 15 April 1899. LDA, orange folder.

93 Murphy–Welsh, 16 April. Idem.

94 *Limerick Echo*, 14 Nov. 1899.

95 Idem.

96 Idem, also *Echo* of 7 Nov.

97 Idem, 7 Nov. 1899.

98 Idem, 28 Nov.

99 Idem.

100 Idem, 5 Dec. 1899

101 Wm. Nolan, Town Clerk–Dr O'Dwyer, 17 Nov. 1899.

102 O'Dwyer–Sec. of St Mary's Temperance Society, 1 Dec. 1899. LDA, file 74.

103 In reply of Br Maxwell, 23 Nov. 1899. AFCR, f. 2059.

104 Idem.

105 R. Ahern. Art. iam cit. in *O.L.J.*, 1987, p. 23.

106 Welsh–O'Dwyer, 19 April 1900. LDA, orange folder.

107 Cit. Ahern in art. cit.

108 Andrew Murphy–J.P. Dalton, 16 Oct. 1903. LDA, file 74.

109 P.J. Browne. 'The Bruff Agitation' in *O.L.J.*, p. 16.

110 Br Anthony–O'Dwyer, 8 July 1907, from Archives of De La Salle House, Castletown, Mountrath. Copy courtesy S. Rushe.

111 *Evening Echo*, 12 Dec. 1899. Letter from 'Truth' dated 11 Dec.

112 McNamara–Dear Monsignor, July 1915. Archives Irish College Rome.

113 Jim Kemmy–Sean Rushe, 29 Jan. 1975.

14 THE PRELATE AND THE MAN

1 Annie–O'Dwyer 28 Nov. 1889, in Annie's Letters, LDA.

2 Idem, 7 Sept. 1890.

3 Bill from vet. Mr B. O'Donnell, for service to mare and foal, 30 Sept. 1893, and a letter from the bishop to Fr Fenton, 21 August 1911, re. a filly expected to win races. LDA. – in a box on personal and family matters.

4 *Limerick Chronicle*, 5 July 1883: song of the 'Show Week', Limerick, 29 June 1883, to the air of 'The Last Rose of Summer'.
5 Fr John Flanagan–O'Dwyer, 3 May 1895. LDA, Flanagan papers, file 13.
6 Annie–O'Dwyer, 27 Nov. 1892. LDA.
7 Idem, 4 Jan. 1901.
8 Idem, 26 Jan. and 1 Feb. 1893.
9 Idem, 14 Feb. 1893.
10 Idem, 24 Feb. 1895
11 Idem, 17 Nov. 1895
12 Address to Bishop O'Dwyer on his return from Rome, Nov. 1895. LDA, file E.
13 Unfinished letter, 19 Nov. 1887, re. start of St John's Hospital, to 'Dear Count', in LDA, file V; and an undated & incomplete letter, from Rome, from Sister M. Philip on behalf of the Mother General of English Nursing Sisters, Little Company of Mary, in LDA, file S (unfinished letters).
14 'The Sisters of Charity of St Paul the Apostle' in *Our Catholic Life*, 11 (Oct. 1958). Courtesy S. Rushe.
15 Richard Canon O'Kennedy in *Irish Monthly*, vol.45, Nov. 1917, p. 700.
16 O'Dwyer–Donnelly, 23 Jan. 1895. DDA, Walsh/Donnelly papers.
17 Idem, 30 Jan. 1894.
18 O'Kennedy, idem.
19 O'Dwyer–Hallinan, 3 Feb. 1917. LDA in brown beribboned folder, mixed correspondence.
20 Cit. in 'Christmas in the Presentation Parlour' in Kemmy (ed.), *The Limerick anthology* p. 18.
21 Idem, pp. 20–21.
22 Idem, p. 22.
23 School annals or chronicles, 1917, pp. 77–8, courtesy of provincial archivist, F.C.J.
24 Idem, for 1895, pp. 16–21.
25 O'Dwyer–Donnelly, 10 July 1895. DDA. Walsh/Donnelly papers.
26 O'Kennedy in *Irish Monthly* (1917), p. 638.
27 Idem, p. 639.
28 Idem, Nov. 1917, pp. 700–5.
29 Idem, p. 699.
30 Begley, *Diocese of Limerick*, pp. 572–3.
31 O'Kennedy, (1918), pp. 22–3.
32 O'Dwyer–Donnelly, 15 May 1894. DDA.
33 *Irish Catholic Directory 1895*, chronological events of 1894, p. 344.
34 Idem, pp. 356–7.
35 Idem, 14 June, p. 361.
36 Idem, 21 June, pp. 363–4.
37 O'Kennedy. *IM*, vol. 45, p. 779. Italics mine.
38 Bp. of Elphin, John Clancy–O'Dwyer, 24 Feb. 1895. LDA, file 40.
39 Idem.
40 Brownrigg–O'Dwyer, 12 Oct. 1899. LDA, file 50.
41 O'Kennedy. *IM*, vol. 45, p. 777.
42 Idem, p. 779.
43 Idem, pp. 780–81.
44 Diocesan Synod 1916, incomplete Ms. LDA, file 53.
45 Canon Punch in a taped interview conducted by Fr Tim Culhane in 1970s. LDA. Copy available courtesy of Fr Edward P. O'Callaghan, OFM.
46 Idem.
47 Canon Begley's notebook in Limerick City Library, excerpts courtesy S. Rushe. On Fr Carroll see, also, Fr Flanagan–O'Dwyer, 21 Nov. 1900. LDA, file 4.
48 Flanagan–O'Dwyer, 23 Dec. 1895. LDA, Flanagan papers, file 11.
49 Idem, 15 Jan. 1897. Idem, file 20.

50 Idem, 7 August 1897. Idem, file 17.
51 Earl of Dunraven. *Past Time and Pastimes*, vol.1, London 1922, p. 28.
52 Idem.
53 Flanagan–Dunraven, 28 Jan 1899. LDA, file E.
54 Flanagan–O'Dwyer, 3 Feb. 1899. LDA, Flanagan papers, file 3.
55 Idem, 9 Feb. 1899.
56 Idem, 10 Feb. 1899.
57 *Limerick Chronicle*, 11 Feb. 1899. LDA, press cuttings in Flanagan papers.
58 Flanagan–O'Dwyer, 23 Feb. 1899. LDA, Flanagan papers, file 5.
59 *Munster News*, 25 Feb. 1899.
60 O'Dwyer–Dear Monsignor, 4 Dec. 1900. LDA, in separate brown folder.
61 J.K. Fitzgerald–Dear Mon Signore, 6/12/1900. LDA, Flanagan papers, file 3.
62 Flanagan–Mon Signore, 7/12/1900. Idem. 'Nunc dimittis' – 'now I may go in peace',
    Simeon's comment on meeting the child Jesus (Luke 2:29).
63 Dunraven. *Past Times and Pastimes*, p. 28.
64 O'Kennedy. *IM*, vol. 46, 1918, pp. 28–9.
65 LDA, across files 38–49.
66 Abraham Brownrigg of Ossory–O'Dwyer, 31 July 1898. LDA, file 40. Bp. Whiteside of
    Liverpool, 12 Aug. 1898. LDA, file 49. Walter McDonald, Maynooth–O'Dwyer, 11 July
    1915. LDA, file 79. Abp. Thomas Carr of Melbourne–O'Dwyer, 2 Oct. 1886. LDA, file O.
    Bp. Thomas Surline of Hamilton, Canada–O'Dwyer, 18 Dec. 1896. LDA, file O. Bp. J.J.
    Guiness of Christchurch–O'Dwyer, 23 and 29 July 1899. LDA, file 49. Bp. James Duhig,
    Rockhampton, Australia–O'Dwyer, 16 Jan. 1911. LDA, file 49.
67 Bp. Robert Browne–O'Dwyer, 30 July 1894. LDA, file N.
68 Brownrigg–O'Dwyer, 31 July 1898. LDA, file 40.
69 O'Kennedy. *Irish Monthly*, vol. 46, 1918, p. 29.
70 Address of clergy on the return of the bishop from Rome, Nov. 1895. LDA, file E.

15 PRIMARY AND TECHNICAL EDUCATION, ADULT INSTRUCTION, AND TEACHER
    TRAINING

1   O'Kennedy. *Irish Monthly*, vol. 45, Nov. 1917, p. 699.
2   Abp. Wm. Walsh. Address at St Joseph's Blind Asylum, Drumcondra, Oct. 1886, and at
    schools of Srs of Mercy, Goldenbridge, Nov. 1886.
3   P.J. Walsh, *William J. Walsh*, pp. 505–8.
4   Address at Limerick Technical Institute, 14 Dec. 1911, given in *Cork Examiner*, and in *Irish
    Educational Review*, vol. V, no. 4, Jan. 1912.
5   Address in 1900, pamphlet, pp. 20–21. The bishop's distinctions between education and
    instruction tend to vary. Sometimes he uses 'education' in a wide sense to cover
    instruction and general education, sometimes, as in 1900 address he makes a distinction
    within Technical Instruction so that the learning of a practical skill is 'instruction' whereas
    an understanding of the principles behind the skills and the capacity to apply them is
    'education', and seems to be equated with 'science'.
6   Address, 1900, idem, p. 22.
7   Address 1911. He probably intended to exclude Trinity College as he had described it in
    his 1900 address as having 'done nothing for the country', p. 23.
8   Address, 1900, pp. 18–19.
9   Idem, pp. 17–19.   10 Idem, p. 8.
11 Trevor West. *Horace Plunkett, co-operation and politics* (Washington DC), 1986, pp. 61–2.
12 Address, 1900, p, 9.
13 Horace Plunkett diary in Plunkett Foundation Oxford. Transcription courtesy of Ms. Kate
    Targett. The diaries have been transcribed only from 1881–95, 1917–18.

14 Plunkett–O'Dwyer, 19 Feb. 1896. LDA, file K.
15 Trevor West, op. cit., pp. 29–30, 64.
16 C.W. Shaw–Lord Monteagle, 5 Nov. 1896. In T.P. Gill papers, Ms.13,509 (6), NLI. There is no further information on the matter mentioned in relation to the bishop.
17 Plunkett–O'Dwyer, 11 Oct. 1903. LDA, file K.
18 Lecture, 1900, pp. 106–7.
19 Plunkett, *Ireland in the new century* (London 1904), p. 110.
20 Idem, pp. 110–11, 116.
21 O'Dwyer–Plunkett, 21 Feb., ref. in letter of Plunkett to O'Dwyer, 8 March 1904. LDA, file K.
22 Plunkett–O'Dwyer, 8 March 1904. LDA, file K.
23 Idem.
24 O'Dwyer–O'Riordan, 19 June 1905, Archives Irish College Rome, O'Riordan papers.
25 Pastoral Letter 1906, p. 10.
26 Idem, pp. 11, 14.
27 Idem, pp. 17–18.
28 Idem, p. 15.
29 O'Dwyer–Commissioners of National Education, 9 Nov. 1905. LDA, file 84.
30 Lecture on 'Technical Instruction',1900, p. 14.
31 Idem, p. 15.
32 JD Daly–O'Dwyer, 26 March 1901. LDA, file 73.
33 Ms. draft submission on Model Schools in LDA, file p.
34 D.H. Akenson. *The Irish education experiment* (London 1970), p. 305.
35 M. O'Riordan. *Catholicity and progress in Ireland* (London 1905), p. 454.
36 Akenson, op. cit., pp. 356–7.
37 Sr Loreto O'Connor, *Passing on the torch: a history of Mary Immaculate College, 1898–1998*, printed centenary publication, 1998, p. 5. LDA.
38 Idem, p. 6.
39 Cit. idem, pp. 6–7.
40 Idem, pp. 8–9.
41 LDA, file 55. Mr P. Molloy, Limerick, was clerk of works, not the contractor as stated in O'Connor above.
42 Wm. Byrne–O'Dwyer, 7 April 1901. LDA, file 55.
43 *The Nation*, 9 Dec. 1899. Ref. in S. Rushe, 6.55.
44 O'Dwyer–Commissioners, 28 Feb. 1906. LDA, file 58.
45 H. Henry–O'Dwyer, 10 Aug. 1897. LDA, file 27.
46 Henry–O'Dwyer, 10 Dec. 1900. LDA, file 27.
47 LDA, file 58.
48 Redmond–O'Dwyer, 17 May 1911. LDA. also in Killaloe Diocesan Archives, Bishop Fogarty papers, O'Dwyer–Bp. Ml. Fogarty, 17 May 1911.
49 *Freeman's Journal*, 17 May 1902.
50 Cit. L. O'Connor, *Passing on the torch*, p. 10.
51 Idem, pp. 11–12.
52 LDA, file 55.
53 O'Connor, pp. 12–13.
54 Idem, p. 19.

16 STRUGGLING FOR EQUALITY IN UNIVERSITY EDUCATION, 1889–1903

1 Royal Commission on University Education in Ireland, *Second Report,* Appendix, pp. 384–5; cit. Rushe 7.45.
2 *Freeman's Journal*, 1 July 1890; cit. Rushe 7.45–46.

3   Patrick J. Walsh, *William J. Walsh* p. 491.
4   Kirby–O'Dwyer, 12 Jan. 1890. LDA, file J.
5   Walsh–Kirby, 30 July 1890. Kirby papers, Irish College Rome, and in *Archiv. Hib.*, 32, no. 281, and O'Dwyer–Kirby, 5 Aug. 1890, no. 289.
6   Walsh–Kirby, 1 Dec. 1891; ICR, Kirby papers.
7   *Irish Catholic Directory (ICD)* 1893, with register of events 1892, 21 Jan., p. 296.
8   O'Dwyer–Donnelly, 28 Nov. 1892; DDA, and p. J. Walsh, op. cit., p. 431.
9   Account in P. J. Walsh, op. cit., footnote pp. 431–2
10 Bp. Gillooly–O'Dwyer, 24 Feb. 1893; LDA, file 32 (yellow folder).
11 Election Result: Conservatives 323, Liberal Unionists 67, Liberals 176. In Ireland, Nationalists – 81 (12 Parnellites, 69 others), 17 Unionists, 4 Liberal Unionists, 1 Liberal. One elected nationalist, John Daly, was debarred from the House of Commons as a convict undergoing imprisonment.
12 Flanagan–O'Dwyer, 22 & 23 Dec. 1895; LDA, Flanagan letters.
13 Major John Ross–O'Dwyer, 31 Dec. 1895; LDA, file 46.
14 Idem, 4 Jan. 1896; LDA, letters of Sir John Ross.
15 Idem, 5 Feb. 1896; LDA, file 46.
16 E. Dease–O'Dwyer, 19 Jan. 1896; LDA, file 45.
17 Letters of Fr Flanagan, 30 Jan. to 3 Feb. 1896; LDA, file 60.
18 Horace Plunkett–O'Dwyer, 19 Feb. 1896; LDA, file K.   19 Idem.
20 Ross–O'Dwyer, 9 April 1896; LDA, file 46.
21 *Seventy years young*. Memories of Elizabeth countess of Fingall, (London; 1991 Dublin ed.), pp. 39–40.
22 A.J. Balfour–O'Dwyer, 26 March 1895; LDA, in brown folder, no number.
23 The falling out between the archbishop and Healy originated in the former acting as arbitrator between the directors of the *Freeman's Journal* and of the *National Press*. Despite a previous commitment, Healy and William Martin Murphy refused to abide by his Grace's decision. Healy and Murphy had been directors of the *National Press* now being amalgamated in the *Freeman's Journal*, of which John Dillon was a director and the moving spirit in the negotiations! See for further information: Thomas Morrissey, *William Martin Murphy*, pp. 25–7.
24 TM Healy–O'Dwyer, 24 Oct. 1896; LDA.
25 *ICD* 1897, register for 1896, 14 Oct. 1896, pp. 370–374.
26 *Newcastle Leader*, 23 Jan. 1897.
27 *Glasgow Herald*, 23 Jan. 1897.
28 *Tablet*, 31 Jan. 1897.
29 *New Saturday*, 30 Jan. 1897; LDA, file J.
30 *Newcastle Leader*, 23 Jan. 1897.
31 A.J. Balfour–O'Dwyer, 19 Feb. 1897; LDA, brown folder.
32 Logue–Walsh, 22 Feb. 1897; DDA, Walsh papers.
33 TM Healy–O'Dwyer, 6 March 1897; LDA.
34 Idem, 11 March 1897 (see also 18 March); LDA.
35 Logue–O'Dwyer, 23 March 1897; LDA.
36 Sheehan–O'Dwyer, 14 & 28 Feb. 1897; LDA, file 37.
37 Donnelly–O'Dwyer, 25 March 1897; DDA, Walsh/Donnelly papers.
38 O'Dwyer–Donnelly, 27 March 1897; idem.
39 T.M. Healy–O'Dwyer, 5 April 1897; LDA, file 80.
40 J.M. Harty–Monsignor Kelly, 12 April 1897; ICR, Kelly papers, box 12, no. 248.
41 *ICD* 1898, register for 1897, 23 June, pp. 374–8.
42 T.J. Morrissey, *William J. Walsh*, p. 161.
43 O'Dwyer–Donnelly, 7 Aug. '97; DDA, Walsh/Donnelly papers.
44 *ICD* 1898, register for 1897, 24 Nov. 1897, pp. 394–5.
45 Idem, 8 Nov. '97, p. 385.

46 *Cork Daily Herald*, 24 Dec. 1897.
47 Walsh–O'Dwyer, 31 Dec. 1897; LDA, file N.
48 John Healy, Clonfert; Richard Sheehan, Waterford; Patrick O'Donnell, Raphoe; Patrick Foley, Kildare and Leighlin.
49 Printed Agenda in LDA.
50 Ross–O'Dwyer, 25 Jan. 1898; LDA, file 46
51 Idem, 2 Feb. 1898.
52 Donnelly–O'Dwyer, 2 Feb. 1898; LDA.
53 Logue–O'Dwyer, 23 Feb. 1898; LDA, file N.
54 Ross–O'Dwyer, 3 May 1898, praising his contribution. LDA.
55 Sheehan–O'Dwyer, 31 May 1898; LDA, file 38.
56 Idem, 8 June 1898.
57 Logue–O'Dwyer, 22 Oct. 1898; LDA, file N.
58 Morrissey. *Towards a National University*, p. 168.
59 'Letter to a Manchester constituent', NUI pamphlet; also see *Towards a National University*, p. 169.
60 Haldane–Walsh, 7 Feb. 1899; DDA, box 371, file 364/6.
61 *Towards a Nat. Univ.*, p. 170.
62 Idem, p. 171.
63 O'Dwyer–Donnelly, 27 Mar. 1899; DDA, file 373/4
64 Idem, 9 May 1899.
65 Walsh–Logue, 21 June 1899; Archives Diocese of Armagh (ADA), Toner transcripts, p. 149.
66 *A university for Catholics* ..., pp. 5–6.
67 Idem, pp. 8–9.
68 Idem, pp. 11–12.
69 Idem, p. 71.
70 Idem, p. 72.
71 O'Dwyer–Donnelly, 26 Mar. 1900; DDA, Walsh/Donnelly papers.
72 *ICD* 1901; register for 1900, p. 441.
73 Idem, pp. 442–3.
74 Idem, pp. 449–53.
75 Letters on 13, 16, 18 Feb. 1900; Irish Jesuit Archives (IJA).
76 Meeting of Senate, Thus. 21 Feb. 1901; LDA, file 81.
77 O'Dwyer–Delany, 26 Feb. 1901; IJ A.
78 Idem, 26 Feb. 1901.
79 Bishop Healy–Walsh, 10 March 1901; DDA, box 373 , file 351/1.
80 O'Dwyer–Delany, 20 March 1901; IJA. See also *Towards a National University* pp. 176–7
81 Bp. Healy–Walsh, 14 July 1901; DDA, box 373, file 351/1
82 Logue–O'Dwyer, 5 Sept. 1901; LDA.
83 Dr Foley–O'Dwyer, 12/9/1901; LDA, file 24.
84 Bp. Healy–O'Dwyer, 5 Sept. 1901; LDA, file 26.
85 Maisie Ward. *Insurrection versus resurrection*, p. 63.
86 Idem, pp. 65–7; also Morrissey. *Towards a Nat. Univ.*, p. 181.
87 O'Dwyer–Donnelly, 19 Nov. (?) 1901; DDA, Walsh/Donnelly papers. Dr Christopher Nixon, prominent Dublin doctor, on senate of Royal University, later knighted. 'Ross' was Major John Ross, later Sir John Ross.
88 M. Ward, op. cit., p. 68.
89 Idem.
90 *Royal Commission on University Education in Ireland*, First Report, p. 14, Q. 320
91 Idem, Reports 1–2, 1901, 19 Sept. 1901, pp. 16 f., 20.
92 Idem, pp. 19–20.
93 Idem, pp. 20–1.
94 Idem, p. 25.

95 Idem.
96 Idem, p. 29.
97 Idem, p. 26.
98 Idem, pp. 29–30.
99 First Report, p. 30.
100 Idem, p. 31.
101 Idem.
102 Idem, p. 37.
103 Idem, p. 27.
104 Idem, p. 49, Q. 650.
105 Idem, Q. 648.
106 Machail, J.W. and Wyndham, Guy, *Life and letters of George Wyndham*, ii, pp. 426–7.
107 Bp. Foley–O'Dwyer, 25 Nov. 1901; LDA, file 24, letters of Bp. Foley.
108 Incomplete, undated letter in LDA. See *Towards a National Univ.*, p. 182.
109 M. Ward. op. cit., p. 59.
110 *Towards a National University*, p. 187.
111 O'Dwyer–Donnelly, 9 March 1902; DDA, f. 373/4.
112 *Towards a National University* p. 187.
113 Walsh–O'Dwyer, 26 Nov. 1901; LDA, file on the University. The reference to a predecessor, was to Dr Daniel Murray who had been prepared to work with the Queen's Colleges, as he had done successfully with the National School System, but was opposed by a majority of bishops and by Rome.
114 *Towards a National Univ.*, pp. 188–90.
115 Maisie Ward. op. cit., p. 61.
116 Logue–O'Dwyer, 30 Nov., 11, 14 Dec. 1901; LDA, file N.
117 O'Dwyer–Donnelly, 9 March 1902; DDA, Walsh/Donnelly papers.
118 M. Ward, pp. 73–4.
119 Idem, pp. 74–5.
120 Prof. Dickie did not sign because he claimed the recommended scheme was denominational and out of harmony with all legislation since 1869.
121 *A page of Irish history*, pp. 520–21; *Towards a National University* p. 194.
122 M. Ward. p. 59.
123 Idem, p. 79.
124 Idem, p. 77.
125 *Hansard*, 4, clxxxvi, 30 March to 4 May 1908.
126 M. Ward, p. 74–6, 78; Royal Commission, *3rd Report*, p. 588 – written submission of E. Thompson Esq., MP, and elsewhere.
127 M. Ward, p. 53.
128 Idem, p. 72.
129 Idem, p. 54. Italics mine.

17 TOWARDS A UNIVERSITY SOLUTION – *MANQUÉ*, 1903–1908

1 *ICD* 1903, register of event for 1902.
2 Idem 1904, register for 1903, p. 448.
3 Idem 1905, register for 1904.
4 *Irish Independent* and *Nation*, 30 Nov. 1903. 'Hence those tears'.
5 John Biggs–Davison. *George Wyndham: a study in toryism*, London 1951, p. 135.
6 Idem, p. 145.
7 Idem, p. 140.
8 Walsh–MacDonnell, 28 Oct. 1903; DDA, box 375, f. 305/3.
9 Idem.

10   *Irish Catholic*, 21 Nov. 1903; cit. Miller, *Church, state and nation*, pp. 103–4.
11   *ICD* 1905, register for 1904, p. 434.
12   O'Dwyer–MacDonnell, 6 Jan. 1904; McDonnell papers C.350, ff 11–14, cit. Miller p. 106.
13   Walsh–MacDonnell, 7 Jan. 1904; idem C. 351, ff.149–50, cit. Miller p. 106.
14   Idem.
15   Cit. Miller, p. 108.
16   Idem.
17   MacDonnell–Bryce, 27 Jan. 1906; Bryce papers, Ms. 11,012 (1), NLI.
18   *ICD* 1905, register for 1904, p. 435.
19   *Freeman's Journal*, 14 Jan. 1904.
20   Cit. Miller, p. 112.
21   *ICD* 1905, for 1904, p. 437.
22   Idem, p. 438.
23   Idem, p. 439
24   *Freeman's Journal*, 20 Feb. 1904. 'Ignis fatuus'– a foolish fire.
25   Idem 24 Feb.1904.
26   IJA. Also in Morrissey. *Towards a National University*, p. 203.
27   'The present condition of university education …', p. 19.
28   Wyndham–Delany, 13, 30 October 1904; IJA.
29   TCD had 1,338 students in 1881; in 1891, 1,162; in 1901, 976 students. Rushe's thesis, 7. 152.
30   *Freeman's Journal*, 28 Jan. 1905. Address at St Philomena's, the preparatory school to Laurel Hill.
31   *ICD* 1906, register for 1905, p. 440.
32   IJA, and in *Towards a National University*, p. 215.
33   O'Dwyer–Delany, 14 Sept. 1905; IJA.
34   O'Dwyer–Delany, 5 Oct. 1905; IJA.
35   *Towards a Natl. Univ.*, pp. 216–17
36   O'Dwyer–Delany, 5 March 1904; IJA.
37   Delany's summary notes on his efforts to secure a governing body for UCD, in IJA.
38   Walsh–Redmond, 13 Jan. 1904; in P.J.Walsh, *William J. Walsh*, pp. 556–7
39   Miller, op. cit., p. 148.
40   Redmond–Bryce, 29 Jan. 1906; NLI. Bryce papers, Ms 11,012, in Miller, p. 148.
41   *ICD* 1907, register 1906, pp. 459–60.
42   R.U.I. Ms. vol. v, pp. 394–7.
43   Miller, p. 456.
44   Mackail, J.W. & Wyndham, Gay, *Life and letters of George Wyndham*, vol. 2, pp. 544–5.
45   Mac Donnell papers, C.350, f.29; Bodleian Library; in Dr A. O'Reilly's Med. thesis 'Sir Anthony MacDonnell and University Reform, 1902–1908', NUI, p. 85. And MacDonnell–Bryce, 18 Aug. 1906; Bryce papers, Ms. 11,013, in O'Reilly, p. 85.
46   Bryce papers, Ms 11,012; cit. Miller p. 148.
47   Bourne–Redmond, 15 Jan. 1906; Redmond papers, NUI, cit. Miller p. 156.
48   *ICD* 1907, register 1906, p. 462.
49   *Freeman's Journal*, 30 Nov. 1906.
50   Idem, 15 Dec. 1906.
51   Redmond papers, statement accompanying Bourne to Redmond, 4 Dec. 1906, cit. Miller pp. 169–171.
52   Bourne–O'Dwyer, 17 Dec. 1906; LDA, folder O.
53   Birrell, *Things past redress*, p. 191.
54   O'Dwyer–Fogarty, 18 Dec. 1906; Killaloe Diocesan Archives (KDA).
55   O'Dwyer–O'Riordan, 28 Dec. 1906; O'Riordan papers, ICR 403.
56   Appendix to Final Report of the Royal Commission on Trinity College Dublin, p. 271.
57   Windle–O'Dwyer, 27 Dec. 1906; LDA, folder L.
58   *ICD* 1908, register 1907, pp. 453–4.

59 *Hansard*, 4 clxix, 72–3.

60 *ICD* 1908, register 1907, pp. 453–4.

61 Incomplete and undated letter, LDA, folder 33A.

62 Ross–O'Dwyer, 27 January 1907; LDA.

63 O'Dwyer–Ross, 27 Jan. 1907; IJA, Delany papers. Ross passed the letter to Delany.

64 Idem, 16 Feb. 1907; ICR. Italics mine.

65 Windle–O'Dwyer, 9 April 1907; LDA, folder L.   66 Idem, 2 May 1907.

67 DDA, f. 132/2. Dublin University petitions to the House of Commons.

68 Windle–O'Dwyer, 23 May 1907; LDA, folder L.

69 See in more recent times: L. O'Broin, *The chief secretary. Augustine Birrell in Ireland* (London, 1969); D.W. Miller; *Church, state and nation in Ireland 1898–1921* (Dublin, 1973); T.J. Morrissey, *Towards a National University: William Delany SJ (1835–1924)* (Dublin, 1983) and *William J. Walsh, archbishop of Dublin, 1841–1921* (Dublin 2000).

70 *ICD* 1909, register 1908, pp. 46 ff.

71 Idem, pp. 466, 469.

72 O'Dwyer–O'Riordan, 24 Jan. 1908; ICR, O'Riordan papers, file no.8.

73 T.M. Healy–O'Dwyer, 25 May 1908; LDA, folder K.

74 *ICD* 1909, register 1908, pp. 513–14.

75 Italics mine.

76 *Things past redress*, pp. 201–2.

77 Cardinal Logue in an address at the Marist College, Dundalk, 8 June 1909, in *ICD* 1910, register for 1909, pp. 478–9.

78 Minutes of Limerick Co. Council's Scholarship Committee meeting, 10 Aug. 1912.

79 Document in envelope in LDA, drawer 2. 'Address to Scholarship Committee', no date.

18 A MEDLEY OF EVENTS, 1900–1912: THE BISHOP AND TEMPERANCE, THE JEWS, THE GAELIC MOVEMENT, MODERNISM, A SILVER JUBILEE, AND OTHER ISSUES

1 Frank Corr, *Limerick Association Year Book 1891*, cit. in Kemmy (ed.), *The Limerick anthology*, pp. 333–4.

2 Amalgamated Society of Pork Butchers–Fr Murphy, 22 Feb., 11 March, 31 July 1902, in Fr Andrew Murphy's letters in O'Dwyer papers, LDA.

3 Gen. Sec. (name illegible)–O'Dwyer, 3 Feb. 1902. Orange file on labour disputes in LDA.

4 LDA, special brown folder with a copy of the arbitration decision in favour of the men, 23 March 1917.

5 *Limerick anthology*, p. 353, from *A pilgrimage through Ireland or the Island of Saints* (Chas. Griffin & Co., 1860).

6 'Housing conditions in 1909' in *Limerick anthology*, pp. 319–20, from J.A. Gaughan. *Thomas Johnson, 1872–1963* (Dublin 1980), pp. 319–20.

7 LDA, file 74. 'City Court House 14 March 1890', typed account.

8 LDA, file P. Handwritten text of the address.

9 Pastoral Letter, 1900, p. 11. LDA.

10 LDA, file 65. Parts of 3 typed sermons.

11 LDA, small yellow cardboard file.

12 *ICD* 1907, annals for 1906. 19 Sept. 1906, p. 469.

13 *ICD* 1904, annals for 1903, p. 448.

14 Dermot Keogh, *The Jews in 20th century Ireland* (Cork, 1998), p. 17.

15 Cutting from *Limerick Journal* 13 Jan. 1904, in Holy Family Chronicles, Limerick, cit. Keogh, op. cit., pp. 27–30.

16 Keogh, idem, p. 31.

17 Cit. Keogh, note 27, p. 251.

18 *Munster News*, 20 Jan. 1904.

19 Adler–O'Dwyer, 29 Jan. 1904. LDA, orange, unmarked folder of miscel. papers.
20 Idem.
21 In Holy Family Chronicles, a two page excerpt entitled 'An excerpt from the Provincial Chronicles 1904', cit. Keogh, p. 38.
22 O'Hara's report, 18 Jan. 1904, CSORP, 1905/23538, NAI, cit. Keogh, p. 34. Emphasis added by Dublin Castle.
23 Idem, emphasis idem.
24 *Munster News*, 23 April 1904.
25 *Freeman's Journal*, 16 April, cit. Keogh p. 48.
26 O'Hara's report, 22 April 1904, CSORP, 1905/23538, NAI. Cit Keogh, p. 48.
27 *Munster News*, 23 April.
28 Idem.
29 Keogh, p. 45.
30 O'Hara's report, 13 April 1904, idem, cit. Keogh, pp. 45–6.
31 Keogh, p. 38.
32 Alexander–O'Dwyer, 25 April 1904, LDA, file 35. Also see Keogh, pp. 38–9.
33 *Limerick anthology,* pp. 13–14.
34 Mt. St Alphonsus, Domestic Chronicle, vol. 3 (1899–1911), Redemptorist Archives, Limerick, cit. Keogh, p. 39.
35 O'Hara report, 12 March 1905, idem, cit. Keogh, p. 39.
36 Excerpt entitled 'An extract from the Provincial Chronicles 1904' in Holy Family Chronicles, Limerick, cit Keogh, p. 39.
37 Letter from P. Hayes, sec. of Mechanics Institute, Bank Place, 22 Jan., in Holy Family Chronicles, cit. Keogh, p. 39.
38 *ICD* 1913, account of 30 Nov. 1911.
39 *ICD*, 1906, account for 1905, pp. 461–2.
40 Cutting in Holy Family Chronicles, cit. Keogh, p. 53.
41 Idem.
42 On the divisions in the community see letters of M.J. Blond, 9 Jan. 1901 and of Louis Goldberg, 10 Jan. 1901, to *Limerick Leader,* in 'Jewish immigrants in Limerick – a divided community' by Des Ryan, in *Remembering Limerick* (Limerick, 1997), pp. 168–9. On Rabbi Levin's departure and subsequent history, see Keogh, p. 51.
43 'My native place' in *My Ireland* (London, 1962), cit. *Limerick anthology*, p. 332.
44 *Limerick anthology*, p. 319.
45 *ICD* 1907, annals for 1906, 7 July 1906, p. 464.
46 Annual for Mary Immaculate Training College, 1950, p. 114.
47 Monteagle–O'Dwyer, 31 Oct. 1888, 7 June 1889, 8 Feb. 1897, 24 Jan. no year; O'Dwyer–Monteagle, no date, offering apologies, esp. to Lady Monteagle, for not calling. LDA, file K.
48 LDA. File M.I.T.C. Secord Report and Third Report, 1903–4, to Dr O'Dwyer.
49 *Freeman's Journal*, 20 Dec. 1901.
50 Idem, 24 June 1907.
51 Fogarty–O'Dwyer, 1 Aug. 1909. LDA, file O.
52 T.J. Morrissey, *William J. Walsh*, p. 233.
53 Walter MacDonald, *Reminiscences of a Maynooth professor* (London, 1925), pp. 376–7.
54 MacDonald, op. cit., pp. 373–4.
55 Idem, pp. 375–7.
56 Idem, pp. 377–8. The reference to a Father of the Church related to Dr Fogarty's eulogy of O'Dwyer at the latter's funeral.
57 *Freeman*, 2 Feb. 1914.
58 O'Laoghaire–O'Dwyer, 25 Sept. 1916. LDA, folder G.
59 Idem, 22 Nov. 1916. LDA, idem.
60 MacDonald, op. cit., p. 316.
61 Idem, p. 156.

62 MacDonald–O'Dwyer, 26 Oct. 1899, LDA, file 79 – Letters from W. MacDonald 1899–1917.

63 Idem, 15/11/1899.

64 Idem, 27/11/1899.

65 MacDonald, *Reminiscences*, pp. 324–28.

66 MacDonald–O'Dwyer, 6 June 1905, LDA, file 79.

67 Idem, 9 Sept. 1908.   68 Idem, 11 Oct.   69 Idem.

70 Idem, 1 and 11 July 1915.

71 Idem.

72 Idem, 22 June 1917.

73 These documents are in LDA, file 54.

74 MacDonald, *Reminiscences*, pp. 328–9.

75 *ICD* 1908. Register for 1907, p. 478.

76 Idem, pp. 418–19.

77 Maisie Ward. *Insurrection versus Resurrection*, Appendix B, p. 559.

78 Idem, p. 265.

79 Idem, p. 293.

80 Idem, p. 287.

81 See pp. 12–17, 20–23, p. 40.

82 *Cork Examiner,* 27 Jan. 1908.

83 ICR O'Riordan papers. O'Dwyer–O'Riordan, 27 Feb. 1908.

84 From a translation in *Catholic Life*, July 1954, p. 19. The full translation is given on the inside page of O'Dwyer's pamphlet – *Cardinal Newman and the encyclical Pascendi Domini Gregis* (London, 1908).

85 Wm Barry, D.D.–O'Dwyer, 23 March 1908. LDA, file 34.

86 ICR O'Dwyer–O'Riordan, 21 March 1908. Italics in text.

87 O'Riordan–O'Dwyer, 17 July 1909, LDA, file I.

88 Account in *Limerick Leader*, 30 Dec. 2000.

89 *Limerick Leader*, 30 Dec. 2000, based on D. O'Shaughnessy, *Limerick: one hundred stories of the century.*

90 O'Dwyer–O'Riordan, 2 April 1910. ICR Box XI.

91 Idem, 7 Sept. 1911. ICR Box 13.

92 *ICD* 1911, register for 1910, p. 458.

93 Idem, 1912, for 1911, 22 Oct. 1911, p. 526.

94 Wm. Barry–O'Dwyer, 11 Nov. 1911. LDA, file F, miscel. docs. & letters.

95 *ICD* 1912, for 1911, 19 Nov. 1911, p. 536.

96 ICR O'Dwyer–O'Riordan, 22 Jan. 1912. '98' refers to the patriotic ballad, 'Who Fears to Speak of '98' referring to the rebellion of 1798. V.G. = Vicar General.

97 ICR O'Dwyer–O'Riordan, 29 Jan. 1912. Only part of the letter remains.

98 A. O'L.–O'Riordan, 5 June 1911. ICR. Italics mine.

99 *ICD* 1912, register 1911, 8 June 1911, p. 498.

100 Idem, for 29 June 1911, pp. 503–4.

101 O'Dwyer–Fogarty, 29 June 1911. Kilalloe Diocesan Archives. (KDA).

102 *Munster News*, 28 June 1911. Cutting in LDA, file 78.

103 O'Dwyer–Fogarty 27 Nov. 1911, see also 22 Nov. KDA.

104 KDA, Fogarty papers, no date.   105 Idem.

106 O'Dea–O'Dwyer, 7 Dec. 1911. LDA file 32.

19 THE BISHOP AND NATIONALIST POLITICS AT HOME AND AT ROME, 1900–1915

1 O'Dwyer–Murphy, 21, 28 May 1900. LDA, file 78.

2 *Limerick Chronicle*, 2 Oct. 1900, cit. O'Callaghan Ms.

3　Idem.

4　Idem, 3 Oct. 1900.

5　Idem, 4 Sept. 1900. The United Irish League was founded by O'Brien in 1898 to agitate for the redistribution of land and the buying out of ranches.

6　*Limerick Leader*, 29 Oct. 1900.

7　Royal Commiss. University Education Ireland, report p. 233.

8　Terence de Vere White, *The road of excess*, p. 260, cit. O'Callaghan Ms.

9　Walsh–Jn. Redmond 13 Jan. 1904, quoted in a letter to Sir Christopher Nixon, 29 Feb. 1904. DDA. See Patrick J. Walsh, *William J. Walsh*, p. 556.

10　O'Dwyer–Redmond, 17 March 1904. Redmond papers, NLI, and 29 July 1904.

11　*Freeman's Journal*, 13 Feb. 1905.

12　Meaning = nothing beyond, nothing above, the best.

13　O'Dwyer–O'Riordan, 8 Nov. 1905. ICR. Box 5, file I.

14　*Freeman's Journal*, 22 Jan 1906. *Limerick Leader*, 21 Feb. 1906.

15　Dillon–Redmond, 15 Dec. 1906. Redmond papers, NLI.

16　Dillon–Fleming, 17 Dec. 1906, Fleming papers, OFM (England) Archives, cit. O'Callaghan.

17　Idem, 30 Dec. 1906.

18　O'Dwyer–O'Riordan, 14 March 1906. ICR, box 5, file I.

19　*Limerick Leader*, 15 May 1907.

20　'The University Question' *Irish Educational Review*, 1, no. 1 (Oct. 1907), pp. 1–13.

21　*Freeman*, 13 June 1908; *Limerick Leader*, 1 July 1908.

22　*Limerick Leader*, 19 Oct. 1908.

23　*Dublin Daily Press,* 22 Oct. 1908.

24　D.W. Miller, *Church, state and nation*, p. 246.

25　Dillon–Fr Fleming, 24 Oct. 1909, Fleming papers, as above.

26　Miller, op. cit., idem.

27　O'Riordan–O'Dwyer, 10 Feb. 1910. LDA.

28　Idem, 24 June 1910. LDA. Italics in text.

29　*Limerick Leader*, 12 Sept. 1910.

30　Idem, 23 Dec. 1910.

31　Idem, 30 Jan. 1911.

32　O'Dwyer–Fogarty, 21 May 1911. Fogarty papers, KDA.

33　Idem, 21 Dec. 1911.

34　Des Ryan. 'Women's suffrage associations in Limerick, 1912–1914' in *Old Limerick Journal*, (winter 1993), pp. 41, 43–4.

35　O'Riordan–O'Dwyer, 23 Feb. 1912, LDA.

36　O'Dwyer–Fogarty, 26 Feb. 1912. KDA.

37　Redmond–O'Dwyer, 9 March 1912. LDA.

38　O'Dwyer–Redmond, 10 March 1912. Redmond papers, NLI.

39　*Limerick Leader*, 20 Dec. 1912.

40　M.J. Curran–M. O'Riordan, 20 Dec. 1912. O'Riordan papers, ICR, box 13, no. 192.

41　Cit. F.S.L. Lyons, *Ireland since the Famine*, p. 301.

42　Idem, p. 303.

43　Pastoral letter, pp. 6–7.

44　Idem, pp. 16–17.

45　*Limerick Leader*, 3 Oct. 1913.

46　Idem, 8 Oct. 1913.

47　*Limerick Leader*, 19 Dec. 1913.

48　Abp. Harty–O'Riordan, 19–7–1914, O'Riordan papers, ICR, box 14, no. 163; see also O'Dwyer–O'Riordan, 13 June 1914, no. 140.

49　Bp. Foley–O'Dwyer, 7–2–1914, LDA, file O.

50　Fergus D'Arcy. 'Larkin and the historians' in D. Nevin (ed.), *James Larkin. Lion of the fold* (Dublin 1980) pp. 375–6.

51 Donnelly–O'Dwyer, 1913, no further date available. LDA.
52 Ciaran O Griofa. 'John Daly, the Fenian mayor of Limerick' in D. Lee (ed.), *Remembering Limerick*, pp. 197 ff.
53 *Limerick Leader*, 27 Aug. 1917.
54 Idem, 29 Aug. 1917.   55 Idem, 12 Feb. 1913.
56 O'Dwyer–O'Riordan, 11 Jan. 1914. ICR.
57 *ICD* 1915, record of documents for 1914, pp. 54 ff. Also see *Limerick Leader*, editorial, 'The labour problem', 23 Feb. 1914.
58 Bp. Foley–O'Dwyer, 7 Feb. 1914. LDA, file O.
59 T.D. Williams. ed. *The Irish struggle*, p. 96.
60 F.X. Martin (ed.), *Leaders and men of the Easter Rising*, p. 217.
61 T.J. Morrissey, *William J. Walsh*, pp. 271.
62 F.X. Martin, op. cit., p. 217.
63 Dillon–Fleming, 17 Oct. 1914. Fleming papers, OFM (E) A.
64 F.X. Martin. op. cit., p. 218; O'Callaghan Ms. p. 323.
65 Redmond–Asquith, 7 June 1915. Bodl. Library, Asquith Ms. 36/94; and copy of Fogarty–Redmond, 3 June 1915, idem, 36/98–9; in Miller. op. cit. p. 315.
66 *Limerick Leader*, 12 July 1915.
67 O'Riordan–O'Dwyer, 3 March 1910. LDA. Italics in text.
68 Idem, 27 April 1914.
69 Gasquet–Redmond, 7 Nov. 1914, Redmond papers, Ms. 15188, NLI, cit. Jerome aan de Wiel in 'Monsignor O'Riordan, Bishop O'Dwyer, and the Shaping of New Relations between Nationalist Ireland and the Vatican during the World War One', *Archiv. Hib.*, liii (1999), p. 98.
70 Aan de Wiel, idem, p. 97.
71 De Wiel, art. cit., op. cit., p. 97; Dermot Keogh. *The Vatican, the bishops, and Irish politics, 1914–1939* (Cambridge, 1986), p. 11; *Catholic Bulletin* (Jan. 1913), 'Notes from Rome', pp. 32–3; on Gasquet's benign attitude, see Shane Leslie–O'Riordan, 3 April 1915, ICR, who considered Gasquet 'an old dear with the smallest capacity for intrigue', and who defended 'the cause of Ireland in the most unsympathetic drawing rooms in London'.
72 Hagan–O'Riordan, 25 Oct. 1914. ICR.
73 Idem, 2 Nov. 1914.
74 O'Riordan–O'Dwyer, 28 Dec. 1914. LDA. Italics in text.   75 Idem, 3 Jan. 1915.
76 O'Riordan–'Dear Monsignor' [perhaps Monsignor Hallinan], 6 Jan. 1915. LDA.
77 O'Riordan–O'Dwyer, 13 July 1915. LDA.
78 Pastoral Letter 1915 in LDA.
79 O'Riordan–O'Dwyer, 20 March 1915. LDA.
80 Idem, 6 June 1915.
81 O'Dwyer–O'Riordan, 8 Sept. 1915. ICR.
82 O'Dwyer–Redmond, 4 Aug. 1915. LDA.
83 Redmond–O'Dwyer, 9 Aug. 1915. LDA, special brown folder.
84 O'Dwyer–O'Riordan, 13 Aug. 1915. ICR.
85 O'Dwyer–Fogarty, 14 Aug. 1915. KDA.
86 Fogarty–O'Dwyer, 21 Aug. 1915. LDA.
87 21 Aug. 1915, cit. de Wiel in paper 'Bishop O'Dwyer's rise in the nationalist opposition movement during the First World War', p. 4. Text courtesy of author.
88 O'Dwyer–Fogarty, 22 Aug. 1915. KDA.
89 O'Dwyer–O'Riordan, 28 Dec. 1914. LDA.
90 O'Riordan–O'Dwyer, 28 Dec. 1914. LDA.
91 Idem, 18 Sept. 1915.
92 O'Dwyer–O'Riordan, 3 Nov. 1915. ICR, box 16, no. 150.
93 E.T. O'Dwyer. 'The Pope's Plan for Peace' in *Irish Ecclesiastical Review*, iii, no. 6 (Dec. 1915), pp. 631–6.

94 O'Riordan–O'Dwyer, 24 Dec. 1915; and 5 Jan. 1916.
95 *Limerick Chronicle*, 9 Nov. 1915.
96 *Munster News*, 10 Nov. 1915.
97 Mentioned as from the *Guardian* in a newspaper cutting that does not carry the paper's name, LDA.
98 Cit. J.M. McCarthy, *Limerick's fighting story*, p. 43, in O'Callaghan Ms.
99 O'Mahony–O'Dwyer, 16 Nov. 1915, in LDA in an unnumbered file on Land and Social issues that contains an envelope marked 1915.
100 O'Riordan–Monsignor, 29 Nov. 1915. LDA. O'Riordan letters. Italics in text.
101 Fogarty–O'Dwyer, 9 Dec. 1915. LDA. Episcopal letters, file O.
102 *Limerick Leader*, 11 Feb. 1916.
103 *Limerick Chronicle*, 25 May 1915.

20 1916: CHALLENGING CARNAGE ABROAD AND OPPRESSION AT HOME

1 *Freeman's Journal,* 15 Dec. 1906, cit. Miller, *Church, state and nation*, p. 172.
2 O'Dwyer–O'Riordan, 8 Sept. 1915. ICR.
3 Idem, 12 Jan. 1916.
4 O'Riordan–O'Dwyer, 5 Jan. 1916. LDA, file I
5 O'Dwyer–O'Riordan, 12 Jan. 1916. ICR.
6 O'Riordan–Mr Wolfe, 22 Jan. 1916. ICR.
7 Fogarty–O'Dwyer, 22 March 1916. LDA, file O. Fogarty Letters.
8 Pastoral Letter 1916, pp. 3,4,7,11,12. LDA.
9 Idem, p. 14.
10 O'Riordan–O'Dwyer, 24 July 1916. LDA, file I.
11 Pastoral … pp. 4–5.
12 O'Donnell–O'Dwyer, 4 March 1916. LDA, file F.
13 *Sinn Fein Rebellion Handbook. Easter 1916.* Compiled by *Weekly Irish Times* (1917 issue), p. 52.
14 Idem, p. 42.
15 Idem, p. 239.
16 Colivet–Bp. of Limerick, 1 May 1916. LDA, in untitled yellow folder.
17 R. O'Shaughnessy–O'Riordan, 23 July 1916, also O'Dwyer–O'Riordan, 10 May 1916. ICR, O'Riordan papers.
18 Curran Ms. p. 71, in Curran papers, Ms. 27,278, vol. 1, Statement to Bureau of Military History, Ms. in 3 vols. based mainly on Curran's diaries in Sean T. O'Ceallaigh papers, special list A 9, NLI. All references for 1916 are in vol. 1, written Ms. 27, 728 (1). Also see Morrissey, *William J. Walsh* pp. 286–7. Italics mine.
19 Reproduced in *Evening Mail*, 30 May 1916.
20 Idem.
21 LDA, file 'Gen. Maxwell and 1916'.
22 Wall–O'Dwyer, 18 May 1916. LDA, file M.
23 J. aan de Wiel. 'Bishop O'Dwyer's rise in the nationalist opposition movement during the First World War', in *History Studies*, Univ. Limerick, p. 6.
24 *Evening Mail*, 30 May 1916. LDA. In the published letter the names of the two priests were omitted.
25 O'Dwyer–O'Riordan, 18 May 1916. ICR. Italics in text.
26 Monsignor Curran's memoirs, 'Dr O'Dwyer's famous letter to General Maxwell', in S.T. O'Ceallaigh papers, Ms. 27,728 (1), NLI.
27 O'Riordan–O'Dwyer, 27 May 1916. LDA, file I.
28 M.J. Curran–O'Riordan, 29 May. ICR.
29 Fr T.A. Murphy, CSSR–O'Dwyer, 27 July, from Philippines. LDA, file 36.
30 Kate O'Donnell–O'Dwyer, 10 June 1916. LDA, file M.

31 Resolution dated 2 June 1916. LDA, file on 'Gen. Maxwell and 1916'.
32 O'Riordan–O'Dwyer, 10 June 1916. LDA.
33 *Evening Herald*, 3 June 1916. LDA.
34 Report on his 'Mission to Ireland', 8–20 June 1916, p. 125, in French Embassy London, courtesy of Jerome aan de Wiel.
35 P.J. Roughan–O'Riordan, 9 June, ICR.
36 L. O'Broin. *The Chief Secretary*, p. 189.
37 Fogarty–O'Riordan, 16 June 1916. ICR.
38 O'Dwyer–O'Riordan, 15 June. ICR.
39 O'Dwyer–O'Riordan, 24 June 1916. ICR.   40 Idem, 27 June 1916.
41 H.W. Cleary–O'Riordan, 25 June. ICR.
42 File F and also in file 'General Maxwell and 1916'. LDA.
43 T. Carey–O'Riordan, 30 June 1916. ICR.
44 R. O'Shaughnessy–O'Riordan, 23 July. ICR.
45 O'Dwyer–Sr. Catherine, 30 June 1916. LDA, small brown folder.
46 O'Dwyer–O'Riordan, 22 July. ICR. '*Dolce far niente*' = Doing sweet nothing.
47 S.J. Darwin Fox–O'Dwyer, 11 July 1916. LDA, file L.
48 Fogarty–O'Dwyer, 31 July 1916. LDA, file O.
49 O'Dwyer–Fogarty, 2 Aug. 1916, Killaloe Diocesan Archives (KDA).
50 L. Ginnell–O'Dwyer, 11 Aug. 1916. LDA, file M.
51 O'Dwyer–O'Riordan, 31 Aug. 1916. ICR.
52 *Irish Independent*, 21 Aug. 1917.
53 O'Dwyer–Fogarty, 9 Sept. 1916. KDA.   54 Idem, 11 Sept.
55 *Cork Examiner*, 15 Sept. 1916.
56 Idem. The Italics occur in the printed leaflet version.
57 Fogarty–O'Dwyer, 10 Sept. 1916. LDA, file O.   58 Idem, 12 Sept.
59 O'Dwyer–Fogarty, 16 Sept. 1916. KDA.
60 Fogarty–O'Dwyer, 17 Sept. 1916. LDA, file O.
61 Letters relating to the speech in LDA.
62 O'Dwyer–O'Riordan, 24 Sept. 1916. ICR.
63 Idem, 30 Sept. 1916. ICR, Box 17.
64 Edward P. O'Callaghan, O.F.M., who provides an introduction and commentary, in *Collectanea Hibernica*, 18 & 19 (1976–7).
65 O'Dwyer–Foley, 14 Dec. 1916. Archives Kildare & Leighlin.
66 Curran–Fr John Hagan, 15 Oct. 1916. ICR, Hagan papers, 1916, letter no. 100, cit. by J. aan de Wiel in 'From "Castle" Bishop to "Moral Leader"? Edward O'Dwyer and Irish Nationalism 1914–1917' in *History Studies*, Univ. Limerick, vol. 2, p. 65.
67 O'Callaghan Ms. for M.A., pp. 372–3.
68 Fogarty–O'Dwyer, 14 Nov. 1916. LDA, file O.
69 O'Dwyer–Fogarty, 16 Nov. KDA.
70 Miller, op. iam cit. p. 345.   71 Idem, p. 346.
72 Fogarty–O'Dwyer, 14 Nov. 1916. LDA, file O.
73 O'Dwyer–Fogarty, 16 Nov. KDA.
74 Curran–O'Riordan, 24 Sept. 1916. ICR.
75 R. O'Shaughnessy–O'Riordan, 23 Nov. ICR.
76 Curran–O'Riordan, 16 Dec. 1916. ICR.   77 Idem, 22 Dec. 1916.

21 1917: *NUNC DIMITTUS* – 'IN HARNESS AND IN A BLAZE OF GLORY'

1 R. O'Shaughnessy–O'Riordan, 12 Jan. 1917. ICR.
2 T.P. Coogan. *Michael Collins*, p. 64.

3 LDA, yellow untitled folder.
4 O'Dwyer–O'Riordan, 20 Jan. 1917. ICR.
5 O'Dwyer–Monsignor Hallinan, 3 Feb. 1917. LDA.
6 O'Dwyer–Fogarty, 17 Feb. KDA.
7 Fogarty–O'Dwyer, 19 Feb. LDA.
8 Pastoral Letter 1917, pp. 7–8. LDA.
9 Idem, pp. 12–13.
10 Idem, p. 14.
11 Idem, pp. 5–6.
12 Idem, p. 12.
13 Fogarty–O'Dwyer, 25 Feb. 1917. LDA, file O.
14 Literally: 'That man has a head' – great ability.
15 O'Riordan–O'Dwyer, 25 March 1917. LDA, file I.
16 *ICD 1918*. Register of events 1917, 2 March, p. 511.
17 O'Dwyer–O'Riordan, 3 April. ICR.
18 O'Dwyer–O'Riordan, 11 March 1917. ICR, box 18.
19 O'Riordan–O'Dwyer, 26 March. LDA, file F.
20 O'Dwyer–Hallinan, 1 April 1917. LDA, brown folder.
21 Printed leaflet, 1 May 1917. LDA.
22 T.J. Morrissey. *A man called Hughes* (Dublin 1991), pp. 72–79. Seamus Hughes was a prisoner at Lewes.
23 O'Dwyer–Fogarty, 4 May 1917. KDA.
24 T.J. Morrissey, *William J. Walsh* p. 301.
25 Idem.
26 Italics mine.
27 *Freeman's Journal*, 25 May 1917.
28 *Evening Herald,* 26 May 1917. LDA.
29 *Freeman*, 2 June 1917.
30 Ignatius Kelly, a paid organiser for the United Irish League, in *Evening Herald*, 26 May 1917.
31 O'Dwyer–O'Riordan, 6 June 1917. ICR.
32 Idem, 22 June.
33 Idem, 3 July.
34 *Limerick Leader*, 20 August 1917.
35 De Valera in a speech at Crossmaglen, cit. *Armagh Guardian*, 1 Feb. 1918, cit. Miller. op. iam cit. p. 395.
36 Dillon to Redmond, June and July 1917, Redmond papers, Ms. 15,182 (24), NLI.
37 O'Dwyer–Fogarty, 13 July 1917. KDA.
38 O'Dwyer–O'Riordan, 27 July. ICR.
39 W. McDonald–O'Dwyer, 29 July 1917. LDA, file F.
40 O'Dwyer–O'Riordan, 4 Aug. 1917. ICR. Italics in text.
41 O'Riordan–O'Dwyer, 5 Aug. 1917. LDA, yellow file.
42 T. Quain(?)–O'Riordan, 18 August 1917, ICR.
43 O'Riordan–Dear Monsignor, 22 August. LDA, yellow file. Italics mine.
44 *Munster News*, 22 Aug. 1917. LDA.
45 Taped interview with Archdeacon Ryan, 1973.
46 M. O'Donnell–O'Riordan, 24 Aug. 1917. ICR.
47 *Munster News*, 22 Aug. 1917.
48 John Lee–O'Riordan, 19 August. ICR.
49 H.W. Cleary–O'Riordan, 21 Aug. ICR. Italics in text.
50 Unknown author–O'Riordan, 24 August 1917. ICR.
51 Thomas Carey (?)–O'Riordan, 22 August. ICR.

52 M. O'Donnell–O'Riordan, 24 August. ICR.
53 *Irish Independent*, 20 August 1917.
54 *Limerick Leader*, 20 August 1917.
55 *ICD 1918*. Register of Eccles. Events 1917, p. 538b.

CONCLUSION

1   Miller. op. cit., pp. 344–5.
2   T.J. Morrissey, *William Martin Murphy* (Dundalk, 1997), pp. 66ff.
3   Richard O'Kennedy. 'The Most Rev. E.T. O'Dwyer, DD' in *IM*, 46 (1918), p. 29.
4   Incident related to the author by Sean Rushe, MA.
5   See Denis O'Shaughnessy. Limerick. *100 stories of the century* (Limerick 2000), 'The caustic
    wit of Bishop O'Dwyer', pp. 46–7.
6   Taped interview with Archdeacon Ryan, 1973, by Rev. Edward P. O'Callaghan, O.F.M.
    refers to 'a dirty little tyrant'. The quotation from Bishop O'Neill is from a comment by
    Monsignor Tynan, a well-known priest and Irish historian, which was found by Rev.
    Donagh O'Malley as an insert in a book owned by Fr Wall of 1916 reputation, entitled
    The Pursuit of Diarmuid and Grainne. Tynan's fuller comment was: 'I began my circulation
    among the clergy in 1943 what time many of the parish priests had served under
    O'Dwyer. The memory the bishop had left to his clergy was not a pleasant one; they had
    all been afraid of him – Bishop O'Neill's summary was succint: 'a terrible little man!'
    [courtesy rev. D. O'Malley]. Bishop O'Neill was born in 1891, and was bishop from 1946
    to 1958.
7   J. Fleming & S. O'Grady. *St Munchin's College*, p. 79.
8   M. O'Donnell–O'Dwyer, 17 July 1917. LDA, file E.
9   *Sunday Press*, 2 Jan. 1977.
10 James G. Barry in article by R. O'Kennedy in *IM*, 1918, p. 29.
11 Idem, p. 28.
12 Archdeacon Ryan tape.
13 Lord Monteagle, in art. cit. In *IM*, pp. 28–9.
14 Taped interview with Dean Punch by Rev. Tim Culhane in 1970s. LDA. There is also an
    interview taped and held by Rev. E.P. O'Callaghan. Dean Punch, born 1884, was presi-
    dent of the first Sinn Fein court at Newcastle West. A great admirer of Dr O'Dwyer, as
    has been seen. From the O'Callaghan tape, the one area where he had reservations about
    the bishop was in his handling of the Mungret College issue. Punch became parish priest
    in the Mungret area.
15 J.G. Barry in art. cit. in *IM*, p. 30.
16 Monteagle, idem, p. 28.
17 Kate O'Brien. *Sunday Press*, 2 Jan. 1977.
18 Monsignor Moloney. ' A Memory of Bishop O'Dwyer' in *Limerick Leader,* 21 Nov. 1940.
19 H.W. Cleary–O'Riordan, 21 Aug. 1917. ICR.
20 D. O'Shaughnessy, op. iam cit. 'Bishop O'Dwyer "a very queer man".' pp. 105–6.

Bibliography

Ireland

Limerick Diocesan Archives
> Bishop George Butler's Papers, O'Dwyer papers, which include collections of letters from the bishop's sister, Annie, from the Revd John S. Flanagan and the Revd Walter McDonald, in addition to letters from many bishops and churchmen, from prominent educationalists, and from public men such as Isaac Butt, T.M. Healy, Horace Plunkett, Aubrey de Vere, T.P. Gill, Wilfrid Ward, Arthur and Gerald Balfour, and General Sir John Maxwell
> Monsignor Denis Hallinan's diary

Dublin Diocesan Archives
> Archbishop McCabe's papers
> Archbishop Walsh papers
> Bishop Donnelly's papers
> Bishop Woodlock's papers

Armagh Diocesan Archives
> Cardinal Logue papers

Killaloe Diocesan Archives
> Bishop McRedmond papers
> Bishop Fogarty papers

Cashel Diocesan Archives
> Archbishop Croke papers
> Papers of Frs Philip Fogarty and John Meagher

Irish Jesuit Archives
> William Delany papers
> Mungret Apostolic School papers
> Minute Book of Province Consultors

Glenstal Abbey Archives
> Copies of Archbishop Croke and John Dillon papers

Laurel Hill School
> Chronicles and annals, Limerick, courtesy of Archives of Sisters of the Faithful Companions of Jesus

National Library of Ireland
> William Monsell (Lord Emly) papers
> John Redmond papers
> Aubrey de Vere papers
> Archbishop Croke papers (also copies at Glenstal Abbey Archives, Co. Limerick)
> Monsignor Michael Curran papers in Sean T. O'Ceallaigh papers, special list A 9

Dublin University
> John Dillon papers and diary (copies of papers also in Glenstal)

National University of Ireland Office, Dublin
> Minute-books of the Royal University of Ireland

Rome

Irish College Rome
> Monsignor O'Riordan Papers
> Monsignor Kirby papers

Archives Fratelli Christiani
> Archives of Irish Christian Brothers in relation to their School at Bruff, Co. Limerick

Archives of Propaganda Fide
> Acts S.C. de Propaganda Fide

Archivo Segreto Vaticano
> The Persico Report

Oxford

Plunkett Foundation
> Diaries of Sir Horace Plunkett (from such transcripts are as available)

PRINTED EDITIONS OF MANUSCRIPT MATERIAL

Monsignor Persico's letters from Archivo Segreto Vaticano in *Collectanea Hibernica*, 24 and 25, ed. Edward P. O'Callaghan, OFM.

Papers of Thomas William Croke, Archbishop of Cashel, ed. M. Tierney, in *Collectanea Hibernica*, 11, 13, 16 and 17

Papers of Monsignor Tobias Kirby, Irish College Rome, ed. P.J. Corish, in *Archivium Hibernicum*, 30 and 32

Edward P. O'Callaghan, OFM (ed.), 'Correspondence between Bishop O'Dwyer and Bishop Foley on the Dublin Rising, 1916–1917,' in *Collectanea Hibernica*, 18 & 19

NEWSPAPERS AND PERIODICALS

Cork Daily Herald	*Daily Telegraph*
Cork Examiner	*Evening Echo*
Daily Express	*Freeman's Journal*
Daily News (Dublin)	*Irish Independent*

Limerick Chronicle	*The Times*
Limerick Leader	*The United Irishman*
Limerick Reporter and Tipperary Vindicator	
Munster News	*Archivium Hibernicum*
The Nation	*Catholic Bulletin*
New Ireland (1917)	*Collectanea Hibernica*
Newcastle Leader	*Irish Ecclesiastical Record*
New Saturday	*Irish Monthly*
New Statesman	*Mungret Annual*
The Tablet	*Old Limerick Journal*

SELECT BIBLIOGRAPHY

Ahern, Richard, 'A history of the Christian Brothers in Limerick' in *Old Limerick Journal*, 22 (1987)

Akenson, D.H., *The Irish education experiment* (London, 1970)

Begley, John, *The diocese of Limerick from 1691 to the present time* (Dublin, 1938)

Birrell, Augustine, *Things past redress* (London, 1937)

Biggs-Davison, John, *George Wyndham: a study in toryism* (London, 1951).

Blunt, Wilfrid Scawen, *The land war in Ireland: a personal narrative of events* (London, 1912)

Browne, Pius J.A, 'The Bruff Agitation. A brief history, 1897–1907' in *Old Limerick Journal*, 11 (1982).

Callanan, Martin, *Records of four Tipperary septs* (Galway, 1938)

Canning, B.J., *Bishops of Ireland, 1870–1987* (Ballyshannon, 1987)

Christian Brothers' Educational Record (Dublin, 1914, 1952)

Coogan, Tim Pat, *De Valera. Long Fellow, long shadow* (London, 1995)

——, *Michael Collins* (London, 1991)

Corish, P.J., *Maynooth College, 1795–1995* (Dublin, 1995)

De Vere, Aubrey, *The Recollections of Aubrey de Vere* (London, 1897)

de Wiel, Jerome aan, 'From "Castle" bishop to "moral leader"? Edward O'Dwyer and Irish nationalism 1914–17' in *History Study*, 2 (History Society publication, 2000)

——, 'Monsignor O'Riordan, Bishop O'Dwyer, and the shaping of new relations between nationalist Ireland and the Vatican during World War One' in *Archiv. Hib.*, 51 (1999)

——, 'Bishop O'Dwyer's rise in the nationalist opposition movement during the First World War', unpublished ms.

Digby, M., *Horace Plunkett: an Anglo-American Irishman* (Oxford, 1949)

Dunraven, earl of, *Past time and pastimes* (London, 1922)

Fathers of the Society of Jesus, *A page of Irish history: the story of University College Dublin 1883–1909* (Dublin, 1930)

Finnegan, Francis, SJ, *Limerick Jesuit Centenary Record, 1859–1959* (Limerick, 1959)

Fleming, John and O'Grady, Sean, *St Munchin's College, Limerick, 1796–1996* (Limerick, 1996)

Fogarty, Bishop Michael, *The great bishop of Limerick*, panegyric, 18 Sept. 1917, published as a pamphlet

Geary, Laurence M., *The Plan of Campaign, 1886–1891* (Cork, 1986)

Hansard's parliamentary debates, esp. fourth series, vol. 187

Healy, T.M., *Letters and leaders of my day*, 2 vols. (London, 1928)

Hurley, Thomas, SJ, *Father Michael Browne, SJ* (Dublin, 1949).

Joyce, P.J., *John Healy, archbishop of Tuam* (Dublin, 1931)

Kemmy, James (ed.), *Old Limerick anthology* (Dublin, 1996)

Keogh, Dermot, *The Jews in 20th century Ireland* (Cork, 1998)

Larkin, Emmet, *The Roman Catholic Church and the Plan of Campaign, 1886–1888* (Cork, 1978)

——, *The Roman Catholic Church and the fall of Parnell, 1888–1891* (Chapel Hill, 1979)

——, *The Roman Catholic Church and the emergence of the modern Irish political system, 1874–1878* (Dublin, 1996)

Lee, David, *Remembering Limerick* (Limerick, 1997).

Leslie, Shane, *Henry Edward Manning. His life and labours* (London, 1921)

Lyons, F.S.L., *Ireland since the Famine* (Glasgow, 1976)

——, *John Dillon* (Chicago, 1968)

——, 'John Dillon and the Plan of Campaign', *Irish Historical Studies*, 14 (1965)

——, *Charles Stewart Parnell* (London, 1977)

Macauley, Ambrose, *The Holy See, British policy and the Plan of Campaign in Ireland, 1885–1893* (Dublin, 2002)

MacDonald, Walter, *Reminiscences of a Maynooth professor* (London, 1925)

McCaffrey, L.J., 'Home Rule and the General Election of 1874 in Ireland', *Irish Historical Studies*, 9:34 (Sept. 1954)

McEvoy, Dermot, 'The scandal at Bruff', *Old Limerick Journal*, 6 (spring 1981)

Machail, J.W. & Wyndham, Guy, *Life and letters of George Wyndham* (London 1939)

Martin, F.X., *Leaders and men of the Easter Rising: Dublin 1916* (London 1967)

Miller, David W., *Church, state, and nation in Ireland, 1898–1921* (Dublin, 1973)

Morrissey, Thomas J., *Towards a national university. William Delany, SJ, 1835–1924* (Dublin, 1983)

——, *A man called Hughes* (Dublin, 1991)

——, *William Martin Murphy* (Dundalk, 1997)

——, *William J. Walsh, archbishop of Dublin, 1841–1921* (Dublin, 2000)

Murphy, Ignatius, *The diocese of Killaloe, 1850–1904* (Dublin, 1995)

O'Brien, Kate, *Land of spices* (London, 1941)

——, 'Christmas in the Presentation parlour', excerpt from *Presentation Parlour* (London, 1963) in Jim Kemmy (ed.) *The Limerick anthology* (Dublin, 1996)

O'Brien, William, *Irish ideas* (London, 1893)

O'Broin, Leon, *The chief secretary. Augustine Birrell in Ireland* (London, 1969)

O'Callaghan, Edward P., OFM, 'Bishop Edward Thomas O'Dwyer and the Course of Irish politics, 1870–1917' (MA thesis, University College Galway, 1976)

O'Conbhuidhe, Colmcille, OCSO, *The Cistercian abbeys of Tipperary*, ed. F. Donovan (Dublin, 1999)

O'Connor, Sr Loreto, *Passing on the torch: a history of Mary Immaculate College, 1898–1998* (private centenary publication)

O'Kennedy, Richard Canon, 'The Most Rev. E.T. O'Dwyer, D.D.' in *Irish Monthly* (1917 and 1918): a detailed sketch by a contemporary

O'Dwyer, Bishop E.T., 'University education for Irish Catholics' in *Nineteenth Century* (Jan., 1999)

——, *The present condition of university education in Ireland: a wrong to the country and an insult to Catholics* (Dublin, 1904)

——, *Cardinal Newman and the encyclical Pascendi Dominici Gregis* (London, 1908)

——, *On the office of bishop*, printed sermon (Dublin, 1894)

——, *Technical instruction*, pamphlet (Dublin, 1900)

——, *Month's Mind* (1886), printed sermon in honour of Bishop Butler (pamphlet)

——, Panegyric at obsequies of Rt Hon. Lord Emly, 25 April 1894 (pamphlet)

——, Preface to vol. 1 of Canon Begley's three-volume *History of the diocese of Limerick*

——, 'The university question' in *Irish Educational Review*, 1 (Oct. 1907)

——, 'Marlborough House – The unjust discrimination between training colleges', *Irish Educational Review*, 2 (Oct. 1908)

——, *Irish Ecclesiastical Record*, review articles: Aug. & Sept. 1880; and regularly from 1882 to 1884

——, various printed pastoral letters

O'Dwyer, Sir Michael, *The O'Dwyers of Kilnamanagh. The history of an Irish sept* (London, 1933)

O'Riordan, Michael, *Catholicity and progress in Ireland* (London, 1905)

O'Shaughnessy, Denis, *Limerick. 100 stories of the century* (Limerick, 2000)

O'Sullivan, T.F., *The Young Irelanders* (Tralee, 1944)

Plunkett, Horace, *Ireland in the new century* (London, 1904)

Prendergast, Frank, *St Michael's parish, Limerick: its life and times* (Limerick, 2000)

Punch, Edward, dean of Limerick, taped interview conducted by Edward P. O'Callaghan, OFM (1973) and in his possession

——, taped interview (1970s) conducted by Revd Tim Culhane, which is in Limerick Diocesan Archives

Report of Educational Endowments (Ireland) Commission, 1887–8 and down to 1891

Report of the Royal Commission (Robertson) on University Education in Ireland, 1902–3

Reports on Catholic Church affairs in *Irish Catholic Directory* from 1886

Rushe, John, 'Bishop O'Dwyer of Limerick 1886–1917 and the educational issues of his time' (MA thesis, University College Galway, 1980)

——, 'Edward Thomas O'Dwyer' in *Old Limerick Journal*, no. 2 (March 1980)

——, 'The early years of Bishop O'Dwyer', idem, no. 6 (spring 1981)

——, 'Edward Thomas O'Dwyer and the Temperance Movement', idem, 8 (Autumn 1981)

——, 'Rev. Edward Thomas O'Dwyer and the Artisans' Dwellings Company; the election of 1874', idem, no. 9 (winter 1981)

Ryan, archdeacon of Co. Limerick, conducted by Rev. Edward P. O'Callaghan, O.F.M. (1973) and in his possession

Ryan, Des, 'Women's Suffrage Associations in Limerick, 1912–14', *Old Limerick Anthology* (Winter, 1993)

Thornly, David, *Isaac Butt and Home Rule* (London, 1964)

Tierney, Mark, OSB, *Croke of Cashel. The life of Archbishop Thomas William Croke, 1823–1902* (Dublin, 1976)

Walsh, Aisling, 'Michael Cardinal Logue' in *Seanchas Ard Mhaca* (2000)

Walsh, Patrick J., *William J. Walsh, archbishop of Dublin* (Dublin, 1928)

Index